A LIBRARY OF LITERARY CRITICISM

A LIBRARY

Volume III
Q - Z

Frederick Ungar Publishing Co., New York

OF LITERARY CRITICISM

Modern British Literature

Compiled and edited by
RUTH Z. TEMPLE
Professor of English
The City University of New York
(*Brooklyn College*)

MARTIN TUCKER
Assistant Professor of English
Long Island University

All selections in these volumes are included by permission of the copyright owners and may not be quoted elsewhere without their approval. The exact reference is given with each quotation. For full acknowledgment to the critics, literary executors, literary agents, and book and periodicals publishers who permitted their material to be included, see the listings starting on page 439, Volume III.

Third Printing, 1972

Copyright © 1966 by Frederick Ungar Publishing Co., Inc.
Printed in the United States of America
Library of Congress Catalog Card Number 65-28048

ISBN 0-8044-3276-7   Vol. I
ISBN 0-8044-3277-5   Vol. II
ISBN 0-8044-3278-3   Vol. III
ISBN 0-8044-3275-9   (Set)

PERIODICALS USED

Listed below are their titles, their abbreviations, if any, place of publication, and, for the British journals, dates of publication. If no place is indicated, *London* is to be understood.

	The Academy and Literature. 1869-1916 (The Academy, 1869, absorbed Literature, 1902)
Adam	Adam International Review, 1932—
Adel	The Adelphi, 1923-55
Am. Hist. R.	The American Historical Review, New York
AmS	The American Scholar, Washington, D. C.
	The Anglo-Welsh Review, Wales, 1949—
AQ	The Arizona Quarterly, University of Arizona, Tucson, Arizona
Ath	The Athenæum, 1828-1921 (merged with The Nation)
At	The Atlantic Monthly, Boston, Mass.
BkmL	The Bookman, 1891-1934 (absorbed by The London Mercury)
Bkm	The Bookman, New York
Cal. Mod. Letters	The Calendar of Modern Letters, 1925-27
CJ	The Cambridge Journal, Cambridge, 1947-54
	The Central Literary Magazine, Birmingham, 1873—
	The Chicago Daily Tribune
CC	The Christian Century, Chicago, Ill.
	Colophon, The Monthly Magazine for Booklovers, 1950-51
The Colophon (N.Y.)	The Colophon, A Quarterly for Bookmen, New York (subtitle varies)
Cmty	Commentary, New York
Com	The Commonweal, New York
CR	The Contemporary Review, 1866—
	The Cornell University Library Readers' Report, Ithaca, N. Y.

PERIODICALS USED

Cnh	The Cornhill Magazine, 1860—
Crit	The Criterion, 1922-39 (title varies)
CQ	The Critical Quarterly, University of Hull, Hull, 1959—
	The Daily Telegraph
	The Dalhousie Review, Halifax, N. S., 1921—
	The Dial, Chicago, Ill., then New York
	Drama, 1919—
DM	The Dublin Magazine, Dublin, 1923—
DR	The Dublin Review, Dublin, 1936— (since 1961 The Wiseman Review, London)
Eg	The Egoist, 1914-19
	Encore, 1954—
Enc	Encounter, 1953—
Eng.	English, The Magazine of the English Association, 1936—
EJ	The English Journal, National Council of Teachers of English, Chicago, Ill., 1912— (title varies)
Eng.R.	The English Review, 1908-37 (merged with The National Review)
ES	English Studies, Amsterdam, Holland, 1919—
	Envoy, 1955—
EC	Essays in Criticism, Oxford, 1951—
Essays and Studies	Essays and Studies by Members of the English Association, Oxford, 1910— (annual)
	Ethics, Chicago, Ill., 1890—
FR	The Fortnightly Review, 1865-1934, The Fortnightly, 1934-54 (absorbed by The Contemporary Review)
	The Forum, Philadelphia, Penna., 1886-1950
	The Golden Blade, 1949—(annual)
	The Griffin, New York
G	The Guardian (see Manchester Guardian)
Hor	Horizon, 1940-50
HdR	The Hudson Review, New York
ILN	The Illustrated London News, 1842—
Irish Monthly	The Irish Monthly Magazine, Dublin, 1873—
JOL	John O'London's Weekly, 1919-54 (merged with Time and Tide)
KR	The Kenyon Review, Kenyon College, Gambier, Ohio
LL	Life and Letters, 1928-35, Life and Letters Today, 1935-50
List	The Listener, 1929— (now The Listener and BBC Television Review)
	The Living Age, Boston, Mass.

L	The London Magazine, 1954—
LM	The London Mercury, 1919-39 (merged with Life and Letters Today)
LQR	The London Quarterly Review, 1853-1931 (title changed: see next item)
LQHR	The London Quarterly and Holborn Review, 1932—
MG, G	The Manchester Guardian, Manchester, 1821— (title changed to The Guardian, 1959)
MGW	The Manchester Guardian Weekly, Manchester, 1919—
	The Mid-Century, New York
MFS	Modern Fiction Studies, Purdue University, Lafayette, Ind.
	The Month, 1863—(title varies)
NationL	The Nation, 1907-21 (merged with The Athenæum)
Nation	The Nation, New York
NA	The Nation and Athenæum, 1921-31 (merged with The New Statesman)
Nat. and Eng. R.	The National and English Review, 1937—
NR	The New Republic, Washington, D. C.
	New Saltire, Edinburgh, 1961—
NS	The New Statesman, 1913-February, 1931, June 1957—(see next item)
NSN	The New Statesman and Nation, February, 1931-June, 1957
NYEP	The New York Evening Post
NYHT	The New York Herald Tribune: Book Week, 1924— (title varies)
NYT	The New York Times Book Review
NYTts	The New York Times Theatre Section
TNY	The New Yorker
	Nimbus, 1951-58
	Nine, A Magazine of Literature and the Arts, 1950-52
NC	The Nineteenth Century, 1877-1901, then The Nineteenth Century and After, 1901-50, then see TC
Obs	The Observer, 1791—
OutL	The Outlook, a Weekly Review of Politics, Art, Literature and Finance, 1898-1928 (title varies)
Paris R.	The Paris Review, Paris, 1953—
PR	Partisan Review, New York
	Phoenix, Liverpool, 1960—
	Poetry, Chicago, Ill.

PERIODICALS USED

Poetry R.	The Poetry Review, 1912—
	The Proceedings of the British Academy, 1902— (annual)
	The Reflex, Chicago, Ill.
	The Review, 1962—
	Samhain, Dublin, 1901-8
SR	The Saturday Review of Politics, Literature, Science, and Art, 1885-1938
Sat	The Saturday Review of Literature, then The Saturday Review, New York
Scy	Scrutiny, 1932-53
SwR	The Sewanee Review, University of the South, Sewanee, Tenn.
SoR	The Southern Review, Louisiana State University, Baton Rouge, La.
Spec	The Spectator, 1828—
Strand	The Strand Magazine, 1891-1950
TA	Theatre Arts, New York
TW	Theatre World, 1925—
	Thought, Fordham University, New York
TT	Time and Tide, 1920— (incorporated John O'London's Weekly, 1954)
TL	The Times, 1785—
TLS	The Times Literary Supplement, 1902—
	Transformation, 1943-47(?)
TC	The Twentieth Century, 1951— (continuation of The Nineteenth Century and After)
TCL	Twentieth Century Literature, Denver, Colo.
VQR	The Virginia Quarterly Review, University of Virginia, Charlottesville, Va.
WHR	The Western Humanities Review, University of Utah, Salt Lake City, Utah
	The Windmill, 1944—
	The World Today, 1923-32 (continuation of *The World's Work,* 1902-22)
YR	The Yale Review, Yale University, New Haven, Conn.
YWES	The Year's Work in English Studies (English Association), 1920— (annual)

NOTE: In citations of books throughout the text, the place of publication is to be understood as London if no other place is indicated.—The abbreviation BC/Longmans, Green means: published for the British Council by Longmans, Green.

QUENNELL, PETER (1905–   )

Mr. Quennell is still a very young man, and if, as it seems to me, his two masques [*Masques and Poems*] constitute something like a *péché de jeunesse,* it is some consolation to reflect that the sinner is really young, and not a middle-aged gentleman trying to create a mild sensation. After all, a cheek is not an inelegant situation for a youthful tongue. Mr. Quennell will almost certainly regret these two masques some day. For the poems in this book he will not have the same regrets, though the verses will hardly satisfy his maturer judgement. They are fragmentary and frequently obscure, but they show that the poet has imagination and a gift of observation. Frequently he achieves an arresting phrase, as, for instance, "the divine emptiness of a keen spring sky."
I. A. Williams. LM. March, 1923, p. 543

Mr. Peter Quennell . . . has attempted the difficult task of transposing all his experience into a realm of complete symbolism. The result (as in the case of Mallarmé, who attempted the same thing in France) demands a special feat of attention on the part of the reader, and I, for one, am not sure that I know what Mr. Quennell is talking about, though he seems to be better as a craftsman and inferior in human interest to an American poet whom he considerably resembles, Mr. Hart Crane.
John Gould Fletcher. Crit. June, 1929, p. 133

Mr. Quennell, in his new critical volume, *Baudelaire and the Symbolists,* writes in an artificial and clumsy style; not beyond suspicion of "Came-the-Dawnishness." It is nonetheless a valuable series of studies; for here within a single cover are portraits of eight tragic poets whose work has deeply influenced modern literature; and the high colour and strain of Mr. Quennell's style does not deprive him of delicacy of discrimination and interpretation.
Spec. Dec. 28, 1929, p. 987

The word Phœnix suggests fire and intensity; thus Mr. Quennell's title [*The Phoenix Kind*] is unsuitable, for his novel is chilly. It is also extremely clever, sophisticated, and what an older generation would have called "thoughtful," but even the thought is reflective rather than intense. The prose has a close, flowing texture, not unlike Mr. Sachaverell Sitwell's, in which day slides into night and weeks into months, without chapter-divisions, without a change of movement or of tone, without a jar; and in this prose incidents and snatches of dialogue are embedded almost with an effect of protective colouring.

One can make any novel sound flat by giving a résumé of its plot. The point here is that the flatness is deliberate. It is inherent in the scheme of the book, whereby everything is revealed to us toned down by the sluggishness of the kindly, sickly, introspective Paul. Paul's emotions are faint, his perceptions only moderately acute, his life almost entirely vicarious. He lives Julian's life, dimly and at a distance: signs cheques for Julian to spend, goes to a party as his shadow and (his one sign of independence) gets drunk, watches him write reviews, and finally, in the same dream, takes his place upon Virginia's pillow. It is a convincing portrait. But the trouble is that there is nothing and nobody adjacent to Paul by which to measure him: Julian and Virginia are equally faint, not providing a bright background for his dusky foreground figure, but drifting in the same medium. And their love cannot burn itself out because, as Virginia herself avows, it has never burnt at all.

This, however, would not matter—a picture of futility could be moving without the introduction of a single significant character—were the reader able to detect in the writer, or in Paul, even if unknown to himself, a scale of values. Futility cannot be interesting unless there is somewhere in its neighbourhood an implied knowledge that this is not all. Mr. Quennell's talents have therefore, on this occasion, been thrown away. But it is only his first novel.

E. B. C. Jones. *Adel.* Aug., 1931, pp. 450–51

Mr. Quennell has written a book [*Byron: The Years of Fame*] which is worthy to be set beside Mr. Harold Nicolson's *Byron, The Last Journey,* and the excellent volumes of Miss Ethel Coburn Mayne. All of them are examples of what historical writing which aims at a popular audience should be: learned, yet alive—not through an artificial infusion of feeling, or through meretricious details, but because their authors have studied them with a sympathetic, yet disciplined, imagination.

. . . He tells very straightforwardly in simple, but beautifully written, English the strange story of Byron's rise to fame, of the furore that he provoked in London, of his perverse marriage and its disastrous results. Both his presentment of the personalities involved and his descriptions of their various backgrounds are excellent: yet never lacking or false in character.

. . . his book is free from the attempt to shock, to excite by disgusting or delight by horrifying, for which the life of Byron offers such an ample opportunity. . . .

It is a proof of the merit of Mr. Quennell's book that we put it down with a desire to probe further into the facts that he brilliantly analyses, and to do so with his book by our side to be perpetually used as a commentary on them.

John Sparrow. *Spec.* Oct. 18, 1935, p. 615

In writing Hogarth's life [*Hogarth's Progress*] Mr. Quennell has had a task which few will envy. Hard-working craftsmen give little scope for the biographer. All that can be told of Hogarth's affairs is contained in Austen Dobson's admirable article in the *Dictionary of National Biography*. His full-length study, which until now has held the field, is largely padding. So, indeed, inevitably, is Mr. Quennell's. The difference is that whereas Dobson's padding makes rather dull reading, Mr. Quennell's is entirely enjoyable. He knows eighteenth century London, particularly its underworld, very well indeed. Any account of Hogarth's day to day existence must be largely conjectural. Mr. Quennell has taken the occasion to give a rich, detailed conspectus of the streets and taverns, theatres and political controversies, in which Hogarth worked and from which he drew his illustrations. Often there are pages on end with no direct reference to the hero of the story, but they are vivid, elegant pages and they help us to an understanding of his art.

Evelyn Waugh. *TT*. July 9, 1955, p. 906

Mr. Quennell is all for the artifice of style; but, he says, we should not imagine that an author develops a style merely to lend additional interest to his work. Style is not clothes, but skin and muscle beneath it.

One cannot quarrel with such propaganda for mandarin literature. The point is that with such qualification, there is no longer any argument. If style really is muscle, then it is also content. And surely an artist can, according to his temperament, write in mandarin or vernacular so long as his form and content are married in significance.

Perhaps, unconsciously, Mr. Quennell is trying to tell us, by concentrating his attention on mandarin writing and ignoring the vernacular, that he doesn't like angry young men and that he appreciates good manners. Certainly his conscious and his unconscious intentions seem in conflict; for, in spite of all his sermons on style [*The Sign of the Fish*], he does not practise what he preaches. In practice he reduces good writing to good manners.

Oswell Blakeston. *JOL*. July 21, 1960, p. 83

QUILLER-COUCH, A. T. (1863–1944)

Mr. Quiller Couch was a poet before he left Clifton College. One of his poems, "Athens," was privately printed in Bodmin in 1881, and is treasured in the British Museum. It is not miraculous—not a "Blessed Damozel"—but it is remarkable work for a schoolboy. At Oxford he distinguished himself by the ingenious and spirited parodies collected (with other verses) under the title of *Green Bays* (1893). Up to this point, however, his verse denoted general literary capacity rather than specially poetic endowment. It is on his single volume of *Poems and Ballads* (1896) that his position as a poet is based, and based, I think, very firmly.

The journalist in Mr. Couch has done some injustice to the poet. It is much to be regretted that a man who can write such admirable verse should write so little. But the time that he gives to prose is not all a dead loss to poetry; for several of his short stories in *Noughts and Crosses, The Delectable Duchy,* and *Wandering Heath,* are as true poems as any in the language. My present business, however, is not with the prose poems. Whatever the compensations, one cannot but regret that Mr. Couch's verse should be so scant in quantity, for in quality it is individual and often delightful. Poetry is an art which demands more leisure and a less pre-occupied mind than Mr. Couch, I suspect, is in a position to bring to it. . . . The poet who cultivates the Muse only in his leisure moments may do good work, but scarcely great. In a word, if Mr. Couch wrote more verse he would write it still better. But for what we have received I, for my part, am truly thankful.

Along with his many qualities, Mr. Couch has two limitations. The first is a lack of metrical impulse, manifesting itself in a preference for short, staccato measures, often very cunningly woven, but lacking in swing and sonority. The second limitation is an odd one in so excellent a storyteller—several of his poems do not tell their own story, or tell it but obscurely.

William Archer. *Poets of the Younger Generation*
(John Lane, 1902), pp. 94–95

Never perhaps has Mr. Quiller Couch displayed so deep a tenderness as in this story of one of the most interesting members of the great Wesley family [*Hetty Wesley*]. How far he has used his novelist's privilege and departed from actual happenings matters not at all. His story has the haunting power of truth. It is the story of a woman's soul. With what delicate and intuitive sympathy does he penetrate into the heart of that complex personality Hetty Wesley. Here is no fancy portrait of an ideal heroine, but a woman of flesh and blood. . . . Seldom has biographer more successfully selected from the mass of material to his hands the things that really matter.

SR. Nov. 21, 1903, Supplement p. vi

It is in . . . [the] eternal spirit of youth that a great part of Q's force lies. He would not, we are sure, rob an orchard, but he feels the temptation; an apple says as much to him as it ever did. Not "the Bachelor," but the boy Q, persists, and, reinforced with the grown man's culture and experience, is able to cloud the mood of his reader till he, too, begins to recover some gleam from the "great days of the distance enchanted"; to go adventuring with the belated Sir John Constantine and his oddly assorted company; to thrill at the sight of the deserted village and the herd of masterless hogs; almost to quarrel with the author for his ruthless elimination of poor Nat Fiennes [in *Sir John Constantine*]. As adventure there has been no better story for a long time; and there is many a laugh in it too. It ends, indeed, on a pathetic note, in sorrow and regret; the adult reasserts himself. But the pathos is wholesome and dignified, the regret manly. Still, we are not quite sure that it comes with perfect fitness at the end of a fantasy, just when we are expecting those who have survived the catastrophe to "live happily ever afterwards."

Ath. Dec. 1, 1906, pp. 687–88

This summer a familiar figure has been absent from the narrow streets and quayside of the little port of Fowey. For "Q" is dead: the Mayor of "Troy Town" has gone to his rest. On 12 May Cornwall lost a most devoted son, and Cambridge a Professor of English Literature she will not lightly replace: he had filled the Edward VII Chair with distinction since those almost legendary days of Verrall in 1912. Only a few months earlier the Everyman Library had paid tribute to the blend of sound scholarship and rich humanity in his Cambridge work by adding to its shelves a volume of his lectures; and at the time of his death, at the request of the Cambridge University Press, and "very much against the grain," as he confessed, he was engaged in writing his Memoirs. Yet it is not in the restricted, if significant, academic field that "Q" primarily made his reputation—though only Professor Dover Wilson, perhaps, can really tell us of the painstaking study and care "Q" brought, over twenty years, to their joint editorship of play after play in *The New Cambridge Shakespeare* series. But the world at large knows him chiefly as the writer of those delightful and unpretentious Stevensonian novels like *Dead Man's Rock,* hilarious pen-portraits of his native Fowey like

QUILLER-COUCH, A. T.

The Astonishing History of Troy Town, and sketches and stories of his home county that have made him as surely the father of modern Cornish "regionalism" as Hardy is of that of "Wessex."

His kindly good humour, his wise and generous sympathy entered into everything he did—whether it was the encouraging of some obscure literary talent, the staging of open-air Shakespeare in some remote Cornish village, or his daily intercourse with the seafaring folk of Fowey where he was both Harbourmaster and Mayor. He knew and talked to everyone in the little town, entered into all its activities, and was universally beloved. And it is just that breadth of vision, that catholicity of interest, that makes others of us mourn one of the soundest critics of his time.

I am not primarily referring to *The Oxford Book of English Verse,* by common consent the greatest major anthology in our tongue; nor to the infinitely harder task (compare the failures!) so excellently accomplished in *The Oxford Book of English Prose,* but to those successive little green volumes that came to us from the Cambridge Press— the "cheap editions" of *The Art of Writing, The Art of Reading, Shakespeare's Workmanship,* the three series of *Studies in Literature,* and similar works which have given to a wider world than is usually privileged to share such things the cream of his Cambridge and other lectures over the last thirty years. The thing which distinguishes the critical work of Quiller-Couch is neither a deep originality nor an aptitude to avail himself of the latest discoveries of psychological research: his *Shakespeare's Workmanship,* for example, contains few of Bradley's brilliant psychological guesses about the plays—brilliant because we feel them to be intuitively right—but he is a safer guide in that world for which Shakespeare primarily wrote: the theatre. His criticism is rather the result of a selective sensitivity applied to his wide range of reading: there seems no age except the Anglo-Saxon, and to a lesser degree the eighteenth century, in which he is not readily at home. The catholicity within his circumscribed selection is astonishing; the fewness of his prejudices remarkable.

Hermann Peschmann. *Eng.* Autumn, 1944, pp. 85–86

Sir Arthur Quiller-Couch reluctantly consented at last to write his life, but unfortunately too late to complete it. S. C. Roberts does something to supply the lack of the later years in *Memories and Opinions* [*an Unfinished Autobiography by Q,* ed. with an introd. by S. C. Roberts] and in his Introduction writes with great sympathy of Q's work in Cambridge. . . . Q's reminiscences of Cornwall, Clifton, and Oxford, are written with his usual happy blend of humour and sentiment.

Ethel Seaton. *YWES,* 1944, p. 21

It would have been unfitting if he had died anywhere but in Cornwall, for he loved the county of his birth so much, absorbed its spirit so fully and wrote about it so extensively that his name and the name of Cornwall can never be separated.

Yet his was no narrow county feeling. His devotion to Cornwall was in fact the foundation of an equal devotion to his country. He loved the history, the scenery, the institutions and the people of England as much as he loved its language and its literature, even though it was for his devotion to these last two that his name became known throughout the world. . . .

Q's steadfast championship of humanity and the spiritual world in an age when both were being repeatedly attacked was the inevitable outcome of his chivalrous nature. It is a significant fact that his own favourite among all his novels was *Sir John Constantine,* the hero of which is a Cornish knight-errant of the eighteenth century. "If," he says in his preface, "you would know anything of the writer who has so often addressed you under an initial, you may find as much of him here as in any of his books"; and anyone who knew Q can scarcely fail to see that in Sir John Constantine he drew a portrait of himself as he would have liked to be.

No more appropriate honour could have been conferred on him than the knighthood that he received in 1910. Consciously or unconsciously, he was actuated all his life by the principles of knighthood as they had been laid down by medieval theorists, even if theory in the Middle Ages remained untranslated into fact as often as not—the principles, that is to say, of loyalty, of courtesy, of defending the right, of helping the weak and the oppressed. Those who knew him can recall numerous instances of his quiet but life-long devotion to these principles. Others can find it scattered throughout his writings. It runs, for instance, right through *Major Vigoureux,* through his *Memories and Opinions,* and through innumerable short stories, such as "The Spinster's Maying," "The Paupers," "Colonel Baigent's Christmas," and "Corporal Sam." His chivalrous heroes are frequently poor people. That was characteristic of Q: he was not one of those who imagine that chivalry cannot exist apart from money or high social position. None of his characters has more of the knight-errant in him than the unlettered Corporal Sam, who knowingly throws away his life to avenge the honour of a poor Spanish woman whom he had never seen alive.

Fred Brittain. *Arthur Quiller-Couch; a Biographical Study of Q* (Cambridge Univ. Pr., 1948), pp. 156–57

RAINE, KATHLEEN (1908–   )

Only the greatest pantheistic verse is able to resolve discordant forms within the magic retorts of art. This calibre the work of Kathleen Raine does not possess.

In a somewhat like fashion her mystical poems too often appear to lack that double discipline—that twin concentration—of thought and speech. Her subject swallows her up, and then her verse loses shape; is engulfed in waves of feeling. But now and again Kathleen Raine has her triumphs: poetic statements that seem to appeal as much by their poignant naturalness as by any earnestly laboured at.

Derek Stanford. The Freedom of Poetry
(Falcon Press, 1947), p. 223

Kathleen Raine is precise even in her mysticism, delicate in her choice of words. In her little book, *The Year One,* she showed signs of escaping from a quasi-mysticism which seemed likely to sterilize her poetry, and in coming down to earth she gained in force and attractiveness.

R. A. Scott-James. Fifty Years of English Literature:
1900-1950 (Longmans, 1951), p. 252

There is only one cause for regret at the appearance of Kathleen Raine's *Collected Poems*—that it is given to us after three or four years' silence instead of a book of new work. . . .

To re-read the poetry in its chronological sequence as here presented, is to be confirmed in admiration at its integrity, purity and musical beauty. Essentially it has not changed: the symbols drawn from Nature ("who is always in the Year One") appear throughout—only the symbol of the angel, which was once powerful, practically disappears, presumably because it is the product of "fallen man," whom Miss Raine has somewhat scornfully discarded as a subject for her poetry. More superficial differences can be traced to the influence of her reading at one time or another—Jung perhaps giving place to Graves, Blake recurring throughout, with sometimes too plain an influence on the style. The latest work does not surpass the best of *Stone and Flower*—perhaps indeed there are now fewer of the pregnant single lines for which she is remarkable, such as, "It is not birds that speak, but men learn silence—" but the work is of more even quality. There were times in the earlier books when her use of words like *eternity* in an emotive rather than an intellectual way, and her reliance on much-worn symbols, such as that of the rose, without revivifying them, led to vagueness, even to sentimentality. It is still occasionally true that the actual words do not carry all that they are meant to convey. . . . Yet as always with the language of true vision, it seems that no conscious attention to technique could have produced better workmanship: her ear is impeccable, and the form of each poem seems unobtrusively right. She uses the blank verse line with a sure instinct. . . .

Anne Ridler. L. June, 1956, pp. 83–84

RATTIGAN, TERENCE (1911–)

Few people, unless they are theatrical historians with their oddly-stacked jackdaw-minds, will remember a play called *First Episode*. It was written by two Oxford undergraduates. It had a short run at the Comedy Theatre during the early 'thirties and passed into darkness. Today it ought to be remembered because it was the First Episode in the stage life of Terence Rattigan, the young man who is now one of the most commercially successful dramatists in Britain.

"Commercially successful" is an embarrassing, slightly snobbish phrase. There is an overtone of distaste. It hints that a dramatist with this kind of success has no real right to his fame: he is a mayfly, and the great writers of the future are to be discovered in cellars off the Strand or in teacup-theatres near Notting Hill. Anyone with that idea must find Rattigan troublesome. He is a commercially successful dramatist who has written good plays. So, for that matter, have Noel Coward, Somerset Maugham, and a line of other dramatists with the misfortune to win commercial success.

I mention Coward and Maugham first of all because Rattigan is still nearer to them than to any other writers. He is now thirty-nine years of age. He was educated at Harrow and Trinity College, Oxford; his father had been acting High Commissioner in Turkey and British Minister in Rumania: it seemed certain that Terence Rattigan would become a diplomatist. He did not; but we can see from the farce of *French Without Tears* and an amusing few moments at the opening of *Who Is Sylvia?*—that is, at both ends of his theatrical span—that diplomacy can still aid him as a dramatist even if he evaded it neatly as a career. . . .

Until 1942 Rattigan was still the author of *French Without Tears* and not much else, though we can find in his record the titles of at least three other plays that, like *First Episode,* are now all but forgotten. Then *Flare Path* arrived in the summer of 1942. . . .

So to *The Winslow Boy* (1946), which some hold to be the dramatist's best play. There must always be dissension between its supporters and others who back *The Browning Version*. . . .

What would Rattigan do next? *The Winslow Boy* ran for more than a year. It was two years before the dramatist returned to the stage. When he did it was with the daring experiment of a double bill: two plays, each in a long single act of the unfashionable length of about an hour. The first of them, *The Browning Version,* was again something that Rattigan had never tried before. He had written a pair of farces, a light comedy, and two strong dramas very different in their treatment. And now *The Browning Version,* as grim a study in psychology as the stage had known for years. It is not one of those carefully-carpentered school stories about a Mr. Chips. By no means. Crocker-Harris, who is retiring, is a failure in his profession as in his marriage. He has nothing of an Old Master's benign varnish: rather, he is like some barbed and rusty wire ready to be destroyed. His wife, at the limit of her resources, is a despicable figure. The conflict between the two has an extraordinary tension. Rattigan's theme might have spluttered thinly across a full evening; in its single charged act every line seems to detonate. . . .

When we have been through a record of fifteen years, there is no need to hunt for elaborate inferences. The plain facts are that Rattigan is a highly successful commercial dramatist; that he knows how to work in all moods; that he is steadily increasing his range; and that, in his failures as in his triumphs, he shows always a sense of the theatre and a gift for persuasive dialogue to serve him well in years ahead. He knows, none better, how to get on the right side of an audience. We may well say that, even if he turned his gaze from the Foreign Office, he is now at the head and front of the Diplomatic Service in the British theatre.

J. C. Trewin. *Adel.* May, 1951, pp. 222–28

Reading Terence Rattigan's ten collected plays is an experience not unlike reclining on the bank of a suavely trickling stream in hot weather. One basks, stretches, is lulled by the swift, interminable, murmur; one's reflexes are neutralised, and life pauses. Except when, at long intervals, the roar of a distant waterfall obtrudes, one's pleasure is negative, derived wholly from that marketable quality known to cynics as ingratiation and to romantics as charm.

It is a charm closely related to that of Bing Crosby, in that it looks deceptively, guilelessly imitable; indeed, it would not be too unfair to call Rattigan the bathtub baritone of the drama. So steadily does he aim to please that in his whole *oeuvre* there is but one "unpleasant" character—the rapacious Mrs. Crocker-Harris in *The Browning Version,* which stands beside the first two acts of *The Deep Blue Sea* as his most impressive work for the theatre. Elsewhere the negative virtues predominate: tact, understatement, avoidance of cliché—the hallmarks, in fact, of the "gentleman code" which holds so much of West End playwrighting in curious thrall. [1954]

Kenneth Tynan. *Curtains* (N.Y., Atheneum, 1961), p. 74

Terence Rattigan keeps trembling on the edge of the really good, and then spoiling it all. He did this in *The Deep Blue Sea,* and in *Separate Tables;* he has done it again in *Variations on a Theme.* . . . The theme is very broadly that of *The Lady of the Camellias.* His heroine, Rose Fish, is a modern courtesan. . . . Since Mr. Rattigan is not the man to take shelter behind the skirts of a club theatre, he has been forced to treat his variations with a certain reserve, not to say timidity; but his portrait of Rose Fish is a full and fond one. . . .

J. W. Lambert. *Drama.* Autumn, 1958, p. 20

Now England's most successful, and perhaps most skillful, playwright presents T. E. Lawrence [*Ross*] to this new generation. What will they make of him and his legend? Mr. Rattigan has done his best to show, within the limits of his medium, the extreme complexity of Lawrence's accidie of spirit. It is to be hoped that his audience will not interpret this as a study of an angry young man soured by success who found a negative solace in cynicism after a traumatic experience in a Turkish guardroom. But that is probably too uninteresting an image to grow into a myth, too uninteresting and above all too old-fashioned. On the other hand there is another *Hero of Our Time* whose lineaments seem to be vaguely outlined in Terence Rattigan's character, a *purely* negative figure, the man whose claim to our attention is not what he does, not what he is, but what he doesn't and isn't, the anti-hero. It would indeed be paradoxical if Lawrence of Arabia should appeal to a new generation as a military, social, and sexual failure pure and simple, a sort of Colonel Beckett-Godot. But why not?

Constantine FitzGibbon. *Enc.* Nov., 1960, p. 56

The picture of Terence Rattigan as the prototype of the old school—the school of the nineteen-thirties drawingroom comedy, of elegant flippancy and everything detested by the new school of Osborne, Wesker, Pinter and company—is too good to be true.

The fact is that, in 27 years, Mr. Rattigan has written 16 plays (only 3 of them in the thirties) of which 9 have not been comedies at all. In the decade since his occasional piece for the Coronation—*The Sleeping Prince*—he has written no comedies. His two principal creations in that period, *Separate Tables* and *Ross,* were wholly serious, and his latest, *Man and Boy,* he describes as "very black, indeed". . . .

Mr. Rattigan defends vigorously the right of the playwright to seek the largest audience possible, so long as he does not pander. He does not believe in minority plays. "The minority play is simply the one that cannot fill the theater."

Ten years ago, in a preface to a volume of his plays, he invented "Aunt Edna," who has been with him ever since. She is the audience norm, not a matinee matron (as she has sometimes been misinterpreted) but the middle-brow theatrelover who is essential to the theater's continued existence. Today, he says, "Aunt Edna" hasn't changed. She goes to the Royal Court (headquarters of the new school of theater), and she likes a lot of what goes on there. She doesn't mind being mystified—she wants not to know what's coming next—but she refuses to be baffled. She gladly accepts that she has to do some interpreting for herself, but bafflement has no satisfactions—it is simply the failure of the author to communicate and she rejects it.

"She will still enjoy a French-windows play if it is good. But I'll bet that at the new National Theatre's *Hamlet* you'll find her side by side with the sweaters and blue jeans, and they'll be both leaning forward intently at the same moments. The point about Aunt Edna is that she adores the theater and usually what she likes is good."

Stephen Watts. *NYT ts.* Nov. 10, 1963, p. 5

READ, HERBERT (1893–   )

Last year Mr. Richards, a psychologist, presented his *Principles of Literary Criticism* to the literary world as (in his own words) a machine to think with. Hardly have we cranked it up when Mr. Herbert Read, an intellectual poet and a convert to the psychological method, arrives, and takes the machine for a few trial runs over the field of literary criticism.

It will hardly be denied even by those who have the bitterest objections to calling in Freud or Jung to hold the ring at literary rows that in *Reason and Romanticism* Mr. Read makes his machine work. These essays are austere, learned, compact, and brief. There is here no easy floating on the tide of emotional appreciation to nowhere in particular. The writing is as scientifically precise as the union between a science and an art will allow. When Mr. Read is driven to use one of the really soiled coins of critical currency, such as "imagination" in reference to Charlotte Brontë, he turns it out fresh from his psychological mint. This virtue, and the unwonted amount of intellectual labour he must do to keep up with Mr. Read at all, make hard going for the unwary reader. Sometimes Mr. Read definitely overloads his machine. There is a limit to the amount of intellectual territory that can profitably be covered in thirty pages.

NA. Aug. 7, 1926, p. 532

Mr. Read is an anti-Romantic and a champion of the intellectual revival. He would like criticism to become less emotional and more scientific. He regards St. Thomas Aquinas as the greatest representative of European thought and professes an adoration for the leader of the French Thomists, M. Maritain. . . . When on concreter ground, Mr. Read (especially in the essay on the Brontës [*Reason and Romanticism*]) shows himself a genuine and subtle critic, but the whole book is written in an exasperatingly obscure manner, giving the impression that the principal things are left unsaid.

D. S. Mirsky. *LM.* Nov., 1926, p. 101

Mr. Read marches with his pack of scientific implements clean over the frontier between Prose and Poetry, with small attention to the traditions prevailing there, and without a sign, beyond a bow to Aristotle, that he recognises how many of his predecessors have been detained at that juncture for the better part of their lives. He says nothing binding until he is safely planted among undeniable prose specimens, and his atitude then, for nine chapters, is that of Dr. Johnson before the stone at Harwich. Prose is what he shows us chunks of; that glint over the horizon may or may not be Poetry. As for Style, he has chosen the chunks he shows us particularly to illustrate the subject. He grinds, magnifies and pronounces upon a number of these in each sort and then leaves us alone with others to do our own assaying. In fact, he has compiled an anthology of English prose to illustrate its main varieties in Style, good and bad, from Wycliffe to Joyce, and has kept up between the extracts a running and cumulative exposition of a method of classification and appraisal. The result is a grammar of pure and inspired English usage. No one previously appears to have got far enough past the delights and exasperations of the frontier-barriers even to perceive that such a work might be possible—except "Vernon Lee," from whom little touching this matter has been completely hidden. . . . It is clear that Mr. Read was driven into the writing of his book [*English Prose Style*] by what, speaking of Henry James, he calls "a sacred rage." He is reverent before the mystery of the written and combined word in all its aspects; but it is the reverence of the scientist and not that of the high-priest. . . . His own embodying prose is carefully and deliberately dull. There is no doubt that the dullness, or rather the abstraction that gives rise to it, is intentional. Nobody could accuse Mr. Read's poetry of being dull or indistinct, or his mind of working ponderously either, when once his words have been pierced and one has come at it. And every now and then, when he is announcing results from the very thick of a job, there is nothing but vitality in his style. But often during the longer movements, when he is gathering the materials for a definition or making a deliberate pronouncement point by point, one is vaguely reminded on the surface of Wordsworth obeying a preface.

E. G. Twitchett. *LM*. Sept., 1928, pp. 508–9, 511

If any art criticism can fairly be called initiation, Herbert Read's *Art Now* can be. What Herbert Read does in effect is to assert the value of "modern" art and to provide fascinating theories and vocabularies with which you can rationalize your enthusiasm for it if you happen to accept his view or agree with him already. At no point throughout the book does he relate his enjoyment to any visible part of any picture. Instead we are given a haze of intellectual theory whose main effect on a docile reader will be to make him feel comfortable with a new fashion in painting without ever having to come face to face with the pictures and commit himself to a direct response.

It is best to admit at once that no one can state finally where the "direct response" ends, at what point the theory behind painting becomes irrelevant, or how much exactly is "visible" in a picture. It would be some help if art critics even recognized the existence of these problems. But few people will doubt that in *Art Now* the connection between the theories (whatever we may think of them) and the pictures has become altogether too tenuous.

J. M. Harding and D. W. Harding.
Scy. Dec., 1933, p. 394

In reviewing Mr. Herbert Read [*A World Within a War*] I am conscious of two worlds warring within his breast, and I am tempted to take sides in this struggle. One of these worlds is very close to Edmund Blunden. There is much in Mr. Read of the quiet observer of nature who relates his experience of the millstream and the "wild-bird's voice" to his books. After reading Blunden, much of *A World Within a War* reads like notes for a Blunden poem. . . . Probably this volume of Mr. Read's is a transitional one in which he is turning to rhyme and music, and also to the integrity of his "innocent eye." There are certainly things of beauty in it: notably the poems of the Spanish War, "The Third," "Summer Rain" and "The Labyrinth." One of the curious limitations of Mr. Read is that he cannot think and argue in poetry. What he can do is observe and illustrate. The poems in which he is dispassionately observing nature or illustrating an idea or a feeling are successful. Where he tries to sustain an argument he fails and is reduced to what appear to be lapses into a mystical faith in beauty. If Mr. Read believes that the realisation of the intrinsic nature of the self and of nature and of poetic beauty is the answer to destruction, it is not quite easy to see why he often argues so ideologically. . . . Here I think there is something unresolved in Mr. Read's philosophy. These poems seem to have emphasised this problem, and I should expect his next volume to be very different from this one.

Stephen Spender. *NSN*. Jan. 13, 1945, pp. 29–30

When Mr. Read, writing of his youth, remarks that "in a few years there was scarcely any poem of any worth in my own language which I had not read"; when he writes of religion in a few dogmatic sentences as the phantasy of an after-life conceived in the fear of death, we have travelled a long way with him—too far—from the objective light of childhood. . . .

We have travelled too far, but we should never have known without *The Innocent Eye* quite how far we had travelled. That is the astounding thing—Mr. Read was able to go back, back from the intellectual atmosphere personified in Freud, Bergson, Croce, Dewey, Vivante, Scheller . . . And if we examine his work there have always been phases when he has returned: the creative spirit has been more than usually separated in his case from the critical mind. (He admits himself in one essay that submitting to the creative impulse he has written poetry which owes nothing to his critical theories.) The critic, one feels, has sometimes been at pains to adopt the latest psychological theories before they have proved their validity. But the creative spirit has remained tied to innocence. . . . In future there was to be no future: as a critic he was to be sometimes pantingly contemporary, and when he was most an artist he was to be furthest removed from his time.

"When most an artist": we are not permanently interested in any other aspect of Mr. Read's work. Anarchism means more to him than it will ever mean to his readers (in spite of that vigorous and sometimes deeply moving book, *Poetry and Anarchism*)—sometimes we suspect that it means little more to him than an attempt to show his Marxist critics that he too is a political animal, to give a kind of practical everyday expression to the "sense of glory" which has served him ever since youth in place of a religious faith; and I cannot share his belief that criticism with the help of Freud will become a science, and a critical opinion have the universality of a scientific law. As an artist he will be assessed, it seems to me, by *The Innocent Eye,* by his only novel, *The Green Child,* by a few poems— notably "The End of a War," by his study of Wordsworth, informed as it is by so personal a passion that it is lifted out of the category of criticism ("we both spring from the same yeoman stock of the Yorkshire dales, and I think I have a certain "empathetic" understanding of his personality which gives a sense of betrayal to anything I write about him"), and some scattered essays in which, too, the note of "betrayal" is evident—the essays on Froissart, Malory and Vauvenargues in particular.

It is that author with whom we wish to dwell—however much lip service we may pay to books like *Art and Society, Art Now, Art and Industry* and the rest—the author who describes himself: "In spite of my intellectual pretensions, I am by birth and tradition a peasant." Even his political thought at its most appealing comes back to that sense of soil, is tethered to the Yorkshire farm—"real politics are local politics." The result of separating Mr. Read's creative from his critical work has an odd effect—there is colour, warmth, glow, the passion which surrounds the "sense of glory," and we seem far removed from the rather dry critic with his eyes fixed on the distinctions between the ego and the id.

Graham Greene. *The Lost Childhood* (N.Y., Viking, 1951), pp. 138–39

We should remember that behind the involved, complex, highly theoretical and sometimes dry manner of Herbert Read, educationist, President of the I.C.A. and proud apologist for everything that he thinks to be *avant-garde*, there is the sensibility of a most delicate, often moving poet. . . . If he is over-tolerant towards nonsense, it is because he credits everyone with his own sincerity. If he words his bitter attacks on the nature of our society and culture mildly, it is because he considers he can thus achieve more for the ideals he believes in than by being a Jeremiah. Naive? No, innocent; despite the scholarly quotations, the aloofness of manner, the public honours, he has preserved his belief in his duty, if not all his faith in the success, of working for "the ultimate harmony of the world."

We should value Herbert Read because he asks questions which most of us in our narrowness or complacency wrongly consider answered.

John Berger. *NSN*. Nov. 26, 1955, p. 714

A distinguished teacher and critic, a man always in advance of the ideas of his time, Sir Herbert has written prolifically and memorably on art, aesthetics, education, politics and sociology as well as on literature. He has brought the same restless energy and sincerity to the poetry he has been publishing since the First World War (see "The Mutations of the Phoenix," and "The End of a War" which W. B. Yeats included in the *Oxford Book of Modern Verse*). Yet for all his hard work and seriousness Sir Herbert has, but for a handful of poems, always seemed more of a thinker expressing himself in verse than a true poet. . . . Only in the long title poem of *Moon's Farm* (originally written for broadcasting and therefore rather flat on the page) does Sir Herbert seem to approach the attractive simplicity of his best work.

Geoffrey Moore. *Poetry Today* (BC/Longmans, 1958), pp. 20–21

Not only the title poem, but the other work in *Moon's Farm* stands as caution to others like myself who had supposed that the foundations for an advance beyond the achievement of the *Collected Poems* (1945) hardly existed. For this reason I let my earlier paragraphs stand, but revise the judgement to the extent of now happily believing that this man, gathering strength from his "return" to the sources of strength, but now equipped with the riches of experiences gained in time, so that he may hold "dialogue" with them, is in a position to develop a vein of philosophical poetry of a kind peculiarly interesting, the more so since it is a vein in which English poetry is generally deficient. Recent poems published in periodicals support this. . . .

When successful as a poet, Read has satisfied his instinct for making the form of each poem the manifestation of the meaning it communicates. The continually advanced, and expanded, theory of poetic form in his literary criticism has thus an empirical basis.

An early major statement, *Form in Modern Poetry,* was published as far back as 1932. We can now see it to have been a bold piece of writing whose main conclusions have been assumed into subsequent critical thought.

In that essay he first thoroughly established for himself an identifiable critical position, and makes it clear that the two authorities on whom he is mainly to depend are the Coleridge of the *Biographia Literaria* and the Keats of the *Letters*. . . . But in addition to Coleridge and Keats there were the possibilities inherent in modern psychology. Read, by an act of co-adunation (to use Coleridge's word), was to make the postulates of this new science support and fertilize his thinking as a literary critic. He has been profoundly affected by Jung. . . .

And here is the place to remark briefly on Herbert Read's single play, *The Parliament of Women* (published in a limited edition, 1961).

Possibly it will never become widely known, but, widely known or not, it is of extreme interest to the student of Read, for here the themes and principles informing his writings on aesthetics, social politics and education are applied to—or inform—an episode in the history of Greece in the twelfth century. Partly in prose and partly in verse, it deserves a performance before its worth is realized. One ought to be able to say this of any play, but it is perhaps particularly true here because the dramatist here is a leading theorist of the visual and plastic arts, and a sensibility long trained to re-act to pictorial composition governs the groupings and scene designs of this play.

Francis Berry. *Herbert Read* (B/C Longmans, rev. 1961), pp. 28–29

Some of the material here assembled [*The Contrary Experience*] has been published before—the opening section, the boyhood memories of life on a farm in the North Riding, and the third section, with its famous war pieces, the raid and the retreat from Saint Quentin. The second part, a war diary extracted from letters home, appears for the first time, as does the last, a disquisition on the history and topography of Stonegrave: for in 1949 Sir Herbert returned to live in the country of his childhood. . . . The result is one of the most impressive and satisfying books Sir Herbert has written. His prose has a moorland strength, its contours clear and firm, yet the mists creep in suddenly, as in the prose and landscapes of the great English romantics who are his mentors. . . .

Sir Herbert recalls the prophets and thinkers who have helped to form his mind—Ruskin, Freud, James, Coleridge, Kierkegaard, Croce, Kropotkin, Sorel. . . . He has always been in the cultural vanguard, yet in this book he romanticises the sense of the past. It is the antiquary not the aesthetician who here has the last word, the English poets not the international revolutionaries who inspire the eloquent attack on modern life and the passionate celebration of nature.

Like all the steps Sir Herbert has taken this one is both carefully reasoned and deeply felt, and if one has sometimes had doubts about where he was leading us in the past, one has none now.

K. W. Gransden. *MGW*. May 30, 1963, p. 11

REID, FORREST (1876–1947)

To call Mr. Forrest Reid the novelist of this region would give a false idea of his art, for he is only concerned incidentally with topography. But it does so happen that most of his scenes take place in or near Belfast and that his art itself contains the two elements indicated above: there is squalor and there is beauty, and both of them are haunted. Haunted by what? It would take some time to answer the question. Certainly not by fairies ninety miles high. But in nearly every chapter, if we look closely, there are hints of that indwelling power seen, sometimes clearly, sometimes remotely. Despite the realism of his method and the prevalence of football matches, razor-strops, and all that, we are conscious of an underlying note that is sometimes sinister and always sad. . . . Behind vulgarity, as behind rarity, there is a presence—of what kind and blending into what Mr. Reid does not choose to say.

Over this profound and equivocal background is stretched a world that bears sufficient resemblance to the present to solace a novel-reading public. It is not the present world, if only for the predominance given in it to youth. Few of the protagonists have seen eighteen summers, while their elders exist mainly as sympathizers, tyrants, and choruses. . . . The author believes that a man's great decisions and experiences occur in boyhood, and that his subsequent career is of little more than recollection—a belief which . . . has significance in his own literary development. Here one must note that this belief necessarily restricts his canvas as a novelist and that, regarded as a transcript of human activities, his novels are a failure. They cover too small a field. . . . They must be classed not as transcripts but as visions before they can be appreciated, and their vision is that of the hierophant who sees what lies behind objects rather than what lies between them, and who is not interested in the pageants of society or history. . . .

More important than the realism is the strong ethical tendency. Questions of loyalty, courage, chastity, and personal decency, are always occurring; indeed, the author tells us that the highest beauty he knows is "a kind of moral fragrance." Such a fragrance is rooted, however remotely, in Christianity and the books approach nearer to the Gospel spirit than appears on the first reading. Complementary to moral fragrance is the odour of sin, and here (perhaps one is stupid or callous) one feels that Mr. Reid makes too much fuss; he is almost as much upset by sin as Nathaniel Hawthorne. He never preaches, he is never puritanical. But he is always a puritan, and he regards it as of absolute and eternal importance that youth should reach maturity unscathed. . . .

His two best novels, *The Bracknells* and *Following Darkness,* probably neighbour some spiritual experience into which the "supernatural," as we crudely call it, entered. They are intensely passionate beneath their surface calm. . . . He is always harking back to some lonely garden or sombre grove, to some deserted house whose entrance is indeed narrow but whose passages stretch to infinity, and when his genius gains the recognition that has so strangely been withheld from it, he will be ranked with the artists who have preferred to see life steadily rather than to see it whole, and who have concentrated their regard upon a single point which Mr. Reid's new novel [*Peter Waring*] has been fashioned—with landscape intelligible. [1919]

E. M. Forster. *Abinger Harvest* (Edward Arnold, 1936), pp. 93–98

A great many years ago a critic compared *Following Darkness*—from which Mr. Reid's new novel [*Peter Waring*] has been fashioned—with *Wuthering Heights*. If the comparison is sound, a change in kind has occurred since Mr. Reid's revision, for *Peter Waring's* ancestry, like that of so much Irish fiction, is in Turgenev's Russia. The story is a typical Turgenev study of very young love, but the early morning mist which sparkles in the background of all such stories in Turgenev is here deprived of its erotic languor by the severe puritan idealism and athleticism of the County Down. There is no living writer in English who can describe growing boyhood as Mr. Forrest Reid does. The puritan childhood is a delicate history of the constant adjustments of constraint and natural passion, and Mr. Reid knows every one of them; his success springs from the fact that he has the kind of sensibility which this knowledge presupposes, and that he avoids the common danger of letting his sensibility outrun the sensibility of his characters. . . . I see only two dubious things in the book: the character of Peter's patroness who is shadowy, and a hint of spookiness here and there. Mr. Reid has always had this preoccupation. One meets it often in Irish writers and with him it is subdued. But the rest is austere, real, delicate and yet firm, free from the more facile kinds of nostalgia, and the maladies of sensibility.

V. S. Pritchett. *NSN.* Sept. 11, 1937, p. 377

Whatever that battered term, *artist,* fully and truly means—shorn, that is, of the so-called "artistic temperament" (an easy refuge) and all pretentiousness and pose—*that* Forrest Reid *was.* We both loved—an excellent thing in moderation—talking shop. And a remarkable shop it is—with the strangest contents—that has Literature inscribed over its window! There lurked, too, beyond the shop itself, and well beyond the till and the invoices, the shop-parlour; where his genius looked after the fire, and his candour cleaned the windows. And beyond *that,* the small walled old garden, with its whitethorn and willows and yew, and its twisted orchard, which had been familiar to him since his earliest years, and whose memories haunt one of his last and of the loveliest and wisest of his books, *The Milk of Paradise.*

Walter de la Mare in *Forrest Reid Memorial* (Foxton, Eng., Burlington Press, 1952), pp. 7–8

Since Forrest Reid died some of the younger writers here have tended rather to talk down his work. They say he doesn't write about life as it is in Ulster. They speak as if all that is graceful and beautiful in literature were unrealistic, escapist.

There is, of course, a sordid side to Ulster life. Forrest Reid dealt with it in *Peter Waring, The Bracknels, At the Door of the Gate*. The fact that he writes about it in beautiful, rhythmic prose only makes his illumination of it more clear. His fault from their point of view is that he saw the other side as well. There was and *is* another side and surely it is for that other side we should prefer to be remembered.

Forrest Reid himself said that his field was narrow and in so doing put a weapon into the hands of his detractors. It is quite true that he took the subjects of most—though not all—of his novels from a narrow field, but the curious thing is that if you really examine these novels you find vividly portrayed typical Ulster characters in great variety. He is most at home with middle classes, from the lowest of the lower middle classes to the two peaks of the upper middle class—immensely rich business people and lapsed aristocrats. He knew them through and through, and though many of his best characters are only incidental to the stories he is telling, they are all completely there—as solid and alive as any characters in the works of any novelist. He wasn't so good with manual workers: they tend to be seen from one side only—from above—and in the same way he saw the aristocracy—if he saw it at all —from below.

Some people have found it strange that Forrest Reid, who had strong spiritual affinities with Ancient Greece and Renaissance Italy, should have appeared and lived in modern Belfast. To me it doesn't seem at all strange because Belfast to-day has a lot in common with the cities of Ancient Greece and Renaissance Italy.

Stephen Gilbert in *Forrest Reid Memorial*
(Foxton, Eng., Burlington Press, 1952), pp. 11–12

Forrest Reid's position as a critic was almost as unique as the place he made for himself by his novels.

It was not such an important position, but its implications are quite as interesting. His standpoint was one very rarely met with today, because he subjected everything he read to the test of his own personal sensibility. For the schools of "applied" literary criticism so fashionable today he had little use; an approach to literature that ignored the flame of beauty which must burn at the heart of all genuinely imaginative writing was of no interest or significance for him; he passed it by. "As I am always preaching, the mind behind the work is what really matters, what makes that work sympathetic or just the opposite. Cleverness in itself is nothing." Nor was mere truth to life enough; to be memorable the writer's work had to be infused with something deeper than accuracy of observation, important though this was, and with something more sustained than technical virtuosity. "If fiction is to be an art I think it must be more than mere realistic reporting, must be a source of inspiration, emotion, vision. . . . Nobody, I dare say, found beauty in the monotonous dripping of rain till Verlaine wrote his poem about it, nobody found beauty in fogs until Whistler painted them." An imaginative work, he believed, "if it is to be first-rate, must possess three qualities—beauty of subject, beauty of treatment, beauty of writing."

Beauty there had to be; otherwise there could be no art. To care for art for its own sake was, after all, only to care for the beauty which that art enshrined. Art for art's sake—abused in practice as the phrase had become—meant art for beauty's sake, no more and no less; and the pursuit of poetry for its own sake was "the pursuit both of truth and of goodness," for, in Andrew Bradley's words, "wherever the imagination is satisfied, there, if we had a knowledge we have not, we should discover no idle fancy but the image of a truth."

Such a view of literature must have its limitations, but the limitations it imposes are self-limitations, and what is lost in breadth has its compensations in deeper insight and sympathy. This he recognized himself, for after all, as he pointed out, "the personal appeal in poetry is everything, because without it, for the particular reader concerned, there *is* no poetry." (*The Milk of Paradise,* p. 7). Here for him was the crux of the whole matter: the critic was only qualified to judge a work of art—as a work of art—if he could feel it on his pulses. That was the final test.

Roger Burlingham. *Forrest Reid*
(Faber and Faber, 1953), pp. 182–83

RICHARDS, I. A. (1893–   )

It seems a little anomalous that Mr. I. A. Richards, that least academic of critical writers, should be set pedagogically aloft on the strength of his *Principles of Literary Criticism* as something between headmaster and chief consulting engineer of the modern scientific school of critics. For it happens that in this country scientific criticism has been unavoidably identified with the claims of a narrower classicism while it would not be amiss or unjustifiable to suggest that Mr. Richards has more in common with the neo-romanticism of Mr. Middleton Murry than with the neo-Catholic classicism of Mr. Eliot upon the one hand and Mr.

Wyndham Lewis on the other. The fact is that in a world of writers who strive to be intellectually honest to the last degree Mr. Richards has restricted recognition and appreciation of what he stands for by the very completeness of his own integrity. Too many, approving or opposing, have sought to label him the critical equivalent of atheist, whereas he is that even rarer figure, the true critical agnostic, essentially not denying but only refusing to affirm beyond the scope of his actual knowledge, and intent in an age increasingly agnostic in temper upon the urgent and truly critical task of erecting a scheme of values dependent not upon some heaven-born inspiration (at whatever distant remove), but springing directly from and constantly returning to the individual in his own common experience. Since what he sought was a purely psychological account of value, he had necessarily to accept the restriction of the subject to a field available to psychological analysis. He himself has always been at pains to stress this essential limitation, and to point out that his results appeared somewhat negative in effect is not at all to impeach their validity so far as they went. He had settled his terms of reference, and to move beyond them could only be to defeat his own aims.

In point of fact *Principles of Literary Criticism* had an effect of being a limiting work because it did not sufficiently define its limits. *Practical Criticism,* on the other hand, recognizes its limits clearly and specifically, and so is not limiting. The new volume, though in some ways less fundamental than its forerunner (in that it largely seeks to apply the principles there originated), in other respects seems more so, and therefore perhaps the more valuable of the two. Mr. Richards has never assumed the rationality of reality, or assumed rational thought to be the sole instrument of apprehension, but what makes this later work especially notable is his explicit recognition that the emotional world of feelings and attitudes is neither rational nor subject to rational control or analysis.

TLS. July 25, 1929, p. 588

Coleridge's doctrine of the Imagination is admittedly difficult, but it is not one half so difficult as Mr. Richards's exposition of it [*Coleridge on Imagination.*] Possibly he has the mysterious secret of the doctrine itself, but after a third careful reading of his book we are persuaded that he has not the secret of conveying it. . . .

If we are to believe him, the art of literary criticism is on the brink of a complete revolution. "Coleridge succeeded in bringing his suggestions to a point from which, with a little care and pertinacity, they can be taken on to become a new science." Probably Mr. Richards's book is to be regarded as prolegomena to the new science. If so, it is lamentably abstruse, and we sigh for a glimpse of those "important practical utilities" which we are encouraged to expect of its operations.

TLS. April 4, 1935, p. 224

I. A. Richards was so hot for mental certainties in *Principles of Literary Criticism* (1925) and *Practical Criticism* (1929) that Pegasus was in momentary peril of being turned into a dray-horse pulling a psychological load. Pure enjoyment became suspect in academic circles and among the coteries. Aesthetic pleasure and emotional satisfaction were lumped together as "escapism," and to be an escapist was to be among the damned.

A. C. Ward. *Twentieth-Century Literature, 1901-1940*, (Methuen, 1940), p. 221

Mr. Richards is a psychologist, and what he is concerned with is the effect of poetry on the mind. He holds that this approach to poetry is, or can sometime hope to be, scientifically sound. In thinking this he is supported by his faith in the future of neurology. . . . The mind, Mr. Richards holds, is the nervous system; not, that is to say, primarily a directing intelligence, but a system of multitudinous responses. Mr. Richards pictures it as "an arrangement of many magnetic needles, large and small, swung so that they influence one another, some able only to swing horizontally, others vertically, others hung freely." . . . Amid all this commotion there is "a final position of rest for all the needles into which they will in the end settle down, a general poise for the whole system."

Now it is the function of poetry, according to Mr. Richards, to produce this harmonious though fleeting state; to bring such order among the needles that they cease from waggling and are at rest. Any poetry can start them waggling; but only the best poetry can stop them waggling. This is the neurological account of the operation of poetry which, Mr. Richards says, "must frankly be admitted to be only a degree less fictitious than one in terms of spiritual happenings." But by A.D. 3000 (if all goes well) the assumption is that it will be several degrees less fictitious.

The chief anomaly of a theory which conceives poetry as a means to make the nervous system function properly is that it ignores or regards as irrelevant the explicit meaning of poetry, in other words, what the poet says. . . . For what the poet sees in general Mr. Richards has invented a class of statements which he calls "pseudo-statements." These are without actual truth, yet without actual falsehood either, for even the nervous system would hardly allow itself to be soothed by a lie. In his later book on Coleridge Mr. Richards seems to modify his attitude on this point; how far it is difficult to say. If imagination is a general mode of apprehension, and what it apprehends is the world "of whole and indefeasible objects," as Mr. John Crowe Ransom says, then without some truth it can have no serious value, and cannot be very good for the nervous system. The great fault of *Principles of Literary Criticism,* as Mr. D. G. James points out in his excellent book, *Scepticism and Poetry,* is that it ignores the fact that poetry is a way of apprehending the world through imagination. In *Coleridge on Imagination* Mr. Richards tries to supply this omission, but he still clings to his "materialist associationism."

The value of Richards's work does not lie in the principles he lays down, which are derived from a particular conception of science whose validity will not be demonstrable until A.D. 3000 (if all goes well), but in his realisation of the many meanings implicit in poetry, and the closeness with which he pursues these meanings. His chief disciple in this particular line, William Empson, excels him both in fineness and intricacy of perception, and his book, *The Seven Types of Ambiguity,* is almost exasperatingly subtle, like his poetry. Yet it may be claimed that Richards's practice has led to a greater accuracy in criticism, as distinct from theory, and a fuller perception of what may be implied by a poem. The hunting of these implications has sometimes become a game very like the hunting of the Snark, but it is an interesting and often useful one.

Edwin Muir. *The Present Age from 1914*
(N.Y., Robert McBride, 1940), pp. 173–75

Psychologistic critics hold that poetry is addressed primarily to the feelings and motor impulses; they remind us frequently of its contrast with the coldness, the un-emotionality of science, which is supposed to address itself to the pure cognitive mind. Mr. Richards came out spectacularly for the doctrine, and furnished it with detail of the greatest ingenuity. He very nearly severed the dependence of poetic effect upon any standard of objective knowledge or belief. But the feelings and impulses which he represented as gratified by the poetry were too tiny and numerous to be named. He never identified them; they seemed not so much psychological as infra-psychological. His was an esoteric poetic; it could not be disproved. But neither could it be proved, . . . and I think it is safe at this distance to say that eventually his readers, and Richards himself, lost interest in it as being an improvisation, much too unrelated to the public sense of a poetic experience.

John Crowe Ransom in *The Intent of the Critic,*
ed. Donald A. Stauffer (Princeton, N. J.,
Princeton Univ. Pr., 1941), p. 95

From 1926, the publication of *Science and Poetry,* he has come a long way. It is perhaps not an extravagant claim to make for Mr. Richards's intellectual history, that it will probably turn out to be the most instructive, among critics, of our age. His great intellectual power, his learning, his devotion to poetry—a devotion somewhat frustrated but as marked fifteen years ago as now—are qualities of an intellectual honesty rare in any age. In exactly ten years, from 1926, he arrived, in *The Philosophy of Rhetoric,* at such a statement as this: "So far from verbal language being a 'compromise for a language of intuition'—a thin, but better-than-nothing substitute for real experience—language, well used, is a *completion* and does what the intuitions of sensations by themselves cannot do. . . . It is no mere signalling system. It is the instrument of all our distinctively human development, of everything in which we go beyond the animals." These words should be read and re-read with the greatest care by critics who still cite the early Richards as the continuing head of a positivist tradition in criticism. There is, in this passage, first of all, an implicit repudiation of the leading doctrine of *The Principles of Literary Criticism.* . . .

Language, says Mr. Richardson, "is no mere signalling system." With that sentence the early psychological doctrine is discreetly put away. [1941]

Allen Tate. *Collected Essays*
(Denver, Colo., Alan Swallow, 1959), pp. 43–44

If it be indeed true, as has been occasionally insinuated by followers of Mr. Richards, that his is a theory that ends all theories except itself and the better thought about language we may look for in the future, then the objections we have brought against his program for the reform of interpretation are not only irrelevant but philosophically unsound—expressions of our wishes that carry over into a new age the fictions and magic-charged concepts of the past. Our examination of Mr. Richards's views will perhaps have been justified if it has revealed the essential circularity of all such retorts. For what is the force of an appeal to the nature of things against rival doctrines of language or discourse when that nature itself has been determined by a decision, prior to any inquiry, to identify reality only with what can be signified in a particular fixed relationship among three equivocal words [logic, grammar, rhetoric]? And what is there to compel an abandonment of the distinctions of traditional grammar or logic in an argument which derives all its negative cogency from a metaphor so admirably adapted to the end of destroying such distinctions as that upon which Mr. Richards's system is based?

R. S. Crane. *Ethics.* Jan., 1949, p. 26

It is perfectly true that Dr. Richards has never been either a groupish man or even a man with the urge to boss groups. There are Leavisians, there are Empsonians, but, as an embattled band, preaching and practising the Master's doctrine, there are no Richardians. Dr. Richards's favourite pastime is the lonely and dangerous sport of mountain-climbing, and there is perhaps something symbolic in that. Nor is it possible with Dr. Richards, as it sometimes is with men even of a solitary temperament, for organized groups to use him as a mascot. His allegiance to science scares off religious propagandists; his respect for religion and poetry puzzles the more philistine kind of scientist; he is a pioneer in examining in detail how language works, but in a way that has nothing in common with the way of the logical analysts. Mere men of letters, finally, are often scared off him by his interest in psychology and semantics. It would be difficult even for the politicians to pin him down. He takes longer views than they do, and cheers himself up by arguments that would startle them. . . . Dr. Richards himself has said that some of his early books were essentially sermons disguised as science. And when he went to China, he found his own basic ideas very beautifully presented to him in the pre-scientific, essentially religious or poetic psychology of Mencius. . . .

Of what has Dr. Richards been speaking, all his working life, whether the ostensible pretext was poetry or teaching or psychology or how language works, except the mind of man? And he is a kind of sage himself and has Confucius's awe of it: "No one knows its country." Whatever topic he has started from, he has in fact been teaching wisdom; and that explains the solitary quality of his thinking.

TLS. May 1, 1959, p. 256

Some critics have remarked unfavourably about the explanatory introduction and notes to this comparatively short book [*Goodbye Earth*], on the tough puzzle element in the poems themselves. I think such things are of little importance. It is language, after all, we say to ourselves tritely, as we close the book, that determines what is and what is not poetry. How extraordinary that a critic who helped to shape the modern movement should clothe his poetic ideas in Hardyesque reach-me-downs!

One says Hardyesque, but only that poet's quaint grammatical forms (the askantlys and so forth), elaborate stanzas and gnarled provincial philosophizing aura are there: absent the narration, the observation of nature, the sense of tangled human relations. Here and there in *Goodbye Earth* (a neat villanelle, for example, and a reference to Newton buying a prism) one receives an impression of the impulse that must have gone to make these ingenious poems, but what comes out on the page is in too dry a tongue for speech. One is glad in the end of that introduction and those notes.

Roy Fuller. *L.* June, 1959, pp. 77, 79

Certainly a good argument can be put up for the view that the New Criticism is a peculiar combination of Richards and T. S. Eliot. But Richards is an Englishman—though he has been at the other Cambridge for thirty years—and most of his writings precede 1945. Neither his only new critical book, *Speculative Instruments,* nor a few scattered articles constitute a substantial change in his point of view. Richards has merely recognized that his earlier trust in the advances of neurology was irrelevant: he still expounds the view of art as a sort of emotional therapy, of the work as a pattern of impulses, of poetry as emotive language, pseudo-statement, or myth. Richards, like Dewey, denies any difference between aesthetic and ordinary experience and upholds a radical psychologism and hedonistic naturalism. Richards's interest in the meaning of meaning, in semantics, has proved his most fruitful contribution to criticism proper. Such a critic as Cleanth Brooks, who does not share Richards's philosophical assumptions, still uses his key terms: attitudes, tensions, ambiguities, and irony.

René Wellek. *Concepts of Criticism* (New Haven, Conn. and London: Yale Univ. Pr., 1963), p. 324

RICHARDSON, DOROTHY (1872–1957)

By imposing very strict limitations on herself she has brought her art, her method, to a high pitch of perfection, so that her form seems to be newer than it perhaps is. She herself is unaware of the perfection of her method. She would probably deny that she had written with any deliberate method at all. . . . Obviously, she must not interfere; she must not analyse or comment or explain. Rather less obviously, she must not tell a story or handle a situation or set a scene; she must avoid drama as she avoids narration. And there are some things she must not be. She must not be the wise, all-knowing author. She must be Miriam Henderson. . . . She has taken Miriam's nature upon hers. . . . Of the persons who move through Miriam's world you know nothing but what Miriam knows. If Miriam is mistaken, well, she is not Miss Richardson is mistaken. Miriam is an acute observer, but she is very far from seeing the whole of these people. They are presented to us in the same vivid but fragmentary way in which they appeared to Miriam, the fragmentary way in which some people appear to most of us. Miss Richardson has only imposed on herself the conditions that life imposes on us all. . . .

To me these three novels show an art and method and form carried to punctilious perfection. [*Pointed Roofs, Backwater, Honeycomb*, Pts. I-III of *Pilgrimage*].

May Sinclair. Eg. April, 1918, p. 58

It seems to us that a comparison between M. Proust and Miss Richardson is not really very profitable—their work does not cover in the least the same ground. In certain ways their methods are alike. For instance, in the books of both authors it is often a little difficult to find out the outward circumstances of the person the working of whose mind we are shown. Both authors realize that it is not so much outward happenings that shape people's lives as the way in which these happenings are interpreted by the persons concerned. But while M. Proust's men and women are active, often restless in shaping their own destinies, altering, re-arranging, striving, Miss Richardson's derive a kind of ecstasy from passivity. It is, perhaps, this passivity that differentiates her work from that of Mr. James Joyce, which, however, it much more closely resembles than that of M. Proust. M. Proust has made what will probably remain for many generations of writers the ultimate analysis of one complete layer of life, not quite the intellectual layer, but what we might call the commensense active layer. . . .

Mr. Joyce's ambitions take him down far below this daylight level to some strange, deep, passionate cave of consciousness. He storms into it, a revealing invader, flashing his lamp here and there on the beautiful and the grotesque and the obscene. But he is always the active explorer, finding things out, and is often in his own despite denunciatory. Miss Richardson, passive and still, sinks through events and states of mind quiet and dumb, and in this ecstasy of listening and waiting she reaches a layer of personality which is different to that either of Mr. James Joyce or M. Proust. . . .

Revolving Lights suffers more than do some of the other books from Miss Richardson's besetting sin—her tiresome twist towards feminism. It is the one blot upon her exquisite fairness and detachment. The reader cannot help constantly wishing that she would see how much any twist takes away from the value of her testimony on other points—Socialism, the territorial classes, Jews, Russians and what not.

Spec. June 30, 1923, pp. 1084–85

Miss Richardson's work is unique in fiction (none of her disciples has ever dared the full implications of her theory) and has a metaphysical value that is absent in Proust or Joyce. For neither of these writers is inspired by the mystical quality that is peculiar to Miss Richardson. . . . Dorothy Richardson has assumed the existence of a soul to which the consciousness has much the same relation that the intelligence has to the consciousness. . . . The great moments of Miriam's experience are not found in moving adventures nor in moments of physical stress, but at those times when she is most keenly aware of herself in relation to the spirit that moves beneath and animates every phenomenon of the great phantasmagoria we know as life and matter.

J. D. Beresford. *Tradition and Experiment in Present-Day Literature* (Oxford Univ. Pr., 1929), p. 47

Dorothy Richardson is our first pioneer in a completely new direction. What she has done has never been done before. She has drawn her inspiration neither from man-imitating cleverness nor from narcissistic feminine charm but *from the abyss of the feminine subconscious.* . . . These quiet and penetrating books represent, in fact, the only attempt I am aware of to put into psychological fiction the real "philosophy," moral, aethetic, spiritual, and that which underlies all these and escapes from all these and mocks at all these—of women where they differ most from men. . . . Miss Richardson is a far more original writer, a far greater writer, than the clever philistine-culture of our age has the sensitivity to understand. She is an authentic philosopher. . . . She has carried this philosophy of the "a-logical, innocent eye" into a new dimension, the dimension of women's secret, instinctive sensitiveness to the mystery of life.

J. C. Powys. *Dorothy Richardson* (Joiner and Steele, 1931), pp. 8, 17–18

She is perhaps the most perfect incarnation that has ever existed of one of the warring elements in the eternal sex war. Hers is—or perhaps I had better say appears to be—the authentic voice of essential woman using the distinctively feminine faculties to express the world. No doubt it was not by chance that she was first trying her hand at writing at the moment when the militant suffragette movement was at its height. Not that the suffragette way was her way. It was not by attempting to do what men do, or by "assimilating masculine culture" that women (according to Miriam) acted in their own true part. Miriam's part was to act, think, feel and experience life with the sentience that belongs to the feminine side of human nature and to do so in full consciousness of what she was doing. . . . Mrs. Virginia Woolf has immense power of presenting the feminine point of view, but she is not herself controlled by it, as Miss Richardson is. Miss Richardson not merely presents the feminine point of view; she is it. She is conscious of the fact, glories in it, and wages (through Miriam) relentless war on the amusing monstrosity of the male intelligence. . . . It is evident that the distinctive excellence for which Miss Richardson stands made it desirable for her to have just such a vehicle as she has chosen; her technique exactly serves her purpose. It lends itself—one might add—to artistic laziness—possibly a feminine defect?—to following the least line of resistance in recording the unordered flow of impressions as they pass through the mind.

R. A. Scott-James. *LM*. Dec., 1935, pp. 202–3

The long trainload [*Pilgrimage*] draws by our platform, passes us with an inimical flash of female eyes, and proceeds on into how many more dry and gritty years. It set out in 1915 with some acclamation, carrying its embarrassing cargo—the stream of consciousness—saluted by many prominent bystanders—Miss West and Mrs. Woolf, Mr. Wells, Mr. Beresford, Mr. Swinnerton and Mr. Hugh Walpole.

Who could have foreseen in the first ordinary phrases this gigantic work which has now reached its two thousandth page, without any indication of a close? The Saratoga trunk becomes progressively more worn and labelled. There is no reason why the pilgrimage should ever end, except with the author's life, for she is attempting to represent the whole effect of every experience—friendship, politics, tea-parties, books, weather, what you will—on a woman's sensibility.

I am uncertain of my dates, but I should imagine Miss Richardson in her ponderous unwitty way has had an immense influence on such writers as Mrs. Woolf and Miss Stein, and through them on their disciples. Her novel, therefore, has something in common with Bowles's Sonnets. She herself became influenced about halfway through these four volumes (comprising twelve novels or instalments) by the later novels of Henry James—the result, though it increased the obscurity of her sensibility, was to the good, for she began to shed the adjectives which in the first volume disguise any muscles her prose may possess. . . . Or was it simply that Miriam became a little older, unhappier, less lyrical? In the monstrous subjectivity of this novel the author is absorbed into her character. There is no longer a Miss Richardson: only Miriam. . . .

There are passages of admirable description, characters do sometimes emerge clearly from the stream of consciousness. . . . But the final effect, I fear, is one of weariness (that may be a tribute to Miss Richardson's integrity), the weariness of the best years of life shared with an earnest, rather sentimental and complacent woman. For one of the drawbacks of Miss Richardson's unironic and undetached method is that the compliments paid so frequently to the wit or intellect of Miriam seem addressed to the author herself. (We are reminded of those

American women who remark to strangers, "They simply worshipped me.") And as for the method—it must have seemed in 1915 a revivifying change from the tyranny of the "plot." But time has taken its revenge: after twenty years of subjectivity, we are turning back with relief to the old dictatorship, to the detached and objective treatment. . . .

Graham Greene. *The Lost Childhood*
(N.Y., Viking, 1951), pp. 84–85

The death of Dorothy Miller Richardson at eighty-four last June 17, in England, removed from our literary scene the last of the experimenters who in the century's opening years created the "inside-looking-out" novel—what we more commonly speak of as the "stream of consciousness" novel. The least read and the most unobtrusive of the experimenters, she had outlived them all, outlived, indeed, her own work and her own modest reputation. . . . Literary history bids fair to use *Pilgrimage* not so much for its exploration of the inner consciousness as for its vivid portraits of certain identifiable figures and its reflection of a certain era in English life and letters. For it is also, to a degree, a *livre à clé* and certain readers have already recognized the marked resemblance between Hypo Wilson and H. G. Wells. . . .

Certainly there can be no question of placing her now on an equality of footing with Proust and Joyce. Miss Richardson was a journeyman beside the nimble-minded Irishman, nor did she have the Frenchman's capacity for discovering a universe in a perfume. She must be written down rather as one of the hardy and plodding experimenters of literature, the axe-swingers and stump-pullers, those who have a single moment of vision which suffices for a lifetime. There was a kind of Zola in Miss Richardson, not in her work but in herself as the artist-type—the immense recording of data, the observation and note-taking, weight and solidity, the carrying out of a major project according to plan. . . . To re-read Miss Richardson now and to re-appraise her in her four thick volumes which embody her twelve novels or "chapters," is to marvel at her unflagging zeal: the book is a victory of resolution, patience, and sensibility over limited artistic means. *Pilgrimage* for all its sprawling minuteness, its endless internal monologue sensitively alert to sunlight and shadow, London streets and rooms, contains distinct qualities of strength, insight and feeling, and above all vitality —the vitality of a purposeful individual who cannot be swerved from a creative task, who indeed converts the task into a self-education.

In the novel we learn how Miss Richardson discovered *The Ambassadors* (Miriam reads it with intense excitement) and learned from Henry James the proper use of "point of view." The fascination of putting the reader into a given angle of vision and keeping him there: this was the lesson of the Master for Miss Richardson and she learned it well; it became the guiding light by which she worked. . . . Today we would call this the "camera eye," so accustomed are we to seeing it done in the cinema. Miss Richardson anticipated the moving picture camera; from the first she brought everything into the orbit of Miriam's eyes and her senses and sought to capture within a book the *ewige Weibliche*— not as men might express it, but as women experienced it. In undertaking to write "point of view" on so large a scale, Miss Richardson set herself a much more difficult task than Proust. . . .

Few men—few critics of their sex—have been willing to climb into Miss Richardson's boat; the journey is long, the "stream of consciousness" difficult—raw unabstracted data, the absence of the omniscient author to serve as guide, the consequent need to become the author so as to bring some order into the great grab-bag of feminine experience offered us; and then the need, Orlando-like, to become the girl or woman, to become Miriam if we are to be her consciousness. Few writers have placed so double-weighted a burden upon their readers. And yet if the challenge is met and the empathy achieved, Dorothy Richardson offers us, on certain pages, a remarkable emotional luminescence—as well as, historically speaking, a record of the trying out of a new technique, the opportunity to examine a turning point in the modern English novel. There is a distinct possibility that a new generation of readers—if there will continue to be readers at all—may truly discover Dorothy Richardson for the first time.

Leon Edel. *MFS*. Summer, 1958, pp. 165–68

RICKWORD, EDGELL (1898–   )

He . . . writes [*Behind the Eyes*] an ingenious little trench piece, in the manner of Mr. Robert Graves, about Hauptmann Kälte and Colonel Cold, who wear "tabs of rime and spurs of ice." He also writes about "the Hippogrif, with wrinkled ivory snout and agate feet," and desires "to pelt slim girls among Sicilian vines." In other words this is an immature book, much of which had better not have been printed. But beneath these integuments one catches glimpses of a real Mr. Rickword who has imagination and eloquence. . . .

OutL. Jan. 21, 1922, p. 56

Some of Mr. Rickword's poems have already been seen by our readers. These are among the clearer of them [*Behind the Eyes*]. In "Such Thoughts," "Lovers," "Passion," "Winter Warfare," "Trench Poets," and "Regret for the Passing of the Entire Scheme of Things" his thought is generally subtle and difficult and his imagery his own; yet he manages to make his conceptions and feelings plain to the reader in every particular, and in good verse. A characteristic poem in his midway manner is "Singing at Night," where not every word has been sufficiently thought on (the alternative being complete spontaneity), but the idea comes through. The attempt has been made to seize a difficult state of consciousness which has moved the poet to wonder and fear. Elsewhere Mr. Rickword tends to go over the border into a chaos of half-expressed thoughts and half-authenticated images; sometimes, even, one cannot be sure that his sentiments are his own and not out of the French.

J. C. Squire. *LM.* April, 1922, p. 656

This collection [*New Signatures*] shows how strong has been the satiric impulse carried down from the post-war reaction, and intensified by the social dissatisfaction of today, but that is not to say that these poets are revolutionaries of the spirit. Yet where is the traditional English humour which no foreigner ever understood? . . . Modern political humbug, the sentimental cult of a rapidly disappearing countryside, the displeasing activities of certain literary coteries—these are the three themes—and the last explains the omission of some good satirists. Mr. Richard Aldington, Mr. Edgell Rickword . . . amid poetic din, will be found here on the roundabouts and swings, or cracking whips in the great tent.

Austin Clarke. *LL.* June, 1932, p. 236

The young man who reached an uneasy maturity in the last despairing years of the 1914 war was very like the young men of to-day who are transfixed in the deeper horrors of the whoring forties of American intervention, and ". . . seeing cool nurses move on tireless feet/To do abominable things with grace . . ." might be lines written yesterday by Louis MacNeice, and not the work of Edgell Rickword more than a quarter of a century ago.

Edgell Rickword is a considerable poet with a very small output. If we ignore his satire on Non-Intervention in the Spanish Civil War written in 1938, the compass of his work is in three slim volumes issued between 1921 and 1931. Yet his poems to-day wear a new looking sophistication which has outlived the more serious works of many of his contemporaries.

Primarily he is a satirist and like most satirists he is frustrated from the beginning by being unable to pierce the thick hides and heads of the wicked and the foolish he flagellates, and his satire is appreciated only by those already in accord with his way of thinking. . . .

So, in a series of brilliant and still readable satires, Edgell Rickword mirrored his age. But as such satire belongs to History rather than to Poetry, I turn to his lyrics to find his true stature. They are excellent—and one in particular . . . reminded me of an older lyric-poet who spent much of his time on politics and satire. Marvell was too large-hearted to object to such comparison.

Denis Botterill. *LL.* Feb., 1949, pp. 113–14

RIDLER, ANNE (1912–   )

Mrs. Ridler's *Poems* are a far cry from the gracefully drawn, athletic line of Mr. MacNeice. She seems to work much too hard for her effects. The pressure of her hand makes a crabbed style of overloaded imagery and awkwardly inverted syntax, so that one feels a lack of elbow-room in the densely packed texture. But perhaps this is a characteristic of a first volume, which will pass with greater practice. . . .

Mrs. Ridler's intention is certainly uncommon and talented. Her language is underivative and fresh, and she used it with precision and the ability to fuse it with sharply articulated feelings. . . . One catches traces of Donne, and occasional lines have the air of early lyric . . . but Mrs. Ridler makes her own material and stamps it with the mark of a firmly independent, although still immature, poet.

Desmond Hawkins. *Spec.* June 30, 1939, p. 1140

Other poems in this volume [*The Golden Bird*]—as in all Anne Ridler's previous books—disarm the critic who is about to protest that she is a little too much under the influence of T. S. Eliot and George Herbert, too often apt to embark upon themes too large for her talent. But often she writes with exquisite delicacy of feeling, rich and true, though within the framework of a convention that includes occasional poems to her Head Mistress, and to her parents on their golden wedding. Amazing that domestic feelings and virtues still keep their flavour and ring true in such a world as this, as they do in Anne Ridler's best poems.

Kathleen Raine. *NR.* June 23, 1952, p. 20

Mrs. Ridler's dignified and moving play [*The Trial of Thomas Cranmer*] has simplicity, exclusion and a somewhat expensive tie-up with its modern corollary. The work is disarmingly modest in tone and she has stuck cleanly to her story. She has far too overtly commended her moral to our current woe. Her characters are believable, especially her hero . . . and we are all for the moment too vulnerable to the martyr-for-conscience theme to fail in our response to her spirit. The unwelcome fact remains that the total result is oddly thin, and that it falls between the loneliness of the majestic and the blood-knowledge of the common. . . .

One would guess Mrs. Ridler to be more dramatist than poet. There are indications that her sense of motion, of single purpose, of human values, might take her much further as a playwright. Poetry is another matter.

Josephine Jacobsen. Poetry. March, 1957, pp. 380–82

ROBERTS, MICHAEL (1902–1948)

Mr. Roberts is a younger critic who makes the ageing generation of literary folk feel insecure. He drives them to the mirror to search for signs of hardening sensibility and senile indifference. For he has all the gifts and most of the acquirements. He has imagination, patience, and respect. He has scholarship, intellectual vigour, and a mature prose style.

What is so disturbing is that with all his accomplishments, his enthusiasm and chief interest are restricted mostly to the poetry fashionable amongst his own generation; the poetry of T. S. Eliot, Ezra Pound, E. E. Cummings, W. H. Auden, Laura Riding, and others. . . . It would be quite easy to ignore him if he were merely an irresponsible undergraduate noisily defending the members of his own set. But he is not that. His *Critique of Poetry* is astonishingly full of insight, sound judgment, and that inspiration which one recognises instinctively as being true and permanent. . . .

It is a pity; because by the restriction of his practice Mr. Roberts is in danger of being claimed by those lily-minded and fatuous people, the highbrows and fashionables, as one of themselves. He is not that; he is a critic who commands serious attention. He has worked, and thought, and he has a lot to teach. I for one am grateful to him. I have learned, from his book, to renew my sensibility and disinterestedness towards poetry, and to throw off that dreadful unsuspected indifference which creeps over us as we pass from bright youthfulness into the fogs of middle-aged affairs and greedy fears.

Richard Church. NSN. Feb. 10, 1934, pp. 198, 200

Mr. Roberts' useful anthology [*Elizabethan Prose*] should do more than remind the general reader that Elizabethan Prose is not confined to a few patches of fine writing. A careful reading of his extracts from journalists alone is sufficient to increase our understanding of Eliza-

bethan verse to suggest an important approach to the culture of the period.
L. C. Knights. *Scy.* March, 1934, p. 438

All that Mr. Roberts has to say [*The Modern Mind*] is interesting, but in his later chapters, on modern philosophy and science, there is not much that is original. . . .

The subject of Mr. Roberts's book, namely the influence of science on language, is an interesting one, and so long as he is dealing with this subject what he has to say is well worth reading. But there is too much of general philosophy, and a somewhat too facile acceptance of the interpretations of science which are favoured by the school to which the author belongs. The consequence is that, in spite of much that is excellent, the book as a whole is unequal and lacking in unity.
Bertrand Russell. *NSN.* June 26, 1937, p. 1048

Michael Roberts is better known as critic and editor than as poet, and those who know his suggestive *Critique of Poetry,* his illuminating study *The Modern Mind,* his thoughtful exposition of T. E. Hulme, and the admirable collection of modern verse he edited . . . (not to mention his too little known anthology of Elizabethan prose, with its provocative, if brief, introduction) will have recognized a keen mind and a fine imagination. But a keen mind and a fine imagination, admirable qualities as they are for the critic and editor, do not suffice to make a poet, and in this volume of verse, as in his earlier 1936 collection, the poetic quality is very uneven, and, though there are a few quite satisfying pieces, most of the poems lack conviction in expression.

The fact is that Roberts, greatly talented though he is, has no sustained power of poetic vision, no way of shaping and compelling his insights into memorable poetic units. His imagination is sensitive and subtle, but it exceeds his ability to embody it in wholly adequate poetry [*Orion Marches*]. . . .

It is not enough to have fine conceptions. No, not even if these are coupled with an unusual ability to handle language. In the poetic imagination language, as it were, is in at the birth; it does not come, as that of Roberts and of so many modern poets seems to come, at a later stage, to "clothe" the conception or "express" the mood. Sometimes Roberts seems to feel that if he has his subject, sees his vision, then the validity of the subject, the quality of the vision, will guarantee that any language used to express them will be poetically adequate. How else can we explain . . . [his] insensitivity.
David Daiches. *Poetry.* March, 1940, pp. 335–36

When Michael Roberts died in 1948 at the age of forty-six, well might it have been said, "Now cracks a noble heart." A man of singular intellectual virtuosity, the three salient facts to be remembered about him are that he was a poet, a Christian, and a mountaineer. He was an authority upon the Cambridge Platonists of the seventeenth century, and the qualities which marked this school—moral and intellectual integrity, philosophical aptitude, and spiritual serenity—were also possessed by him. His mountaineering adventures, which inspired some of his best poems ("Kanchenjunga," "Levanna," and "Elegy for the Fallen Climbers" are three examples), together with his love of exploration, made solitude habitual and congenial, engendering within his mind a certain objectivity, if not remoteness. On account of his having edited *New Signatures* and *New Country* he is still regarded as one of the leaders of the Left-wing movement in poetry of twenty years ago, but this is an error. He was an adherent to no movement, school, or party (save for the Communist party, which he soon quitted), remaining a steadfast individualist to the end, following his own star. To a degree, his technique was influenced by that of such contemporaries as W. H. Auden and Cecil Day Lewis. His talent, however, was too potent for him to remain beholden to any other poet for long, and his finest work—and it is very fine—is unmistakably though unobtrusively his own.

Ralph Lawrence. *Eng.* Summer, 1958, p. 69

ROBINSON, LENNOX (1886–1958)

Mr. Robinson's new play [*Patriots*] is not so good as *Harvest*. He has a fine idea; and he has worked it out successfully up to a point. . . . But the play is the work of a writer whose imagination is not yet working at full pressure, and whose craftsmanship is quite elementary. Mr. Robinson is imaginatively gifted. Frequently there are touches of character carefully observed and beautifully expressed, and a keen realisation of dramatic effect, which show that it is well within the author's capacity to rise considerably above the level of his present achievement. But there is yet only the merest hint of Mr. Robinson's capacity for really great work.

John Palmer. *SR*. June 15, 1912, p. 744

Still in his thirties, he is one of the most noteworthy of the coterie influenced by Synge to turn their talents to the interpretation of contemporary Irish life. Like Synge, Mr. Robinson has done the greater part of his work for the theatre. At the outset of his career he showed unusual dramatic ability, and he has now developed firm technique. Even ten years ago Lady Gregory and Mr. Yeats had so high an opinion of the young playwright that they asked him to accompany them to this country [U.S.A.]; he has since become manager of the Abbey Theatre, and his new play has not only been given in Ireland but has been one of the recent successes in London. Lennox Robinson is a dramatist of assured position.

Mr. Robinson's plays may be divided into two groups: those describing rural and small-town life in Ireland, and those dealing more or less remotely with Irish politics. To the first group belongs his earliest play, *The Clancy Name,* succeeded by *The Crossroads, Harvest,* and *The White-Headed Boy,* the last produced originally in Dublin, on December 13th, 1916. Between *The Crossroads* and *The White-Headed Boy* come the political plays, *Patriots* and *The Dreamers.* Mr. Robinson's latest play, *The Lost Leader,* is likewise of this class. . . .

Mr. Robinson portrays not only the hardships of Irish life, of peasant farmer, small shopkeeper, politician, but the idealism of Irish character, often a prey to its own defects. Timothy Hurley, in *Harvest,* because he has brought himself to the verge of ruin by educating his children and starting them in positions in life superior to that he occupies, burns his own property to obtain the insurance; the idealism of James Nugent's associates in *Patriots* is undermined by material prosperity. By showing Irishmen dissatisfied with their condition in life, with their fellow-countrymen, yet struggling to hold a vision always before, although beyond, them, Mr. Robinson helps to explain why Sinn Fein, despite contradictions and illogicalities, has made such headway in Ireland. He is the dramatist of Irish discontent.

A comparison between Robinson and Synge has already been suggested. Both have written of the Ireland of their day, yet Mr. Robinson is the more faithful realist, for he does not stamp his personality upon his plays as did Synge. This may be due somewhat to the greater variety of people in Mr. Robinson's plays; he writes not only of the country but of the town, whereas Synge dealt almost exclusively with peasant life in remote districts. Synge, moreover, was always a protestant against circumstance; in all his work he stressed the aspirations rather than the failures of his characters; in the last analysis he is a romanticist, or an idealist, rather than a complete realist. Mr. Robinson, on the other hand, although he shows the dreams of his characters, shows with equal emphasis their thwarting; he stands outside his people, almost indifferent to their fate; circumstance leads them whither it will. Perhaps Synge's extraordinary ear for prose cadence was partly responsible for the emphasis he placed upon the imaginings of his people, who speak in a language that is a garnering of picturesque phrases rather than a faithful rendering of common speech. Nobly struggling against Destiny, Synge's figures have passionate poetic utterance; crushed by the monotony of every day, Mr. Robinson's men and women confine themselves to the less vivid words of familiar intercourse.

N. O'Connor. *SwR*. July, 1922, p. 280

Mr. Lennox Robinson, for some years manager of the Irish company [Irish National Theatre at Abbey Theatre, Dublin], has given two very noteworthy plays not only to the Irish but to the English-speaking stage. *The Lost Leader* is one of the most imaginative plays of our time, utilising with admirable tact and skill a legend (wholly groundless I believe) which clings to the memory of the Uncrowned King of Ireland, Charles Stewart Parnell. . . .

Mr. Robinson's later play, *The White-Headed Boy,* may be compendiously described as the perfection of peasant comedy. It has not its rival in the English language. It continues and consummates the tradition established at the very birth of the Irish Theatre, showing all the merits and none of the defects of earlier plays by Robinson himself and other writers of his school. Not only in observation and in humour, but also in construction, it is above reproach—a work of which any literature may be proud.

William Archer. *The Old Drama and the New*
(Boston, Small, Maynard and Co., 1923), pp. 370, 374

Amusing, very far from being pointless, light and well-acted, it is surprising that *The Round Table* should not be at the beginning of a decent run. . . . Well, well, it is another warning not to write plays. This one was very much better than most and far more amusing. It was original; it was pointful; it was light. . . .

Desmond MacCarthy. *NS*. May 30, 1925, p. 198

Here is a technically imperfect play [*The Round Table*] which is many miles, streets, oceans . . . better than 99 per cent of West End successes. Yet this piece—all shame to playgoers—is not doing roaring business. Why? Because, presumably, it does not deal with life as it is lived in gilded cages by vulgar little singing-birds. Because the life with which it has the temerity to deal is the middle-class life known to thousands of families in these islands. Because it keys up that life to a nice pitch of comedy and exaggeration. Because half the characters are first-class comic creations, and the other half, being familiar, amuse without fatiguing. Because the dialogue is uniformly witty. Because the whole piece is *exceedingly good fun.* Because for about ten minutes we are asked to use about one hundredth part of our brains. The last, of course, is the snag. No audience has ever cared tuppence about technical imperfections. . . .

. . . . I shall be told that Mr. Robinson has attempted to make an amalgam out of two compounds each of which, though good in itself, can never have anything to do with the other. . . . But my point is that it is better to dine off alternate slices of perfectly good onion and perfectly good peach than on some homogeneous scrap of offensiveness picked up in the gutter. Do I quite believe in Daisy? No. . . . Does she interest me? Yes. Do I believe in Mr. [Noel] Coward's fallen angels? Yes. Would they get drunk and deceive their husbands? Yes. Do I care if they do? Can *anything* they do interest me? No. Very well, then!

James Agate. The Contemporary Theatre, 1925
(Chapman and Hall, 1926), pp. 119, 121-22

The decline of ancient families in an alien age is still a popular theme, and our emotional response to it is almost ready made. Mr. Lennox Robinson has been attracted by this popular theme for some years and to a gift for dialogue which is always entertaining, even when it amounts to very little, he adds the charm of a twilight mood. But for all this charm of a lingering Celtic twilight, there is a shrewdness in his delineation of character which stimulates our minds, even though the dramatist avoids unpleasant consequences, preferring to leave his comedies in the fairy-land of happy endings.

TLS. April 1, 1939, p. 800

Killycreggs in Twilight is a bitter-sweet comedy suffused with Southern Irish charm suggesting, as a line in it almost says, that it is complementary to Mr. Robinson's stronger play, *The Big House*. Someday . . . comparison must be made of the Southern Ireland country-house plays with the Southern States country-house plays of Mr. Paul Green.

Harold Brighouse. MG. May 12, 1939, p. 8

RODGERS, W. R. (1909–)

The poems themselves [*Awake! and Other Wartime Poems*], noisy, verbose, eloquent and intellectually rather adolescent, achieve most of their effects by means no less violent than the man who murdered his wife by tearing her arm out of its socket and beating her over the head with it. Mr. Rodgers is at present obsessed with assonance to the point where it sticks like a plum in his throat and impedes almost all utterance. . . . But this obsession with the word as machinery is acknowledgedly the healthiest of propensities in the young poet: for instance,

Tennyson's earliest experiments in assonance and dissonance made it impossible for him, finally, to write a technically shabby line. I do not think that Rodgers is a Tennyson, but I am sure he is better than Rupert Brooke.

. . . . As I see it, Mr. Rodgers has only to take a deep breath and clear his throat of technical matter in order to say things both comprehensibly and memorably. Then he will probably write poems comparable with the best being written now.

George Barker. *NR*. April 13, 1942, pp. 517–18

Here, says Mr. Mark Van Doren, is "the war poet of the war." But premature classifications do not serve the cause of literary criticism. I don't think, in spite of the title [*Awake! and Other Wartime Poems*], that Mr. Rodgers would thank us to call him a war poet. And what do we mean by "*the* war poet"? In England, G. W. Stonier accepts Mr. Rodgers as "this war's Brooke." Well, it will be better if we forget about Brooke and the war for a moment and think about the poetry (for that matter quite a number of these poems were written before the war started). Just what we have got here?

This is the poetry, not of diagnosis, but of clarification. In the 1930s the younger English poets were busy answering the question, "What do you think of England, this country of ours where nobody is well?" They were diagnosing the ills of their time by means of a rather confused mixture of Freud, Marx, the English Public School, and a handful of minor prophets; their imagery was often ambivalent to the point of self-contradiction, they were confused about their audience, and they had a tendency to equate diagnosis with cure. Employing rich and involved techniques derived from Donne, Hopkins, the French Symbolists, Eliot, Pound, and a few personal choices, they tried to express in crowded verse their view of the nature of the present discontents. They produced some exciting poetry, but they never stopped sounding like experimentalists. Now Mr. Rodgers, though these are his first poems, doesn't sound like an experimentalist at all; nevertheless his poetry is fresh and original. One reason for this difference is that the young English poet of ten years ago had too much theoretical knowledge to be able to apply it successfully in a diagnosis of any contemporary ill.

. . . . Influenced . . . more by MacNeice and Spender than by Auden, and not so very much by any of them, his ideas are simple but not silly, his verse limpid but not trite. His characteristic fault is a kind of dead plainness—a good fault in a poet who comes after a decade of poetry that inclined to pedantic obfuscation. His characteristic virtue is speed and light. When I say that his ideas are simple, I mean that they are unified, coherent, communicable, which is not to say that they are easy. And he holds his words steadily in a cool palm. . . .

His most successful poems are constructed in a series of well-planned verse paragraphs, where the lines have a fine elasticity (occasionally overdone to the point of disturbing looseness) and the stanza is rounded to a genuine pause, sudden or slow, or . . . balanced savagely on a short, rhyming line.

David Daiches. *Poetry*. May, 1942, pp. 97–98

About this time, the poetry of W. R. Rodgers began to appear in magazines. Although it is easy to write extensively about Barker and Thomas and still say something important, it is not so easy to do with Rodgers, and that is just the point. There is nothing spectacular about him. In fact his verse has a sort of dogged earnestness about it, although it is far from pedestrian. His great virtue is that he speaks for himself. He is relatively free of the fashionable influences of the day, and he has almost no visible connection with the previous generation. His work is as simple and profound as he can make it. His effects are achieved quietly, and they are always the direct outcome of integral experience. He never depends upon secondary references to chic reading matter and current postures. One of his peculiar virtues is a special sonority—a sort of gong and woodwind depth and color of long vowel and labial, sibilant, and nasal music which is, as it were, a kind of counter Hopkins. Hopkins' baroque irritability expressed itself in staccato vowels and plosives and stops and a restive metrical distortion. Rodgers has the confidence of Solesmes or the pre-Bach organists—the marching, sure, unperturbed musical development of Byrd and Gibbons and Frescobaldi —a Protestant, or at least pre-Tridentine answer to Hopkins. The quality I associate most clearly with his work is a rugged, protestant magnanimity, courteous and polished enough superficially, but with, still underneath, a certain strongly masculine gaucherie. The comparison that springs to mind is Andrew Marvell.

Kenneth Rexroth. Introd. in *New British Poets,* ed. Kenneth Rexroth (N.Y., New Directions, 1949), p. xxi

Bringing only critical faculties to bear on them, I find a good deal to object to in Mr. Rodgers' poems. It seems to me that Mr. Rodgers assaults the reader with an armory of poetic blunderbusses. He is more sensitive to alliteration and onomatopoeia than to words, and more intoxicated by sensations than exact in metaphor and imagery. . . .

However insensitive his methods, Mr. Rodgers writes the kind of poetry he wants to write, and in a long poem . . . produces the effect of a big design, like a long-stretched roughed-in cartoon. . . .

Add to this, the whole poem [*Europa and the Bull*] is erotic, sensual, and genuinely exciting both as narrative and as a procession of sensations. Mr. Rodgers has also a certain wittiness—not altogether unlike that which gives so much pleasure to the admirers of Christopher Fry's plays—which sparkles from line to line. . . .

. . . . Rodgers is an uneven poet, sometimes extremely vivid and visual, sometimes . . . vulgar. Everyone though should read him, because he is a poetic phenomenon. Those like myself who find a good deal to object to cannot afford to ignore such an energetic talent. And those who not so particular will be stimulated by the energy which manages to retain simplicity while tying a great many verbal knots. There is a good deal of pleasure to be got from this book; and, whatever critical judgment may finally say about Mr. Rodgers, he can now straightaway, be enjoyed.

Stephen Spender. *NR*. March 23, 1953, pp. 19–20

ROLFE, FREDERICK (1860–1913)

Rolfe has no fame and few friends. Even with publishers he carried on acid controversies in green and heliotrope inks as to whether "Sixtus and Sixtine" were only corrupt forms of "Xystus and Xystine." On a point of medieval spelling or of wilful indentation he would challenge a legion of printers' devils. Artifex rather than artist, he was not a Lord of Language, but a would-be tyrant of words, and, words seemed to turn and tyrannise over him. His classical verbalisms amused scholars, but none dared to ask what he meant by "tygendis" or "technikrym." Ouche, birth-flare, lickerishly, liripipe, fylfot, noluntary, solert or talpine are good English, though rare. But tolutiloquent, contortuplication, fumificables (for tobacco), zaimph, aseity, purrothrixine, banaysically, remain to trouble commentators. The only meaning attachable to "rose-alexanrolith" might occur to a Chinese mind as a portmanteau-word for the London pavements on Alexandra Day. He was very fond of the word *precipitevolissimevolmente,* which would have made his literary epitaph. . . .

It is difficult to place his morbid sense of the picturesque and garish. His history never rose above the following: "So the Senior Branch in the line of the direct descendants of the murdered Duke of Gandia, bastard of the Lord Alexander P. P. VI, withered in sumptuous obscurity." His epigrams caught fire; single words blazed. He summed up Savonarola as a director turned dictator, the subtlety of which he urged in hectic and violent correspondence. As he grew older and lonelier he ceased hurling his gaudy books at a public who ignored him. In Venice he retired upon himself, and rumour said that he was occupied as a gondolier. Certainly his private craft, silken-sailed and fantastically painted, appeared in the canals. He died fearless and unforgiving, a defeated soul, who might have done much had he been born into the proper era. The Byronic pose would have suited him even better than the Borgian. In the curious game of "Parentage" he might have been placed as a fiery cross between Gilles de Retz and Marie Bashkirtseff. He died quite alone, and there was none to overhear if he muttered *"Qualis artifex pero!"* As he wrote of hero Hadrian VII: "Pray for the repose of his soul. He was so tired."

Shane Leslie. *LM.* Sept., 1923, pp. 509–10

In 1904 Baron Corvo abandoned his Barony and reverted to his natal name, though he gave it a deceptive twist by writing the first two letters of Frederick so that they might be read as Father (Fr. Rolfe). Appropriately, he first used his own name on his masterpiece, *Hadrian the Seventh.* It is an autobiographical drama, in which the hero throughout fulfils Rolfe's dreams. Like him, a rejected candidate for Holy Orders, the force of George Arthur Rose's vocation is recognized after twenty years of starvation and oppression have embittered him. Belatedly admitted to the priesthood, tardy amends are made for his sufferings, mental and financial. And then, by a combination of circumstance made to seem probable by astonishing art, he who was so recently the despised and rejected of men is elected to the Papacy, choosing the dignity of Hadrian the Seventh. Then the fun begins. Rolfe really lets himself go. Instead of becoming obedient to his cardinals, the new Pope lives up to his position of infallible autocrat. His sufferings have taught him command, not obedience. Half the delight is in the thinly veiled personalities, the palpable truth to fact. Hadrian appoints his early friends (all recognizable among Rolfe's acquaintances) as Bishops and Cardinals, and issues an astonishing Epistle to All Christians, admirable extracts from which are set before the reader. There is an interview between Hadrian and the Kaiser, and another with the King of Italy. All the dialogues ring out loud in the ear. On every page are metaphors like lightning, similes that shine, and appositions that linger in the mind like verse; but the comparisons out-top all in point, as in the descriptions of the Pope's "cold white candent voice, which was more caustic than silver nitrate, and more thrilling than a scream." . . . Rolfe's phrases tell as much as the paragraphs of others. Hadrian reconciles the papal and temporal powers in Italy by a Bull on the text, "My Kingdom is not of this World," and by relinquishing all claims to temporal dominion; and he sells the art treasures of the Vatican for thirty-three millions sterling, which is applied to the benefit of the Italian people. Finally, he is assassinated as he walks in procession through Rome, and the last words of the book are: "Pray for the repose of his soul. He was so tired."

Hadrian the Seventh is Rolfe's testament. There is no precedent for it in English literature, and even if his lost manuscripts are never recovered, it will assure him an exalted place in the appreciation of those who cherish good writing.

A. J. A. Symons. *LL*. July, 1928, pp. 92–93

The Quest for Corvo apparently continues on more levels than one: here, for instance, is yet another book by Corvo himself, hitherto unpublished (how many, one wonders, are still to come?); and a novel [*The Unspeakable Skipton*] by Miss Hansford Johnson in which Corvo's disreputable career is taken as the text for a study of literary paranoia. Why do we continue to find him so interesting? The answer is, I think, quite simply that Corvo was lucky enough (twenty-odd years after his death) to find the perfect Boswell: a better one, indeed—as some may think—than he deserved. The A.J.A. Symons's *Quest* was not only an admirable book in itself, but created a new genre in biography; it also, having aroused our interest and curiosity in Corvo, left a number of questions unanswered. But for Symons, one feels the self-styled Baron would have been long since forgotten; his talent was of the slenderest, and of a kind that wears badly; much of it, too, was dissipated in works which were really beyond his compass. He worked best on a small scale, and, apart from *Hadrian VII,* a notable if rather overblown tour de force, his longer books suffer from a poverty of imagination which no amount of windy rhetoric can conceal. He was also insanely vindictive and, his malicious gibes at his enemies become, by constant repetition and overemphasis, merely tedious. The sad truth is that Corvo, both as a man and as a writer, was really rather a bore, and—whatever his addicts may assert to the contrary—the posthumous cult, occasioned by Symons's biography, has been largely a success of scandal.

Nicholas Crabbe, like most of its predecessors, is crypto-autobiographical, and deals with Corvo's London years around the turn of the century. Much of it is a flat, factual account, very thinly disguised, of his quarrels with his publishers, John Lane and Grant Richards; the malice is more vitriolic than ever, but the freakish, quasi-Firbankian quality which distinguishes Corvo at his best is here largely absent, and the book makes dullish reading.

Jocelyn Brooke. *L*. May, 1959, pp. 68–69

ROSENBERG, ISAAC (1890–1918)

Of the many young poets who gave their lives in the war, Isaac Rosenberg was not the least gifted. Adverse circumstances, imperfect education, want of opportunity, impeded and obscured his genius; but whatever criticism be made of his poetry, its faults are plainly those of excess rather than deficiency. His writing was often difficult and obscure, because he instinctively thought in images and did not sufficiently appreciate the limitations of language. Also, a continual fear of being empty or thin led him to an over-intricate complexity. But there was no incoherence in his mind. . . .

The poems . . . speak for themselves. The obscurities, the straining and tormenting of language in the effort to find the right expression, the immaturities of style and taste, are apparent on the surface. The imaginative conceptions and the frequent gleam of imaginative phrasing should be equally apparent. But what does not appear on the surface is the fine intention, the ardent toil, and the continual self-criticism which underlay his work. Rosenberg's aim was, in his own words, a kind of poetry "where an interesting complexity of thought is kept in tone and right value to the dominating idea so that it is understandable and still ungraspable."

Laurence Binyon. Introd. in Isaac Rosenberg. Poems
(Heinemann, 1922), pp. 1, 11

Isaac Rosenberg was in direct line of descent from the Prophets. His upbringing had colored his life and his poetry was a reflection of his life. The intense ghetto-Jewish upbringing of his parents had bred in him a like acceptance of Jewish things. In him there is not apparent the struggle with outside influences that we find in earlier Jewish writers, as we find in Zangwill, that expressed itself in the aggressive-apologetic attitude. For, with Rosenberg, the time for the revolt from things Jewish had gone, its place taken by pride of race and a desire for the continuity of the best traditions of the Jews. . . .

It is from the viewpoint of his Jewishness that we must judge Rosenberg. Edward Shanks in his review of the *Poems* for the *Daily News,* June, 1924, realized this. He wrote, "In the pages of this book we discern a face no less alien than that which looks at us out of the frontispiece." But most of the other critics have failed to realize that to approach to an understanding of Rosenberg's work, one must first know and understand the Hebraicism which underlies everything he has written.

Beth Z. Lask. The Reflex. Dec., 1929, pp. 45–46

What most distinguishes Isaac Rosenberg from other English poets who wrote of the last war is the intense significance he saw in the kind of living effort the war called out, and the way in which his technique enabled him to present both the suffering and the waste as inseparable aspects of life in war. Further, there is in his work, without the least touch of coldness, nevertheless a certain impersonality: he tried to feel in the war a significance for life as such rather than seeing only its convulsion of the human life he knew. . . .

The significance which the war held for Rosenberg might have been anticipated from his dissatisfaction with the pre-war social order (especially acute, it seems, in South Africa where he was living when the war came). . . .

It was because of this attitude to the pre-war world that Rosenberg, hating the war, was yet unable to set against it the possibilities of ordinary civilian life and regret those in the way, for instance, that Wilfred Owen could regret them in "Strange Meeting." When Rosenberg wanted to refer to an achieved culture—rather than merely human possibilities—against which to measure the work of war he had to go back to remote and idealized Jewish history, producing "The Burning of the Temple" and "The Destruction of Jerusalem by the Babylonian Hordes." More usually he opposed both to war and to the triviality of contemporary civilization only a belief in the possibilities of life and a hope derived from its more primitive aspects. . . .

Rosenberg seems to have been specially impressed by the destruction of men at the moment of a simplified greatness which they could never have reached before, their destruction by the very forces that had made human strength and endurance more vividly impressive than ever. This conception of the war he tried to express through the fiction of some intention being fulfilled in the destruction. . . . From this it was a short inevitable step to the suggestion of some vague immortality for these lives. . . .

This immortality and the value he glimpses in the living effort of war in no way mitigate his suffering at the human pain and waste. The value of what was destroyed seemed to him to have been brought into sight only by the destruction, and he had to respond to both facts without allowing either to neutralize the other. It is this which is most impressive in Rosenberg: the complexity of experience which he was strong enough to permit himself and which his technique was fine enough to reveal. Naturally there were some aspects of the war which he was not able to compass in his response: maiming and lingering death he never treats of—he thinks only in terms of death which comes quickly enough to be regarded as a single living experience. Nevertheless the complexity he did achieve constituted a large part of his importance as a poet.

D. W. Harding. *Scy*. March, 1935, pp. 358–63

In reading and re-reading these poems I have been strongly impressed by their depth and integrity. I have found a sensitive and vigorous mind energetically interested in experimenting with language, and I have recognised in Rosenberg a fruitful fusion between English and Hebrew culture. Behind all his poetry there is a racial quality—biblical and prophetic. Scriptural and sculptural are the epithets I would apply to him. His experiments were a strenuous effort for impassioned expression; his imagination had a sinewy and muscular aliveness; often he saw things in terms of sculpture, but he did not carve or chisel; he *modelled* words with fierce energy and aspiration, finding ecstasy in form, dreaming in grandeurs of superb light and deep shadow; his poetic visions are mostly in sombre colours and looming sculptural masses, molten and amply wrought. Watching him working with words, I find him a poet of movement; words which express movement are often used by him and are essential to his natural utterance.

Rosenberg was not consciously a "war poet." But the war destroyed him. . . . "Break of Day in the Trenches" has for me a poignant and nostalgic quality which eliminates critical anaylsis. Sensuous front-line existence is there hateful and repellent, unforgettable and inescapable. And beyond this poem I see the poems he might have written after the war, and the life he might have lived when life began again behind those trenches which were the limbo of all sane humanity and world-improving imagination. For the spirit of poetry looks beyond life's trench-lines. And Isaac Rosenberg was naturally empowered with something of the divine spirit which touches our human clay to sublimity of this expression.

Siegfried Sassoon. Foreword in *Collected Works of Isaac Rosenberg* (Chatto and Windus, 1937), pp. ix, x

ROSS, ALAN (1922–   )

The Derelict Day . . . is a return to the reality that the Americans who were at home during the two wars never knew. These poems were written by a naval officer in Western Germany between June 1945 and July 1946. Thus they owe their inspiration to the first year of occupation; the atmosphere, sombre, desolate, hopeless, is poignantly conveyed from that land where the "cratered cities are already history" and so acute is the poet's power of observation that his handling of other themes, not merely for escapist reasons, is anticipated.

FR. Nov., 1947, p. 399

In *Time Was Away* Mr. Alan Ross and John Minton, his romantic illustrator, go to Corsica; and this, also, is a book on a high level: poetic, personal, the pungent effect of travel on keen senses. The book suffers in tone, however, from a hatred of Merimée's island; and this tone, which owes much to the dust bin smells of post-war Europe, is in danger of becoming a convention. . . .

Like Mr. William Sansom, Mr. Ross over-writes, also without vulgarity; given a taste for life and an individual feeling for the scene, this is not a bad way at all of writing books of travel, for it conveys strongly the sense (which highly-strung travellers have) of a fruitful conflict between themselves and the country. . . . As a present *Time Was Away* would be a pleasure to have; it is informative, excites envy of the travellers.

V. S. Pritchett. NSN. Dec. 4, 1948, p. 507

Mr. Alan Ross has an eye for colour and a feeling for atmosphere and his facility for calling up a picture by an arresting simile has established him as one of the most vivid of modern prose writers. But the qualities which distinguished *Time Was Away* and *The Bandit on the Billiard Table* as travel books come out less well as poetry.

His descriptions, for instance . . . are these truly poetry or the prose work of a brilliant journalist re-arranged? I do not use the word "journalist" with any derogatory implication. From the seventeenth century to the present day much of the best English prose has been written by journalists. But poetry must surely convey an idea or an impression which could not be so well conveyed in prose, and the recollection of Mr. Ross's resolute prose sometimes prevents enjoyment of his verse. The same qualities are there, a little weakened by transmutation, but there is rarely anything more.

C. V. Wedgwood. L. Sept., 1954, pp. 88, 91

His most obvious gift is one for vivid, impressionistic imagery. He is like a tourist passing through life who conscientiously, and effectively, ticks off the sensory qualities of things, detail by detail. When he wishes to go beyond the sensuous surface of his experience, however, his chief resource seems to be flat expository statement. Several of his poems . . . are little more than inventories of striking, detailed impressions. On the other hand, there are a few . . . which are little more than prose discourse. More frequently Mr. Ross encloses a richly figured texture in a prose framework. Some of these have a kind of innocent charm but most of them produce the effect of an immature art, of poetry not fully realized [*Something of the Sea: Poems 1942-52*].

Ernest Sandeen. *Poetry*. July, 1956, p. 270

Mr. Ross has an extremely sharp eye and nose for places, but oddly enough his purely descriptive pieces rarely make the impact that their material would seem to warrant. Perhaps there is too much material. . . .

So many notions (most of them excellent) scramble for places that too many lines are enjambed, have feminine endings, and often the verse seems to have no time to breathe—to sing, rather. Indeed such poems are on the whole less poetic, because more constrained, than many equivalent passages in the author's prose books.

But the present collection [*To Whom It May Concern*] which represents Mr. Ross's verse from 1952-57, contains several new departures and these are very much more interesting and successful. Most notable is a series of love poems towards the end of the book. In these, the trained senses of the observer report most acutely the physical aspects of the affair, and it is good to find what is so infrequently done in such poetry—the clothes, the flesh, the fard, the precise *mise-en-scène*. . . .

And even more important, these poems usually fall into a convincing form, much more melodious and memorable than the topographical pieces. No doubt the heightened emotion accounts for this, for though in his less personal verse Mr. Ross is not lacking in general ideas they do not seem passionately held. The coalescing into inevitable form happens, too, in a number of lighter, anecdotal poems which, again, I think, represent a fresh development. . . . In short, this is an uneven collection, but one which shows the author capable of going on to poetry of even greater feeling and control.

Roy Fuller. *L.* Oct., 1958, p. 73

Poetic journalism has its place, and Mr. Alan Ross is good at it. He always stays on the surface wherever he is, and he is ubiquitous. If male critics were not always making this most boring of dichotomies, I would never mention a poet's sex. But Mr. Ross's strike me as a wholly masculine world—not only, that is, an exclusive world, but selecting things to be exclusive about, like cricket and ward-rooms. . . . And all the love-poems seem to take place in bed which also counts as on the surface.

Kathleen Nott. *Enc.* Nov., 1958, p. 92

ROWSE, A. L. (1903–   )

How can every event and factor in England's evolution be rendered in 128 pages? Especially when a historian is no longer content to deal in reigns and campaigns only, but wishes to honour Hooker, Harvey, Hogarth, and Handel? Mr. Rowse [in *The Spirit of English History*] has managed this feat because his scholarship is not merely organised but canalised. It springs into channels so natural in appearance that the art of their arrangement is concealed. He may pack seemingly half a century into a paragraph, but then we find that was only a political summary; next comes a piece of the essential economic changes of the time, then an array of religious, literary, scientific, architectural interpretation. The current flows, never clogged with controversy or brought up against great locks like "the end of an age." With continuity, clearness and proportion are the virtues of what is in scope no more than an essay. As the centuries approach our own, each is treated with a little more complexity and a little more length than the one that went before. Always there is the suggestion of a reserve of learning, making us sure that Mr. Rowse could extemporaneously expand any given paragraph into a lecture or a chapter.

Spec. Dec. 17, 1943, p. 586

Mr. Rowse's collection [*The English Spirit*] falls into two or three main groups. There are the historical studies: here he shows his equipment. There are the pages on the poetry of Herbert and Swift: there he goes farther and shows his sensibility; and Mr. Rowse is richer, I think, in his evocative pages than in his argumentative ones. And then there are the more generalised pages on the English spirit, where he is a mixture of historian, poet and journalist. If it is true—but I do not think it is—that the English are modest and self-deprecating about their virtue and achievement, they are well served by the obliging Celts, the Welsh, Irish, the Scots and Cornishmen like Mr. Rowse, who remind the world that the Englishman is not a decadent because he is a peaceful man who admires above all the middle way. . . .

Mr. Rowse is at his best among the Elizabethans, not only because there he is soaked in knowledge, but because they, above all, fill the ardent side of his imagination; the more sensitive and reflective side is taken by the last peaceful decade before the Civil War, the years of Herbert, Vaughan and Traherne.

V. S. Pritchett. *NSN.* Nov. 18, 1944, p. 339

He combines a fiery local patriotism with a restless and imaginative antiquarian curiosity. No doubt he would claim that the two aspects of his faith are inseparable, and indeed in the best of his stories [*West Country Stories*] they often seem to be so. But there is, in fact, a certain stridency, an excess of protestation in his devotion to Cornwall which one never hears in the wiser and gentler tones of Mr. Rowse the historian. It is the declamatory patriotism of the Anglo-Indian, and Mr. Rowse is himself half an exile from his beloved Cornwall. . . .

But fortunately less than a third of the book is marred by this weakness. In such simpler and more direct anecdotes as How Dick Stephens Fought the Bear Mr. Rowse's imagination and curiosity run harmoniously together with the happiest results. And for the restrained passion of the antiquarian and historical sketches which fill more than half the book, I have felt that intimate admiration which is also an affection for the writer. Here he is a master. He has Trevelyan's genius for making the past as vivid and actual to us as the present, and love of his native place adds a lyrical quality which is rare indeed in a historian. The chapters on "The Duchy of Cornwall" and "Cornwall in the Civil War" are as exciting as most ghost stories. They are subjects with a minimum of intrinsic interest for me, yet the writer's enthusiasm is contagious and irresistible. It is fact and not fiction which fires Mr. Rowse, and the fact is never dry, but living, mysterious and poetic.

Philip Toynbee. *NSN*. Jan. 26, 1946, pp. 68–69

Mr. Rowse's *The Spirit of English History* is a pleasantly written brief survey of many aspects of English life from the beginning to modern times. There is not as much philosophy in it as in Trevelyan's *English Social History* or in Williamson's *The Evolution of England,* but there are many wise comments, a nice feeling for the English countryside, and an agreeable prejudice for the author's own Cornwall. Mr. Rowse's pervasive and complacent nationalism will prove a trifle tedious to American readers. When he says, for example, that Elizabeth was forced to undertake the conquest of Ireland "at great expense and the cost of infinite misery" because Philip of Spain had intervened there, he is carrying his justification of English policy too far. But he does manage to put into the shortest of short histories of the English people a great deal of varied information about English living and work without making it a manual or a textbook. Mr. Rowse is at all times readable.

He makes a few slips. Cromwell was not an East Anglian squire but a cadet member of a wealthy and new Huntingdonshire family. Sir John Eliot was not by any means the leader of the House of Commons. Many of Rowse's literary judgments would be disputed. But these are small matters.

Wallace Notestein. *YR*. Winter, 1946, p. 347

A. L. Rowse, eminent historian, loves his Shakespeare well but not wisely. Like a husband who claims to understand his wife and then proceeds to prove the opposite, Rowse tackles the subject possessively. His biography suffers from this proprietary attitude. Although distinguished by insight and fullness of vision, it makes assertions which simply are not proven [*William Shakespeare*]. . . .

Sometimes he can be brilliant in his psychological insights, as in his discussion of Marlowe and Shakespeare. Shakespeare offered less of an embrace to reason than to passion in his work, while Marlowe always fired his poetry from his head. Yet Marlowe died in a tavern brawl while Shakespeare lived out his life by means of calculated, rational compromises.

There is no reason why a great historian should not be a great literary critic, but I don't think Rowse has closed the gap. His volume is immensely loud. Declaration and self-confidence, however, are only the beginning of accomplishment.

Martin Tucker. *NYEP*. Jan. 19, 1964, p. 43

ROYDE-SMITH, NAOMI (? –1964)

The weakness of the piece [*Mafro, Darling*] is its hesitation between comedy of manners, for which Mafro is too fantastic, and frank farce from which Miss Royde-Smith and the company were constantly turning away. It is possible to argue, of course, that the fantastication should be diminished and even abolished, Mafro toned down, and the delicate comedy, always inherent in the theme, developed. Undoubtedly Miss Royde-Smith could do that very nicely in a novel; probably she could have so succeeded in a play of gentle comedy, as she proved by the writing of one or two of the episodes. But I am not at all sure that a large theatre in Shaftesbury Avenue is tactically the right place for it.

Ivor Brown. *SR*. March 2, 1929, pp. 282–83

Some novels show such distinguished qualities that one begins at once to scold them for not being first-class. *The Island* shows many distinguished qualities, but they belong rather to the author's mind than to her book. . . . Thwarted in her normal impulse, she [the heroine] falls in love with a vain, beautiful and selfish girl. . . .

Such a story should be deeply moving, or even unbearably depressing. The last chapters strike home, but it is hard to respond to the story as a whole. . . . Miss Royde-Smith is fond of cat images and will, perhaps, pardon us if we follow her effort to find out what is wrong. Like a mother-cat with her kittens, she will not let her characters alone. She sets them down, and invites the reader to observe them; and then, impatient of their efforts, she picks them up, gives them a good explanatory wash, and puts them down again, shaken and blinking, somewhere else. *The Island* is full of good things; but it ought to have been first-class.

L. A. G. Strong. *Spec.* July 12, 1930, p. 60

"When there's a conflict the first thing to do is realize both sides of the contest—and then to find a bridge between them," says one of the characters in *The Bridge,* and in doing so states the central theme of Miss Royde-Smith's book. . . . There is at times a startling loveliness about this novel, with its slow opening, the sudden swift contrast of place and persons forced on Andra, and the final return to a slower tempo.

Brian Roberts. *LL.* Dec., 1932, p. 481

All Star Cast is an ingenious but not a very satisfactory novel. . . . Miss Royde-Smith writes with considerable knowledge of the theatre and with considerable animus against old-fashioned dramatic critics. The book begins well; but Miss Royde-Smith never succeeds in convincing us that we should like to see the play.

Peter Quennell. *NSN.* Aug. 22, 1936, p. 259

There is . . . no room for preaching in Miss Royde-Smith's *For Us in the Dark,* which is a crime story treated realistically. It is a rather dreadful book, because its subject is dreadful, and no attempt is made to conceal the sordidness or mitigate the horror. . . . It is a long work, with a complicated plot, and it is very well done, except for what occasionally strikes one as a note of exaggeration, a wilful piling of horror upon horror. . . . Readers with stout nerves and a curiosity to meet the criminal soul face to face will not be disappointed.

Forrest Reid. *Spec.* Oct. 1, 1937, p. 558

The readers to whom this title recalls Caponsacchi's apologia [*For Us in the Dark*] will find his suspicions confirmed by the note: "The story of this novel is based on the published reports of a famous trial, and all the characters in it are drawn from life." In effect Miss Smith has cast Browning's *The Ring and the Book* in modern English dress. She has accomplished this feat with extraordinary skill. Every character in Browning's masterpiece finds a counterpart in the translation. . . . At times the reader forgets the magnificent authority of Browning, and abandons himself to melodrama of the type fixed by Ouida or Marie Corelli. Nor is the book worse for that.

R.M.L. NR. Jan. 19, 1938, p. 319

RUSSELL, BERTRAND (1872–   )

Mr. Russell's lectures on psychology [*The Analysis of Mind*] are, as you would expect, brilliant in form and radically critical in intention. He has approached the subject, the most abused in all philosophy, with the frame of mind belonging to a general philosopher, and has sought rather to arrange and simplify modern thought upon it than to advance theories of his own, though theories of his own he certainly enjoys.

H. C. Harwood. LM. April, 1922, p. 668

The Scientific Outlook . . . should be read at the same time as *Brave New World* [by Aldous Huxley]. Mr. Russell, a prophet of a different calibre, corroborates Mr. Huxley at several points. He, too, imagines that the commonweal may take over the organization of human breeding, that certain categories may be reared for certain tasks, and supervised and strictly controlled during their leisure. . . . He, too, sees in the removal of all suffering the shipwreck of the restless human soul; while his vision of the scientific world-oligarchy is even more appalling and fraught with terror.

Peter Quennell. LL. March, 1932, pp. 115–16

Lord Russell, as everybody knows, is an extremely witty writer. His wit is, however, peculiar in being due less to the appositiveness of verbal connections than to the logical drive of his thought seeking expression. . . . Lord Russell's manner of writing more closely resembles the style of the eighteenth-century than that of any other writer. As in Hume and Gibbon, the mildness of the manner is in inverse proportion to the pungency of the sense. Lord Russell writes with a velvet pen. It is only at the close of the unemphatic paragraphs that the claws appear and some touch of cat-like malice enchants or scarifies the reader. . . .

But if the manner is that of Hume and Gibbon, the attitude is that of Voltaire. Intolerance, cant, hypocrisy, stupidity—to Russell, as to Voltaire, these things are intolerable; above all, stupidity. . . .

Like Pareto, Lord Russell exhibits human behavior for our inspection with an air of scientific detachment. . . . In fact, however, the air of objectivity is delusive. Judgment is implicit in every line, and almost always it is adverse. . . .

Lord Russell's own creed . . . appears to be that of an eighteenth-century rationalist. Kindliness and tolerance are the great virtues: live and let live the only possible rules of conduct: the provision of comfortable leisure for individuals the object of politics: the knowledge of how rightly to employ it the end of ethics. Possibly! But, admiring them as ends, Lord Russell seems to have a poor opinion of these things as means. Never have I known tolerance advocated with such venom, or good nature praised so bitterly.

C. E. M. Joad. *NSN*. Oct. 12, 1935, pp. 527–28

On Sunday Bertrand Russell will be eighty. He ought, by this time, to seem "venerable," especially as he is, after all, a philosopher, and indeed the greatest philosopher alive. But he is too full of life, youth, hope, wit, and provocation to assume the tranquil dignity of age. He is very much *not* retired. Since he was seventy, he has published ten new books—the tenth, called *The Impact of Science on Society,* appears this week—and several of those books are as controversial as any he has written. He broadcasts and lectures regularly and sends an occasional scorching letter to the Press. A year or two ago he hit the sea in a Scandinavian air-crash, but swam with Socratic calm and more than Socratic energy to safety. His appearance is immensely distinguished: a trim, erect figure with a fine head of white hair and a face that is at once sharply Voltairean and gently humane. At a time in which pessimism is an almost universal faith, and orthodox religion is reclaiming so many intellectuals, Lord Russell remains adamantly optimistic, anti-clerical, utilitarian; he is unwavering in his belief in reason, in the necessity, and the practicability, of rational solutions to the problems of mankind. . . .

As a philosopher, Lord Russell has no patience with theoretical ethics, but as a publicist he has had much to say about contemporary morals. His views on marriage and education inevitably attracted attention. The book that was taken by careless readers to advocate adultery suggested in fact that sexual impulse should be "trained instead of thwarted," and that voluntary self-sacrifice, prompted by love, should take the place of repression based on taboo. In education, Lord Russell has never suggested that children should have no discipline, but rather that the element of force in education should be reduced to the barest minimum. To discover that barest minimum, he ran a school in collaboration with his second wife, Dora Russell. After this experiment he returned to university teaching, first in America and then at Cambridge, where he was reinstated as a Fellow of Trinity during the Second World War.

Maurice Cranston. *Spec.* May 16, 1952, pp. 635–36

When Bertrand Russell published a book of short stories a year or so ago, it seemed a trifle odd that this distinguished philospher and social critic should have turned, at his age, to writing mildly amusing fiction. It now appears that in *Satan in the Suburbs* Lord Russell was merely getting the range. With his latest book, *Nightmares of Eminent Persons,* he lays down the real barrage and sweeps the enemy right off the field.

Everything Lord Russell learned about storytelling in his earlier experiment is now used to build up and enliven a group of satirical fables which demolish, and in some cases, positively atomize, a number of the author's bêtes noires. Semantics, the prudish censorship that assumes knowledge must be sinful, the dismal resignation that psychiatry calls adjustment, existentialism, modern power politics, and finally the whole mechanical world of the future collapse into rubble under his fire.

Although the pieces are witty, unpredictable, and wildly fantastic, they are written in a formal, even severe prose which achieves a note of timeless authority. . . .

I suspect that Lord Russell, for all his cynicism and despite his habit of smashing idols, is a romantic at heart. History and observation tell him that the folly, vanity, cowardice and cruelty of the human race are all but unlimited. He will not, however, resign himself to this fact, and clings stubbornly to the dream of a world ruled by kindness, intelligence, and dignity. As Dr. Bombasticus would say, he refuses to adjust. His refusal may be somewhat uncomfortable for Lord Russell, but when he puts it into comic terms, it is sheer joy for his readers.

Phoebe Adams. *At.* Sept., 1955, pp. 80–81

At ninety, George Bernard Shaw was merely a grand old man, safe and senile on the shelf of public adulation. But Russell can galvanize a police court, write books that are read for what they say, irrespective of the age of the person saying it, and be refused the use of the London Festival Hall for his ninetieth birthday party—in case the celebrations might lead to a breach of the peace. Yet in an age which prizes the false bonhomie of the television personality, Russell's crisp and emphatic answers have a Victorian manliness which is quite alien to the medium in which they appear.

In this respect, he reminds one more of a latter-day J. S. Mill than of any contemporary type. Nor is this merely fanciful comparison. Russell has said that he is in complete agreement with Mill's values, especially in the emphasis placed upon the liberty of the individual;

and one has only to recall the now celebrated broadcast debate between Russell and the Jesuit Fr. Copleston to see that what Russell has said of Mill can be said of himself: his intellectual integrity is impeccable. Until he went to Cambridge, Russell, like Mill, was "solitary, shy and priggish." But Mill was never a university man, whereas Cambridge fitted Russell like a glove, and he became a Fellow of Trinity in 1895.

If Mill can be described as having a joyless knowledge of the sources of joy, this cannot be said of Russell whose sheer exuberance has helped to make him the best-seller he is. He admitted to Alfred North Whitehead, with whom he collaborated on *Principia Mathematica* from 1910-13, that he loved words; they seemed, said Whitehead, to satisfy his craving for expression. Yet beneath the wit is an edge of deep intellectual penetration. . . .

Russell remains, as he admitted on his eightieth birthday, an optimist, refusing to accept fatalistically that man is born for trouble; and this is precisely where he disappoints most deeply—in the vision of the Paradise, as he calls it, that man can and will achieve, if only he banishes the threat of nuclear warfare. No man's solution can rise above his analysis, and a distinct limitation is revealed by Russell's constant, even breezy, denial of that fuller understanding of human nature which dawned upon Mill when, in asking himself the question, "if all your objects in life were realized, would this be a great joy and happiness to you?," he found that an irrepressible self-consciousness distinctly answered "No!"

John Coulson. *Com.* June 15, 1962, pp. 301, 303

Though publication of this volume [*Political Ideas*] adds nothing to what is already known of Bertrand Russell's political views, it is interesting as showing how early his style and thought matured. It consists of pieces on capitalism, socialism, individual liberty and national independence which were intended to be given as lectures during the First World War, but the Government did not allow them to be delivered. They were published in 1917 in the United States and the first lecture, which gives a title to the book, was actually delivered in Glasgow by Robert Smillie, President of the Miners' Federation.

TLS. Dec. 5, 1963, p. 1002

RUSSELL, GEORGE WILLIAM (1867–1935)

Repetition . . . spoils the discursive charm of *A Londoner's Logbook,* a reproduction of one of those monthly gossipings which one reads on their appearance in the *Cornhill* with a good deal of pleasure further enhanced by the certainty that they would not be a lasting burden on the memory. In these Mr. Russell repeats not himself but others. . . . It is not unlikely that in a hundred years or so the book may be of some value. Suburbia is not badly sketched and the names of eminent people drop out with the allusive grace that would please the people he sketches. Future historians may not improbably look on Mr. Russell as diarist somewhat as they now regard Horace Walpole's letters. The Logbook is inferior to the letters in that it was written to please a mass of people rather than a succession of units; but Mr. Russell even when he is telling a very old story or spreading his month's store of humour most thin has the light touch. He can express his mild satire with something of the same success as Mr. [Augustine] Birrell his mild criticism; and we prefer them both in a magazine.

SR. Jan. 24, 1903, pp. 112–13

This delightful little book [*Cooperation and Nationality*] appears very opportunely, at a moment when the forces of rural reform are, in Ireland and elsewhere, coming to grips with certain "vested interests" which block their way. In thirteen vivid chapters Mr. Russell defines what is gradually coming to be known as the problem of rural life, describes the conditions which have produced it, and, as his main task, indicates a solution. He is primarily concerned with Ireland, but makes it clear that the causes of rural decay, though they act with peculiar intensity in Ireland, are much the same all over the world, and need the same remedies everywhere.

OutL. April 13, 1912, p. 551

The evolution of George W. Russell, the economist, from "Æ.," the mystic poet, has been gradual. The one has so slowly merged into the other that it is now difficult to dissociate them. In the beginning, "Æ." came forward primarily as an exponent of mysticism, though in such an early pamphlet as *Priest or Hero?* one can discern the later polemicist on behalf of intellectual freedom. With "John Eglinton," Charles Johnston, W. B. Yeats, and Charles Weekes, he was one of a group of young men who met together in Dublin, some twenty to twenty-five years ago, for the discussion and reading of the Vedas and Upanishads. These young enthusiasts created in time a regular centre of intellectual activity, which was translated in part into some of the most interesting literature of the Irish Revival. Their journals, *The Irish Theosophist, The Internationalist,* and *The International Theosophist,* contained a great deal of matter which has since taken a high place in modern Anglo-Irish literature. It was in the pages of those reviews that the first poems of "Æ." were published, and to them we owe a number of essays afterwards collected by "John Eglinton" under the title, *Pebbles From a Brook*. Of all who contributed to that intellectual awakening few remain, in the Hermetic Society, as it is now called. But "Æ." is still the mystic teacher, the ardent seer, whose visions and eloquence continue to influence those about him. One no longer enjoys the spectacle described by Standish O'Grady, of the youthful "Æ.," his hair flying in the wind, perched on the hillside preaching pantheism to the idle crowd. His friends Johnston and Weekes are elsewhere, the heroic days of intellectual and spiritual revolt have passed; but "Æ." may yet be seen, in less romantic surroundings, constantly preaching the gospel of freedom and idealism.

Ernest A. Boyd. *Appreciations and Depreciations*
(T. Fisher Unwin, 1917), pp. 27–28

His appeal, to the bright modern whose prophets are Sitwells and Huxleys, may not be immediate, but to any who can and will accept his mood, it will be profound and permanent. This submission to "the Vedic seers," this concern with the flesh only as the clay envelope of the kaleidoscopic rainbow spirit, may suggest a blunting of that sharp immediacy of secular experience found, especially, in some of Mr. [Aldous] Huxley's work, but none can deny, when the surface is penetrated, the presence of a deeper and more enduring beauty, a beauty of that intelligence which is the soul, flowering in the grave and lovely poetry of a man who has pondered deeply upon life in quest for an enduring reality, and who in his quest has passed beyond revolt to understanding of the mystery of pain as the condition of joy. . . .

Geoffrey West. *Adel.* Aug., 1931, p. 44

Æ's book, *Song and Its Fountains,* may be taken either as a curiosity or an unusual experiment in creative criticism. It is a book which should eventually stimulate arguments because of its implications and challenge to psychological usage; unfortunately, for the moment it has been only accorded a reverential welcome by those who uncover their heads and look pious whenever the word "soul" or "mystic" is mentioned. It is probable that Æ's mystical ideas would surprise those amiable critics if they pursued them. Here, however, we are concerned with the literary implications of his book. The comments of poets upon their intimations and moods of inspiration have been but jottings and scribblings. . . . Æ, in *The Candle of Vision,* attempted to trace the workings of the imagination, and he began, like Bergson in his study of dreams, with that moment when we shut our eyes and encounter the void of darkness. In this book he takes a number of his own poems, not as object lessons but, so to speak, as gins to catch the unsuspecting visitants of mind. . . . Æ analyses that passive mood of the waking consciousness, which the plain man dismisses as day-dreaming or mooning—the creative mood of poetry—and surmises a commerce between the inner being and the outer being. This vivifying method of setting a poem to catch its own tail is, at least, a stimulating variation on critical means. But the book is more than criticism—it is the revelation of a poet's imaginative life and his visual experiences attained by a disciplined concentration which belongs to the East.

Austin Clarke. LL. June, 1932, pp. 228, 230

Æ . . . has a metaphysical theme for his long poem, *The House of the Titans;* it is an allegory of the heavenly descent of the soul. It has not the power nor the psychological depth of Mr. [Conrad] Aiken's poem [*Landscape West of Eden*], but it is free also from his (perhaps) necessary obscurity. The blank verse of *The House of the Titans* is clear and quiet, and the poem lives by the nobility of the theme, seen through the words rather than in them, and by the poet's subservience to it. The slight, sometimes beautiful, shorter poems in this volume, though they have many subjects, constantly return, in a word or phrase, to the same theme, as though it were the water that nourished their existence.

LL. Jan., 1935, p. 481

Though really belonging to what is called, in the vocabulary of the moment, the petty bourgeoisie, Æ was an aristocrat, with all those qualities that have been so impressively summarized by the Russian philosopher Berdyaev as marks of an aristocracy: he was magnanimous, he was unenvious, he was courageous, he had no prejudices, he was a free being. I never knew him to take personal offense, though he sometimes showed a fury like a god in a rage at things said against his country or his countrymen. His open letter to Rudyard Kipling, who had jibed at Irish nationalism, was such a reproof and on such a large-minded plane that Kipling's reputation as a writer was shaken, even unjustly shaken. . . .

His was never the biting Dublin wit—sometimes Dublin wit was nothing but plain downright malice—but Æ's had always something affectionate and whimsical in it, and one remembered it like a caress. It was this, I think, that helped to make him, along with his great magnanimity, the most popular, next to Douglas Hyde, of the men of the Irish Renaissance. His appearance is familiar to Americans, for he came here often to lecture and was widely photographed. The sudden entrance of this tall, broad-shouldered, bearded man into any assembly would give a thrill to the beholders, for he looked a prophet, a seer, a high priest of some divinity. He was a familiar figure in many milieus, for he mingled in all the activity of his country, whatever form they took —politics, art, literature, education, the theater, the labor movement— the last indeed with passion. During the bitter and revolutionary transport workers' strike of 1913 he took the platform for the workers and made a sensation by announcing, in that beautiful voice of his, "All the real manhood of this city is to be found amongst those who earn less than a pound a week." His sympathy with labor was not the literary and sentimental attitude and attitudinizing now common among writers, but of such a nature that the workers looked to him as one of their spokesmen and counselors.

Mary Colum. Life and the Dream
(Garden City, N. Y., Doubleday, 1947), pp. 171–73

Perhaps the most isolated literary figure of the beginning of this century is Æ (George William Russell). Æ does not, like Blake, create his own mythology, but his poetry is inspired by a tradition to which modern western civilization is diametrically opposed: a combination of theosophy with Celtic mythology. Whereas Yeats was influenced by French symbolism and other literary movements, Æ remained faithful to his essentially religious sources. His poetry does not reach the perfection achieved by Yeats, and he considered life to be much more important than poetry. It has been said that, among great Irishmen, Yeats was the poet, and Æ the saint. Æ dismisses Christianity as a belief which has been artificially grafted on the Irish soil while the cosmic consciousness was dwindling and replaced by individual perception. Christianity, according to Æ, is but a moral code, whereas three things are required of a religion: a cosmogony, a psychology and a moral code. Æ's doctrine might be summed up by saying that he believed in the divinity of both Man and the Earth, and that the purpose of life is to re-unite with the Ancestral Self; for Æ admits the Fall of man. His aim in his poems is to communicate with the divine beings who are still present in the Memory of Earth, and in this respect his poetry may be regarded as fervently religious: "I believe that most of what was said of God was in reality said of that Spirit whose body is Earth." . . .

Human suffering, according to Æ, derives from the fact that the earth is a place of exile where the vision of eternity is a release from pain. This is why his poems are so human and so touching (cf. the poem entitled "Pain"). Moreover, they are full of a warm sympathy towards nature, for in his eyes nature is not impersonal but the very face of the spirit.

Almost all his poems express communion with the spirit of life which endows all things and beings with the halo of a magic presence, as if they reopened the dried-up source of primitive, myth-creating poetry. The world seems new and wonderful when the humblest things have a soul, and a scientific mind is bound to be startled by this transfigured world.

Raymond Tschumi. *Thought in Twentieth-Century English Poetry* (Routledge and Kegan Paul, 1951), pp. 251–53

Æ was neither a fraud nor a failure, though Sean O'Casey has lengthily accused him of being both. Paradoxically for one often loosely described as a "mystic," Æ would have regarded his inability to deserve that title as his greatest shortcoming; in a letter of 1894 he confessed, "I am not capable of leading the pure ascetic life in thought and act which alone can develop any spiritual insight worth acquiring." On the other hand, he felt no regret at not having developed a systematic philosophy: "You see my life has been made up of a series of visions and intuitions, and each of these (has) appeared to me so precious that I never thought of making a system out of these intuitions." Nor did he care to perfect his artistry in any medium ". . . literature does not interest me enough to make me anxious to work hard at it. I simply want to live a natural energetic life. . . . I am working for causes I feel to be good." Æ's success lay in being himself, a pre-eminently good man. Now that he is dead, we can find but little of him in his poems, his prose or his paintings; if we are to reach him at all, it must be through . . . [his] letters or in the writings of men who themselves were far from good—George Moore, for instance.

Vivian Mercier. *NYT*. Dec. 24, 1961, p. 11

SACKVILLE-WEST, EDWARD (1901-1965)

The Ruin, Mr. Sackville-West's new novel, has its weaknesses, but a hasty recourse to cynicism is not among them. He calls his novel Gothic, and it is true that the physical attitudes in which the characters find or put themselves are always strange, generally angular, and often beautiful, but subject and treatment recall the Elizabethan rather than the Middle Age. Many readers will remember Mr. Sackville-West's *Piano Quintet.* In that remarkable book he succeeded, by an imaginative interpretation of the minute facts of human experience, by dwelling always on the inexplicit and unarticulated, in conveying the effect of an intense spiritual drama. One might hazard a guess that *The Ruin* is an earlier work; in style it is often immature and often awkward, its dialogue is frequently unnatural and conforms to no convention, even of the author's own, its texture is uneven and its touch undecided. Unlike its predecessor, it is emphatically not an accomplished book. . . .

Intensity is the chief characteristic of Mr. Sackville-West's art: it never relaxes, persisting in season and out of season, sometimes with a ludicrous effect. He overcharges the common moments of life; he makes the characters equally capable of emotion, so that they seem to evolve out of each other. But though for small occasions this is a positive defect, for the passionate scenes which occupy the second half of the book it is an enormous gain: for the dialect of despair, which is common to all men, rises unerringly to the characters' lips. The greater the demands Mr. Sackville-West makes upon his talent, the more readily it responds until . . . it is indistinguishable from genius. As a complete work *The Ruin* cannot be counted a success. . . . But it contains passages that are almost unique: passages in which the mind and soul are stretched and amplified to their extreme capacity, passages in which beauty, love, and terror have found a new and livelier expression, and in which splendour of conception is matched by nobility of language.
L. P. Hartley. *SR.* Sept. 18, 1926, pp. 317–18

. . . he has not lost sight of the quality which makes lasting biographies—the essayist's touch which draws from all these details and references a recurrent music. . . .

The undertaking [*A Flame in Sunlight: The Life and Work of Thomas de Quincey*] was valiant, and the result is attractive; even where opinions will differ, Mr. Sackville-West pleases us with his earnest search for the truth. . . . In any case Mr. Sackville-West has not shunned what as an artist of ideas he might have disrelished, the underlying labours of good biography.

Edmund Blunden. *Spec.* April 17, 1936, p. 711

During the past decade Mr. Edward Sackville-West has, deservedly, earned for himself a considerable reputation as a critic equally authoritative on painting, literature, music, and even radio; the understanding of these art-forms has, for many, been both clarified and enriched by the powerful searchlight trained upon them by this keen, discerning mind. The individuality and soundness of his views, together with the extreme felicity of phrase in which these views are expressed, combine to make his work remarkable in an age where constructive criticism is a comparative rarity, and where, as he himself has commented, the critical apparatus has become, owing to a general lowering of standards, woefully unstable. . . .

It was not until the publication of *The Ruin* in 1926, however, that Mr. Sackville-West's general trends and highly personal myth began to show their outline. *The Ruin* is sub-titled "A Gothic Novel," which is in itself revelatory, for Mr. Sackville-West shares the preoccupation with the *roman noir* expressed by the surrealist, many of whose methods and basic tenets were to be incorporated in the revolutionary organization of *The Sun in Capricorn:* the relation of Gothic standards to the fabric of contemporary reality is a major feature of his work, though in its initial manifestation the conventional ingredients are deftly modernized, and the setting, the huge grey country house Vair, bears, apart from its antiquity, no resemblance to a crumbling House of Usher or Castle of Otranto. . . .

. . . [*The Sun In Capricorn*] must be considered his greatest triumph: a work astonishing, in its enormous scope and complexity, from an author so young at the time of writing. To examine it in detail would require a separate essay, for it is conceived on a multitude of different planes all of which converge to a central point, the node of the novel. It can be read as an allegory, a novel of action or of ideas (attaining frequently, on these levels, to the stature of *The Possessed,* from which perhaps it originally derived), a work of political and social significance, or a love-story; the fusion of these seemingly disparate trends is accomplished with consummate dexterity and a serious single-mindedness of purpose comparable to Conrad's, whose *Under Western Eyes* may be suggested as another formative influence.

TLS. May 11, 1951, p. 292

Edward Sackville-West is, to my mind, one of the subtlest and most interesting of living novelists; yet he has, as a writer of fiction, been unduly neglected in recent years, and it is perhaps worthwhile to enquire, briefly, into the reasons for this.

In the first place he is, without a doubt, one of the most *variously* talented men of his age. Consider the range of his activities: he is a brilliant amateur pianist, as well as being a learned authority on musical history; he has been, in his time, a poet, a radio-dramatist and a biographer; and has lately published a volume of essays [*Inclinations*] which establishes him as one of the most sensitive and penetrating critics of our day. Thus to distinguish oneself in so many fields is, in an age of specialists, a very remarkable achievement; too often, nowadays, a man thus brilliantly equipped will either be compelled (from economic or other motives) to concentrate, to his disadvantage, upon a single activity, or (which is worse) will tend to lapse into a facile amateurism. Mr. Sackville-West has avoided both those pitfalls; and if his output as a novelist has been comparatively slight, the reason is, I think, not that he has dissipated his talent in other directions, but that his finely-developed critical sense has prevented him from publishing work which fails to conform with his own high standards.

This stringent self-criticism has, perhaps, been indirectly responsible for his recent comparative neglect: he has not published a novel for seventeen years, and so long a silence is liable to prove damaging. . . . But there are . . . more important reasons why Mr. Sackville-West should, in recent years, have been overlooked; it is not merely that he lacks the qualities which go to make a "popular" novelist—so, after all, did Joyce and Virginia Woolf; it is rather, I should say, the highly personal and idiosyncratic nature of his writing which has tended to alienate the critics—and especially those whose influence has been in the ascendant since the nineteen-thirties. His whole attitude to writing—as well as his writing itself—is deplorably "unfashionable"; he is, for instance, a romantic. . . . Moreover, he is essentially a religious writer, though this is usually implicit in his work rather than explicit; and finally there is his style—as individual and as personal to himself as that of any other modern writer. Mr. Sackville-West could never have become (in the sense that, say, Joyce or Hemingway became) a *chef d'école;* he stands as a novelist entirely apart, and the special quality of his writing is far too personal and (as I think) too subtle to be easily imitable.

Jocelyn Brooke. *Month.* Aug., 1951, pp. 99–100

SACKVILLE-WEST, V. (1892–1962)

Miss Sackville-West has already shown in her poetry and her first novel, *Heritage,* how deep and true is her passion for beauty, especially the beauty of the English country-side. She has interpreted the peculiar splendour of the Kentish weald admirably. In *The Dragon in Shallow Waters* she gave us terror, purgings through pity . . . but of all her work I think the most characteristic, the most memorable is her short story (not so very short, one hundred and twenty pages), *The Heir: A Love Story.* It is one of the world's perfect love stories . . . the growth of love in a man for a house. . . .

There is an amazing sense of quiet satisfaction to be got out of this story. We are made to feel that it really is one of the world's great love stories.

Miss Sackville-West's prose is a clarion call to slack Englishmen to look to the rock whence they were hewn and to make some effort to stem the foreign invasion. The old squirearchy are being displaced by commercial plutocrats who know nothing of, and care nothing for, the beauty of the English country-side. She strives to make us realise the heritage that is ours in such places as Knole before they are dismantled and changed.

S. P. B. Mais. *Some Modern Authors*
(Grant Richards, 1923), pp. 142, 144

She has done everything in her life, I imagine, simply because she thought it would be a delightful thing to do. The result of this is that she has made her own atmosphere, by collecting around her, quite unconsciously, a number of other atmospheres; first the atmosphere of Knole, English fields, houses, hills and rivers; the atmosphere of Persia and the East; the atmosphere of a certain kind of English society; the atmosphere of certain friends who seemed to her delightful people and therefore good friends to have. I would say that she has never definitely chosen anything or anybody all her life long, but that when a place or a person or a book has appeared close to her and has seemed the sort of place or person or book natural to her, she has attached it to herself without consciously thinking about it. This makes inevitably her position romantic, whether she wishes it or no, because the essence of romantic living is to find pleasure in the things around one, and she has found intense pleasure in them. This intensity of approach is at the basis of all her work.

I do not think that before *The Edwardians* she was a very good novelist. *The Dragon in Shallow Waters, Heritage* and *The Heir* are works of atmosphere, not of character creation, philosophical ideas or narrative force. Her cleverest book of this kind, *Seducers in Equador,* is a brilliant imitation rather than an original creation. Nevertheless I believe *The Heir* to be one of the best of modern long short-stories and I thought for some time that that was where her talent lay—in the creation of a beautiful place, its loveliness evoked by a poet, the figures in it like statues in a garden. . . .

Seducers in Equador was one of the earliest pupils in Mrs. Woolf's school for good writing. I do not know how highly Miss Sackville-West values this amusing little book. She may indignantly protest that it owes nothing at all to Mrs. Woolf. Authors are given to these indignations, but it is a further fact that Mrs. Woolf is Miss Sackville-West's closest friend among writers; they meet constantly and understand each other perfectly. All the more remarkable then that Miss Sackville-West has kept her independence, that most precious of her gifts, so resolutely, for *Seducers in Equador* is the only one of her books that shows any sign of Mrs. Woolf's influence. . . .

I do not think that I am claiming for Miss Sackville-West any of the extravagant things that personal friendship and interest sometimes blind one to claiming. I think that she is only in mid-career, but I must confess that I find among all the writers in England no one else who has achieved such distinction in so many different directions. The novelists who are also poets, the poets who are also novelists, are very rare always. Among the novelists now that Hardy is dead, Rudyard Kipling (who is not really a novelist), Ford Madox Ford and Rose Macaulay are almost the only examples of whom I can think as poets, and among the poets only Osbert Sitwell and Martin Armstrong as novelists.

Hugh Walpole. *Bkm.* Sept., 1930, pp. 23, 26

Joan of Arc, as Miss Sackville-West truly says, "makes us think, makes us question; she uncovers the dark places into which we may fear to look." . . .

To settle the obstinate questionings of these invisible things, she determined to go through the whole tragic history in all its tedious details, and to set it down as objectively as possible. Rightly, she has deliberately lowered the tone. Her style is as far removed from the rhapsody of De Quincey as from the ribaldry of Voltaire while it yet avoids the involuntary panegyrics of Anatole France and the curiously dubious admiration of Bernard Shaw. She shuns all poetry, and of set purpose keeps to the prose of the investigating historian. This is the correct attitude for one like her, who confesses that she is in "the position of anybody torn between an instinctive reliance on instinct and a reasonable reliance on reason." [*Saint Joan of Arc*]

E. E. Kellett. *Spec*. June 19, 1936, p. 1141

. . . Miss Sackville-West is traditional, even old-fashioned, both in matter and manner, and it may be said at once that this reluctance frequently fetters the spirit of her work, and encourages a personal timidity through which it is the duty of an artist to break. At its most repressive moments, it piles up poetic phrases in her work, conventionalises emotions, and dodges behind literary echoes of form and diction. . . .

Indeed no lights are burning in the ivory tower. But that is not the only tower which this poet inhabits. I should say that it is a place where she retreats during certain moods of weariness of mind, of defeatism, when confidence falls low, and her sense of purpose wavers. She is not often to be found there. Her more natural place is in a tower not of ivory, but of brick, a richly coloured house set in a richly coloured land, and furnished with a collection of treasures gathered by her as she has ranged over time, scholarship, and life. This tower, not pallid and circular, but eight-sided, represents at each angle an idiosyncrasy of the persons within, whose vigour, sensuality, passion, practicalness, and common-sense are gathered thereby. . . .

Throughout her work . . . [the] quality of personal elegy, the celebration of emotions that at the time seemed inexhaustible and insurmountable, yet have been survived by her, persists as a sort of ground-bass, giving a deep tone to her verse, a Roman quality which has perhaps much to do with her attraction toward the work of Virgil, and the conscious modelling of *The Land* on the form and mood of *The Georgics*. . . .

Through that restriction of theme . . . she has mastered more than her subject. She has mastered also the waywardness and turbulence of her moods, bit down their vagueness to a precision that is hard and objective, given them a universal out of a personal value. She has put her hand to the plough in more senses than one. She says that "the country habit has me by the heart," and her heart, under that discipline, works the more harmoniously with her mind. This process, a hard one which cannot be mastered merely by willing, needs time, patience and experience before it can be acquired. Once acquired, however, it produces that essential poetry which is content with simple words, unliterary associations, and humble effects.

Richard Church. *FR*. Dec., 1940, pp. 600–5

Ultimately what her work poses is a religious question: the validity of "order," determining or determined by qualities of the heart. Order has a repetitive motion in time; it keeps a social form in being; it is a vehicle for culture. Above and around the social order are those other orders of which she is acutely aware: the soil through the seasons, and the monastic, contemplative order, generating graces impalpable but potent. While the social order changes, is continually breaking down and reforming, the two other orders, those of the soil and the soul remain constant—the root of life and its ultimate flower. In *Pepita* Miss Sackville-West disclaims the title of novelist. "I hated writing novels," she tells her mother, "really only cared about writing poetry and other things." One need not take her too literally to see her as fulfilling her clearest intentions in her poetry and, of the "other things," in *The Eagle and the Dove,* also her *Saint Joan of Arc.* . . .

In her poetry Miss Sackville-West at times dreams of a hotter sun than ours. "But in this dear delusion of a South. . . . We northerners must turn towards our flowers." And so she turns to make bloom her Wealden clay of "yeavy spite." "The country habit has me by the heart." Emerging from the order of the great house in its heyday, she has based her poetry and her life latterly on the order of nature, with its wintry austerities, its flowery rewards; a type it may be of other orders, but in an age of doubt at least a sure footing and foundation for a belief in life. Miss Sackville-West is fascinated by problems of the integral self and its sources. Like Keats she is "capable of being in uncertainties, mysteries, doubts, without any irritable reaching after fact and reason." Rather, in a mood of devout uncertainty she continues to develop and deepen.

TLS. Feb. 6, 1953, p. 88

Miss Victoria Sackville-West prefaces her life of *La Grande Mademoiselle* with some sensible remarks about translation, and the difficulties of retaining the style of a past epoch even when the words themselves seem most easy to render into another language. . . . Miss Sackville-West has been right to approach her subject in an entirely unpretentious, easy-going manner. She never presents Mademoiselle as anything but a goose, and by the end one has a clear idea of just the sort of goose she was. . . .

. . . Miss Sackville-West has produced a sympathetic and convincing picture—perhaps one should say tapestry.

Anthony Powell. *Spec.* April 10, 1959, p. 518

SAINTSBURY, GEORGE (1845–1933)

With this third volume, *From Blake to Swinburne,* Professor Saintsbury completes his great history, and sets English Prosody firmly and finally (in more than one sense) on its feet. For the Professor, in his general conclusions, is entirely convincing, and we do not think we shall hear much more of the rival theorists with whom he has such incidental fun. The fact that the learned writer does get fun out of so serious a subject as the technical study of English poetry will probably scandalise the less poetical critics, and we can imagine pompous people declaring that many a sentence in this book is "neither good grammar nor good criticism." But the fact is that a *History of English Prosody* by any one else would probably be unreadable, while Professor Saintsbury, with his personal asides, his intimate footnotes, and his breezy dogmatism, is always stimulating (if only *quia multum amat*) and often brilliantly right. The most serious fault in the book is the dismissal of Meredith's poetry in half a page, probably because Professor Saintsbury (who is nothing if not partial) does not like it. . . . But if authors were to suppress their personal likes and dislikes for the sake of Procrustes, their books would be very dull. Whereas Professor Saintsbury's work is delightful to read and invaluable to all students of poetry.

Eng. R. July, 1910, p. 763

Now, the great, and perhaps peculiar, glory of Professor Saintsbury is that he has retained this gusto, this central flame of literary enthusiasm, throughout a long career (be it noted that he is treated here as a writer) devoted to the chronicling of literary history and similar ventures. Note, first, the sheer bulk of his work: several volumes of essays on individual writers, periods, styles, and what not; anthologies and various editing work; biographies; histories of English, French, European literatures; histories of criticism, English prosody, English prose rhythm; the novel, English and French; and so forth. The list is amazing: the mere sight of it intimidates one and makes the more indolent of us wonder what we do with our time. But mere bulk tells us comparatively little. As some ubiquitous contemporaries have shown us, it is not difficult to suggest solid achievement, at least in the catalogues, by dint of hashing and rehashing. I have heard of a certain tradesman, now dead, who had a passion for collecting execrable verse and making books of it, until at last he took up more space in the literary reference books than almost any living writer. But if we examine some of the volumes in this list, and think of what went to the making of them, our wonder and admiration can only grow. To say, as Professor Saintsbury himself does somewhere, that he has "undertaken some tough literary ventures" in his time is only to understate the matter. With the audacity of an Elizabethan sea-captain, he has put out his cockle-boats into vast uncharted oceans of literature, and returned triumphant, laden with glittering spoil and odorous

with strange spices. . . . Throughout he never declines from the critic proper, apt to appreciate and compare, to the mere recorder with his blunted palate and lack-lustre eye. Hardly ever do we meet with the weary gesture, so familiar elsewhere, that directs the author and his work to their appointed pigeon-hole, the particular kind. . . . And it is this almost unique combination of extraordinarily wide reading and research and unflagging appreciation, gusto (call it what you will), that makes him so rare a critic, so delightful a guide and companion in letters, for these and any other times. There is such a brave and human spirit shining through everything that he has written that one is stupefied at the queer epithets—"academic," "pedantic," and the like—that have been hurled at him by novelists turned critics and others; . . . .
J. B. Priestley. Figures in Modern Literature
(John Lane, 1924), pp. 145–47

His long life, sixty years of which we may estimate to have been entirely devoted to the service of literature, does fall, as symmetrically as he could have wished, into three literary generations. In the first of these, if we neglect infancy and apprenticeship, he made his reputation not, one gathers, without dust and heat; in the second, having gained a secure and dignified academic position, he wrote his biggest books and taught with increasing authority and widening influence; the third was a kind of St. Martin's summer in the course of which it was given him to complete . . . all his remaining literary projects except a History of the English Scholastics which perhaps few would prefer to have in exchange for what he accomplished towards his History of Wine. In the seventeen or eighteen years of the last phase, between his resignation of the Editor's chair and his death a few weeks ago, he had attained while still alive the quasi-historic status due to his great achievements and his immense learning. He had also attracted to himself the personal affection not only of the survivors of the first two generations but of many who belonged entirely to the third and who knew him chiefly, and often only, by his writings and by his fame.
Sir George Chrystal. LM. March, 1933, p. 434

Saintsbury, since his death, has come more and more to stand out as the sole English literary critic of the late-nineteenth and early-twentieth centuries, the sole full-length professional critic, who is really of first-rate stature. He is perhaps the only English critic, with the possible exception of Leslie Stephen, whose work is comparable, for comprehensiveness and brilliance, to the great French critics of the nineteenth century. Unlike them, he has no interest in ideas. In religion he was Church of England and in politics an extreme Tory, but his prejudices were rarely allowed to interfere with his appetite for good literature, wherever and by whomever written. He was probably the greatest connoisseur of literature—in the same sense that he was a connoisseur of wines, about which he also wrote—that we have ever had in English. In this, he stood quite outside the academic tradition. Though he contributed to the *Encyclopaedia* and to *The Cambridge History of English Literature,* he has always more or less the air of a man who is showing a friend the sights of some well-studied and loved locality. . . .

Reading *The Peace of the Augustans,* I came at last to realize that Saintsbury, besides being a great critic and scholar, was one of the best English *writers* of his time. The spell that he can cast in his more mature work is of a kind that is not common in literary criticism; it is more like the spell of fiction or memoirs— . . . . What he has done is create an imaginative world composed almost exclusively of books and their makers, with an admixture of foods and wines. In this world, his ostensible occupation is tasting and digesting the authors (as well as the vintages and dinners) and appraising them with scrupulous fairness from the point of view of the enjoyment they afford; but this record becomes an adventure story and a commentary on human experience, ...

Edmund Wilson. *Classics and Commercials*
(N.Y., Farrar, Straus, 1950), pp. 306–7, 366–67

SAKI (1870–1916)

"Saki" has given us many good things but nothing quite so good as this. It is with a sense of very real pleasure that we are able to pay tribute to its high excellence [*The Unbearable Bassington*]. Mr. Muñro's craftsmanship is remarkable. In the present story he works in froth, in the flippant, frivolous, bridge-playing, much-talking, much-shopping, killing-time world of a certain section of London society. Yet in the end the froth turns out to be almost unbearably solid. We do not remember any book which has left us more saddened and more obsessed by a sense of dreary intolerable pain. At once cynical, witty, and debonair, Mr. Munro's epigrams are like the stars of the sky for multitude. But so light and polished are they that they never become tiresome. . . . A great book.

OutL. Nov. 16, 1912, p. 671

Within the narrow limits of his few score of short stories and his single brief novel, Saki achieved a remarkable individuality and perfection.

His stories, often little more than expanded anecdotes, or satirical essays cast into dialogue, are usually farcical, though here and there a gruesome little horror tale challenges comparison with his spine-chilling contemporaries, Arthur Machen and Montague Rhodes James. It is noteworthy that these stories by Saki are usually based on the werewolf theme or some other abnormal interplay between the human and the animal worlds.

His comic stories, however, reveal a sardonic view of human nature and a cold intellectual cruelty which perhaps in the long run render them more horrifying than the stories of terror which are interspersed. A transitional species of story is that which uses the supernatural for comic effect, such as "Tobermory" and "Ministers of Grace"—a device later exploited by Thorne Smith, who may be described as the Wodehouse of fantasy. But the main stream of Saki's characteristic work is to be seen in the stories wherein his favorite spokesmen, Clovis Sangrail or Reginald, amuse themselves by concocting some outrageous and circumstantial lie to befuddle a credulous listener or to rout a tedious one. Often, as in "The Unrest Cure," "The Lull," "The She Wolf," and "The Stampeding of Lady Bastable," the lie is not merely verbal, but becomes a complicated plot for terrorizing an unwanted guest or for mortifying a complacent egotist.

In these two basic ingredients—deception and sadism—Saki's stories point directly back to the plots and characters of the Jonsonian and Restoration comedies. The author's supercilious air of mockery is so well sustained that the reader is never sure how much of the satire is directed toward the clever and unprincipled young men who inflict the torture and how much toward their victims. But the attribution of "sadism" to the stories is justified by a reading of Saki's one novel, *The Unbearable Bassington,* which depicts the same social scene and the same types of personality, with an unexpected absence of farce. Comus Bassington is definitely a pathological sadist, and the author tries to analyze his behavior in the perspectives of his family, his school, and his caste.

Lionel Stevenson. *AQ.* Autumn, 1949, pp. 232–33

Mr. E. V. Lucas, expert on both mirth and grimness, long ago described the perfect hostess as one who puts by the guestroom bed "a volume either of O. Henry or Saki or both." It is all right to put it there, but one hopes it will be brought downstairs the next morning, for Saki's most perfect felicity is to be read aloud in a house-party setting. The bracketing with O. Henry is not just casual; though the two are as different as Texas and Surrey, both are instinctive story-tellers dealing perfectly with their chosen material. (Both also did all their best work for newspapers.) . . . Both Saki and O. Henry are masters of the park-bench setting. Saki was less insistent on twisting the story's tail, but an equal master of surprise when he chose. . . . He could purge the decorous amenities of an English weekend party with blasts of cyclone farce. He could show the conversation of a few ladies at bridge as deadly and quick on the trigger of concealed weapons as a Western barroom brawl.

Christopher Morley. Introd. in *Short Stories of Saki* (N.Y., Modern Library, 1958), pp. v-vi

The new worlds that were being explored by Edwardian writers like Wells and Bennett, the social problems investigated by Galsworthy, the scandalous social situations that provided subjects for Mr. Maugham, were either uninteresting or repulsive to him.

Perhaps it is chiefly for this reason that there is little serious criticism of him, and that little is unsatisfactory. He has been compared with Max Beerbohm, O. Henry and John Oliver Hobbes, and Mr. Evelyn Waugh has said that he "stands in succession between Wilde and Firbank in the extinct line of literary dandies." Such comparisons seem not wrong but incomplete, because they ignore so much that can be found in his writing. It is true that some of his stories end with the snap of a tale by O. Henry—one in this selection is "The Reticence of Lady Anne," in which a husband enters a drawing room where his wife is sitting in an armchair, and carries on an argument with her in monologue form. The last line of the story reveals that she has been dead for two hours. Another theme used more than once puts a man in an embarrassing position in the presence of a woman who is finally discovered to be blind. But such tricks are the least part of Saki, and are found in comparatively few stories. He lacks the urbanity of Beerbohm, the good humour of Wilde and the irresponsible gaiety of Firbank. The chief characteristics of his writing are its casualness, flawed wit and cruelty.

The casualness sprang from the circumstances in which the stories were written. They appeared in weekly periodicals and were cut to the length (or rather the brevity) that was required. It does not seem that Saki took them seriously. There is no indication that he ever talked about his own art, or about art at all, to his friends. Saki was a wit by nature, an artist by accident, and he was unlucky in the time at which his talent came to flower. Edwardian writers almost all show the touch of vulgarity that makes the whole world kin, and Saki is not immune from it. At its finest, his wit is the kind of verbal explosion that would sound even better on the stage than it looks in print. The stories are comic, ingenious, interesting, witty: but it is *The Unbearable Bassington* . . . that justifies a belief in Saki as a writer with a major talent that was repressed into minor manifestations.

TLS. Nov. 21, 1963, p. 946

SANSOM, WILLIAM (1912–   )

He is not interested in character for its own sake as [Henry] Green is; he picks out in his characters' minds only those few instants in which they are being immediately reacted upon by some impersonal power, fire or water or steam, by which they are in danger of being controlled. In this way Green's more orthodox picture of human action against the background of the blitz is replaced by a disturbing vision of dwarfed human insignificance before the elemental onset of fire or explosion or vertigo or pressure of water. Smoke billows up, flames crackle, pumps roar, jets play, walls fall; and in the eyes and mind of the helpless firemen the imagination transfers the terrifying dynamism to the inanimate object. "The Wall" can be taken as the perfect example and epitome of Sansom's instinctive imaginative approach to contemporary activity; and he has repeated this unashamedly enlarged realism in later studies, notably "In the Morning" and "The Boiler Room," in both of which the destructive power latent in certain objects, a storage tank full of petrol and a boiler on the point of bursting, supplies the motive force for what little human action there is.

Sansom clearly finds a diabolical fascination in the machinery which clutters up our particular corner of modern existence. The trailer-pumps which chug through his stories, the hoses that snake and coil through them, the dynamos that hum and the ladders that sway, are all given lurid life in the flickering flames and drifting smoke, crashing walls and blazing roofs. Life with Sansom is a kind of animated Wadsworth landscape dancing devils' tattoos in a fearsome reek that Wadsworth's flat functionalism never visualized. Perhaps a more illuminating comparison is with Graham Sutherland; and the calling shapes and beckoning shadows dire, which his view of our age has impelled Sutherland to mass into his pictures, are closely enough akin to Sansom's mechanical familiars to make the artist express in his own medium very much what the writer expresses in his. . . . I dwell on Sansom's preoccupation with this suggestive symbolism because it is to be regarded as symptomatic of the profound unease that he shares, perhaps unusually sensitively, with all sensitive people today.

Ronald Mason in *Modern British Writing,* ed. D. V. Baker (N.Y., Vanguard, 1947), pp. 284–85

Perhaps the best story here [*Three*] is "The Cleaner's Story." It is an elaborate, lyrical and highly original performance. We are shown the life of a French provincial town through the eyes of a being who is down on her knees scrubbing a café floor. . . .

When all this has been said—still no impression of Mr. Sansom's story is given whatsoever. And to tell the truth, it is as difficult to catch hold of this author's texture, to expound his spiritual pyrotechnics, as it would be to put salt on the tails of a great herd of unicorns and fireflies—should one ever endeavor to do so. Yet as a matter of fact Mr. Sansom's individual gift does lie, not in the plots of his allegorical tales, but indeed in their texture. That is to say, in the flickering of his poetical green fingers, which have only to point to our platitudinous everyday things—boots and shoes, railway trucks, dirty teacups, luxury flats, bits of grey fluff on the floor—to make them at once stir in their profound sleep, sit up, grimace and chirrup, come unexpectedly clattering at us—or sing *arias* in the grand manner, perhaps discourse on metaphysical points, wrestle and dance, sing beautiful love songs—and disappear again like the famous spectre, with a perfume and a most melodious twang. (Such green blood ran also in the veins of Strindberg and Maeterlinck. And by the same token I should much like to see Mr. Sansom attempt a play.)

Julia Strachey. *Hor.* May, 1946, p. 357

There has been a curious change in William Sansom. *The Body,* his first novel, is a break with his own past. He belonged to the group of young British writers who work in the Kafka tradition, presumably in the hope of creating a new, major art form. Sansom's short stories (*Fireman Flower*) had reached a point where great expectations were not unreasonable. He had availed himself of the beat in Kafka, the structure that can be turned any way to fit modern life, the analogues of experience, the philosophical tone. But he has dropped all this, just when one might have expected him to carry it further. . . .

The strange thing is that this break-through into actual experience should leave Sansom's writing not richer, but thinner than before. The abundance of sensations is no gain. In throwing off Kafka, he has deprived himself of a ready-made ordering principle, the intellectual form that the latter's style provides. He freed himself with a vengeance; in his eagerness to write a novel redeeming experience, he cast away the earlier concepts, forgetting to provide any of his own. But there is not only an intellectual vacancy; *The Body* lacks directness, it comes at experience obliquely, from the surface, with a glancing blow and a shower of words that seldom pierce through. The oblique is an endemic disease of contemporary English fiction, it is the style of the lowered capacity for life, and *The Body,* like all the other novels, is thoroughly spotted with it.

Isaac Rosenfeld. *PR*. Sept., 1949, pp. 950–51

The Face of Innocence . . . is a new departure by a writer of already proven talent. William Sansom has so far written about a highly individual, almost private vision of life; it is as if he had fulfilled the child's dream of being three inches high and able to walk through the field grass, seeing the commonplace herbs transformed into a fantastic jungle. Most of his work has been dominated by the poetic lyricism of an entirely fresh and uncorrupted eye focussed on the familiar—seeing the side of a house, its hallway, the vest of the man who lives in it, and the light fixture on its stairway, as if such things had never been seen before. His novel *The Body* was an astonishing treatment of the optics of jealousy, a story almost entirely developed in terms of things seen rather than things heard or felt. His new novel develops largely through conversation, and the poetic vision survives in only a few passages, though in all its crystalline and limpid beauty. . . . What takes its place is a gay, if somewhat acid, humor, a tone of light mockery.

. . . There is a pleasant edge—approaching satire—to it when the three chief characters go to the south of France and Tunis for a tense and unwise holiday: seldom has the discomfort and unease of a particular kind of British traveller been better drawn. Mr. Sansom's new manner has created something odd and enjoyable, a combination of emotional penetration and delicacy with comedy that recalls the good-natured frolicking of the best Wodehouse.

Anthony West. *TNY*. Sept. 8, 1951, pp. 110, 113–14

Mr. Sansom's new novel [*A Bed of Roses*] seems to be a study in cruelty. It opens with a vivid and very effective description of the claustrophobic horror of a girl locked in a cupboard by her bullying lover, and continues, it seems, on a course of deliberate degradation. . . .

If Mr. Sansom intended to teach the lesson that there is an unpleasant side to all of us which plays no small part in the mixed motives of human attraction, he has got his emphasis wrong, and his story reads as the triumph of egoism and exhibitionism over all instinctive as well as conventional standards of decency. Perhaps he intends it as a warning, but if so it is little needed, since it is only in a novel that one would have the patience to put up with so unpleasant a character as Guy for so long a time. In the background is much pleasing description of travel in Spain, and it is only regrettable that Mr. Sansom did not leave his readers to enjoy it without involving them in the unrewarding crossplay of Guy and Louise.

TLS. Jan. 29, 1954, p. 69

William Sansom's new novel is the best thing he has written since *The Body* which perhaps it even surpasses. He is one of the few novelists practising today whose books are read for the writing, who can excite and move by selecting a particular word and placing it in a particular position in a sentence, whose style is elastic and can be adapted to the various moods it expresses. In the past this virtuosity has occasionally involved a sense of strain; reading *The Loving Eye* one is constantly startled by the originality of his observation and the exactitude with which his prose conveys it, but the technique is so consummate that the total effect is delectably smooth. His subject is the mysterious world of London back-gardens, which he evokes with poetry and humor: across these a man sees a strange girl at her window, falls in love with her, gets to know her, marries her. In fact, not much happens, but like Eudora Welty Mr. Sansom can create a scene in such sensuous detail that the minimum of incident is needed to animate it. . . . The success of this London romance proves again that Mr. Sansom is more happily inspired by the English scene than by more obviously exotic "foreign parts."

Francis Wyndham. *L.* Dec., 1956, pp. 75, 77

Of his particular faculty, one is most aware when (as so often in the novels and stories) he makes the officially "ordinary" his province. In part, indeed, the hold on us of his fiction lies in that conjury which transmutes the banal—the suburban street, the stale little city park with its asphalt margin, the overlit trite café, the too-glossy living room. This forceful, at times all but hallucinated, imagination kindles at just those scenes from which others shrink. How will such a writer fare when what confronts him is in itself exotic?

The prestige of the Sansom travel books is the answer. I admit to finding *Blue Skies, Brown Studies* less dazzling, as a whole, than its predecessor, the Scandinavian *The Icicle and the Sun,* though as vicarious travel it is as satisfactory, and as a performance no less adroit—in one aspect, even, possibly more so. Mileage is greater (we range from the Mediterranean up to the Baltic); and with that, the general subject is more comprehensive. . . .

This writer's strength, apart from his way of seeing, is his style—subtle, alert, concrete, racy, poetic. Living style nourished by all five senses, bold in its metaphors—roof tiles of Provençal hill towns likened to "apricot-colored Donegal tweed," the restored Vienna Opera House to "a giant white-and-gold powder compact of exquisite workmanship," distant Italian cypresses to "tomb-green ice-lollies," and so on.

Elizabeth Bowen. *NYT.* June 18, 1961, p. 1

SASSOON, SIEGFRIED (1886–   )

He is the personification of the intellectual attitude toward modern warfare. Those "low-jargoning men" who were temporary soldiers haunt him, and they swarm through his book [*War Poems*] querying every detail of that Fate which, against most of their feelings, made of them something new, incongruous, in every way at variance with intellectual ideas. He loves them passionately. . . .

We have still to learn whether Siegfried Sassoon, with his red anger, his queer understanding of men, his sensitiveness, his pride, his facility in spinning a song, the absurd ingenuousness of his rhythm, but the great force and interest of his present production, will be sufficiently inspired by other subjects in the future to engage our sympathies in Peace as he has stirred our emotions in War.

Harold Monro. Some Contemporary Poets
(Leonard Parsons, 1920), pp. 130, 137

One takes up today a volume of verse like *Georgian Poetry, 1918-19.* Here are poems by Mr. de la Mare, Mr. Wilfred Wilson Gibson, Mr. W. H. Davies, none of them without lyrical feeling or felicity of expression. But the poems that stand out in this volume are the war poems of Mr. Siegfried Sassoon. Beside them most of the other poems in the volume become dim and insubstantial—a pretty cloaking of conceits with words, a flight for refuge into private fantasies. The mutinous passion of Mr. Sassoon's poems hovers on the edge of hysteria and unendurable pain —"I'm going crazy; I'm going stark, staring mad because of the guns"— but what is left in the end is a piercing sense of tragedy, of loss and agony and bitter destruction. From Mr. Sassoon's impassioned testimony to the pity of war, its waste and desolation, his pride in the endurance of men, his lament for the singing that will never be done—from this one turns to the singing of other poets in wartime. Here are delicate and consoling fancies in plenty, reassuring thoughts and comforting images. . . . Alas! There is no beauty in talking about beauty. There is no poetry in invoking poetic conventions.

Robert D. Charques. Contemporary Literature and the
Social Revolution (Secker, 1933), pp. 68–69

Mr. Sassoon turned in disgust from the "dying heroes and their deathless deeds" to *Suicide in Trenches,* remorse after killing, "unmanly" collapses, physical horrors. He excelled in the terse colloquial anecdote.

Worse than military blunders, however, were the crass ignorance of civilians, the belief "That chivalry redeems the war's disgrace," that the wounded were "longing to go out again," that all was well with uncomplaining heroes. In *Song Books of the War* he foresaw the oblivion that falls on the public mind, and the return of the romantic view of war against which he was striving.

Such pieces are too acid for the popular anthologists, who prefer the radiant "Everyone Sang." Yet they are Mr. Sassoon's gift to modern poetry; they reveal the Georgian turning from the lyrical moment to the socially significant, shedding his romance under the compulsion of disillusionment and sympathy, freeing himself from rhetoric, and achieving by forthright rhythm, a new, often epigrammatic, pungency.

After the War, Mr. Sassoon continued to batter the shallow façades of complacency. His technique changed little. Occasionally a tedious mock-pedantry and an excessive alliteration went hand in hand with a certain peevishness. The best of these later poems are those in which a light Byronic influence is uppermost; for instance, "Lines Written in Anticipation of a London Paper attaining a Guaranteed Circulation of Ten Million Daily," in which with apparently casual wit he traces the history of the press-peer, comments on the News Value of the Bible, and congratulates all those whose activities have led to an expansion of circulation.

Geoffrey Bullough. *The Trend of Modern Poetry*
(Oliver and Boyd, 1934), pp. 97–98

Siegfried Sassoon, like those authors whom Charles Lamb loved, is above all a *person*. You cannot fit his works into any of the neat critical pigeonholes. He is the "non-attached" writer, a type which in these days of regimentation is becoming increasingly rare. The best of his writings are "the language of the heart," expressing no "ideology" but simply conveying to the reader the vision and the wisdom of a fine, sensitive personality, at once imaginative and humorous. W. B. Yeats once called William Morris the happiest of poets. It may seem paradoxical to apply this phrase to the author of the terrible war poems of 1918, but Sassoon's later books are the work of one of those rare minds which good fortune cannot spoil, and which can enjoy without complacency. The publication of his new prose work, *The Old Century,* perhaps the most carefully wrought, and in some ways the most beautiful of his books, provides a fitting occasion for a short survey of his writings.

The son of a member of a distinguished Anglo-Jewish family and of the sister of Hamo Thorneycroft, the sculptor, herself an accomplished painter, Siegfried Sassoon was brought up in a household full of artistic associations, and in his boyhood dreamed of writing poems which would be a counterpart to G. F. Watt's pictures. His earliest publications were slim volumes of richly decorated verse of the Pre-Raphaelite kind (printed at his own expense), but the beginning of his really important and characteristic poetry is to be found in that remarkable poem, now unfortunately unobtainable, called *The Daffodil Murderer,* published anonymously in 1913. . . .

His new book, *The Old Century,* is a "straight" autobiography, a series of pictures of the author's boyhood and early manhood; "pictures," however, is an inadequate term to describe what Sassoon does in these pages. He seems not so much to delineate the past as to live through it again, and to take his reader with him on a kind of enchanted voyage to his mother's house in Kent, to the Norfolk rectory where the family holidays were spent, to Marlborough and Cambridge and other places in that queer remote pre-War England which knew nothing of the blessings of bombing aeroplanes or poison gas. The writing of this book has the quality of "gusto" which Hazlitt admired in prose, the power of making the reader share the writer's enjoyment. It belongs not so much to the class of autobiographies as to that of works of wise and happy contemplation of the past, such as certain of Hazlitt's essays, Gissing's *The Private Papers of Henry Ryecroft,* Somerset Maugham's travel books, and some parts of George Moore's reminiscences.

Sassoon's achievement is twofold, and it is difficult to say which part of it is the more admirable or likely to be more enduring. His early work was a notable part of that testimony of English poetry against war in the twentieth century which is comparable with the testimony of Byron and Shelley against tyranny in the nineteenth. In his later years he has created an island of peace where the spirit can find refreshment in a world of turbulence and chaos; and this refreshment is given not by the easy method of escape into a world of fantasy, but by the delighted contemplation of life through the medium of a poet's wisdom.

V. De Sola Pinto. *Eng.* Spring, 1939, pp. 215, 224

The instinct which has led him to project now in verse, now in admirable prose, his past experience, has been a sure one. At first it may seem strange that a poet should have spent so large a part of his life in writing autobiography. He has gone over as a memoirist the same ground, though, of course, with fresh detail, which he had covered in *Memoirs of a Fox-Hunting Man* and the Sherston series. *The Weald of Youth, The Old Century,* and now *Siegfried's Journey* together cover his life from childhood to 1920. But it has been worthwhile. For apart from that literary skill and fineness of observation which give intense pleasure to readers, his temperament and adventures enabled him to help us understand our own times.

Desmond MacCarthy. *Memories* (Macgibbon and Kee, 1953), pp. 143–44

Mr. Sassoon, one of our elders in the magic, has written little over the last few years. His values are those of a different age. If poets are makers now, they were *seers* then, skryers; and his work still bathes in a warm afterglow of Yeats. His new book [*Sequences*] is full of the ripeness of contemplation and his lyric vein is still the grave and tender instrument it always was; but the sharp sense of aphorism which made him the best satirical poet of the first world war is still there and the ideal still fits its envelope of form perfectly. His themes have changed, however, and he has become the poet of sadness, inhabiting memories of better(worse?) days. His place in our poetry is a secure one for those who value such compassionate thoughtfulness and ripeness of experience.

Lawrence Durrell. *TT*. Dec. 8, 1956, p. 1533

SAVAGE, D. S. (1917–   )

Originally greatly under the influence of D. H. Lawrence, D. S. Savage has developed along similar lines. He makes the rather acute point that a thoroughly integrated person would not go about calling himself a "personalist," but his book, *The Personal Principle,* is a review of the masters of a generation, Lawrence, Yeats, Eliot, Crane, Auden, in terms of their ability to achieve personal integration or integral personality. The fact that he gives critical approval only to Harold Monro casts a certain suspicion on his method, but the book has some penetrating insights and has been very influential. His poetry certainly shows forth an integral personality lost in the violent, noisy, squalid darkness of a depersonalized and collapsing society. Savage, once the British editor of the forthrightly Lawrentian magazine *Phoenix,* is one of the possible channels through which D. H. Lawrence has re-emerged as a powerful, even dominant influence.

Kenneth Rexroth. Introd. in *New British Poets*, ed. Kenneth Rexroth (N.Y., New Directions, 1949), pp. xxiii-xxiv

D. S. Savage is an excellent, original, and sometimes infuriating critic. These six essays [*The Withered Branch*] on E. M. Forster, Virginia Woolf, Aldous Huxley, Hemingway, Joyce, and Margiad Evans . . . contain some of the best things I have read lately in the field of literary criticism. Mr. Savage is distressing, I suppose, because just on the edge of real achievement, he will take a dizzy jump into the absolute.

Part of the book's brilliance and value comes from its complete repudiation of the so-called New Critics. . . . Mr. Savage disposes of the question of "technique" straight off by comparing it with "a much more primary and fundamental activity, which I propose to call *vision*." . . .

What counts is how the critic operates in these areas. And I might add that it is good to have the solid, durable elements of both art and criticism stressed again . . . with the eloquence and insight that Mr. Savage has at his command.

Maxwell Geismar. *Sat.* Aug. 2, 1952, p. 10

Mr. Savage, like Mr. Wyndham Lewis, might be said to judge from the point of view of the absolute, though it is an absolute of a different flavour. He tends to dismiss writers of such different types as Mr. Forster, Joyce, and Yeats, for fundamentally the same religious reasons: Mr. Forster sins against whatever to Mr. Savage is the Truth and his failure to discover a new one, except in art, and Yeats by his proud posing and his reactionary politics. Later writers tend to be dismissed as one-sided adherents of "politicism" or "estheticism," both shallow fallacies. The severe gusto with which Mr. Savage sets about his task of universal destruction makes one hope that he will in the long run tell us what the Truth is which he has found, and so many of the rest of us seem to have missed; but so far, in his critical work, the Absolute is assumed rather than expounded.

G. S. Fraser. *The Modern Writer and His World*
(Derek Verschoyle, 1953), p. 341

SAYERS, DOROTHY (1893–1957)

. . . Miss Dorothy Sayers is an adept at the perfection of form demanded, in *Have His Carcase,* for the creation and elucidation of her purely terrestrial mysteries.

Viola Meynell. *LL.* June, 1932, p. 247

There are certain writers who have made their success in a genre remote from playwriting and yet have displayed a dramatic flair which has perhaps surprised no one more than themselves. Dorothy Sayers is certainly an example, for she has been long established in the field of detective fiction where her careful confections concerning Lord Peter Wimsey have been relished by peer and peasant. Her first venture into the drama, in fact, was a pleasant, if rather mild, melodrama, *Busman's Honeymoon,* in which she portrayed her favorite hero with the collaborative efforts of M. St. Clare Byrne. A year later she revealed her true interest in the stage in her composition of *The Zeal of Thy House,* a poetic and religious drama written for production at Canterbury. This has high

quality, sensitiveness of expression, and dramatic sweep. The same may be extended to *The Devil to Pay* (1939), . . .
George Freedley in A History of Modern Drama,
ed. Barrett H. Clark and George Freedley (N.Y.,
D. Appleton-Century, 1947), p. 216

The first volume of Dorothy L. Sayers's version of *The Divine Comedy* shows her returning to her old love—medieval literature. She has produced the most rapidly moving and apparently effortless translation, with a valuable introduction and notes which with maps and diagrams (by C. W. Scott-Giles) help to make clear both story and allegory.
Geoffrey Bullough. YWES. 1949, p. 15

What Dorothy Sayers is about in this slim collection of pamphlets and addresses [*Creed or Chaos?*] is a definition of Christianity as "a religion for adult minds." The adult mind, she feels, is what Christianity's attackers, and all too frequently its defenders, lack. . . .

Miss Sayers has no comforting illusions. She speaks out against tawdry church art, against Christian tolerance of mammon and ungraciousness toward publicans, but most of all against nominal Christians, "both lay and clerical." In her view every problem and every struggle is at base a question of theology. She sees the chief problem of theology (or rather *about* theology) today as the doctrine of Christ, the God-man.
Riley Hughes. Sat. July 16, 1949, p. 15

Whether Mr. [C. S.] Lewis regards himself as a serious creative writer I do not know. Miss Sayers certainly so regards herself, and this not only on the basis of her religious plays, but also of her detective fiction which . . . she uses as the material of aesthetic theory, with insufficient attention (though in this field alone) to the other creative productions of mankind. She seems to be well versed in the *Divine Comedy;* and if she had chosen this work, let us say, instead of her own novel *Gaudy Night* as the material for her analysis of the creative process [in *Unpopular Essays*] . . . such objectivity might have saved her from the great risk of confusing the introspective and the creative, which always besets the writer of projected fantasies. . . . there is no reason why Miss Sayers should not write detective fiction. There is a legitimate market for competent entertainment. But since there is no doubt that Miss Sayers at least takes her Wimsey phase rather too seriously, we have some ground for suspecting that the preference of both these writers for abstraction is significant. Their later theological development illuminates an incapacity or a dislike for analysing and comprehending concrete individual human character, which was always characteristic of them.

Kathleen Nott. *The Emperor's Clothes*
(Bloomington, Ind., Indiana Univ. Pr., 1954), pp. 254–56

It is now twenty years ago since Lord Peter Wimsey popped the question to Miss Harriet Vane bang under the Warden of New College's windows. " *'Placetne magistra?'*—*'Placet!'* " (how that dreadful scene sticks in the memory). . . .

Re-reading Miss Sayers again this week, I remembered how we loved it all at thirteen, and how sophisticated we felt on the train that took us back to the grim Warwickshire prep school. . . . Lord Peter struck it rich in the sexual imaginings of my generation. His *dicta* preceded the chivalrous infantilism of G.K.C. (the white nights of an adolescent flirting with Rome) by about one year. . . . All that is by the by. For, of course, we all enjoyed Miss Sayers' stories themselves egregiously, revelling in the Bradshawnmanship of *The Five Red Herrings,* the campanalogy and fen-flooding in *The Nine Tailors,* Puffet, the comic sweep in *Busman's Honeymoon,* the Duke's trial scene in the Lords, the Mitfordian splendours of Duke's Denver, the tramps and gigolos of *Have His Carcase.* I am afraid we even delighted in that dreadful capping of literary quotations.

In a sense, my generation grew up with Lord Peter. . . . As we aged, Lord Peter grew almost wholly serious. By *Gaudy Night* the only traits remaining from the old unregenerate bachelor Wimsey were his taste in port and his passion for incunabula.

John Raymond. *NSN.* June 30, 1956, pp. 756, 758

Dorothy Sayers died in 1957; and as a period of disesteem normally follows hard on the death of writers and composers, this collection of twelve addresses [*The Poetry of Search and the Poetry of Statement*] is a timely reminder of her remarkable achievements. Having earned a world-wide fame as writer of detective stories, which often threw an entertaining and informative light on the milieu in which the ingenious plot was laid, she gained so great a success by her religious play, *A Man Born to be King,* that it outsold all her detective stories put together. Then she found yet a third and wholly absorbing outlet for her skills, and enthusiasm in the study and translation of Dante's *Commedia,* while her version of *The Song of Roland* bore witness to her early training as a medieval linguist. . . .

Half the addresses bear directly or indirectly on the *Commedia,* and in them, together with her two volumes of *Introductory Papers,* she has given the English student of Dante a stimulus and a guide not to be found elsewhere. Besides their interpretational value, they retain that fervour which made her lectures a spiritual tonic. . . .

Certainly her listeners enjoyed themselves, and readers of these "Essays of Statement" will have cause to wish they had been there, too.

TLS. Sept. 13, 1963, p. 690

SCARFE, FRANCIS (1911–   )

Another pleasurable poet is Francis Scarfe. His poems [*Inscapes*] are more visual, gayer than those of [Vernon] Watkins. Watkins seems to live absorbed in a world of poetry; Scarfe to go round with a pair of scissors cutting up reality into brightly colored montages.

Stephen Spender. *Hor*. Feb., 1942, p. 100

Francis Scarfe tends in the same direction [dramatized reports and not imaginative recreation], though his greater technical ability than many of his fellows makes him correspondingly more agreeable to read, and he has an ironic wit, which can produce neat parodies of workers' songs [*Forty Poems and a Ballad*].

Robert Herring. *LL*. April, 1942, p. 16

In *Transformation I,* the poet Francis Scarfe writes in a manner that indicates clearly his spiritual suffering: He speaks out for a large number of young writers who begin to see that our life is something more than a political game or an economic gamble. He comments upon Stephen Spender's *Ruins and Visions:* "I find them immeasurably sad (and beautiful) because they are defeatist, that is to say because the writer is disillusioned with both himself and society. Is this the universal treason, this universal disgust? I think so. Looking at Spender's fine monument to chaos and unbelief, I cannot but feel that a *more spiritual conception of life is needed among the younger generation as a whole.*" The italics are mine, for while I am not at all sure about the truth of the statement relating to Spender's alleged unbelief, I am certain that most of the younger writers [—like Scarfe—] need to meditate about spiritual things.

E. W. Martin. *Transformation 3,* 1945?, p. 187

A vein of reminiscence and brooding description runs through much of Scarfe's poetry, which is sometimes marred by an emotional facility, but at its best it is authentic and moving.

David Daiches. *The Present Age in British Literature* (Bloomington, Ind., Indiana Univ. Pr., 1958), p. 230

SHANKS, EDWARD (1892–1953)

A year after the first shock of pleasure occasioned by *The Queen of China,* one had started wondering whether the author was, after all, just another of the cultured and very clever young men with which the universities seem to supply modern literature in embarrassing profusion. Recently and almost simultaneously appear two self-contradictory answers to the half-formed question: Mr. Shanks' *First Essays on Literature* . . . and his fourth book of verse, *The Island of Youth.*

Besides confirming a former suspicion that Mr. Shanks as a poet was over-sophisticated, his latest volume of poetry enables us to justify rationally our pleasure at the publication of *The Queen of China.* And the appearance of two novels during the interregnum of only three years serves to explain the narrative element in his poetry as something fundamental to the man's mind even while underlining the too constant facility of the poetry.

The sophistication of *The Island of Youth* has produced an extension of the facility which in the previous volume was already replacing the restraint and shyness of an artist intensely conscious of what his forerunners had accomplished. The change may also be due to an intellectual conviction that modern poets are too fearful of stretching themselves out full-length. Mr. Shanks is no longer fearful. "The Island of Youth," which lends its title to the volume containing it, is a well-told story in verse, moving with not quite sufficient impetus, but to the tune of delicate cadences. . . .

Just as Mr. Shanks is a poet, he is also a subtle thinker. These terms are deliberately selected, because a careful consideration of his poetry produces the conviction that he has not yet put his intellect into it, though he is very close to the stage which Keats had reached at the recasting of *Hyperion.* "A good job too!" you exclaim? But every poet must reach this crisis, and surmount it, or else become an echo of himself. And profundity in poetry is not didactic preaching, nor philosophical thought-spinning, nor the obscure humour which generally spoils Mr. Sacheverell Sitwell's most promising work. . . .

An unexpected conclusion, however, results from a reading of the essays. Mr. Shanks as critic is better in sorting out philosophical ideas and attitudes in his authors than in outlining and weighing esthetic values. When he deals with W. B. Yeats, or Keats, or Shelley, he will illustrate platitudes originally. When he writes of Mr. H. G. Wells he amply justifies Benedetto Croce's warning to critics that they must not confuse biography, even mental biography, with criticism of literature. . . .

A wrong impression will be conveyed to the reader if *First Essays* is left on this note. To recapture our pleasure in the subtlety and wealth of Mr. Shanks's mind we have merely to continue reading this fascinating volume. . . . Mr. Shanks is never less than entertaining, and he is not always too busy or too prejudiced to be profoundly wise. At least one reader looks hopefully and with pleasant anticipation for his next work, whether this be criticism, or poetry, or a novel. In the novel Mr. Shanks may produce the *Erewhon* of this generation.

R. L. Mégroz. *Living Age*. June 30, 1923, pp. 786–90

Mr. Shanks' long and crowded novel *Queer Street* will extend his reputation. Its centre is the Bran Pie Club in Soho, its interest the lives of those who frequent it. . . . With the possible exception of Couan Carteret, Mr. Shanks' characters are members of a new Bohemia, for which the qualification is not artistic or literary proclivity, but residence, temporary or permanent, in Queer Street. He studies with great lucidity the interplay of his varied characters, and every now and then a brilliant exactitude of phrase reminds us that he has written fine poetry and makes us wish that he would go on doing so. The one objection to this most important book is that Mr. Shanks carries his detachment from his characters a little too far, reducing to penny plain an area so large that we feel bits of it at least should be twopence coloured; but that is an effect conveyed by the whole rather than by any of the parts.

L. A. G. Strong. *Spec*. Oct. 8, 1932, p. 456

Mr. Edward Shanks is a poet and a critic. He is also very much of an Englishman. And the combination, in his case, has produced the type of poetry and of criticism that we long ago were familiar with in the writings of Sir Edmund Gosse, and that has of recent years again been brought into nauseating prominence in the writings of Sir John Squire. These critics, from their vast eminence on the leather-covered seats of the Athenaeum and other literary clubs ("It is only the clubs that have ever produced any good literature," once observed Sir John Squire) have long since acquired the habit of bestowing their patronage on outsiders. As Dukes and Earls and Knights of letters, they can and do always unbend from the contemplation of their own loftily perfect creations to give a few pats on the back and an occasional scolding to an American. Their position is secure. Now that the last English outsider, D. H. Lawrence, has been dead these seven years, and the few others —Wyndham Lewis, Roy Campbell, Ezra Pound—are either silenced or in exile, Squire and Shanks and their ilk are the undisputed masters of English literature. In order to escape from their insidious influence one has to be born a Scots Nationalist or an Irishman, to proclaim oneself a Communist or to give up the idea of writing for an English audience altogether. Mr. Eliot of recent years has not escaped—nor have the Sitwells.

Mr. Shanks has now delivered himself of a book on Edgar Allan Poe. The book tells us nothing that we did not previously know. It tells us that here, in America, we have never been able to see Poe for the great literary artist he was because he borrowed money, drank, and acted absurdly—but that in France on the other hand, where Poe's works and influence penetrated at a time when no one knew anything of his life, he became the spiritual parent of an entire school of writers—a school which completely transformed French literature from 1870 down to 1914. . . .

The English have a strange sense of humor. They never appear funny to themselves, except occasionally when they license some jester like Bernard Shaw to give them sport. Their own literature, their own art, their own statesmanship, they have taken with portentous gravity ever since Queen Victoria made a laureate out of Tennyson. They pride themselves on their craftsmanship, their moral dignity, their honor and their honesty. As a matter of sober fact, they have few of these qualities. Mr. Shanks' book is ill-written and badly put together. He wastes pages describing Poe's attempt to write a novel, and has little to say about the poems or the tales, except incidentally. And then always with the avowed purpose of finding flaws in them.

John Gould Fletcher. *Poetry*. Sept., 1937, pp. 353–56

In writing this review I feel I am probably being unfair; and this is due to my having swallowed in a week-end more Poe than was good for me. Well, I had never really read him before, and Mr. Shanks' book [*Edgar Allan Poe*] offered the chance. How much better if I had waited until the day when perhaps a voice would have prompted—"Now, I think, we'll read a little Poe." Mr. Shanks, himself, I feel sure, has been reading Poe gingerly for years; he takes, at any rate, a balanced view. I recommend his book as an admirably sound piece of criticism which does not overrate its subject or puff the legend or his life. . . . True, Mr. Shanks takes a rather more favourable view of the stories; but his quotations, it seems to me, damage his case. They are good, nothing more.

G. W. Stonier. *NSN*. Feb 13, 1937, pp. 250–51

SHAW, GEORGE BERNARD (1856–1950)

The promptest notice of *Mrs. Warren's Profession* would have been too late to guide anyone as to whether he should or should not go to see the play. And the belatedness of my notice matters the less because the play, though performed only twice, lives lustily in book-form, and will assuredly live so for many years. Not that it seems to me "a masterpiece —yes! with all reservations, a masterpiece," as Mr. Archer hastily acclaimed it. Indeed, having seen it acted, I am confirmed in my heresy that it is, as a work of art, a failure. But the failure of such a man as "G. B. S." is of more value than a score of ordinary men's neat and cheap successes, even as the "failure" of a Brummell is worthier than a score of made-up bows in the gleaming window of the hosier. *Mrs. Warren* is a powerful and stimulating, even an ennobling, piece of work—a great failure, if you like, but also a failure with elements of greatness in it. It is decried as unpleasant by those who cannot bear to be told publicly about things which in private they can discuss, and even tolerate, without a qualm. Such people are the majority. For me, I confess, a play with an unpleasant subject, written sincerely and fearlessly by a man who has a keenly active brain and a keenly active interest in the life around him, is much less unpleasant than that milk-and-water romance (brewed of skimmed milk and stale water) which is the fare commonly provided for me in the theatre. It seems to me not only less unpleasant, but also less unwholesome. I am thankful for it.

Gratitude, however, does not benumb my other faculties. With all due deference to Mr. Archer, "Not a masterpiece, no! with all reservations, not a masterpiece" is my cry. The play is in Mr. Shaw's earlier manner —his 'prentice manner. It was written in the period when he had not yet found the proper form for expressing himself in drama. He has found that form now. He has come through experiment to the loose form of *Caesar and Cleopatra*, of *The Devil's Disciple*—that large and variegated form wherein there is elbow-room for all his irresponsible complexities. In *Mrs. Warren* he was still making tentative steps along the strait and narrow way of Ibsen. To exhaust a theme in four single acts requires tremendous artistic concentration. When the acts are split up loosely in scenes the author may divagate with impunity. But in four single acts there is no room for anything that is not strictly to the point. Any irrelevancy offends us. And irrelevancy is of the essence of Mr. Shaw's genius.

Max Beerbohm. SR. Feb. 1, 1902, pp. 139–40

An intelligent critic of George Bernard Shaw's *Man and Superman*—without doubt the author's most notable and mature book—entitled his article "The New St. Bernard." There was a certain felicity in this emphasis of the resemblance between Shaw's attitude and that of the great saint with whom he is so closely connected. The famous Christian ascetics of mediaeval times, and very notably St. Bernard, delighted to disrobe beauty of its garment of illusion; with cold hands and ironical smile they undertook the task of analysing its skin-deep fascination, and presented, for the salutary contemplation of those affected by the lust of the eyes, the vision of what seemed to them the real Woman, deprived of her skin. In the same spirit Shaw—developing certain utterances in Nietzsche's *Zarathustra*—has sought to analyse the fascination of women as an illusion of which the reality is the future mother's search of a husband for her child; and hell for Shaw is a place where people talk about beauty and the ideal.

While, however, it may be admitted that there is a very real affinity between Shaw's point of view in this matter and that of the old ascetics —who, it may be remarked, were often men of keen analytic intelligence and a passionately ironic view of life—it seems doubtful whether on the whole he is most accurately classified among the saints. It is probable that he is more fittingly placed among the prophets, an allied but still distinct species. The prophet, as we may study him in his numerous manifestations during several thousand years, is usually something of an artist and something of a scientist, but he is altogether a moralist. He foresees the future, it is true—and so far the vulgar definition of the prophet is correct—but he does not necessarily foresee it accurately. [1904]

Havelock Ellis. *From Marlowe to Shaw*
(Williams and Norgate, 1950), p. 291

The announcement that Bernard Shaw, moralist, Fabianite, vegetarian, playwright, critic, Wagnerite, Ibsenite, jester to the cosmos, and the most serious man on the planet, had written a play on the subject of Don Juan did not surprise his admirers. As Nietzsche philosophized with a hammer, so G.B.S. hammers popular myths. If you have read his *Caesar and Cleopatra* you will know what I mean. This witty, sarcastic piece is the most daring he has attempted. Some years ago I described the Shaw literary pedigree as—W. S. Gilbert out of Ibsen. His plays are full of modern-odds-and-ends, and in form are anything from the Robertsonian comedy to the Gilbertian extravaganza. They may be called physical force, an intellectual *comédie rosse*—for his people are mostly a blackguard crew of lively marionettes all talking pure Shaw-ese. Mr. Shaw has invented a new individual in literature who for want of a better name could be called the *Super-Cad;* he is Nietzsche's Superman turned "bounder"—and sometimes the sex is feminine.

James Huneker. *Iconoclasts* (T. Werner Laurie, 1908),
pp. 233-34

Most people either say that they agree with Bernard Shaw or that they do not understand him. I am the only person who understands him, and I do not agree with him.

Gilbert K. Chesterton. *George Bernard Shaw*
(John Lane, 1910), Introd.

Shaw's analysis of Ibsenism [*The Quintessence of Ibsenism*] holds out a large, sane, tolerant standard of life as the inevitable lesson of Ibsen's plays. Lies, pretences, and hypocrisies avail not against the strong man, fortified in the resolution to find himself, to attain self-realization, through fulfillment of the will. However much one may regret that Shaw, by preserving his *postulata* in concrete terms, has to some extent diverted our attention from the whole formidable significance of the Ibsenic drama, it is idle to deny that the book is at once caustically powerful and unflaggingly brilliant. Certainly Shaw has seen Ibsen clearly, even if he has not seen him whole. Ibsen cannot be summed up in a thesis . . . this is Shaw's last assurance to us that he has not reduced Ibsen to a formula. . . .

Archibald Henderson. *George Bernard Shaw*
(Cincinnati, Stewart & Kidd, 1911), p. 275

In the last act [*Candida*] Mr. Shaw, with any amount of alertness and audacity, makes a feint at extricating himself from the odd hole into which his plot has led him, but the play does not really complete itself, it merely apologizes for not going on, and the apology has a touch of the sentimentality which is Mr. Shaw's dread, or one of his dreads. Still, the play, though broken off short as a play, is a finished masterpiece of satiric observation, not through books, newspapers, and other plays, as is commonest in our theatre, but at first hand.

The only trouble for the spectator, apart from the weak ending, is that Mr. Shaw cannot make Marchbanks talk up to his part. Marchbanks is to be a young Shelley; his talk is to be Shelleyan, at any rate poetic, and Mr. Shaw sees this and does his best to write non-metrical poetry for Marchbanks to speak. But Mr. Shaw's writing, while it has no stupidities, has no beauties; the fairies seem to have made a very strict arrangement, before his birth, that the ones with force, lucidity and mordacity to give away to new-born infants should all be there, and that all the ones with sensuous loveliness of any kind in their gift should stay away. So when Mr. Shaw makes his young poet talk "softly and musically, but sadly and longingly" of a "tiny shallop to sail away in, far from the world, where the marble floors are washed by the rain and dried by the sun; where the south wind dusts the beautiful green and purple carpets," we salute an honest effort, but also we feel that, as Holofernes said of Biron's verses, "Here are only numbers ratified; but, for the elegancy, facility, and golden cadence of poesy, caret." It is as if a master of positive clearness and directness like Huxley had attempted, with that equipment, to do Keats's work, or as if Comte had tried to write a Song of Solomon. When Mr. Shaw, the rationalist, the determinist, the literalist, the man who thinks, as Tybalt fenced, "by the book of arithmetic," essays the description of golden dreams, the result is a chill or a bewilderment.

C. E. Montague. Dramatic Values
(Methuen, 2nd ed., 1911), pp. 78–79

With characterization and dialogue to his credit, we may add that he has a gift, over and above all that industry can do to develop it, for the dramatic nexus of a story blossoming in scene and situation: and we might define a situation as a scene at its tensest moment of interest. All the reiterated careless talk about Shaw's having no theatre sense for curtains and climaxes is comically erroneous . . . it overlooks his constant and brilliant control and manipulation of the raw material of the theatre in such wise as to give us scenes of all but unexampled power. Even in a play like *Getting Married,* which might be named as the least dramatic of his repertory, when we have listened straight through to the vivid battledore and shuttlecock of an argument which curiously neither tires nor bores, is not the scene when the mayoress turns mystic one that has very great stage value—allowing, of course, for the genre of the piece, namely, satiric high comedy?

Richard Burton. Bernard Shaw (N.Y., Holt, 1916),
pp. 285–86

Bernard Shaw has confessed that he prefers Englishmen to Irishmen, "no doubt because they make more of me," yet he cannot refrain from adding that he never thinks of the English as fellow-countrymen. This is the quintessence of what Ireland knows as "West Britonism." Our West Britons are so enamoured of England that they desire above all things to mix with Englishmen, their children are educated, if possible, in English schools, and everything is done to eliminate the "vulgar Irish" element from their lives. These people are, for the most part, rewarded like Shaw, by finding West Britonism more profitable than Nationalism. Yet nobody who has lived among them can have failed to get an occasional glimpse of this underlying sense of alienism to which Shaw alludes. Sometimes the feeling comes out in the form of violent Irish patriotism, when in England, on the part of men whose contempt for Ireland, when at home, never lacks an excuse for its expression. At other times more discretion is shown, the outwardly staunch loyalist admitting, in private, that whenever he goes to England he feels himself a foreigner. . . .

English people have been disconcerted by Shaw's ability to view them from the outside, as it were. They should remember that he is merely exercising the privilege of the expatriate. Denationalised Irishmen are all capable of similarly disinterested criticism, and do not refrain from it, even in Ireland, where their position imposes obligations of caution. Shaw has no such obligations, and is, therefore, in a position to say more freely and more generally, what the others have whispered or felt, at least in some particular connection. . . .

Shaw is never more faithful to Irish Protestant tradition than when he exhibits scepticism towards the virtues of England, without, however, turning definitely against her. He is sufficiently aloof to be critical, but his instincts draw him so inevitably to the English people that he cannot be really inimical. In short, he is that perfect type of *sans patrie* which the anglicisation of Ireland has produced; men who cannot understand their own compatriots, and must necessarily take refuge among a people with whom they are condemned to be aliens.

Many critics of Bernard Shaw, struggling with the postulate that he is a puritan, have pointed out flaws in the theory. The contradictions can be resolved by reference to his Protestantism. Irish Protestantism differs considerably from English puritanism, although their lines coincide at certain points. The former has the advantage of presenting an undivided religious front, whereas the latter, by the exclusion of the Anglican Church, loses its homogeneity. Shaw himself has explained this solidarity of Episcopalian and Dissenter in Ireland, which enabled him to be educated at a Methodist College, where the minority of pupils belonged to that sect. Social and political circumstances make cohesion possible amongst Irish Protestants. The negative virtue of being non-Catholic dispenses with those dogmatic *nuances* which render intercourse between Anglican and Nonconformist a different problem in England. Shaw had the typical school life of his class, and justly boasts that, in consequence, his is the true Protestantism.

Ernest A. Boyd. *Appreciations and Depreciations*
(T. Fisher Unwin, 1917), pp. 111–13

Socialist though he is, he does not hold to any views that would give the democracy complete control of its affairs. He recognises the fundamental inequality of the human ego whilst denying the necessity for economic inequality. Democracy he calls "the last refuge of cheap misgovernment," and he can by no stretch of the imagination be reckoned a "government of the people, by the people, for the people" reformer. He would certainly have the people governed for the people but by those who know not only their business as governors, but who know and are determined to minister to the welfare of the whole state with no other class distinction than that of character.

Holbrook Jackson. *Bernard Shaw*
(E. Grant Richards, 1917), p. 138

Four hours of persistent button-holing at the Court Theatre convinced the dramatic critics that as a simple entertainment *Heartbreak House* was a failure. But what else it might be they did not try to find out. They hurled at the author the quite meaningless epithet of "Shavian"—as though it were his business to be Tchekovian or Dickensian or anybodyelsian except himself—and then ran away like children playing a game of "tick." What is there about Mr. Shaw that he should break so many heads as well as hearts? In and out of season, from his preface-tops, he has proclaimed that he is no leisurely horticulturist, pottering about Nature's garden and pruning it into trim shapes. The tragedy and comedy of life, he has shouted, come from founding our institutions—and in these he certainly includes our plays—on half-satisfied passions instead of on a genuinely scientific natural history. Well, here is natural history preached with all the fury of the Salvationist. With Shaw fanaticism means the blind espousal of reason, a marriage which, in the theatre, turns out to be rather a joyless one. What, this disciple would ask, in comparison with truth and reason are such petty virtues as good playwriting, good manners and good taste? Truth, like everything else, is relative; and what is truth to the sentimental, loose-reasoning playgoer is not necessarily truth to the unsentimental, logical playwright. "A fool sees not the same tree that a wise man sees." If a man can be partaker of God's theatre, he shall likewise be partaker of God's rest, says Bacon. But if truth be the thing which Shaw will have most, rest is that which he will have not at all. If we will be partakers of Shaw's theatre we must be prepared to be partakers of his fierce unrest.

But then no thinker would ever desire to lay up any other reward. When Whitman writes: "I have said that the soul is not more than the body, And I have said that the body is not more than the soul, And nothing, not God, is greater to one than oneself is," we must either assent or dissent. Simply to cry out "Whitmanesque!" is no way out of the difficulty. When Ibsen writes a play to prove that building happy homes for happy human beings is not the highest peak of human endeavour, leaving us to find out what higher summit there may be, he intends us to use our brains. It is beside the point to cry out "How like Ibsen!" *Heartbreak House* is a restatement of these two themes. You have to get Ibsen thoroughly in mind if you are not to find the Zeppelin at the end of Shaw's play merely monstrous. It has already destroyed the people who achieve; it is to come again to lighten the talkers' darkness, and at the peril of all the happy homes in the neighbourhood. You will do well to keep Whitman in mind when you hear the old sea-captain bellowing with a thousand different intonations and qualities of emphasis: Be yourself, do not sleep. I do not mean, of course, that Shaw had these two themes actually in mind when he set about this rather maundering, Tchekovian rhapsody. But they have long been part of his mental make-up, and he cannot escape them or their implications. The difficulty seems to be in the implications. Is a man to persist in being himself if that self run counter to God or the interests of parish, nation, the community at large? The characters in this play are nearer to apes and goats than to men and women. Shall they nevertheless persist in being themselves, or shall they pray to be Zeppelin-destroyed and born again?

James Agate. *Alarums and Excursions*
(N.Y., George H. Doran, 1922), pp. 187–89

There is a kind of shy, embarrassed man of merit who cannot keep or even reach to his proper position in the world without making some sort of pretence about himself. Mr. Bernard Shaw is such a man. He has created his legend with such extraordinary skill that those who know him well have great difficulty in persuading the general public, which has neither the time nor the intelligence to understand a man of marked personality, to believe that the legend *is* a legend, that the reputed Bernard Shaw is not the real Bernard Shaw. The common notion is that he has an insatiable craving for publicity, is immensely conceited and self-centred, and does not care what folly of thought or conduct he commits if by so doing he draws attention to himself. The truth about him is that he is a shy and nervous man, singularly humble-minded and sincere, very courageous and full of quick, penetrating wisdom, and so generous and kindly that he may be said to be willing to do more for his friends than his friends will do for themselves. He is a Don Quixote without illusions. When he tilts at windmills, he does so because they are *wind*mills in private ownership, and he wishes them to be driven by electricity and owned by the local authority. In print and on platforms, Mr. Shaw brags and boasts and lays claim to an omniscience that would scandalize most deities, but no one who has the ability to distinguish between sincerity and mere capering is in the least deceived by his platform conceit. He is one of the very few men in the world who can brag in public without being offensive to his auditors. He can even insult his audience without hurting its feelings. There is a quality of geniality and kindliness in his most violent and denunciatory utterance that reconciles all but the completely fat-headed to a patient submission to his chastisement; and his most perverse statements are so swiftly followed by things profoundly true and sincerely said that those who listen to him are less conscious of his platform tricks than are those who merely read newspaper reports of his speeches.

St John G. Ervine. *Some Impressions of My Elders* (N.Y., Macmillan, 1922), pp. 189–90

To His Worship The Mayor of Stratford-on-Avon, Mr. Mayor of Shakespeare's Town: I am sure that many thousands of my countrymen were as much surprised as myself to find that Mr. George Bernard Shaw was chosen to be the chief guest of your town at your annual Shakespeare Festival this year. You will allow, sir, that one of the qualifications for proposing the memory of Shakespeare on such an occasion is the possession of some small amount of respect and admiration for the poet. The following passage in Mr. Shaw's own words shows that he has an unbounded contempt for Shakespeare: "With the single exception of Homer, there is no eminent writer, not even Sir Walter Scott, whom I despise so utterly as I despise Shakespeare when I measure my mind against his. The intensity of my impatience with him reaches such a pitch that it would positively be a relief to me to dig him up and throw stones at him, knowing as I do how incapable he and his worshippers are of understanding any less obvious forms of indignity."

I do not know, Mr. Mayor of Shakespeare's town, what are your personal feelings towards Shakespeare, nor after Stratford's hospitality to Mr. Bernard Shaw, am I able to estimate how much love and reverence for Shakespeare are still to be found among his fellow townsmen. But I think a majority of my countrymen will agree with me that a further main qualification for proposing the memory of Shakespeare in any gathering of Englishmen, is a feeling of fellowship and kinship with him in his passionate love for England. . . . Surely we may expect that his sponsors will take care to select some man who, even though he is not of English blood, shall yet have declared in his life and work a warm sympathy with the body of English traditions, beliefs, aspirations, customs, ideals, all the wild tingling enthusiasm, all the enticements to clear sane thought, chivalrous deeds, and proud English citizenship which the name of Shakespeare kindles in the heart of every truly begotten son of Shakespeare's land.

> Henry Arthur Jones. *Mr. Mayor of Shakespeare's Town* [*: A Protest Against the Visit of Mr. Bernard Shaw to Stratford-on-Avon for the Shakespeare Memorial Meeting, April 23, 1925*] (British Museum, 1925), pp. 15–17

I get the keenest pleasure watching Shaw squirm through a tattooed subject. He confesses he couldn't write words Joyce uses: "My prudish hand would refuse to form the letters; and I can find no interest in his infantile clinical incontinences, or in the flatulations which he thinks worth mentioning. But if they were worth mentioning I should not object to mentioning them, though, as you see, I should dress up his popular locutions in a little Latinity. For all we know, they may be peppered freely over the pages of the lady novelists of ten years hence; and Frank Harris's autobiography may be on all the bookstalls."

You will observe that he can find no interest in these matters, yet he appears to have read them all and remembers them pretty well; which would seem to belie his lack of interest in them. When I find no interest in a thing I simply drop it and forget it, but Shaw is made of sterner stuff. Like reformers and censors and smut-hounds generally, he wallows in what he likes to call dirt, not from pleasure, but as duty. This completely contradicts his simile that pornographic novels are like offering a hungry man a description of dinner, and that, even if the description was very lifelike, it could not satisfy his hunger. All I can reply is that these descriptions seem to have satisfied Shaw's hunger, for he seems to have read them all and gone without his dinner.

> Frank Harris. *On Bernard Shaw* (Victor Gollancz, 1931), pp. 229–30

Two curious events have lately happened in connection with Mr. Bernard Shaw. An edition, in thirty volumes, of his collected writings, from his novels upwards, has been announced at the price of £31 10s. a set, and practically sold out before issue, and an "omnibus book" containing a complete edition of his plays in over 1,100 large pages has, at 12s. 6d. (net), apparently enjoyed all the prosperity of a "best seller." Seldom, surely, has been seen a more striking proof of the worldly wisdom of courting unpopularity. If there is one thing more than another which, by some mysterious force of his being, Mr. Shaw has seemed most furiously to detest and despise, it is what his old hero, Ibsen, once called the "compact majority." During the fifty years or so in which, as a journalist and platform orator, he has been addressing England there has hardly been a native sentiment of any notable breadth or depth upon which he has not poured his derision. A wave of any sort of public opinion had only to manifest itself, and forth came his flaming *Vox Populi, Vox Diaboli,* like the blast from a dragon's jaws. Public mourning brought forth his joke, public rejoicing his mockery, public anxiety his gayest two-step. And now, when, as the most juvenile of septuagenarians, he issues his works at prices calculated to suit all pockets, forth rush the people of whom he has made such fun, chequebook in hand, and pay him the most "practical" tribute the human mind can conceive.

H. M. Walbrook. *Eng.R.* Sept., 1931, p. 446

One feels, indeed, that Shaw was always at his happiest when he left his own period and lived for a while with the people of another age; that although *Heartbreak House, John Bull's Other Island* and *The Doctor's Dilemma* may be revived as "period pieces" quite as often as *The School for Scandal, She Stoops to Conquer* and *The Importance of Being Earnest,* yet the most natural, most convincing, most imaginative, least self-conscious of his works are *Caesar and Cleopatra, Androcles and the Lion,* and *Saint Joan.* These will live as long as there is an English stage devoted to anything better than the sort of play from which he redeemed it. For reasons we have seen, most of his characters do not get far enough away from himself to attain a life of their own, and the really vital ones, the religious and self-conscious types, come straight from their creator. But in the three plays just mentioned the subsidiary characters catch some of the radiance spread by the protagonists and the strings of the puppet-master are fainter. Shaw must have felt where his real weakness lay as a dramatist of contemporary life; for he confessed that he had always been a sojourner on this planet rather than a native of it; that his kingdom was not of this world; that he was at home only in the realm of his imagination, and at ease only with the mighty dead: with Bunyan, with Blake and with Shelley; with Beethoven, Bach and Mozart.

Hesketh Pearson. *Bernard Shaw* (Collins, 1942), p. 394

Anybody who was one of the younger generation in 1900 can never forget or pay his debt to G.B.S. It was he and Samuel Butler who were the pathfinders and led that younger generation so bravely and gaily out of the wilderness of the nineteenth century, though neither the leader nor the led, of course, realised that they were heading for the infinitely worse horrors of the twentieth century wilderness. In reading and before criticising his latest book, it is well to recall this and to begin in the spirit of "Let us now praise famous men" and Bernard Shaw among them. For he was a great iconoclast and the images which he threw down were those of Moloch, Belial, Pecksniff, and a thousand other nameless gods whose damp and downcast looks are recorded in the first book of *Paradise Lost*. But it would be a poor compliment to Shaw to review his book [*Everybody's Political What's What*] published in 1944 merely by praising the books which he had published before 1900. It is true that the injunction "de mortuo nil nisi bonum" is only to be followed if the dead man is still alive, and therefore does apply to most authors above the age of 60. But at 88 Shaw is less dead than most thinkers are at 58, and still therefore deserves to be treated seriously.

It is, no doubt, a wonderful book to have been written by a man of his age, yet one can hardly fail to regret that he should have written it. It is a kind of "Shorter Shaw," a compendium of his most important or persistent doctrines and dogmas. What he says here has almost always been said by him before in his plays and prefaces, and said better. The humour and wit are still there and the acrobatic nimbleness of mind; also the sound sense beneath the nonsense. Yet it reminds one of a gramophone record of a famous soprano, singing, when she was almost but not quite too old to sing, Schubert's *Nussbaum*—"What a lovely voice she had!" some one says, as the last note of the piano dies away and the needle grates into the groove.

Leonard Woolf. *NSN*. Sept. 16, 1944, p. 188

When we turn to Shaw's range of theme or subject it is like passing from a very deep (even bottomless) inland lake to the Atlantic Ocean. In subject alone no other dramatist has ever had such a range with the possible exception of Shakespeare. Nothing human is alien to that old gentleman whether he understands it or not. He is afraid of nothing but erotic emotion and he sits on the fence and puts out his tongue at it. He believes that every picture should tell a story and a moral story at that. He is probably the leader of the revolution against the theory of Art for Art's Sake that so prevailed in the studios and garrets in the beginning of this century.

James Bridie in *G. B. S. 90,* ed. Stephen Winsten
(Hutchinson, 1946), p. 88

I am myself a Victorian, and am conscious in my bones of what he has done to me: for better or worse I am not the man I should have been had Shaw not tackled me, before I made his personal acquaintance, while I was still in my twenties. Let me own frankly that I began by disliking him; he was constantly offending my taste; and taste is often a protective extra skin which we have acquired from our parents, or have put on, to keep us from disturbing thought about things which are unpleasant. Sometimes he offends me still by his gratuitous exaggerations—not of facts, but of phrases; using, for instance, that worn-out cliché about grown-up lack of intelligence over things which "the mind of any child of ten could master." But I can still remember the characteristic Victorian statement which came out of my mouth in his hearing (the first time we ever met) at a small social debate, that, if the working class were paid better wages, they wouldn't know how to spend them properly, and how jovially he felled me to earth for it, and made it impossible for me ever again to defend an unjust wage system by that sort of argument.

It is worth noting, I think, that in his fight for the recovery of right values, in a social order which had become so mentally and morally defective under its veneer of Christianity, Shaw (though much more a Christian in principle than most of us) was entirely secular in his method of attack on the social conscience; and it was not until he wrote his preface to *Androcles and the Lion* that he openly championed Christianity against the charge that it had become a proved failure, and declared that it had not failed because it had never yet been tried, and that it was about time that it *was* tried. It was a case of the Humanist once again (as has happened before) coming to the rescue of Christian realism from the cold formalism of other-wordliness.

Laurence Housman in *G. B. S. 90, ed. Stephen Winsten* (Hutchinson, 1946), pp. 48–49

One of George Bernard Shaw's outstanding characteristics is his versatility. And what can illustrate this better than the fact that this remarkable man, known to most people as a playwright and author, and to some as a musician, is an enthusiast for a subject which some may consider outlandish—phonetics? His interest in the subject dates from long ago, and has always taken a practical and constructive shape. He is an expert shorthand writer, and it was presumably the phonetic principles involved in shorthand that opened his eyes to other possibilities offered by this science.

So convinced did Shaw become of the valuable potentialities of the subject that some twenty-eight years ago he conceived the idea of making the general public aware, by means of a play, of what phonetic science is and what can be done with it. Hence his *Pygmalion,* which he tells me is the most popular of his plays. One of the purposes of this comedy was to show up the somewhat disagreeable fact that under the present conditions people's manner of speaking has much to do with their success or failure in life (in the material sense). A second was to call attention to phonetics as a means of enabling a dialect speaker to change his accent. In *Pygmalion* phonetics is represented as providing a key to social advancement—a function which it may be hoped it will not be called upon to perform indefinitely. Those who have seen the play and have given thought to the principles demonstrated in it will no doubt have inferred that the methods of phonetics are of more general application—that they enable a person with a definitely local accent to speak, if he so desires, with a pronunciation more widely current and not necessarily that of a particular social class, and that they give us a means of learning to pronounce foreign languages far more intelligibly than was possible in pre-phonetic days.

Mention must be made here of services in the phonetic line which Shaw has rendered to the B.B.C. For several years he was chairman of a special committee charged with the duty of making recommendations for the guidance of announcers. These recommendations related to uncommon words of which the pronunciation was doubtful, to words which are pronounced in more than one way, to English proper names which announcers might not ordinarily be expected to know, and to suitable anglicizations of foreign words and names which either had occurred or were thought likely to occur in the news. . . . Under his guidance much good work was achieved, as the remarkable series of booklets *Broadcast English* shows.

Dr. Daniel Jones in *G. B. S. 90*, ed. Stephen Winsten
(Hutchinson, 1946), pp. 158–59

If Shaw's plays are in the first place the meeting-ground of vitality and artificial system and in the second of male and female they are in the third place an arena for the problem of human ideals and their relation to practice. His characters may be ranged on a scale of mind, ideas, aspirations, beliefs and on a scale of action, practicality, effectiveness. At one extreme there are men of mind who make as little contact with the world of action as possible. Such are most of Shaw's artists. At the other extreme are men of action who lack all speculative interests and ideal impulses. Such are Shaw's professional men: soldiers, politicians, doctors. At a little distance from the one extreme are the men of mind who are interested in this world even if they can do nothing about it. Such, in their different ways, are Tanner, Cusins, Keegan, Shotover, and Magnus. At a little distance from the other extreme are certain practical men with a deep intellectual interest in the meaning of action. Such are the businessmen Undershaft and Tarleton, the soldiers Napoleon and Caesar.

The conversations which all these men, of mind or of action, have with each other have, perhaps, more nervous energy, a more galvanic rhythm, than any other disquisitory passages in all Shaw. For they are all pushing, probing towards the solution of the problem of morals in action. They are all part of the search for the philosopher-king. Keegan talks with the politician Broadbent, Shotover with the businessman Mangan, Magnus with his cabinet. Most strikingly, perhaps, Undershaft talks with his Professor Cusins. They are agreed that there is no hope until the millionaires are professors of Greek and the professors of Greek are millionaires.

Although the problem enters in all Shaw's plays there is one special repository for it: the history play. We have seen that *Caesar and Cleopatra* is a melodrama and one of the *Three Plays for Puritans*. It is also the second of three history plays—*The Man of Destiny,* and *Saint Joan* are the other two—in which Shaw worked at his problem by connecting it with great historical figures. One must however be very clear about the fact that Shaw never tried to do the job of the historical figures. As his way is, he informs everybody that his plays are utterly historical and defends their most whimsical anachronisms in notes that are not uniformly funny. However, there were scholars who fell for it and earnestly corrected Shaw's facts in solemn articles. A whole book was written to "refute" *Saint Joan*.

Shaw's claim was that he knew history intuitively! He writes his plays, reads the history books afterwards, and finds—so he says—that he was right all along, for "given Caesar and a certain set of circumstances I know what would happen." Those who think this a naive confession are themselves naive. . . . He retains his right to be absurd in everything but psychology. And he recognizes a limitation in all historical writing which our historians would be wise to grant: that our understanding of an historical character is a highly subjective affair.

Shaw differs from a sound historian not in being more subjective but in not being a historian at all. Shaw was not interested in the peculiar character of each period—Napoleonic, ancient, or medieval—but in indicating what has not changed. Seeing and hearing people much like ourselves (or better) the audience learns that no progress has been made during historical time.

Eric Bentley. Bernard Shaw (N.Y., New Directions,
1947), pp. 158–60

Shaw postulates a universe containing or consisting of two factors, life and matter. Admittedly, he sometimes speaks of life as creating matter as when, by willing to use our arms in a certain way, we bring into existence a roll of muscle, but the general rule is that matter is, as it were, there to begin with. Thus, matter is spoken of as life's "enemy." "I brought life into the whirlpool of force, and compelled my enemy,

Matter, to obey a living soul," says Lilith at the end of *Back to Methuselah*. Regarding matter in the light of an enemy, life seeks to dominate and subdue it. Partly to this end, partly because of its innate drive to self-expression, life enters into and animates matter. The result of this animation of matter by life is a living organism. A living organism, then, derives from and bears witness to the presence of both the fundamental constituents of which the universe is composed; it is life expressed in matter. Shaw suggests rather than explicitly states that life cannot evolve or develop *unless* it enters into matter to create organisms; these are, in fact, the indispensable instruments wherewith it promotes its own development.

C. E. M. Joad. *Shaw* (Victor Gollancz, 1949), pp. 177–78

The *Methuselah* cycle, together with *Man and Superman,* may be taken as the Testament of Shaw's religious beliefs; and in *Saint Joan* and the other religious plays the same faith is implicit, though in these it is not placed in the centre of interest. . . .

What we must gratefully recognize in him is his faith in life, the positive manner in which he affirms its value, his declaration that it has meaning and a purpose, his rousing summons to every man to whom the precious gifts of life and consciousness have been given to further its highest ends and to add all his strength to the sum-total of creative effort. Life, and life more abundantly, always at its best and always raising itself to a higher pitch—that is the way of salvation that he preaches to us all. Heretic he may be, but to him the deadliest of all sins is scepticism, the most certain of all truths is that we are saved by faith. His mind has been nourished on the Bible and on Bunyan. He is at one with them in his conviction that the supreme enemies of God and of man are the life-deniers—the pessimists, the shirkers, and the cowards. His condemnation of them is the condemnation of the Apocalypse: "For the fearful and the unbelieving, their part shall be in the lake which burneth with fire and brimstone; which is the second death." Few people will agree with all his opinions; some of them we may even detest; but in the end it is not his opinions that matter. It is the positive affirmation of a magnificent faith, faith in the value of life. That is the last word of *Back to Methuselah,* spoken through the lips of Lilith.

W. S. Handley Jones. *LQHR*. April, 1949, p. 145

Certainly whatever impact Shaw has made upon any of the numerous generations who have been exposed to his work has been in his role as dramatist. Though he no doubt would scream in denial, I contend that the prose polemics in his body of work are footnotes, even if some of the notes seem longer than the text. With the plays, however, I include the prefaces. They stand distinctly apart from the rest of his polemical writing, taking a life and spark from their juxtaposition to the plays.

But the Fabian essays and addresses, *The Intelligent Woman's Guide to Socialism and Capitalism, Everybody's Political What's What* and so forth, are more important to Shaw than to his public. They have their place in an exhaustive study and they may be cited, from time to time, in our discussion. Beyond this they would obscure, rather than clarify, our attempt to see Shaw, as thinker, in the whole. Essentially these other works repeat what is said in the plays and prefaces and repeat it weakly.

This decision takes some justification from Shaw's own insistence that truthtelling is better done by the creative imagination than by literal account. "You may read the Annual Register from end to end and be no wiser. But read *Pilgrim's Progress* and *Gulliver's Travels* and you will know as much human history as you need, if not more."

The novels, which in general I think are better than they are commonly supposed to be, nevertheless are not of great importance to his matured thought which found its natural vehicle in drama. *The Adventures of the Black Girl in Her Search for God,* a fable of great charm, does not go, in content, beyond the discussions of religion in *Androcles and the Lion, Back to Methuselah,* and *Saint Joan.*

I have divided the plays into First, Second and Third periods, which prove to be remarkably balanced as to volume of output, although this did not enter into consideration.

The plays of what I call the first period begin with *Widower's Houses* and end with *Captain Brassbound's Conversion.* They mark the establishment of Shaw's success and the development of most of his characteristics. Had he written nothing more he would have been, on the strength of these plays, still the leading English-speaking dramatist of his time, though in the light of what was to come, it is almost impossible to conceive of such a termination.

I mark a second period with *Man and Superman,* for it seems to me that this play makes a forward leap in stature out of all ordinary relation to his previous rate of growth. This immense surge of creative power is sustained phenomenally through such master works as *Heartbreak House, Back to Methuselah,* and *Saint Joan.*

After *Saint Joan,* however, in the third period which begins with *The Apple Cart,* there is a steady diminution of power, though scarcely one of production.

Edmund Fuller. *George Bernard Shaw*
(N.Y., Scribner's, 1950), pp. 16–17

The next period of Shaw's life [from 1876] has naturally been the subject of criticism in that he lived on his mother for nine years. It can be defended in more ways than one. The Shaw family, apparently so cold to one another, had nevertheless a rock-like loyalty that was taken for granted. When, later in life, Shaw's mother retired from teaching and his sister was unable to earn a living, they both lived in comfort, in separate establishments, on Shaw. It never occurred to any of them that it could be otherwise. Another explanation is that Shaw had the intuition that his ability craved food, must be fed, and was of such quality as to justify his living on his mother. . . . In fairness to Shaw it ought to be remembered that many a young person has accepted the sacrifice of parents while he went to school and university. This is really what happened in Shaw's case. . . . He read hard in libraries; he studied pictures in art galleries; he studied the best music. In essence, Shaw had a prolonged university career, only perhaps of a better kind.

Robert F. Rattray. *Bernard Shaw: A Chronicle*
(Luton, England: The Leagrave Press; distributed
by Dennis Dobson, Ltd., London, 1951), pp. 28–29

He struck a mortal blow at melodrama, both within and outside the theatre—even the popular socialist form of it called the Class War. On the whole he did well, though we may consider whether melodrama is not after all as necessary to life as mythology seems to be necessary to religion. I have said that he was the most nutritious of writers, and also that his world was not quite a sane world; the contradiction is only a seeming one—just as vegetables are the most healthful of foods, but consistent vegetarianism is a craze. He did not understand that excess is a part of health or that a sense of evil is an element of sanity; nevertheless to an age drunk with romanticism he came as a healer. Partly for evil, but I think more for good, he has taught us to take politics less seriously. . . .

Arland Ussher. *Three Great Irishmen*
(Victor Gollancz, 1952), p. 60

Next to his optimism and his energy, the most striking thing about Shaw was his furious eclecticism. He felt no necessity to choose between the various modern prophets. He would take something from them all, and moreover he would reconcile the most disparate. He was an Ibsenite of course. But he was also, or was soon to become, a disciple of Marx, of Nietzsche, of Bergson, of Wagner, of Samuel Butler, and of John Bunyan. Besides becoming a socialist, he was also a nonsmoker, a teetotaler, a vegetarian, an antivaccinationist, an antivivisectionist and an advocate of reformed spelling.

All this would have been more than enough to give a serious case of intellectual indigestion to anyone else, but for him it was merely very stimulating and very nourishing. Sooner or later the teaching of all his masters was synthesized, one furnishing an economic system, another a moral system, a third a metaphysic, and a fourth a religion. Though he never wrote it all down in systematic form, Shaw has at one time or another propounded the parts of what is probably the most inclusive body of doctrine since Thomas Aquinas.

One thing which made this possible was a sort of cheerful optimism enabling him to temper the more intransigent doctrines of his various masters and to fall back upon the formula "What this really means is . . ." Moreover, what it really meant was usually something less intransigent as well as frequently gentler and more kindly than the doctrine of his masters is generally assumed to be.

In the plays of the first decade especially, this cheerful determination to tame the wild men and to draw the fangs of revolution seems particularly striking. Nietzsche's doctrine of the superman—which might seem to others to foreshadow a blond beast, amoral and ruthless—tends to become no more than a rather extravagant method of recommending self-help and improvement. *The Revolutionist's Handbook,* supposed to have been written by the rebellious John Tanner, hero of *Man and Superman,* begins by breathing fire and then carefully explains that in democratic England there is all the revolution necessary every time the voters have recourse to the ballot box. In the same book a shocking section ridiculing sexual morality and especially the sentimental word "purity" ends by demonstrating that, since the number of men and women in England is approximately equal, monogamy is the only sensible system. In that same play even Strindberg's battle of the sexes, described by Tanner in the first scene as a remorseless struggle where the only question is which party shall destroy the other, turns out to be but a sort of sham battle in the course of which the Life Force makes the hero and heroine temporarily irrational in order that it may benevolently trick them into sacrificing what they believe to be their desires in favor of their deepest impulse—which is to try to create better offspring.

Joseph Wood Krutch. Modernism in Modern Drama
(Ithaca, Cornell Univ. Pr., 1953), pp. 50–51

You might say that he made up his mind too early, which gave him an immense advantage in debate, arming him at all points, but cost him something in wisdom. Bertrand Russell, who had known him a long time, said that G. B. S. was an immensely clever man but not a wise man. He seemed to me to have a sort of natural wisdom in his ordinary dealings with life (he must have given people in private more really good advice than any other man of his time), but to be perverse, obstinate, cranky, wrong-headed, in his positive philosophy. He was, in fact—and came at just the right moment—a great destroyer, head of the Victorian rubbish disposal squad. He hid any doubts he might have about his positive wisdom in quick mocking laughter, just as he hid so much of his face behind a beard, red and white at the proper seasons. But because he was an iconoclast, this does not mean, as many people imagine, that all his work will "date" itself into obscurity. I suspect that all the "dating" that can happen has already happened. His best pieces, those comedies unique in style and spirit, have the vitality that defies time and all social changes. Their character, their appeal, may be different—for notice how early plays like *Arms and the Man* and *You Never Can Tell,* once thought to be grimly shocking, now seem to bubble and sparkle with wit and delicious nonsense—but they will be alive. And existing still behind the work will be the memory and the legend of the man, half saint and half clown, preposterous in his Jaeger outfit and assorted fads, glorious in his long stride towards some kingdom worthy of the spirit—the wittiest of all pilgrims, humming an air by Mozart.

J. B. Priestley. *Thoughts in the Wilderness*
(Heinemann, 1957), pp. 186–87

SHERRIFF, R. C. (1896–   )

Literature about the war has been plentiful and very little of it has been any good. Quite lately Mr. Sassoon and Mr. Blunden have written books about it that will live as history, as literature, as works of art, and Mr. R. C. Sherriff has accomplished an even harder task. He has put the war on the stage and he has done it once and for all. . . . Mr. Sherriff has put a three-act play into a support-line dug-out in front of St. Quentin, and no one need ever try to do it again. . . .

The Peace Societies of England ought to join together and send *Journey's End* on tour throughout the length and breadth of the country. It is worth fifty times more than all their propaganda, which consists mainly of reprinting out-of-date speeches by elderly gentlemen.

A. G. Macdonell. *LM*. Jan., 1929, pp. 314–15

To the soldier *Journey's End* is a record, remarkable in its fidelity, of his own experience of war. The play recaptures for him the very atmosphere of days half-forgotten but most worthy of remembrance. On that if on no other account it is to him a great play. The more fortunate generation which has already succeeded us will find here material which will enable them, if they will, to sit in judgment. It may well be that their judgment will be unfavourable; the men of yesterday bear no aureole of romance. *"Magnanimi heroes nati melioribus annis"* could not have been written by a poet of today. But perhaps we may hope that, though the future may rightly lay claim to the better years, England will not wholly forget the men of an ill-starred generation who, when the darkness closed round them, were great of heart.

C. O. G. Douie. *NC*. June, 1929, p. 848

Yet I cannot say that the play [*Journey's End*] is entirely satisfactory as a work of art. It is enormously impressive and stirring, and in the matters of dialogue and selection it is beyond praise. But I find that, in my own case and in the case of others who saw it at this dress rehearsal, it excites rather than purifies; and I fancy this is because its inspiration is neurotic. Decidedly it is lit by Plutonic fires rather than by the daylight of Apollo. To begin with, it is one more expression of the desperate infantilism characteristic of the modern young Englishman. I do not mean by that to quarrel with his emphasis on the tragedy of murdered youth which was the war's foulest offence, for that is legitimate and most beautifully contrived, particularly at one moment. . . . That *Journey's End* contains memorable indictments of the world's guilt in this respect one does not complain; but one is disquieted by Mr. Sherriff's assumption that immaturity is the most important phase of existence. The older men in the play are represented as being not only protective to the boys, but deferential to them, as to people of obviously greater importance; and their references to the lives they have left in England are so perfunctory that one realizes the author himself is incapable of believing they could include experiences as exciting and profound as the relationship between the boy of twenty-one and the boy of eighteen, which started at school.

The significance of this can be seen when one considers that there have been three first-rate plays written by young Englishmen since the war—*Prisoners of War,* by J. R. Ackerley; *Young Woodley,* by John Van Druten; and this *Journey's End;* and they all have this obsession with immaturity. . . .

Infantilism is not a happy state. The childhood of the individual and the race is full of fears, and panic-stricken attempts to avert what is feared by placating the gods with painful sacrifices. For this reason *Journey's End* is a sad play, sadder even than a war play ought to be.

Rebecca West. *Ending in Earnest*
(N.Y., Doubleday, Doran, 1931), pp. 47–50

Mr. Sherriff wins our confidence very quickly. There is nothing at all showy about his craftsmanship but we are aware, somehow, that we can rely on it, that he is not going to let us down. Nor does he. . . .

. . . Mr. Sherriff's invention and felicity never fail him, and we come away from the theatre conscious of having seen a piece of work [*Miss Mabel*] which is, in its unambitious, unpretentious way, something of a minor *tour de force*.

Peter Fleming. *Spec.* Nov. 26, 1948, p. 694

. . . when he comes up for public examination, the result of all the judging, the valuing, the sounding, is to put Sherriff in the place he held during 1929: as the author of *Journey's End*. Not, perhaps, in precisely the same place, for fashion has veered: it is no longer proper to call the play the noblest modern war drama yet written. It is an Ancient Monument: we can speak of it today with respectful interest, pointing to this and that beauty, this and that flaw, and observing how much better some of the war plays have been that have followed it. . . .

Since 1929, Sherriff, in the theatre, has been known principally as a good-mannered dramatist, who never patronizes the small-town and suburban people of whom he prefers to write. This is why he has sometimes to endure the label of "matinee dramatist," one of the sillier tags: here the gum, fortunately, is by no means imperishable. There is no reason why one should condemn a quiet little play that does what it seeks to achieve, and does it with sense and good taste. . . . Sherriff cannot be an exhibitionist; and for this, in some quarters, his reputation has suffered.

J. C. Trewin. *Dramatists of Today*
(Staples Press, 1953), pp. 144–46

However much the play [*Journey's End*] may seem to protest against the futility of war, there is, in fact, an acceptance of the values which make war possible. The nearest approach to a statement about war is Raleigh's "It all seems rather—*silly,* doesn't it?" Silly—but the only decent thing a man can do. *Journey's End* is, in its total effect, a pathetic tribute to the virtues of conformity.

Which, perhaps, explains why Sherriff is so concerned to conform to the tastes of his after-dinner audience. Raleigh's death is the ultimate evasion. For the real horror of war is that people are killed, senselessly, and die in great pain. Death is ugly. . . .

I can't help feel that Owen's ghosts, cringing in holes in "the poignant misery of dawn" deserved a little more real attention than Sherriff has paid them.

Albert Hunt. *Encore.* Dec., 1959, pp. 8–9

SHUTE, NEVIL (1899–1960)

One thing more certain than fatigue in metals is the absence of fatigue in reading Mr. Shute's novels. He has the knack of leading the reader quietly yet breathlessly from one suspense to another. The plot of *No Highway* is ingenious, even for its author, who has invented many such in his time; it builds absorbing as well as literate entertainment, and probably no author now writing can make better fictional use of scientific technology. To which is added a somewhat synthetic love story which no one need believe in who doesn't want, and an American female movie star whom no one should believe in at all. She illustrates Mr. Shute's strength by exploring his weakness—that combined with a superb gift of narrative he has an imagination that probes situations more easily than emotions. For this reason he portrays with effortless verisimilitude the surface-values of English character—notably that gift of understatement which is no mere verbal trick but a code of manners for the mind, impressing its own pattern of predictable behavior on some millions of Englishmen.

James Hilton. *NYHT*. Sept. 5, 1948, p. vii

Mr. Shute, too, has an alternative profession. You probably know of him only as a robust and successful novelist, but his real name is Norway and for many years he was an aircraft engineer. *Slide Rule* is concerned with this side of life and little else. Childhood and youth—he is the son of a former secretary to the Irish Post Office and witnessed the Dublin Easter Rising at uncomfortably close quarters—and experiences in the first world war, are done in a few pages. His big inside story is about the airships R100, on the design and construction of which he worked and in which he flew to Canada, and the R101, with whose disaster airship endeavour in England came to an end. . . . This interesting, mildly eccentric and not always totally responsible person, an example of the rare but dangerous cultivated soldier-charmer type, cast a spell over the susceptible Ramsay Macdonald. He appears to have known as much about flying as a dandelion clock. After airships, Mr. Shute helped to launch a new aircraft enterprise, now part of De Havilland's. He leaves us abruptly in 1938, celebrating the sale of the film rights of one of his novels. His writing is crisp and accomplished. He, too, tells us singularly little about himself, but self-revelation is not his purpose.

Maurice Richardson. *NSN*. July 10, 1954, p. 48

For excellent, rattling workman that he is, his characters remain novelist's characters, good or bad, old or young, male or female. When he is dealing with aircraft or engineers Mr. Shute remains exciting. *No Highway* and *Round the Bend* are both, on their own terms, highly successful. But in *Requiem for a Wren* the hangars and slide-rules are one uncomfortable remove away. . . . If Mr. Shute would stay in the air he would be more entertaining. As it is he is simply mawkish and provincial.

John Metcalf. *Spec*. April 8, 1955, p. 452

The towering success of Mr. Nevil Shute is not in the least mysterious. He is an excellent spinner of stories as such . . . he understands the technique of tension; and having been himself a good and original engineer, taps a whole new public of engineers, technologists, etc., who may otherwise find the straight novel lacking in interest for themselves. His is largely a masculine public, a public with no fancy aesthetic ideas and no desire to be troubled by those psychological depth-charges with which some writers cause disturbance, guilt and longing in the souls of their readers. It is a public with a streak of disciplined romance and a good-humoured capacity to believe six impossible things before breakfast, if those things are allied to the power of the planchette-board, extra-sensory perception and the rest of it—white man's magic, rather light-hearted stuff, not to be taken too seriously. . . .

I have never forgotten Mr. Shute's very early book, *The Pied Piper*, or his penultimate book, *On the Beach*. One, I thought, was extremely touching, the other pretty courageous. And in neither of them has he played this heaven-and-earth-Horatio trick. Why *will* he do it? Mr. C. S. Forester, a fine exponent of the action story, does not think of stepping outside the probabilities, and his strength lies there. But I suspect that for Mr. Shute's admirers, or a great number of them, the wild romantic excursions have a special appeal. I have known men of action, technical men, practical men, men who are always tinkering with machines, who yearn for a touch of the small-scale supernatural and are quite gullible in the search for it.

Pamela Hansford Johnson. *NS*. Aug. 16, 1958, p. 200

It is a very sad thought that in *Trustee from the Toolroom* we have Nevil Shute's last novel. No one in modern literature is quite like him. Nevil Shute was in the first place a stunt writer; that is to say, an author who writes from personal skill of a technical craft; and who writes with such an intensity of understanding that he infects his readers with a degree of interest scarcely less than his own. . . .

Such are the uses and indeed the infectious charm of good stunt writers. But Nevil Shute had far greater literary qualities to back his documentary knowledge than most stunt writers. He had an imaginative choice of very unusual subjects, and the selective power of the true artist in fitting all his characters into appropriate incidents. His novels are beautifully constructed and his characters convincing.

He has perhaps less drama and even less poetic imagination than Kipling; but both writers had the same blend of intensity with accuracy that gives their readers fellow feeling and the fullest confidence in their author. Neither novelist would have used their documentary knowledge, as many novelists do now, in order to lead you up the path of neurotic sentimentalism.

Chequerboard is perhaps his most imaginative and therefore, in a psychological sense, the truest of his novels; but *No Highway, Requiem for a Wren* and *Pied Piper* are all three deeply moving and sincere studies of those caught up in our long life and death struggle.

What made Shute a major novelist was that he had acquired this double faculty. Technical knowledge was a passion with him; but imagination was the bread of his life.

Shute wanted to understand why human beings act as they do in a given situation, and his vivid faithful imagination supplied him with situations that exactly exposed and expressed the characters he had found for them. He was not always an equal writer, and he made one or two great mistakes in his choice of subjects.

Phyllis Bottome. *JOL.* April 7, 1960, p. 397

SIDGWICK, ETHEL (1877–   )

The three novels [*Promise, Le Gentleman, Herself*] thus suddenly in hand are, it seems, all that this new English "discovery" has to her credit. She is not an altogether surprising discovery. Miss Ethel Sidgwick is daughter of an Oxford scholar, Arthur Sidgwick; niece of the late Professor Henry Sidgwick of Cambridge; and cousin of the Bensons. She has been a teacher in a number of girls' schools, in England and France: a fact which accounts in part, perhaps, for the subtly Brontesque flavor of these stories, especially the last of them, *Herself.*

The American publishers state that these three novels were written in two years. At all events they were published in England within that time, and scored an immediate and unusual success. We have not had to wait so long for them as we often do for English successes, and it is to be hoped that we may not have to wait at all for whatever this writer may do in the future. For her work is of unusual quality, remarkable not only as the work of a new writer, but on its own merits.

SIDGWICK, ETHEL

Promise, the first of the novels in order of publication, treads dangerous ground. We have had frequent occasion to complain recently of the feeble and enfeebling attempts of current novelists to interpret "the artistic temperament." Repeatedly, we have been asked to interest ourselves in essential weakness and pusillanimity, for the sake of a merely alleged merit. This is the result of a general confusion, fostered by feminine novelists, of the unconventional and the irresponsible. Miss Sidgwick's young genius is queer from the view of the parent and the schoolmaster, freakish in the eyes of the ordinary way. But this, we are gradually led to see, is due not to lack of balance, but to an instinct towards what is big and natural.

Nation. Nov. 28, 1912, pp. 508–9

Succession is a finished literary performance which, regarded from many points of view, is remarkable. It may be argued that it shares the limitations of genre music, and that, just as the eminence of a Grieg eludes comparison with the music-makers of the rest of the Western world, so, in relation to the great human family, the music-steeped Lemaures are isolated, specialized, even localized. To this extent it might be urged that this is not a great human novel. Having said this, we may express our admiration for the rare skill with which a succession of three generations of a gifted family, viewed merely in their physical relationship one to another, or in their artistic inheritance, is handled. . . . The technical quality of the dialogue and the restrained yet profound emotional interest show the artistry of the writer.

Ath. May 3, 1913, p. 489

Miss Sidgwick, her American publishers, Small, Maynard & Co., are at some pains to explain, comes of a distinguished Oxford family. One might have divined this for one's self. Not that she takes her background solemnly, after Mrs. Ward's manner. She takes it evasively, with delicious lightness. It is her lightness of touch that gives her away. This is the almost dangerous cleverness, one feels, this is the sure, sophisticated talent, that grows easily and naturally out of inherited opportunity and complicated social intercourse. Yet there is nothing derived about Miss Sidgwick's point of view. Beguiled by all sorts, conditions and races of men—with a sympathetic preference for the French cook, or the Irish vagabond, or the German Hausfrau, as against the Oxford exquisite—she is as far from British superiority as she is from imitation. Mr. Henry James, her literary father, had not to sigh over *Promise,* as he must have done these last years over a good many feminine first books, "Am I as like that as that?" It is merely that she seems to have been born to good talk—her method is largely conversational—and to a great variety of civilized human relations. Like Mr. James, she conceives such relations as thrilling in themselves, even when they are the inevitable ones, and whether or not they are dependent on sex. Sex is not her primary concern, social or cosmic problems do not touch her, raw realism is not what she seeks. In short, she does not belong to the Five Towns or the Wellsian schools. Her interest lies in the intricate relations and reactions of character, manners, and nationality. Human character is obviously what she cares most for; after that for music and for France.

Promise, later followed by a long sequel, *Succession,* leaps into the heart of these three absorbing passions. It is a carefully wrought study of the development of a musical genius, and a French one at that. . . .

Her France is not *"pastiche"*; it goes far beyond the observations of the curious traveller. I can think of nothing to match it for penetration and completeness in recent English or American literature. Arnold Bennett has, of course, given us some inimitable French types, and Henry James some still more famous ones, but they have chiefly portrayed foreigners in a French setting, and that is also true of Mrs. Wharton. Yet, after all, the important point is not that Miss Sidgwick feels France, but that within the definite limits of her intuitive talent she does feel. There is no telling where her zest for human analysis may take her next. We can be sure at least that her line will always be adventurously cast into the psychological undercurrents of the stream of life.

Elizabeth Shepley Sergeant. NR. April 17, 1915,
Supplement, pp. 5–6

Miss Ethel Sidgwick is one of the most individual of the English novelists of our day. Of course any first-rate novelist is individual; no one would read *These Twain* fancying even for a moment that it was by Mr. Wells, or *Victory* with the idea that it was by Mr. Galsworthy. Mr. Hugh Walpole, Mr. D. H. Lawrence, Mr. J. D. Beresford, Mr. Compton MacKenzie—to name a few others—are individual enough to keep each one in his own particular sphere. Miss Sidgwick, however, has a character rather more marked than any of them, or at least her books have. Superficially she reminds one of Henry James, but any such resemblance is as unimportant as in the case of Mrs. Edith Wharton. Miss Sidgwick is preëminently what is called "a novelist of marked distinction"; she has to a very high degree her own view of life and her own way of expressing this view, and both are excellent. . . .

Hatchways, though it does not give us so clear a notion of its author's world and her view of it as Miss Sidgwick's other books, gives it to us in much their manner. People and things are presented much as they are—without much direct narration, that is—and we are left to gather what we can. That is, of course, in the main, the method of life itself; we see people and hear them talk, but it is rarely that anybody tells us a finished story of his life and adventures. Miss Sidgwick is selective; she tells only those things that hang together; but she explains little, and, as a rule, is content to jot down things that are said and done and leave the rest to us. When one remembers that she is dealing with people who by habit and tradition do not express their emotional life openly, and who, when they do express themselves, have not the gift of eloquence that belongs to some other races, one can understand why Miss Sidgwick may be called subtle. But subtle or not she is always worth reading, and here, though there are no figures like Violet Ashwin and John Ingestre, there is yet much to interest and charm.

E. E. Hale. *Dial.* Dec. 14, 1916, pp. 535–36

The essence of Miss Sidgwick is her instinct for Literature. Sometimes, like her own Charles, "she teases the language, and fidgets her phrases: but her aim is precise in general, and her taste pure." Our appreciation depends on a quick intellect, familiarity with art atmosphere and book-language, a love of the fine shades. In structure and style she is not realistic; she frankly composes; yet, in her own way, lays bare the soul. She is modern: because she does not concern herself with single emotions, whole characters, a crude clash of black and white. She is never melodramatic. Nor does the narrative make up one centralised plot. It grows out of the immense complexities and interchange which super-civilisation imposes on human-nature. The persons of the drama are pulled in a thousand different directions, by circumstances, place, and standards; growing out of intellectual activity, a cultured outlook, inherited standards. They are in touch with that new morality which our ancestors would have dismissed as a perverse confusion between right and wrong, a curious twisting of emotion, and a conception, rather morbid, if not decadent, of human nature. Over the brilliant surface Miss Sidgwick moves with ease and precision: manipulating her high-spirited team with a cool, strong hand: drawing the picture in firm, fine, lines: never losing our attention, or ceasing to charm. Beneath the surface lurks Truth: real emotion, and vivid humanity.

It is supreme art, admirably controlled.

R. B. Johnson. *Some Contemporary Novelists* (Leonard Parsons, 1920), pp 105–6

The blatant inadequacy of her work [*Restoration*] is not her fault. Her style is witty, delicate, and allusive, and her sentiments comprise all that is desirable. Not talents are lacking her, but a drawing-room, and the drawing-room spirit is dead. To pretend that it is not, to pretend that an especial class of intelligent and unoccupied women have a place to which men, after scraping and combing, may bring grave topics to be turned to delicate gossip, is beyond the powers of even Miss Sidgwick. The world has lost its water-tight compartments. Miss Sidgwick shows that this is rather regrettable, and her *Restoration* may temporarily take the place of one.

H. C. Harwood. *OutL.* May 26, 1923, p. 431

SILKIN, JON (1930–   )

A number of young poets do exist who can be called "romantic" (if that term any longer means anything), but they have tended to be neglected. . . . The two best are Jon Silkin and Geoffrey Hill. Silkin has been compared to D. H. Lawrence, largely because both poets employ animals as symbols of the human condition; but whereas Lawrence almost always used them as emblems to illustrate the gulf between them and humans or between their appearance and their "meaning" . . . Silkin uses them as living parables of decency, tolerance and love, creatures removed from ourselves by only a tiny fraction. . . . What this implies is a great compassion, a great tenderness for the dumb struggling of all life, whether human or animal; responsibilities begin when such concern becomes a rule of conduct. The technical equipment Silkin uses is crude, often naive, but the crudity and the naivete keep out the worse faults of glibness and oversophistication; his concern with innocence, with cruelty and with death—large, dangerous themes—is warm and human.

Anthony Thwaite. *Essays on Contemporary English Poetry* (Tokyo, Kenkyusha Ltd., 1957), p. 170

What Jon Silkin lacks in *The Two Freedoms* is . . . control. . . . Mr. Silkin is only able to deal adequately with the childishly simple: "Death of a Bird" is the one poem in the book that really comes off. The rest simply fall to pieces. Mr. Silkin seems to be losing what power over language he did have in his first book: the choice of adjectives is particularly unfortunate. . . . Images are blurred throughout, and in very few poems is even the basic structure clear. Apparently Mr. Silkin often feels about half-way through a poem that he ought to turn it into a statement about mystical experience. But the statement remains unmade, and we are only aware of a breathy striving toward something very vague.

Thom Gunn. *Spec.* Aug. 8, 1958, p. 200

There are strange and beautiful passages in Mr. Silkin's poems [*The Two Freedoms*], profound feeling, unusual integrity, and a sense of breaking through to a vision which is only now and then attained. They impress even when they confuse or disappoint. The title poem is very fine, and makes one feel that Mr. Silkin will become one of the best poets of his generation.

Edwin Muir. *NS*. Sept. 20, 1958, p. 387

One might . . . subdivide poets into those of the inner and the outer voice. Mr. Jon Silkin . . . is trying to strike a balance between them, but, to me at least, seems at present most successful with the internal voice.

Kathleen Nott. *Enc.* Nov., 1958, p. 92

Mr. Silkin, despite idiosyncratic efforts at concentration, is diffuse and his method of writing leads him into strange non-sequiturs, apt to be comic when he least means it. His poems tend to ask enigmatic, seemingly irrelevant questions, and certain lines read as if they had got in by mistake from some other poem. There is intensity of feeling, gravity, a continual preoccupation with technique, but they do not as yet reduce to much. One feels simply that either these are not the right words, or that Mr. Silkin is not clear about the kind of poems he wants to write. Reading him is like looking through binoculars, each lens of which is differently focused.

James Stern. *L.* Sept., 1958, p. 73

SILLITOE, ALAN (1928–   )

But for all of Arthur's [the hero of *Saturday Night and Sunday Morning*] energy, his life is sadly limited in scope and value. It is a life bound by ritualistic practice and unexamined assumption, for in the absence of a genuine consciousness, his freedom comes to little more than a repetition of familiar acts with increasing violence. Yet Mr. Sillitoe makes a particular point of "accepting" Arthur; indeed he strongly implies that there is a special sort of realistic virtue in "accepting" him as he is, and not expecting him to become anything different . . . despite my pleasure in the novel, [this attitude] leaves me with some doubts.

Mr. Sillitoe's attitude toward Arthur is notably free from moral naggings or political exhortation; but it may be that in its hard-headed and undeluded way it is not quite free from sentimentality, the kind of sentimentality which, passing as cultural relativism or a respect for variant mores, one sometimes finds among anthropologists who celebrate the odd behaviour of "their" tribes. It is an attitude which tempts the observer—in this case the writer—to abandon a little too easily his own standards, his own judgments. It is an attitude that fits a little too conveniently current intellectual and middle class feelings about workers:— *see yonder tamed and vivid beast, munching his fish and chips, frolicking with his beer and telly.* And should not this capacity of a novel for copying the dominant moods of the moment be at least some cause for uneasiness?

Irving Howe. NR. Aug. 24, 1959, pp. 27–28

His new novel [*The General*] is a fable. . . . The moral is impeccable. . . . But it is not the moral that makes a fable but the fable the moral, and Mr. Sillitoe's fable is unconvincing. Because it lacks what James called density of specification it imposes on the reader no illusion of any kind of reality. . . . Mr. Sillitoe has made his gesture. Its bravery demands praise; but having recognized the bravery all one can do in honesty is to adapt an earlier critic on an earlier writer and say, "Back to your factory-hands and Borstal boys, Mr. Sillitoe!"

Walter Allen. NS. May 21, 1960, p. 765

To trade too heavily on a book's topical appeal is to invite swift critical retribution. A case in point is Mr. Alan Sillitoe's first novel, *Saturday Night and Sunday Morning,* which has just appeared in a paperback edition, decked out with tributes from the reviewers and a still from the film version. Does Mr. Sillitoe represent a significant new departure, the true voice of proletarian feeling coming at last after so many disgruntled arts-graduate fakes, or is it going to seem incredible in a few years' time that intelligent adults were ever persuaded to take his saga of beer, bed and brawls at all seriously?

Mr. Sillitoe's Nottinghamshire setting is authentic enough, and so is his skilful handling of a difficult dialect without ever becoming self-consciously "regional" or clogging the action of his story. But his hero, a two-fisted, hard-drinking Casanova of the factory-floor with the constitution of Popeye the Sailor, has the synthetic stamina of a comic-strip rather than real vitality or even plausibility. And does it not now seem that there is something altogether too calculated about his outbursts against authority in every shape or the complacent cynicism of the book's closing pages? There are many good touches in the course of Mr. Sillitoe's squalid story . . . which suggest that the fuss has not been altogether about nothing; but it seems a pity, not least for the author's sake, that uneven promise has been taken for solid achievement.

TLS. Sept. 2, 1960, p. 562

Alan Sillitoe's first novel, *Saturday Night and Sunday Morning,* appeared less than four years ago and it is some sort of comment on the whimsies of the literary market that one should already be concerned to disinter his reputation. Since that book ("If he never writes anything more, he has assured himself a place in the history of the English novel," *New Yorker*), he has, in fact, written two or three more and, if one is to judge from the Sunday reviews of his latest, he runs the present danger of being less written about than written off.

Saturday Night met with the large acclaim that usually signals either a work of genius or the satisfaction of a contemporary need. The truth, as so often with the truth, seems in retrospect to have lain somewhere in between. . . . What hindsight allows is that the book's main achievement was to have caught and rendered a class context unfamiliar to most readers, and writers, of novels. We are so prey to fashion that a couple of decent novels about industrial communities north of the Thames is enough to set off talk of a proletarian movement in English fiction, with knowing nods towards Lawrence and Arnold Bennett: four such novels, and the "movement" is felt to have usefully run its course. There isn't, after all, so much to know about the proles (so runs the insidious argument) and the healthy shudder of confronting a kitchen sink, cracks and all, has its therapeutic moment and fades. Against this arrogant nonsense *Saturday Night* stands firm. To afford a sense of physical entry into unknown terrain is not the least of the novelist's capacities and Mr. Sillitoe's first book did this with freshness and urgency.

As much was true for *The Loneliness of the Long-distance Runner,* the collection of short stories that followed. The title-piece took one with some guile into the mind of a pistoning cross-country Borstal boy, and into a more coherent revolt than Arthur Seaton's: conscientiously throwing a race the Governor wanted him to win. . . .

To be kind, if not fulsome, one would gloss over the book of poems, *The Rats,* that succeeded this, but it would do no one any sort of service, least of all their author. The tone and tenor of these extraordinarily incompetent verses have been fairly paralleled all too recently in those maniac home-thoughts from abroad of Osborne's: they issue from a strangulating anger that jettisons all considerations of intelligence and responsibility. Mr. Sillitoe is unlikely to be remembered as a thinker. . . .

John Coleman. *NS.* Oct. 27, 1961, p. 610

Alan Sillitoe has not abandoned the characters and themes of his first fiction. His people are still the recalcitrant and casually criminal poor. Nottingham is still the place. In the title story of his new collection [*The Ragman's Daughter*] there is the familiar thieving hero who steals not only for kicks but on principle. . . . What seems clear is how powerfully these books have acted on the general nostalgia for the working class which has spread through the culture, the new and mainly salutary wish to think well of its departing ways. . . .

Close analysis is likely to get drowned in his characteristic style of flowing, roaring, worming reminiscence. . . . A buttonholing Whitmanesque loquacity is the rule, which comes to grief when the novel as a whole lasts too long. . . . He is the archivist of the sly, battling Sillitoes and in his foremost works he has done them proud. But one is entitled to a few doubts. "The Long-Distance Runner" contains a distinction between "In-laws" ("In-law blokes like you and them," he explains to the reader) and "Out-laws," like the writer himself and his hard cases. Society is reduced to these two categories, with the focus on the charming madhead delinquents and their relatives, and with the others cartooned as "pig-faced snotty-nosed dukes and ladies." Those who belong to neither group, who neither break the law nor live off it in some privileged or parasitic state, are nowhere. Mr. Sillitoe should be informed that they are the ones who read his novels.

Karl Miller. *NS*. Oct. 18, 1963, p. 530

SINCLAIR, MAY (1865–1946)

A novel has recently been published—*The Helpmate,* by Miss May Sinclair—which appears to fall exactly into the category of those works in which the Edinburgh Reviewer traces most clearly the blight of the Convention. It is a novel, that is to say—written by an author whose performance, brilliant though it be, falls in some respects short of its promise—a novel which, though abounding in cleverness, must for various reasons be held to have missed a success very nearly attained, must on the whole be regarded as a brilliant failure. . . .

Now I will venture to say that this book, for all its cleverness, does not deserve the high praise it has received nor the kind of praise it has received. And I strongly suspect that most of the reviewers in the leading newspapers know that it does not. I seem to trace in all these reviews the restraining finger-prints of a Convention—not the British Convention. Here and there a bold spirit dares to find the story dull, improbable, irritating—but I observe in almost all these reviews a curious coincidence: the reviewers concentrate on the very dull and not a little improbable figure of the respectable wife, whilst her far more interesting and more lifelike husband is left severely alone, save for a few approving allusions that might have been dictated by the novelist:

"dignified indulgence," "loving mildness," "unfailing tenderness," and the like.

Lady Eleanor Cecil. *Living Age.* Sept. 21, 1907, pp. 579, 588

Miss May Sinclair has not failed to write an interesting book on Charlotte, Emily, and Anne Brontë [*The Brontë Sisters*]. How could she? After covering all the ground from Mrs. Gaskell to the Abbé Dimnet, she has remained herself; and this volume is the story of her experiences among the Brontës and their critics, written for those who are as well up in the matter as herself, but still eager to exchange opinions. It is part of the justification for books that they facilitate such exchange of opinions; yet to us it seems not wholly necessary that every stage in their formation should be perpetuated in print. Miss Sinclair's book is too long. She quotes a great number of Emily Brontë's verses in a manner more suited to a newspaper discussion. She should have quoted much more to arrest the ignoramous; far less would have been sufficient for the devotee. The book has only reached a half-way stage to finality.

Evidently Miss Sinclair set to work with some excitement, and that is well; but she must have continued when the excitement had abated, and not waited long enough for after-thoughts. She is too often unsettled without being strongly moved, tired without being calm. Not but what she has put good things into every part of the book, and more than good things. . . . But the whole is an exercise, not an achievement. It is rather the expression of a point of view than really individual. We feel that Miss Sinclair has sacrificed much to a desire to be impressive.

Ath. July 13, 1912, p. 33

Miss Sinclair's work is quite good enough to stand on its own merits without any apologia. She has undoubted power and sincerity. She is intensely sensitive, and is especially apt in dealing with the subtle emotions and fine-drawn distinctions, varying shades of light and colour. It would be absurd to pretend that the eight stories which make up this volume [*The Judgment of Eve*] are Miss Sinclair's best work. All are readable, but from the standpoint of the author's high achievement several are negligible.

SR. April 25, 1914, pp. 542–43

It would be hard to find a better illustration of the gulf that divides Georgian from mid-Victorian fiction than that which is furnished by Miss Sinclair's choice of a hero [*Tasker Jevons*]. The heroes of fifty or sixty years ago were generally of the Admirable Crichton type: handsome, athletic, and distinguished. They took Double Firsts, played in the University Eleven, and rowed in the University Eight. James Tasker Jevons did none of these things. He had no social or educational advantages; he was undersized, and was only redeemed from physical vulgarity by the freakish irregularity of his features and his fine eyes. . . . But he was a genius, and he knew it; he had mapped out his career in advance and carried out his plans to the letter. . . . Miss Sinclair has given us a brilliantly written and extremely interesting book with a new type of hero, for whom, if we cannot love him, we come in the long run to entertain a feeling of intermittent affection.

Spec. April 15, 1916, p. 504

In *The Divine Fire* . . . Miss Sinclair gave no indication of her dissatisfaction with the traditional method of novel-writing; she did no more in that book than give her readers a glimpse of under-currents. Her other novels, arresting pieces of work, were the well-told stories of the competent craftsman. *The Three Sisters, The Combined Maze, The Tree of Heaven,* were good in matter and in manner. . . . Miss Sinclair was one of a golden fellowship, but until she wrote *Mary Olivier* she did not stand out from among them as definitely critical of tradition.

Dissatisfaction, however, was in the air. A number of writers, weary of the iterated tale, of the melange of sentimentality, convention, faked incident and false psychology known as the popular novel, were making experiments of one sort and another; and when Miss Sinclair published *Mary Olivier,* she ranged herself definitely with the pioneers. Her position as a writer who has had the courage to look at life from an individual standpoint will be strengthened by her forthcoming book. In *The Romantic* she uses the direct method, presenting her story through the mind of one of the characters. This method is also employed by others of the group to which she belongs, for instance, Dorothy Richardson; but to say that Miss Sinclair derives from this writer would be doing her less than justice. For one thing, Miss Sinclair was experimenting with this method before Miss Richardson began to write, and for another their work has nothing else in common. Miss Richardson's is monumental. Having chosen a dumping-ground she is pouring on to it novel-load after novel-load of heterogeneous objects, and by so doing is raising an immense, an almost Cyclopean, mound. Miss Sinclair, on the contrary, is selective. She produces an effect of lightning, of concentrated seeing, of extraordinary and sudden brilliancy, and this effect is particularly apparent in her presentation of John Roden Conway in *The Romantic*. I do not know of any piece of writing more subtly forcible than the lifting of veil after veil from the man's personality until the creature stands revealed in pitiable nakedness. Miss Sinclair presents him to us, and the reader is left to find the pity of humanity for a soul so marred, to murmur in fear and trembling, "Can such things be?" and to acknowledge unwillingly, sorrowfully, that they are.

C. A. Dawson-Scott. *Bkm.* Nov., 1920, p. 248

Like *Mr. Waddington of Wyck,* Miss Sinclair's new book [*Life and Death of Harriet Frean*] is a study of the psychopathology of Peter Pan. Neither Mr. Waddington nor Miss Frean ever grew up. In the earlier book it takes the form of conceited selfishness. In the latter it takes the form of conceited unselfishness. And since we live in a post-Butler world, it is of course the unselfishness which causes the most unhappiness. . . .

The old army of psychological novelists, with Henry James at their head, left no act of their characters without a clear and conscious cause for it, and thereby justly deserved to be called academic. For life isn't like that. The new army, with Miss Sinclair not to be far from the van, are apt to leave no act without a clear cause for it in the subconsciousness. This novel in consequence resembles an X-ray photograph—the facts are there but not the likeness.

Miss Sinclair's skill is astounding, her brilliance never failing, but she writes *a priori.* She is an academic artist in the truest and least insulting sense.

Raymond Mortimer. *Dial.* May, 1922, pp. 531, 534

. . . [May Sinclair] is too rebellious to see quite straight as an artist. *Anne Severn and the Fieldings* is, in any case, not one of Miss Sinclair's best books because, although it contains the essential truth about all its characters, it is not true enough to the appearances of the world. The myth she has designed to express her discovery hardly holds together. There is reality in the theme of Jerrold, the man who is everything that is noble and fine, but who is evasive and turns his back on unpleasantness. . . . But the circumstances of the book are so casually imagined that the mind is sceptical. . . . But more damaging to the effect of *Anne Severn and the Fieldings* than . . . mechanical defects is Miss Sinclair's reaction against the fluffy, feminine ideal. . . . Anne Severn is her author's declaration that a woman can be passionate and sexual and yet a cool and dignified human being. She is rather more that than she is a person. She has something of the almost priggish open-airiness and self-reliance that the early pioneers of the higher education of women strove to inculcate in their pupils. She interrupts the story to say "Yea" to a "Nay" that was uttered in controversy outside it. When she intervenes in the processes of the tractor . . . there is a surface on the description of her action, a glossy surface such as one sees on those big advertisements that hang in railway stations, which proceeds from Miss

Sinclair's consciousness that many people have alleged from time to time that the things that women do with levers may be mysterious but are not efficient. It is this slight disingenuousness in the conception of the principal character that makes the book distinctly less impressive than Miss Sinclair's novels usually are. For it is primarily a novel about passion; and when one is shown Anne consumed by passion, the very power of her creator makes us shocked and incredulous. This is the real thing; but how startling it is that Anne should have felt it. One feels as a headmistress might if she discovered that the head prefect was engaged in an ardent love affair. This is not to say that Miss Sinclair is not a gifted and delightful artist. She has shown herself that in other volumes; she shows herself that here, in the description of the peace of Wyck on the Cotswolds, and in the characterization of the Fieldings. But perhaps just because here is a romantic theme, that might well involve its writer in adherence to the romantic conception of women, she has forfeited one tiny part of her artistry.

Rebecca West. *NS*. Dec. 2, 1922, pp. 270-72

The unifying factor in the work of May Sinclair is its humanity. The emotions are controlled by the intelligence, but ever and again we find them claiming their inalienable rights, and it is then that the author produces her finest work. This is not sentimental, but there is about it a naked truthfulness quite free from that conventional rhetoric which is the evil tradition of most writers in dealing with emotions.

Nowhere have I found more convincing truth than in *Mary Olivier*. This book is undoubtedly the toughest, the most compact of Miss Sinclair's works. It is built of even, well-laid bricks, bound together by a mortar which is consistently good in quality. The whole is a harmonious composition. *The Three Sisters* is Miss Sinclair's masterpiece, but *Mary Olivier,* equally among her works and among the best literary productions of the last few years, holds a special position. It is the model of modern romance, and is as far removed from the old convention as are the novels of Dorothy Richardson and James Joyce, except where it shows too great a respect for certain dead institutions or laughable professions of faith. But this defect is its sole weakness, and is weakness, moreover, only to the philosopher or anarchist. In avoiding cynicism, the author is sometimes betrayed into the use of ancient currencies. In any case, she is the least conventional of women writers.

The form of *Mary Olivier* is new; it is an experiment—a sudden intellectual gesture of the author. This experiment is a complete success. Besides being solid and compact, the book contains a quick succession of pictures. One gets the impression of an album of highly finished engravings, filled with useful details, well grouped, and not interfering one with another. Moreover—and this is most remarkable considering the complete revolution in Miss Sinclair's style—these pictures have her old perfection of finish.

Jean de Bosschère. YR. Oct., 1924, pp. 82–83

Miss Sinclair's *The Dark Night* is the novel in verse (free of a kind) of an accomplished novelist who has already expressed herself again and again in her natural medium, and is now trying an experiment in a medium not naturally her own. The flavour of her poem is what might be known as *modern,* though the word has a shifting value, and perhaps a more fitting expression is *up to date.* . . .

Miss Sinclair . . . has, as her primary consideration, a story to tell. Her imagination moves in terms of personality, reaction, plot, the interplay of character upon character. *The Dark Night* is conceived primarily as a story, and could have been told, without any loss of interest, in the usual manner of the novel. Most readers will be instinctively disposed to judge it by the standards of criticism usually applied to the superior novel. Her motive, therefore, in substituting free verse for her excellent prose is open to conjecture.

Harold Monro. Crit. April, 1925, p. 145

Poetry and metaphysics were her first lines of activity. She produced books of verse in 1887 and 1890, wrote reviews and articles for philosophical journals, and came only after some years to the art of fiction. Her first short story was published in 1895, and her first novel, *Audrey Craven,* the following year. It showed no very clear signs of genius; and neither did its two successors. The first novel which gave her the beginning of a reputation was *The Divine Fire.* She was a realist and at first tended to show the drabness and futility of life rather than the brighter aspects. *The Creators, The Life and Death of Harriet Frean, The Flaw in the Crystal,* and various short stories helped to consolidate a reputation that became so high that in 1916 William Lyon Phelps called her "the foremost living writer among English-speaking women." . . .

Her later novels were, perhaps, more finely contrived, surer in delineation, more subtle in character drawing, than anything she had done before. The short book, *A Cure of Souls,* is a delicious, mildly ironical portrait of a lethargic, comfort-loving rector, which perhaps shows Miss Sinclair at her best. It is complete, rounded, and humourous.

TL. Nov. 15, 1946, p. 7

A student of psychology and philosophy—it was she who, reviewing *Pilgrimage* in 1918, first borrowed the term "stream of consciousness" from William James—she must have been among the earliest English novelists to have been aware of the work of Freud. Neither *Mary Olivier: a Life* nor *The Life and Death of Harriet Frean* could have been written without a knowledge of psychoanalysis. Both describe the upbringing of young women during the second half of the Victorian age. The general attitude towards the age, at any rate as seen in the middle-class family, is akin to Samuel Butler's in *The Way of All Flesh,* though the modern reader may also see in them foreshadowings of the matter, though not the manner, of the fiction of Ivy Compton-Burnett.

Especially interesting now is May Sinclair's technique. Throughout the novel we are placed as it were in Mary's consciousness, but there is no stream-of-consciousness as such. Her thoughts are reported for the most part in *oratio obliqua,* usually in the second person: . . . At the same time, though not going anywhere as far as Joyce in *Portrait of the Artist,* May Sinclair very ably renders the increasing complexity of the mind from the simple terms of childhood.

Walter Allen. The Modern Novel in Britain and the United States (N.Y., Dutton, 1964), pp. 15–16

SITWELL, EDITH (1887–1964)

Whatever may ultimately be said of the permanent value of their work, few will deny that, while they [the Sitwells] were fighting for new values, they did pull down the Gates of Gaza, perfectly willing to break their own heads along with those of the Philistines . . . . in some sort they have won now, the gates are down, and the Philistines are at their oldest and most dangerous trick of attempting to persuade themselves (and the Sitwells) that they were on the side of the rebels all the time, and, indeed, that there was never any rebellion at all. . . . The Sitwells have not done more than prove that they have a vision, and they have not yet imposed it on their own minds. They are all young, and are all developing. . . . As a family and as individuals they have invented a new idiom, but if they do not now adapt it to express a new truth it will become a dead invention in their own hands.

SR. March 26, 1927, p. 474

A summarised view, then, of the prolific fifteen or sixteen years of her activity suggest that she is no pioneer anarch building on tradition, but a romantic compelled by time-tyranny to be unromantic; that she is a verse-writer of talent (which may be called the feminine of genius); that she has had experiences varying from the valueless to the slightly valuable, but that on few occasions only has she succeeded in organizing them; that her limited class of experience has produced poems little more varied than the uprights of a circular railing and damaged by an unreasonable excess of irrationality.

Geoffrey Grigson. BkmL. Aug., 1931, p. 245

Her book [*The English Eccentrics*] is a friendly excursion rather than a guide, and fuller of acknowledgements than of references. The lesson to be drawn from it—if so heavy a draught as a lesson be required—is that eccentricity ranks as a national asset, and that so long as it is respected there is some hope that our country will not go mad as a whole. . . . Those of us who assume (perhaps wrongly) that we are sane, can learn from her pages the lesson most necessary for a sane man; the need of a tolerance which is touched by pity but untouched by contempt.

E. M. Forster. Spec. May 19, 1933, p. 716

Miss Sitwell . . . has done her pioneering, and we are now able to regard her work, not as controversy, but as poetry. The fact remains that she was one of the writers who bridged the gap between the sterile years of the early war and the post-war years of excited experiment; that she helped to keep the interest in poetry alive when it was near extinction. . . .

Society has declared itself the modern Vanity Fair. The English countryside has proved bucolic beyond endurance. In the present there seems no haven for this acute and irritable mind; there remains the past. And in the past she finds the elegance, the grace, the soft civilized beauty which she vainly seeks in the present. It is to her own childhood that she turns for solace. . . . And in *The Sleeping Beauty* (1924) and *Troy Park* (1925) she looks back to the dreaming summers of youth. . . . The "Troy Park" of the collected edition is almost entirely autobiographical. . . . Within those walls it is always summer. . . . She has never really left Troy Park; or, if from time to time she has left it, the brutality and treachery without drove her hastily back. So, living herself within the veil of a dream, the dream which was her own childhood, she looks out at the external world and sees that, too, as a dream. Her view of life remains in essence that of a child, a sensitive child seeing everything in terms of its own private world. . . . Miss Sitwell has retained a child's imagination while acquiring an adult's power of voluptuous expression. . . . She has not merely recreated, she has created a world. . . . In her verse the discords which torment her as a person suffer metamorphosis; they become poetry. And so for once we really are confronted with the romantic poetry of escape.

Dilys Powell. Descent from Parnassus
(N.Y., Macmillan, 1934), pp. xiii, 111–12, 127–34

One cannot think of her in any other age or country. She has transformed with her metrical virtuosity traditional metres reborn not to be read but spoken, exaggerating metaphors into mythology, carrying them from poem to poem, compelling us to go backward to some first usage for the birth of the myth. . . . Nature appears before us in a hashish-eater's dream. This dream is double; in its first half, through separate metaphor, through mythology, she creates, amid crowds and scenery that suggest the Russian Ballet and Aubrey Beardsley's final phases a perpetual metamorphosis that seems an elegant, artificial childhood; in the other half, driven by a necessity of contrast, a nightmare vision like that of Webster, of the emblems of mortality.

William Butler Yeats. Preface to *Oxford Book of Modern Verse* (Oxford Univ. Pr., 1936), pp. xviii-xix

With the appearance of *Street Songs* and *Green Song,* those who cared for poetry recognized a true poetic and prophetic cry which had not been heard in England since the death of Yeats. This was not merely exquisite poetry: it was great poetry; we felt once more the excitement of having amongst us a poet who could give us back our sight and our belief in the human heart, a poet on Shelley's definition.

Throughout Miss Sitwell's poetry a Swinburnian element persists. We are conscious of it in her elaborate technique, in her uncanny sensibility to the texture of language; and also, I dare say, in an occasional diffuseness, and in a feeling that the central core of her meaning is veiled in mist, and will dissolve if we approach it too closely. Miss Sitwell herself has accepted this kinship with Swinburne, . . . [Her] appreciation of Swinburne's verbal mastery is one of the most illuminating of all her critical studies, and one of the most personal. Many young people adored Swinburne in the early years of this century, but few mature poets would have admitted to an equal admiration in 1932.

After *Gold Coast Customs,* it is not surprising to find that Miss Sitwell wrote no poetry for many years. She was re-creating her spirit, seeking a belief or a vision which would enable her to transcend the evil and misery in the world; and during these years, evil was moving towards its catastrophe. We must suppose that much of her time was passed in reading, for these are the years of her anthologies of poetry with their critical introductions. And here I may say in parentheses that these introductions seem to me, with their self-imposed limits, to be among the most valuable pieces of modern criticism, and a merciful relief from that sheep in wolf's clothing, Taine's English Literature in a new disguise, the sociological criticism of Marxism. It is true that they endow the reader with a very subtle ear and demand from him very strict attention; and few readers, perhaps, can have followed Miss Sitwell in her discrimination of every nuance of sound. But anyone who has attempted to do so, must have had his capacity for enjoying poetry increased beyond measure; and what more can we ask of criticism?

In spite of Swinburnian and symbolist characteristics, it is clear from her latest poems that Miss Sitwell's place in English literature is with the religious poets of the seventeenth century. Again and again the audacity of her sensuous images reminds us of Crashaw; she has Traherne's rapture at created things, and Vaughan's sense of eternity. . . . Miss Sitwell is essentially a religious poet; that is to say, she has experienced imaginatively, not merely intellectually, the evil and misery of the world and has overcome that experience by the conviction—the full, imaginative conviction—that all creation is under the Divine Love.

Kenneth Clark in Celebration for Edith Sitwell,
ed. J. G. Villa (N.Y., New Directions, 1948),
pp. 56–59, 66

With the publication of *Street Songs* in 1942 and *Green Song* in 1944 Miss Sitwell has not only won an almost unique place for herself among the poets of this war but abundantly fulfilled the highest hopes which her admirers have had of her. This great flowering of her genius is her reward for years of devoted and patient labour at her art. From her first beginnings she possessed an instinctive sense for the true essence of poetry and a sensibility so fine and delicate that it can detect all the subtle echoes and associations which float around the sounds of human speech. She set herself a hard task when she made up her mind to restore to English poetry the richness of texture which had been largely lost in the Edwardian and Georgian epochs. For this reason much of her early work was experimental. . . . Of this preparatory work, in many ways so brilliant and so fascinating, she is herself a stern critic. When she published her *Collected Poems* in 1930, she omitted many pieces that others would wish to be included. . . . Yet even in this remarkable volume she had not found the full range of her gifts. Though *The Sleeping Beauty* showed of what enchanting fancy and haunting melody she was capable and *Gold Coast Customs* showed what tragic power and prophetical fury were hers, it was not until the Second World War that she fused all her different gifts into a single kind of poetry and combined in noble harmony her delicate fancy, her uncommon visual sense, her tender sympathy, her heroic courage in the face of a shattered world and her deep religious trust in the ultimate goodness of life.

The imagery of rain is developed with enormous power in "Still Falls the Rain," which has claims to be the most profound and most moving poem yet written in English about the war. It was inspired by the air-raids of 1940, but it has nothing transitory or merely contemporary about it. It is an intense, highly imaginative and tragic poem on the sufferings of man. . . . The destruction wrought by the air-raids is transformed into an example of man's wickedness and punishment and redemption. He brings his own sufferings upon himself, but through them he may be redeemed. So Miss Sitwell passes beyond the horror of the present moment to a vision of its significance in the spiritual history of man and through her compassion for him finds a ray of hope for his future.

This assertion of positive values in the face of corruption and destruction is fundamental to Miss Sitwell's poetry and gives to it a special coherence and harmony. Against "Lullaby" and "Serenade" we must set such poems as "Harvest" and "Holiday." We shall then see how Miss Sitwell passes through the harrowing doubts and despairs of war to a constructive outlook. This outlook is religious. . . . Whatever wounds mankind may inflict upon itself, whatever it may suffer from decay and destitution, it can in the end be healed by finding itself in harmony with the poses of nature and with the light and the love that inform them.

Maurice Bowra in *Celebration for Edith Sitwell*,
ed. J. G. Villa (N.Y., New Directions, 1948), pp. 20–31

Edith Sitwell has . . . written many books of prose, notable among them a biographical study of Alexander Pope and a novel based on the tragic life-story of Jonathan Swift, *I Live Under a Black Sun*. She has also been an indefatigable and highly original anthologist, and has combined the chosen comments of others with her own *obiter dicta* in two unique anthology-journals, *A Poet's Notebook* and *A Notebook on William Shakespeare*. In all these works, or in the introductions to them, she has provided a great deal of valuable light on her views of what the lives of poets mean, what poetry is for and how it works; so that they are not only fascinating in themselves but also important for anyone who wishes fully to appreciate the *oeuvre* of this remarkable poet. . . .

I have remarked before on the fact that, though each phase of Edith Sitwell's poetry seems distinctly marked off from those that preceded it, the more carefully one studies them the more closely one sees that they are related. They are like a continuing argument between the two poles of her inspiration, between romance and satire, affirmation and irony; now one gains the ascendancy, now the other, in method as in content. In her poems from "Still Falls the Rain" to "The Canticle of the Rose" they seem to find a resolution within a larger synthesis: the depth of tenderness and compassion, the understanding of human desolation that so poignantly informed "The Little Ghost Who Died for Love" are there, and at the same time the savage mockery of *Gold Coast Customs;*

the dream-like incantations of *The Sleeping Beauty* and the hard drumbeat of rhythms first evolved in *Nursery Rhymes*.
John Lehmann. *Edith Sitwell* (BC/Longmans, 1952), pp. 7, 31

As Oscar Wilde once said: "The English and Americans share one illusion; both think they speak the same language." His remark applies to British collections of American poetry. Dame Edith's selection [*The Atlantic Book of British and American Poetry*, ed. Dame Edith Sitwell] (and this without quarreling with her omissions and inclusions) is scarcely an exception to Wilde's rule. Her remarks on Eliot and Pound are refreshing and inspired, but her authority in the selection of verse loses much of its originality and firm footing. She is not "at home" with her understanding of American poetry; one feels that she plays safe by including Eliot's *The Waste Land* and only in her selection of translations by Arthur Waley from the Chinese and Eliot's adaptations from Saint-John Perse does the original force of her poetic genius shed light in the last 200 pages of *The Atlantic Book*. A modest inclusion of a few of her own poems in the final section shows her superiority over so many of her contemporaries. . . . Compared to many recent collections in the field, its flaws are minor, and during a grey decade in England, the book restores the splendor, the color, the vivacity, and memorable endurance of British poetry.
Horace Gregory. *VQR*. Spring, 1959, p. 309

It has been firmly maintained by her critics that *Façade* derives its chief interest from the technical acrobatics of the work; that this collection of poems is noteworthy not so much for what it says as for the way in which it says it, not so much for its meaning as for its abstract quality, the sound patterns it makes from words. Yet this does not constitute the poetic totality of *Façade*. These poems are not merely impressionistic exercises in poetic technique. Had they been so, not even William Walton's scintillating musical accompaniment could have enhanced their literary value. . . . The dazzling virtuosity and concentrated brevity of the music provides a pungent, allusive commentary, and is a perfect embellishment of Dame Edith's incisive wit and parody.
Geoffrey Singleton. *Edith Sitwell: The Hymn to Life*, (Fortune Pr., 1960), p. 48

SITWELL, OSBERT (1892–   )

Mr. Osbert Sitwell has two or three distinct styles. The first and most obviously popular is the ironic political satire. Here he has achieved individuality. It makes no difference whether he signs them with his own name or with a pseudonym, or leaves these satires unsigned. Anybody who has read one of them can immediately detect his hand in the others as they appear in the *Nation* and the *Herald.* I don't suggest that they are the last word in lyric poetry, but they are very satisfactory as satires; even that hobbling rhythm, which leaves one uncertain as to whether he is writing prose or *vers libre,* is particularly apt for this conversational irony.

Mr. Sitwell has not reprinted many of these in book-form, and they would be rather out of place in a book containing poems designed to produce an effect of beauty; but in a separate volume they would be entertaining. The book should be called *England's Conscience,* or something of that sort. Mr. Sitwell's social satire is much lighter than Mr. Sassoon's, and therefore, I think, preferable. No one else has made such devastating fun of the perplexed, muddleheaded English "good people." Their faculty for "doing the dirty" with words of peace and love on their lips is a legacy from the good old days when their ancestors spread civilization with the Bible and brandy. . . .

When Mr. Osbert Sitwell is attempting to create beauty he is less sure of himself than in satire; one can see that he is experimenting carefully, and trace a development from the method of a poem like "Clavicords," with its pure emotionalism, to the fantastic decoration and irony of "De Luxe." In his more recent poems I seem to trace the effect of that aspect of Laforgue which has been so admirably developed by Mr. Eliot. I notice this development with great interest, since Laforgue strikes me as one of the most dangerous influences one can imagine; his style is sometimes very confused, and his cynicism is so frequently a mere confession of his sentimentalism.

Richard Aldington. *Poetry*. Dec., 1920, pp. 163–64

Mr. Sitwell is exceedingly accomplished: he is terribly accomplished: he is erudite, witty, dexterous, eloquent: he has a sharp eye, and that special sort of fair-haired obtuse shrewdness which is almost a prerogative of the English: he knows his history, and can refer as easily to Ur and the Chaldees as to the Brookes of Borneo: he knows the English language, and tosses it and catches it with a conjurer's virtuosity. And nevertheless, in this book [*England Reclaimed*] of charming eclogues, one questions whether anywhere is precisely that "wisdom of the blood" for which one always has so famished a craving. Here are some delicious thumb-nail portraits—or perhaps one would better describe them as Kate Greenaway watercolors; for they have a good deal of Kate Greenaway's Botticelli primness and precision. One thinks of those absurd little hillocks, of the color of spinach, starred all over with daisies and primroses, very much as the spinach is mooned with slices of egg; the petals, the twigs, the very blades of grass are counted; it is as primitive as Cimabue, but it is also self-conscious. Mr. Sitwell's poetry is like that. It is very precise, very meticulous. Every detail is put in, and every detail has its ingenious epithet. It is all very *soigné,* very detached, very witty: a sort of embroidery world, exact and yet unreal. These flowers and trees and country scenes are not flowers and trees and country scenes; they are quaint pictures done in bright-colored wools, and all of them smelling of lavender. It is a kind of polite English Spoon River, or Rother, done bucolically on a counterpane.

In short, Mr. Sitwell is extremely clever, but he is, at bottom, one guesses, lacking in that ultimate *vox et praeterea nihil* of the poet who is a poet by instinct and necessity. He amuses us, he delights us—but he never disturbs us, he never reveals. Technically speaking, he is adroit, if a little prolix and over-descriptive: he has that inordinateness, that inability to know when to stop, which is so often, alas, a characteristic of the clever.

Conrad Aiken. NR. April 11, 1928, pp. 252–53

I think here we come to Osbert Sitwell's distinctive merit in fiction and the essay, that with depth of feeling and perception there is an extraordinary capacity for being interested in people and things. . . . Sitwell has an exceptional capacity for being interested and, notwithstanding a manner that often seems and occasionally is careless, he has command of a most effective style for conveying impressions and ideas. One might expect him to seem sophisticated, rather blasé, after all his sightseeing and his innumerable personal contacts with other people. But read that extraordinarily eloquent passage (in which there is no "fine writing") on Mrs. Slowcombe, in *Happy Endings* and see how a rush of fervent sympathy has enabled the author to move his reader. . . . This directness of vision which imparts to his prose its special quality is what we should attribute to the poet keeping his eye on the object, if it occurred in verse. (Curiously, it is not a special quality of his verse except where, as in *England Reclaimed,* the verse contains a considerable prosaic element, which perhaps justified his own view of his fiction as that of a poet manqué, though in verse alone I think he can hold his own with the majority of the well-known contemporary poets.)

R. L. Mégroz. *Five Novelist Poets of Today*
(Joiner and Steele, 1933), pp. 184–86

Wit was noticeably absent from Osbert Sitwell's earlier satires. From 1919 onwards, however, a new intellectual intensity entered his work. At first his irony remained heavy: as when he hailed the return of the social climbers to their pre-war activities (*War-Horses*). With an enthusiasm worthy of a larger game he pursued these aristocratic pretenders and their parasites. Meanwhile he was developing, with his sister Edith and his brother Sacheverell, the rococo imagery which is a feature of their côterie. To this and to the influence of Ezra Pound and T. S. Eliot we may attribute the remarkable change of manner apparent in the best of these satires. He now alternated generalisation with the invention of typical characters. His studies of Mrs. Freudenthal and of Mrs. Kinfoot —some in *vers libre,* the best in rhyming quatrains of four-stressed lines —show a great advance in accuracy and economy.

In another series he turned his attention to the middle class and the peculiar limitations, as he thought them, of the conventional Anglican view of life. His most original satires are those in which the treatment of imagery is determined by a predominant emotion, as in *English Gothic,* where the description of a cathedral, outside which "Stone bishops scale a stone façade," is made to suggest the petrifaction of belief and habit among the worshippers. In "Anglican Hymn in Foreign Parts," he parodied "Through Greenland's Icy Mountains" in a style adapted to the English view of the world as a mechanical plaything invented for English enjoyment—a world in which birds sing "clockwork songs of calf-love" while "The ocean at a toy shore/Yaps like a Pekinese"—a daring assimilation of external description into the attitude criticised.

Osbert Sitwell has significance in the history of satire for still another experiment; he was one of the leaders in the revival of the heroic couplet.

Geoffrey Bullough. *The Trend of Modern Poetry*
(Oliver and Boyd, 1934), pp. 102–3

The Scarlet Tree, by Osbert Sitwell, has an advantage over many autobiographies: it is written by an experienced novelist, who is here turning into art a richer material than he has used elsewhere, and who is partly employing the novelist's craft in shaping it. Who else but a novelist would contrive the checks upon racing Time which we find in this book, the disposition of a heavy emphasis here, a light one there, the holding back of an explanation till "later," the anticipations, the use of suspense, and above all the carefully-timed entrances and re-entrances of the characters? In biography Sir Osbert Sitwell's contrivances would be intolerable; in autobiography they are a blessing. There is something else which strikes one as one compares this book with a novel: because this is life, and not fiction, certain characters with traits which would in a novel be unacceptable outside the broadest farce are acceptable here. Where, in a novel, after our acquaintance with a character has extended over several hundred pages, could we believe the statement that he had "invented a musical toothbrush which played 'Annie Laurie' as you brushed your teeth, and a small revolver for shooting wasps?" Sir George Sitwell, the author's father, is said to have invented both of these; perhaps they worked; but we should be rather incensed by the idea in a novel. So that, throughout, *The Scarlet Tree* has all the virtues of a large-scale discursive *roman fleuve,* with none of the restrictions of probability that a serious novelist has to impose on himself.

Henry Reed. *NSN*. Aug. 31, 1946, p. 155

It is to Sir Osbert Sitwell's credit that he has never pretended to be other than he is: a member of the upper classes, with an amused and leisurely attitude which comes out in his manner of writing, and which could only be the product of an expensive upbringing. Probably, so far as his memory serves him, he records his likes and dislikes accurately, which always needs moral courage. How easy it would have been to write of Eton or the Grenadier Guards in a spirit of sneering superiority, with the implication that from earliest youth he was the holder of enlightened sentiments which, in fact, no comfortably-placed person did hold a generation ago. Or how easy, on the other hand, to stand on the defensive and try to argue away the injustice and inequality of the world in which he grew up. He has done neither, with the result that these three volumes *(Left Hand, Right Hand, The Scarlet Tree,* and *Great Morning),* although the range they cover is narrow, must be among the best autobiographies of our time.

George Orwell. *Adel*. July-Sept., 1948, p. 250

. . . it would be a mistake in considering his poetry to suppose that beauty and poetic feeling are completely jostled out by wit and satire. To go back to Pope—many people think of him only as the scourge of the literary dolts and dullards of his generation: they forget, for example, his beautiful Pastorals. So with Sir Osbert. The beauty of such a poem as "Winter the Huntsman," the splendid imagery in "Fox Trot" . . . and the powers of imagination in the opening lines of "Cornucopia" will be missed by no sensitive reader. Nor could readers study his short poem "Night" without sensing that they were enjoying poetry of a singularly high order.

During the 1920's Sir Osbert published three important books of prose—*Triple Fugue* in 1924, *Discursions on Travel, Art and Life* in 1925, and *Before the Bombardment* in 1927. *Triple Fugue* consists of six long studies of human behaviour and of human eccentricity—an amusing and fascinating collection. But the reader will notice the serious motive lying behind this book: his purpose has been well defined as "to satirize the scientific, political and social tendencies which seem to him today to threaten individuality in a machine-run civilization." The threat of 1924 has moved perceptibly nearer in 1951 and that is perhaps one of the reasons why Sir Osbert's prose writings keep their sparkle and freshness.

Before the Bombardment, undoubtedly, after the autobiography, Sir Osbert's finest book, is a satirical novel and describes Scarborough before 1914, and the unexpected shelling of the town by German cruisers at the close of that year. . . . He himself has described it as "the foundation of my whole reputation."

Discursions is a most memorable and original account of Southern Italy and some parts of Germany. . . .

Roger Fulford. *Osbert Sitwell*
(BC/Longmans, 1951), pp. 11–12

Sir Osbert Sitwell's new book of verse portraits [*Wrack at Tidesend*] does not fit neatly into any traditional category. The total effect . . . is an oddly paradoxical one, of elegiac satire, comic pathos, and realistic pastoral; and the mood in which these sketches from a north-eastern seaside town in the Edwardian decade are written—one of wry homesickness—is paradoxical, too. . . .

His approach is, however, partly a collector's. He is determined to have at least one good specimen of each Edwardian balnearic type. . . . What he is homesick for is, perhaps, his own childhood. His characters are certainly seen with a child's mercilessly accurate eye, the eye that does not rub away individual edges into a grey, vaguely apprehended "social background"; and also with a child's way of giving perfectly ordinary personages a legendary, larger-than-life quality. The portraits seem at once more hollow and more significant than their originals can have been. They are full of an energy oddly limited in scope. . . .

Sir Osbert's verse, like his prose, has an accumulative richness, making its points with a lingering amplitude rather than by sudden concentration. Taken individually, some of his portraits might seem almost aggressively trivial, but as a set they impress. The scene is shot with gleams of cold light, the sea glitters in the background. One closes the book with a sense of pity for these secure, petty, self-assertive lives, but also with a longing for the brilliant childhood place, familiar and remote as an old snapshot, to which one can no longer return.

G. S. Fraser. *NSN.* June 7, 1952, p. 679

SITWELL, SACHEVERELL (1897–   )

I find Mr. Sacheverell Sitwell extremely satisfactory at times. He has an exquisite sense of beauty and he can create a mood. I like his use of words. When he says: "Silence, the cape of Death, lies heavy Round the bare shoulders of the hills," he really "does the trick" for me. It is poetry, or rather it is the kind of poetry I most enjoy. He has a gift for precise observation and description.

Richard Aldington. *Poetry*. Dec., 1920, p. 166

Sacheverell's sole volume, published last year, *The 101 Harlequins,* attracted, I fear, little notice from the mandarins. Ninety-three harlequins were omitted from it (why?); but despite the vast omission, it appeared to me to be a wonderful portent. It is most damnably difficult, though it seems less difficult to me this year than it did last. I can still make scarcely anything of the sixth Harlequin, for example, or of several other pieces. And when you have finished the book you feel like nothing at all. But I will stand till I fall dead by the positive assertion that there is a very considerable amount of new beauty in this book. You don't see it clearly. It tantalizes you by its shyness. You see it moving dimly at the ends of misty glades. It exists, however. It is a characteristically Sitwellian beauty. And more than any other Sitwell book or manifestation *The 101 Harlequins* persuades you to be convinced that the Sitwells live in a world of perceptions and sensations of their own— in a "dimension" of their own, extraordinarily, insultingly, different from anybody else's. Their idiom, perhaps, comprises too many unicorns, harlequins, and Kinfoots; it perhaps is too busy with the mischief of making one sense do the work of another (seeing sounds, hearing colours, etc., etc.); but the idiom may be modified, is being modified; and anyhow it is only the vehicle, not the content.

Arnold Bennett. *Adel.* Aug., 1923, pp. 236–37

One of the most interesting phenomena of the literary world today is the advent of the Sitwell brothers and sister. That the children of one father, bred in an aristocratic family, should each exhibit a personality so pronounced as to command public excitement is, indeed, extraordinary. But that one of them should go still further and show himself to be truly an artist of originality of temperament and technique; well, that is a miracle. I think *All Summer in a Day* presents us with that miracle. . . .

To read his book is to be bewildered, angered, convinced, abused; and over and above this, enriched with a ceaseless tropical rain of energy expressed in a new prose rhythm. The book stands for a distinct advance in the technique of English prose. The analyst might say that it bears evidence of the influence of Joyce, George Moore, and Yeats. That would be true; but it has something else, a sigular speed, a nervous lateral spread, a vertical billowing, that one can compare only to the art of Berlioz and Stravinsky. And that is to say, perhaps, that here is an instrument, a technique absolutely modern, the very flesh and blood of the Spirit of the Age. What the jazz-musicians are expressing through a parodied form of the old paraphernalia of sentimentality, Mr. Sitwell is doing masterfully through the more permanent vehicle of consious psychological method. . . .

For Mr. Sitwell, poetry has a panic, faunal power, that breaks through political culture and moral rule.

Richard Church. *Cal. of Mod. Letters.* Jan., 1927, pp. 326–27, 329

His book [*The Visit of the Gypsies*] leaves the reader with an enriched vision of the Middle Ages, a pointed world of pale-haired ladies and scaphandroid knights, with chequered squires and tapering hounds, and chess-board castles showing through the trees. But *The Visit of the Gypsies* is poetry not criticism, and though it contains interesting comments upon Gothic art, the chief interest is the style and imagination of the author. Mr. Sitwell may be compared to a man who peers at an Old Master, and sees his own features reflected in its glass.

In his sensibility he is kin to Breughel and Constantin Guys as well as to Beckford and Drummond of Hawthornden. Pageantry has to become, as it were, neurotic in its conceits before it excites him. He is peculiarly aware of water and sound. Like a dowser, he finds streams everywhere, and the boughs a continual accompaniment of his visions. Then he translates the reports of his five senses into terms of one another, so that songs give off scent and colours taste like honey. His prose is full of startling images. . . . He loves the medieval world for its dewey meadows and winding horns. . . . But this serves to remind the reader of the deliberately subjective character of the book. Its theme is not Gothic art, but the effect of Gothic art upon the writer's imagination and memory. . . .

The Visit of the Gypsies is a dashing experiment in the most elaborate sort of English imaginative prose. Indeed, it suggests that Mr. Sitwell is equalled in this pursuit only by Virginia Woolf and James Joyce.

Raymond Mortimer. *NA*. May 25, 1929, p. 276

Mr. Sacheverell Sitwell in his best poems is not capable of such extended metaphysical flights as those of Mr. Graves, though his poems mostly cover more space in print. His scope, at the best, is only that of a pastoral poet: unfortunately this limitation of talent sets the stamp of minor verse on almost all that he writes. . . . One is rather at a loss to account for the public interest in Mr. Sitwell. He lacks the hard brilliance, the violent juxtaposition of fancy and fact that prevail in the work of his elder brother and sister; his mind is at once more sensitive and more shrinking from brute force than theirs, and whenever he attempts a long poem, he painfully over-elaborates his theme.

John Gould Fletcher. Crit. Aug., 1929, p. 169

It is not necessary (or perhaps even desirable) to be an architect or a painter to be perturbed by Mr. Sacheverell Sitwell's "Defence of the North" embodied in these first two volumes [*The Visit of the Gipsies, These Sad Ruins*] of his trilogy. It is not necessary because there never before was a book on architecture seen primarily through the eyes of a painter, of painting seen through the eyes of a poet. Here, indeed, is that incurable habit which sees out of dimensions, and by virtue of that vision invests all in a hobgoblin light as of an innocent and fertile Puck. Mr. Sitwell, descending for an instant to what is almost prose, observes of the object of this work "that it has been written, not as concatenation of facts, or to confute the learned, but for the exercise of other faculties, which not even the most prolific of poets can expect perpetually to bear fruit." This is unusually direct self-criticism. . . .

All this may be, as Mr. Sitwell suggests, a holiday from verse. But if it be prose, indeed, then he is more than entitled to share M. Jourdain's astonishments.

But because the book, as a whole, bears the same relation to prose as a swallow to a hen, it must not be imagined that it does not contain a world of insight and erudition. . . . Mr. Sitwell has a thesis. His book is a study "if not a defence, of the fair-haired races that have imposed themselves for a thousand years upon all the countries of Northern Europe." . . . A single tapestry ["The Visit of the Gipsies"] stands half-way between the Middle Age and agelessness. Mr. Sitwell by the odd paradox of his creative imagination finds more motion in the stillest of fabrics than the rest of us in a gale. He feels a great wind racing through a quiet room. It blows away a hundred dusty records of painting and architecture, but when it has settled down all these, long dead, have the freshness of colour and a virginity of outline with which the painter and the architect first saw them. These books are hardly criticism at all. Indeed, they are worse than that. They are mere re-creation.

Humbert Wolfe. SR. Oct. 12, 1929, pp. 421–22

If the eighteenth century from time to time appears in Miss [Edith] Sitwell's poems, the manners, the retired self-consciousness, it is an earlier period that her brother Sacheverell recalls. He has been compared to the Elizabethans often, and necessarily, enough; the richness and freshness of some of his lyrics are a complete justification. But the difference is there too—he is their antitype in manner. For most of the

Elizabethan songs, however complicated, are simple enough in sense; they riddle gaily. It was not till nearer the Carolines that the shadow of the intellect fell on the lyric and its strength began to enter. Mr. Sitwell's lyrics are rich and beautiful, but not gay. Nor is it only the intellect that makes them difficult. They are aromatic gums, but hardly flowers. . . .

His world is larger than his sister's, but less entrancing. Larger, for it deals much more often and definitely with the present external world; it has a greater medley of things, natural, and fabulous, and of great art. But larger also because it is striving with philosophy, and asking itself intellectual questions.

Charles Williams. Poetry At Present
(Oxford, Clarendon Pr., 1930), pp. 184–85

Mr. Sitwell's feeling of texture seems never to fail him, and it is always born of his subject, and is absolutely controlled, conveying the visual sense, the oral sense, that he possesses in such a remarkable degree. . . .

Mr. Sitwell's verse is full of exquisite and sharply apprehended visual impressions, born into a texture, a movement, that fits them perfectly. . . .

These sensual impressions, so accurate, so acute, add to our experience. Although Mr. Sitwell's green world of happy growing things is unruffled by any violence, so that the charge of inhumanity is brought against him by persons who dislike any poetry excepting that which is based only upon emotion, he yet gives us the world that we see, but do not know that we see—he increases our sense values.

Edith Sitwell. Aspects of Modern Poetry
(Duckworth, 1934), pp. 172, 175–77

I am prepared to admit that the impact of metrical modernism has been so vigorous and so well-timed that it will be difficult for a poet henceforth to feel himself quite at his ease within the forms transmitted to us by our ancestors. But are there any others available? . . . Conceive now a poet who needs a full line; who, being a poet, cannot sing unless he knows his chorus are following him; and, being modern, cannot fit himself into even the stateliest measures of the past. What will he do? One need not ask, because he has done it: he has written the *Canons of Giant Art*.

G. M. Young. Daylight and Champaign
(Jonathan Cape, 1937), pp. 205–6

A philistine detractor of Mr. Sitwell's work once complained that, in his poetry and in his prose, nothing was ever presented to us on its own merits—everything was "like" something else and usually (he added) something extremely unlikely. For more appreciative and discriminating critics, however, Mr. Sitwell's gift of finding analogies is one of the pleasantest features of his literary style. His eye is apt to reflect a double image; in any given work of art, he distinguishes not only the object itself but its connection with other fields of aesthetic achievement, with its historical origins and its racial background. This faculty has been of great advantage to him in his present book. Roumania is, no doubt, a delightful country; but, considered as material, it is much inferior to the various countries of which Mr. Sitwell has already written. *Roumanian Journey* has a two-fold interest. It contains some fascinating impressions of the Roumanian scene (presented with Mr. Sitwell's customary vividness) and it makes those impressions doubly memorable by relating them to his memories of other landscapes—both landscapes of the terrestial and the imaginative order. Mr. Sitwell, as always, is acute and sensitive. . . .

During his stay in Roumania, Mr. Sitwell received much support and encouragement from the Roumanian authorities; and the tone of the narrative is rather too consistently eulogistic—the Jewish problem is glanced at and gracefully skirted—but the whole effect of the book is lively and readable.

Peter Quennell. *NSN*. May 28, 1938, pp. 920–22

He has . . . the rare quality of being able to write the kind of book which is needed. He can be as discursive, poetic, personal, satirical, macabre as anyone else when he wants to be, but he does not feel the fatal itch of exhibiting all his talents all the time. *Roumanian Journey* is practical and even prosaic. . . . It is a guide book written by a traveller who knows just where guidebooks usually let one down. He keeps himself and his travelling companions austerely in the background. His theme is the country itself, its aspect and sound and smell. He eschews politics, with the result that his book will be of value long after the particular combinations of Danubian Powers which excite notice today.

Evelyn Waugh. *Spec*. May 20, 1938, p. 925

Mr. Sitwell is a rare phenomenon. He is a traveler with a purpose, but he relishes the picaresque incidents of his travels. He is a passionate lover of art and architecture, but he is also a scholar. And he is a creative artist, a poet, and writer driven to bear witness, as he phrases it himself, to "the splendors and miseries of the world and the glory of being alive."

This book [*Arabesque and Honeycomb*] is in the first place about Mr. Sitwell's impressions on his recent travels in the Lebanon, Syria,

Iran, Jordan, Egypt, and Turkey. It is also a comparison of Islamic architecture and culture in general with the products of that other world civilization, the Roman, backed by memories of earlier travels and much reading. And finally it can be seen as part of Mr. Sitwell's autobiography, the latest record of his experiences in his journey through life.

Its major merit is that it illuminates what otherwise would remain mere guidebook *Sehenswürdigkeiten* with the light of acute sensibility, scholarly knowledge and wide experience.

Julian Huxley. *Sat.* April 26, 1958, p. 26

Mr. Sitwell has been to the Andes, in a hurry. Also to Guatemala and Yucatan. He writes of churches, sculpture, flowers and so on, by a self-contained process of aesthetic thrill according to which something encountered must be described or evaluated by something previously encountered somewhere else; a llama by a yak, Cuzco by Lhasa, Machu Picchu by Petra, a Peruvian drink by a French one, Peruvian megalithic walls by the Amsterdam bricks in the paintings of Jan van der Heyden. It is too bad if you have never seen a van der Heyden, have never drunk that French drink, have never been to Petra, or Lhasa, and never watched a yak; and nothing as a result seems to have much existence, let alone human weight or density, or salt—or even sugar. He doesn't pause much, he doesn't enlarge, verbs are weak, views are "superb," experiences are "unforgettable." After reading this book [*Golden Wall and Mirador*] with some care I only remember a story that quetzals are caught when they are asleep after eating too many avocado pears and swallowing the large stones. I can't think what Mr. Sitwell thinks of his publishers' thoughts about how to illustrate.

Geoffrey Grigson. *Spec.* June 30, 1961, p. 961

SMITH, LOGAN PEARSALL (1865–1946)

"You cannot," runs the last of these aphorisms [*Afterthoughts*], "be too fastidious." Certainly Mr. Logan Pearsall Smith himself has always preferred the small and the exquisite to the large, the loose, the facile. In his own work he has cultivated the single thought rather than the essay; he has even been fastidious enough, in the Treasuries that he has compiled, to prefer prose to verse and thereby has won the gratitude of all who have discovered for themselves what a fine art prose can be and how the reserve of its appeal lends to it, in these days, a distinction that, passing for the most part undetected, is denied to metre. . . .

As usual, to my thinking, the most objective aphorisms are the best, the worst those in which the writer sticks pins into himself. The whole collection is the fruit of disillusion, trying to recover gaiety by a smile at its own expense. The background, the circle, the friends, and the circumstances can be inferred between the lines, but in the midst of this aridity survives a faith in the pursuit of some perfection in order that the savour of life may not be lost.

This savour, for him, would be to write a perfect prose, and, for a reason to be given in a moment, I do not think that he will reach it by writing aphorisms. English is not the best language for that, and in the single sentence may we not detect a certain timidity, as if the writer hesitated to spread his wings? I dare to say so because from the two previous books of *Trivia* one passage lingers in my mind: the best that Mr. Pearsall Smith has written and very unlike the rest. . . . Were he not diffident of showing his feelings, his thoughts might be dissolved in such a way as would make them touch us and at the same time achieve for him the prose that he would like "to distil."

Osbert Burdett. *SR*. Feb. 21, 1931, pp. 277–78

I have hinted that all of Mr. Smith's aphorisms [*Afterthoughts*] are not successful. Even his best are doubtless not gems of the first water. But if he has produced no pearls or rubies, he has fashioned a few semi-precious stones not to be despised. Nowhere is it more necessary than here to be grateful to a writer for his successes and not condemn him for his failures. Perhaps it is harder today to write a good aphorism than a good sonnet. The field of general truths about human nature is not unlimited. . . . If Mr. Smith has added a few permanent grains to the world's store of gnomic wisdom, he is indeed a writer to be envied.

Henry Hazlitt. *Nation*. April 29, 1931, p. 479

Its chief merit . . . [*On Reading Shakespeare*] is as an anthology of critical opinion arranged in the light of a personal appreciation. There is a great deal of the personal appreciation, which tells us much about Mr. Pearsall Smith, a little about Shakespeare, and almost nothing about reading him. The title of the book should have been *After,* not *On Reading Shakespeare.* . . .

Mr. Pearsall Smith's taste is unexceptionable and his personal preferences well chosen. He pays warm and thoroughly documented tributes to Shakespeare's poetry and his powers of characterization, he has a little clean fun with the more vulnerable schools of criticism, and he indicates, if he does not attempt to solve, the problems which beset the scholar and the connoisseur alike. He tells us, very often indeed, and sometimes with a naive emotionalism, what a splendid experience reading Shakespeare can be. But he does not tell us how to savour that

experience to the full. His book, accordingly, is aimless. His raptures we could have taken for granted; we should have welcomed his advice.
Peter Fleming. *Spec.* April 21, 1933, p. 576

No one who is interested in contemporary attitudes toward Shakespeare, or who supposes, perchance, that the last words upon the subject were said by Goethe or Brandes, Bradley or Lee, should miss . . . [*On Reading Shakespeare*]. In . . . [*On Reading Shakespeare*], a cultivated amateur, thoroughly familiar with . . . other common-sense approaches to the "mystery" of Shakespeare, eludes them as best he can and makes an often convincing case for the kind of idolatry against which Professor [E. E.] Stoll's works are a reaction. Mr. Smith has not, perhaps, either the strength of such another champion of his attitude as Dover Wilson or such a powerful system-building imagination as G. Wilson Knight, but he knows his Shakespeare and will defend apologetically, when he cannot defend aggressively, his right to read *Hamlet* as something more than a curious example of Elizabethan stage conventions.
Joseph Wood Krutch. *Nation.* Oct. 11, 1933, p. 414

To Mr. Pearsall Smith, high on the terrace of his ivory gazebo, their [the critics'] discordant, contentious voices have come vaguely drifting. The result—a slender volume [*Milton and His Modern Critics*] of protest and appreciation—is designed both as an essay in controversy and a recall to order.

The effect of the book, however, is only mildly interesting. One of two courses was open to Milton's modern champion. Either he might have embarked on a detailed analysis of these contemporary attacks, seeking to understand the point of view that has inspired them, or—better still—have attempted a fresh survey of his hero's genius. Mr. Pearsall Smith takes both courses but succeeds in pursuing neither of them very far. He gives a slight sketch of each of the offensive critics, makes some harmless fun of Mr. Pound's translations . . . and darts a puzzled glance in the direction of Mr. Eliot's poetry. . . .

Mr. Pearsall Smith loves Milton because he is a lover of language, because he has been fascinated always by the colour and rhythm of words, and Milton's conscious artistry gives his estheticism the scope it needs. Here and there, the estheticism seems a trifle negative; and one or two of his statements sound almost silly.
Peter Quennell. *NSN.* Nov. 16, 1940, pp. 496–98

"I don't want respect," he would say: "treat me with affectionate derision." . . .

In [his letters] as much as in *All Trivia* and the masterly ellipses of

Unforgotten Years, we glimpse a long lifetime of unbroken literary activity. . . . The literature he liked was, on the whole, the literature of amenity; next to the greatest masters, Homer, Virgil, Dante and Shakespeare, he preferred writers whose work was small in scale and perfect in form . . . and for himself he devised the minute forms of *Trivia.* He never doubted, I think, that these would afford the completest fulfilment of his gifts; . . .

Logan was by temperament a spectator, not a participant, and his life was peculiarly free from outward incident. For eighty years he did exactly as he liked. A winter in Venice; March and April at Settignano; a few unhurried weeks at the British Museum library, and back to Sussex for the buddleia season—such was his life at the age of forty. . . .

Mr. Cyril Connolly has referred to the "Logan-note, which resounded like the ring of a fine glass through his mutations of personality"; . . . Logan loved gossip: he was extremely credulous: and he loved to embroider . . . even Henry James and George Santayana, the two writers whose suffrage would have meant most to him, were slow to accept him as anything more than an agreeable amateur. . . .

In religion, he was a sceptic of the purest Voltairean sort; and he professed to regard the sexual instincts as merely a source of delicious absurdities. Literature and Society are the themes of his letters, as they were of his life. . . .

To have been the intimate of Berenson and Roger Fry, and the friend of Whistler and Durand-Ruel is a felicity which no picture-fancier of our own generation can aspire to rival. . . .

The impact of England, France and Italy was neither dulled nor heightened by the thought of his American childhood. Except, indeed, for his nomadic summers in Colorado, there is no feature of his earliest years that seems to have survived the tremendous exclusive excitement of the European adventure. His dislike for America was so intense as to resemble a physical reflex rather than an act of criticism. . . . His own truancies began in earliest childhood; and when he made the definite break with America, in 1888, he sailed for Europe with all the sensations of a bridegroom. Not England alone, but the whole of Europe was to be his bride; nor did he ever repent of his choice. He enjoyed a sixty-years' intoxication; and he embodied in himself the attitude of mind which was elevated, in *The Ambassadors,* to the loftiest plane of art. . . . Logan liked to see himself as moving freely between the great world and the world of ideas. . . .

So far from gushing forth uncontrollably, his work was strained off, drop by drop, through the muslin of a super-sensitive critical sense . . . by 1897 he was turning towards the form which he brought to perfection —the "separate page or paragraph of prose." In *Unforgotten Years* he admitted to have received the definitive thrust in this direction while perusing Baudelaire's *Le Spleen de Paris*. . . . It may seem incongruous to invoke the patronage of Flaubert . . . for *Trivia,* one of the most diminutive books since the Microcosmographie of Earle. But the question is one of quality, not of scale. The resonance of *Trivia* corresponds not to the importance of its subjects but to the perfection of its style. . . . The elaboration of *Trivia* was Logan's preferred employment during a great part of his life.

John Russell. Introd. in *A Portrait of Logan Pearsall Smith Drawn from His Letters and Diaries* (Dropmore Pr., 1950), pp. 2–3, 6–8, 10–11, 15, 17–22

SMITH, STEVIE (1902–)

. . . it has been interesting to find that a novelist, Stevie Smith, who made a success before the war with *Novel on Yellow Paper* (1936)— seriously gay, grimly comic, exquisitely inconsequent—has gone on since the war to achieve a greater (literary) success with *The Holiday* (1949). It is less effervescent in comicality but still has a lightheartedness which carries with it a terrifying burden of serious import, of apprehension, of awareness of the tragic problem of the individual and the corresponding problem of the human race in its present perplexities. A book amusing, serious and at moments profound.

R. A. Scott-James. *Fifty Years of English Literature: 1900-1950* (Longmans, 1951), p. 187

It would be a manifest exaggeration to call her a neglected poet, yet as one of the most original women poets now writing she seems to have missed most of the public accolades bestowed by critics and anthologists. One reason may be that not only does she belong to no "school"— whether real or invented as they usually are—but her work is so completely different from anyone else's that it is all but impossible to discuss her poems in relation to those of her contemporaries. The dismissing adjective usually tacked to her verse is "fey," which is accurate enough for her less successful pieces—and she is a very uneven poet. Her poems either come off magnificently or collapse absolutely. Then she is that extremely rare bird, a great comic poet—though the word "comic" has in this connection an unfortunately pejorative connotation (one thinks of Thomas Hood, W. S. Gilbert, Ogden Nash). It will not do, either, though it is much nearer the mark, to classify her poems as "light" in the sense that Auden defined the word in the preface to his *Oxford Book of Light Verse.* Perhaps her nearest equivalent among contemporary poets is John Betjeman, who surfaces with deceptive gaiety an inherent gloom, except that in the case of Stevie Smith the gaiety is fundamental and does not deceive the gloom but defines it. A concise example is the comic-sinister title of her book: *Not Waving But Drowning,* taken from a poem about a drowned man (in this case no relation of that worn out upper-case archetype, The Drowned Man). . . .

The uninhibited wit and gaiety which she brings to her best poems plus the optimism they often express provides an appearance of frivolity which is in reality a mask worn to further the impact of truth which, were it declaimed from a lugubrious tripod, would be vitiated or diluted. The apparent geniality of many of her poems is in fact more frightening than the solemn keening and sentimental despair of other poets, for it is based on a clearsighted acceptance, by a mind neither obtuse nor unimaginative, but sharp and serious, innocent but far from naïve, and because feminine having a bias towards life and survival, of the facts as they are and the world as it is.

David Wright. *Poetry*. Aug., 1958, pp. 311–12

SMITH, SYDNEY GOODSIR (1915–   )

"Sydney Slugabed Godless Smith" upon whom "Auld Oblomov has nocht on," has written in *Under the Eildon Tree* a poem in Twenty-four Elegies in praise of his Love. . . . The very gusto, the good-humoured cynicism, the sentimental display of some classical learning, and the sudden seriousness, give his elegies the qualities of drunkenness. They are exhilarating, stagger and come to sudden and often laughable conclusions, and the red light of his "Sandra the cow o the auld Black Bull" dances a furious jig from one end of the line to the other.

Denis Botterill. *LL*. July, 1949, p. 56

Sydney Goodsir Smith is the clearest lyric voice arising from the British Isles today. This is not said in dispraise of other poets in those islands. We all know there are other good poets there, at least two great ones. But for pure song I know none excelling him.

Although born in New Zealand, he has been writing for more than a decade in Lallans, the Lowlands Scots language now enjoying somewhat of a literary Renaissance; but I do not wish to compare him here with his co-revivalists, such as Tom Scott, Lallans poet and translator of Villon, and the father of the modern Lallans Revival, Hugh MacDiarmid (Christopher Murray Grieve), except to remark that he is a much more personal poet than MacDiarmid, whose most personal lyrics seldom have the urgency of personal statement (and who most often writes in a vein of philosophic generality and in a polyglot mixture, most recently, of Lallans, German, Greek, etc.) and that, in this latest phase of Smith's work—his flowering, so to speak—he does not deal with themes of Scottish Nationalism, although one can find poems by Smith on these themes in earlier issues of *Poetry Scotland*. . . .

Edith Sitwell, in her preface to *So Late into the Night,* rightly compares Smith to Blake and the best of Dickinson and Burns. He especially shares the earlier Blake's deceptively simple surface that opens into incredible depths of meaning. Any reader can find a poem there. The more the reader's insight, the more of a poem he will find, but the simplest attentive reader can at least enjoy these songs. This is not said in dispraise of difficult poetry—far from it. Most other modern poems of any worth tend to be difficult, even at the surface. But it's nice that poetry as good as this is at least superficially accessible to anyone able and willing occasionally to refer to a glossary. . . .

His poems are far more condensed than Burns ever was or wanted to be. His two "ballants," *King and Queen o the Fowr Airts,* and *The Wraith o Johnnie Calvin,* though ballads right enough, do not have those lines and lines of dispensable matter that weary us so often not only in Burns's ballads. And though he uses anapestic and dactylic substitutions freely, they seldom degenerate into the mere hippity-hop that Burns was so apt to fall into. But as in Burns, there's a "God's plenty o' deils" in his poems and a great lot of "lemanrie" and "luve."

Jackson MacLow. *Poetry*. April, 1955, pp. 52–54

Linguistically, Sydney Goodsir Smith has followed MacDiarmid's lead, though he has not gone so far; and it is very much to his credit that this is the only respect in which he may be said to have been influenced by the older writer. He uses the language of the street, the countryside, and the Makars—not, of course, in a witless hugger-mugger of the vernacular and the mandarin, but with very considerable art indeed.

The resultant language is learned, but not sophisticated. This suits Smith's talent and temperament excellently well, for he is at once bookish and helplessly (not hopelessly) romantic: it is still possible to speak in this language of the heart and the soul without seeming mawkish and of drunks and whores without seeming adolescent. At a time when poetry in English is so guardedly tight-lipped, so donnish, so cagily "witty," Smith can write love poems of direct and outspoken passion, political poems (like most Scottish poets he has strong Nationalist feelings—this bamboozles the English) which need no disguise of symbol or parable, and poems about the wild boys in the bars which are made poems by the extraordinary expressiveness of the language and his equally extraordinary tact in translating speech rhythms into the rhythms of verse.

Figs and Thistles contains poems of all these sorts, as well as two translations (of Blok's *The Twelve* and Corbière's *La Rapsode Foraine et le Pardon de Sainte-Anne*) which are tours de force.

These poems belong to no school: any two lines are immediately recognizable as Smith's and that is because they are idiosyncratic, not eccentric. Sometimes they fall into the typically Scottish faults of sentimentalism and rhetoric, but these faults are the excesses of its virtues. For this is a poetry of the passions, not the intellect. If one goes to it for perceptions of refined subtlety or for teased-out "metaphysics" or for any daring formal experimentalism, one will be disappointed. What is there to be found is a poetry of great variety, of energy, intensity, humor, and passion. It has not much to do with manners. But it is poetry you will not go to sleep on.

Norman MacCaig. *Poetry*. Aug., 1960, pp. 320–22

Sidney Goodsir Smith's Festival play *The Wallace* has all the qualities that make Schiller unacceptable to English audiences. It is Romantic, it is unsophisticated and it is written with all the stops pulled right out. The passion only just stops short of being sentimental, the dramatic climaxes of being melodramatic and the rhetoric of being rant, while the brawny, bearded, belligerent hero narrowly avoids being a parody Scotsman who might start tossing cabers at any minute. But close as it comes to the edge of the precipice, the play never topples into absurdity, and for something written on such a big scale with so little in either its style or its content to connect it with the twentieth century, it is quite a feat that it doesn't.

NS. Sept. 3, 1960, p. 305

The atmosphere, the tone and temper, in which his great work [*Carotid*] is conceived and carried through is that in which our guest has his life and being. He speaks Carotides fluently—especially at times where he would have no little difficulty in using at all what is absurdly known as standard English. One of his rarest most admirable qualities is the way in which he squares precept and practice. He doesn't merely praise Stand-fast. He stands or falls by it with the most commendable consistency. . . .

Where else but in Sydney's poetry in all the corpus of Scottish verse, are you so insistently reminded of the ironclad rule that if the ankles are more than half as big round as the calves that settles it and one can no longer maintain any interest whatever? Being trained to observe details even at a glance, the outstanding characteristics of members of the other sex who come under his observation—as few of them can fail to do—and qualities such as youth, shapeliness, and shallow depressions of the temples, which happen to appeal to him, inform his verses to a much greater extent than in the work of any other Scots poet.

Hugh MacDiarmid. *Sydney Goodsir Smith* [Presidential Address given in Old College, Edinburgh, for Edinburgh Univ. Scottish Renaissance Society, Dec. 14, 1964] (Edinburgh, Colin H. Hamilton, 1962), pp. 10–11

SNOW, C. P. (1905–   )

The Conscience of the Rich is printed out of turn; it should be taken as coming second in the series. It does not belong with *Time of Hope* and *Homecomings,* which dealt with Eliot's own experience, but with those others in which his observation of friends and acquaintances introduces him to passions and conflicts which are to be echoed and amplified in his personal life. Committed to the first person, the author cannot quite avoid in this book giving the impression that Eliot is unnaturally absorbed in his friend's affairs; he also manages to be present at some scenes which would be more convincing if they occurred in private. Eliot's pervasive participation mars, I think, the particular effect of this novel, but is no doubt necessary to the group as a whole. As always, the author gradually leads his hero and his readers towards a moral dilemma, subtly balanced and of some complexity, which is dramatically and satisfactorily solved. Once the dilemma is distantly sighted, the book becomes gripping; the early stages, however, are not immediately attractive. C. P. Snow is not a sensuous writer; I find it hard to visualize his characters and to catch their individual intonations, although each is fully realized on the social and the moral levels. His description of an Anglo-Jewish family (conservative, exclusive, proud, rich but not blatantly so, distinguished in politics but not in the arts) is accurate; it is an intellectual conception, so that we know all about these people but do not feel that we know *them*. An attempt is made to turn "Mr. L" into a "character" in the more superficial sense; he has some eccentricities and repeats certain idiosyncratic expressions, but he is only a shade more palpable than the others as a result. None of this, however, matters; the author must be given time before the absence of decor is seen to be irrelevant; his characters exist on the moral plane or not at all. There they have drama and life.

Francis Wyndham. *L.* June, 1958, p. 71

When the war was over Snow was invited to become a Civil Service Commissioner with special responsibility for scientific appointments.

... Snow's rôle in affairs from 1945 has been considerable, yet not easy to define. He has, of course, participated in all the major appointments of scientists to the government service; and he has acted as an essential point of reference in questions of official policy relating to scientific manpower and technological education. But one may presume that his major contribution, less formal and more permeating, has been to bridge the gap between scientists, whose professional training tends not to encourage them in making human judgments, and men of affairs, whose professional training may leave them something short of adequate when making scientific judgments. For his services to the country in public affairs a knighthood was conferred on him in 1957.

Meanwhile, since 1947, Snow has published seven more novels of the projected eleven which will complete the *Strangers and Brothers* cycle. It is quite different from a chronicle-sequence, or a *roman fleuve*. In content it is essentially a personal story—the story of a man's life, through which is revealed his psychological and his moral structure—yet by extension and implication it is an enquiry into the psychological and moral structure of a large fraction of the society of our times. As further volumes appear its form is disclosed as massive and intricate, yet fundamentally simple.

William Cooper. C. P. Snow (BC/Longmans, 1959), pp. 10–11

All the familiar merits of C. P. Snow are somewhere in evidence [*The Affair*]. The pace is beautifully even. The general discussions and the private chats are well handled, the underlying uneasinesses admirably suggested. The C. P. Snow faults are also present. People still feel things in their fibres, and on occasion the fibres speak. Possibly as a result of the Proust studies, a new sprinkling of French words has appeared, some of them not in Larousse. On the other hand, with the passage of time, Eliot's Latin genders have gone to pot. . . . The talk of power, responsibility and so on has become more automatic, even rather smug. . . .

It cannot be said that one looks forward to the remaining volumes with the unshaken confidence one maintained at any rate up to *The New Men*. . . .

One now has a feeling that the structure has in some obscure but not quite real sense been abandoned. The present contrivance does not quite belong with it. We may not have sympathized with Eliot's former struggles, but at least we recognized them as real. . . . Now Eliot has arrived. There are no more struggles, no more examinations to pass. And one has the uncomfortable feeling that experience has also ceased, that no "resonance" can take place in this over-upholstered, acoustically "dead" space. It is perhaps of some little relevance here that in the present work Eliot describes himself as tone-deaf.

TLS. April 15, 1960, p. 237

The prime importance of the *Strangers and Brothers* series is surely its loving concern with bureaucratic man. The plots of *The Masters* and *The Affair* deal with the decisions to be taken by dons at a Cambridge college about, in the first case the election of a new Master and in the second the expulsion of a Fellow; *The New Men* is much concerned with departmental argument and internecine warfare between the scientists working on the development of the atomic bomb and the administrators handling the project; similar problems appear in the background of other books. It is plain that the whole atmosphere and procedure of jockeying for power holds a fascination for Snow. His lobbyists are always calculating votes and possibilities. "Nightingale can't cross over again . . . you're also counting on Gay, but I set him off against Pilbrow." *The New Men,* and part of *Time of Hope,* show the dangers of generalization, for the first gives a brilliant picture of the attempts to make the atomic pile work, and the second suggests admirably the atmosphere of life in a barrister's chambers. Here, undoubtedly, is an English novelist writing from the inside of men at work, but they are in both cases technicians, of science and the law, and they do not really provide exceptions to the rule that our novelists never deal from the inside with ordinary working-class occupations.

TLS. Sept. 9, 1960, p. vii

Sir Charles Snow's views on the Two Cultures make me wonder what sort of people he thinks people are. . . . He thinks that the way to deal with the cultural split is instructional: both cultures must be taught about each other's specialties.

It is this very objective and behaviouristic approach, combined with certain features of his later collection, the Godkin lectures, given at Harvard, and published as *Science and Government,* which makes me wonder whether he does not miss an essential part of the meaning of "culture": and whether indeed the underlying aim, not perhaps sufficiently reflected, is not unification but *gleichschaltung*. . . .

In *Science and Government* Sir Charles gives his reasons for believing that we want more scientists at every level of our administration. I do not find his reasons either convincing or clear. . . . Sir Charles himself says that scientists are not necessarily good administrators. And even in technical situations which may be literally a matter of life and death for the rest of us, the chances that their judgment will be wrong seems to be about fifty-fifty. Sir Charles is fascinated by the relations of intrigue and power in scientific and academic life. In spite of the fact, or maybe because of it, that petty competition takes up a great deal of their time, compared with the problems of the outer human world, or even of their scientific work, the scientists do not often enough appear as solid and quirky moral beings. It is true that Sir Charles gives his scientists problems of social morality to bite upon which, in themselves, must seem to many of us of genuine importance. For example, what should be done about dropping the bomb they have spent the war making, or the problem of secrecy as posed by patriotic commitment *(The New Men);* or the problem of scientific integrity *(The Affair)*?

But this reads generally like a paper-discussion: and weight for weight, the characters are in too much of a tizzy about where their next honour is coming from. It is instructive to follow the careers of one or two of the Snow-Saga men between *The Masters* and *The New Men,* via *The Affair.* Walter Luke, for one, a tough-spoken young prole boffin-Fellow (hardly ever with less than four letters to his name, or blanks, anyway, for Sir Charles is delicate about this) has moved, by way of bomb-research and radiation-sickness, to his knighthood. Nightingale, whom in *The Masters* nobody could endure, a lonely bachelor reduced to spinsterish spite through having wandered up the wrong power-corridors, has not indeed achieved either a title, or the F.R.S. which has haunted him for years, but at least he has a wartime gong and the college bursary, plus, what nobody could have foreseen, a highly satisfactory wife. (For, if his characters have missed the honorific bus, Sir Charles will sometimes reward them himself, after we have given up all hope, with a psychological boost.) And lots of "bright young men have made their reputation."

But the characters seldom have real insides or real and convincing passions: and one wonders whether the narrator-device which Lewis Eliot provides, is, not so much a convenient god's eye view, as a way of dodging the problems of subjectivity, a reversal that is of our whole artistic development, towards a more primitive or juvenile concern with "humours" or the kind of personage one meets in a morality-play.

The abstract and passionless quality reminds one more than anything of Science Fiction or the best quality Whodunit—without the thrills. In fact, after reading a good deal of Sir Charles's fiction, one is driven to ponder on Dr. Leavis's insistence on "relevant life," and the serious novelist's duty to surround his characters with it. . . . I cannot think that the boffin as depicted by Sir Charles is the type to which the whole creation moves. Even if his picture, or rather diagram, of the status-struck scientific world is accurate, the best treatment of this adolescent situation might well have been *satirical.*

Kathleen Nott. *Enc.* Feb., 1962, pp. 87, 94–6

The line which he takes in *The Two Cultures* is so far from the actuality of his temperament in this respect that we can only suppose that he doesn't mean it, not in all the extravagance of its literalness. Or we suppose that he means it at the behest of some large preoccupation of whose goodness he is so entirely convinced that he will seek to affirm it even in ways that would take him aback if the preoccupation were not in control of his thought. And this, I think, is the case. I believe that the position of *The Two Cultures* is to be explained by Sir Charles's preoccupation—it has become almost the best-known thing about him— with a good and necessary aim, with the assuring of peace, which is to say, with the compounding of differences between the West and the Soviet Union. It is an aim which, in itself, can of course only do Sir Charles credit, yet it would seem to have implicit in it a strange desperate method of implementing itself.

For the real message of *The Two Cultures* is that an understanding between the West and the Soviet Union could be achieved by the culture of scientists, which reaches over factitious national and ideological differences. The field of agreement would be the scientists' common perception of the need for coming together to put the possibilities of the scientific revolution at the disposal of the disadvantaged of all nations. The bond between scientists, Sir Charles has told us, is virtually biological: they all have the future in their bones. . . .

In this denial of the actuality of politics, Sir Charles is at one with the temper of intellectuals today—we all want politics not to exist, we all want that statement of Hegel's to be absolutely and immediately true, we dream of Reason taking over the whole management of the world, and soon. No doubt a beneficent eventuality, but our impatience for it is dangerous if it leads us to deny the actuality of politics in the present. . . . What is gained by describing the resistance to Reason as other than it is, by thinking in the specious terms of two opposing "cultures"?

Lionel Trilling. *Cmty.* June, 1962, pp. 469–70

I suppose everyone has been more or less forcibly acquainted with the facts. In 1959 Sir Charles Snow, a well-known British novelist and spokesman for the sciences, delivered a Rede lecture at Cambridge, which he named *The Two Cultures*. His theme was, briefly, that the split, the gap in communication, between the "two cultures," of the sciences and the humanities, was already wide and would, unless steps were taken, continue to widen; that this was an unhappy, indeed, a potentially perilous thing; and that it was everyone's concern to try and do something about it. The theme, if neither very original, nor very deeply thought out, nor very memorably expressed, seemed at least meritorious. Coming from someone in the public position that Sir

Charles enjoys, its tenets (one felt), though no doubt on the woolly side to begin with, and destined to be filtered through many, many tons more of Establishment wool before they penetrated to any vital spot, would culminate in effects that would be, if marginally, more useful than not. But in 1962, in another endowed lecture of the usually cozy Cambridge sort (the Richmond), the critic F. R. Leavis attacked both Sir Charles and his lecture with an uncontrolled virulence of fury that had hardly been seen in England since the days of *The Edinburgh Review* nearly a century and a half earlier. . . .

Sir Charles is very much what it is fashionable to call a figure of the Establishment. Quite typically, too, he was not born to it but "came up from the ranks" by way of a state school in Leicester. At Cambridge he was a molecular physicist and elected a Fellow of his college in that subject at the age of twenty-five. The war took him, ten years later, out of the university into the Civil Service. At the same time he turned seriously to the novel, and has more or less divided his time between these two latter callings since. . . . More serious students of literature no doubt think of Snow as respectable rather than brilliant, a conscientious writer of the second rank who has astutely made an unfamiliar but important piece of territory his own. They certainly do not in general regard him as anything remotely in the nature of a menacing portent or bogey. His is in fact the type of mind, wide but comparatively shallow, that is usually underestimated, rather than the reverse, by the professional critic—whose own mind will tend to cut pretty deep but, in his case, on a front that is comparatively narrow. A paragraph of a Snow novel yields nothing whatever to deep analysis; his merits lie in the structure and ordering of the whole. His is a typical administrator's mind, not very perceptive over details, but capable of forming and retaining a well-balanced picture of the entire field. . . .

No, the rest of us can just sit back and have a quiet ironic laugh at the spectacle of these two gladiators—but no again, indeed we can't. For only one gladiator is in the ring. To the whole of Leavis' onslaught Snow has answered—precisely nothing. He has answered nothing but rather, a few months later, on the occasion of his induction to the honorary Rectorship of a Scottish university, delivered a lecture upon "Magnanimity."

Hilary Corke. NR. April 13, 1963, pp. 27, 30

Sir Charles Snow is quite satisfied to take over, entirely unaltered, the machinery devised by Trollope. Sir Charles's interests are those of a practical man; he is concerned primarily with how the world works and how things get done. Since this kind of preoccupation has not altered very much in the last century, there is no reason why Sir Charles should trouble himself to adapt the Trollopian form; it will do as it stands; Galsworthy in *The Forsyte Saga* found that form perfectly suited to the task of describing the Edwardian social scene and Sir Charles finds it equally suited, for his own special purposes, to the mid-twentieth century. And indeed it may be that this kind of copious realistic novel, generously inventive as to episode and detail but entirely uninventive in regard to everything that concerns the art of the novel, can usefully be written in each generation. But there seems to be no possibility of any give and take between Snow and any other contemporary English novelist; he, like them, is "encased" in his talent; it is perhaps significant that he finds less affinity with anything in contemporary English literature than with the literature of Soviet Russia, which he seems to admire with strikingly few reservations.

John Wain. *Essays on Literature and Ideas*
(Macmillan, 1963), p. 40

There are times when the style is the man and when the hero is closely related to the creator. I find it hard to know whether the creator of the "Strangers and Brothers" sequence is a very modest man or a very self-satisfied one. Self-satisfied, because of the pervasive smugness, the transparent if subfuse gratification which the author derives from his acquaintance with men who matter and his intimacy with the ins and outs of the corridors which they walk. . . . The stock explanation is that, neither modest nor self-satisfied, Sir Charles Snow is simply the detached historian of the British Establishment. So. This Establishment had hitherto inspired me with more respect, or more fear, or more *something,* than does Snow's epic portrayal of it.

"When she wrote"—a minor character engaged on a biography of her late husband—"she didn't fuss, she just wrote." The same can be said of Snow, and perhaps—which is not to ask that his personages should talk like Durrellian diplomats—he ought to try to fuss just a little. He employs clichés as such; not (for better or worse) wittily, or questioningly, no, he has the courage of his clichés. His style has been praised on the grounds that it doesn't exist (like the only good German, etc.) and his use of commonplaces has been defended as sound naturalistic practice. That is to say, people (politicians, civil servants, scientists especially?) talk in clichés, and life consists largely of banal situations, and Snow's themes are of such public moment that the artist's fine Italian hand may not be allowed to distort the account. It is a decent scruple, which novelists of a documentary sort can honestly feel; and it is best conciliated by the reminder that a novel is only a novel, after all, or, better still, that a novel *is* a novel.

In one way and another I found *Corridors of Power* a lowering experience.

D. J. Enright. *NS.* Nov. 6, 1964, p. 698

Corridors of Power claims to be a political novel, a rare, though respectable form. . . . In my opinion, only Hilaire Belloc achieved complete success. No one else seems to think so. His best novels are mostly unobtainable and are never read.

Snow approaches the theme from a special angle. This is a novel about civil servants as well as about politicians. The narrator is a civil servant: so are many of the principal characters. I have read only one of Snow's previous books, *The Masters,* and the characters here allude to previous happenings which are to me unknown. Even more mysterious, this is a closed world. . . .

Apart from the unreality of the central theme, I cannot believe in the characters. They are too intense. They never stop being civil servants or politicians. I had the same difficulty with *The Masters,* which deals with the election of the head of a college. I could only murmur: "Not like the life of the dear Fellows of Magdalen." I have experienced two such elections. The Fellows felt strongly when they applied their minds to the question, which was for about one hour a week. The rest of the time they taught pupils, read books, gossiped, or did whatever Fellows do. Civil servants may be different. I know too few to judge, though the conversations I have heard in the Athenaeum are not at all like those recorded by Snow. Politicians, I am sure, are just like dons: individual human beings with a particular activity which sometimes stirs their interest. They are a great deal more loyal to each other than Snow suggests, and a great deal more simple-minded also. They do not really settle high politics at cocktail parties or at glittering dinners. If they ever talk politics there, it is for fun—to tease each other or to entertain the company. There is not a single laugh in Snow's book. There are many laughs in life, among politicians and even among scientists. . . . Snow seems to think that great political events are determined by mutterings in dark corridors. Really they can all be followed in the light of day, and any well-informed observer can describe in detail what is happening. Snow's novel might make sense if it took place in the Kremlin, though even there events are much less mysterious than is often supposed. Set in this country it is not a political novel at all. It is a Victorian melodrama, told in stodgy 20th-century prose. The experienced novel-reader, who is trained to follow clues, may perhaps make some sense of it. For my part, back to Belloc.

A. J. P. Taylor. NS. Nov. 6, 1964, p. 698

SORLEY, CHARLES (1895–1915)

His language is poor and thin, but it moves powerfully, and constantly suggests organic forms. This is most unlooked-for in a tyro. Sensuous images are extraordinarily persisted in and as strangely few. Rain, wind, running, one particular spot on the downs where four grass tracks separate east, west, south, and north, from a tall weathered signpost and the "red-capped town" of Marlborough, where he was at school—these images return and return, ever freshly applied; but there is no hint of the neighbouring Savernake forest, it had too much the character of hostility to free movement. This young mind runs tirelessly, with ever-revived pleasure, through an open, wet, bleak, grey land. . . .

Words halt behind thought and feeling. After vision and inspiration have been aroused by experience, even the best poetry may seem lame. But Sorley was conscious of another reason why "Beauty is better not expressed." He knew that it would not be welcomed. He had reached that stage when the soul reacts against parents, masters, and the world that has fostered it. He was a rebel, an unusually clear-eyed and affectionate rebel, who did not only feel that things were wrong, but could point them out with an unerring finger.

T. Sturge Moore. *Eng. R.* Oct., 1918, pp. 259, 261

The lives of Rupert Brooke and Charles Hamilton Sorley afford an interesting, if obvious, contrast and comparison. There is so much to say about Rupert Brooke and comparatively so little about his poetry. His life was so manifestly incomplete, so provocative, so full of promise rather than production, his verse so finished, and so often entirely achieving its limited object, that his life seems to have been designed to write about, his verse to enjoy.

One is tempted, for the sake of symmetry, to say that the exact opposite is true of Charles Sorley. But that would not be correct, for though Sorley's verse is far more provocative of comment than Brooke's (just as it is far inferior in achievement), his life is not at all uninteresting, as the present letter-autobiography shows [*Letters*]. Still, there is more to say of Sorley's verse than of his life, and readers of his *Marlborough, and Other Poems* must not expect a prose equivalent to the intense originality and vigour of such poems as "The Song of the Ungirt Runners."

Spec. March 13, 1920, p. 351

As John Masefield considered Sorley the most promising of the English poets killed in the war, these letters of his come highly recommended. One approaches them prepared to find little beyond promise—a hint of something fine cut down before fulfillment; they turn out to be very much more than mere promise; they are in themselves achievement, the expression of a rarely independent mind, humorous, rich and wise far beyond its years. For though Sorley died when only a few months over twenty, in reading these letters there is no need to discount his age. Indeed the average run of life's critics are rather childish by comparison with his detached judgment—and at the same time their chief cause for envy should be his spontaneous youth. . . .

He is no more impressed by the giants of foreign literature, *qua* giants, than by English ones. "Rotters like Swinburne and Tennyson" he naturally despises. And even of his god of the moment, the prophet who succeeds Masefield and Hardy in his affections, he remains calm enough to say: "If Goethe really died saying 'more light,' it was very silly of him: what he wanted was more warmth." In such criticism there is evident no perverse dislike of orthodoxy, no impulse to demolish idols simply because they are enthroned, but a simple desire and keen ability to pierce the haze of centuries of opinion and appraise the "great man" at his naked face-to-face value.

R.L. *NR*. July 21, 1920, p. 232

One who knew him better than the mere reader of his letters can pretend to know him declares that, in spite of his poems, which are among the most remarkable of those of the boy-poets killed in the war, Sorley would not have been a man of letters. The evidence of the letters themselves is heavy against the view; they insist upon being regarded as the letters of a potential writer. But a passionate interest in literature is not the inevitable prelude to a life as a writer, and although it is impossible to consider any thread in Sorley's letters as of importance comparable to that which joins the enthronement and dethronement of his literary idols, we shall regard it as the record of a movement of souls which might as easily find expression (as did Keeling's) in other than literary activities. It takes more than literary men to make a generation, after all.

And Sorley was typical above all in this, that, passionate and penetrating as was his devotion to literature, he never looked upon it as a thing existing in and for itself. It was, to him and his kind, the satisfaction of an impulse other and more complex than the æsthetic. Art was a means and not an end to him, and it is perhaps the apprehension of this that has led one who endeavoured in vain to reconcile Sorley to Pater into rash prognostication. Sorley would never have been an artist in Pater's way; he belonged to his own generation, to which *l'art pour l'art* had ceased to have meaning.

Ath. Jan. 30, 1920, p. 137

It has been said that the death, in action, of Charles Hamilton Sorley constituted the greatest loss of the war to English Literature. There may be some, perhaps, who will hardly commit themselves to this; but none will be so foolish as to deny that more than sufficient interest in his personality was kindled by the publication, in 1916, of his *Marlborough and Other Poems* to justify the present appearance of this volume [*Letters*]. These letters, edited by his parents with admirable restraint, form an invaluable commentary on the Poems themselves. Having read them we feel that we understand not only the Poems, but also their author as we never could have done had we had only the Poems to guide us. Indeed, were we forced to decide between Poems and Letters we would choose the latter.

The Letters really divide themselves into three groups: those written while at school at Marlborough; those while staying (and studying) in Germany, first at Schwerin in Mecklenburg and then at the University of Jena; and, lastly, those while in the Army at home and in France.

Charles Sorley was a born letter-writer. As we read we feel ourselves to be wandering pleasantly among the green places of earth, with a brilliantly discursive boy at our side. Now we are roaming the bare face of the Wiltshire Downs, under swift skies and in racing winds; now we are in Germany, intellectually happy, but soon longing again for an English heaven above us; now in camp at Shorncliffe; now by a shell-torn roadside in France. And always the boy at our side is sparkling with humour and enthusiasm. . . .

While fighting for England he rebelled against English hypocrisy and ignorance, as he had earlier against the hypocrisy and futility of much of the public-school system. All insincerities he loathed, and all false sentiment. Thus he came to criticise Rupert Brooke's "1914," finding its glorification of the act of dying for one's country too sentimental and sententious. To his un-selfconscious kind of patriotism such behaviour was actually not a piece of self-sacrifice, but a duty. His patriotism was warm not with the fire of the fanatic or the romantic, but with the warmth of mother earth. He would have prayed not that earth might approximate to heaven, but that heaven might approximate to earth.

SR. March 20, 1920, pp. 281–82

SPARK, MURIEL (1918–   )

Memento Mori is an exceedingly adroit book but, in its rather conscientious heartlessness, not an entirely likeable one. Miss Spark is clearly on the side of some characters as against others. But there is a certain glee about the precipitation with which they are all jumbled together in their common fate. Miss Spark manages to get a large number of sharply defined and entirely convincing characters, of a wide range of human and social varieties, into her picture. The life of an old people's ward in a hospital is described with gruesome convincingness, especially when one end of it is filled with "geriatric cases," who come in like some wild medieval carnival. But for all its smoothness and precision *Memento Mori* never quite loses the flavour of being a gratuitous curiosity.

Anthony Quinton. *L.* Sept., 1959, p. 85

Miss Spark has shown in previous books how workmanlike is her study of the society she describes: sometimes, indeed, she gives the impression that she is more sociologist than novelist. Certainly there has been no funnier or more revealing picture of spiritualist circles than this. [*The Bachelors*]

Many readers relish Miss Spark's novels chiefly for this: her characters may be improbably sinister, but they are larger than life and much funnier. Yet surely her talent is more original; it has something to do with a quick and in many ways unfeminine intelligence (her logic is ruthless) allied to a matter-of-fact acceptance of metaphysical thoughts which most of us ignore or fear. The tension thus created, between her sharp hilarious exposure of trivialities and the underlying mysteries of the soul, intrigues and baffles the reader, and is in itself a sort of satire.

The Bachelors is less baffling, less extraordinary, than *Memento Mori,* but the tension is still there, because even bachelors need to know what happens after the free meals and free love. Miss Spark may not encourage "the amendment of vices," but she makes it refreshingly clear that modern satire can be more than anger or tittle-tattle.

TLS. Oct. 14, 1960, p. 657

The Prime of Miss Jean Brodie is a gloriously witty and polished vignette, and why, since the author has herself said she cannot help finding almost everything in life slightly ridiculous, should she not feel the same about the sombre problems which beset society, and Roman Catholics in particular, in this troubled and insecure age of ours? . . . One may argue that Mrs. Spark is at her best in avoiding bulky themes, but if her admirers are right in thinking *Memento Mori* the most serious of her books, by far her best, it will not be long before she must tackle material tougher than the vaguely symbolic portrait of a memorable eccentric lady of the 1960's.

TLS. Nov. 3, 1961, p. 785

She enjoys certain evident advantages: wit, high-fantastic humour, a sense of style, a capacity to communicate human oddity and solitude. She is also fashionable in being a Roman Catholic, and a convert too. . . . Next, Mrs. Spark is a stylist, and this allows her to skim deliciously over the surface of things, using elegance as a device for holding anything incoherent, inchoate, or disagreeable at arm's length, even while acknowledging its presence. It also allows her, by the wit and precision of so many of her words, to conceal the fact that her novels tend to be static and even, by a paradox, circumlocutory. . . .

The remark "neurotics never go mad" occurs in two of her books, and is the prime consolation accorded Mrs. Spark's characters in their daily struggle not to appear too eccentric to others or too disturbing to themselves. It is because she can convey this and so persuade us to find it comic, that Mrs. Spark has, in twelve years of writing, become a minor monument.

Anne Duchene. MGW. May 2, 1963, p. 11

If this book [*The Girls of Slender Means*], shrewd, economical and funny as it is, misses being absolutely top-notch Spark it is, I think, because she has caught the gaiety of the times but missed something equally important: their moral earnestness. . . . Muriel Spark's glittering surface poison always needs one deep incision to make it run in the veins. . . . Mrs. Spark has the wit, the Catholicism and the unkindness of Evelyn Waugh, but she has not yet mastered his skill at heartbreaking jungle deaths.

Katharine Whitehorn. Enc. Dec. 1963, pp. 80–81

A writer who interests me more [than Golding], and whose books are less allegories than moral or religious fables, is Muriel Spark. Her characters and backgrounds, and her use of dialogue, all have an authentic ring, but her purposes are those of the ordinary realistic novelist. She is a devout Roman Catholic (Golding's metaphysics are also Christian) and Mrs. Spark's gift for comedy is made portentous by her sense of the eternal significance of all human choices. . . .

Mrs. Spark's novels are at once very amusing and harrowingly penetrating; she is compassionately aware of how much of life is distraction in Pascal's sense, the search for trivialities and disguises that will divert our minds from the soul's sadness and loneliness, from life's uncertainty and transcience, from the abyss.

G. S. Fraser. The Modern Writer and His World
(Penguin Bks., 1964 [rev. ed.; first pub. Derek
Verschoyle, 1953]), pp. 171–72

SPENCER, BERNARD (1909–1963)

Perhaps the most pleasurable poetry written during the war was that by a group of civilian friends in Cairo, Lawrence Durrell, Bernard Spencer, and Terence Tiller. This was primarily personal in tone and descriptive in manner. Durrell and Spencer, who had both lived in Greek islands in the years before the war, were chiefly concerned with the landscape and the atmosphere of the eastern Mediterranean, particularly the Hellenic, world. Of the two, Spencer was the better poet of pure landscape, but Durrell could perhaps convey historical atmosphere in a richer fashion.

G. S. Fraser. *The Modern Writer and His World*
(Derek Verschoyle, 1953), p. 264

His moments of intensity tend to start from the visual object, like a painter's sketches picking out shapes and colours that combine and testify. Testify to what, though? With a facility of expression that runs ahead of him, Mr. Spencer has the genuine wish to speak a language with some broadly moral meaning that he cannot always drag from the vivid scene [*With Luck Lasting*]. . . .

Mr. Spencer is a poet worth watching. He already commands an enticing freedom and delicacy of utterance; given a more sharply focused content, his poems will have real power.

TLS. July 26, 1963, p. 556

In all this [the business of getting material collected and printed for the magazine called *Personal Landscape,* edited in Cairo with Lawrence Durrell and others] Bernard played an attentive if somewhat lackadaisical part; he was a man impossible to harry or fluster. Nor was this mere laziness; it was a kind of inherent belief that if you hurried things too much you couldn't observe them with the necessary attention and extract from them their vital juices. He was always reproving me for my lack of what he called "a respect for the Object" and I accepted his mild reproofs with attention. I had discovered something in his poetry and his conversation which interested me and fired me—because it was a quality I felt I lacked. He had a sort of piercing yet undogmatic irony of approach to people and things; as if he had taken up some sort of quiet vantage-point inside himself from which with unerring fidelity he pronounced upon the world—not in the form of grandiose generalizations, aphorisms, or epigrams, but in small strict pronouncements which hit home. His best poetry is like that—a succession of plain, almost nude, statements which somehow give one the feeling of incontrovertibility. The feeling, the tenderness is all the purer for not being orchestrated too richly; in the fine grain of his poetry there is much that reminds me of Edward Thomas, and his best poems will certainly live as long as the best of Thomas. I told him this once; he neither agreed nor disagreed. He put on his most quizzical expression and said: "Have a beer." The real truth was, I think, that his poetry was so bracketed to his private vision that he didn't care whether it *was* better or worse than Thomas or Keats or anyone else. . . . It was good Spencer, that was what mattered.

Lawrence Durrell. *L.* Jan., 1964, pp. 42–43

SPENDER, STEPHEN (1909–   )

Mr. Spender's *Poems* received more genuine praise and roused higher hopes than any first book of poetry since the eclipse of the Georgians. They were informed with a passionate awareness rare among his contemporaries, they were intensely individual and they achieved the memorable line (still one of the final tests of true poetry) with quite exceptional frequency. But would so sensitive a lyricism survive, in this harsh age, beyond a first volume? *Vienna* is Mr. Spender's answer. The social and political perception which was hinted at in the *Poems* is here vastly expanded but not by any means at the expense of his impassioned lyricism. In this long poem the author has set an individual relationship, a personal adjustment, against the social and political background of a revolutionary Vienna. It has already been complained, by those who would apparently wish Mr. Spender to go on repeating his earlier success, that *Vienna* fails because its characters are particularized (Dollfuss, Fey, Wallisch, etc.) and because its hold on the reader is therefore conditioned at the outset by partial considerations. But Mr. Spender has contrived to fuse the general with the particular in an altogether remarkable manner; and his method, moreover, has enabled him to show up the personal theme in his poem the more poignantly because of the hideous social background against which it is set. Thus nothing has been lost of the poet's first success and at the same time his poetry is made to march forward with the continual expansion of his experience.

C. Henry Warren. *FR.* Feb., 1935, p. 250

Spender's poems similarly are often difficult because the meaning itself is intricate, though this intricacy is not due so much as in Auden to an adaptation or syncretism of specialist-theories, but rather to Spender's own very equivocal view of the world in which he lives. In speaking of imagery I suggested that Spender's images pull more than their own weight, tend to become as factual as his properties. And many things in his poems seem, like Yeats's Tower, to exist on two planes of reality at once. . . .

Spender's view of the world, as I said, is equivocal—but honest. Adopting Marxist doctrine he yet sympathizes with the Anarchists and this poetic anarchism glosses his writing with fantasy. Compare a novel, which Spender very much admires, Ramon Sender's *Seven Red Sundays*.

Louis MacNeice. *Modern Poetry*
(Oxford Univ. Pr., 1938), pp. 173–74

Mr. Spender has always met with indulgence from publishers and reviewers. Respectable names can be quoted in support of the view that each of his works is a masterpiece, or at least points towards a more glorious future. Whereas, in fact, as is known to readers of this journal, almost the opposite is the case. Yet his most recent work [*Trial of a Judge*] is announced by the publishers as "a tragic statement," and by himself (presumably) on the title-page as a "tragedy." (Mr. Auden, we remember, was content with calling *Paid on Both Sides* a charade.)

In examining the pretensions of this poetical drama it will be convenient to start from the notion of "tragic *statement*." For the most notable portion of the play—and the only one in which the author writes with any clarity and force—occurs in the fifth act. Here various barely disguised versions of the author discuss their points of view. There is a Communist, a Liberal judge and later a "Fascist" leader. But the kind of clarity and force which their statements have adequately place the pretensions. For they are no more than could be attributed to his own prose work on the same theme—the position of Liberalism between the two more rigid "theologies." He puts the well-known arguments in such a way that no one could mistake them. Nor does he seek to favour (or so it seems) the Communist more than the Liberal, and the Fascists once the stylization is admitted are creditably drawn. It is clear from various remarks uttered by Mr. Spender that he has been working towards this style for a long time and attributes to it remarkable virtues. Yet it does not force conviction on us by any poetical means. Nor do the arguments penetrate far enough into the problems involved to convince us intellectually. The blurb asserts: "The material is political, but the readers and the audience will, according to their abilities, find deeper levels of meaning." Apart from a passing tribute to the beauty of this piece of advertisement, the attentive reader will quickly recognize it as bluff. The meaning in this portion is on the surface and when read leaves you exactly where you were.

H. A. Mason. *Scy*. Sept., 1938, p. 219

The curious thing about Mr. Spender is that he can be soft and arduous at the same time; despite lapses, there is a continuity which carries over from one poem to another and makes his work, as a whole, more remarkable than single examples of it. He aims at being truthful, whatever the cost, about himself and about the world he lives in. He gives us in the first place personal history. There is the lover, with an air of "Look, we are coming through!" whose past mistakes and failures clog the present. The poems at the beginning of *Ruins and Visions* entitled "A Separation," communicate vividly a sense of loss. Despair, pity and self-pity, the uselessness as well as the inevitability of regret, rise tardily to the surface out of regions of pain. The blow is softened (this is the condition of Mr. Spender's advances in self-knowledge), but not so completely as to muffle impact. . . .

Mr. Spender, perhaps, is the poet of muddle; but even slipshod sentences and hazy feelings are justified so far as they enable him to prod experience a little further. Reading his poems, one may be reminded of a journey through one of those pleasure caves in a Luna Park. We take our seats in the bumping and slowly revolving tub, to drift awhile in darkness before shooting rapids; a brightly lit grotto confronts us round a corner, or a spider hanging in mid-air unexpectedly tickles our faces; more rapids, a skeleton or two, a pastoral tableau, and we are back again, rubbing our eyes, in daylight. The journey may seem to have let us down, but, after all, it provided the excitements we now belittle. So with a Spender poem I often feel, "How much more might have happened, and very nearly *did* happen!" Unsatisfactory? Maybe. But by always edging towards greater things *Ruins and Visions,* in fact, enlarges its poetry, and in general Mr. Spender is better worth reading than the safe writer who compounds at a lower level.

G. W. Stonier. *NSN*. Aug. 1, 1942, p. 79

Mr. Spender must subject himself to his own judgment at some point. If he chooses to publish books like *Life and the Poet,* the danger is that the occasional penetrating pieces of insight—and these are nearly always of a human kind—will be overlooked among the pages of scanty scholarship and loose thinking. For there are more readers who will find scanty scholarship and loose thinking to their minds than will value the occasional moments of something better. It is possible that Stephen Spender will, at a certain moment, find himself, as Yeats did, in such a way that his solution will illuminate in retrospect his present confusion. From Yeats's early work, no one could have foreseen the distance that he would travel, but only the direction. But not all acorns grow into oaks, and it remains to be seen whether Stephen Spender's subsequent writings will give a significance to much that he is writing at present; which as it stands is less experimental than feeling in the dark.

Perhaps this is put too strongly. Stephen Spender has already gone a certain way, touched a certain depth; far enough to assure him a place as one of the best younger poets of this time, but not far enough or deeply enough to make his searchings significant; as they can only be in the necessary context of a real solution.

Kathleen Raine. *Hor.* Sept., 1942, pp. 211–12

Of these fashionable poets Stephen Spender is next best [to Auden] and somewhat more orthodox. Toward the end of *Poems* (1933) are several revolutionary lyrics, threatening death to exploiters, pitying the unemployed, and, in their imagery of aerodromes and railways, looking to a Wellsian future. Advising "young comrades" to forsake their fathers' houses, Spender points to dawns "exploding like a shell" and to new roots seeking water. These poems, mostly in free verse, show lyric intelligence and Spender's admiration of Whitman and Lawrence. Aside from "Pylons," "The Funeral" is worthiest of notice and most original. Here Russian workers carry to a grave (while red flags wave) a dead worker, "one cog in a golden and singing hive." Revolutionary enthusiasm may excuse the presence of cogs in the hive and explain the general looseness of these poems, which were, however, a welcome change from Eliot.

William York Tindall. *Forces in Modern British Literature, 1885–1946* (N.Y., Knopf, 1947), p. 58

I find Stephen Spender's *Collected Poems* awkward, woolly-minded and lame: I also find that they produce upon me the unquestionable exhilaration of a veritable poetry itself. A man who stammers has at least got something to stammer about; he has been demonstrably affected by whatever inflicted his stammer. But only too often the poet who produces a book of collected poems merely reveals the fact that in truth he has written none at all. Moving among the fragmentary masonry of Spender's *Poems,* the egomaniacal columns and the doors that don't fit, the staircases that end in mid-air and the attics in which there are too many mirrors, among all this miscellaneous and often half-baked bric-à-brac, the true presence itself dominates, moves and operates. These poems almost restore to us the dignity that properly pertains to those who believe because it is impossible. What is to Spender's honour is that he has written bad poems but almost never phoney ones. There is no danger of his poems going to Hollywood but a reasonable likelihood that they will finish up in hospital. Thus if you come upon a cripple walking you can be fairly sure that he wants to get somewhere. And Stephen Spender has reached the point of no return. He has now to show us what the mature poems are like of a man whose youth was so easy that it was too hard. His destiny is to prove that a poem with an impediment of speech, a club foot, and butterfingers, can neverthe-

less enunciate, hold and pursue the poetic affirmation. His poems are thus good poems because and in spite of the fact that they are bad ones.
George Barker. *Nimbus.* Summer, 1955, p. 93

Spender was a less intellectual, more emotionally subjective poet than either of these two. Auden and MacNeice typically used either a fairly regular if slightly roughened or jolting blank verse, or fairly strict stanza forms, made modern-seeming by a certain amount of rhythmical syncopation, but avoided free verse; Spender liked free verse and often gave the effect of writing it even when he was attempting to write in blank verse or rhymed stanzas. His verse was a slow-moving, rather dense medium in which long and contorted sentences, expressing a painful groping of the mind, would lead suddenly up to lines of great lyrical concentration and poise. . . .

It is hard to find between the styles and temperaments and attitudes of these four poets [Auden, Spender, Day Lewis, MacNeice] the obvious affinities that reviewers found so easily in the 1930s. Yet the habit of grouping them together made sense in relation to their beginnings. They did work in couples and influence each other. They appeared in the same magazines and anthologies. Their work first became familiar in an anthology, *New Signatures,* edited by Michael Roberts, an important critic and interesting poet who died prematurely in 1949. Roberts did more for them than merely publish their work. To many of them he was an elder brother, whose approval and admiration mattered a great deal to them. Roberts was a skilled mountaineer and it was largely under his influence . . . that the image of the hero as pioneer or explorer played such an important part in the group. Some of their imagery also comes from a close attachment to the atmosphere of English public-school life; there is sometimes what might be called a "boy scout" flavour about their writing, an emphasis on the small group and its daring leader with a background of the boy's adventure story. . . . It is worth noting that Isherwood took no degree, and Spender and Auden very poor degrees at Oxford, because the continuation of school boy fantasy-attitudes, or of the habit of escape and rebellion through fantasy, prevented them from acquiring the mental discipline, the provisional acceptance of conventional frameworks of thought, and the willingness to work hard over small areas, that makes for student success. . . .

But the fantasy of Auden and Spender, even at its most extreme, was a symbol of, a metaphor for, reality. They saw around them a world of apparent safety and real drift from which they turned to images of danger courageously faced and of conscious human purpose. They felt that England was flabby and dead so they wanted to awaken those around them to the tensions and dangers of the time, to its strength and beauty.

Machinery with its controlled power fascinated them: Spender in particular wrote about pylons and railway engines with simple lyrical enthusiasm, as an older poet might have written about clouds, swans, or roses. Machinery signified energy, and what a weak and drifting time needed was to "Drink here of energy, and only energy": Spender's phrase summed up the central drive of the whole group.

What is also notable about Auden and Spender is the masculine tone of their poetry which almost excluded family life, domestic affection, or the great traditional theme of unhappy romantic love. Tenderness or awe for a woman as a person hardly appears: for they idealized a thinking, acting group of male leaders.

G. S. Fraser. The Modern Writer and His World
(Penguin Bks., 1964) [Derek Verschoyle, 1953],
pp. 300–2

SQUIRE, J. C. (1884–1958)

These [*Imaginary Speeches*] are very clever and entertaining parodies. They are, too, genuine parodies. They are not merely rather vaguely jocular or farcical, as is much which passes for good parody; they do aim to be criticism by slight exaggeration. Mr. Squire has caught to perfection not only the mannerisms but the style of thought of his politicians. There is a speech by Mr. Balfour defending a Unionist Budget in 1919 which provides for the 50 per cent taxation of land values. It contains one glorious Balfourian sentence, over a page in length, with no fewer than nine relative clauses. Then there is a magnificent oration by Lord Roseberry attacking a Liberal Finance Bill, the only feature of which is the repeal of the license duty on dogs. These are the best things in the book—both perfect parodies.

OutL. April 27, 1912, p. 623

He is one of those poets who appeal in the first place by their rhythm, just as others appeal mainly by vowel melody, and others by the evocation of pictures. I do not mean that any good poet does neglect any one of these three constituents of good verse. They are indispensable channels through which feeling is conveyed or aroused; but any given poet will appeal chiefly by one of them, and with Mr. Squire it is rhythm. He is one of the few living men (Dr. Bridges and Mr. De La Mare are others) of whom it can be said that he has made definite and genuine discoveries in this direction. Most of our poets . . . prefer to perform on the instruments which their predecessors have left them. Others, whom I like less, merely sit on the keyboard, as Liszt said. But Mr. Squire has made real discoveries of real value. The lovely, fluent stanza

of "Rivers," capable of assuming innumerable different shapes without losing its individuality, proves the worth of his metrical invention.
Edward Shanks. *Dial.* Jan., 1920, p. 130

I want to talk of J. C. Squire the poet, but two things stand in the way, *Books in General* and *Tricks of the Trade,* neither of which can be classed as poetry. This most versatile of our younger writers refuses to be classified as a mere poet: whatever he touches he adorns, and therefore it is necessary to notice briefly his achievement as a critic and a parodist before we aspire to place him in his proper category. Under the pseudonym of "Solomon Eagle" he discourses glibly week by week on "Books in General" in *The New Statesman,* and under his own name on the same subject in *Land and Water.* He is perhaps the ablest literary critic alive and does for literature today much what Shaw did for the theatre in *The Saturday Review* of several years ago. . . .

But it is, I imagine, as a poet that Mr. Squire would have us finally pass judgement upon him. In March 1918 he issued a volume of poetry which, in his own words, "contains all that I do not wish to destroy of the contents of four volumes of verse." . . .

The most obvious criticism to make on turning over the pages is that there is, as we should have expected, always evidence of a sharpened intellect, but by no means always a sense of beauty in these verses. He tries all kinds of tricks with metres, and almost his most ambitious poem "Rivers" relies very little on rhyme for its success. This, of course, puts a large burden on to the thought and vocabulary, and sometimes the thought and the vocabulary are not strong enough to stand the extra strain.
S. P. B. Mais. *Books and their Writers*
(N.Y., Dodd, Mead, 1920), pp. 114, 120–21

Poems: First Series was a selection from the verse he had written up to 1918; *Poems: Second Series* contains all the poems he has written since, and a group of poems called *An Epilogue* (1917), which in 1918 he apparently did not think worthy to be included. Mr. Squire as a critic, unless a book contains downright follies, when no one can underline them more neatly, or is harsh, or contains suggestions of lust, is not an exacting judge; and that sympathetic generosity of temperament extends, perhaps inevitably, a measure of its indulgence to his own. He is not self-critical. The inclusion of some of these poems in a series destined to represent him as a poet is only explicable on the supposition that he valued them, first and foremost, for the feelings which inspired them. . . .

He is not a prolific poet; yet, comparatively small as his production is, no modern poetry requires more careful sifting than his; for, when he fails, his failures never show uncoordinated strength, but the droop of weakness. . . . His easy . . . descriptions, while evoking the obvious, can at times—and without the help of one unexpected word or far-fetched simile—convey also the finer shade and even the exotic; but, failing to do so, his description becomes merely conventional; and that intimate note of his which woos its gentle way into the affections as well as the imagination of the reader is ever but a semi-tone off sentimentality, often the more pronounced for being cloaked by apparently casual or sensitive under-statement. The temptation he should particularly guard against is that of heightening, when imagination flags, the emotional appeal by faltering into the affectionately "natural." . . .

That human, all too human, element in Mr. Squire's work which makes it hard for him to keep, as an artist must, the spontaneous expression of sympathy and sensibility at a certain distance, has saved him from the modern fault of pursuing incommunicable idiosyncrasies of sensation, or dredging his subconscious for any old boots and mussel-shells which may be lying there, and presenting them as treasure-trove.

Desmond MacCarthy. NS. May 13, 1922, pp. 150–52

The position of Mr. J. C. Squire in contemporary poetry is very curious. Traditionalists and persons who have a horror of innovation in poetry have regarded him as a dangerous rebel, a man out to destroy the ease and comeliness, the old beauty of our verse; whereas, on the other hand, the wild young men, who believe that poetry was born again when they first set down their obscure reactions in jerky prose, have seen in Mr. Squire a mere slave of empty tradition and have suggested that he can hardly be considered a poet at all. Further, not being a member of any school or group (for the so-called "Georgians," about whom there has been far too much talk, are not really a school or group) and not being easy to "place," he has been rather neglected by those critics who have written little books on modern verse, its tendencies, its revolt, its Vision and Idealism, its want of Vision and Idealism; he has been left to himself. Yet he has been consistently enjoyed and praised by persons who take the poetry of their own time seriously and examine it curiously in their search for original minds and fine craftsmen, and such persons have looked forward to every succeeding volume of work that Mr. Squire has given them, secure in the knowledge that in him they have discovered both an original mind and a fine craftsman. Actually, the explanation of this curious position of his lies in the fact that he is original, one of the most original poets we have; the rigid conservatives and the wild rebels have both assailed him simply because he is in neither of their camps; he is in his own camp; he has done what every original poet has always done, he has not broken away from tradition, but he has modified it to suit his own purposes. He is an experimenter, and . . . a successful experimenter. Having new matter to his hand, he has fashioned new and fit forms in order that such matter might be expressed scrupulously.

J. B. Priestley. *Figures in Modern Literature* (John Lane, 1924), pp. 188–89

A legend has grown up round him. For some he has become a morose keeper of a petrified Royal Academy of Poetry. For others, his shadow lies across the whole field of contemporary verse, darkening what is bright in it, and underlining in black what is dull. For others still he is the captain of the forces of light. And in all this argument and controversy the original Mr. Squire has been obliterated, the Squire, who made no particular claim except to be allowed to address "The Moon" and "The Birds" in language tranquilly apposite to those endearing objects. Indeed, Mr. Squire who, I am sure, asked nothing better than to take his place modestly at the gate of Olympus, has by some malign destiny been converted into, or at any rate regarded as, the janitor of contemporary immortality. It is possible that he is himself to blame for having had thrust upon him the harsh functions of Cerberus, or he may not be to blame. But for my part I do not very much care because I am far more interested in the author of "The Birds" than in the adjudicator of the Hawthornden, far more disturbed by the composition of "The Rugger Match" than by the decomposition of contemporary reputations and claims. Mr. Squire, it seems to me, in the period of Rupert Brooke, Flecker, and the earlier de la Mare and Davies, was quite definitely entitled to a place by such poems as "Harlequin" and "The Moon." And not only that. As a satirist he promised to take very high rank indeed, though he has not yet cared to claim the chair between Belloc and Chesterton left vacant for him. It was not his fault, if, as the ultimate darkness quenched star after star, his became the dominant luminary in the impoverished sky. Nor did he in fact step into the dead men's flying shoes. He stuck manfully to his own, until he let himself be swept into the marshes of Free Verse. And as long as he claimed only the winged feet of Mercury, and did not aspire to other pinions, he was in my view justified of verse, and verse of him. He was in the tradition, and was not afraid of it, and his courage had its reward.

Humbert Wolfe. *Crit.* Jan., 1926, p. 596

. . . It is surprising to find that he died only two years ago. He writes out of the late Victorian tradition lingering on, inept and genteely Epicurean, into the time of Rupert Brooke. John Betjeman in his introduction, a model of diffidence, wisely makes few claims for him as a poet. "This book displays the things Jack Squire held dear—his friends, his children, his native Devon, his dogs and English life and scenery in the country and London." One may be excused, perhaps, for not feeling over-excited by such a range of interests. Moreover the style of the poems is painfully dated. . . . However, the book is instructive, if for no other reason, in that the style, which appears so transparently bad to us today, was fashionable and could still be taken seriously thirty or forty years ago. It is no worse than most of the writing that appeared in *Poetry London* during the forties; and there are fashionable styles around now that are equally bad. But most of us do not see through fashionable styles until the fashion that bred them no longer exists. [*Collected Poems*]

Thom Gunn. Poetry. Jan., 1961, pp. 260–61

STANDISH, ROBERT (1898–)

In a recent review I attacked sociological novels on the grounds that the information could be better and more briefly imparted in pamphlet form. Mr. Standish compels a revision of that judgment. . . .

My ignorance of Japan makes it impossible to vouch for the accuracy of Mr. Standish's picture [*The Three Bamboos*] but I can vouch for the conviction which it carries.

The book traces four generations of a Samurai family, from Commodore Perry's first expedition to Japan in 1853 to the aerial attack on Pearl Harbour. With an odious logic the whole psychological and economic development of the country is unrolled. . . . It is impossible to see how Mr. Standish could have told us so much in any other form, and he avoids the irritation of unnecessary plot and laborious psychology. This is a frankly two-dimensional picture of a people and period which are of absorbing topical interest.

Philip Toynbee. NSN. Aug. 1, 1942, p. 80

Mr. Standish has more than once in the past turned his knowledge of Japan and Japanese to excellent popular advantage. Never a very stylish or individual writer, he has deserved attention for what he had to say if not for his way of saying it. *A Worthy Man,* however, is a toothache of a book. The setting of a Chinese treaty port on the Yangtse is perfunctory, the story is crude and sentimental, and I wince at the memory—the telling is a quite excruciating proliferation of *clichés.*

R. D. Charques. Spec. Aug. 8, 1952, p. 198

Portraying the once-glamorous life of Occidentals on the China coast, this novel [*Gentlemen of China*] focuses on Shanghai twenty years ago. The well-documented narrative winds, with nostalgic interest, along such crowded thoroughfares as The Bund and Nanking, Bubbley Well and North Szechuan Roads, past the Astor House, the British Consulate and the Customs Building, over the Whangpoo River, Sonchow Creek and the Grand Canal.

Mr. Standish achieves his effects through an approach which, although fictional, seems the most discerning this reader has ever encountered in his work so far. It's almost as if the author had taken his text from the seventh page of the first chapter of his own writing and then preached an admirably perceptive sermon on the basic reason for the present misunderstanding between this country and China.

Henry Cavendish. *NYT*. March 1, 1953, p. 4

STANFORD, DEREK (1918–   )

He treats of ten young poets in clear and sober fashion [*The Freedom of Poetry*], attaining a synthesis for each by the critic's usual method of selecting quotations suitable for his purpose, and building them up methodically until a clear picture of the poet and his work emerges. He makes a very fair assortment of some—notably Gascoyne, Keyes, Norman Nicholson, and Ruthven Todd—but he also writes in a major key about some very minor poets. His persuasiveness cannot be denied, but when I checked up some of the quotations in relation to their context, I gained a suspicion of special pleading. It seems to me that although he had been at great pains to emphasize the admitted and half-hidden excellences of Nicholas Moore, he damaged his case by being oblivious of his striking weaknesses. Moore has more desert than oasis; is more interested in himself than poetry. . . .

I do not suggest that any of the ten poets Derek Stanford explains are unworthy of attention; only that the book is premature—too premature to be helpful to any but the poets themselves and their immediate acquaintance. The method and care which Middleton Murry gave to his studies of Keats, when used by Mr. Stanford to illuminate and illustrate his selected poets, tends to mesmerize the reader into accepting his conclusions regarding their value and validity. Francis Scarfe's more faulty but less pretentious *Auden and After* is in my opinion a more useful handbook.

Denis Botterill. *LL*. Feb., 1949, pp. 115–16

Mr. Stanford believes that from the beginning the work of Christopher Fry has been largely subjected to critical misinterpretation, and I agree with him. . . . For this reason, the very thorough examination which he has made of the poet's work [*Christopher Fry*] is timely. He has grasped, as few other critics have done, the paradoxical seriousness of purpose in Christopher Fry's comedy, his intensely interesting philosophical attitude and the deliberate and skillful craftsmanship which lie beneath the apparently effortless glitter. It is only a pity that, with the perception he shows in this book, his presentation should be so very earnest—almost, in places, dull. There is hardly a smile, hardly a change of note in the monotonous voice. A dash of Tynan would have worked wonders. For all that, Mr. Stanford has many penetrating things to say, and he is especially acute in his analysis of Christopher Fry's individual brand of metaphysics, his "emotional apprehension of thought."

John Guest. Spec. July 13, 1951, p. 71

Any book published on Thomas at this time is bound to be regarded with some suspicion. Mr. Stanford's [*Dylan Thomas*], however, is a serious work of criticism, an honest attempt to come to terms with his subject. He is not at all an undiscriminating admirer. . . . But his tone is always modest and his judgments tentative. His book needs to be read with the poems themselves at the reader's elbow—that is the index of its value. . . .

Mr. Stanford is not a particularly felicitous writer: his book shows some signs of hasty composition, and some of his references are not quite comprehensible—the parallel he seeks to make between Thomas and Gray seems especially far-fetched. . . . All the same, as an interim report on Thomas's work, his book has value.

NSN. Jan. 15, 1955, p. 82

STARK, FREYA (1893–   )

Fourteen years ago Freya Stark wrote a book called *The Valleys of the Assassins,* which seemed to me then and still seems one of the rare and lovely travel books fortuitously thrown up from time to time by professional travellers, to take their place in the stream of English literature. . . .

Perseus in the Wind is the plump fruit now hanging on the boughs after the probationary blossom of her early experience. It should have been easy to foresee that if she could already write in those terms in 1934, by 1948 she would still be writing in the same strain. . . . Miss

Stark is a serious person, and these essays must represent the philosophy she has worked out for herself after years of dangerous and adventurous living. Whether she has commanded happiness is only for herself to say; beauty she has recognized to the point, I should judge, of poignant pain; death she has valued at its proper estimate; enjoyment has always been richly hers; and as for the conquest of fear—well, that, like happiness, must remain for her to say. The reader has no business to pry into such private things; and Freya Stark is not only a serious person but is also a private person, whose last recesses of secrecy demand respect. . . .

These essays, then, must stand for the summing-up of a life's creed worked out in lonely and often perilous places. They reflect a fundamental optimism, if by optimism we mean a belief in all which is generous, beautiful, permanent and true, "such delicate goods as justice, love and honour, courtesy, and indeed all the things we care for."

V. Sackville-West. *Spec.* Nov. 26, 1948, p. 704

She has given much pleasure to many people. She has scholarship enough to give some plausible reason for venturing into places so remote that even the R.A.F. has been put to some trouble to extricate her; she has communicated her enthusiasm for such places with marked success—but one has always feared her awful promise to strangle a book with fine writing. On the whole her travel books escape with no worse injury than a wry neck. What happens when she tackles a more tractable *genre* is all too sadly evident in her new book.

Perseus in the Wind is a volume of twenty essays in which Miss Stark gives her reflections on such subjects as Service, Happiness, Education, Beauty, Death, Memory, Love, Sorrow, and Courage. It has to be confessed that her bearing in the presence of these abstractions is irreproachable; indeed, it is frequently admirable. But it is hardly original. . . . We could accept these reflections in the spirit with which they were offered (for Miss Stark modestly disclaims all intention of being original) were it not that she smothers most simple statements with figurative language. . . .

P. H. Newby. *NSN.* Jan. 1, 1949, p. 17

Miss Freya Stark's writing seems to me wholly admirable; and so are her aims, her side-shows and her digressions. "Curiosity led me," she states, "pure, disinterested curiosity," and she adds that "if we are to criticise the British for anything, as we cannot get out of the habit of doing, even now that we are poor—it would be for lack of this virtue." Fortunately Miss Stark has always possessed the virtue in full measure, and one is glad to note her pronouncement that "curiosity ought to increase as one gets older."

Certainly in this new book [*Ionia: a Quest*] she has chosen a theme worthy of her own virtues and abilities. For the coast-line of Ionia is, as it were, the birthplace of curiosity. . . .

It shall be said that whether Miss Stark is looking for history or not, she is constantly looking at it, constantly plunging into it with the zest of a diver, and emerging with rare finds which she displays or strings together in an admirable pattern and in accordance with her "accuracy of a different mood." The severest professional historian may well be delighted at and even instructed by her manner of discovery and presentation, however much he may sometimes be shocked by her rapid generalisations. These are always forceful and fresh, like the rest of the writing, and may appear at any time. . . .

To have brought into clear light with love and knowledge, so much of what might have faded, to have so insisted on the concrete reality of what is immortal and with an accurate style to have transmitted to others, in detail and extent, the rarity of her own fine experience—these are great achievements, and many other readers besides myself will be grateful to Miss Stark for what she has accomplished.

Rex Warner. *Spec.* Nov. 12, 1954, pp. 583–84

"This book" [*The Lycian Shore*], she says, "lays no claim to learning, but roams through space and time as books of travel should do." The reader may fairly complain that it devotes rather too much length to learning and does not roam through space or time half enough. In the case of so eminent and well-loved a writer of travel books, such a complaint would be based only on the excellence of her past achievement, and disappointment is no more than relative. It is what is missing that disappoints, not what is here; and perhaps what is most obviously missing is sympathy with her subject. Miss Stark does not hold the Turks in the same affection as she does the Arabs and Persians; and if, like other Britons, at heart she prefers the Greeks, like other Britons she is not going to say so.

C. M. Woodhouse. *TT*. May 12, 1956, p. 557

STEPHENS, JAMES (1882–1950)

There are poets who cannot write with half their being, and who must write with their whole being, and they bring their poor relation, the body, with them wherever they go, and are not ashamed of it. They are not at warfare with the spirit, but have a kind of instinct that the clan of human powers ought to cling together as one family. . . . James

Stephens, as he chanted his *Insurrections,* sang with his whole being. Let no one say I am comparing him with Shakespeare. . . . But how refreshing it was to find somebody who was a poet without a formula, who did not ransack dictionaries for dead words, as Rossetti did to get living speech, whose natural passions declared themselves without the least idea that they ought to be ashamed of themselves, or be thrice refined in the crucible by the careful alchemist before they could appear in the drawing-room. . . .

We have a second volume of poetry from James Stephens, *The Hill of Vision.* He has climbed a hill, indeed, but has found cross-roads there leading in many directions, and seems to be a little perplexed whether the storm of things was his destiny after all. . . .

The Hill of Vision is a very unequal book. There are many verses full of power, which move with the free easy motion of the literary athlete. Others betray awkwardness, and stumble as if the writer had stepped too suddenly into the sunlight of his power, and was dazed and bewildered. There is some diffusion of his faculties in what I feel are byways of his mind, but the main current of his energies will, I am convinced, urge him on to his inevitable portrayal of humanity. With writers like Synge and Stephens, the Celtic imagination is leaving its Tienanoges, its Ildathachs, its Many Coloured Lands and impersonal moods, and is coming down to earth intent on vigorous life and individual humanity.

G. W. Russell. *Imaginations and Reveries*
(Dublin, Maunsel, 1915), pp. 35–36, 41–43

Mr. James Stephens was not born of woman, nor did he "just grow" as Topsy did. He descended upon this world, completely adult, exactly as the angels in *The Demi-Gods* descended on the hill where Patsy McCann and his daughter Mary found them. I have heard and I believe it to be true, that Mr. Stephens (it seems ridiculous to call an angel *Mister!*) was found by AE the great Irish poet and greater Irish man, clinging to the branches of a tree in Stephen's Green, Dublin. AE instantly hauled him off his perch (for he is very familiar in his manner with angels and the like) and informed him that the only occupation fit for a heavenly being was that of a lecturer on Cooperation under the director of the Irish Agricultural Organisation Society; and people say that Stephens was so scared by this statement that he wrote two books in his hurry and alarm and then bolted to Paris where he now sits congratulating himself on his escape from affairs. But that was a mistake. In running away from AE, he also ran away from Ireland.

And let this be noted: the two books which he wrote in Ireland are better than the two books he wrote in France. I will not deny that *Here*

Are Ladies and *The Demi-Gods* are full of good stuff; indeed I will affirm that they are; but they are without that salty, Irish quality which makes *The Charwoman's Daughter* and *The Crock of Gold* such tasty reading. One feels that the angel, unaware of sex when he made these two books, in the sense that the neurotic novelists are aware of it, had become very conscious by the time he reaches *Here Are Ladies* and *The Demi-Gods* that "male and female created He them." One feels too when one reads *The Charwoman's Daughter* and *The Crock of Gold* that the angel, in his flight to Stephen's Green, contrived to see the whole of Ireland very clearly, but when one reads the later books one feels that wingless, he is now squatting on the pavement in front of a Parisian cafe looking at Ireland through liqueur glasses. And Paris is the very devil of a place for an Irishman to live in. . . .

In addition to the four prose works named above, Mr. Stephens has written two volumes of poems: *Insurrections* and *The Hill of Vision*. They are full of that roaring rebellion against set things which is in everything that he writes, which, indeed, makes his tendency to moralise all the more remarkable. Perhaps the most considerable of his poems is "The Lonely God," a piece which is full of the beauty of the disconsolate. It is when one reads "The Lonely God" and *The Charwoman's Daughter* that one realises how dreadful a thing it was for Mr. Stephens to fly to France, and how urgent a thing it is that he should instantly return to Ireland. If Puck must preach to the multitude, let him take his pack and go tramping the roads in Donegal and Connacht and the Middle West. AE's instinct was right: Mr. Stephens can expend his preacher's energy in propagating the principle of cooperation among the Irish peasants; and having rid himself of rhetoric in this fashion, he can settle down in comfort to write the fine stuff with which he began his career as a writer. He may be certain that that is the only stuff his admirers desire from him.

St. John G. Ervine. *BkmL*. April, 1915, pp. 5–6

Kindness and good humor . . . are the essence of James Stephens. The whole man is in his writings, from the impish irreverence of *Insurrections* to the haunting pathos of *Reincarnations* with all the expense of child-like fancy in *The Charwoman's Daughter* and the grotesque laughter of *The Crock of Gold* between. Pity and suffering, too, have gone into the making of him, and have sharpened that uncanny faculty of his, which enables him to establish himself on the friendliest terms with dumb animals, whose thoughts he can record with a whimsical tenderness. His soft brown eyes are lit at once by the highest intelligence and by that profound, inarticulate love, which none ever sees unmoved, in the eyes of the finest animals. This gnome, this elfin wit, the James

Stephens of quips and fancies that bubble into laughter, of sensitive emotions that soar into prose and poetry of freshest beauty, is the James Stephens, above all, who has a fine soul.

Ernest Boyd. Portraits Real and Imaginary
(N.Y., George H. Doran Co., 1924), p. 254

The poetic genius of James Stephens has won recognition slowly but it was never better founded than during the past two years in America. His wonderful aptitude for prose-romance tends to distract attention from his no less important poetic gifts. Nobody has ever written simpler poetry. His work may be said scarcely to deal with ideas at all. A bird's cry, the cry of a snared rabbit and the vital, overwhelming desire to release it, the crooked windings of a goat-path on the side of a hill—these and such as these are his themes. He seeks only to convey the feeling of an experience, never to describe it in any realistic sense. And, rarest of attributes among the serious poets of today, he has a certain tint of humor that comes to glitter on the edges of his happier moods with such a brightness as belongs only to poetry. . . .

Stephens has definite limitations, but they are the limitations of a fairy. He is an elf among the modern poets and no line that he has written could discredit the art of Shakespeare himself.

Edward Davison. EJ. May, 1926, pp. 334–36

Etched in Moonlight is a volume of short stories told in a delicate, sometimes rather affected style. They at once obtain the hearing which anything so well written must procure, and reveal a tragic insight into life which needs only the slightest of material to obtain its effects. Mr. Stephens seems trying to find the lowest percentage of spirit and curiosity with which a man can live and seems appalled by the degradations he has discovered. . . . All the stories are good, some rather in the manner of *Celibate Lives,* others more purely Celtic pieces of poetic imagery. The style is lyric and precise, and admirably suited for this kind of story.

Cyril Connolly. NS. March 17, 1928, p. 730

STERN, G. B. (1890–   )

Larry Munro is for other readers. Is this Miss G. B. Stern the author of *Children of No Man's Land?* In that novel she packed so many talents that it would not hold together; it flew apart and was all brilliant pieces, but in this! Larry Munro, we repeat, and once again Larry Munro. That is all there is to be said for it. Miss Stern herself strings a quality of more or less bright little beads in between, but they are scarcely visible for the flashing, all-a-quivering Larry Munros of which her claim is composed. It is not stupid—it is silly; not clever—but bright; and it is so sentimental that it makes the reader hang his head.

K[athleen] M[ansfield]. *Ath*. Oct. 8, 1920, p. 472

Miss Stern has one of the queerest talents among contemporary novelists, for she lives by choice on a mental desert rich in natural beauties but unvisited by culture. One can imagine her sitting up among the palm branches, shamelessly clad only in the bright hibiscus flowers of her innate gifts, dropping cocoanuts on the heads of a party of missionaries from the *Times Literary Supplement* and the *London Mercury*, who had landed to try and get her to listen to the good news about Flaubert. She simply does care for any of the literary conventions of to-day. Now, that is very unusual. . . . That is why she makes no attempt to stamp *The Room* with what are recognised to-day as the hallmarks of a good book. She writes jauntily; anybody who hastily turned over the leaves might jump to the conclusion that here was a respectable artisan of the Berta Ruck type. . . . But the literary snob would lose a good deal. For *The Room* is a very rich and jolly book. It shows Miss Stern's power of creating real people at its very best.

Rebecca West. *NS*. April 1, 1922, p. 734

It is possible sometimes to wish that Miss Stern had a little less cleverness, a little less talent for light and amusing flippancy. She has other qualities which these sometimes obscure. She draws character originally and she really does see into the minds of her persons. But at the same time she has a light and facile pen and a distinct gift for making amusing phrases. It is a pity indeed that one side of her should seem to interfere with the other. But so it is. Her natural talent for psychology really ought to be developed even at the expense of her ability in inventing conversations and scenes which are as unsubstantial, though they are as pleasant, as meringues.

Edward Shanks. *LM*. May, 1922, p. 97

With her usual sureness of touch, her capacity for communicating experience, and her wide cosmopolitan outlook, this author presents not only the intriguing Toni Rakonitz in her relations with her English husband, Giles Stoddard, but the whole Rakonitz clan in their relations with each other. . . . The book [*A Deputy Was King*], indeed, may be said to represent Europe through the medium of this family, which, to a certain extent, at least, is chameleon-like in its adaptation to environment. . . . As for the odd entanglements of the central married couple curiously innocent as entanglements go, they are as nothing against the intricate tribal ramifications which Miss Stern has known how to weave into a pattern of living reality.

J. A. T. Lloyd. *FR.* May, 1927, p. 718

There have been many actresses among the lively characters with whom Miss Stern has beguiled her admirers. She catches their glamour and their fallibility, the hard work in the glare of the footlights and their gay fascination in private life as few contemporary novelists have done. In *The Donkey Shoe* she adds to her theatrical gallery the entrancing Jessica Marwood. . . .

G. B. Stern has never written and surely never intended to write profound novels; but she has never failed to entertain. If the peculiar enchantment of the actresses she writes about is convincing, her sympathetic portraits of the young are just as persuasive. It is the ability to present the beguiling and baffled Jessica with as much understanding as she does the unhappy Damaris [Jessica's daughter] which puts on this latest of her novels Miss Stern's own inimitable stamp.

Pamela Taylor. *Sat.* June 7, 1952, p. 23

Wooden is the last word for G. B. Stern, an elastic stylist if ever there was one. I remember at an early age being stunned into admiration of her nerve for daring to write something as solemn as a book in a style of tea-party gossip. On and on she goes—interjections, asides, explosions, slang, an overwhelming gush of reminiscence, anecdote, nonsense and chit-chat about nothing in particular, but all extremely well-done. She is, stylistically, what used to be called "a rattle," and rather refreshing it is, among so many prudent stylists, to meet someone as exuberantly verbose. But what is it all *about?* Well, *For All We Know* (a suitably airy title) is about one of those brilliant, fictional families with ramifications so complex that even with a family tree at the beginning you can hardly tell by the end exactly who is whose great-aunt or grandmother or second cousin. But it doesn't really matter; what does is the frightful, fascinating buoyancy of plot, characters, conversations, and, of course, plain narrative. It struck me as wildly untrue to life, but so have a lot of better books—and very agreeably so, if you are a fast reader and can speed up into the spirit of the thing.

Isabel Quigley. *Spec.* Jan. 13, 1956, p. 58

STRACHEY, LYTTON (1880–1932)

In *Eminent Victorians* Mr. Strachey did two things for biography: he humanized it by irony, he gave it form. He went out in search not of great figures and noble characters, but of human nature, and he always found it. Having found it, he set it out in his own terms. All his characters passed through his eighteenth century work shop, and emerged in the ironically appropriate costumes he had devised for them. They emerged, if not in their own shape, then in some shape which revealed it.

Impartiality is one of Mr. Strachey's chief virtues. Every stroke of irony in his books is weighed not for its effectiveness but for its justice; and accordingly every stroke tells. He conventionalizes his themes, certainly; he expresses them in terms of his eighteenth-century intellect and his modern imagination; but he does not falsify them. He gains more in effect by ignoring an obvious advantage than Mr. Philip Guedalla, for example, gains by seizing it. He has the eighteenth-century instinct for the judgment which can be reasonably defended, and the eighteenth-century knowledge that an inessential piece of cleverness is always foolish, for it will be found out. A witty writer, there is very little of his wit that can be detached without detaching a valuable piece of characterization or injuring a perfectly serious judgment.

He seems at first glance to be completely outside the current of modern literature; and a clever writer calls him a Voltaire who has reached the age of two hundred odd years. There is little resemblance between the author of *Queen Victoria* and the author of *La Pucelle*. Mr. Strachey's sensibility is modern; his imagination is romantic; only by his cool rationality does he belong to the eighteenth century. His *Cardinal Manning* and *Queen Victoria* would have appeared very novel if not quite incomprehensible to Dr. Johnson; their sceptical imagination and compassionate irony would have disturbed the lexicographer's mind. The truth is that Mr. Strachey has a very modern temperament and sensibility, and that he would be more completely at a loss than almost any other writer if he were transported into the eighteenth century. If he appears out of place in our time it is not because his intelligence is unmodern; it is because his temperament is unique. He is an inimitable writer, but he belongs as certainly to this age as Lamb did to his.

Edwin Muir. *Transition* (N.Y., Viking, 1926), pp. 119–20, 126–27

Throughout the sketch ["Florence Nightingale" in *Eminent Victorians*], his imaginative incidents and touches all go to heighten the portrait, as for the purposes of popular and entertaining biography it has been recreated. The woman who has been made a plaster saint is to be shown, without regard to mere evidence, as possessed by a demon of rage and fury, which is done partly by rewriting passages of the original which are not spicy enough. Sir Edward Cook's *Life* disposed of the mythical figure and left in its place a very human personality. But the *Life* was not for the many, and Mr. Strachey could not resist the temptation to go a step further. What fun, he seems to have said to himself, to turn the saint into a fiend! Such an attempt, one would suppose, might overreach itself, but he has made it. This is Mr. Strachey's "angle of view." Is the result biography?

Rosalind Nash. *NC*. Feb., 1928, p. 265

We may admit that the whole of modern biography is in this beautiful economy attained by silent suppression here and there, "manipulations" reduced to a minimum. But let the biographer stick to his last and, above all, make no concession to pedantry. At the end of *Elizabeth and Essex* there is a bibliography which is disturbing to the creeping critic—the pedant—who reads such things; for it omits at least five of the most important sources for the life of Essex. But, doubtless, with the general reader *Elizabeth and Essex* will enhance Mr. Lytton Strachey's great reputation.

G. B. Harrison. *Spec.* Nov. 24, 1928, p. 777

The figure of Lytton Strachey is so important a figure in the history of biography that it compels a pause. For his three famous books, *Eminent Victorians, Queen Victoria,* and *Elizabeth and Essex,* are of a stature to show both what biography can do and what biography cannot do. Thus they suggest many possible answers to the question whether biography is an art, and if not why it fails.

Lytton Strachey came to birth as an author at a lucky moment. In 1918, when he made his first attempt, biography, with its new liberties, was a form that offered great attractions. To a writer like himself, who had wished to write poetry or plays but was doubtful of his creative power, biography seemed to offer a promising alternative. For at last it was possible to tell the truth about the dead; and the Victorian age was rich in remarkable figures many of whom had been grossly deformed by the effigies that had been plastered over them. To recreate them, to show them as they really were, was a task that called for gifts analogous to the poet's or the novelist's, yet did not ask that inventive power in which he found himself lacking.

It was well worth trying. And the anger and the interest that his short studies of Eminent Victorians aroused showed that he was able to make Manning, Florence Nightingale, Gordon, and the rest live as they had not lived since they were actually in the flesh. Once more they were the centre of a buzz of discussion. Did Gordon really drink, or was that an invention? Had Florence Nightingale received the Order of Merit in her bedroom or in her sitting room? He stirred the public, even though a European war was raging, to an astonishing interest in such minute matters. Anger and laughter mixed; and editions multiplied.

But these were short studies with something of the overemphasis and the foreshortening of caricatures. In the lives of the two great Queens, Elizabeth and Victoria, he attempted a far more ambitious task. Biography had never had a fairer chance of showing what it could do. For it was now being put to the test by a writer who was capable of making use of all the liberties that biography had won; he was fearless; he had proved his brilliance; and he had learned his job. The result throws great light upon the nature of biography. For who can doubt after reading the two books again, one after the other, that the *Victoria* is a triumphant success, and that the *Elizabeth* by comparison is a failure? But it seems too, as we compare them, that it was not Lytton Strachey who failed; it was the art of biography. In the *Victoria* he treated biography as an art; he flouted its limitations.

Virginia Woolf. *At.* April, 1939, p. 507

Strachey's looks are important because this idiosyncrasy of person takes its final colour from an idiosyncrasy of mind. Neither is likely to recur; and if today, fifteen years after his death, there seems no general disposition to regret this, it may be due in part to his intermediary station, midway between history and art. We know what to expect when the great historians of the nineteenth century become themselves a part of history. Their rendezvous is with Dr. G. P. Gooch, whose hand, like that of a country grocer, is never far from his scales and balances. Strachey came too late for this. He could not even be said to have closed or perhaps opened) the age of the amateur, since J. A. Froude had won some such title nearly fifty years earlier; and though he was, as much as Gibbon or Grote, a dedicated professional, he might not at first have appeared in this light. His choice of sources, for instance, could not have pleased the tribunal. Where Stubbs had spent his school holidays deciphering rolls in the Court House at Knaresborough, Strachey made notes from Greville and de Catt; where Motley had toiled among "black-letter folios in half a dozen languages, dark, grimy and cheerless as coal-pits," Strachey was confessedly, indeed exultantly happier with Sainte-Beuve and Saint-Simon. Then again, there would have emerged a grave conflict of ultimate intentions. Ever since Gibbon launched his last impieties from the terraces of Lausanne, English historians have striven to put things back as they had been before. In 1866 Stubbs had proclaimed that "the study of modern history is, next to theology itself, the most thoroughly religious training the mind can receive." Religion appeared to Strachey in the guise of a fantastic and comical deformity, and he opposed to it a lucid pessimism, an undistressed acceptance of what, in his first published essay, he called "the whole dismal fatality of things." Agnostics of the previous generation had bequeathed to the squares of Bloomsbury a legacy of honest and tormented doubt from which these plane-shaded retreats have still to recover; but one could say of Lytton Strachey what a French critic has written of Bayle—"Il n'accuse pas Dieu; il l'embarrasse." . . .

History, for Lytton Strachey, was a series of *tête-à-têtes* with chosen persons—a thing not so much written as talked over; and from the record of his talks one can picture the outward and inward parts, the hide and the heart, not only of his subjects but also of their interlocutor. Strachey is in fact the great *intimiste* among historians. Other writers have used portraits to give pause to their narratives; but with Strachey the narrative is all portrait, and if we look into the eyes of his Voltaire or, more surprisingly, of his Prince Consort, we seem to see, reflected in their pupils, the gaze of their bland inquisitor. All the other facts of history are dimmed and thrust backward by this intense and continuous scrutiny of individuals. Such was the fixity of his regard that the great public events of history often take at best a tertiary place, . . .

Lytton Strachey set out to remedy the lack, as he saw it, of any English counterpart to the great short biographers of France—"the Fontenelles and Condorcets, with their incomparable *éloges,* compressing into a few shining pages the manifold existences of men." This he considered "the most delicate and humane of all the branches of the art of writing." While conceding a certain grandeur to this tribute, one must assert that, on the contrary, the art of Fontenelle and Condorcet does find its parallel in English, and that, moreover, Lytton Strachey's work is really not very like the *éloges* to which he has offered so personal a wreath.

John Russell. Hor. Feb., 1947, pp. 92–94

Strachey with his long russet brown beard and his high squeaky voice was certainly the most astonishing of the Bloomsbury group. He combined strikingly their gaiety with their intermittent chilliness. Sometimes he would play childish games . . .; often he would discourse brilliantly and maliciously; at times there was something insidiously suggestive about his giggling manner; at times he would sit in his chair without saying a word to anyone. He was delicate and hypochondriacal. But despite his oddness, his invalidism, his facetiousness, there was a devotion for his friends which commanded their loyalty so much that his death was a greater blow than any other to those who knew him well.

Stephen Spender. PR. Jan., 1949, p. 62

. . . in *The Lives of the Poets* (1906), we are told that "Johnson's aesthetic judgments are almost invariably subtle, or solid, or bold; they have always some good quality to recommend them—except one: they are never right. That is an unfortunate deficiency; but . . ." "Except one"—that is ony admissible as a *constructio ad sensum*. There are two *surprises,* each qualifying what has gone before. This kind of thing is to be found in his writing at all periods. We might even conclude that the whole sentence has the triviality of:

> Men have many faults,
> Women only two;
> Nothing's right they say,
> Nothing's right they do.

were it not for the fact that Strachey's apparently absurd words carry some truth, and pave the way for sound and suggestive criticism.

"The greatest misfortune," he says in the first of the essays just mentioned, "that can happen to a witty man is to be born out of France." His own achievement proves the contrary. His wit has triumphed over the difficulties of the English language and enabled him in this country to become supreme in his own kind. Of course he was helped by steeping himself in French literature. The epigrammatic style which he discovered in such different writers as La Rochefoucauld, Pascal and Voltaire was congenial to his fastidious and ironic mind and no doubt helped to mould his own. He admired what was "polished, pregnant, and concise." The qualities of "lucidity, balance, precision" which he finds in Gibbon were among the virtues of eighteenth-century French prose, and the fact that they were shared by many English writers in the eighteenth century is one of the things that draw him to the England of Pope and Swift and Hume. But language, literature, style are not suspended in the void; they spring out of or fit themselves to a certain kind of life, a mode of thought, a prevailing sentiment or emotion; and Strachey is drawn to the literature of both England and France in the eighteenth century because the habits of that age attract him. . . . The eighteenth century, on its more decorative side, with the elegant conventions which it observed and its unawareness of our more recent conventions—with its personalities, its loves, its scandals, its wit—all of it that has been preserved in poetry and in prose, in letters and diaries, in buildings and in gardens—even grottoes—this was enchanting and nourishing to the spirit of Strachey. But if this is what he shows he liked, what about his dislikes? The essays no less than the biographies leave us in no doubt. "The Age of Victoria was, somehow or other, unaesthetic to its marrow-bones . . . it will never loom through history with the glamour that hangs about the Age of Pericles or the brilliance that sparkles round the eighteenth century." . . .

His air of detachment is only a technical device sometimes but not always employed by him. He admits explicitly that what is written by a historian (the biographer being one kind of historian) is governed always by a "point of view." History, he says in the essay on Gibbon, is not a science; it is an art.

R. A. Scott-James. *Lytton Strachey*
(BC/Longmans, 1955), pp. 12–16

Lytton was a very strange character already when he came up to Cambridge in 1899. There was a mixture of arrogance and diffidence in him. His mind had already formed in a Voltairean mould, and his inclinations, his passions, the framework of his thought belonged to the eighteenth century, and particularly to eighteenth-century France. His body was long, thin, and rather ungainly; all his movements, including his walk, were slow and slightly hesitant—I never remember to have seen him run. When he sat in a chair, he appeared to have tied his body, and particularly his legs, into what I always called a Strachean knot. There was a Strachean voice, common to him and to all his nine brothers and sisters.... It was mainly derived, I think, from the mother and consisted in an unusual stress accent, heavy emphasis on words here and there in a sentence, combined with an unusual tonic accent, so that emphasis and pitch continually changed, often in a kind of syncopated rhythm. It was extremely catching, and most people who saw much of Lytton acquired the Strachey voice and never completely lost it. Lytton himself added another peculiarity to the family cadence. Normally his voice was low and fairly deep, but every now and again it went up into a falsetto, almost a squeak.

This squeak added to the effect of his characteristic style of wit. He was one of the most amusing conversationalists I have ever known. He was not a monologuist or a raconteur. Except when he was with one or a few intimate friends, he did not say very much and his silences were often long. They were often broken by a Strachean witticism, probably a devastating *reductio ad absurdum*—the wit and the devastation owing much to the perfect turn of the sentence and the delicate stiletto stab of the falsetto voice. Many, particularly among the young, as I said, caught his method of talking and ever afterwards spoke in the Strachey voice; so too, many caught his method of thinking and thought ever after with a squeak in their minds. The unwary stranger, seeing Lytton contortedly collapsed in a tangle of his own arms and legs in the depths of an armchair, his eyes gazing in fixed abstraction through his strong glasses on his toes which had corkscrewed themselves up and round to within a foot of his nose, the unwary stranger might and sometimes did dismiss him as a gentle, inarticulate, nervous, awkward intellectual. All these adjectives were correct, but woe betide the man or woman who thought that they were the end of the matter and of Lytton Strachey. I used to tell him that, when he came to see us and we were not alone, I proposed to put a notice on the arm of his chair: BE CARE-FUL, THIS ANIMAL BITES.

The animal bit because, behind the gentleness, the nervousness, and the cynicism, there were very considerable passions. They were the passions of the artist and of the man who is passionately attached to standards of intellectual integrity. This may sound priggish to some people, but no man has ever been less of a prig than he was. He suffered the stupid and stupidity and the philistine and philistinism with unconcealed irritation which might take the form either of the blackest, profoundest silence or of a mordant witticism.

Leonard Woolf, Sowing (N.Y., Harcourt, Brace, 1960), pp. 133–35

STRONG, L. A. G. (1896–1958)

Ambition is a laudable quality in a writer. Yet the first novel that is inspired by big aims is likely to be a less satisfying product in itself than one which attempts no heights or profundities. This statement applies emphatically to *Dewer Rides,* which is remarkably interesting as promise, but very imperfect as fulfillment. Mr. Strong has essayed a novel on the epic scale. A disciple of Thomas Hardy, or perhaps still more of the modern peasant novelists of Scandinavia, he has sought to present the tragic development of a man of the soil against a grim—almost a determining—background of Nature. The scene is a village, representing the last human stronghold, on a wild fringe of Dartmoor, where spring does not triumph until weeks after it has established itself in the valleys, and where every civilizing influence has won a tardy and precarious victory.

.... It is not that Mr. Strong has no sense of character. He has a very true and lively sense of it; he already excels, indeed, in still portraiture. But he cannot make his characters develop. They do not move naturally, but jump violently from one phase to another. If Mr. Strong can overcome this difficulty he should do notably good work. His vision is both large and minute; he conveys atmosphere; and his descriptive gifts are far above the average.

Gilbert Thomas. Spec. June 22, 1929, p. 982

Mr. Strong is in danger of being choked with butter by his critics. And this is a pity. He is a poet with a poet's command of language; as a novelist he is virile as well as sensitive; and it is not improbable that some time in the not distant future he will write a piece of fiction of the first order. When that time comes, the people who are now bellowing about his "genius" will be out of breath. And if not out of breath, they will have found someone else to bellow about. And if they have found no one else, they will certainly have exhausted their vocabulary of laudation. It is a poor look-out for Mr. Strong. I, for one, have too much respect for his rich talent to suppose that he does himself justice in *The Brothers*. . . . If cruelty and violence were the measure of greatness (and they are sometimes accounted so), this book would be a masterpiece. There is, indeed, far more in it than that: some admirable writing, lyrical descriptions of Nature, and good dramatic narrative. But violence (rather than strength) is the keynote. It is less its violence, however, than the casual take-it-or-leave-it manner in which the violence is presented that impairs the story as a work of art. Mr. Strong is at no pains to make incredibilities credible. His people are drawn in the flat: they have little human substance, and all that they do has the air of being forced on them by their author. All that they do, and all that they suffer too. Natural death seems to be almost unknown in the Western Highlands. Mary is murdered; the genial Captain M'Grath is drowned; Ferus drinks himself to death; John is gored by a bull. It is true that the elder Macraes die in their bed, but even two swallows do not make a summer.

Gerald Bullett. *NSN*. Jan. 23, 1932, p. 96

Mr. L. A. G. Strong was born in 1896. He was up at Oxford in 1919. He is therefore contemporary with such Georgian poets as Edmund Blunden, Robert Graves, and Richard Hughes. Unlike these however he did not become generally known until 1929; and then it was his prose, and not his poetry, which brought him before the public eye. Indeed although Mr. Strong began as a poet and still (with increasing maturity) practises that art, it is as a novelist that he has won, on both sides of the Atlantic, his considerable claim to fame. It was perhaps natural that, although last year saw the publication of both *The Garden* and of the *Selected Poems,* it was the former which made the year historic for him, though the latter finally "placed" him for discriminating readers. For he is first of all a poet; and it is the poet in him paradoxically which gives him rank and dignity as a novelist. He does not seem to possess a novelist's innate sense of form or architecture; he is not essentially dramatic; and he is sometimes weak and conventional in his character drawing: his novels live, in fact, mainly by virtue of the quality given them by the poet's seeing eye and the poet's sensitive heart.

C. Henry Warren. *BkmL*. Feb., 1932, p. 266

Having recently read or re-read the whole of Mr. Strong's work I would suggest that there is undoubtedly a mysterious division in him, which is injurious to the dramatic accumulation of power in his novels and destruction of that highly valuable element, the narrator's rightness of manner and attitude. In so far as his novels are nevertheless to be ranked as works of art, though imperfect works of art, his triumphs are due to a poet's keen visualisation and a corresponding verbal skill.

After reading *The Garden* and some of the short stories you get a vision and a feeling for Dublin and the coast, hills and villages near it that seem to satisfy the mind as if the scenes described had been specially visited. The same thing is true of the beautiful scenes from the West Highland Coast of Scotland in *The Jealous Ghost,* and except for a few rather melodramatic touches, it is true of the wild Dartmoor scenery in *Dewer Rides.* No reader of Mr. Strong needs to be told with what relish he records fishing expeditions. He gives you the changing sights and sounds of the sea water, the angler's feelings, and the fish's. You feel the captured conger's teeth, see the glistening white belly, smell the sea-slime, watch the last muscular contortions with pity and fear. . . .

In retrospect I find most suggestive his confession to me about the inspirational phase that precedes the working out of a new novel.

"I see a new novel as a landscape first," he said, "with hills and perhaps a sea-coast and bays and promontories. There are one or two clouds obscuring features of the picture. Presently the clouds begin to clear away, and then I have the main events, represented by the chief landmarks." . . .

Mr. Strong's art as an essayist is most easily seen in some of the tales. Pieces like "Storm," "Travellers" and "The Rook" in *The English Captain* have the very minimum of "story," all depends upon the manner and the style which on such occasions are good enough to dispense with any sort of plot. Only readers whose minds have been poisoned by our popular fiction magazines (which, glory be, are one by one going to rack and ruin) would complain of the author's freedom here. If any cause of complaint against him exists it is only that "and other stories" added to the title of *The English Captain* needs the further phrase "and sketches." His versatility as a tale teller makes Mr. Strong a valuable ally of the modern story as art and an influential enemy of the story as a brand of groceries, to be labelled and ticked off by editors who lack both the intelligence and the energy to think for themselves when considering manuscripts for publication. Keats was described as the poet's poet. Perhaps Mr. Strong may be described as the tale writer's writer. His chief contemporary rival for that distinction is I think Mr. Osbert Sitwell. I assume of course that A. E. Coppard is outside the competition. He stands by himself.

R. L. Mégroz. *DM*. July, 1932, pp. 30–33

L. A. G. Strong's new novel, *Corporal Tune,* is being hailed in London for its great beauty, and it is certainly one of the most sensitive and delicate of all his books. Its theme is simple, the writing exquisite without affectation, the implications innumerable. And at the same time the novel has both perfect detachment and a quite personal intimacy which make it unique.

Mr. Strong, as is known, was very ill some time ago (it is good news that he is now fully recovered); and the tale describes many of the thoughts and feelings of a sick man. But it is, for all that, a work of imagination and the work of a considerable artist.

The chief character is a writer whose wife has died in childbirth; and the writer himself is in reality at the point of death. Accordingly it might be thought that the note of *Corporal Tune* is one of melancholy. This is not the case. There are frets, of course, and discoveries of all sorts of hidden thoughts such as may arise in the mind of a dying man; but the quality of the book lies in its calm understandings and its poetic interpretations of the soul of man.

A very good book, which seems slight at first reading and grows in strength as one remembers it. Not for everybody, but for those to whom beauty in a novel—limpid beauty, for there is nothing obscure or affected in Mr. Strong's outlook—is a delicious experience.

Frank Swinnerton. *Chicago Daily Tribune.*
July 28, 1934, p. 12

With an armchair for each and teacup a-tinkle, Mr. Strong gathers his guests close about him for a chat on "the drama." The time is certainly late afternoon. Beginning impressively but somewhat frighteningly with the sentence "In the Beginning Was The Word," he hustles on to a safer quotation "All the World's a Stage." His pinkie lifted, Mr. Strong confidentially tells his companions why he has been courageous enough to witness several hundred stage productions, fifty of them by Shakespeare, and why his life has grown richer and fuller as a result. . . .

So Mr. Strong chats on with his friends (never failing to infuse a *soupçon* of learning when the moment is auspicious), the tea grows cold, and everyone yawns to leave. . . .

So Mr. Strong's little volume, with all its baggage of good intentions, has few new things to tell the old audiences. It is predictable that the number of new audiences to whom it can tell old things will be rather below estimate [*Common Sense About Drama*].

Walt Crane. *TA.* Nov., 1937, p. 906

Of the welter of words that have been published about James Joyce and his life's work, there has been no study more informative, more lucid and more intelligent than *The Sacred River*. Although Mr. Strong appears not to have known Joyce personally, nevertheless as a judge of his production, he is probably better qualified than any other writer who has so far attempted to plumb the depths and obscurities of *Ulysses* and *Finnegans Wake*. Of the eight main reasons that Mr. Strong gives for adding to the mass already written about Joyce, three would seem to be of outstanding importance. First, he is himself an Irish poet and novelist who knew Dublin when and after Joyce knew it; second, he has always taken a technical interest in singing and in singers. As the biographer of John McCormack, with whom Joyce once competed in a concert, Strong believes that "no one can get the full sense of Joyce's phrasing who has not studied to sing a legato phrase." Third, one of Mr. Strong's main interests for many years has been the theory and practice of several distinguished psychologists, including, of course, Freud and Jung.

James Stern. NYHT. April 15, 1951, p. 4

STUART, FRANCIS (1902–   )

Mr. Francis Stuart's *Glory,* which begins as a novel in its scene laid in Ireland, transports us, as it continues, to the other side of the world and to the sphere of romantic allegory as well. The Irish have been compared to the Russians, and Mr. Stuart's presentation of them will cause the comparison to be made again; his characters, in their charm and fickleness, seem distantly related to the characters of Chekhov, and they tend to live largely in their imaginations. . . . Perhaps Mr. Stuart himself is "one of the legion of outcasts of the machine-age, of romanticists," of those who seek to avoid becoming "obsessed by flesh and steel." Whether there is any salvation for the world or not, it is comforting to think of all those whose worldly failure implies a spiritual success, those who, like these characters of Mr. Stuart's, . . . may be bankrupts and wasters and nobodies and daydreamers, but are capable of heroic devotions. They are the salt of the earth, and we owe gratitude to those who can recognize their savour.

William Plomer. Spec. Sept. 1, 1933, p. 292

Mr. Francis Stuart is a novelist, and able to find a philosophical justification for his temperament, but possessed by the . . . romantic passion for adventure. . . . But Mr. Stuart's great fastidiousness gives higher value to his experiences.

Racing, flying, love-making, and the religious emotion are in his eyes among the chief "things to live for." His book [*Things to Live For*] ends with him at Lourdes, tending the dying and reading the list of starters in the next day's Derby. "How good life is," he cries, "How good in its prodigality and exuberance so that in the midst of suffering and death there are also great games." He is a good Catholic, but his scale of values is more romantic than Catholicism. It is the complete abandonment of St. Thérèse de Lisieux that he admires, as he might admire the sensuality of an adulteress or the virtuosity of Steve Donoghue. The importance of an act lies in the intensity behind it rather than in the object in front of it. Such self-consciousness in the pursuit of the various orders of ecstasy may seem too intentional and antagonise some readers. And Mr. Stuart in turn would probably despise some of the persons I most admire as bloodless intellectuals. For it is usual for romantics to ignore the wild exhilaration to be derived from the intellect when abandoning every interest it fights its way to the discovery and exploration of the truth.

Raymond Mortimer. *NSN*. Oct. 20, 1934, pp. 558–60

The three "younger hopes" of Irish literature are the novelists Seán O'Faoláin, Frank O'Connor, and Francis Stuart. Whatever their ranks, O'Faoláin and O'Connor are serious writers, but how Stuart crept in is difficult to say. Presumably it was due to Yeats's ridiculously high estimate of his work (presumably due, in turn, to Mr. Stuart's liberal use, in and out of quotation marks, of Yeats's poetry). Francis Stuart has made no contribution to the literature of that kind of struggle I am concerned with—having risen far above such trivialities—but his contribution to the cess-pool of "mystical" messiness is far from inconsiderable. *Try the Sky* (in the foreword to which Compton MacKenzie writes, "I suggest that Francis Stuart has a message for the modern world of infinitely greater importance than anything offered by D. H. Lawrence") is really the maximum mush, all about Old Mother Earth, a continental quasi-Goddess (very amoral, very romantic), and a quasi-Indian Princess called Buttercup, who curiously enough is half a beast (see Lawrence) and half a wave (see Yeats). I hasten to mention that *Try the Sky* is in no way about Ireland or the Irish (except that the "narrator" of the story happens to be an Irish youth who had been better employed earthing-up his potatoes). But Stuart's well-known "Irish" novel, *The White Hare*—a revolting mixture of treacle and sherbet, something like Yeats's Noble Women posing for a psychoanalyst—is only a little less nauseating.

D. J. Enright. *Scy*. Spring, 1943, p. 184

Mr. Stuart is an Irishman who spent World War II teaching at the University of Berlin. The destruction he saw there has evidently been etched in vitriol on his mind and heart. Unfortunately his attempts to perform a kind of Irish Dostoievsky have produced a cross between D. H. Lawrence and Hermann Hesse [*Redemption*].

Anne Fremantle. *NYT*. Jan. 21, 1951, p. 21

SUTRO, ALFRED (1863–1933)

Considered in the clear light of criticism, *The Builder of Bridges,* by Mr. Alfred Sutro, is seen to be the best of all his plays—better even than that powerful and popular work, *The Walls of Jericho*. The present piece is strong in story, well-studied and consistent in characterization, neat and firm in structure, and written in dialogue that is fluent, graceful, and often deft and witty. As a representation of life, it has the ring of reality; and as an instance of theatric art, it is an admirable technical achievement, and may be recommended heartily to students of the stage. Yet it was reviewed adversely by nearly all the newspapers of New York, and has also failed to make money with the public.

Clayton Hamilton. *Forum*. Dec., 1909, p. 576

Sutro has a sense of the stage, but very little of life. He is bound by the traditions. He must have stock figures, stock plots. He is clever at manipulation. He has nothing to say that matters, but his stagecraft is good. He entertains, but leaves no permanent impression on the mind.

He represents, best of all contemporary writers, what is bound to happen when you compel men of intelligence and ideas to limit their output to inconsequential and wholly artificial themes. Mr. Sutro has wit; he appears also to have sufficient wits to go with the stream and give the actor-managers what they think the public likes.

S. P. B. Mais. *Some Modern Authors* (Grant Richards, 1923), p. 324

Mr. Sutro has not had a very good Press for his *Living Together*. All the brilliant old men have dubbed him out of date. Mr. Sutro, in trying to be advanced, has not been nearly advanced enough, and has given a description of modern *liaisons* in terms not of the stable. This is very shocking, and *Living Together* has been given away with a pound of tea. As a matter of fact, this is, in many ways, very unfair. Mr. Sutro puts a play together very well; his dialogue is slick and amusing; he knows what people are like, and why they get into difficulties. . . .

Yet . . . for all its merits, there *is* something wrong with *Living Together*. Mr. Sutro has tried to put too much new wine into his old bottles. He has tried to sing songs of Cowardice in the tempo of Sardou. . . . The shapelessness of modern life, the chaos of its moral standards cannot be jammed into a neat Sardou box. Hence we have come to hate the well-made play, the "strong" scene, what the French police call *"la confrontation des témoins"*; we look rather for similarity of key, for suggestions of feelings, for looseness of construction. A play almost becomes good, if it is "untheatrical."

Francis Birrell. NA. Feb. 9, 1929, p. 652

The name of Alfred Sutro, who died last month at the age of seventy, may possibly survive as that of the translator of Maeterlinck's *Life of the Bee*—a great translation of a great book. It is hardly surprising to learn that he rewrote it seven times before he was satisfied with it, so easy and apparently effortless is the result. In Mr. Sutro's book of reminiscences, *Celebrities and Simple Souls*, . . . published a few days after his death, there is a pen picture of Maeterlinck. . . .

But Sutro's early days of enthusiasm in Paris, and his championship of Maeterlinck (then suspect and unpopular in England) soon gave place to the triumph of Sutro as a popular dramatist. Though *The Walls of Jericho* had a great success, his plays are uniformly worthless. The reason for his failure (though he did not put it like that) he gave in one sentence in one of his lectures: "The dramatist should keep one eye raised to heaven and the other on the box-office." This is an infallible recipe for bad work. The dramatist (or any other artist) should keep both eyes fixed either on heaven or on the box-office—which only means writing either for a future audience or for a present one. Genuine work will result in each case. The result of Sutro's method was to produce, merely from the box-office standpoint, more failures than successes, and to write nothing that survived even his lifetime.

BkmL. Oct., 1933, p. 7

SWINNERTON, FRANK (1884–   )

Mr. Swinnerton has written four or five other novels before this one [*Nocturne*], but none of them compares with it in quality. His earlier books were strongly influenced by the work of George Gissing; they have something of the same fatigued grayness of texture and little of the same artistic completeness and intense vision of *Nocturne*. He has also made two admirable and very shrewd and thorough studies of the work and lives of Robert Louis Stevenson and George Gissing. Like these two, he has had great experience of illness. . . . It was in connection with his Gissing volume, for which I possessed some material he needed, that I first made his acquaintance. He has had something of Gissing's restricted and gray experiences, but he has nothing of Gissing's almost perverse gloom and despondency. . . .

This is a book that will not die. It is perfect, authentic, and alive. Whether a large and immediate popularity will fall to it, I cannot say, but certainly the discriminating will find it and keep it and keep it alive. If Mr. Swinnerton were never to write another word I think he might count on this much of his work living, when many of the more portentous reputations of today may have served their purpose in the world and become no more than fading names.

H. G. Wells. Introd. in *Nocturne* (N.Y., George H. Doran, 1917), pp. xiii-xiv

I now know Swinnerton—probably as well as any man knows him; I have penetrated into the interior of the shop. He has done several things since I first knew him—rounded the corner of thirty, grown a beard, under the orders of a doctor, and physically matured. Indeed he looks decidedly stronger than in fact he is—he was never able to pass the medical examination for the army. He is still in the business of publishing, being one of the principal personages in the ancient and well-tried firm of Chatto and Windus. . . . He reads manuscripts, including his own—and including mine. . . . He tells authors what they ought to do and ought not to do. . . .

Nevertheless, publishing is only a sideline of his. He writes for himself in the evenings and at week-ends—his office never sees him on Saturdays. Among the chief literary events of nineteen-seventeen was *Nocturne,* which he wrote in the evenings and at week-ends. It is a short book, but the time in which he wrote it was even shorter. He had scarcely begun it when it was finished. . . . You can say what you like about *Nocturne,* but you cannot say that on its own scale it is not perfect, consummate. At least I cannot. . . .

Swinnerton's other gift is the critical. It has been said that an author cannot be at once a first-class critic and a first-class creative artist. To which absurdity I reply: What about William Dean Howells? And what about Henry James, to name no other names? Anyhow, if Swinnerton excels in fiction he also excels in literary criticism. . . .

It was Swinnerton's work on R. L. Stevenson that made the trouble in London. It is a destructive work. It is very bland and impartial, and not bereft of laudatory passages, but since its appearance Stevenson's reputation has never been the same. Those who wish to preserve their illusions about the greatness of Stevenson should refrain from reading it. Few recent books of criticism have aroused more hostility than Swinnerton's *Stevenson.* There is a powerful Stevenson cult in England, as there is in America. And in London there are sundry persons who cannot get far into any conversation without using the phrase, "As dear old R. L. S. used to say." Some of these persons are personages. They rage at the mention of Swinnerton. One of them on a celebrated occasion, exclaimed in fury: "Never let me hear that man's name!" This detail alone shows that Swinnerton is a real critic. Sham criticism, however violent,—and Swinnerton is incapable of violence—does not and cannot arouse such passion.

Arnold Bennett. *Frank Swinnerton*
(N.Y., George H. Doran, 1920), pp. 10–13

Mr. Swinnerton has already nine novels to his credit, all of them masterpieces of style, and is still comparatively unknown. Yet he is as well able to reproduce the atmosphere of life in the successful and unsuccessful suburbs of Weybridge and Kennington as Stephen McKenna is in the aristocratic world of Mayfair and Kensington. . . . He is far more alive than Mr. McKenna: his vision is larger, his sympathies broader.

S. P. B. Mais. *Books and Their Writers*
(N.Y., Dodd, Mead, 1920), p. 37

This, we believe, is the real weakness of *Coquette*. When Mr. Swinnerton is spinning out this unreal substance the defects of his writing appear in all their nakedness—sometimes journalistic, sometimes pompous, sometimes vulgar. But when he is pushing his way into the heart of his subject all these defects are forgotten; they serve only to emphasize the reality of his achievement.

If we had to define that achievement more closely we should invoke the name of Gissing. Mr. Swinnerton is sometimes as pontifical as Gissing, without Gissing's scholarly restraint in the use of words. He has not that queer, smouldering passion of hatred for the sordid which burns dully through Gissing's work. But he has some of Gissing's real qualities; he has his patience, his determination, his honesty. With great travail he builds something which has solid foundations, however flimsy the superstructure. Of which of his coevals can so much be said?

John Middleton Murry. *NA*. Oct. 1, 1921, p. 23

It was as an analyst of lovers, I think, that Frank Swinnerton claims and holds his place among those whom we still sometimes call the younger novelists of England.

I do not say this because his fame was achieved at a bound with *Nocturne,* but because all his novels show a natural preoccupation with the theme of love between the sexes. Usually it is a pair of young lovers or contrasted pairs, but sometimes this is interestingly varied, as in *September,* where we have a study of love that comes to a woman in middle life.

The unique character of *Nocturne* makes it very hard to write about Swinnerton. It is true that Arnold Bennett wrote: "I am prepared to say to the judicious reader unacquainted with Swinnerton's work, 'Read *Nocturne*' and to stand or fall, and to let him stand or fall by the result." At the same time . . . it is not entirely just to estimate the living writer by a single unique performance, an extraordinary piece of virtuosity which *Nocturne* unquestionably is. For anyone who wishes to understand and appreciate Swinnerton, I would recommend that he begin with *Coquette,* follow it with *September,* follow that with *Shops and Houses* and then read *Nocturne.*

G. M. Overton. *Authors of the Day*
(N.Y., George H. Doran, 1922), pp. 327–28

The first thing to be said about Mr. Swinnerton's "panorama" [*The Georgian Scene*] is that it is a thoroughly good show. He knows what he is writing about. . . . Intermittently his pages (of which there are more than 500) offer the easier charm of autobiography or reminiscence. The reader is given brief but vivid and taking glimpses of Chesterton and Belloc on the lecture platform, of Wells, Bennett and A. A. Milne at home, and portraits of Shaw, Barrie, James Stephens, H. M. Tomlinson, Galsworthy and many others, including, rather by the way, Sir Harry Johnston. These things seem dashed off unelaborately but effectively. . . .

Geoffrey West. *FR.* May, 1935, p. 637

Mr. Swinnerton is an admirable gossip, despite his rather irritating habit of addressing the reader [*Background With Chorus*] in the manner of an after-dinner speaker; his literary judgments are less valuable and occasionally one is startled by an almost incredible lack of discrimination: thus, he will refer to Gilbert Frankau (as a poet) in the same breath as Brooke, Flecker, etc. Yet his remarks on Lawrence are wise and to the point and a good corrective to much of the nonsense that has been written about that overrated master. It is to be hoped that in the next instalment Mr. Swinnerton will be equally commonsensical—and disrepectful—about some of the figures of the *entre deux guerres.*

Jocelyn Brooke. *TT.* June 30, 1956, p. 785

Frank Swinnerton describes his new book [*Background with Chorus*] as "a footnote to changes in English literary fashion between 1900 and 1917." His models are the great anecdotalists, Boswell, Hazlitt, Haydon,

Crabb Robinson. He has written, not literary history, but a book to which future literary historians and biographers of the period will turn with gratitude. And who is better qualified to do so? Swinnerton is now 72: as publisher's reader and editor, novelist and journalist, he has been round and about literary London for as long as the century itself, for he started his first job on Jan. 14, 1901. . . .

It is through the minor and now often minuscule figures that Swinnerton most successfully brings his period to life, no doubt because the bigger men he deals with, from James to D. H. Lawrence, are familiar to us through scores of other men's books and articles as well as their own writings. But as ever he is excellent on his two great friends and heroes, Arnold Bennett and H. G. Wells; and he writes all the time with a demureness that is a most effective foil to the feline in his style and with a sharpness of perception that goes hand in hand with an engaging modesty.

Walter Allen. *NYT*. March 10, 1957, p. 5

SYMONS, ARTHUR (1865–1945)

To find the real Symons, we must turn to *Silhouettes, London Nights,* and *Amoris Victima*. Here we encounter a distinct personality, an individual note, and a restricted, but far from insignificant, technical accomplishment. Unfortunately, the individual note is at the same time insistently monotonous. The poet, even in recording his many moods, reveals himself as a man of one mood—a sensual melancholy. His verses impress us, one and all, as the metrical diary of a sensation-hunter; and though he disclaims all concern with morality, he is a moralist in spite of himself, inasmuch as the picture he presents of a sensation-hunter's life is distinctly deterrent. I do not doubt that a good deal of Mr. Symons's work—the *Amoris Victima* sequence, for example—is dramatic. In other words, Mr. Symons does not merely record his own actual sensations and experiences, but gives them an imaginative extension; working out in detail the data they provide, the possibilities implicit in them. This, however, is not true drama. It is only self-dramatisation, Byronism. . . . These three booklets might be grouped together under the title of Turgueneff's first book: *Memories of a Sportsman;* and one is harrassed with doubts as to whether the memoirs are always quite sportsmanlike.

William Archer. *Poets of the Younger Generation*
(John Lane, 1902), p. 412

In one branch of theatrical criticism, Mr. Symons is more knowing, more meticulous, than almost any of the regular critics. . . . I can imagine that any young mime, reading attentively what Mr. Symons has to say of Coquelin and Bernhardt and Hading, would derive real profit for his or her own work. I do not agree with all Mr. Symons's estimates. But the point is that they are estimates—keen and patient observations, made from a sound basis of first principles, and not merely the usual peppering of fortuitous epithets.

One reason why this book [*Plays, Acting and Music*] is so fresh and welcome is that we see for the first time the Pateresque manner and method of criticism applied to dramatic art. "Pateresque" is no slight on Mr. Symons. . . . Essentially, he is himself, and that self merely happens to have been Pater's—a sensitive, fastidious, ever-ruminating self. The quietism of his style is, not less than Pater's, a genuine growth from within. The most salient point of likeness between the two men, that which is at once their cardinal strength and their cardinal weakness, is that for each of them (as, indeed, for every quietist) art matters more than life, and form in art more than meaning. . . .

When he writes . . . of the cities that he has visited, and tells us, with very delicate art, of the many impressions they made on him, I always feel that they are, somehow, cities of the dead. . . . If Mr. Symons were not such a quietist, he would not be, on the whole, so patient and penetrating an art-critic. He would not, moreover, be himself. A definite self—that is what one most needs in a critic. . . . And the habit of demanding all kinds in one man is a stupid habit, due, no doubt, to that modern spirit of hurry-skurry which makes us so impatient of all learning that cannot be absorbed quickly and easily from one compendious source. Every quality has its defect, and it is only by eclectic reading that we can behold that monster, the perfect critic. [Sept., 1903]

Max Beerbohm. *Around Theatres*
(Rupert Hart-Davis, 1953), pp. 273–74, 276

One is led by the mention of Arthur Symons to the recollection of the now slightly unfashionable but once significant period called by us the "eighteen-nineties," of which Symons as a critic may fairly be presented as the interpreter, and as a poet the exponent. One remembers that for a short but brilliant twelve months he edited the *Savoy,* that bolder rival of the *Yellow Book;* one remembers, too, his admirably judged pronouncements on the artistic and literary tendencies of his day. . . . In spite of the trees, in spite of being himself one of the trees, he was yet able to see the wood. Although he himself elected to follow the prevailing fashion as a man of letters, he remained as a critic fully alive to the faults which might and would be found with his age by its detractors. . . .

As the interpreter of the 'nineties Arthur Symons cannot be forgotten. If in his own poems he parades less of the exotic than many of his contemporaries, he at least represents supremely one facet of the taste of his day: he is the poet of the town. . . . Unfortunately for one who was born a graceful and supple rhymer, his work is likely to suffer from the urbane dandyism he affected, and from being read in the future not so much for its own merits as out of a literary curiosity.

V. Sackville-West. *NA*. June 28, 1924, pp. 414–15

At the risk of seeming severe, I venture to assert that Mr. Symons's translations are the best of the verse that he has given to us. By his metrical translations and his criticism he was the strongest link between English literature and French influences. But he was not a poet born; he brought to poetry every gift that can be acquired without the specific poetical endowment. Consequently his verse is at its best when it seeks to render into English the quality of foreign thought and rhythm. When once the indispensable element is supplied, all his gifts of scholarship, craftsmanship and imaginative sympathy can accomplish wonders. It therefore follows that he was designed to be an artist in prose, and particularly in that kind of interpretative prose, itself a form of translation, which we call criticism. . . . Mr. Symons, not being, except at one remove, a creative artist, was at his best as a translator of verse, and most at ease as a translator in criticism. . . .

When we consider the range, the sensitiveness, the extent, and the thoroughness of his work, he stands alone in our criticism and literature. None has had the various qualities that produce good criticism so evenly balanced as he. . . . Mr. Symons is a man of imaginative insight, and of catholic knowledge, not only of the arts but of artists, who has devoted himself without wavering to criticism almost alone. We go to his writings, therefore, not in search of independent essays on the subject of their titles . . . but for an imaginatively precise definition of the particular quality of the work of art in question. . . . The aspect with which he deals is the simplest and enduring aspect, and wherever he has been able to discern it rightly and to make it clear, he has achieved a piece of criticism that will always be revealing. His work, indeed, is the most solid contribution in prose that the Beardsley period produced. . . . He has an extraordinary power of giving definition to elusive qualities, which Pater, being less intellectually minded, was content to suggest emotionally.

Osbert Burdett. *The Beardsley Period*
(John Lane, The Bodley Head, 1925), pp. 161–62, 200–1

The duration, the literary importance, and the influence of the decadence, with us, have all been frequently exaggerated. Mr. Symons for a few years seemed to have his place in it, but he had begun writing well before it developed, he did much of his finest work after it was at an end, and always he stood in an important sense aloof. With its curiosity, its concern to capture passing impressions and moods, its desire to be modern, to accept as material the artificiality of modern life, he was in sympathy; of the cruder part of its moral error he was the severest critic. . . .

The critic . . . is broader, is more nearly the whole man, than the poet in Mr. Symons, but the two coexist, and that they do so in harmony, co-operating to make his imaginative world, is his distinction. A few minor aberrations apart, they are not out of accord; and though at one time Mr. Symons wrote some pieces of verse open perhaps to mild reproach on his own principle, he was decadent only as Baudelaire was. In the great bulk of his poetry, that is, certainly in all the finest of it, if he at all used the material offered by the decadence in its widest sense, by the sophisticated, corrupted, self-doubting life of his age, and not merely of the 'nineties, he did so otherwise than as a decadent.

Will anyone tell me how to date a dozen of the best songs and brief lyrics made by Mr. Symons? They connect him on the one hand with the Elizabethans, and on the other with Verlaine, and are his own. They belong, beyond possibility of question, to the eternal now of our poetry. . . . The diction . . . is pure; the construction of the sentences of a distinguished simplicity; the writing delicately taut, the music coaxed out of words instead of extorted from them. There are no tricks, of the 'nineties or of any other period; there are no baits for the public of that day or any.

T. Earle Welby. *Arthur Symons: a Critical Study*
(A. M. Philpot, 1925), pp. 122–23, 126–27

I myself owe Mr. Symons a great debt. But for having read his book [*The Symbolist Movement in Literature*] I should not, in the year 1908, have heard of Laforgue and Rimbaud; I should probably not have begun to read Verlaine, and but for reading Verlaine, I should not have heard of Corbière. So the Symons book is one of those which have affected the course of my life.

T. S. Eliot. *For Lancelot Andrewes*
(Garden City, N. Y., Doubleday, Doran, 1929), p. 100

He, more explicitly and more influentially than any of his contemporaries, saw how to synthesise the earlier English tradition—particularly Blake, on whom he wrote a good, and in this connexion revealing, book —with Pater and those European Symbolists he knew so well. Symons also had considerable part in the associated revival of interest in Donne and the Jacobean dramatic poets. But above all he wrote the book out of which the impressionist poets of the early twentieth century learnt the elements of French Symbolist poetic.

> Frank Kermode. *Romantic Image*
> (Routledge and Kegan Paul, 1957), p. 107

In 1899 two new books, one psychological and one literary, fastened on the word *symbolism:* Freud's *Interpretation of Dreams,* which appeared in Vienna in November, and Symons's *The Symbolist Movement in Literature,* published in September in London. Although unlike in method, both recorded the search for a psychic reality which had little to do with exterior reality. Symons's book, like Freud's, gave a name to the preoccupation with modes of half-uttered or half-glimpsed meaning which, as we can see clearly enough now sixty years have passed, was a principal direction in modern thought. . . .

It was no doubt a little embarrassing to Symons that he had to represent as his avant-garde a group of writers who were anything but young. Of those he discusses, Nerval was not so much Symbolism's father as its grandfather (its father was Baudelaire), having died in 1855; five of Symons's other examples (Laforgue, Villiers, Rimbaud, Verlaine, and Mallarmé) had died between 1887 and 1898. The only two living exponents of Symbolism with whom he dealt were Maeterlinck and Huysmans, neither of them fledglings. But the lives and works of all these writers retained enough tumult to satisfy the demand for strangeness and novelty, and Symons turned the scandal that hung over them into a glamor previously reserved for the English romantic poets. . . .

That it should have been Symons who wrote the first book in English expressly devoted to the French Symbolists was not strange. A Cornishman born in Wales, who prided himself on not being English, he came to London while still young and set himself promptly to the task of showing that the English, rather than himself, were the provincials. . . . All the arts attracted him; he played the piano, went to concerts, studied Whistler and the French impressionists, attended music halls, ballets, plays. . . . His critical articles, witty, informed, sensible, and graceful, as befitted a friend and admirer of Pater, and somewhat lacking in emphasis too, were soon appearing in the *Athenaeum* and elsewhere. When he became editor of the *Savoy* in 1896, at the age of 31, he occupied a position in England as the principal interpreter of contemporary writers, which was like that of Valéry Larbaud in Paris in 1920.

> Richard Ellmann. Introd. in Arthur Symons,
> *The Symbolist Movement in Literature*
> (N.Y., Dutton, 1958), pp. vii–x

SYMONS, JULIAN (1912–)

The poems of Julian Symons [*Confusions About X*] are competent and rather charming and really not very original. Here, again, it is a trifle disappointing to observe how a talented individual can succumb to the prevailing idiom of the time and lose most of his own characteristics in too strict an emulation of fashionable tones of voice. Symons produces poems which are not literally interchangeable with those of W. H. Auden, but from any couple of lines I happen to turn up it is obvious how near to an echo he manages to be.

George Barker. *LL.* July, 1939, p. 149

Surrealism, the spontaneity of Dylan Thomas, the Left propaganda and music-hall aspects of Auden, are the most dangerous reefs for the younger poets at the present time, being methods easily adopted but liable to stunt a follower's own gifts if he has any. In the face of these dangers it is reassuring to find stabilizing, though experimental, elements in many of the new poets, including Allott, Symons and Ruthven Todd.

Julian Symons is an interesting subject, because not only has he never hesitated to express his opinions, so that it is clear enough where he stands, but because he successfully edited his own magazine, *Twentieth Century Verse,* and did much to encourage talent which could find little expression elsewhere. The very time of the birth of his magazine is not a bad clue to its editor: it appeared when *New Verse* was becoming doctrinal, and was in at the death of that amusing Surrealist and Communist adventure *Contemporary Poetry and Prose.* The direct ancestor of *Twentieth Century Verse* was no doubt *New Verse,* but in Symons's fathering of so many of the younger poets he is no doubt hatching a dangerous brood which might do more than continue what *New Verse* stood for. . . .

Apart from questions of language, . . . [the] ability . . . to develop a theme is the ultimate quality we have the right to demand of a poet. Symons has this . . . quality for lack of which many young poets are now hopelessly floundering. The presence of this ability, even though he has exploited it only in a minor way up till now, is Symons's surest claim to the reading public's attention in the next few years. [1940]

Francis Scarfe. *Auden and After*
(Routledge and Sons, 1942), pp. 131, 144

"Sir," said Dr. Johnson, "the man who should read *Tristam Shandy* for the story would hang himself." And so he might; but in misreading *Tristam Shandy* he would also miss a pleasure of a very special kind. So it is with *The Thirty-First of February.* Its real subject is not who—

if anybody—killed Mrs. Anderson. It is how close hysteria lies under farce, savagery under passion, a whole *Walpurgisnacht* under the veneer of civilization. It is how a number of events and persons . . . can push a man over the edge. For our [American] word "thriller," the English say "shocker." This is neither a whodunit nor a thriller. But the shock in it is one of a very special kind.

Basil Davenport. NYT. Feb. 4, 1951, p. 24

Popular biography and popular appreciation . . . still lag behind the findings of criticism equipped with knowledge of the insights derived by depth psychology, and it is the first merit of Mr. Symons's short critical biography [*Charles Dickens*] . . . that its point of departure is [Edmund] Wilson's essay. Not that Mr. Symons has not much of his own to contribute. His interpretation of the character of Dickens in terms of Kraepelin's *Manic-Depressive Insanity and Paranoia* is fascinating and, as far as it goes, truly revealing; and his analysis of Dickens's visual sense, admirably illustrated by comparison with the film and with surrealist painting, is as good as anything that has been written on this aspect of the novelist. . . . All in all, this little book must be considered the best short introduction to the greatest of English novelists that exists; indeed, it is so good that one hopes Mr. Symons will one day give us a full-length study.

NSN. Oct. 27, 1951, pp. 471–72

Mr. Julian Symons has now provided us with a twentieth-century account of the nineteenth-century colossus. His *Thomas Carlyle,* if competent rather than inspiring, has the merit of being honest, straightforward and, within its terms of reference, intelligent. It adds nothing to what was already known about Carlyle, but expounds him in contemporary terms. Given Mr. Symons's own point of view, it was inevitable that he should at times convey the impression of apologizing for his subject. Carlyle, he writes, "is likely to appear uncongenial to most contemporary readers," the reason being, apparently, that though he started off on the moving stairway leading up to the Century of the Common Man, he lost heart or was seduced away, and started furiously trying to step downward—an undignified, futile and enraging enterprise. . . .

Mr. Symons, that is to say, is inclined to make excuses for what in Carlyle least required it—his deep awareness of the essential fallacy in the utopianism which, gathering momentum in his day, is still working itself out to its melancholy and, in terms of human suffering, tragic conclusion. . . .

Apart from his basic assumption that Carlyle went wrong where in fact he went right, Mr. Symons's account of Carlyle's life is sympathetic, and holds a just balance in the matrimonial controversy which has played so large a role in biographical writing about him.

TLS. Feb. 15, 1952, p. 124

SYNGE, J. M. (1871–1909)

His work has something of the quality of folk-poetry; but he got by an austere eclecticism the effect which the best folk-poetry has gained from generations of selection and rejection. He was as consciously an artist as the decadents from whom he escaped, and more eclectic even than they; for they made their choice now from life or its outer garments, and now from other men's fancies, while he refused all but life only. He could feel with the best of them an "exquisite satisfaction" to find himself "making away from civilisation" in a primitive canoe, and his eyes were always open for artistic effects. . . .

The observer never quite identified himself with his [Aran] island friends, but stood a little aloof, not so far as to lose his vision. "On some days," he writes, "I feel this island as a perfect home and resting place; on other days I feel that I am a waif among people. I can feel more with them than they can with me." Thus and not otherwise could he have been the artist he was.

Francis Bickley. NationL. April 3, 1909, p. 18

At the time of his first visit to Coole he had written some poems, not very good for the most part, and a play which was not good at all. I read it again after his death . . . and again it seemed but of slight merit. But a year later he brought us his two plays *In the Shadow of the Glen* and *Riders to the Sea,* both masterpieces, both perfect in their way. He had gathered emotion, the driving force he needed, from his life among the people, and it was the working in dialect that had set free his style. . . .

I remember his bringing the play [*The Playboy of the Western World*] to us in Dublin, but he was too hoarse to read it, and it was read by Mr. Fay. We were almost bewildered by its abundance and fantasy, but we felt—and Mr. Yeats said very plainly—that there was far too much "bad language," there were too many violent oaths, and the play itself was marred by this. I did not think it was fit to be put on the stage without cutting. It was agreed that it should be cut in rehearsal.

Lady Gregory. Eng.R. March, 1910, pp. 559, 563

No such gift has been made to modern Ireland by any of her children as Synge's disengagement of the essence, the differentiating virtue of the native imagination in Irish country folk. Such services help to make nations, for they render national qualities apprehensible and sensuous, so that the idea of them can be grasped and cherished by plain minds. Commonly it is tough work to keep a modern country from kicking away any quite great work of art that is laid at her feet. Shelleys, Ibsens, Whistlers—their own receive them not, and when Ireland's turn came she did as the rest, or part of her did. But soon the hooting is over. Already from Galway to Prague Synge's eager and glowing genius has entered at open minds. To them the august and quiet sadness of *Riders to the Sea* has made the word "tragedy" mean something yet more stirring and cleansing to the spirit than it did. In his harsh, sane, earthen humour, biting as carbolic acid to slight minds, they find a disinfectant well worth having, at the lowest, in an ailing theatre.

C. E. Montague. *Dramatic Values*
(Methuen, 1911), pp. 14–15

"There was something very nice about Synge." The friend who said this to me, added that "though the plays are cynical, he was not cynical in himself." I do not feel that the plays are cynical. They seem heartless to me at first sight. The abundant malicious zest in them gives them an air of cruelty. But in the plays, Synge did with his personality as he did in daily life. He buried his meaning deep. He covered his tragedy with mockeries. . . .

I never heard him mention his early life nor what he endured in his struggles to find a form. I believe he never spoke about his writings, except to say that he wrote them slowly, many times over. His talk was always about vivid, picturesque, wild life. He took greater joy in what some frantic soul from Joyce's country said when the policeman hit him than in anything of his own. Knowing almost nothing of England he disliked her. . . .

. . . His relish of the savagery made me feel that he was a dying man clutching at life, and clutching most wildly at violent life, as the sick man does.

John Masefield. *CR*. April, 1911, pp. 473–74, 475, 477

This strange Irishman was a solitary, who cared to talk with peasants, and was interested in things rather than ideas. . . .

Irishmen had written well before Synge, but they had written well by casting off Ireland; but here was a man inspired by Ireland, a country that had not inspired any art since the tenth or twelfth century, a country to which it was fatal to return. Was Synge the exception, and was he going to find his fortune in Ireland? . . .

I am sorry to say that Yeats fell into the mistake of attributing much reading to Synge; he had little love of character and could not keep himself from putting rouge on Synge's face and touching up his eyebrows. He showed greater discrimination when he said, "You will never know as much about French poetry as Arthur Symons. Come to Ireland and write plays for me." And for his great instinct we must forgive him his little sins of reason. He very rightly speaks of Synge as a solitary, and it is interesting to speculate what made him a solitary. Was it the sense that death was lurking round the corner always, and the sense that he possessed no social gifts that helped to drive him out into the Aran Islands, where he knew nobody, and to the Latin Quarter behind the Luxembourg Gardens, where nobody knew him? A man soon perceives if he be interested in others and if others be interested in him, and if he contribute nothing and get nothing, he will slink away as Synge did.

George Moore. *Eng.R.* Feb., 1914, pp. 353, 358, 363–64

Mr. [P. P.] Howe, who wrote a sincere and able book on Synge, may be taken as a representative apostle of the Synge cult. He sets before us a god, not a man—a creator of absolute beauty—and he asks us to accept the common view that *The Playboy of the Western World* is his masterpiece. There can never be any true criticism of Synge till we have got rid of all these obsessions and idolatries. Synge was an extraordinary man of genius, but he was not an extraordinarily great man of genius. He is not the peer of Shakespeare; he is not the peer of Shelley: he is the peer, say, of Stevenson. His was a byway, not a high-road, of genius. That is why he has an immensely more enthusiastic following among clever people than among simple people.

Once and only once Synge achieved a piece of art that was universal in its appeal, satisfying equally the artistic formula of Pater and the artistic formula of Tolstoi. This was *Riders to the Sea. Riders to the Sea,* a lyrical pageant of pity made out of the destinies of fisher-folk, is a play that would have been understood in ancient Athens or in Elizabethan London, as well as by an audience of Irish peasants today.

Robert Lynd. *Old and New Masters*
(N.Y., Charles Scribner's Sons, 1919), pp. 94–95

In Paris Synge once said to me, "We should unite stoicism, asceticism and ecstasy. Two of them have often come together, but the three never." . . .

He had that egotism of genius which Nietzsche compares to that of a woman with child. Neither I nor Lady Gregory had ever a compliment from him. After *Hyacinth* Lady Gregory went home the moment the curtain fell, not waiting for the congratulation of friends, to get his supper ready. He was always ailing and weakly. All he said of the triumphant *Hyacinth* was, "I expected to like it better." He had . . . charming and modest manners, in almost all things of life, a complete absorption in his own dream. I have never heard him praise any writer, living or dead, but some old French farce writer. For him nothing existed but his thought. He claimed nothing for it aloud. He never said any of those self-confident things I am enraged into saying, but one knew that he valued nothing else. He was too confident for self-assertion. I once said to George Moore, "Synge has always the better of you, for you have brief but ghastly moments during which you admit the existence of other writers; Synge never has." I do not think he disliked other writers—they did not exist. One does not think of him as an egotist. He was too sympathetic in the ordinary affairs of life and too simple. In the arts he knew no language but his own.

I have often envied him his absorption as I have envied Verlaine his vice. Can a man of genius make that complete renunciation of the world necessary to the full expression of himself without some vice or some deficiency?

W. B. Yeats. *LM*. April, 1928, pp. 642–44

Synge was born in 1871, of an old Wicklow family. By the end of the century he was in Paris, ill, very poor, doing hack work for various journals. He met Mr. W. B. Yeats, who in a happy moment urged him to return to Ireland, and seek inspiration there. It was at the time of the Irish literary renascence, when a number of cultured Irishmen were labouring to create a national art. Synge went to the Aran Islands. Almost at once he began to write with authority, and by 1903 he had entered upon the six years of creative life to which his fame is due. . . .

Synge's poetry has no startling intrinsic merit, yet it is of the utmost importance to the study of himself, and to other poets. Great as his influence has been upon the theatre, it may well be that as a poet he will best prove to have been the prophet of a new time. His verses were written at odd occasions over a period of twenty years, to please himself. He had strong theories on poetry in the abstract, and more definitely upon the particular function of poetry in his own time: but apart from these theories his verse is a kind of diary, in which freed from professional loyalties and restraints, he could ease his soul without fear of an audience. Thus, although he shows that he had a command of a powerful technique . . . he wrote his verses as it were in his shirt-sleeves, when the day's work was over. Yet this work has influenced almost all his successors in Ireland, including Mr. Yeats, whose *Responsibilities* (1913) shows strongly the impress of his friend's mind. This influence upon the greater of the less is a commonplace of literature: but in this case it was not Synge's comparatively slender technique

which was the cause, but his clear vision of the state of poetry and the measures needed for its cure. The few critical judgments he expressed in his maturity are as authoritative as any in the history of criticism.
L. A. G. Strong. *DM*. April, 1932, pp. 12, 16

Synge is undoubtedly the most remarkable English-speaking prose dramatist of the century, in the same way, and for much the same reason, that the Abbey Theatre is the most remarkable development in the theatrical history of these islands for some three centuries. Certain aspects of his work, as of the Irish dramatic movement as a whole, offer some of the best material we have for a study of the place of drama in the total culture of a modern society. . . .

. . . Synge's achievement, in his short space, is notable; the more so when one distinguishes it from the general cultural movement of which it forms a part. It is important to emphasize the very real differences of level in his work, and to estimate accurately both the virtues and the limitations of his dramatic language. The account which I have suggested makes Synge a somewhat different figure from the name in the usual list of regional dramatists. His work is small in compass, but it is, if not itself major drama, at the very least an important re-discovery of major dramatic possibilities.
Raymond Williams. *Drama from Ibsen to Eliot*
(Chatto and Windus, 1952), pp. 154, 168

Synge once wrote in his notebook that originality was not enough unless it had the characteristic of a particular time and locality and the life that was in it. He had had the good fortune to live in an Ireland where even men of mediocre talent were fired by the enthusiasms of the day to write better than they were able to. . . .

To some Irish people he was—and still is—a suspicious visitor bearing dubious gifts from the Big House, and this explains why his short career was so tempestuous. Yeats wrote, "Synge is invaluable to us because he has that kind of intense, narrow personality which necessarily raises the whole issue." Which is to say that his work more than that of any of his contemporaries comes closer to achieving the assimilation of the Gaelic past which the Irish Renaissance stood for. Whether he was dramatizing a tragic fact or incident of violence in contemporary Irish life, exploring the applications of ancient folk tale or heroic myth, or merely describing in unpretentious language the daily life of the tinker, the farmer or the fisherman, he was interpreting the traditional life of Ireland. It is to him more than to any other Irishman writing in English that we go for an insight into this life.
David H. Greene and Edward Stephens. *J. M. Synge*
(N.Y., Macmillan, 1959), p. 302

THIRKELL, ANGELA (1890–1961)

If there is any criticism to be made of *Ankle Deep* it is that the author has fallen a victim to the modern vice of facetiousness and refused to take her sentiment seriously. Constantly the lovers are being called "this pair of imbeciles" or the like, which prevents one from feeling the pity as well as the ludicrousness of their situation. But I hesitate to say anything that would suggest that Angela Thirkell has not the nicest taste in satire—or it may be irony—and gives the greatest promise of being a first-class writer of light humour. But she must keep in the background of her stories. Her opinions we should be glad to see in essay form. In a novel—I regret to appear ungracious—it is her characters we want, not herself.

Sean O'Faolain. *NSN*. Jan. 21, 1933, p. 76

Mrs. Thirkell's volume [*The Demon in the House*] about that plague of a little boy, Tony Morland, has a most distressing verisimilitude. No man can read it, if he be honest, without recalling his own capabilities of being tiresome to his elders, no woman without wondering at her sex's miraculous patience with the blunt-headed pertinacity of the human male. . . . He is the best boy in fiction since Mr. [Hugh] Walpole's Jeremy, and Mrs. Thirkell has none of Mr. Walpole's desperately avuncular conviction that grown-ups know better than the boy what is good for the boy: her Mrs. Morland is content—and oh! how justly—to know what is more convenient for mothers.

LL. Dec., 1934, p. 361

The peace which breaks over Mrs. Thirkell's lovingly chronicled Barsetshire families is . . . dilapidated. Just as war was for them, in the previous novels, more a question of annoyance and patient contriving than horror and privation, so peace is almost frustration—the commission nearly won, the skimping and make-do prolonged. Peace has failed to come as a great, dramatic climax; even its announcement is confused, its celebrations aggravating as all the bakers are closed.

If Mrs. Thirkell's legions of admirers have worried lest a Brave New World alter or disturb her county families they may relax and enjoy this new story [*Peace Breaks Out*] as usual. Life goes on much as before in village and close (Mrs. Thirkell is, to my knowledge, the only

English novelist who has dared to draw a Bishop universally disliked), bazaars are held, tennis matches arranged, house parties achieved. . . .

When problems and grim realities confront us on every side, it is perhaps ungrateful to complain of such undemanding entertainment. Yet at the risk of seeming captious, a plea is entered for a new field for Mrs. Thirkell's delicious and penetrating talents. She has now evolved such a well-recorded circle that there are no surprises left. The nonsequitur (of which she is undoubtedly the most ingenious creator); the old lady who never gets to her feet but in a landslide of impedimenta; the innocent and beautiful young women, or the hearty and wholesome ones, still, figuratively at least, brandishing their hockey sticks; the gallant young men, the equally gallant older ones, bungling a bit but adroitly managed by their wives; the snobberies of the servants' hall; the lower classes who may be kind, courageous, or difficult but who may never, never escape from their vulgarity—Mrs. Thirkell has drawn them all so neatly that one almost feels she is playing with stock figures from a kind of Pollock's Penny Plain and Tuppence Colored Children's Theatre. They may be manipulated into different positions but they never vary. And, too, she has developed a style which, while (deceptively) easy and confidential, has now become so involved that it verges on tea-table conversation with an elderly, delightful, but just faintly tedious aunt.

Pamela Taylor. *Sat.*, May 24, 1947, p. 14

Never too Late, if my calculations are accurate, is the twenty-fifth volume of Angela Thirkell's Barsetshire chronicle. Its characters are nearly all old friends. Its settings are wholly familiar to Thirkell readers. . . .

Mrs. Thirkell, like her own Mrs. Morland, whose experiences, sentiments and "snipe-flights" of observation one often feels she shares, has never professed to take her novels seriously. They are her bread-and-butter work, her annual habit, the means by which she earns or supplements her living. She rates them, as writing, far lower than her first book *Three Houses,* a collection of childhood memories associated with her grandfather, the painter Burne-Jones, and his circle. In this she shows clear judgment, for the now rare and little-known *Three Houses* is a small jewel, beside which the interlocking units of the Barsetshire chronicle seem like a bright string of Poppit beads.

And yet it does not do to dismiss the Barsetshire stories lightly. Not only have they given pleasure to thousands of readers on both sides of the Atlantic, but they have set out a pattern of a certain sort of English life in the first half of the twentieth century, which social historians of the future would be foolish not to follow.

C. A. Lejeune. *TT.* June 9, 1956, p. 685

Even Angela Thirkell and Barsetshire have finally conceded that times have changed. This is a memorable admission, but not to be rated as a defeat. It simply means that Mrs. Thirkell has become the most relaxed social historian in England, and Barsetshire natives, freed from years of martyrdom to the stiff upper lip, are more like their best selves than at any time since peace was declared.

The army of occupation has come to stay in Thirkell Land. New ideas, strange words, unfamiliar attitudes and bizarre combinations of possessed and dispossessed gentry are accepted as fixtures in a world where change once spelled treason. Released from her Emily Post-duties, the author is at her best as a shrewd rocking-chair critic. True, the scene [*Close Quarters*] is set in one of those peculiarly depressing English summers. . . . Yet the general effect is of deep contentment and simplicity. Barsetshire has gone back to first causes and likes it. So, needless to add, will every reader who prefers the Barsetshire variety of the past to the present. . . .

Perhaps Mrs. Thirkell herself has been suffering from the exigencies of a stiff upper lip in recent years. Certainly this candid-camera shot of Barsetshire unmasked has put it right back into its niche of immortality.

Isabelle Mallet. *NYT*. Sept. 21, 1958, p. 40

Mrs. Morland, not the least agreeable of Mrs. Thirkell's permanent *dramatis personae,* admits to writing the same book year after year because her public likes it. If Mrs. Thirkell's own admirers were to voice a criticism it would not be that her books are all identical, for they do vary considerably according to which part of Barsetshire she happens to be visiting, but that she constantly repeats herself in little things. The same quotations appear in book after book, and even in the mouths of totally different people in the same book. And she will not let sleeping dogs lie. It is quite a while now since Noel Merton flirted with Peggy Arbuthnot, but we are reminded of it with unfailing regularity every time the Mertons appear on the scene.

Many old friends appear, some briefly, in *Love at All Ages,* but as Lady Graham's youngest daughter is now married to a clergyman who is also a Duke's son we are introduced to a new household, that of the Duke of Towers, with his American wife. Mrs. Thirkell is perhaps a little perfunctory with them; they are not as interesting as the Pomfrets or even the Omniums.

TLS. July 7, 1959, p. 421

THOMAS, DYLAN (1914–1953)

Mr. Dylan Thomas is I believe, twenty-one years of age. He has very great gifts, though they are not as yet completely resolved. He is, at moments, a prey to his subconscious self, and consequently to obscurity; but from that subconscious self rise, time after time, lines which are transmuted by his conscious self into really great poetry, whose truth has been lived with the most profound intensity, until it could be fused, concentrated into this strange greatness.

It would be impossible to exaggerate my feeling of excitement when I read this poem ["A Grief Ago" in October issue of *Programme*], so beautiful and moving for all its obscurities. Here, I said to myself, is a young man who has every likelihood of becoming a great poet, if only he will work hard enough at subduing his obscurity: I know of no young poet of our time whose poetic gifts are on such great lines.

The poem I have quoted shows an enormous advance on those contained in *18 Poems* (published by the *Sunday Referee* and the Parton Bookshop); but these, too, contained many beauties.

Edith Sitwell. LM. Feb., 1936, pp. 386, 388

Dylan Thomas is one of the most promising of the poets under 30, but he has suffered through catching the public eye a little too early, which resulted in unfounded criticism by both his supporters and detractors. He was promising in 1934 (*18 Poems*) and promising in 1936 (*25 Poems*). To those who have followed his production since then he is still promising, and this premature estimate of him is being made to clarify the nature of that promise.

For many people his poems are puzzles, seeming to offer at first reading no more than a forbidding cliff, impenetrable to reason, from which there jut great crags of capricious imagery. Some people (notably Miss Sitwell) read him for his sound, but though the words peal fully and roundly, the rhythms are monotonous enough to make this pall. . . . The dominant points of contact seem to be James Joyce, the Bible, and Freud. The personal habits of language and mythology of Dylan Thomas can readily be identified through these three sources. The first is linguistic, the second mythological, the third psycho-pathological, the key to his interpretation of his world. . . .

"Poetry must drag further into the clear nakedness of light more even of the hidden causes than Freud could realize." So wrote Dylan Thomas in his admission that he had been influenced by Freud. The influence is first of all general, understandable in a poet whose chief preoccupation is to explore childhood and adolescence. Only a reader of Freud can receive the full impact, which is enormous, of Dylan Thomas's predominantly sexual imagery. The influence of Freud would seem to go even further in view of the poet's acknowledgement that his activity as a poet is one of self-discovery rather than self-expression or even self-analysis. In their finished state the poems suggest that self-analysis could be undertaken by such a poet only by analyzing what he had written. That is to say, they are not the product of analysis, but the very raw material for it. They are in the fullest sense documents: they are intellectual or cerebral, but so spontaneous that the poet himself might well be amazed and bewildered in face of them. . . . He seeks the world in himself, and consequently his work is entirely autobiographical.

Francis Scarfe. *Hor.* Nov., 1940, pp. 226, 235

Dylan Thomas is another "opaque" poet who writes poetry for poetry's sake.

Unlike Mr. Graves, he does not extract the pure poetry from experience; unlike Miss Sitwell, his poems are not the hymns of an inner poetic experience within which a lifetime of wider experience has been transcended. To Thomas, simply, every vivid impression for which he can find a suitable image is poetry. In a way, his prose reveals his poetic method even better than his poetry does. For in his prose we see him as he is, a kind of poetic roving camera, who snaps up everything and puts it down as a brilliant poetic image in words as tasty and as full of local sea-flavour as winkles which one buys from a stall on the coast. The obscurity of his early poems was due to the fact that they were poems written without any strong principle of selection to guide the reader through the thick images and the loquacious sounds. They were often just collections of wonderful poetic insights, sustained by no unifying thought or experience behind them. The difficulty at once disappeared wherever there was a unifying theme, as in the well-known lines in memory of Ann Jones.

Probably Thomas is the poet who has gained more than any other (if any others have at all gained) from having to do war work. Writing scripts, broadcasts, and so on, has given him the sense of a theme, without taking away from the forcefulness of his imagery. There is no fundamental divorce between his prose and his verse rhythms, and this has enabled him to invent new rhythms in his verse, which owe much to prose, without having the diffuseness which vitiates entirely free verse. One must not be misled by the elaborate patterns which some of the poems make on the printed page, to think this part of a reversion to regular form similar to the reversion of Auden in his later work. The principle of Thomas's poetry is entirely free, and the patterns which he has arrived at are obtained by listening to the rhythms that come most naturally to him in ordinary speech, and slightly emphasizing and conventionalizing them. Thus, hearing him read a talk about memories of Christmas on the wireless, I understood at once the patterns of his recent poetry which are essentially patterns of speech, the music of rhetoric.

Stephen Spender. *Hor.* April, 1946, pp. 233–34

One day recently this writer met Dylan Thomas at a Third Avenue bar and grill. . . . Thomas is a little short, a little round and round-eyed, a little fair, very unruly-haired. His strongly modeled but no longer cherubic face (as Augustus John drew it) bears a male resemblance to Elsa Lanchester's. He said: "Say I am thirty-five years older, small, slim, dark, intelligent, and darting-doting-dotting-eyed. Say I am balding and toothlessing. I am also well-dressed." Mr. Thomas was wearing rumpled tweeds and was coatless. "Do you think that an invisible coat is well dressed? It is absolutely essential that I wear an invisible coat. Visible overcoats make you feel proprietorial."

Avoiding the sartorial question, I asked Thomas if he ever read American poetry. He replied with mock eloquence: "Whenever the day is dull and the rain is falling and the feet of the heron are battering against my window, and whenever the Garnetts (who are a literary family) or the gannets (who I believe are a bird) are gossiping in the bay, then what do I do but count my beads and then: a volume of American verse edited by Oscar Williams!"

What, one wanted to know, were Mr. Thomas' conclusions after such an immersion? "I suddenly have the death wish," he said, "which is what I started with. And then it all begins again: the melancholy, gay, euphoric roundabout."

Thomas drank his whisky and beer a little moodily. "Any possible success that could happen to me is bad for me," he said, apparently thinking of his audiences. To pursue the thought: Was it "success" if people liked his work?

"If people like my poetry, if they like my reading of it, if they like me, that is success, and that is bad for me. I should be what I was," Mr. Thomas replied. Did Mr. Thomas mean thirty-five years ago? "No, twenty years ago," he said. "Then I was arrogant and lost. Now I am humble and found. I prefer that other." [May 14, 1950]

Harvey Breit. *The Writer Observed*
(Alvin Redman, 1957), pp. 124–25

He was only 39, and had been world-famous for half that time. It was not simply his poetry, nor his wonderful voice that accounted for his renown. But the whole man. He was not only a great poem, in contradistinction to almost all the others, spare, marcid, and atrabilious in appearance, whose manner of poetry leaves an impression of barrenness, as if their words were only the skeleton of a structure of speech, but he looked it. There was nothing niggardly or narrow or ungenerous either in his appearance or in his "walk and conversation." His was a magnificent outgoing spirit, abundantly manifested in all that he did and was in no matter what connection. Had I been ignorant of his writings and his broadcastings, and even of his name, I could not have been ten minutes in his company without recognizing in him a man of genius.

Hugh MacDiarmid. Adam. 1953, p. 35

The poet is great; the prose-writer, despite many evident marks of genius, merely competent; but the prose-writer is far more versatile than the poet. The prose-writer assumes many characters, devises many characters, plays upon emotions which range from the serious to the comic. The poet assumes a single character; and, strictly speaking, he is a poet only of the most exalted emotions, the emotions of grief or joy. Call him what you will, tragic poet, bardic poet of sublimity; the point is that his proper character is a lofty and heroic one. . . .

Although he comes through love to his faith, we never see him, in the poems, really thinking how others think or feel; they exist simply as objects of his emotion. . . . He can enter into worm and animal, but he will look out through his own eyes. He can create worlds; but he creates his worlds in his own image, and remains the center of his thought and feeling. . . .

These two limitations—his restriction to certain ranges of emotion and his restriction to one character—amount to this: that he was a lyric poet of the loftiest kind. But also they cannot be disregarded; a poet so restricted must either aim at and achieve the sublime, or he fails. . . . His art demands great energy of thought and passion and all the accoutrements of the grand style; when the high conception is wanting, energy becomes violence and noise, the tragic passions become the melodramatic or the morbid, ecstasy becomes hysteria, and the high style becomes obscure bombast. . . . When Thomas is not master of his tricks, his tricks master him.

Elder Olsen. Dylan Thomas (Chicago, Ill.,
Univ. of Chicago Pr., 1954) pp. 22–24

Certain English newspaper critics were very quick to say that we, the Americans, had in our usual thoughtless way destroyed a great poet by tempting him with our easy money to work himself to death traveling about exhibiting himself. It was not easy money, to begin with, and after he was here the poet confessed that he hated his public readings and suffered fearful anxieties on account of them. But he needed money desperately and this was something he could do well. It is perhaps true that he came here out of despair, in his poverty and distraction. This may have been the jumping-off place, but there was going to be one soon, anywhere at all—time was closing in on him; he was probably as well off here as he would have been anywhere at that exact time, for the simple reason that he was not going to be well off anywhere ever again. . . .

Dylan Thomas was at the top of his fame, he had achieved what turned out to be his life work, and though his first youthful poetic fervor had passed, he appeared to be in a cycle of change for further development; yet, as all artists do at that time, he feared a waning of his powers. He needed a radical change by way of rest and refreshment; and he would make enough money to go back to Wales to his fishing village, his wife and three extraordinarily beautiful children, and go on writing poetry. . . .

No man can be explained by his personal history, least of all a poet. Dylan Thomas' life was formed by his temperament, his genius, in relation—in collision—with his particular human situation. . . . A drunken poet is not more interesting than any other drunken man behaving badly and stupidly. His daily, personal life in fact was no better than that of tens of thousands of dull alcoholics who never wrote a line of poetry. His poetry made the difference, and that is all the difference in this world.
Katherine Anne Porter. *NYT*. Nov. 20, 1955, p. 5

The critical issues arising from Thomas' work are nothing like settled; and there is, besides, the fascinating speculation about what he would have done if he had lived another thirty years. I myself am quite certain that he would have gone on writing, though his impulse as a purely lyrical poet seemed to have spent itself. He was becoming more and more interested in various dramatic forms—theatre, radio, film, opera: a very natural development in his case. The collaboration with Stravinsky could obviously have been a highly fruitful one; and perhaps Thomas himself (who, it will be recalled, once turned down an offer to play the lead in a Broadway comedy) would have developed into one of those executant-artists like Cocteau, who take an active part in the presentation of their work, so much so that the work is not fully itself in their absence. Thomas was so full of originality and creativity that the slander about his being an extinct volcano, "finished," played out, that one began to hear some five years before his death, always struck me as the refuge of little, negative minds. . . . There are certain uses of the "aside" in Thomas' poems that point unmistakably to the theatre. That is why, in spite of the wealth of his achievement, one still thinks of Thomas as a "promising" poet, because his promise was so huge; whereas George Herbert (say), who died at the same age, seems fulfilled; he did what he had to do, and it was enough. Dylan Thomas, I am sure, died while still at the beginning.

John Wain. *Enc.* March, 1961, p. 82

The importance of the words "Cry joy" draws our attention to a singular feature of Thomas's poetry: it is optimistic, or at least celebratory. Most of the poetry of this century that is worth re-reading is understandably and expectedly pessimistic or tragic. Thomas himself, as his letters and poems show, was well aware of the "horrors & hells" of the world in which he lived. (According to Brinnin, he once claimed to have seen the gates of hell, and as far as I know there is no valid reason for disbelieving Thomas.) We can scarcely call his early poems cheerful, but on the other hand neither are they professionally grim in the standard manner of the nineteen-thirties. And more and more as he matured do the notes of exultation and celebration, first heard clearly in the poem in memory of Ann Jones, become dominant in his poetry. . . .

Thomas's unique ability to find proper reason for celebration and exultation in the contemporary world of "horrors & hells" is most succinctly expressed in Polly Garter's famous remark, "Oh, isn't life a terrible thing, thank God?"—a remark that looks merely silly quoted on its own and out of context like that, but which in its context is both moving and meaningful.

"Cry joy," Thomas said, were the most important words in the most personally urgent poem he had written to date and one written in a desperate time. And at the untimely time of his death, he was working on what was to be his loudest cry of joy, the ambitiously-conceived long poem, "In Country Heaven." . . .

Paradoxically, the only published film-script by Thomas is one of a film that was never made. This is *The Doctor and the Devils,* based on a story by Donald Taylor about Burke and Hare, the notorious body-snatchers and murderers of nineteenth-century Edinburgh. . . .

This film-script and many of the radio-scripts may be regarded as preliminary exercises for Thomas's most widely-known work, the "Play for Voices," *Under Milk Wood.* The origin of this goes back to 1939. . . .

He had actually been asked in the previous year by a producer on the Welsh B.B.C. to write a dramatic feature in verse, and had replied that he doubted his ability to do it, because he wrote so slowly, "and the result, dramatically, is too often like a man shouting under the sea." The idea, however, continued to fascinate him. The story of the gradual evolution of *Under Milk Wood* is told by Daniel Jones in his preface to the published work. Its immediate origin lay in the development of "Quite Early one Morning," which was broadcast in 1945. At first, this was to be combined with the idea of "The Town that was Mad" which Thomas had first propounded to Richard Hughes in 1939. In October 1951, he sent to Marguerite Caetani, the editor of *Botteghe Oscure,* the manuscript of *Llareggub. A Piece for Radio perhaps.* . . . (Thomas eventually changed the title because he felt that the joke in the coined name, Llareggub—which he had first used in his story "The Orchards" —was a small one, and because he feared the name would be forbidding to American audiences. The spelling "Llaregyb" in the published version simply removes the joke and is quite pointless.)

Under Milk Wood is not a play at all in any strict sense of the word. . . .

No dramatic conflict, no development of character, no action in the usual dramatic sense (though there is a surprising amount of movement, from character to character, from one part of the village to another, from the present to the past and back again)—it is all too easy to list qualities that are missing from *Under Milk Wood* if we insist on regarding it as a play. On the other hand, its virtues are even more obvious: the brilliant use of language and imagery to create atmosphere and character (though this is occasionally overdone), the rollicking sense of humour, the joyful bawdy. The great virtue of the work, however, is none of these, but its informing sense of compassion, a compassion which is extended to all the characters, not merely to such an obviously sympathetic one as Captain Cat. . . .

In *Under Milk Wood* he presents us with a vision of a world that is completely good, where there is no evil and no sin, and yet it is a world very human, very fallible, and extremely interesting both to its inhabitants and to us.

T. H. Jones. *Dylan Thomas.* (N.Y, Grove, 1963), pp. 48–49, 87–91, 93, 95

THOMAS, EDWARD (1878–1917)

There has for some time been need of just such a book as this about Maeterlinck [*Maurice Maeterlinck*]. Mr. Thomas steers a clever course between the drawing-room enthusiasts who have made the success of *The Blue Bird* a little ridiculous, and, on the other hand, those members of the Committee on the Dramatic Censorship who spent humorous days implying the worst of other members who confessed to liking *Monna Vanna*. . . . It will be seen that Mr. Thomas takes his own way with Maeterlinck; but, like the excellent critic he is, he never allows his own personality to obtrude upon that of the subject he is studying.

OutL. Feb. 10, 1912, p. 214

His poetry is a phenomenon as singular, in its own way, as that of Mr. A. E. Housman. . . . Thomas wrote no verse between quite early life and the middle thirties. Then, in 1913, he began to pour out a great number of queer, rather fierce, very intense poems, disconcerting in content and form, and unlike anything ever written by anyone else. I have been told that the poetry of Mr. Robert Frost gave him his first impulse; and that may be so, though the impulse never became an influence. However it may be, Thomas continued to write verses during the last four years of his life; and when he was killed in April on the first day of the battle for the Vimy Ridge, he left a considerable number of pieces behind him. The first of these (sixteen or so of them) had been published only a few weeks before in an *Annual of New Poetry* over the signature "Edward Eastaway"; and the literary public had not bestirred itself sufficiently to take any interest in them, when suddenly it heard that the author was Thomas and that he was dead. . . .

I suggested . . . Thomas was a disillusioned and somewhat embittered man. He spent the best of his youth over critical essays and books of literary travel which, though he did them as well as he could, that is to say, very well indeed, were not meant for permanence and will not be permanent. His was the minor tragedy of a man who, consenting to write for the market, was kept on the very margin of popularity by an uncompromising conscience and insisted on putting his best work into books for which, in themselves, he cared very little. The tone of his poetry conveys the impression that he felt that the gift for it had come to him too late. The poems deal throughout with the things which, as I suppose, made life endurable to him; but they alternate between the feeling that the loveliness of these things can only increase his own discontent and the other feeling that they are at best only attempts to hide the misery of life. It is as though he treated this stubborn and late-won talent with a certain disdain, holding it less in awe because it had come after the time to give him pleasure. And in his seeming indifference, he handles verse brusquely and carelessly and so gets out of it, again and again, effects of rhythm and description novel and marvelously penetrating. . . .

Thomas was not perhaps, probably never would have been, a great poet; but he was a poet exquisitely true and exquisitely individual.

Edward Shanks. *Dial*. Dec. 20, 1917, pp. 631–32

I always considered his criticism the best part of his literary work. He was about the best critic of poetry in his time. His learning was as profound as his taste was unerring. As regards prose, his book on *Walter Pater* is the best on the subject. One sentence alone shows a wonderful sense of what makes for style: "Only when a word has become necessary to him can a man use it safely; if he try to impress words by force on a sudden occasion, they will either perish of his violence or betray him." The book was a failure because the British public does not want judicial criticism. To the literary snob Pater was a fetish, and fetishes are not meant to be the subject of intelligent discussion.

Much the same drawback applied to Thomas's deep and sympathetic interest in human beings as such. He chose types which do not excite general interest. Our urban population likes to read of dukes and Prime Ministers and millionaires, with a female complement of duchesses and adventuresses. An intensive study of Welsh farmers and rustic milkmaids and tramps excites but little curiosity. And Thomas perhaps felt that there was not so much demand for his writing as it deserved, without realising that in this imperfect world a man has often to begin by creating a demand for himself. All this, however, aggravated a natural melancholy of temperament, which was not cured by various abstinences either from meat or drink or tobacco. His health suffered much as Shelley's did when removed from the robust influence of Peacock.

E. S. P. Hynes. *Eng.R*. June, 1917, pp. 528–29

The poetry of Edward Thomas affects one morally as well as aesthetically and intellectually. We have grown rather shy, in these days of pure aestheticism, of speaking of those consoling or strengthening qualities of poetry on which critics of another generation took pleasure in dwelling. Thomas's poetry is strengthening and consoling, not because it justifies God's ways to man or whispers of reunions beyond the grave, not because it presents great moral truths in memorable numbers, but in a more subtle and very much more effective way. . . .

The secret of Thomas's influence lies in the fact that he is genuinely what so many others of our time quite unjustifiably claim to be, a nature poet. To be a nature poet it is not enough to affirm vaguely that God made the country and man made the town, it is not enough to talk sympathetically about familiar rural objects, it is not enough to be sonorously poetical about mountains and trees; it is not even enough to speak of these things with the precision of real knowledge and love. To be a nature poet a man must have felt profoundly and intimately those peculiar emotions which nature can inspire, and must be able to express them in such a way that his reader feels them.

Aldous Huxley. *On The Margin*
(N.Y., George H. Doran, 1923), pp. 143–44

There was something of the Byzantine angel about him; ethereal, refined, aloof. Thomas was so austere in the matter of food and drink, so conscientious, so incurably monogamous, that, differing fundamentally from each other, we agreed perfectly....

Although a Welshman (of an unusual variety, he was careful to explain) Thomas was more English than many an Englishman; too English altogether; and also too much of a hack writer. He talked and wrote of books, and of books about books, till the lyrical core of his mind was submerged, imprisoned, encysted in an inpenetrable capsule. His poems —if only he could have published one slender volume every two years, and nothing else whatever! Instead of that, he told me (I think) that since the age of seventeen, when his first book appeared, he had written three of them every year. Three books a year—a dog's life. I would sooner have been blacking boots. I, too, like Richard Jefferies, but Thomas liked him too much; he has the same limitations as has the countryside he so lovingly describes....

What Thomas lacked was a little touch of bestiality, a little *je-m'en-fous-t-ism*. He was too scrupulous. Often, sitting at the Horse Shoe or some such place—often I told him that it was no use trying to be a gentleman if you are a professional writer. You are not dealing with gentlemen; why place yourself at a disadvantage? They'll flay you alive, if they can. Whereupon he would smile wistfully, and say that another pint of Burton would be my ruin.

And then he was blown to pieces in the War.

Norman Douglas. *Looking Back*
(N.Y., Harcourt, Brace, 1933), pp. 143–47

Some of the profound melancholy that overcame Edward at intervals was no doubt due to a tinge of that Celtic temperament inherited from his parents, both Welsh by origin, though living far from Wales. But I always knew there was a far deeper cause than the straits of poverty or the influence of race. When first he came to me, I said to myself, "Yet another poet!" for in those days we were all publishing thin volumes of verse.... Till the war fell upon us and he volunteered for service, he had never written poetry. One of the few blessings of that war was that it gave his genius release. In the army he was released from other people's books and could allow his own genius to fulfil itself. As to livelihood, he and his wife and children were then fairly secure. To a man of his self-distrust and want of confidence, there was some advantage, too, in being under orders which admitted of no hesitation. The daemon of melancholy left him. The last time I saw him he was in uniform, calm, confident, and courageous of heart. The energy of his soul had found its line of excellence. He was writing or had already written those poems which after his death on the field were to give him a high place in the English literature which he knew and loved so well.

Henry W. Nevinson. LL. March, 1940, pp. 272–73

During and immediately following the war years a great many people who were not conspicuously fond of, or well acquainted with, English literature, found new inspiration and increasing pleasure in a poet who died as long ago as 1917. He was Edward Thomas, a man who had always been part of the very stuff of our heritage of the soil and whose voice, always true yet always quiet, was now being heard again with growing significance. Today, he stands as the only one of the Georgians who remains widely popular. The passing of the years has brought him nearer today to a vaster public than he ever dreamt of, and in the verse of this simple, clear, unaffected man continuing generations are finding refreshment and a justification of almost all they hold dear in life. . . .

Quite suddenly his torn and tormented life resolved itself as he had never thought it would. War broke out, and after little hesitation, he became a soldier. What is more important, he began to write verse, and almost at once emerged as a true poet, writing with a grasp of words which came, technically mature, at once, no doubt thanks to the long apprenticeship he had sentenced himself to endure. His friendship with the American poet Robert Frost encouraged him, and soon, as the war moved on, he was writing first-class poems by the dozen. All his poetic work is crammed into those few years he had left to him. He began diffident as ever—and a certain serene yet somehow confident shyness never left him—under the pseudonym of Edward Eastaway. He sent his new poems round to his literary friends, Frost, Edward Garnett, W. H. Hudson, Eleanor Farjeon who typed them, for him, and although a few were published during the war years, most were spurned by editors and publishers who later came to print them with avidity. It is ironical that they earned more money after his death than when he really needed it.

David Gunston. Colophon. Jan., 1951, p. 32

I suppose I had met Edward Thomas in the anthologies, and admired the pieces anthologies always choose, such as "Out in the Dark" and "Lights Out," some time before he began to speak to me with a voice that seemed to respond more and more subtly to my own feelings about *things*—old houses, hidden streams, woods under rain, bonfires in gardens and twisting country lanes—than that of any other poet I had read. I cannot now date the change and the revelation for myself; I only know there was a time when he was one among twenty or thirty Georgian poets I was reading with enthusiasm in the first flush of my discovery of what was then modern poetry, and that he is now one of the only three or four of those poets I still read and come back to again and again with delight and wonder.

John Lehmann. The Open Night (Longmans, 1952), p. 76

We turn from his clear, abstemious, unemphatic prose to the verse of the *Poems,* and it is as if a wind had suddenly come out of the south, setting the waters free. Thomas had been criticizing other men's poetry for twenty years, and all these years had been steadily storing up his own. It is a poetry that not only breaks away from poetic convention, into a verse in which the rhymes are the faintest of echoes, the metre at times scarcely distinguishable, and form as insubstantial as a ghost's, but much of it is "about" what most poets leave unremarked, or, at any rate, unrecorded. We listen to a kind of monologue, like that of one of his own nightingales softly practising over its song, as though in utmost secrecy we were overhearing a man talking quietly to himself, or to some friend strangely silent and understanding, pouring out his reveries, ruminations, remembrances. Yet these are not remembrances only of what has happened in the past, but of what is almost insupportably real and near and present, taking the aspect of the past on the eve of a long farewell.

Walter de la Mare. Private View
(Faber and Faber, 1953), p. 119

THOMAS, R. S. (1913–   )

R. S. Thomas is Welsh, was born in Wales, and is the rector of a country parish there. He has published in Montgomeryshire three books of poetry, *The Stones of the Field* (1946), *An Acre of Land* (1952), *The Minister* (1953). He has now united the three books, discarding some poems and adding new ones to make this composite volume. He is a regional poet of much more than regional interest. His poetry is born of a sympathy and a struggle with his fellow-countrymen. A poet is liable to be a kind of exile in his own country or time: the consciousness of difference, and the effort to communicate it, may provide his emotive power as a poet. . . .

Mr. Thomas's poems are a country priest's response to the atmosphere and look of his parish, and more especially to his parishioners; they are the product of his exploration of their lives, of his understanding and compassion as a man and as a priest. . . . Living in a non-industrialized environment, Mr. Thomas sees and hears natural phenomena, perceives their effect upon those beings who live nearest to them, and is conscious, as a townsman cannot be, of the fertility and fruitfulness of the soil and of the beauties of growth. At the same time he is deeply troubled by the apparently stunting and impoverishing effect upon the human spirit of wringing a living from the soil by incessant hard work. But if his toiling peasants, he seems to say, are thus spiritually gnarled and emotionally starved, if they do not show in their lives the exuberance, joyfulness, playfulness, spontaneous warmth or passion of nature, that is not only the fault of grubbing about in stony ground, it is a consequence of the puritanical and life-denying Welsh tradition of Calvinistic Methodism that has done much to form them.

William Plomer. *L*. March, 1956, pp. 74–75

The poetry of R. S. Thomas conveys the prime impression of a single force directed to one carefully limited theme, the isolation of the natural rhythm of man's life ("Rhythm of the long scythe") in the natural order, seen with irony, occasional bitterness, with urbane control of word and metric, and a tautness of mind, the fruit of a particular urbanity. Indeed, there is especial irony in attributing this urbane quality to a poet who so passionately repudiates the urban.

For all the complexity of Thomas's tone and attitudes, it seemed that his craft had declared itself in full stature in the first volume, *The Stones of the Field,* in 1946, and then for nine years, through *An Acre of Land* (1952), the long broadcast poem, *The Minister* (1953) to the first collected edition, *Song at the Year's Turning* in 1955, had done no more than amplify the few original themes, turning them over, handling them with the deftness of a surgeon, revealing a few more strands of their texture but demonstrating no conspicuously new powers. And we should have been quite content with another thirty years of this detached compassion, united to a self-critical craftsmanship as great as any shown in English verse to-day. But *Poetry for Supper,* published in 1958, and the few poems that have appeared in the journals since, are different in tone and range from the earlier works. The same subjects are treated and with the same attitudes, but the emotional range has greatly increased; the ironic comment has deepened (and with a lancing bitterness rarely heard before), while the compassion is wider. Above all R. S. Thomas has become more explicit in statement; while he forces no acceptable conclusion, makes no assumption of dogma, the credal implications always present in his work are now less allusive in statement. . . . The strenuous intelligence of this parson-poet would appear to have a suitable point of rest in that closing identification of the believer with the crucified Christ; it would be dangerous in fact to expect any point of rest at this moment in the work of an exploratory mind which is as astringent in renouncing easy attitudes for itself as it is compassionately ruthless in analysing his neigbours.

W. Moelwyn Merchant. *CQ*. Winter, 1960, pp. 341, 351

THOMPSON, SYLVIA (1902–   )

The Hounds of Spring is a moderately competent novel of pre-war, wartime, and post-war England. It is diffuse and contains much matter, especially in the dialogue, that could be well left out: and its plot, which entails the loss, by a very deserving if pompous and unimaginative soldier, of two wives, is decidedly artificial. But Miss Thompson, whatever scene she describes, or whatever character she portrays, never goes far wrong. Her novel gives the effect of having been written, as Browne says, "on one legg"; it deserved a firmer stance. She has a kind of indolent insight into the workings of many minds; but her penetration suffers from the carelessness of her presentation. The book is too informal: but it is full of promise. Miss Thompson is never taken in by her characters, her judgment is rarely at fault: but the want of intensity which so often accompanies wide sympathies and a central position makes her work less effective than it should be. Her art is less mature than her experience, but her experience is remarkable.

L. P. Hartley. *SR*. April 3, 1926, p. 456

In *Summer's Night* the different races are the rich and the not-so-rich. Miss Thompson makes one have doubts, at first, as to the discrimination of her detail: she thinks, for instance, to give reality to the selling of Melcombe, the Bitternes's ancestral home, to the manufacturing parvenu, Lord Whichford, by reproducing the perfunctory correspondence exchanged by the parties on the subject. Here the letter killeth indeed. But it is not long before detail, coming to the telling and exquisite moments of a young passion, is well embarked on a very delicate and understanding study of a young man and woman—she the daughter of the parvenu, he the artist-son of the impoverished ancestral home.... She has, indeed, a distinct place among younger novelists; she possesses something more than the power cleverly to reflect her time; she is moved by beauty in too positive a sense merely to depict its absence; and these young lovers in their happiness and later in their married estrangement are certainly figures of beauty.

Viola Meynell. *NSN*. April 9, 1932, p. 455

Miss Thompson in her interesting new book [*Unfinished Symphony*] sets the problem as to whether a girl educated quite outside of this structure and without the slightest knowledge of it could learn to adjust herself when, later on, she is inevitably thrown into contact with the world of men. In one sense *Unfinished Symphony* derives from the Mowgli stories and all the other books in which children of the jungle are suddenly and devastatingly launched into unsuspecting civilised society; but Helena, its heroine, is in no sense a daughter of the wild. . . .

The premises . . . are wild—for it seems incredible that in this age a girl should grow up as the heroine is supposed to and speak with such a quaint mixture of pedantry and innocence. Granted these premises, however, the story is a very moving one of the loss of youth's illusions, effective because written with all Miss Thompson's usual smoothness. It is lighted up by vivid, malicious pictures of a fashionable society similar to that described in *Summer's Night.* . . .

Elizabeth L. Brown. *NYT*. March 19, 1933, p. 7

Miss Sylvia Thompson persists in diluting her shrewd and delicate talent with too much glamour. It is a pity that she does not, even for once, try the experiment of ignoring or chancing the look of things. The exercise of writing of her elegant and charming people from the unstated, implicit assumption of their elegance and charm should be fruitful for her, because she understands human motives, can be charmingly witty, and writes some passages with an admirable, wise detachment. But she will have *décor*—and of a kind that really does not need to be laboured. This new book [*The Gulls Fly Inland*] is overcharged with meditative sippings of old cognac and the smell of little yellow roses; there is too much of the whiteness of magnolia trees and the bronze beauty of men seen against the turquoise-blue of painted walls. This kind of thing only shows up the central weakness of the whole book, which is in the author's nervous leniency with the passion of love, to which she can allow only two moods, sweetness and pain. . . . If she would only turn her fine, deft talents away awhile from brilliant asides about elderly people, babies, governesses and servants, and direct them without fear or favour on to her central theme of attractive-seeming people in love, she could hardly fail to produce something highly individual and moving. If she could chance beauty for awhile, forget it, how deftly she might establish it!

Kate O'Brien. *Spec.* Sept. 5, 1941, p. 244

TILLER, TERENCE (1916–)

To preserve some sense of discrimination amongst the poets whom I like, I am reduced to having to give marks and places. Purely for convenience's sake, in dealing with these dozens of poets, and not because I believe in a Stock Exchange of the arts, I place the poet I now come to first of the younger writers. This is Terence Tiller. Having read his poems several times, I think that they combine the merits of the other younger writers on this list, and lack their defects. Mr. Tiller is as accomplished as Vernon Watkins, without being so literary. He can use effective and violent imagery, and can think, in addition to this. His poems strike one as whole, and as well organized. He can write about the present without reminding one of the headlines of the morning newspaper, full of "certain hazy abstractions" such as "Iceland, Singapore and the Near East." . . . Mr. Tiller is still a little under the influence of Auden, and his poetry has not got that precision of observation which strikes home again and again, as do the early poems of Eliot. All the same, these musical and thoughtful poems grow on one as something genuine, without being subjective and personal.

Stephen Spender. *Hor.* Feb., 1942, pp. 100–1

Mr. Terence Tiller's new collection *Reading a Medal* (his first for ten years) is, in its blend of the subtle and the lyrical, the most polished and mature of the books under review. His singing line, while always original, contains profound echoes from the silver age of English Romanticism which few of his younger contemporaries would risk (or bring off, if they did risk it) and which come to us like zephyrs in a desert. . . .

In his best work Mr. Tiller allows nothing to interfere with his exceptional lyrical gift. He knows there is no real alternative to what he calls, in "Resolutions of a Committee," "virginal wrestling . . . for possession of the lunar nine-quetzal-class muses, and their return." And in the three lyrics called "Brompton Cemetery," . . . the muses return in triumph.

K. W. Gransden. *Enc.* March, 1958, pp. 82–83

TODD, RUTHVEN (1914–)

Over the Mountain suffers from a division of style and purpose. . . . It is a sort of allegory: the story of a young man named Michael . . . who lives in a village at the foot of the Pale Peak . . . and longs to conquer the summit and discover what is on the other side. The adventurous part of the book comes . . . at the beginning; Mr. Todd's account of the climb is really exciting, in spite of a tendency to rely too much on the nightmares and fantasies of the exhausted climber. . . . When Michael has descended the other side of the Peak, the interest, for me, dropped rapidly. The unknown land is discovered to be a parody of his own country (in fact, a parody of contemporary Europe) with caricatured inhabitants . . . the political satire, though aimed at objects which badly need it, is of the order which relies for its effect on the simplest exaggerations, like those highbrow romps which on Sunday evenings put the dictators through it with a smile and a song.

Desmond Shawe-Taylor. NSN. March 11, 1939, p. 390

Ruthven Todd's brand of rusticity is not that of the Georgian weekend. Instead, it is a sense of the land's longevity; its immemorial usage. Nor is this habit of observation limited only to the country of his birth [Scotland]; for in the poem "Various Places" he conveys the impression of an English country with the same topographical character-drawing as we find in his poems of home. It would, however, be time to say that these descriptions are the result of a visual closeness to the subject rather than of any strong identification.

Just this more simple background of the soil was what assisted the poet to understand, by a process of contrast, the nature of the city; its own distinct pattern of social living. For Ruthven Todd the metropolis appears as an incubator of hate, a vast vat of anxiety, the very seat and source of war. Residing in the city, where one lives beneath a constant bombardment of news, close to the dynamos of policy and law, produces and strengthens a sense of history. Thus in the verse of Ruthven Todd the evil muse is history; and his lines are heavy with its presence; cast in the shadow of its prophecies.

Derek Stanford. The Freedom of Poetry
(Falcon Pr., 1947), pp. 226–27

Mr. Todd, keeping the easy, competent tone of the British amateur, fittingly chooses his title [*Tracks in the Snow*] from the elegant Edward Gibbon, whose taste for the sciences, he believed, enabled the anatomist and chemist to track him "in their own snow."

Eighteenth-century science was, of course, imperfectly experimental and often injudicious in its curiosity about "phlogiston," its evidence on the Druids and the Flood, and its harebrained regard of orangutans, wild girls, and all those outlandish creatures the Scottish Lord Monboddo pursued for a lifetime—Dr. Johnson: "I am *afraid* (chuckling and laughing) Monboddo does not know he is talking nonsense." This uncertain, occultist science, in the "rational" eighteenth century, inspired in the arts visions we can only call nocturnal. Maybe Mr. Todd's largest service is forcing us again to recognize what we have too often forgotten—the nocturnal, Gothic eighteenth century rediscovered by the surrealists.

Wylie Sypher. Nation. June 14, 1947, p. 720

Ruthven Todd's poems [*A Mantelpiece of Shells*] have a certain hard quality which may be more British than American. His poems tend to be definite, scholarly and occasional. He writes in strict forms. There is a strong feeling of place or of person in his work, a struggle to synthesize his life in America with his background in Britain. . . .

Mr. Todd has sometimes a decisive turn of phrase. His poem about Blake, entitled "Excess," ends: "That all the words of William Blake/ Proved justly that the world was mad." His feelings break the shell of intellect in "A Narrow Sanctuary" and "The Perfect Now," both poems of emotional understanding. His range is considerable, his writing is firm, and there is often wit.

Richard Eberhardt. NYT. Dec. 18, 1953, p. 4

TOLKIEN, J. R. R. (1892–   )

Methodical persons who prefer to plan their reading may find some difficulty in "placing" Dr. J. R. R. Tolkien's massy prose epic, *The Fellowship of the Ring*. Spenser, Malory, and Ariosto are named among its progenitors, but the pedigree would appear to include *Beowulf,* the *Gondal Saga, Goblin Market, The Water Babies,* and *The Idylls of the King*. In an age of rather sordid realism it is pleasant to see a new fairy mythology in process of creation, and even more pleasant to perceive that many readers willingly join in this game of make-believe.

D. M. Stuart. Eng. Autumn, 1954, p. 114

I suppose readers exist who do not enjoy Heroic Quests, but I have never met them. For many of us they are so much the most delicious form of literature that we can devour one even when our critical faculties tell us it is trash. Those who remember *The Hobbit* as the best children's story written in the last fifty years will open any new work by Professor Tolkien with high hopes, but *The Fellowship of the Ring* [pt. I of *The Lord of the Rings*] is better than their wildest dreams could have foreseen; if he is not a rich man by next Christmas, I shall be surprised.

In discussing a book of this type, a reviewer is at a disadvantage because he must not spoil the reader's pleasure by giving away what happens, which—in this case—is at least as exciting as the story of *The Thirty-Nine Steps*. In the normal Quest plot there is a numinous object which has either fallen into the hands of the Enemy or is protected from the unworthy by terrifying guardians; none but the predestined hero can find it, but it is good that he should. In *The Fellowship of the Ring* the numinous object, which is like the Ring of the Niebelungs only even more sinister, is in the possession of the hero at the start. . . .

This quest takes place in an imaginary world of Mr. Tolkien's invention with its own landscape, history, and inhabitants. In its general characteristics this world is Celtic and Scandinavian rather than Mediterranean. . . .

Perhaps Mr. Tolkien's greatest achievement is to have written a heroic romance which seems wholly relevant to the realities of our concrete historical existence. When reading medieval examples of this genre, enjoyable as they are, one is sometimes tempted to ask the Knightly hero—"Is your trip necessary?" Even in the Quest for the San Graal, success or failure is only of importance to those who undertake it. One cannot altogether escape the suspicion that, in relation to such knights, the word "vocation" is a high-faluting term for a game which gentlemen with private means are free to play while the real work of the real world is done by "villains."

In *The Fellowship of the Ring,* on the other hand, the fate of the Ring will affect the daily lives of thousands who have never heard of its existence. Further, as in the Bible and many fairy stories, the hero is not a Knight, endowed by birth and breeding with exceptional *areté,* but only a hobbit pretty much like all other hobbits. It is not the wise Gandalf or the mighty Aragorn but Frodo Baggins who is called to undertake this deadly dangerous mission which he would much rather avoid, and if one asks why he and not one of a hundred others like him, the only answer is that chance, or Providence, has chosen, and he must obey.

W. H. Auden. *Enc.* Nov., 1954, pp. 59–62

Now it seems clear that *The Lord of the Rings* is fairy-story according to Professor Tolkien's understanding of the term. And though it may be urged that the theory is not intrinsically a very interesting or important one, at least we must fairly take account of it in the present connection. Let us then consider the book for a moment in terms of the criteria Professor Tolkien has offered us. Marks for Fantasy, say eight out of ten: one cannot deny that to keep going throughout three large volumes the story of the difficulties and obstacles which had to be overcome before the Ring could be destroyed was a considerable feat of endurance, and within limits the Other-world created has the internal consistency claimed for it. "Within limits" because in fact considerable advantage is taken of our ignorance: we don't really know anything about the wonders that may take place in this Other-world, and not infrequently wonders are sprung on us that we have no reason to believe possible. Again we sometimes find ourselves wondering why some difficult things should be possible when some other things, that would seem by comparison quite easy, are not. . . .

Thus far, we have had to admit that *The Lord of the Rings* is an unusually successful book. One's doubts begin to stir, however, when one looks for that nameless "value" that Professor Tolkien also mentioned, "that value which, as literature, they [fairy-stories] share with other literary forms." Here, of course, Professor Tolkien offers us no clear guidance and our evaluations must accordingly be more tentative. Nonetheless, the inadequacies that one has to comment on make themselves felt at a very elementary level. It is impossible, for instance, not to notice the peculiar manner of the writing. One cannot very well talk about the style of the book, for the style changes so constantly and so radically. At one moment, for example, we are confronted with an heroic, almost an epic, style; at another we are offered pages of lush Romantic description somewhat redolent of Tennyson, though of course in prose; while in a wholly different style again are those passages in which the hobbits are described (free for the time from serious cares) enjoying their simple jolly selves in characteristically simple and jolly fashion.

Mark Roberts. EC. Oct., 1956, pp. 454–56

TOMLINSON, CHARLES (1927–   )

These poems [*The Necklace*] require no introduction. From one point of view this is the most astonishing thing about them, the way they build up for themselves their own poetic universe. And if the world they inhabit is conspicuously "their own," it is not therefore a private world. On the contrary; we are offered here no private symbolism or *ad hoc* mythology, no projection of conflicts personal to the poet. The world of these poems is a public one, open to any man who has kept clean and in order his own nervous sensitivity to the impact of shape and mass and colour, odour, texture and timbre. The poems appeal outside of themselves only to the world perpetually bodied against our senses. They improve that world. Once we have read them, it appears to us renovated and refreshed, its colours more delicate and clear, its masses more momentous, its sounds and odours sharper, more distinct. Nothing could be less literary, less amenable to discussion in terms of schools and influences.

Donald Davie. Introd. in Charles Tomlinson.
The Necklace (Oxford, Fantasy Press, 1955), p. 3

Seeing Is Believing introduces [into America] the work of a talented young English writer. Charles Tomlinson's theme, as indicated by his title, is how the mind and eye cooperate to build a world—a theme brought into modern poetry by Wordsworth and central to the work of Wallace Stevens (there are traces of Stevens in a few of these poems). To this theme Tomlinson brings a rich rhetoric that is capable of imparting energy to objects in its descriptions of the eye's play. His poetry exhibits thought and an evident delight in massed language. The result is an impressive first volume.

Harvey Shapiro. NYT. June 22, 1958, p. 4

Mr. Tomlinson's remarkable capacity for development is the most salient of his virtues. That he is intensely English, yet at present accessible chiefly to American readers; that he is invariably omitted from London Letters concerning English writing in the fifties, while the paper-doll warfare of the Angry Young Men and the University Wits passes for urgent literary history; that no British publisher's reader has been able to recognize his verse as even competent; that a blurb for the present volume [*Seeing Is Believing*] concocted in a New York publisher's office summarizes his qualities more accurately than any British reviews of *The Necklace;* these are facts for a historian to ponder who would trace the sequel to that now distant age when a Robert Frost was compelled to go abroad and be discovered (by Ezra Pound, it is true) in London.

Hugh Kenner. Poetry. Feb. 1959, p. 340

He is a very cool customer indeed, and very, very precise. Precision, in fact, is what his poems are about: precision of outline, of definition, of intent. . . . He is a poet whose whole business is with getting things clear, saying exactly what they are like and how they fit objectively together. If F. T. Prince is a painter's poet, Tomlinson is a bit of a poet's painter. Essentially not superficially, he is interested in how things look. His landscapes are landscapes *out there,* not symbols of any states of mind. Moods and generalisations are just colours on his palette, more or less useful in painting an accurate picture [*A Peopled Landscape*].

It is all very serious, but at the same time flat and unvarying. Even the experiments don't really alter the singleness of his note; his first book was influenced by Wallace Stevens, his second by Pound, this new one by William Carlos Williams and Marianne Moore. Yet despite the transatlantic clothing, he remains a rather staid English watercolourist, painstaking and a trifle cold-blooded. But if you like treescapes, he is your poet.

A. Alvarez. Obs. July 14, 1963, p. 24

TOMLINSON, H. M. (1873–1958)

Mr. Tomlinson is a born traveller. There are two sorts of travellers—those who do what they are told and those who do what they please. Mr. Tomlinson has never moved about the world in obedience to a guide-book. He would find it almost as difficult to read a guide-book as to write one. He never echoes men's curiosity. He travels for the purpose neither of information nor conversation. He has no motive but whim. His imagination goes roaming; and, his imagination and his temper being such as they are, he is out on his travels even if he gets no farther than Limehouse or the Devonshire coast. He has, indeed, wandered a good deal farther than Limehouse and Devonshire, as readers of *The Sea and the Jungle* know. Even in his more English volumes of sketches, essays, confessions, short stories—how is one to describe them?—he takes us with him to the north coast of Africa, to New York, and to France in war time. But the English sketches—the description of the crowd at a pitmouth after an explosion in a coal mine, the account of a derelict railway station and a grocer's boy in spectacles —almost equally give us the feeling we are reading the narrative of one who has seen nothing except with the fortunate eyes of a stranger. It is all a matter of eyes. To see is to discover, and all Mr. Tomlinson's books are, in this sense, books of discoveries.

As a recorder of the things he has seen he has the three great gifts of imagery, style and humour. He sees the jelly-fish hanging in the transparent deeps "like sunken moons." A boat sailing on a windy day goes skimming over the inflowing ridges of the waves "with exhilarating undulations, light as a sandpiper." . . .

But weather-beaten as Mr. Tomlinson's pages are, there is more in them than the weather. There is an essayish quality in his books, personal, confessional, go-as-you-please. The majority of essays have egotism without personality. Mr. Tomlinson's sketches have personality without egotism. He is economical of discussion of his own tastes. When he does discuss them you know that here is no make-believe of confession. . . .

He picks out from the disordered procession of things treasures that most of us would pass with hardly a glance. His clues to the meaning of the world are all of his own finding. It is this which gives his work the savour and freshness of literature.

Robert Lynd. *Books and Authors*
(N.Y., G. P. Putnam's Sons, 1923), pp. 252–58

He travels because he is by nature a dreamer, and he writes because he is by circumstance a rebel. His mind falls into the order of dreams, the dreams recur and stimulate him again and again to fresh journeys; in the breath of dreams he sees the same images, like figures in smoke, and he returns to the same early country of childhood's memory, the same admired characters and scenes of manhood's memory, repeating what he loves because he loves it and because it revolves and in its turn possesses him again. Yet there is nothing dreamlike in what he tells, and perhaps his best prose is given to the sharp, clear and simple telling of simple matters—of the rust of an anchor, the coldness of seas, the unexpectedness of stairs and passages in rough weather. Of these and a hundred other items he writes as the most businesslike, dreamless alderman would write if he could. For a long while, he says, the steamer was a harsh and foreign thing, unfriendly to the eye, hard to understand; but he learned to know her faults and now would resent any change. . . .

He shows something childlike and candid in his stare at strange things, counting and looking at them—familiar enough to others—as though no one had ever seen them before. It is as if Robinson Crusoe or John Bunyan had gone to sea in a tramp steamer and confronted that anchor, that heavy swell, those stairs and passages, and gazed half in doubt, half in delight. Thus it is that *The Sea and the Jungle* gives you immediately a double view—of what the writer sees with his unaccustomed stare, and of the fresh receptive mind touched by the succession of images and wonders. And all is so simple that there is an effect of cunning in the simplicity, the plain thing being enriched, yet no more complicated than is the tree by its shadow, which as you look becomes indeed a part of the tree.

It may be freely admitted that Mr. Tomlinson's other books are not all equal to *The Sea and the Jungle*. Some are precisely journalism, and the wisdom of collecting the items may be doubted, for when he reviews books . . . he shows that he is less interested in what men say than in what they do and the world they inhabit. Ideas attract little interest and no warmth in his regard, and so his reprinted reviews are not the things to compel a new reader's attention, and perhaps the best to be said for them is that there is nothing to repel it, certainly not that cleverness which, he sees, is craved only by the brainsick, as drink is craved by a morbid body.

John Freeman. *LM*. Aug., 1927, pp. 401–4

Most of his readers, perhaps all but the most astute, would be surprised if they met him. There is nothing of the traveler about H. M. Tomlinson. He is not bronzed, hearty, hail-fellow-well-met, nor does he carry with him any suggestion of great distances and strange suns. Yet his appearance, I think, is significant, revealing not a little of his secret. At a first superficial glance, he looks like a rather hard-bitten city clerk. At a second glance, he looks like a gnome, who has come up from some elfin solitude to observe the stir of things on the bright surface of the world, to see men hurry down long streets, swing up to their navigating bridges, or dive below to their engine rooms, and harry their little ships across the globe to some fantastic heart of darkness. These two contradictory appearances bring us close to the secret of his unique power as an essayist of travel. His work would not have the force it has unless he were at once the city clerk, that is, the man who knows the life of the dark streets, and knows what it is to escape, and the elfin recorder, with such a wealth of exact yet luminous imagery, who travels here, there, and everywhere in search of strangely significant facts. He is not to be confused with those writers—and there are not a few of them—who deal largely in the same wares, the docks and the old clippers, and little ports on the edge of the jungle, for the purpose of achieving cheap romantic effects. Theirs is the way of easy escape. Although, to the casual observer, he may seem to travel the same path, actually his way is very different, for it is that of hard escape. . . .

Romance is there—the strange distant light has never gone out—but it is something seen between bouts of wrestling with hard facts. Remove him from these scenes of heroic routine, touched with fantastic beauty, and you have an ironist of a sardonic and uncompromising temper. His reading is significant, for when he has reluctantly set aside the great simple voyagers, his men are Swift and Heine and Butler and Anatole France. Criticism is not really his business at all, though for some years he was engaged in it. He could probably write about a few books and the authors better than any man living, but for the rest, he is no critic. His demands are too narrow and personal, and he would rather explore the world than other men's minds. He would seem to pass by the light graces of life and literature with a shrug. Sentimentalism makes him angry. . . . But though he may be unduly embittered at times, he is anything but soured, and is far removed from certain contemporary authors who assail the universe and their fellow creatures because vanity is eating out their hearts.

J. B. Priestley. Sat. Jan. 1, 1927, pp. 477–78

When he first emerged as a writer on the sea his emergence happened to coincide with the rise of Joseph Conrad to popular favor; and the fact that they both wrote about these marine matters caused him to be labelled an imitation of Conrad. This is fatuous; for while Conrad is (pardonably enough) a loose and inexact writer of English and gets his strength from the images he pulls somehow (largely by setting hazy phrases side by side) through the tangle of his language and the rhythm with which he arranges them in his tale, Mr. Tomlinson's gift is for the precise use of words which scoop up so much of reality as he desires and leave it on his page. It is, as it were, the art of Turner as against the art of Manet. Their differences in essential character dictated a difference in form.

The rhythm that so pleased Mr. Tomlinson was the quiet, almost imperceptible rhythm of daily life. He is himself almost completely non-neurotic, giving one the impression that he has found the proper sublimation for every impulse he has ever had; and he has not that supreme degree of creative genius which makes him interested and sympathetic in lives that are totally unlike his own. He, therefore, does not get swept into those vortices which rage round the attempts of a person or a group of persons to resolve some quarrel with the universe, as is the customary behavior of Conrad, who was neurotic and who, even if he had not been, would still have been interested and sympathetic in [sic] people who were. In fact, Conrad was a born novelist, and Mr. Tomlinson is a born essayist. And the public will not read essays. Therefore, long he languished unread and when he came into his own, had to do it through *Gallions Reach,* a fine book, but spoiled by the violent insertion into it of the conflicts appropriate to a novel. I wish that everybody who reads it would turn back to an essay on "Earthshine" in Mr. Tomlinson's *Old Junk,* which is unrivalled in its expression of a beauty so subtle that one would have certified it as inexpressible.

Rebecca West. *Bkm.* July, 1929, p. 520

Mr. Tomlinson, who this week attained the age of 80 and who therefore, according to the custom of this country towards its literary men, is on the edge of an assured status, has since 1917 published fewer than thirty books. There are two facts worth notice about his series: the more important is that it did not begin before the writer's style was fully seasoned, and the second follows from the first; fully seasoned, it has not altered, and scarcely been modified. . . .

Accent is Mr. Tomlinson's triumph, and his limitation. In his rare novels, the people face occasions, but they do not grow, and the central figure is often the same. He is a bit of a Marlow, and to those who know the richness of Conrad that is scarcely dispraise. . . .

TLS. June 26, 1953, p. 412

TOYNBEE, PHILIP (1916–)

Mr. Toynbee's novel belongs to the kind that must either be first-rate or else thrown in the waste-paper basket. *The Barricades* is *not* first-rate; and in so far as it is "smart," which is always a fairly awkward thing to be in letters, it sports, alas, the smartness of yesterday, or the day before even—the surest way of all of being dowdy. It is, or seems, a very long book about a schoolboy who in 1937 runs away from school to try to get to Spain with the International Brigade, and about a schoolmaster who gets chucked from his job, for drink and impudence, and hangs about London, Paris and the South of France, acting as some kind of washed-away Mephistopheles both to his own hardly perceptible *alter ego* and to the schoolboy. This is a good theme, but—like any other—it stands or falls in presentation by the significance or not of its exponents, and it seems to me that Mr. Toynbee has failed to give any authority, comic, tragic or symbolic, to either of his leading characters. And if that is so, it is too much to ask us to follow them so very closely, from drink to drink and from pretentious party to still more pretentious private argument, learning only as we go that they are dull, vain exhibitionists, forever repeating themselves and never being really funny or really moving.

Kate O'Brien. *Spec.* Dec. 24, 1943, p. 604

"What *is* it?" seems more than usually difficult to answer about *The Garden to the Sea*. Scrambled novel, poetic monologue, autobiographical figment? All apply, or don't quite. . . .

I had to read *The Garden to the Sea* a second time to rid myself of the mere distraction of finding my way. The first time plunged me into such a whirl as one might meet in a Dylan Thomas poem beginning "I am Adam"; but the poem would be short and intense, whereas Mr. Toynbee, though finely emphatic, is long. What he does succeed in is giving to a tale of passionate disagreement impassioned speech. The question is whether he has not sacrificed too much in the way of clarity, character, detail and "story" to that end, and whether his prose-poetry is sufficient reward.

It seems to me—-but I may be wrong—that he strains after effects. His correllation of a wrecked marriage with the Fall, and of self-vindication with the common lot, assumes significance. Tiresias at the keyhole, Ulysses in the pub, Tristan and Isolde smoking in the garden; in the hands of Eliot, Joyce, Cocteau, they may enchant, though already with Cocteau the oddity, the amusingness of it, begins to pall. For the lesser writer it offers a convenient 3-D. . . .

For me, therefore, *The Garden to the Sea* remains experimental, interesting: a poem-novel or psychological incantation which everyone with a grain of curiosity should read. Whatever its faults or derivations (echoes of Eliot and Auden), it lifts the commonplaces of the novel high out of their usual clutter.

G. W. Stonier. *NSN*. July 25, 1953, pp. 109–10

He spent the Thirties (on the evidence of this book) in a rather stormy process of growing up; not having "found himself" until the silly season was over, he did not have to go through the trying process of losing himself again like his immediate seniors. In any case his book is not about himself but about two young men who really did typify English upper-class life in the Thirties. It is a very good book [*Friends Apart*], one of those documents which manage to transcend their class and become literature without losing their usefulness as documents. . . .

People are more important for what they are than for what they do, and this and other questions arise from Mr. Toynbee's excellent book because he has used his skill to give us a vivid impression of his two friends without ever telling us what we *ought* to think about them. On one ground or another, this book is required reading.

John Wain. *Spec*. March 19, 1954, pp. 332–33

So what is *Pantaloon*? It is really, I suggest, a rag-bag of memories and reflections held together by a character strenuously repudiating the idea that he is Philip Toynbee. Perhaps something is after all gained by Mr. Toynbee's making his hero an octogenarian, because considering how much the whole consciousness of the book is autobiographically tinged, he does somehow succeed in being Philip Toynbeeish without being Philip Toynbee. . . .

I entreat the reader to disregard [its faults], and to read this book from beginning to end, overcoming all the protests which will make him, from time to time, want to throw it out of the window. For poets, it will come as something of a revelation; for it may well be a breakthrough from the dreary academicism into which poetry has sunk in the day of the triumph of those Wagnerian dwarfs of criticism who are responsible for works such as the recent Pelican volume of essays on modern literature. . . . Finally this book is funnier than any poetry since the Auden of the *Orators*.

Stephen Spender. *Enc*. Dec., 1961, p. 81

What *Two Brothers* tries to do is to build a mosaic of insights, a constellation of enlightening moments. Mr. Toynbee writes also, ominously, of finding himself "increasingly anxious to eliminate all sense of narrative from what I write." It is a high ambition: is there any poem in any language of 130 pages which does not tell a story?

The first criticism must be then of the form. It is true that a knowledge of Mr. Toynbee's preceding poem, *Pantaloon,* will offer a good number of clues to the multifarious obscurity of the present poem. He has included references to characters and jokes and literature and history in such an offhand, unhelpful way that some pages look like a section of a German report, rather than a poem, so full are they with capital letters.

A more serious fault than this, and an unusual one in Mr. Toynbee's imaginative writing, is the tiredness of the language: I discover that in all the notes I took while reading the book I have not written down a single striking image. In place of sustained imagery there are clots of adjectives which tend to attenuate immediacy and give the work a curious air of special pleading. This is reinforced by a maddening use of italics to ram home an idea. At times reading the poem is like being shouted at by a man with a bad stutter.

Julian Jebb. *TL.* July 19, 1964, p. 29

TREECE, HENRY (1912–1966)

It is true that he has written a book about [Dylan] Thomas, and that some of his early poems were very like Thomas's. They have a very common background, both being Welshmen, admirers of Hopkins and Joyce, readers of the Bible and ballads, and having the Welsh gift of the gab. But although Treece's twenty-five sonnets in his *Towards a Personal Armageddon* are similar in atmosphere and climate to Thomas's, and similar in texture, it is evident on a closer reading that Treece has adapted Thomas's discoveries to different ends. Treece's early poems were over-rich, but with a richness which is that of a young poet conscious of his own power. Less disciplined than Thomas, his syntax was none the less easier, his vocabulary less disturbing and his rhythms more fluid. . . .

If a poet is not rich when he is young, he will be for ever poor. And this atmosphere of poetry, which creates itself so rapidly in the writing of Treece as in Thomas, is something peculiar to the Welsh and Irish poets, a gift which cannot be acquired save by long acquaintance with a restricted culture. Now Treece is obviously refining the personal mythology which was the whole subject of his "Armageddon" poems, and which is extremely hard to decipher. In his later poems he is coming nearer to folklore, and no doubt discovering that a personal mythology is only strengthened when it is brought to the level of the popular imagination. He has deliberately turned to the legend and fairy-tale of the past, and seems to be engaged in interpreting the present world in terms of them. His later poems are full of princes, magicians, strange old men and suffering girls. And this is, perhaps, the secret of the Celtic imagination, this ability to see people as symbols. . . . His recent poems as a whole show, side by side with this revival of mediaeval legend and atmosphere, a deepening religious sense which might ultimately lead him far away from his first conception of personal myth. But however he develops, allegiance to a movement can neither help nor hinder him: the essential thing is there, that purity and innocence which breathes from some of his poems. . . .

Francis Scarfe. *Auden and After*
(Routledge and Sons, 1942), pp. 164–65

Treece has been a leader of the English Apocalyptic Movement, a literary reaction against the social-realist writing of the Nineteen Thirties, and of a later movement known as Personalism. These movements, rejecting the complexity of modernity, seem to have their counterpart in the American back-to-earth school, where there is also the danger of fundamentalism, a single attitude and not the criss-crossing of many theories of mystical reality made personal by the fact that a person is writing about them.

. . . The language itself, though Treece occasionally employs a distinctive image, is the language of a neutral poetry, burning neither hot nor cold. Unqualified words such as truth and beauty are employed to give a meaning which they do not give. [*Collected Poems*]

The apocalyptic mystic rebel is still possible in modern poetry, as shown in the poems of Robert Lowell, for example. Treece, a respectable poet, cannot match his arms against those poets he presumably opposes, for none of them is respectable. First of all, he does not have the technical fireworks, a sense of language as reality. He seems to think that by referring to a thing, he is creating it quite neatly. There are goose girls with golden hair, witches, rosaries, evil snakes, thinking flowers, innumerable phoenixes, all kinds of beautiful paraphernalia, including Sir Lancelot on his charger and Ophelia drowning. On such matters Treece relies, quite easily. By and by, however, the wary reader wishes for a little social realism, or if not for that, a dazzling metaphysics.

Marguerite Young. *NYT*. Aug. 18 ,1946, p. 23

The literal definition of Apocalypse according to the Oxford Dictionary is Revelation. The rather frenzied flavour of the Book of Revelation, however, has given the word overtones which have replaced the more sober original conception in the modern consciousness. When Henry Treece says that "the writer who senses the chaos, the turbulence, the laughter and the tears, the order and the peace of the world in its entirety, is an Apocalyptic writer," it is not difficult to accept the term. One would expect a violence of expression, an aggressiveness of outlook which would adequately reflect the character of our time. . . . And yet Treece and his colleagues of the new Apocalypse never seem to progress far beyond an acceptable definition. There is an enormous gap between their poetic practice and the programme they profess to observe. . . .

The aim is good. I can also respect Treece's sincerity. But after this is said most of these essays [*How I See Apocalypse*] are spoilt by a hotchpotch of minor blemishes which come from the heart rather than the head. I feel that Treece has adopted a mantle that does not altogether become him. It may be due to bewilderment, a little perhaps to uncertainty. The familiar sentimentality continually thrusts itself forward. His "forlorn princess" and "gaily coloured prince" are such inapt symbols as to make his argument appear unreal and unconvincing. . . . If we could abstract what he has to say from his manner of saying it I believe we would find a sane critic, with a highly-developed capacity of appreciating the best in another's work, but so long as he allows his style to be pocked by these uneasy evidences of self-consciousness he will never command the attention he deserves.

John Atkins. *Adel.* July-Sept., 1947, pp. 234–36

Treece himself has often been called an imitator of Thomas. It is true that Treece wrote an enthusiastic brochure about him when Thomas' total oeuvre was exactly *Eighteen Poems,* but there really is not a great deal of resemblance. Both are Welsh, but Thomas speaks, . . . for the aristocratic underworld of a suppressed civilization. He is always the Druid, passing on his occult wisdom within the sound of the church bells. Treece uses a material much closer to folk art, to the changeless, gnomic tales of the universal peasant, Teuton, Celt or Finn. In fact, his best poems are very Germanic, Märchen poetry, Grimm capsules. In spite of his Personalist professions, it is very difficult to come at the personal core in his poems, they slip away into anonymity, like handicrafts or Gothic woodcarvings.

Kenneth Rexroth. Introd, in *New British Poets,*
ed. Kenneth Rexroth. (N.Y., New Directions, 1949),
p. xxiii

Mr. Henry Treece is a good and practised hand at writing historical stories for children, his favourite periods being Romano-Celtic and

Saxon times, though in *The Bombard* . . . he comes up to the fourteenth century. . . . His method is to write straightforwardly, without affectation, and to strike home with a quick thrust of imagination. For instance, when his Vikings are enjoying a rare smooth patch in mid-North Atlantic, he says the sea is "a sheet of glass as broad as the world, as muscular as a giant's flank." He also has the good habit of writing a brief foreword called "About this Book" which gives the reader a firm background note. There is no harmful cruelty in his books, though there is much bloodshed and tension. I should like to read an older book of his called *The Children's Crusade,* if only to see how he avoids harmful cruelty in a matter so full of it. . . . *Viking's Sunset* is about the supposed voyage of the Viking Sigurdson and his supporters from Norway by way of Iceland and Greenland to the New World and is dedicated to an American boy who told the author that a longship prow had been found in one of the Great Lakes. The author catches the saga-feeling very well and also the mixed Viking characteristics of jolly roving, dash, pluck, seamanship and fireside tale-telling. He gives a particularly fine description of Vikings going berserk. Brotherhood between Northmen, Eskimos and Red Indians finds a loyal place—a shade slippery perhaps—and the villain of the piece, maimed, resentful and murderous, is understandable. Everybody in children's adventure stories seems like little boys . . . perhaps they were.

Rosemary Thompson. *Spec.* June 10, 1960, p. 850

Mr. Treece's interpretation of the myth of Jason's quest for the Golden Fleece [*Jason*] makes compulsive reading; the vigorous emphatic style and the quick succession of appalling adventures ensure it. But the world it displays is not a pleasant one, and at the end the reader may be as much disgusted as sated with thrills. Was the heroic age of Greece really so nasty as this? . . .

Mr. Treece's real fault is a mistake of emphasis. Granted that these myths are full of adultery, incest, and unnatural vice, does it follow that the Hellenic mind dwelt incessantly on these subjects?

TLS. July 7, 1961, p. 413

TRENCH, HERBERT (1865–1923)

Not only "Deirdre Wed," but also several of the shorter poems in Mr. Trench's volume [*Deirdre Wed*] are marked by great intellectual sincerity and frequent felicity of rhythm and phrase. Did space permit, we would gladly quote from his "Ode on a Silver Birch" and the "Song for the Funeral of a Boy." The faults that we have to find with him are mainly on the side of technique. Here he contrasts unfavourably with Mr. Yeats, one of whose greatest charms lies in his power of saying, exactly and with ease, the precise thing which he wants to say. In its absolute freedom from all signs of the workshop his lucid verse has the naturalness and inevitability of a flower. It is not so with Mr. Trench. There is often a slip between his conception and the expression of it. Awkward inversions, uncouth archaisms, and haphazard punctuation suggest an effect of imperfectly smelted ore. The material is not thoroughly fused in the furnace of art. Frankly, at times we fail altogether to catch his meaning. This is in part due to a deliberate straining after novelty of diction, which is one of his dangers; but partly also to an apparent failure to realize that an idea or image clearly outlined to his own mind may not be equally clear to his reader, unless he takes pains to make it so. The most sympathetic reader will not do all the work.

Ath. Jan. 12, 1901, p. 40

"Deirdre Wed" is the title poem of Mr. Herbert Trench's volume. . . . Since Mr. Trench affects an almost Meredithian obscurity of diction, and since Celtic legend at its best is misty in outline, the poem is a difficult one to follow, and we shall make no attempt to describe it, beyond saying that the story is told in sections by bards of several far-separated centuries.

William M. Payne. *Dial.* Oct., 1901, pp. 240–41

For a poet to conceive that it is he who sings his song, and that therefore it matters little in what form it is given, is to miss the essential business of creation. It is for this reason the mind catches the similarity between Mr. Trench and an old-time scop. Such an old-time bard sang his songs; but a modern poet cannot sing his songs. . . . He has to create a form that shall sing his songs for him. And if he fail to create such a form, however worthy its subject, the total product will stumble. It is for this reason Mr. Trench so frequently fails. We feel it is Mr. Trench singing, and that there is something of chance in the fact that he is singing in the particular form we see. Chanted by him to an audience his themes might be inspiriting enough. A dropped word, a redundant syllable, a misplaced cadence, an overflowing meaning, would matter little: the demand for form would be sunk in the inspiration of the subject. But the day of the singer is over; this is the day of the creator. . . .

This is the difficulty of *Deirdre Wed,* strengthened as it is by a finely conceived subject. But when in *Apollo and the Seaman* he turns to a subject far from inspiriting, and bordering on polemic, we receive a poem framed on the model of the *Ancient Mariner,* but with a metre that fails in surefootedness, set in stanzas and defying their setting at one and the same time.

It is rather when we come to his lyrics that we discover Mr. Trench at his best. For a lyric demands form. It refuses to be conceived apart from form. It demands sure-footed metre too. And since Mr. Trench has been confining his attention to lyrics his work has consequently gained just that which it lacked before, conviction.

Darrell Figgis. *Studies and Appreciations*
(J. M. Dent, 1912), pp. 152–53

He wrote almost entirely in metre, a restraint rare enough now, and the bulk of his work is, for a lifetime, comparatively small; nor is it, as one might suppose, all pure, threshed in quality. A few of his happier lyrics have appeared in the passing anthologies, but he belonged to neither movement, nor phase, and doubtless will have no influence. His strength, like that of others who passed through the Eighteen-Nineties, grew from the Victorian period. He adhered rather to the Arnold heresy than to the orthodoxy of Tennyson. Culture and anarchy, if one sought a caption, might be applied to his work. He was a cultured poet, studious of the greater traditions of English literature, unafraid to recall what was best, yet troubled by contrary inclination. He did not originate nor set fire to strange waters. He used the common material and measures of poetry, lending them an individual voice of which the value can be ascertained. Unlike most poets who serve an innocent apprenticeship in public until their voices have found no echo but their own, Trench did not publish until he had found a certain maturity. There is, therefore, no development in the ordinary sense of the word, in his work; his imagination deepens, but it does not amass nor colonise. Influences are to be found to the last in his work, though they are often challenging and in the nature of feudal prerogative. In temperament he was what Arnold would have called an *esprit fort;* his philosophy is intolerant, though it sought to be human, but since a different mood is the tide now—as when eighteenth-century scepticism gave way to transcendentalism—it must seem old-fashioned in its strength. He rarely attained to the lucid quality of the best of Arnold. There is a constant effect of struggle, a lack of fusion between idea and word in his poetry, a failure of coincidence that may be of the age or come from emotional causes, though sometimes it is the mixed smoke and flame that happen when poets go back to the workshops of imagination and words are wrought on the anvil. . . . Curious unreliability, then, a sudden loss of power, remain in his work, due perhaps to too deliberate a discipline of emotion by traditional form, or even to romanticism at variance with scholarship.

He sought the grand style with perhaps overmuch premeditation, though it is interesting to note that he has written but little blank verse, the medium which seems best adapted to that manner.

Austin Clarke. *LM*. June, 1924, pp. 157–58

Dramatic situations with something oddly general and familiar in them, the beauty of Italy, the stress and restlessness of passion, memories of a scholar, thoughtful observation of birds, of the dawn, of the stars, a development of positivist philosophy into an almost religious sense of the immortality and the unity of human life through the family, war and sentiments appropriate to an Englishman—such are the themes of Mr. Trench's poetry—and they are one reason why his verse is poetry. And it is moving not only on account of them, but also because they leave no sense of tranquility; because they are the self-expression of a man who did not find repose in any of them. He knew emotion, and he recollected it, but not in tranquillity. The complexity of the passionate experience is renewed in his meditation on it, and works his mind up to a complexity like its own. There is little simplicity in this poetry: it is highly wrought and intricate: it will never be popular. But it is an extraordinarily interesting development of the tradition of nineteenth-century poetry, poetry like Matthew Arnold's, whose effects Mr. Trench very carefully studied and used, poetry which is haunting because of its restlessness and which has the elusiveness and the distinction of a writer who caught the secret of style from familiarity with Europe's masterpieces. Yet it is not academic, because it is itself art. Mr. Trench was a poet on his own. . . .

He is almost too elusive: by careful attention we may succeed in catching his meaning and his effect, but even then not always. But this is, of course, the very delicacy of art, to be almost ethereal, impalpable, and yet not wholly so.

R. E. Gordon George. *CR*. July, 1924, pp. 76–77

Herbert Trench was born at Avoncore, county Cork, in 1865, went to Haileybury and Oxford, and worked from 1891 to 1908 on the Board of Education. The next two years saw him curiously transformed into the director of the Haymarket Theatre; then his health failed, and the last decade of his life was mainly spent in the neighbourhood of Florence, till he died at Boulogne in June 1923. The bronze bust by Antonio Maraini, reproduced in the *Collected Works,* shows a not unfamiliar, masterful type of man—flannel collar flung wide at the throat, the hair thrown back as by a violent wind all along the line of the high forehead, eyes wide apart and rather defiant, the chin a little over-resolutely set. It becomes easy, after seeing it, to understand how, though his youth produced the inevitable *Deirdre* which it appears to be compulsory for every literary Irishman to produce at some time or other in his life, Trench came to regard the Celtic twilight . . . as "sentimental mystery-mongering." Yet he hugged all the closer a queer, mystical prepossession of his own; the human race, he dreamed, was being safely shepherded by Destiny towards an ever-increasing realisation of the Oneness of the Many, of the absorption of all individuals in the unity of the life of the Universe. . . . The persistence with which Trench rides this hobby-horse of his with a perpetual clanging of "chalices" from its saddlebow, grows a little tiresome to the unconverted. The mystic has always longed in this way for absorption; but the ordinary human mind is not mystical, and is left cold by this passion for getting lost in things. . . .

In fact, Trench was one of those extravagant poets who have beaten out their metal thin to make sieves to hold moonshine; yet the true metal was there. His rigmaroles on the war can be forgotten in the lilt of lyrics like the "Requiem of Archangels for the World," his apotheoses of the family in the pure poetry of "Deirdre Wedded," [sic] and some of the best love poems of their decade. Trench admired Arnold, but he had not Arnold's depth. His long odes echo Meredith, but they have not Meredith's wit. It is Wilfrid Blunt, if any one, that these love lyrics recall—that undertone of fierceness, that slight but stirring sense of the fanatic's bitterness beneath the lover's kiss.

F. L. Lucas. *Authors Dead and Living*
(N.Y., Macmillan, 1926), pp. 140–42

TREVELYAN, G. M. (1876–1962)

What is perhaps most frequently forgotten, or ignored, is the skill of his literary craftsmanship. Trevelyan is a born writer, and a natural storyteller; and this, amongst historians, is a rare gift; only Prescott, amongst the great historians, has his facility in equal or greater measure. In consequence, those episodes of history which were full of dramatic action, with a firm beginning and obvious end, have brought forth some of his best writing—the *Garibaldi* books, *England under the Stuarts,* much of the *History of England,* and perhaps *Blenheim*. As a stylist he cannot be compared with Gibbon, Macaulay, or even Clarendon, and amongst his own generation he would have to concede the first place to R. H. Tawney, but he has written passages of greater lyrical beauty than any of them, when the heart of the poet has been stirred. A poet at large in history is a unique phenomenon of our literature and will create for

Trevelyan a special place in the history of English letters. Certainly, I think, it will secure a permanent niche for *Garibaldi's Defense of the Roman Republic,* which, were it fiction, would live as one of the greatest love-stories, told with exquisite feeling and poetic power. The same poetic temperament has been responsible for some of the best evocations of times past that have been written in our language. They are scattered throughout his works but brought together and continuously sustained in the pages of the *Social History.* If one quality is to be singled out, it should be this, for, of all historians, he is the poet of English history.

His work has one other great and enduring merit, the tradition within which it was written. The Victorian liberals and their Edwardian successors have made one of the greatest contributions to science and to culture ever made by a ruling class. To these by birth and by instinct Trevelyan belonged. Therefore, as time passes, his work will acquire fresh significance and become the material of history itself, for these books of his will show how these liberal humanists considered their past, from whence they derived their tradition, by what they would like themselves judged. And because he has written from such a standpoint, he has helped to inculcate into the hearts of men and women, born in more desperate times, a regard for human justice and personal freedom.

John H. Plumb. *G. M. Trevelyan*
(BC/Longmans, 1951), pp. 33–34

As befits a "layman" [*A Layman's Love of Letters*], Dr. Trevelyan ranges far and wide in these lectures. As befits a scholar, he deals not only with what is well known but also with certain authors and passages which will be unfamiliar to many readers. Among those authors who are too often unfamiliar both because of fashion and neglect . . . is Meredith, to whom Dr. Trevelyan devotes the last, and one of the best, of his lectures. It would indeed seem natural to suppose that the author of *Modern Love* and of *Love in the Valley* should also have written other poetry worth reading; but not everyone has made this supposition. Dr. Trevelyan seems to me peculiarly enlightening and just in his estimate both of Meredith's prose and poetry. But he is enlightening and just throughout. His book is a pleasure to read in itself and it will make the reading of other books more pleasurable. This is the kind of "layman" who should make the clergy look to their cloth.

Rex Warner. *Spec.* March 12, 1954, p. 299

Historians are apt to debate, in their dry academic fashion, the reasons why the books of their colleagues sell. Trevelyan, for his part, has never made a secret of his creed. It is that each generation, in its brief today, longs to know more of its elder brothers and sisters, hid in death's dateless night, how they lived and fought our battles of liberty and made angels weep at their doings—longs for that contact of person with unknown person that poetry achieves on another level. For this, the writer of history must have, besides a love of truth and infinite industry, two instruments, the command of words and the power of narration. Trevelyan once wrote: "The art of history remains always the art of narrative. That is the bed-rock." To that word he has always been faithful, caring not a whit for the murmurs of soured ancients.

No one may call this a facile kind of history. Behind the trilogy of Garibaldi and the volumes of Queen Anne lie years of travel in Italy, years of work in libraries and the British Museum, and a formidable bibliography; behind the *Social History* is a lifetime of reading, reflection and experience. Of this the reader sees nothing. He remembers only a hundred pictures: Garibaldi gazing from the heights upon the groves and palaces of Palermo; Shakespeare passing the gunpowder plotters in Welcombe Woods; Marlborough chafing at Eugene's delay before Blenheim; the great storm of 1703 sweeping over Eddystone; the luminaries of Edinburgh's bench and bar lurching down the murky wynd at midnight, assailed by exhalations whizzing from the skies.

But on an eightieth birthday we do not think of books alone, and indeed to those many who have known Dr. Trevelyan either as teacher or friend or Master of Trinity the books mean less than the man. Some have been surprised at first by the brusque manner, the incisive word, or the silence difficult to break; they have soon come to admire a simplicity of life and speech, and an exquisite courtesy of act as well as of word. They have recognized the deep convictions, the respect for liberty, the love of toleration of the great generation of Liberals. The last three lines of Chaucer's characterisation of his Knight might have been written of Trevelyan.

David Knowles. *Spec.* Feb. 17, 1956, p. 210

TURNER, JAMES (1909–   )

The consequence of . . . [an] absence of limitation is that the poem [*The Pastoral*] makes much less effect than it should. It sprawls. It is as when a dancer, who would be most pleasing on a platform, loses herself by careering over the whole stage.

And secondly there is too much Wit. The images are often far-fetched or sensational or perverse, and sometimes verge upon the unintelligible. And this leads on to the third count against this kind of writing and the most serious. The *Pastoral* is largely a *private* poem. There are many allusions which can only be supposed significant for those who know more of Mr. Turner's secrets than the common reader possibly can do. Mr. Turner holds the view, I do not doubt, that his thoughts are most attractive in the form in which they occurred to him. Many think the same, to whom I can only say that in this form they may have a special sentimental interest for the author, and a high value for the psychologist, but he who claims to read poetry for pleasure (and this claim we of the reading public must never forgo) begs for some pruning, some shaping, some exactitude, and at length some style, some form.

I have tried to deal honestly with the *Pastoral* because it is so full of poetry and so promising, if Mr. Turner is, as I take him to be, a comparatively young man. There is a very wide range within which it is *possible* to write good poetry, but poetry without limits is exceedingly difficult, and perhaps Shakespeare only has achieved it. The "Moderns" may easily justify the abandonment of the old conventions in verse and diction, but unless they can forge some new bonds for themselves they will only effect something good occasionally and by chance. At least I think that is the nature of art in general, and poetry is an art. It is the art of *making* something, and it is only within strict limits, as within the limits of a stage, that words can create a world that holds together.

Adam Fox. *Eng.* Spring, 1943, p. 128

Amateurs of the unusual may be disappointed to find that James Turner's six studies [*The Dolphin's Skin*] in eccentricity include characters who seem to have been less fantastic than unfortunate. . . . Then the author's way of writing up his little biographies is not always helpful. . . . At times one might call it the "let's take a peek" method and the "not too fanciful to assume" approach. Again, Mr. Turner is often naive in his remarks concerning his subject's emotional attachments. Only the story of William Jennens and his fellow misers emerges as a complete success. One will not forget the fire which was suffered to go out at the meagre dinner because eating was deemed an exercise to induce sufficient warmth.

O. B. *TT.* Nov., 1956, p. 1405

TURNER, W. J. (1889–1946)

He undeniably asserts his poetic independence. In its tone, symbolism and interest, his verse has an apartness of its own; it is almost defiantly removed from the scrutiny of experience or ideas. How much this implies of strength or weakness, and what evasiveness, if any, enters into his seemingly elusive poetry, must appear by degrees, if at all. To read him almost anywhere in his work is to get very quickly the sense of a peculiar atmosphere or vision; he is certainly a poet of idiosyncrasy. And if we follow his poetry another interest very definitely reinforces this one, for he shows a development which is not so much change of form as progress. Between his first volume and those which came next there was a marked advance, and the last book which he has published makes a hardly less clear advance upon the others. Discovering himself more truly, as so subjective a poet must do, he has also penetrated farther into the resources of his poetry. . . .

How much more he had written before he published his first book (*The Hunter and Other Poems*) in 1916 one does not know, but he was already writing then with a good deal of accomplishment: an easy rhythm, a facility of phrase and much colour of fancy. These were evidently the expression of a quick and receptive sensitiveness, and they showed that he had a poetic fertility to draw on. But there, on the whole, these verses stopped. The special form of his vision was not distinct in them, and one notices rather their sentimental variety, and their yielding to sensation. The poems which could be read with most contentment were those in which Mr. Turner seemed to allow himself time, and also simplicity. . . .

Mr. Turner's real poetic individuality, as it has developed in *The Dark Fire* (1918) and his succeeding books, is much more interesting than this. That it brings very quickly the sense of a peculiar air or place has been noticed already. This seems to lie far from the usual human stabilities and not less far from the decisive human passions. It is a realm of images where feeling pursues feeling. Yet it is not the witched, still world of magical fantasy, where you are haunted by the beauty or terror of preternatural things. This may be a poetry of escape, but it does not choose that way of substitution. What it suggests, rather, is such a transmutation of our world as happens in dreaming; explicitly at times, and more often with a subtle implication, it shows many of the characteristics of dreams.

Arthur McDowall. LM. Dec., 1924, pp. 158–59

Mr. Turner the poet has often been overshadowed by Mr. Turner the critic, that Playboy of the Music World. He is an artist whose genuine originality has not yet perhaps been fully appreciated and accepted. I think that much of his work, by reason of some quality of vision which it is difficult to define, stands alone, beautiful, heartbreaking. Its principal characteristic is an aloofness that is half-dry and half-contemptuous. Yet the aesthetic high-tuning of which his fastidiousness is a signal, demonstrates itself also by a negative activity. Mr. Turner can turn savagely on human society and even on himself, and the instrument of his genius emits a scream of obscenity. This is not an uncommon result of indignation and the reactionary despair that follows any form of moral or aesthetic revelation. We find the musical counterpart of it in Liszt and Paganini, who periodically insisted on using instruments which were out of tune.

Richard Church. NS. July 12, 1930, p. 448

In Mr. W. J. Turner's work, music and poetry are two different coloured strands of the same thread: to disentangle them and ignore either is to miss the true colour of the whole. That is my excuse, in this simple study of his output, for considering equally Mr. Turner the poet and Mr. Turner the music critic. I may ultimately prefer the poet; but he would not be that poet were it not for his vivid ability in the critcism of music.

Australian by birth, Mr. Turner came to Europe at an early age, and finally settled in England. First impressions abide however and there is no doubt that the somewhat exotic nature of a good deal of the poetic imagery of his earlier poetry derives from the country of his birth. His first written work appeared in the *New Age,* where he did occasional dramatic dialogues. Then came the War. . . .

The War ended and Mr. Turner took the place of Dennis Browne as music critic to the *New Statesman,* a post he has vigorously occupied ever since. His contributions to music criticism were as fresh and individual as his contribution to the new post-War poetry. He had the temerity to break clean away from the pedantic traditions of the profession and write of music *as an experience.* The result, as perhaps might be expected, was abuse from the academicians, and praise from the intelligent amateurs. To the former the gusto of Mr. Turner's sensuous perception seemed rather ill-mannered, the uncompromising honesty of his exposures of flummery and sham an impertinence: to the latter they were a sheer delight—here at last was someone who could talk to them about music as if it were a living art and not a corpse upon the dissecting table.

C. Henry Warren. BkmL. Nov., 1931, p. 107

Mr. W. J. Turner has an original mind and I think improves. He is very good when he is good; but that is not often. Sometimes it looks as though he were guying his own genius. This is sad, because, when he is truly himself, he can make glorious whatever he touches.

Ranjee G. Shahani. Poetry R. Jan.-Feb., 1942, pp. 28–29

Though he had been Literary Editor of this journal only since 1942, he had by then established a recognised reputation as a peculiarly sensitive and sincere musical critic and a poet of a high order. He had also written plays—notably, *The Man Who Ate the Popomack,* which ran for some time at the Savoy in 1923—and was the author of many volumes of poems and several books on musical criticism. As Literary Editor he showed himself a conscientious and discerning reviewer and a wise selector of other reviewers.

Spec. Nov. 22, 1946, p. 535

There is an underlying sense of certainty here—possible to a poet born in 1889 but not to one born in 1922—in the light of which doubt becomes a rhetorical device or a spiritual exercise and emotions are enjoyed for what they are, rather than lived through for what they may arrive at. Turner's poetry is very uneven: from thick rhetorical denunciation (as in the sonnet "Peace and War") to delicate impressionist confessions (as in "Windermere or Winter Haven") he runs through a wide variety of moods and techniques, but always with a sense of excitement, sometimes of exultation, sometimes of gnomic urgency, sometimes purely speculative. The personal note is always urgent: the poetic idiom is direct, individual, often careless. He has a tendency to scatter language too readily, throwing words and images up in the air to see how they look as they come down. . . . Turner wrote as he pleased, belonging to no school: but put his poems besides those of Sidney Keyes and, in spite of himself, he falls into a category—into the category of those who have known what it was to be innocent, and remember all the emotions of innocence outraged and the pangs of innocence educated.

David Daiches. *Poetry.* Oct., 1947, pp. 49–50

TYNAN, KATHARINE (1861–1931)

It was in the pages of *The Irish Monthly* that Katharine Tynan first won recognition as a poet. She was one of that brilliant company that gathered about Father Matthew Russell, and that was first introduced to the world through the pages of this magazine.

It is a far cry to 1885, when Katharine Tynan published her first volume of verse. Now there comes to us for review her *Collected Poems.*

In an age in which literature—and even that branch of literature that is poetry—is wrested from its high purpose and forced to serve as the vehicle of decadent thought and pagan concepts of life, it is a joy to come upon something worthy of so rare a gift as that of the poet. . . .

Katharine Tynan, in her songs, has maintained the Victorian tradition for pure, clear and direct singing—the tradition of Wordsworth and Tennyson. One agrees with AE in his introduction to this volume when he dwells on the natural ease with which she writes poetry. The metre in which the majority of her poems are written is peculiar to herself. It was this metre of hers, if I mistake not, that no less a poet than Francis Thompson praised. The form in which her poems are cast is individual. She created a form to suit her thoughts and moods, just as Tennyson created a form; as Hardy did.

Her subjects are many and varied. She is the poet of human love and longing and loneliness, just as she is the poet of hope and happiness in a spiritual world beyond the stars. Her *Collected Poems* are divided thus: "The Old Country," "Mother and Child," "Songs of Love, Life and Death," "Saints and Angels," "Prayers and Desires," "Heaven and Earth," "In War-time," "Birds and Flowers and Beauty of Earth," "Legends and Fantasies," "The Tree-lover," and "Personalia." . . .

I shall conclude by quoting from AE's Foreword: "Katharine Tynan says of herself that she was born under a kind star. It is true. She is happy in religion, friendship, children, instantly kindling at any beauty in gardens, flowers, in sky and clouds. She has, too, that spiritual bravery which makes beauty out of death or sorrow. A friend passes, and he is sped on his journey, not with despair, but with hope, almost with imaginative gaiety. It is a great gift this, which on a sudden changes our gloom to a glory."

Michael Walsh. *Irish Monthly.* Dec., 1930, pp. 627–31

Although Mrs. Tynan is a modern novelist, we seem to step a long way back in her novels. We are away from the novel, so popular in our own day, which is scarcely a story. We are aeons away from any sordidness, any beastly eroticism, the backwash of so much of our modern fiction. Mrs. Tynan is not in any sense a great novelist. She has no place in the same rank as Sheila Kaye-Smith, she has not a masterly touch of creation, but she can give us a very good story. I do not want to be misunderstood if I say that Mrs. Tynan is more than anything else the type of novelist who gets a rather obvious but good plot. Sometimes we are in danger of forgetting exactly what a plot is. In so much modern fiction, excluding detective fiction, there is no plot at all. We are simply gazing at the map of a mind. But in the stories of Mrs. Tynan we are introduced not only to a good plot but to an exciting tale and a tale which is always perfectly clean. A great deal of the fiction of our era can be best described as perfectly dirty. Mrs. Tynan is clever without being in the least subtle. She is smart without letting her fiction become merely shallow smartness.

Patrick Braybrooke. *Some Catholic Novelists*
(Burns, Oates and Washbourne, 1931), p. 209

W. B. Yeats was twenty and Katharine Tynan twenty-four when they first met. She was the daughter of Andrew Tynan, a strong farmer of Whitehall, Clondalkin, County Dublin; had published her first poem in a Dublin paper when she was seventeen and in that year of 1885 had won considerable notice as a poet with her first book of poems *Louise de la Valliere*. The means of their introduction was Professor Oldham of Trinity College, Dublin who was then editing the *Dublin University Review*. He said to her abruptly one day, much as one might announce the capture of a rare moth, "I've got a queer youth named Yeats," and brought the poet to see her soon afterwards. . . .

It would be a mistake to judge her solely by the mountain of mediocre fiction which she produced. Yeats probably overvalued her poetry, as he overvalued Todhunter's plays, because of friendship and the dominance of a literary tradition which both of them disliked; but his criticism of her work . . . is generally clear about her limitations and he may not have been far out in considering her an Irish Christina Rossetti, with all that this reckoning implies. The selection of twenty-one of her poems which he made for the Dun Emer Press in 1907 shows that she was a considerable minor poet and her anthologies of Irish poetry deserve to be remembered more than they are. George William Russell's [AE] tribute to her the year before she died [Introduction to *Collected Poems of Katharine Tynan*] will be found to coincide in many points with Yeats's view of her. Yet when all this has been said, the respective literary careers of Yeats and of Katharine Tynan, who were both subject to many of the same influences and both often employed upon the same themes, show most clearly the difference between the quality and the singleness of purpose of a major poet and the occasional felicity of a minor one.

Roger McHugh. Introd. in *W. B. Yeats's Letters to Katharine Tynan*, ed. Roger McHugh (Dublin, Clonmore and Reynolds, 1953), pp. 11–14

TYNAN, KENNETH (1927–   )

In *Alec Guinness,* Kenneth Tynan provides a fully illustrated study of this important actor, boldly printing as both dust-jacket and frontispiece the hirsute Hamlet of 1951. About this controversial production, Mr. Tynan, who "took off," as they say, the Player King, is extremely funny. . . .

Mr. Guinness's career is fully dealt with, and an agreeable picture emerges of a most competent (and, in comedy, brilliant) actor, but it is Mr. Tynan who, plainly without intending it, chiefly lingers in the mind when the book is closed. The publishers call him "witty and provocative." Yes, thank Heaven. It is his youthful privilege to be rather rude, but who else would describe Henry Sherek as "the ventripotent impressario" and St. Joan as "the incinerated *franc-tireuse*"? May one hope for further full-length studies of other actors? But they should be prepared for a seat behind a pillar at the very back of the pit.

Arthur Marshall. *NSN*. Dec. 5, 1953, p. 722

Tynan is undoubtedly the most brilliant critic we have. Apart from writing dazzlingly well, he has a sinewy intellect, great erudition, practical experience of writing and directing, and urgent ambitions for the theatre. Where the standards of many critics never develop beyond a wittily disguised form of "I know what I like"—which all too readily reverses into the stultification of "I like what I know"—he writes from the position of "I know what I want." He is never bothered by the occupational doubt about how much a critic should let himself be influenced by his own beliefs: his demands are totally personal, and reflect his own Socialism, atheism, flamboyance and candour. . . . A masterly play with a thesis that Tynan finds disagreeable is in for an icy time; whereas an incompetent play with its heart in the right place will get quite long shrift. Biased towards social realism and unhampered by the fallacious notion that art and propaganda are necessarily antithetical, all the same he has a discreet weakness for the zany play in a vacuum, especially if it is funny, like N. F. Simpson's *A Resounding Tinkle*. "Being as schizophrenic as everyone else, I am partly drawn towards the ideal of Zen Buddhism (i.e. non-thought) and partly towards its antithesis: i.e., progressive social thought. I am fully aware of this split in my attitude. . . ." he has said of himself.

Penelope Gilliatt. *Encore*. Dec., 1959, p. 28

"What, when drunk, one sees in other women, one sees in Garbo sober." Tynan sees the Garbo glow in the theater everywhere. The rave is equally for W. C. Fields and Ruth Draper, Jimmy Cagney and Tennessee Williams, what Stanislavsky said and what Brecht said, Maria Casares as Death in Cocteau's *Orphée*—"I have never seen the imminence of suicide more powerfully conveyed"—and *West Side Story*, which "compromises only on the brink of greatness; and that, surely, is triumph enough."

It isn't that Tynan likes everything, but that he is able so strongly to absorb and to respond to everything theatrical. He knows, from love, why French playwrights reserve their greatest parts for women and why the English have no "heavies." He knows to a decimal point what percentage of the box office goes for theater rent in London and Paris. And just as he is the only writer I have ever heard of who got to interview Garbo, so he is the only drama reviewer who has described himself as present at the frenzied rewriting of a play after a tryout. When he describes Michael Redgrave in *Richard II* as excellent but "still missing the real heights by an inexplicable inch," you recognize the sense of loss; and though he loves to make fun of Sir Ralph Richardson's personal manner, you can see that no one knows it better—"His feathery, yeasty voice, with its single spring-heeled inflection, starved the part of its richness; he moved dully, as if by numbers, and such charm as he possessed was merely a sort of unfocused bluffness, like a teddy-bear snapped in a bad light by a child holding its first camera."

Although Tynan is often glib in enthusiasm, he is never flip in condemnation; a virtuoso performer in journalism, a pro from the minute the curtain goes up, he never makes fun of anyone without establishing a valid point by it. His wisecracks are astonishingly accurate. He says of Orson Welles's production of *Moby-Dick* that "It is absurd to expect Orson Welles to attempt anything less than the impossible," which is so true that you can't imagine another way of saying it; and when he reports of *King Lear* at the Old Vic that "A whole gamut of inaudibility is painstakingly run . . . listening to Stephen Murray's Lear was like lip-reading Shakespeare by flashes of lightning," you can see that he may have lived the play better than the actors did.

So brilliant a critic is easy to read and fun to read, for Tynan throws himself wholeheartedly into the writing of a piece of critical prose. . . . He takes you on a tour of the contemporary theatrical world, and his reactions are so strong and intelligent that it is impossible not to enjoy the writing and to be grateful for the tour.

Alfred Kazin. *Contemporaries* (Boston, Little, Brown, 1962), pp. 486–87

There are two reasons why Mr. Tynan's collected reviews [*Curtains*] are interesting. The first is that they record the history of his own quest; the second, that this quest was concurrent with a similar march in the English theatre. The reviews cover the period from 1950 to 1960, and during this time the transformation of the drama was matched by the transformation of Mr. Tynan. Both transformations are to be applauded, so long as they do not stunt themselves by becoming permanent. Mr. Tynan is more vulnerable than the theatre in this respect because he has reached his goal and made up his mind. The theatre, not having a mind, never reaches any goal and just goes where fashion pushes it.

The fashion when Mr. Tynan began reviewing was perfectly conventional—as it will be again, no doubt, before long. The fashion Mr. Tynan wanted to impose was more exciting: he loved "the theatre of fantasy and shock" and believed that "this sad age needs to be dazzled, shaped, and spurred by the spectacle of heroism. . . . If heroic plays take the stage, life may produce, in honest emulation, its own poor heroes of flesh and fact." Today, ten years later, Mr. Tynan believes he has dropped all this, for he has come to regard the theatre "as a branch of sociology as well as a means of self-expression." The change is not so great as Mr. Tynan thinks, for in both points of view the importance of artistry is less than the importance of being earnest. The shaping of real life heroes is no less sociological than the shaping of radical realists; all that has happened is that the social reformer wishes now to reform in a different way. One stresses this point because it is important to understand that the young missionary's attitude to the arts was the same as the mature missionary's; the playwright's aim must be socially beneficial and a play is to be judged largely by the directions it takes and the conclusions it reaches.

Nigel Dennis. Enc. April, 1962, pp. 52–53

USTINOV, PETER (1921–   )

For Mr. Peter Ustinov, a very young man, old age presents a theme endlessly fascinating. The old caricature themselves, and Mr. Ustinov is a brilliant mimic; they are funny and pathetic, as he sees them, and too often hideously powerful. So *The Banbury Nose* starts in 1943 with the old men firmly in possession. . . . Mr. Ustinov pokes fun at his characters (and there are few dramatists now that can do it better), but he has a heart too.

NSN. Sept. 16, 1944, p. 184

The most discussed playwright in England today is Peter Ustinov. He has achieved this distinction at the age of twenty-three, a fact which seems to have annoyed some of his critics who blame him for his youth, which, after all, is not his fault. They would prefer him to save his thunder for riper years, but apparently Ustinov has thunder and talent enough to last out a lifetime, and has lost no time in beginning his career. During the past three years he has written four long plays, several one-act plays, translated a piece of Jean Sarment, and acted as collaborator with Eric Ambler on the successful film *The Way Ahead,* and now reaches success with a smashing and brilliant hit, *The Banbury Nose*. This play has established him beyond any doubt and elicited from Mr. James Agate, the dean of London's dramatic critics, the assertion that Ustinov is the greatest genius now writing for the English stage. And not only this, but it has been said that he has as much wit as Bernard Shaw but with more warmth and sentiment, that he makes Noel Coward look like an amateur, and that he possesses a knowledge of stagecraft far superior to that of Mr. Priestley.

Richard E. Meyer. *Sat*. Dec. 16, 1944, p .11

Ustinov (born in 1921) has spread himself in all directions: as actor, as producer, and as the author of ten or eleven plays, often of a gay and wise originality. (He is also a witty practitioner in pastiche.) Why seek for influences? He has something of Shaw in him, something of Bridie, a great deal more of himself. . . .

His two major plays—one of which ran for about twelve times as long as the other—are *The Love of Four Colonels* and *The Moment of Truth,* each staged in 1951 [in London]. The first of these, with its alarming and quite untrue opening line, "We seem to have run out of conversation," is, in effect, Ustinov's agreeably original variety bill. He is entitled to call it a play, but it is a group of sketches set in and around a castle in which the Sleeping Beauty wakes. . . .

The Moment of Truth (1951) which was first called—and I think it is the better title, *King Lear's Photographer,* is far more single-minded. Again Ustinov thinks of the old 'un. There was a time . . . when a democratic republic, conquered by its enemy, found itself partitioned and under the nominal rule, as Head of State, of a retired Marshal: an almost legendary figure from the past. With this in mind, we can follow one of Peter Ustinov's parallels. . . .

Ustinov's *Lear* parallel can be hampering, and the play is apt to drift, especially that last scene when the dotard is mad indeed, but not in the apocalyptic grandeur of Lear. . . . But there is a piece here that aims at both mind and heart. . . . It would be twice as impressive if Ustinov had curbed his eloquence, shaved more closely. He writes pondered, close-wrought dialogue that is often near-Shavian in manner and matter, and he has Shaw's trick of running on. It is not often in these days that we have to reproach a dramatist for copiousness, for allowing talker to bear down dramatist. Ustinov speaks always from an overflowing, independent mind; he will be a great name in the English theatre. Indeed, he is nearly that already. Why wait to say so until he is one of his old 'uns?

J. C. Trewin. *Dramatists of Today*
(Staples Press, 1953), pp. 192–97

Peter Ustinov's *The Love of Four Colonels,* received by the London critics with much the same enthusiasm they exhibited in the case of Terence Rattigan's *The Deep Blue Sea* and other plays that have subsequently caused us to scratch our noses, again induces the skeptic itch in that abused organ. It has a few amusing episodes and some intermittently deft bits of dialogue but the bright spots are outweighed by so many more lusterless ones and the whole is so engulfed by a strain for "imagination" and for something approximating authentic fantasy that it suggests a man performing a solo tug-of-war and acquiring the resultant hernia. . . .

And what is the end product of all this mountainous cerebral striving? The molehill thought that man reaches ever for the unattainable, that beauty is incorruptible, and that a man remains himself with the inexorableness of a leopard's spots.

So much for drama criticism. As to theatrical criticism, the report is somewhat more favorable, since something of a show has been maneuvered out of the materials with the help of very attractive performances. . . .

George Jean Nathan. *TA*. March, 1953, pp. 67–68

It is a dozen years since Ustinov launched his first sputnick into the rather uninhabited outer space of modern English drama; and since the acid-tender sketch of *The House of Regrets* his output has mounted steadily in range and maturity of content. Long before Ionesco came into fashion he was experimenting with techniques. *The Banbury Nose* told its story backwards; *The Love of Four Colonels* introduced elements of symbolic fantasy. . . .

He has not greatly moved on from this viewpoint in *Romanoff and Juliet*. Not an "engaged" playwright in any social or political meaning ("I deem it the function of the dramatist to ask questions, not to answer them," he has written), there is nevertheless a serious purpose in all his plays in the wider human sense; and that he chooses to present it not didactically but in a witty, even frivolous, case, as in *Romanoff and Juliet* with its disturbed suggestion of the need for human liaison between east and west, does not invalidate it.

What it does do, of course, is to restate the theatrical truth already exponded by Shaw—that a pill gilded by humour is the more easily swallowed by the public. This gilding has become an unforunate necessity in recent years, with the sharp decline in the proportion of dramatic plays which West End managements will risk placing before the public. Ustinov, like Osborne, has gained from his natural wit; but it is still a reproof to the London theatre that his French Revolution play, *The Empty Chair,* has only been seen in the provinces. For it is in many ways his maturest work to date; an analysis of the rise and fall of personalities, and fundamental changes in revolution, which in the literary sense surpasses any of his other plays.

Audrey Williamson. *Drama.* Summer, 1958, pp. 32–33

What a fascinating study of perpetual creative motion he is, this fellow Peter Ustinov. Writer, actor, producer. Films, theatre, television. How on earth does he do it, when most other people spend a lifetime plugging away at *one* goal, rather badly?

Mind you, he is still The Man Who Never Quite. . . . He has been prematurely tipped for genius for years; but he is still a better playwright than most actors; a better actor than most playwrights; a better talker than most speakers. A man of many parts indeed, and nearly every part better than average good.

I have been reading a collection of his short stories. They are mostly rather bad, and yet it's a very good book. For the answer to which paradox you might be obliged to read *Add a Dash of Pity*.

Most of the characters are quite unbelievable and many of the situations daringly ditto. They seem only to exist at all as vehicles for carrying a message. Not, however, a *precious* message. Ustinov is more interested in humans than in Humanity, and always takes his ideas more seriously than he takes himself. The irony, the satire, the clever stuff is sometimes overdone, and one feels, behind the short stories, the urge to create a serious book called, perhaps, *On Loving Stupid People,* or *The Tyranny of Justice.*

Tom Greenwell. *JOL.* Dec. 3, 1959, p. 288

VACHELL, HORACE ANNESLEY (1861–1955)

This [*Blinds Down*] is perhaps the mildest story with a purpose that has ever been written. In addition, it suffers from a defective plot. Its purpose is to show that girls above the age of fifteen should not be kept in ignorance of some of the primary facts of life. But as the modern girl is hardly likely to be brought up by two such antiquated maiden ladies as the Misses Mauleverer, the force of the lesson is a little lost. . . . If at the end of the story the reader feels that he has gone through a course of Miss Young [E. H. Young], at least Mr. Vachell's latest fiction does not take it out of him mentally.

OutL. July 20, 1912, p. 91

It is as an interpreter of action, or British character in action, that Mr. Vachell interests one most. Power in motion occupies him to the exclusion of power in repose. In this the artist is consistent with the man. A keen rider himself, he writes, you may say, with a close rein, and never loosens it till he has landed his field of characters back under shelter of a logical outcome, cheerful for choice. This passion for energy has preserved him from the morbid, the cheap and the futile, and if he has sometimes flirted with the inadequate, he has not spared himself compensatory pains. A happy fertility has saved him from a common fate. Most writers lavish on their early work material they might have husbanded and turned to advantage later on; that kind of remorse is part of the price incurred in learning a difficult craft. Mr. Vachell attacked it under arduous conditions, in the seventeen years he spent in California, and he has never been gravelled for lack of matter since. It is characteristic of him that he went there to shoot buffalo; having bagged his bull, he took up ranching, and pursued the one as he had pursued the other, to the death. There seemed no chance of war just then, so he gave up his commission in the Rifle Brigade, and alternated steers with stories. He has been heard to say there are early books of his that deserve to be "scrapped"; what is better, he has given us successors enough to wipe them out. I would put in a recommendation to mercy for the first book of all, *The Romance of Judge Ketchum*. . . .

There is internal evidence that Mr. Vachell's writings are rapidly produced, or else that when he revises, if ever, he does it with an eye more to the purport than the text. Taste resents the meaningless christening of a trivial American in *The Face of Clay* with a name like Johnnie

Keats, and there are touches in certain of the other books likely to yield to a corrective pen. But in the main, Mr. Vachell's style is like his heroes, rapid, masterful, resourceful, and more than equal to the situation. It will grace many a twentieth-century anthology of English prose. It would be hard to improve upon it as a vehicle for that temperamental appetite for action which I conceive to be the main characteristic of the man. Like Kipling and Masefield, he interprets British nature faithfully because he graduated early in the school of travel, observation, tenacity.

J. P. Collins. *Bkm.* Sept., 1916, pp. 49–50

Veteran author of more than seventy works, including novels and plays, Mr. Annesley Vachell confesses [*Distant Fields*] that he is completely Victorian; and certainly he is abashed by our modern Eros. Harrow, early years of roughing it in California, theatrical suppers, and War years —so he assembles his good memories and anecdotes. He gives us in ample measure of that public self, genial and practical, into which best-selling authors manage in time to merge their individuality.

LM. July, 1928, p. 654

VAN DRUTEN, JOHN (1901–1957)

Young Woodley shows up one of the greatest evils in our Public School system as we know it today. As far as I am aware, there exists no Public School where the authorities have made some conscientious effort to solve this problem of sex education. . . . That is why I welcome such a play as *Young Woodley*. Let none be debarred from seeing it. . . .

There is nothing crude about it, and if Mr. Van Druten's forthcoming novel is as good as the play it will have a ready sale, and the author can congratulate himself in having done something to mitigate the evil crop of inhibitions and neurasthenias that are such a lamentable feature of our time.

A. C. Gordon Ross. *Spec.* July 14, 1928, p. 52

If literature has any social purpose beyond that of mere diversion, it lies in extending human sympathies by bringing us into contact with the lives and minds of others. . . .

This sociological preamble is evoked by . . . two dramas which see murder and the murderer from the human viewpoint. . . . Mr. Van Druten [in *Diversion*] has more likely been concerned only with carrying on that theme of the tragic growing pains of the soul with which he dealt in *Young Woodley;* but the result has been to give us a companion piece to *To What Red Hell* by Percy Robinson, with the propaganda none the less strong because it is almost unconscious. . . .

It is, indeed, part of the ingenious craftsmanship of these pieces that, despite the terrific tragedy of their time, both succeed in having humour. True, as the tragic climax is approached, this is subjected, but there is none of the self-conscious gloom drama of earnest young playwrights with a mission. . . . In *Diversion* the humour is so excellent that there is every reason to fear Mr. Van Druten's secession to the ranks of the writers of flippant cocktail comedy.

Horace Shipp. *Eng.R.* Dec., 1928, pp. 726–27

Young men in love seem to be a favourite study for Mr. John Van Druten. Are they interesting? Mr. Van Druten certainly interested us in *Young Woodley*. His new hero, Wyn Hayward in *Diversion,* is less "sympathetic." We have seen him so often before!—the respectable youth hopelessly entangled with a far from respectable woman ("actress," as usual). He pleads, he raves, he explains—or rather explains that he can't explain it. We see his eminent Harley Street father offering the vain help of words. We feel that forcible isolation in a nursing home, with perhaps a mild operation for appendicitis, would be the one remedy. But, like the father, we can do nothing except watch and find it incredible that a notorious "actress" should so enslave a young man who has already (he tells us) had his "affairs" and his experience of women.

Richard Jennings. *Spec.* Oct. 13, 1928, p. 481

Van Druten owes much of his success in the theatre to his ability to understand and use actors felicitously and his remarkable comprehension of feminine psychology. Even women have been known to declare that this is *one* dramatist who understands how they function. This was most evident in his drawing of Leonora in *There's Always Juliet* in which he etched her character deftly while keeping aloft his gossamer lines. This tendency toward airy writing is one which may eventually lead him into a mere thinness which most English comic writers share. . . .

The Voice of the Turtle (1943) proved a sheer delight both in writing and in playing. A tour de force employing only three characters, this comedy of love in the spring in Manhattan was the smash dramatic hit of New York's 1943–1944 season. Van Druten's deftness in character depiction was never more apparent. He enlarged the two principals to the point that they were on the stage for an hour and a half without the audience's becoming bored. . . . Many of Van Druten's plays have been American in background. With his home established here we have found him in the 1944–1945 season being more and more American in thought and feeling as well as content. This is certainly proved true in his adaptation of Kathryn Forbes' stories, *Mama's Bank Account,* as *I Remem-*

ber Mama (1944). This is a nostalgic, beautifully textured, deftly fashioned, honestly sentimental comedy-drama.

George Freedley in *A History of Modern Drama,*
ed. Barrett H. Clark and George Freedley
(N.Y., Appleton-Century, 1947), pp. 198–99

Once more Mr. Van Druten has preferred to show his single-minded wizardry with a small cast (five in number) and one set. And even if it is a much better play than most of those that confine themselves so rigidly, we do begin to invent wildly for ourselves. In the past—though not at *Bell, Book, and Candle*—while sitting out these economical pieces, I have often felt that a sudden transformation scene, or ten minutes with the Dagenham Girl Pipers, would round the business off with a pleasing flourish.

J. C. Trewin. *ILN*. Oct. 23, 1954, p. 712

In the academic life, as in the army, personal affairs are a scandal, almost by definition—that is why there is so much gossip in college communities. That a teacher should have a wife or a mother, to say nothing of a vice or a weakness, is *unthinkable* to those who look up to him; his very bodily existence, his shaving, sleeping, going to the toilet, jeopardise his classroom standing from moment to moment. . . . The indecencies of the academic position, the shame of being a man when one would prefer to be a pure omniscience . . . all this is the subject of *The Druid Circle,* a play that would have been better if craftsmanship had not fashioned it so expertly, if it had avoided high climaxes and dramatic confrontations and remained insistently on the plane of the ordinary, where the teacher's tragi-comedy really takes place. The atrocity committed by the professor who makes a student read aloud a very intimate love-letter, is robbed of its proper shabbiness by the hysterical emphasis Mr. Van Druten, the author, puts on it; what is horrible about the academic life is not that a teacher should do such a thing in a crisis of passion and jealousy, but that he would do it as a matter of course, without any sense of emergency, as a routine disciplinary measure. . . . In the professor's *descent* to persecution of the ugly little pair who are his victims lies the play's real pathos and squalor, but a false nimbus of pathos is drawn about this smug couple by the author's inveterate stagecraft, which transforms a timeless study of character into a rather belated defence of youth and its sexual rights. Here, as in *The Voice of the Turtle,* Mr. Van Druten encases a certain amount of realistic observation within a sentimental convention without appearing to notice the leak of meaning that results.

Mary McCarthy. *Sights and Spectacles, 1937-1958*
(Heinemann, 1959), pp. 127–28

VULLIAMY, C. E. (1886–   )

Mr. Vulliamy's *John Wesley* is much more than a life of the founder of the sect. It is also a history of the early years of revivalism in general, and contains a number of Aubreyesque sketches of Wesley's friends and supporters. In fact, Mr. Vulliamy, without appearing to crowd his canvas, has examined the later half of the century through the eyes of the Evangelist. . . . This life of Wesley, written with sympathy and wit and a scholar's knowledge of the period, is bound to find many readers.

R. Strachey. *NSN*. Oct. 31, 1931, p. 550

One hesitates to damn a book like this [*John Wesley*], so obviously the fruit of years of research and containing such an enormous body of fact. Yet it is not sufficiently well written, nor sufficiently well organized, to gain many readers other than those who have a burning interest in Methodism. It is often pedantic, although there are flashes of humour here and there, and the author's attitude, although he does describe episodes in which Wesley appears ridiculous, is one of attenuated hero-worship. Wesley is forever striding through crowds of hostile Englishmen, oblivious of brickbats, stones and rotten eggs. . . . Wesley is shown as sadly deficient in his personal relationships, though he spends his life meddling with other people's affairs. But to Mr. Vulliamy, at any rate, he is "a living character of rare beauty and force."

Geoffrey T. Hellman. *Bkm*. May, 1932, p. 191

Poor Boswell! He has had his day—just such a day as he would have wished, basking at the fireside of tolerance, in the company of great men who anatomized his follies with mercy and were duly grateful for the biography which they helped to produce. Now the world grows cold again for Boswell. After the apologists, the alienists. Mr. Vulliamy thinks Boswell was mad. Macaulay's verdict is qualified, not quashed: guilty, but insane. . . .

The evidence against sanity is strong indeed; Mr. Vulliamy fails to make the most of it only in one instance. . . .

Mr. Vulliamy's attractive, sensible, and only occasionally unimaginative study is especially valuable for its analysis of Boswell's relations with Johnson. The "dog-like devotion" theory is exploded. Mr. Vulliamy's Boswell was something more than a man with a great opportunity; he was a great opportunist [*James Boswell*].

Peter Fleming. *Spec*. Dec. 2, 1932, pp. 796, 798

The portentous title of C. E. Vulliamy's latest production must not cause the reader to suppose that *Mrs. Thrale of Streatham: Her Place in the*

Life of Dr. Samuel Johnson and in the Society of Her Time etc. deserves consideration as a work of scholarship. But the work deserves mention in *The Year's Work* in order that his facile pen may not lead the reader into acceptance of his statements and opinions without further examination of that "newly assembled evidence" upon which he claims that they are based. . . .

Vulliamy may think that only "stiff prigs" commended *Rasselas* or were interested in "such a stilted thing as *The Vanity of Human Wishes*" or cared "much about the prosy moralizing of *Ramblers* and *Idlers*." But *The Rambler* was already in the sixth collected edition by 1763, *Rasselas* was in its third edition, and Johnson's *Shakespeare* appeared in the year 1765. These examples suffice to contradict the above statements and the conclusion that "he was not a figure known to his contemporaries."

The portrait of Mrs. Thrale is similarly painted in colours which make a striking effect, but the drawing is out of focus and the perspective weak.

Edith J. Morley. *YWES,* 1936, pp. 225-26

WAIN, JOHN (1925–   )

If Wain and Amis have been commonly lumped together it is partly their own fault: they have been associated in literary enterprises outside fiction. And they share a common background: both are graduates of Oxford who teach English in provincial universities. . . . Different though their novels are, they seemed informed by similar attitudes. The heroes of both *Hurry on Down* and *Lucky Jim* could be described equally well as tough intellectuals or as intellectual toughs. They seem consciously, even conscientiously, graceless, and their faces seem set in a snarl of exasperation. They are sensitive, but sensitive in a way quite other from that traditional in our fiction: it is to the phoney, the bogus, that their nerve-ends are tremblingly exposed, and it is at the least suspicion of the phoney that they go tough. Conventionally educated, they are at odds with most of the attributes of the conventional English education. They smell rackets everywhere and are determined not to be imposed upon. It is possible to guess at the influences that have produced the attitude behind them. Experience in the Services certainly helped to make them; but I suspect George Orwell, Dr. Leavis, the Logical Positivists and perhaps Robert Graves—or rather, the outlooks these represent—all contributed to their genesis. . . .

In their approach to the novel both these writers appear to be influenced by the eighteenth century. They are anti-romantic, and one of the interesting things about *Hurry on Down* is that it is an experiment in the picaresque. Its hero plunges from Oxford into the "low" and the sordid almost as though these were themselves guarantees of the real. During his career he is a long-distance lorry-driver, window-cleaner, male nurse, chauffeur and radio gagman. Wain is a wholly serious writer who expresses his seriousness through a wild farce. In this, as in the pace and splenetic energy of his prose, together with a fine exasperated fury at the world, he is reminiscent of Smollett.

Walter Allen. *The Novel Today*
(BC/Longmans, 1955), pp. 29–30

Writers of this [satirical] kind have so caught the ear of the serious reading public lately as to provoke the wry comment that they are already a new Establishment. Of them all, John Wain is the most frequent, fluent and varied publicist. His two novels do not display the imaginative power of Iris Murdoch's or the comic sense of Kingsley

Amis', but they are interesting contributions in the new picaresque mode. His "New Academic" poems are sometimes wittily effective, though he cheerfully waives his claims to a leading place as a poet of his kind in favor of Philip Larkin. His criticism is not as promisingly searching as that of Donald Davie, but is more widely engaged, often ranges outside the somewhat restricted field of specific "lit. crit."

This collection of essays [*Preliminary Essays*] strengthens one's hunch that just there—in the range of his intelligent hospitality—may be John Wain's real strength. He seems most likely, of any in his generation, to become that valuable and now rare person, the general man of letters. He is immensely hard-working and almost always extremely competent. He has read very widely and is clearly setting himself steadily to widen his range all the time. . . .

Richard Hoggart. *Nation*. Oct. 27, 1957, p. 285

A novel of character (Mr. Wain's third), a picturesque extravaganza, a social satire, a modern morality, or simply a cautionary tale, *The Contenders* defies classification. But John Wain, who is one of the founding Angry Young Men and winner of the Somerset Maugham Award for 1958, obviously enjoyed himself immensely while writing it. He has a wicked sense of humor and a relentless hatred of pretension and pomposity. Woe betide anyone—from bishops to bartenders—who get in his line of fire. Even when he is shooting from the hip, which is most of the time, his marksmanship is . . . unerring.

Roger Pippett. *NYT*. April 27, 1958, p. 4

I should like . . . to discuss . . . [some of the] contents of Mr. Wain's book [*Preliminary Essays*]: his balanced common sense on "Restoration Comedy and the Modern Critic," where so much writing on the subject is exaggerated and partisan; his "Notes on Four Victorian Poets"; his championship of Arnold Bennett; and his discriminating assessments of Ezra Pound and William Empson; or—the only failure in the book—his thin and unsatisfying review of Dylan Thomas's *Collected Poems*. Common sense, plain speaking, are the outstanding characteristics of Mr. Wain's writing; but these things have their limitations. In dealing with poetry of the complexity of Dylan Thomas's, common sense is not enough; and our conviction of the validity of his opinions is not increased by such phrases as "Miss Sitwell, who is simply not interested in the ordinary process of being intelligent" (where he means, if he means anything, "intelligible," not "intelligent"); or "Meanwhile we want a little less gas about Thomas and some criticism that really talks turkey and gets down to particular instances." Back-slapping mateyness of this kind has little to do with serious criticism, for it is entirely unconstructive; as it is, in the Restoration Comedy essay, to call Charles II "a flop."

H. Peschmann. *Eng.* Summer 1958, p. 45

Mr. Wain, one feels, will push on through eventually. A second, long short story . . . is not very good, but shows that Mr. Wain is pushing—that he knows of the existence of a world of high imagination and fascinating mystery and would like to reach it. Meanwhile the other stories in this collection [*Nuncle and Other Stories*] only show how dull and insignificant his present world is—stories of Manchester, drab little rooms, uninteresting pubs, tedious people. One story has a Swiss setting, and one hopes that the Alps may raise Mr. Wain out of his flat country: instead, the Alps are chopped down, to fit the flatness. All in all, here are humor, brevity and good sense—but still waiting for the magic wand that will remove the lowly cheese roll from their feet.

Nigel Dennis. *NYT*. July 16, 1961, p. 4

Poetry is an impure art, though French poets have purified it more than once seemed possible. British taste has always preferred its poetry full of reverential impurities, and some British poets have agreed about this. John Wain seems to be one. His "Anniversary" [*Weep Before God*] is oratory at its most humane and affecting, most a man speaking to men; "This Above All Is Precious and Remarkable" is oratory at its clearest and boldest; and "Poem" (despite its title) is oratory at its most solemn, urgent and ambitious.

Donald Davie. *NS.* July 21, 1961, p. 91

Strike the Father Dead is John Wain's fifth novel. The two main characters of the book write their own histories in two conflicting, well managed styles—the pedantic, dry, self-exposing prose of the father, a very Hebraising Professor of Classics who adheres to a code of self-discipline, is played off against the slangy, ironic, Holden Caulfieldish self-exposition of the son, who has a freer, less moralistic vision of life and runs away from home to become a jazz pianist. But for his rebellion to be of any real substance it must disclose a system of values that forcefully encounters those of the father. Yet, though the cards are all stacked in the son's favour, his own style is self-deflating. And thus Mr. Wain can't really hit the mystic note; the scenes where he comes to "understand" strike false. What Mr. Wain can do superbly is to evoke the general jazz-playing ethos into which he penetrates, to give precise, clear social detail, and manage a hard commonsense note which destroys all pretences, even the author's own. The whole, however, is given a warm, documentary reality which is its most pleasing quality.

Malcolm Bradbury. *MGW*. March 29, 1962, p. 11

WALKLEY, A. B. (1855–1926)

Under the somewhat ambitious title of *Drama and Life,* Mr. A. B. Walkley has gathered together and reprinted a number of his dramatic criticisms and essays. There is, perhaps, no form of literature more apt to be ephemeral than the review of a theatrical performance written for the daily Press; and it is a convincing proof of the value of Mr. Walkley's critical work that his volume, composed as it is almost entirely of such reviews, may be read with pleasure and profit. To say that the notices strike the reader quite as freshly as when they first appeared would be to commit "a fallacy in proportion." Mr. Walkley at his best puts me in mind of the sparkle and exhilaration of champagne; and champagne, once opened, is a thing that does not keep. But Mr. Walkley's articles are not all effervescence. Besides their smartness and their "modernity," their reiterated appeals to Aristotle, and their innumerable lapses into French slang, they possess a quality which is rare enough in the dramatic criticism of the present time—the quality of thought. To use one of Mr. Walkley's favourite phrases, he is certainly not an "unidea'd" writer. His views, though they do not bear the impress of the vigour and originality of such a critic as Mr. Bernard Shaw, have the compensating merit of a freer play and a wider relevance.

Spec. Nov. 16, 1907, p. 776

There are fifty-two of these little "hurticles" [*More Prejudices*], as Thackeray would have called them, and readers of *The Times* will remember having smiled over them at successive breakfasts. The style of Mr. Walkley is familiar; we all know his easy, mocking, wise and casual touch. He is generally in earnest, but likes to pretend that he is not. He has witnessed so many exhibitions of popular sentiment at the theatre that he has become slightly biased, against sentimentality on the one hand and against pedantry on the other. He has certain foibles which are passions. His feeling for Jane Austen surpasses love, and becomes obsession....

We ought, perhaps, to say more about the theatrical criticism, since, after all, Mr. Walkley is a drama critic before all else. But his readers are familiar with his attitude, and will read once more his useful hints to the public and to the profession without surprise. He abounds in reasons for leniency, and is really rather severe, though always reasonable and just; and after the play is over he always falls back on Miss Austen and M. Proust.

SR. Sept. 29, 1923, p. 361

Excess of emotion made him uncomfortable (to the question why the early nineteenth-century audiences were moved to fainting and floods of tears by plays that leave modern people cold, he replied in one word: "Drink!"); some revelations of the human spirit struck him as indecent; he had a Gallic love of work that was orderly, shapely, and finely finished. Our own Elizabethans (not wholly excluding Shakespeare) and the nineteenth-century Russians, for instance, never appealed very closely to him. On the other hand, he found in Marcel Proust, for all his way of writing, a precision in subtlety, which he found nowhere else except in the novels of his beloved Jane Austen. And in secret he liked some poetry a good deal more than he would admit. A great reader, a great lover of letters, and at the same time a man of the world, he had his own touchstone of reality, and he liked anything that made for reality as he saw it. Vagueness and extravagance in life and in art were foreign to a mind whose ultimate test was always aesthetic.

Charles Morgan. *TL*. Oct. 9, 1926

Knowledge of him was so deep that there was no need for him to sign or initial his work—the Walkley manner was immediately apparent in everything he wrote. His identification was not dependent upon obvious signs. He did, indeed, frequently mention Jane Austen, and was addicted to the repetition of one or two quotations of Dickens. There was a period, too, when he was overfond of foreign phrases in his work. But those were small signs by which he revealed himself. The principal sign was the incommunicable richness of his own personality. In a quite remarkable way he put himself down on paper so that those who had made his acquaintance in the columns of *The Times* could not possibly be in any doubt about his identity. . . . There was wit in his work; his words were well-selected words; his writing was easy (though not easily done) and had thought in it; and he pleased his readers with the suggestion of graceful scholarship in the lightest of his sentences. He abhorred solemnity and was embarrassed by earnest people and enthusiasts. Or so he pretended. His affection was for the rare and subtle thought and for delicate comedy. Tragic things, if they did not actually repel him, acutely disturbed him; he did not care to hear about them. But his liking for comedy was not a sign of a nature which despairs of life. I imagine that he was in his heart a man profoundly pessimistic.

St. John Ervine. *Obs*. Oct. 10, 1926

WALLACE, EDGAR (1875–1932)

It will be of interest to recall the beginnings of this famous sensational writer. He had very little education and entered the Army before the Boer War as a private soldier. He had always a feeling for the use of words, and he had written verse as a schoolboy. As a Tommy he issued a book of poems, *Writ in Barracks*. He was then in Simonstown, South Africa. There was something promising in the little book, and it got a fair press—with one exception. Mr. Jerome K. Jerome wrote a column of ridicule which made Wallace feel entirely foolish and humiliated. He feels that humiliation to the present day, which should be a warning to critics not to hit young authors too hard.

"I could just read and write when I went into the Army," he said to me. "Every book of my own has been an education. The advice I would give all neophytes is to write verse and keep on writing verse (I say this in spite of my own mortification). Secondly, I would recommend a close study of the Book of Job, which as pure literature is to me the finest thing in the Bible. I am immensely taken with its simplicity. It abounds in one- and two-syllable words expressing the most poignant thought—straight, stark English written in old English words.

"I encountered a simplicity without any literary value in the vocabulary of the African natives. The Swahili and the Mobongo have a limitation of words. Getting on to lying—which is a form of literature—the native has no subtlety. He will say to you, 'I lied to you because it was difficult to tell the truth,' and you wouldn't have believed it."

Of course, everyone knows—or ought to know—that Mr. Wallace's African stories dealing with Sanders, Bones, Bosambo, the lying chief, and other choice characters, are entirely different from his crime stories. They have infinite humour, and display a surprising knowledge of native life. Mr. Wallace has just written his tenth book in that vein, called *Sanders,* and has also undertaken a Sanders play. Mr. Wallace has had as much success with these novels as with the others, though they are in an entirely different genre. His knowledge of Africa is obtained at first hand, as he has been through the Dark Continent twice.

Of late years Wallace is giving freer play to his sense of fun. His series of stories about "Educated Evans," a little racing tipster, are extremely diverting. Wallace knows all about the turf. He has a zest for racing, and is the possessor of one of those precious animals which are as delicate as fine ladies—and as a rule much more costly. He admits a moderate passion for gambling, and has certainly done very rash things at Monte Carlo, but he says he is learning some sense with regard to the tables there. He has made very good use of his experiences as sportsman and a gambler, in local colour for his books, which represents compensation for any bad days on the Turf or at the Casino. Two of his racing stories are "The Flying Fifty-Fifty" and "Down Under Donovan."

Mr. Wallace believes a writer should be equipped for life from all possible points, and he holds that the most thorough way of doing this is in being a journalist. In fact he is much prouder of the title of journalist than novelist. He says he owes his whole success as a writer to Mr. Thomas Marlowe, who gave him his first start on the *Daily Mail* and thereafter appointed him War Correspondent and Special Correspondent all over the world. His first important work was in connection with the South African War. He finished the war for the *Mail*. He knows the United States and Europe better than most men know their native county. Morocco was a happy hunting ground for him as regards future fiction. He prophesied the big trouble with the Riffs twenty years back.

Louis McQuilland. *BkmL*. March, 1926, p. 302

Wallace was certainly the only author of our time who had forgotten the titles of thirty-five or forty of his own books.

He had no illusions about his work. He did not believe, as do many of our younger and even more ephemeral authors, that he was creating great and enduring literature. He had a wholesome scorn of novelists with A Message. He was writing stories to make money, and that was the end of it. He had no hope that any of his work would live after him —though in that respect he may have underestimated the merit of some of his stories. Only time will tell.

He hated the sex novel, which, he used to say, was the easiest thing in the world to write provided one's mind were dirty enough.

Robert G. Curtis. *Edgar Wallace—Each Way*
(John Long, 1932), pp. 66–67

The most typical, and by far the largest group, [of his works] are those which depend for their interest almost exclusively on intricate and sensational plot, and in which the characters are little more than puppets. The straightforward "crime thriller," the typical Edgar Wallace book, belongs to this group: *The Crimson Circle, The Green Archer, A King by Night, The Dark Eyes of London, Terror Keep* and *The Man from Morocco* are half a dozen of the more famous titles which come to mind.

Those books which depend primarily on the interest of their central character, and in which plot takes a secondary place, are less numerous, but have been by no means less successful; they are, in fact, considered by many Wallace enthusiasts to be his best work. In this group are all the books written round the characters of Sanders, Bosambo, and Bones; those which follow the adventures of the little Cockney tipster, Educated Evans, and the old-fashioned, spinsterish detective, Mr. J. G. Reeder. The Smithy books, *The Gunner* and *The Orator,* fall into this category. . . . Wallace's characters are all two-dimensional; they have no depth, though their backs and fronts are adorned with as many mannerisms, characteristics and turns of humour as should convince any reader in search of light and exciting entertainment; and his plots, in the same way, are so permeated with the improbable that the reader, once hypnotised by the breathless anxiety to know what happens next, loses all touch with reality and wanders in a maze of confusion and suspense through a hair-raising criminal world built of the purest fantasy. Despite its horrors, though, it is a reassuring world, for the hero always wins in the end, crime never pays, love finds a way, and the heroine is always saved from worse than death. . . .

Subsidiary to these two main groups—the plot novels and the character novels—is a third which has racing as its central theme, though spiced with a pungent criminal flavour. The Educated Evans books are on the fringe of this group. . . .

A fourth group can conveniently be made of those books which were written round an isolated idea, the experiments of which, though successful, he never chose to repeat. These include *Captains of Souls* (a thriller built on the idea of a soul transmigration), *Chick* (the adventures of a bank clerk who inherits a peerage), *The Books of Bart* (a love story), *The Day of Uniting* (the supposed end of the world through collision with a comet), *The Devil Man* (a highly fictionised account of the life of Charles Peace), and *The Northing Tramp,* which is partly a crime story but chiefly concerns the relationship between a spoiled heiress and the tramp whom she marries out of pique, and who is eventually able to add to her happiness by revealing himself as an earl.

Margaret Lane. *Edgar Wallace*
(N.Y., Doubleday, Doran, 1939), pp. 289–91

WALPOLE, HUGH (1884–1941)

Among our younger writers there are few so worthy of critical attention as Mr. Hugh Walpole, who is possessed of qualities and gifts rare in themselves, rarer still in combination. In *Mr. Perrin and Mr. Traill* he showed a singular power of realising and rendering the sordid details of life, and then transfusing them with mystical significance; his latest work is more frankly idealistic, but shows something of the same curious blending of everyday fact with spiritual mysteries. . . . All his portraits of men are good; how admirably, for instance, has he shown the blending of absurdity and heroism in Bunning. *The Prelude to Adventure,* true to its title, leaves the reader questioning, looking forward, conscious of immense purposes to be worked out, and full of desire to follow . . . [the hero] on his quest of atonement.

OutL. May 18, 1912, p. 738

His books, from the first to the last, have not become antiquated; they are as fresh today as they were at any time through the past ten or twelve years; the people in them, true in costume and speech to their various moments, are equally true to that which in man is changeless. They, the novels, are at once provincial, as the best novels invariably are, and universal as any deep penetration of humanity, any considerable artistry, must be. Never merely cosmopolitan, never merely smart—even in his knowledge of smart people—they are sincere without being stupid, serious without a touch of hypocrisy; and, on the other hand, light without vapidity, entertaining with never a compromise nor the least descent from the most dignified of engagements. . . .

Usually great creative writers—gifted, together with pity, with clarity of vision—have dealt in a mood of severity with life; they are largely barred, by their covenant with truth, from the multitude; but Mr. Walpole, not lacking in the final gesture of greatness, has yet the optimism that sees integrity as the master of terrors. Literature, different from painting and music, serves beauty rather by the detestation of ugliness than in the recording of lyrical felicities. But, again, Mr. Walpole has countless passages of approval, of verbal loveliness, that must make him acceptable not only to a few but to many.

In reading, for example, *The Secret City,* there is the satisfaction of realizing that the consequent enjoyment rises from an unquestionably pure source. It is a preoccupation to be followed with utter security—for once an admirable thing, a fine thing, is altogether pleasurable.

Joseph Hergesheimer. *Hugh Walpole*
(N.Y., George H. Doran, 1919), pp. 6–8

Of the general soundness of Mr. Walpole's work I am perfectly convinced. Let no modern and malicious mind take this declaration for a left-handed compliment. Mr. Walpole's soundness is not of conventions but of convictions; and even as to these, let no one suppose that Mr. Walpole's convictions are old-fashioned. He is distinctly a man of his time; and it is just because of that modernity, informed by a sane judgment of urgent problems and wide and deep sympathy with all mankind, that we look forward hopefully to the growth and increased importance of his work. In his style, so level, so consistent, Mr. Hugh Walpole does not seek so much for novel as for individual expression; and this search, this ambition so natural to an artist, is often rewarded by success. Old and young interest him alike and he treats both with a sure touch and in the kindest manner. We see Mr. Walpole grappling with the truth of things spiritual and material with his characteristic earnestness, and we can discern the characteristics of this acute and sympathetic explorer of human nature: his love of adventure and the serious audacity he brings to the task of recording the changes of human fate and the movements of human emotion, in the quiet backwaters or in the tumultuous open streams of existence.

Joseph Conrad. *Appreciations,* ed. Grant Overton
(N.Y., George H. Doran, 1922), p. 1

We cannot, as a whole, regard Mr. Walpole as a typical modern novelist. He works with the old material, character studies from observation, not self-revealing. A composed plot, dramatic construction, a set subject, a defined purpose, almost a moral. He deals with facts, words, appearances, crises and the exceptional. He uses rapid movement, strong local colour or atmosphere, and does not despise melodrama. There is, of course, subtlety in abundance, continual soul analysis, and the Ideal of Self. Only these are symptoms of his age, not the web of his art. As a craftsman he accepts broadly the tradition of novel writing; following it with masterly skill: building thereon great work.

He accepts, too, much from Romance, which Realism holds in derision; gaining thereby an invigorating vitality which we do not find in some, at least, of his contemporaries.

R. Brimley Johnson. *Some Contemporary Novelists*
(Leonard Parsons, 1922), p. 75

Mr. Walpole deals with the naked cruelty and toil of ordinary life. He sees life ever a hard experience, playing with those who pass along its alleys, as though they were mere helpless, humble pawns, driven here, driven there, so fast, so inevitably that none can say whence they come and whither they go. It is perhaps a melancholy picture, but it is the more melancholy in that it is so terribly true.

In the opinion of the writer, the book that is most characteristic of Mr. Walpole, when he is in a mood of passionate sincerity is most certainly *Fortitude*. And the book that shows Mr. Walpole in his other mood, that of a mystic, is most shown in *The Golden Scarecrow*. . . .

In some ways Mr. Walpole is probably the most serious novelist of the present day. It may not be an exaggeration to say that his work is of the very highest quality. There is never the very slightest suggestion of any vulgarity in his work. Mr. Walpole writes of life as it is, he does not *make* a story, the story makes itself. It proceeds naturally and logically to its appointed end.

Patrick Braybrooke. *Novelists: We Are Seven*
(C. W. Daniel, 1926), pp. 77–79

. . . Mr. Walpole has only himself to blame if his claims are sometimes overlooked, for he is, first and last, a novelist, a story-teller, and therefore his work, though intrinsically as valuable, offers a smaller target to the critic. While others were busy setting the universe in order, castigating society, analysing sexual psychology, and making an occasional excursion even into theology, Mr. Walpole, an undaunted pedestrian, has plodded along the main road of English fiction. This single-minded devotion to the matter in hand may and does command our respect, but it does not, in general, excite so much remark as do the activities of those who, disclaiming the novel-form, treat it as a rag-bag into which to stuff their preachments and audacities, their bad tempers and their social remedies. . . . The temptation to neglect good ordinary writers, and thereby to exaggerate the importance of the unusual, is one that, even in the moment of deploring it, is hardly to be resisted. Mr. Walpole happens to be a popular as well as a good writer. A conscientious craftsman, he has produced book after book, every one of which has been in some degree robust, charming, and eminently sensible. His work exhibits, moreover, a surprising versatility. It is a far cry from the playful fantasy of *Maradick at Forty,* and the searching irony of *Mr. Perrin and Mr. Traill,* to *The Dark Forest* and *The Secret City,* stories as rich in atmosphere and suggestive gloom as are their titles; to the quieter charms of *The Cathedral;* or, again, to the almost Flaubertian flavour of *The Old Ladies,* a masterly tale in which the last ounce of significance is extracted from apparently unpromising material. The least one can do is to salute, in passing, an artist who, though clever enough to be able to cut capers, has chosen for himself a less spectacular part.

Gerald Bullett. *Modern English Fiction*
(Herbert Jenkins, 1926), pp. 121–23

Indeed, his whole method is rooted in the group. He uses the family community in his first novel, *The Wooden Horse:* he uses it in his latest novel, *Wintersmoon.* He uses it in eleven out of the eighteen intermediate novels in *Maradick at Forty, Fortitude, The Duchess of Wrexe, The Green Mirror,* the *Jeremy* books, *The Captives, The Young Enchanted, The Cathedral.* In two of the remaining seven he uses the nearest thing to the family group—the school community *(Mr. Perrin and Mr. Traill)* and the college community *(Prelude to Adventure).*

One of the five other volumes is a book of short stories called *The Thirteen Travellers:* the other four are all stories based on the impact of the individual upon a community: *The Old Ladies* gives us a group of elderly women in a lodging house, dominated by one of the inmates: *The Dark Forest* is a study of a military group in Russia during the war: in *Harmer John* we see a town banded against a newcomer whom it has at first welcomed. Indeed it may be said that, except in a privately printed volume of confessions called *The Crystal Box,* Hugh Walpole has never related the history of an individual apart from the crowd: that his individual should be related to the crowd is a condition of his story-telling, as it was a condition of all the traditive novelists before him.

Indeed, even in his mere technical approach to his story, he follows, he does not invent. A favourite opening of the traditive novel is a death in the first pages, with the consequent readjustments in the life of the principal character. One has only to think of *Pamela, The Watsons, Villette, Nicholas Nickleby,* or *Framley Parsonage,* to realize how constantly this opening is used. Hugh Walpole uses it in *Fortitude,* in *The Captives,* and in *The Cathedral.* He is still fonder of that other opening, popular since the days of *Rob Roy,* the arrival of the stranger or the return of the exile. He uses it in *The Wooden Horse, Mr. Perrin and Mr. Traill, The Young Enchanted, The Cathedral, Harmer John,* and, in a very orgy of traditionalism, combines it, in the *Portrait of a Man with Red Hair,* with no less than three other famous openings—the arrival of a stranger in a strange inn in a strange town in a strange country as the preliminary to arrival in a very strange family circle indeed.

These conservatisms might be elaborated endlessly. In one only of his typically traditional impulses does he in form break away from consecrated use. He becomes experimental so soon as he deals with the problem of the introduction of children into his book world. Indeed, before turning to Hugh Walpole's main contribution to the novel today, it may be useful to consider his minor experiment in new handling of familiar material; for unless the reader convinces himself that the *Jeremy* books and *The Golden Scarecrow* are a constructive contribution to the art of the novel as well as a series of pleasant studies of childhood, he is not likely to be interested in the major experiment—the use of a whole range of novels concerning adult life for two distinct purposes at once.

Clemence Dane. *Tradition and Hugh Walpole*
(N.Y., Doubleday, 1929), pp. 88–90

What, then, of the conflict of labour and capital in the poems of Mr. de la Mare, the class struggle in the novels of Mr. Walpole? The question is more pertinent than may appear, and the answer presents less embarrassment than might be expected. Conflict is not less menacing for being ignored, and literature is not imaginative for nothing. It is imaginative either in the obvious sense of preferring imagination to reality—imaginary delights to actual horrors—or, more commonly, in the sense of reproducing reality in ideal forms. The difference or the degree of resemblance between social reality and its idealisation in Mr. Walpole's novels is a measure of his social sympathies. If he has nothing to say of the extremes of privilege and poverty or of the passion of discontent they have bred, it is because, in the last resort, we must suppose, he desires nothing to be said. If his novels do not breathe a syllable of class struggle, it is scarcely because such struggle does not in fact exist, but rather because it has no ideal significance for him. His brand of politics may never appear—he may indeed, as the saying is, have no politics—but what is evident is that Mr. Walpole's sympathies are restricted to materially rosy conditions of society and the outlook upon life which they beget. He would appear to be on the side of existing authority.

Robert D. Charques. *Contemporary Literature and Social Revolution* (Martin Secker, 1933), pp. 37–38

Captain Nicholas is good, but it is also faintly vapid like a dish containing excellent ingredients which a too relaxing atmosphere has caused to melt. . . . Mr. Walpole handles his main idea and his human, if well-known, characters so wisely that one wishes the whole book were not somehow blanketed in a sauce of usualness.

LL. Oct., 1934, p. 124

In *The Bright Pavillions* Hugh Walpole has risen to heights he has not before attained in his Herries Chronicles, if, indeed, he has not done the finest piece of fiction of his long career. I am willing to go even farther and say that *The Bright Pavillions* will rank prominently, and for a long time to come, among novels in the historical genre. It is a dark and frequently sinister story of Elizabethan England of the Virgin Queen and Mary of Scotland. Witchcraft and religious feuds flame through the pages. But nowhere is Mr. Walpole untrue to Elizabethan thought and psychology. . . .

The Bright Pavillions is the very spirit of England; it is the heart's blood of England which pulsates throughout its pages.

Percy Hutchinson. *NYT*. Nov. 10, 1940, p. 7

On May 15, *Anthony Trollope* was published, and Hugh was so encouraged by the favourable opinions of [J. B.] Priestley, and indeed of most people, that he decided to carry out another idea which for some time he had cherished—of making an anthology of his favourite passages in the Waverly novels and prefacing them with a long critical introduction—"if I ever have time! But *what* fun life is!" Time was found at last, and the book appeared four years later [*The Waverley Pageant*].

Two American visitors brought good news. George Doran reported that the American sales of *Wintersmoon* had reached the impressive total of 70,000 copies, and Lee Keedick offered a fee of £1000 (which Hugh accepted) for twenty lectures to be delivered in the States at the beginning of 1930.

Rupert Hart-Davis. *Hugh Walpole*
(N.Y., Macmillan, 1952), p. 291

He found himself in the world of success with a surprise which never quite left him. He had blundered into it by an unbelievable chance, and continued to blunder into it more and more deeply. If he had tried he could not have ever got out. He enjoyed it, as he enjoyed what brought it, the writing of his stories. Yet friendship was always more important to him. His life was a search for a succession of "true friends." He found them, but was sometimes terrified lest he should lose them and not be able to replace them.

Edwin Muir. *Obs*. March 9, 1952, p. 7

Appreciation from those he esteemed, or who counted in the literary hierarchy, made him delirious with joy. And, owing to his engaging, warm-hearted personality, more appreciation was expressed than his books in themselves warranted. They were competent, fluent, serious, well invented; their appeal was mainly to the mass of middlebrow minds over two continents. *Auream mediocritatem:* the golden flow streamed fabulously in his wake as he wrote and lectured on The Novel. He had the Midas touch. It is strange now to read of. One luxurious house, flat and car after another; thousands of pounds' worth of luxurious pictures, till his walls overflowed. A dream life, only marred by the sharp occasional wounds from envious and malicious reviewers, and by the uneasy knowledge that he was not, and was not regarded as, a front-rank writer. "I've got sincerity and vitality, but very little else." One thing he had not got was a feeling for style. I remember saying to him that the shape and sound of a sentence mattered more to me than its sense; he lost his temper and said I was talking "pretentious piffle."

Rose Macaulay. *List*. March 20, 1952, p. 471

WARNER, REX (1905–   )

The actual performance displayed in this first book [*Poems*] is very uneven, a mixture of sensuous observations and dialectics which has not fused into a unity. The reader is continually being brought face to face with acute and accurate images of the natural world, and when politics are introduced, and often when abstractions of any kind appear, a poem goes to pieces. More specifically: the poem "Love" attempts in a purely direct manner to create this fusion, and is half-successful; it is when Warner begins to draw to his conclusion and his generality takes precedence over the details that the words fail to solidify the reader's experience.

Samuel French Morse. *Poetry*.
April, 1938, pp. 36–37

The imagination of Mr. Warner is cold, adventurous, exalted, visionary and sensuous. He sees in our society the failure to love completely; and his women are very conscious of the male failure and, at times, of their own. But one suspects he is persuaded *intellectually* of this; does he really feel it? One sees him arguing that love is the basis of the moral life, but does he *know* that it is? One asks this question simply because Mr. Warner expresses himself with a beguiling and melodious gravity. Like solemn music, his smooth, simple and dilatory prose fills and possesses his subject, so that the mind of the reader is calmed and persuaded. It is strange to find a writer, who began under the influence of *Ulysses* and who continued under the influence of Auden's gift for giving general ideas, and even conventional phrases, a hieratic visual power, now emerging into a measured and classical prose. It is an exultant prose. It is his own. But it is in danger of becoming free verse and of putting a spell upon the writer as well as on the reader. As I have said earlier, Mr. Warner is a Greek scholar and he has learned much from the direct and modulated clarity of the Greeks. There are moments in his later work when one feels he enjoys the music of his own elegies more than he enjoys his invention. And the effect is, oddly enough, that this bold, poetic, abstract mind and really adventurous imagination is in danger of making a negative impression. It is muffling its drums.

V. S. Pritchett in *Modern British Writing*,
ed. Denys Val Baker (N.Y., Vanguard, 1947),
pp. 308–9

Still sympathetic to the Marxist conception of history [*The Cult of Power*], Rex Warner still believes also in propaganda for revolution;

but it is a revolution of ideas, a personal responsibility in which the citizen must evolve for himself new standards and create his own sense of unity in an age bereft of both.

More than any other English writer this one has succeeded in establishing imaginative contact with those forces that shape mankind for a new era of cooperation. His view is a long-term one and not necessarily optimistic; but beyond the revolt of individual against neighbour and community, of nations against the international society, he sees not only an ethic of world-brotherhood but a state of society wherein men work for this ultimate ideal. With the fervour of a moralist and the restraint of an artist, Rex Warner labours to point out that in man is the riddle of the universe to be discovered.

E. W. Martin. *FR*. Jan., 1947, p. 76

In a book of this kind [*The Young Caesar*] the style is as vital an element of characterization as any. There is a monolithic quality in Caesar's writings, a weight and a flatness which are curiously paralleled in Mr. Warner's own. The latter, at any rate, largely ignoring local colour and period detail and concentrating upon his subject's characteristic mode of expression, succeeds to a remarkable degree in catching the Caesarean intellect in action—its attack, its logic, its meticulous ordering of the past. The same device enables him to portray Caesar's contemporaries, Marius, Sulla, Cicero and the rest with a partiality and a bite which are the memoir-writer's privilege, denied to the historian.

Of course by giving us Caesar's own version Mr. Warner has considerably limited his scope. Deceptively candid up to a point, the speaker is always selecting his material: Caesar is the kind of autobiographer who addresses himself to an audience, not to a confessor, and in such a context we cannot expect to learn much either of the great lover or of the bulk buyer of votes.

Ian Scott-Kilvert. *L*. Sept., 1958, p. 66

The past decade has witnessed a remarkable renaissance of the historical novel. The Zeitgeist is of course propitious. . . . But the enhanced status of this genre of novel is largely due to the application of distinguished talents employing intelligently the refinements of historical scholarship and the resources of psychology. Mr. Rex Warner, a fine classical scholar and an accomplished novelist, as old admirers of *The Professor* and *The Aerodrome* are aware, has now come over into Macedonia and rounded off the promise of *Young Caesar* with a brilliant story of Caesar's maturity and achievement. . . .

Mr. Warner's first outstanding achievement is to recapture the quality of Caesar's style. . . . This is a remarkable feat and a nice tribute to the sensitivity of the author's scholarship. His second achievement seems to me to be the convincing revelation of Caesar's psychology. He has created a satisfying picture of a genius. . . .

Anyone with the mildest inclination for *romanitas* will find this novel enthralling.

William Hughes. *NS*. Oct. 1, 1960, p. 484

Warner . . . has much more certainty than Kafka. He believes in goodness making itself apparent in the real world; he believes in the power of love, in brotherhood, and in the integrity of the individual. Furthermore he has definite beliefs about the nature of the social unit, beliefs which range him alongside the Auden-Spender group of the 1930's. . . .

The unification of the masses is of great importance in the Warner canon, for only strength that is morally informed can oppose the strength of evil. Critics fastened early on the superficial resemblances with Kafka and failed to understand that Warner was beginning a development which would ultimately define his intentions in such a way that Kafka's influence would be replaced by the less apparent but more real influence of such English writers of social intention as John Bunyan and Charles Dickens. With each novel he discarded more of the Kafka extravagance and nightmare, defined more clearly his beliefs in terms more social than individual, while examining the religious and political skepticism of the thirties. An investigation of the religious theme as a dominating factor in his novels, one to which the social intention is seconded, will indicate Warner's development as a novelist and the many differences that ultimately distinguish his work from Kafka's. . . .

In the light of Warner's development as an allegorist, one comes ultimately to the conclusion that he is quite removed from Kafka in purpose as well as theme. Those resemblances that do exist—the seeker, the frontier, the extravagance, the nightmares, the "absurdities"—are superficial. No Kafka hero ever reached the point of assurance that Roy does in *The Aerodrome*.

A. A. Devitis. *TCL*. Oct. 1960, pp. 108, 116

WARNER, SYLVIA TOWNSEND (1893–   )

She has no Platonic consolations for her green Dorsetshire world [*The Espalier*], brooded over by the sardonic melancholy of Hardy and Powys, except a wry, good-tempered humour. The fact that she imitates Hardy at times with a closeness within the forbidden degrees, cannot disguise her originality. Less skilful technically than *The Unknown Goddess* [by Humbert Wolfe], her work lends itself less to quotation.

Yet there is the firm impress of a personality one likes and respects in the allegory of "The Virgin and the Scales," or the brief, bold strokes of the narrative in "Nelly Trim," with its swift, Homeric opening. . . . Some will complain that Miss Warner, like most happy possessors of both youth and cleverness, overdoes the second; but time will cure. Some, again, will find her view of life too ironic; but so is life. Miss Warner should be heard of again.

F. L. Lucas. *Authors Dead & Living* (Macmillan, 1926), pp. 253–54

In comparison with Mr. Yeats or Mr. Monro, Miss Sylvia Townsend Warner is occupied with a smaller problem. Her work is infused with that rare quality, a genuine rural sentiment. This is not the faked-up rural sentiment of most of the Georgians, but that more homely and genuine thing, the actual country outlook of Burns, Herrick, Barnes, Herbert, or Hardy. That Miss Warner has to admit a certain indebtedness to these predecessors, goes without saying. Yet her book is a perfectly honest performance, and her craftsmanship is both sure and subtle within its limits. Her general outlook has grown a little more fanciful and less poignantly tragic than when she wrote her earlier book *The Espalier* which was an exceptionally fine performance. Now that Miss Charlotte Mew is dead, I think Miss Warner should be proclaimed the best woman poet in England, outside of Chelsea—which, as we know, has its own ideas.

John Gould Fletcher. *Crit.* June, 1929, p. 133

Miss Townsend Warner has been criticised and is likely to be criticised again for the fact that in her new novel, *The Corner That Held Them,* she views her fourteenth-century nuns through twentieth-century eyes. I can only feel thankful that she does. How bitter this mediaeval concoction would be without the jam of modern wit and irony!

In literature reality is relative only to our willingness to believe, and, because I can believe in them, Miss Warner's nuns are for me much more like fourteenth-century nuns than could be any tedious puppets talking pseudo-Chaucerian. As far as period details are concerned I do not know whether the novel is accurate or not, but it is something more —it is entertaining. Miss Warner's survey of thirty-three years of life in the convent of Oby is from start to finish a mild, sustained delight, never during its three hundred and ten pages jarring one by any obvious error in the drawing of her long pageant of characters. She treats them all with equal insight and interest so that, as far as importance is concerned, they are all much of a size and rouse the same sympathy. The resulting effect is slightly flat but one of complete realism.

Olivia Manning. *Spec.* Dec. 3, 1948, p. 744

Miss Sylvia Townsend Warner . . . is a true professional: she has a style of her own, a distinctive outlook on life, a sly, pungent, poetical way of expressing what she sees. She does not always see anything very new; her imagination turns more readily backwards, preferring to evoke and interpret the atmospheres of the past rather than the tricky materials of our own time. She is one of those writers who have an unmistakable *flavour,* recalled with pleasure long after the story and its persons are forgotten. It is a flavour deceptively smooth, and even prim, for she writes with a grace and polish; but there are undercurrents of earthiness and poetry, and the two things together, the smoothly raked surface and the surprising subsoil, are what give her work its distinctive and pregnant quality.

James Michie. *L.* Jan., 1955, p. 90

WATKINS, VERNON (1907–   )

Vernon Watkins is a young Welsh poet, and that is part of the trouble with his *Selected Poems*. There is apt to be in the young Celt, especially when he is a little over-conscious of himself as such (the real Ur-Welsh, I believe it has been claimed, were not Celtic at all, but never mind) more than a trace of an *überspannt* quality that is hardly distinguishable from the Teutonic. The Welsh, however, usually, have more interested ears; and that this is so Mr. Watkins gives evidence in his use of the spondee in his poem "Thames Forest," written in sapphics, or in the slant rhymes of Yeats's "Tower." In general, the shorter lyrics in this book are the more interesting; Mr. Watkins takes after William Butler Yeats a good deal, and no better practice could be recommended, but he has not yet quite learned how to bring off effects of original terseness. The trouble with the long poems is that they contain too many words. . . .

Rolfe Humphries. *Nation.* Oct. 23, 1948, p. 471

Watkins' poems will never set the times on fire but they will illuminate the intellectual sensibilities of people and the dark passages of human communication; and what is more they will illuminate these odd and ambiguous perspectives without casting shadows. These poems [*The Death Bell*] remind me continually that there are, really, no categories of major and minor poetry; there are simply poems. And they also serve to remind me that, in poems which have truly traversed and emerged from the imaginative machinery of a natural poet, all sorts of crude and undigested elements can be present without serious hurt or damage to the poem. Watkins sometimes employs such tattered phrases as "verdant ground" or "black as pitch"; and he more often permits the shade of Yeats to dictate entire lines. . . . But the impression effected is neither of commonplace carelessness nor of derivative expedience: it is more as though one were being deliberately chided for the suspension of critical tolerance. These occasional dead words and imitative instances do not *spoil* the poems in which they occur: the poems are so intensely innocent that these things look like dirt on children, undesirable but not defects.

George Barker. *L.* Aug., 1954, pp. 88, 90

What will first strike the many readers who now come, perhaps, for the first time to the consideration of a large compact body of Vernon Watkins' verse [*The Death Bell*] is the tremendous change of attitude which must have overtaken English poets since the heyday of Pound and Eliot. During the twenties and even to some extent, the thirties, the poet was concerned with a kind of bitter pin-pricking, a deflation of rhetorical language and high-falutin' ideas. It was done, of course, for the sake of honesty, for the sake of poetry, but much of the public could never get over its initial squeamishness at what appeared to be imaginative crudity and emotional cynicism. With Mr. Watkins there will be no such difficulties. His diction is as lofty as the most confirmed Miltonian could desire and his eyes are always firmly fixed on the "timeless" values of the Christian religion. In this he is typical of a whole generation of poets, whom I shall call "Symbolist," but his sustained virtuosity and precision are typical of nothing but a very unusually exalted sense of the craft of verse.

Burns Singer. *Enc.* Oct., 1954, p. 79

Perhaps the best thing to do is to start by enumerating the weakest qualities of Watkins' verse, in the hope that I shall be able to demonstrate why they finally do not matter when set against the poetry they contain. My first objection is that, when read in bulk, Watkins' poems manifest a monotony of rhythm, in spite of the fact he employs a very wide variety of forms and metres. It is not that the beat falls too often and insistently upon the *expected* syllable, so much as that all the poems, whatever their measure or intention, seem to be set to the same key. With this goes a monotony of style. Watkins' vocabulary appears to be taken consistently from the same wardrobe drawer, no matter what sort of poem he is dressing. In the matter of Watkins' style there is, paradoxically, another objection—it is possible to hear the voices of numerous other poets speaking clearly, too clearly, in the background. Usually it is Yeats, but often it is Hopkins; and even in his latest book one comes across bits of Coleridge. . . .

But his weakness is a tendency to be easily satisfied, and not to mind the darned and shiny phrases he often patches his metre up with—e.g. "breaking wave," "windless air," "hurrying waters," "violent fury." In this he is in exact opposition to Dylan Thomas and George Barker, whose verse often suffers from their dissatisfaction with the obvious. . . .

What I find in Watkins' verse, then, and do not find except in a very few contemporary writers, is the gift and birthmark of poets—the shaping spirit of imagination. It is this quality which, in Watkins' *Ballad of the Mari Lwyd* no less than in Coleridge's *Ancient Mariner,* transmutes what might otherwise have been merely a somewhat complicated allegory into a series of statements that remain true at different levels and in different senses: statements about the dead and the living, the dichotomy of good and evil, about fear and forgiveness, about the relation of poets to people.

David Wright. Nimbus. Spring, 1955, pp. 13–14

With the publication of *The Death Bell* in 1954, Vernon Watkins stepped quietly into the front rank of contemporary British poets, and his new volume [*Cyprus and Acacia*] serves to maintain his ascendancy. There is little in Mr. Watkins's work that excites immediate admiration in the reader's mind: the effect is cumulative, and deeply impressive. Once an overt disciple of Yeats, he is now completely himself, save that here and there one is reminded of Laurence Binyon in his later manner. Mr. Watkins has a potent lyrical gift; but his verse is so impregnated with imaginative thought that even a poem of such apparent spontaneity and with such a dancing rhythm as "Touch with your Fingers" provokes reflection rather than any more facile emotion. Many of his poems—"Call it all Names, but do not call it Rest" and "Before a Birth" are two examples—have a majesty which is rare indeed in modern verse. If such poems are rhetorical, they are rhetorical in the grand manner, and are nobly sustained to the end. Master though Mr. Watkins is of a variety of technical devices, these are nowhere obtrusive, art notably concealing art. Moreover—it can be gratefully added—there is no poem in this collection that is not completely intelligible. This is a volume of outstanding distinction, which it is a privilege to praise.

Ralph Lawrence. Eng. Spring, 1960, p. 29

Vernon Watkins . . . writes very long and very loose. In some odd way, each new book of his seems more old-fashioned than the last. Not that he is traditional in the Georgian manner of, say, Blunden. Watkins goes, instead, right back to a poet like Henry Vaughan: a musing, elderly style, full of queer insights, sensitivity, and longeurs. When he succeeds as in "The Crane" [*Affinities*], he produces verse which is beautiful and wholly his own. But when he fails he is endlessly dull.

A. Alvarez. *Obs*. March 10, 1963, p. 24

WATSON, WILLIAM (1858–1935)

In his introduction to the two-volume selected edition of Mr. Watson's work, Mr. J. A. Spender remarks: "There are writers of a copious and diffuse habit whose best is arrived at by a vigorous process of selection; but Mr. Watson is certainly not one of these. He writes at long intervals, refines, rejects, condenses, with a fastidiousness of self-criticism which is too rare among modern authors. He has, of course, his degrees of excellence, but his work is from the beginning a selection. . . . Mr. Watson has two distinctive qualities. . . . One is the power of conveying illuminative criticism in poetical form, as, incidentally, in his Elegiac Poems, in many of his Sonnets, and in the Epigrams, which last, despite the work of other writers who have practised the aphoristic quatrain, assume in his hands an original and characteristic form. The other is a descriptive and meditative kind of poetry which, though in subject it derives from Wordsworth, departs widely from the Wordsworthian method in its technique. To this class belong many poems which, suggested by some mood or phase of nature, deal with the greater problem of life and death, philosophy and religion." . . . Some critics have had scruples, and perhaps, if the sacred word [poetry] is only to be applied to the inspired moments of Keats and Coleridge, and to such things as are of their kindred, even if not of their quality, then the author of "Lacrymae Musarum" cannot be admitted to the temple. He must be content to stay in the excellent company outside. There is often a fine fire of moral indignation in his verses, and often by sheer burnishing he makes them shine like steel; but neither of these things is the authentic, miraculous flame. But if by poetry one simply means good writing in verse, he is indisputably of the elect. It is nothing but a question of nomenclature. You may deny that Dryden and Pope are poets; you cannot deny that they are among the great writers of English.

Mr. Watson's love of epigram and antithesis suggests comparison with the Augustan age; but, though classical in his economy, he is altogether of the century of Wordsworth, Tennyson and Arnold. He writes in their tradition, and in his outlook on life he is a thorough-going romantic. He considers our forefathers to have been finer fellows than we are, and hopes that our descendants will attain to even loftier summits. It is characteristic of the romantic to believe that he lives in a depression.

Francis Bickley. *BkmL*. April, 1915, p. 8

Watson, in his study of the great writers, seems never to have realized that what matters chiefly, what tells, is not the great phrase, but the personality behind the phrase. He has learned from many writers to make phrases almost as fine as those writers have made; his phrases are never meaningless in themselves, and they can be exquisite in their form. But the phrase, coming with nothing but its own significance behind it, a rootless flower, deriving no life from the soil, fails to convey to us more than an arid, unsatisfying kind of pleasure. There it is, a detached thing; to be taken, you may say, for what it is worth; only, live words will not be so taken. Compare Watson's "Ode to Autumn" with the "Ode to Autumn" of Keats. The poem is one of Watson's best poems; it is full of really poetical phraseology. But the ode of Keats means something in every word, and it means Keats quite as much as autumn. Watson's poem means neither autumn nor Watson; it represents Watson setting himself to describe autumn.

Arthur Symons. *Forum*. June, 1922, p. 488

It is true, one phrase of his—"Abdul the Damned"—lingers in public memory and is familiar even to those who know nothing of Abd-ul-Hamid or the Armenian massacres or William Watson. "Who was Abd-ul-Hamid?" I have heard people ask, "and why was he damned?" . . . That rhetorical sequence of sonnets, *The Purple East*, written at the time of the Armenian massacres, was by no means among the best of his works, but it was probably the most read; for it was produced at a time when his reputation was at its highest, and suiting the purpose of politicians, was much quoted at public meetings and in the Press. It was, in fact, an exaggeration of what was most representative in his work. It was his forte to bring poetry into alliance with public life, more especially the public life of Liberalism and the Nonconformist conscience. He was qualified for this task in the first place by the fact that he spoke the language of poetry. He talked the language of Milton by the same force of habit under which another kind of person might talk the language of the hunting-field or of the movies. He learnt *Paradise Lost* off by heart (as also did Mr. John Burns, and Macaulay, did he not?) when he was a boy; and he went on talking the language of Milton, with a sort of splendid sonorousness, for the rest of his life. . . . He confesses to admiring the "pregnant style," and one has the feeling in reading most of the verse that it is perilously poised on a tightrope of rhythmic splendour, and that if he wished to say "Give me a cup of tea" it would be in lofty blank verse, or perhaps in those hexameters and pentameters, where accent takes the place of quantity, which he used with considerable skill.

R. A. Scott-James. *LM*. Sept., 1935, p. 415

William Watson's death awakens the sort of reflections that are fitting to those who aim at an official rank. Just as Lord Curzon attained large successes yet died disappointed because he was never Prime Minister, so William Watson's life has a pathetic incompleteness because he never attained to be Poet Laureate. . . . Watson wanted recognition for his work as a poet, and in all essentials he had it. What he lacked was the title, which could add nothing to the quality of his achievement. Yet in a sense it was natural that he should feel baulked, for he was cut out to be Laureate almost as perfectly as Tennyson. His thought was not extravagantly individual, but he could give individual distinction to thoughts upon public affairs which were common to the serious minds of his time. The literary forms which he used, the moulds into which his thought was cast, were traditional; he inherited them from Wordsworth and Shelley, adding, as Tennyson did very largely, and Matthew Arnold much less markedly, a new accent of his own. But essentially his verse presented nothing difficult or unfamiliar to anyone who was at home with the English poetry of the nineteenth century, in which what began as a revolt ended as an academic tradition. . . .

Watson had confidence enough in the individual character of his poetry to seek no garb of strangeness. He uttered what he knew that others were thinking and feeling, confident that he could say it for them in a way to win their gratitude. It was, indeed, this lack of strangeness, this easy solidarity with all about him that marked him so specially for the office of laureate, and many regretted that it never fell to him. But they regretted also that he should have allowed this disappointment to prey, as it did, upon his mind, and spoil his talent.

FR. Oct., 1935, pp. 492–94

It is possible that the literary historian of the future will regard the year 1935 as a very significant date in English letters, for he may well take the view that a great phase of poetry, which began with the publication of the *Lyrical Ballads* in 1798, ended with the death of Sir William Watson in August last. It is already manifest that he was the last survivor in the distinct line of inheritance from the great poets of the Victorian age. Whatever the fortunes of English poets may be in the future, that particular succession has now come to an end. . . .

The derivative quality of some of Sir William Watson's verse is not to be denied. He caught much of the manner of his favourite poets—that of Milton and that of Tennyson perhaps most of all. . . . But all this is only to say that in his earlier work Watson was playing the sedulous ape to the great English poets, and what better could a young poet do? . . .

There is individuality enough in Watson's verse, in fact, whenever his feelings are deeply stirred, and wherever he is charged with any depth of intellectual conviction. Doubtless he is not one of the greatest thinkers among our poets; doubtless his powers of expression were in advance both of his intellect and his imagination—a remark which might be made with at least equal truth about Tennyson. But he was a very great artist, and many things that were well worth saying he said nobly and memorably. . . .

Henry Bett. *LQHR*. Jan., 1936, pp. 14, 21–22

WAUGH, ALEC (1898–)

In *The Loom of Youth* we have a truth presented with austere sincerity, with dignity and restraint, yet not without that suggestion of bitterness which is inherent in all expressions of deep feeling. And its total effect upon me is one of acute disillusion. I had grown in the belief that, whatever his faults, the public school boy was always a better sportsman than the Board School cad, more plucky, cleaner-minded, and above all, straighter. And he is not. He is just the same, though wanting the same excuse of poverty and ignorance. I cannot honestly say that I am glad to make his better acquaintance, but I do honestly say that I am glad to make the acquaintance of a new author, of whom one may safely predict such great things in the future. Indeed, this first book of his is in itself a fine achievement, well-conceived, and well done in every way, and wholly praiseworthy alike for the excellence of its writing, and the worthiness of its purpose.

Edwin Pugh. *BkmL*. Sept., 1917, p. 180

To the intentions of Mr. Alec Waugh I have already paid every possible compliment. His short stories showed him as a writer who could start from scratch. He was finding things out for himself. He was recording in language of unaffected simplicity the impact of the world upon a mind of singular clarity and freshness. The result was not in itself remarkable, but the possibilities were unbounded. Therefore even *The Lonely Unicorn* does not make me quite to despair. The advocate for the defence might plead that the mistake lay in the choice of material. He could not, unfortunately, argue that the treatment was good enough to refurbish these rusted weapons of the immature novelist, the walking out, the jilting, the marriage night. Mr. Waugh has attempted a realistic novel without one single quality of a realist. He makes a catalogue instead of a phrase. He suggests the reminiscences of a prosy old bagman instead of creating the illusion of life. He is capable of writing . . . [that]

the hero in a moment of strain noted for the first time the number of roses in a carpet. Whatever he says has been better said before. He offers nothing new. He presents the lamentable spectacle of a young man doing badly old tricks.

H. C. Harwood. OutL. May 13, 1922, p. 382

I think that my favorite of his novels is still *The Loom of Youth*. He has advanced enormously since then in maturity of outlook and polish of style, but his first book has a peculiar fragrance of youth and enthusiasm about it. His later work, like that of all sincere artists, inevitably reflects the passage of time and the twelve years since the war have been difficult and deadening ones. *Cardcastle,* which, oddly enough, was least successful commercially, comes next in my admiration, and after that *Three Score and Ten*. Of his non-fiction works I think that his last book, *The Coloured Countries* . . . comes far and away ahead. If one had to attribute any ancestry to Alec's peculiarly individual style, one would first think of Mr. George Moore, but of Mr. Moore brought up to date, divorced from Paris of the nineties and Dublin of the early nineteen-hundreds and plunged into the insecure world of post-war London; of George Moore disillusioned even of his last inviolable stronghold of belief in the Sanctity of Art. Nothing could be better suited to this style of writing than the compilation of a leisurely, discursive and acutely critical travel book, such as Alec has produced in *The Coloured Countries*. Moreover this book is very much more than the mere daily journal of the novelist on a holiday. It contains in the chapters about Haiti what I think we may predict will be the germ of Alec's future development. It seems to me that he is growing out of novel writing; his narrative poems, his story-teller's instinct for significant detail, his ability to sort out tangled chains of motive, to assess probabilities, to render incidents dramatic and memorable, seem to me all to fit him for the rôle of historian.

Evelyn Waugh. Bkm. June, 1930, p. 300

Alec Waugh gives full value. . . . I mean that Mr. Waugh, who has seven previous novels to his credit, is a professional: a professional story-teller who brings a pure competence to his work, who is unafraid to confront his characters with major problems—of power, of sex, of friendship, of loyalty—and who handles these confrontations deftly. He has drawn . . . at least half a hundred individual and distinctive characters and set them to weaving, before our eyes, the pattern of a book [*Island in the Sun*] that will entertain and inform and be read to the end.

In the main Mr. Waugh's professionalism stands him in good stead.

He has a keen eye and ear for the processes of power, and a real ability to observe both class differences and social mobility. In any public place, the reader comes to feel he is a sound guide, not apt to let one down. . . .

To ask an author to write another kind of book from the one he has produced is unfair, and Mr. Waugh has not set out to probe the intimacies of his characters' emotional responses. But the kind of book he has written is harmed and limited—in a way that Maugham, for instance, escapes—by the fact that these characters never move spontaneously from within. The reader can never forget that they exist to be manipulated by the author. The immediate environment with which we follow this (quite believable) manipulation ends as each episode ends.

Elizabeth Janeway. *NYT*. Jan. 8, 1956, p. 1

This is a thoroughly well-constructed book [*Fuel for the Fire*] with an excellent plot and characters that suit its incidents; but it is not quite good enough. This is not because the novel covers too wide a field and has too many characters. *War and Peace* takes a whole country, and many sections of Russian society, including a whole foreign invading army, into its gigantic stride, without failing to carry its breathless reader with it. Nor is it because the society Alec Waugh describes is middle class and mediocre. Flaubert's *Madame Bovary* only deals with three exceedingly mediocre middle-class characters, and yet Flaubert makes your blood run hot or cold with their hopes and fears. It is the heat of the centre of the novelist himself that makes a really great novel; and the temperature of this novel is lukewarm. . . .

There is nothing slipshod or unlikely in Waugh's book of this island society on the last rungs of a change into "Who knows what?"

Perhaps the partial failure of this interesting book is due to the fact that none of its characters care enough for either God or man; and literature as well as life has something to do with both.

Phyllis Bottome. *JOL*. May 26, 1960, p. 621

This is what happened to me. I wrote my first novel when I was seventeen. Published eighteen months later, it was, in England an immediate success. It has never been out of print. I have no illusions about the quality of my work. I know myself to be a very minor writer. But it was apparent from that novel that I had been endowed at birth with the one essential gift that is possessed equally by the worst novelists and the best, without which nothing can be achieved in fiction; the knack of narrative, the capacity to make a reader turn the page to see what is on the other side. You have to be born with that. You cannot acquire it in a college course of creative writing. Yet even so, as the early chapters of this book will show, it was only through an unusual sequence of circumstances that the book, *The Loom of Youth*, was written. I might never have realized that I had that knack. And even after the book had been written, after I was established as a professional story-teller, it was chance—a cablegram that reached Tahiti on a Wednesday evening instead of on a Thursday morning—that made me the kind of novelist I am, a restless, perchless traveller, avid of change and of the sun, searching for his plots and characters between Capricorn and Cancer.

Alec Waugh. The Early Years
(N.Y., Farrar, Straus, 1963), p. xiii

WAUGH, EVELYN (1903–1966)

The nature of his best fiction; its fantastic gravity in the face of the ridiculous, its levity over accepted forms of seriousness, its high narrative flash-point accompanied by one sleight of hand after another—these admirable gifts of the satirical novelist have frightened even his admirers into the hole-and-corner approval that family men whisper behind their hands about prostitutes, but never admit to their wives. So rubbed away in Waugh's finished work are the pain and labor of the writing, that the artist is condemned as frivolous. He is frowned on for his dexterity. . . . He is mistrusted because he can pull anything from performing seals and oranges to acute major materials out of an air of nonsense at a second's notice, fit them perfectly into narrative place, and flick them out again with none of the second-rate writer's passion for clutching his material.

. . . Where others have shown in a million ways the crushing effect of social form on struggling individuals, Waugh, the lover of inanimate objects, has delighted in showing how valued material may be destroyed at a moment's whim by the wilful use of individual power. Candide is usually Waugh's central character—though his Candide may as easily be a house or a painting or a tradition as a man or woman—and with the blandness of Goldsmith and the sophistication of Trollope he has liked to put rural innocence into the cruel hands of urban wiseguys, and to show, with sadistic pleasure, the helplessness of the intellectual confronted by the brute.

Nigel Dennis. PR. July, 1943, pp. 350–51

The great thing about *Decline and Fall,* written when the author was twenty-five, was its breath-taking spontaneity. The latter part of the book leans a little too heavily on Voltaire's *Candide,* but the early part, that hair-raising harlequinade in a brazenly bad boys' school, has an audacity that is altogether Waugh's and that was to prove the great principle of his art. This audacity is personified here by an hilarious character called Grimes. Though a schoolmaster and a "public-school man," Grimes is frankly and even exultantly everything that is most contrary to the British code of good behavior: he is a bounder, a rotter, a scoundrel, but he never has a moment of compunction. He is supplemented by Philbrick, the butler, a graduate of the underworld, who likes to tell about revolting crimes. This audacity in Waugh's next book, *Vile Bodies,* is the property of the infantile young people who, at a time "in the near future, when existing social tendencies have become more marked," are shown drinking themselves into beggary, entangling themselves in absurd sexual relationships, and getting their heads cracked in motor accidents. The story has the same wild effect of reckless improvisation, which perfectly suits the spirit of the characters; but it is better sustained than *Decline and Fall.* . . .

A Handful of Dust, . . . is, it seems to me, the author's masterpiece. Here he has perfected his method to a point which must command the admiration of another writer even more perhaps than that of the ordinary nonliterary reader—for the latter may be carried from scene to scene of the swift and smooth-running story without being aware of the skill with which the author creates by implication an atmosphere and a set of relations upon which almost any other novelist would spend pages of description and analysis. The title comes from T. S. Eliot's line, "I will show you fear in a handful of dust," but except on the title page, the author nowhere mentions this fear. Yet he manages to convey from beginning to end, from the comfortable country house to the clearing in the Brazilian jungle, the impression of a terror, of a feeling that the bottom is just about to drop out of things, which is the whole motivation of the book but of which the characters are not shown to be conscious and upon which one cannot put one's finger in any specific passage. . . . He has himself made of audacity a literary technique. He exemplifies, like so many of his characters, the great precept of Benjamin Jowett to young Englishmen just starting their careers: "Never apologize, never explain." [1944]

Edmund Wilson. *A Literary Chronicle: 1920-1950*
(N.Y., Doubleday Anchor, 1956), pp. 266–68

Among the world-creators of our time Evelyn Waugh is the most entertaining, and perhaps the most gifted. The world he invented and decorated with extravagant *jeux d'esprit* is a comic world. In it he moves with the blandest security and ease; from within its circumference he can utter any commentary on life, create and manipulate any beings who inhabit there. Brilliantly equipped to direct the radiant and fantastic circus he has called into being, he can stand within it cracking his whip while his creatures leap through his paper hoops with the most engaging levity, the gravest fantastic capers. His command of verbal style is adept and skilled, his characters admirably irresponsible, his wit unfailing. Like Anthony Blanche in *Brideshead Revisited,* he does more than entertain, "transfiguring the party, shedding a vivid, false light of eccentricity upon everyone," so that prosaic people seem to become creatures of his fantasy.

What would occur should he step out of his delightful baroque circus tent into a solid actual world (if indeed any world is this) was not a question which used to trouble the reader, who accepted his unique contribution as a priceless gift. It would seem that he has now stepped out of it; and the airs beyond the ropes breathe on us with something less of rarity, with a lusher, less sharp and exhilarating taste. It must be the desire of his most ardent devotees that he should speedily retrace his steps. . . .

If Mr. Waugh would sternly root out the sentimentalities and adolescent values which have, so deplorably as it seems to many of us, coiled themselves about the enchanting comic spirit which is his supreme asset as a writer, and return to being the drily ironic narrator of the humours of his world and of his lavish inventive fancy, he would thereby increase his stature, he would be not a less but a more serious and considerable figure in contemporary and future letters. His genius and his reputation seem to stand at the crossroads; his admirers can only hope that he will take the right turning. It is possible that he may. The sentimentality that largely vitiates *Brideshead* is a common, perhaps in some degree or another a universal, weakness. There is in nearly every writer, perhaps in nearly every human being, a soft-headed romantic, who will, if allowed, get out of hand.

Rose Macaulay. *Hor.* Dec., 1946, pp. 360–61, 376

As a writer, of course, Mr. Waugh's importance does not depend only on his religious opinions. It depends primarily on his literary ability, and in the development of his style there is much that is interesting. In his early writing he showed a crisp, selective economy that sometimes a little suggested the reticent yet well-displayed Bond Street window, the fashionable couturier's exhibition, all in excellent taste but in a taste dictated by fashion rather than any long-lasting propriety. His dialogue was brief and staccato; often as staccato as Mr. Hemingway's, though to a different tune. For while Mr. Hemingway, in much of his early work, wrote to a rough, blunt, monosyllabic, *faubourien* convention, Mr. Waugh composed in the sharply polished, close-cut yet nicely modulated habit of the upper classes. His development has been steadily towards a style more ample and more clearly akin—though without affectation—to the classical mode of English prose that was established in the eighteenth century. His adoption of a fuller, yet alert and closely disciplined style was very well shown in some chapters of an unfinished novel which he published under the name of *Work Suspended*. Here Mr. Waugh, working with a very perceptible sense of *métier,* wrote some passages of English prose that were, in their quite contemporary way, manifestly in the tradition that began with Addison and Swift and Steele; and in *Brideshead Revisited* he has occasionally filled his sentences more fully still.

Eric Linklater. The Art of Adventure
(Macmillan, 1948), pp. 53–54

When we draw nearer to the present we can observe the process in action. We can watch *The Wasteland* from being *avant-garde* become a classic, or *The Cocktail Party* turn popular. Evelyn Waugh writes a long short story *Helena*. According to one intellectual critic, Raymond Mortimer, this is a little masterpiece, the best thing he has done; in the view of another, Henry Reed, it is but one more proof of the absurdity of considering him as a serious writer. Which estimate will influence posterity? A review, any publisher will tell us, cannot decide the fate of a book: but a long critical article can certainly decide the future of an author. . . .

Now it is clear that many successful writers possess a certain spellbinding quality which is sometimes called a narrative gift, sometimes readability, sometimes charm or suspense or style, but which is in fact the materialization of an author's personality through what he writes. . . . What is happening in Evelyn Waugh's case is that his forcible personality is now manifesting itself more and more through his work and beginning to dominate his public. Under its spell the separate components are united as by the patter in a conjuring trick. Mortimer accepts the trick, while Reed isolates a paragraph to show how fatuous is the dialogue. But when we are under a spell we do not notice a weakness in dialogue. Extracts from books used as examples by hostile critics usually appear worse than they are because the continuous buzz of the author's personality is missing.

Who then is right? Mr. J. Isaacs, who seems to think readability a blemish, gave six omniscient talks on contemporary literature in the Third Programme without mentioning Evelyn Waugh, while on Leo

Myers, Sidney Schiff and Elias Canetti he lavished praise. Which way will posterity jump?

Cyril Connolly. *Ideas and Places*
(Wedenfeld and Nicolson, 1953), pp. 224–25

Now that Mr. Waugh has, in his latest work, *Men at Arms,* returned to the setting of twentieth-century England before and during the Second World War made familiar to us by his earlier novels, it is possible that his retelling of the legend of St. Helen [*Helena*] will be regarded as a momentary episode, an aberration even, in the work of this sharp delineator of the modern social scene—an episode indeed of peculiar entertainment value by reason of the apparent incongruity between the venerable Christian story and the familiar, racy modern idiom in which it is retold. Such apparent incongruity between theme and medium may be felt, according to the taste of the reader, either as an entertaining levity in line with *Hamlet in America* and similar traditional irreverences, or as a rather shocking incursion into the pious field on the part of a writer who would be much better advised to stick to flippant and esoteric social satire. The disproportionate bother caused by the character in *Men at Arms* who referred to Confession as "scrape" . . . is symptomatic of such confusion of critical standards. For it is a critical confusion, since there are not two Mr. Waughs—the serious and the frivolous—but one, and this one writer has in *Helena* achieved a work which is entirely of one piece. The alleged incongruity is in fact a congruity, that between the supernatural and the natural; and as this is a problem which will always face the "Catholic" novel, it is perhaps worthwhile examining how Mr. Waugh does it in detail. To this end it will be useful to draw out some of the threads which link *Helena* with *Brideshead Revisited,* his immediately preceding work, and his first postwar work in which the problem was specially faced. "Technically this is the most ambitious work of a writer who is devoted to the niceties of his trade," said the dust-cover of *Helena,* but when the work appeared the eminently critical task of developing this statement was perhaps rather obscured both for those who approved of the work and those who did not, by a feeling of discomfort resulting from the apparent incongruity between theme and technique. Further reflection at a distance of time may succeed in revealing this incongruity as the key to Mr. Waugh's greatest success.

Frederick J. Stopp. *Month.* Aug., 1953, pp. 69–70

It is an oddity of Mr. Waugh's work that almost all his principal characters have one parent living, but none of them have two. Paul Pennyfeather, it is true, is an exception in the one direction. He has no more than a guardian. So, too, is William Boot with his uncles, but after him trail a large company of the single-parented. Of these, John Beaver, Basil Seal, and Lord Pastmaster have indeed mothers. But Lady Metroland is only incidentally a mother, Lady Seal, a character of minor importance in *Black Mischief,* and Mrs. Beaver, in *A Handful of Dust,* a character whose baseness is lightly sketched. What Mr. Waugh prefers for his characters is a widower father, eccentric, cynical, Tory, anticlerical, amusing and uninterested in his parental responsibilities. Between these eccentric characters there is a distinct resemblance. The fathers of John Plant in *Work Suspended* and Charles Ryder in *Brideshead Revisited* are indeed—doubtless designedly—practically the same characters over again. . . . Mr. Waugh has clearly a marked aversion to the depiction of his characters as the children of two regular and living parents. He tries in *Men at Arms* to give us a portrait of another type of parent, Guy Crouchback's widower father—admirable, pious, modest, unselfish—but the attempt is not altogether successful. . . .

Now this repetition in character after character and book after book of an incomplete family background is clearly no accident. The family is the essential unit of society. He who comes into life from a broken or incomplete family comes into life to that extent an incomplete man, and modern society, as Mr. Waugh sees it, whether he be looking at it in his three-dimensional or in his two-dimensional novels, whether he be engaged in painting a Catholic contrast to secular futility or merely in exposing futility, is essentially a society of incomplete men and women—a society of men and women, who, having renounced the religion for which they were born, are losing rapidly the culture that is based on that religion and the humanity that is based on that culture. I have selected as a turning-point in Mr. Waugh's literary, intellectual, and artistic development, his study of *Edmund Campion* in 1934, and from that study he learnt not so much the truth of the Catholic religion, which he had already accepted a few years before, but rather what he feels more intensely than some other Catholic apologists—the sundering nature of its claims.

Christopher Hollis. *Evelyn Waugh*
(BC/Longmans, 1954), pp. 34–36

Waugh is a writer of a purely brainless genius, which he has amplified by the possession or development of enormous technical skill. He was born with the natural gift for satire. His satires will probably live as long as literature lasts. And he has written several of them! What an achievement that is one may realise by trying to think offhand of seven other comic novels by seven other individual English writers. Being a man of genius he should never, under any circumstances, have opinions, for whenever he has written out of his opinions it becomes all too plain all over again that imagination is a soaring gull and opinions no more than a gaggle of ungainly starlings, chattering angrily on a cornfield. Opinions breed anger, nourish hate, ossify the heart, narrow the mind. . . . He has what Yeats wished for his daughter, a "radical innocence . . . self-delighting, self-appeasing, self-affrighting." He did not receive it from ancestry, or from this class or that, from church or university; he did not build it out of ideas, or theories. It is one of Nature's primal gifts. But it can be lost, and it can commit suicide. It can poison itself. Thinking is pure poison to innocence. Huxley who never knew innocence thrives on thought. Waugh? One recalls what Cocteau said of Mistinguette, that she magnificently reversed Descartes' *Cogito, ergo sum* into *Mais je ne pense jamais! Donc je suis!*

Sean O'Faolain. *The Vanishing Hero*
(Eyre and Spottiswoode, 1956), pp. 68–69

Mr. Evelyn Waugh is among the most deceptive of writers; in an age of self-exhibition he is neither what the public takes him for nor what he gives himself out to be. . . . At the same time there has appeared a new and better-printed edition of his most successful novel, *Brideshead Revisited,* with new chapter-headings, a number of revisions and cuts and a new preface. It is interesting to see how and where Mr. Waugh has changed this least typical of all his books. It is amusing to find how different the effect is from what the preface claims.

"I have modified the grosser passages," he says, and in a purely stylistic sense this is so. All those highly charged rhetorical sections which share something of the moralizing reflectiveness of the Victorians have had the occasional sentence cut. . . . Today it sounds as if Mr. Waugh prefers the altogether drier and less romanticized episodes between the narrator and his father, which recall the fragment *Work Suspended* that he abandoned earlier—to our considerable loss.

. . . Under his supposed snobbery (which is partly mannerism, partly misinterpretation) Mr. Waugh has a fine sensitivity for values and virtues that are now underrated and in danger of disappearing. He might do more to save them by showing realistically where they are to be found in ordinary people—like Hooper—or at least what are the hopeful elements on which such individuals can build. *Hooper Revisited:* that could be a magnificent theme for him, if he would only forget his resentment of the traveling salesman with his "fat wet hand-shake," of the "underdog's snarl," and the rest. He will not promote the qualities in which he believes so long as he presents them as the property of a limited social group.

TLS. May 16, 1960, p. 598

Much of his success depends on the fineness of his style; "fine style" thought of in the old-fashioned way, as felicity of utterance, wit, charm, rather than as a vital union of form and moral content. His *bon-mots* deserve to be repeated exactly. Take away the verbal precision, and you crash down too violently on the meaning. This very risk, however, might remind us of the twin dangers lying in wait for any discussion of a humorist: you can take him too seriously, or you can take him not seriously enough. To accept Waugh's urbane savagery at its face value might seem monstrous; yet his novels are nearer to Aldous Huxley than to P. G. Wodehouse, when all is said. Thinking back over the sequence, one remembers how often he has taken the equivalent of a Hola or a Nyasaland in his stride, without finding any pressing need to cast a vote; how often his leading characters have suffered a total destruction, inadvertently, in which he appears to find nothing objectionable. His very style poses a problem. It is a civilised style, modifying in the act of saying what is being said; guaranteeing, one would imagine, an achieved urbanity beyond the cynicism. Yet Waugh frequently suggests, through his own characters, that such a style can be appearance rather than reality: the *tone* of a polite age, surviving the values that gave birth to it, and remaining as a dangerously misleading façade.

A. E. Dyson. *CQ*. Spring, 1960, p. 72

... passages [from his work] illustrate what is static in Mr. Waugh's expression of his religion. Religion as a man-made answer to pressing human needs disgusts him. . . . The Church is concerned to preserve the truth, solid and palpable as a lump of wood, from the rot of fantasy. It is entirely concerned with fact. . . .

The consistency of Mr. Waugh's opinions is indicated by his admiration for Baroque art, the plastic expression of Tridentine Catholicism and a great European movement that left England almost untouched. His version of English history at large is simply but fairly stated in this way: after being Catholic for nine hundred years, many English families, whether from intellectual confusion or false prudence, apostasized in the sixteenth century to schismatic institutions which were good only in so far as they retained elements of the true worship. The consequence has been modern paganism (at a guess, Mr. Waugh thinks of this as an atavism in degenerating stock); the inevitable end is a restoration of the faith, but the interim is ugly and tragic except in so far as it is redeemed by the suffering of the martyrs and the patience of the faithful. . . . This conservatism is of course reflected in the author's social opinions; the upper classes are good in so far as they hold on to the values and the properties cherished by their families. Aristocracy, like the Church, fights a defensive action, and that which it defends is, in the long run, a Catholic structure. Very intelligent upper-class Englishmen are not common in Waugh, and when they occur (Basil Seal is the notable case) they are not intellectuals. Their brains have nothing solid to work on; not being Catholics they are not in a position to pursue the truth with any seriousness. Yet if they preserve their families and their customs they do as much as they can to maintain the link with those "ancestors—all the ancient priests, bishops, and kings—all that was once the glory of England, the island of saints, and the most devoted child of the See of Peter." The words are [Edmund] Campion's.

Frank Kermode. Puzzles and Epiphanies
(N.Y., Chilmark Press, 1962), pp. 165–66

WEBB, MARY (1881–1927)

Mrs. Webb has not written a *Wuthering Heights,* but she is of contemporary novelists the one least unlikely to do so. If the passions which she describes tear less painfully the poor flesh harbouring them, they are, like Heathcliffe's, rather the spirit of a waste than the comfortable affections of humankind. And Mrs. Webb, like the great Emily, is often at a loss how to reduce to a common formula her appreciation of the homely, solid life of the countryside and her sense of the dark mysteries latent in nature, both organic and inorganic. Unlike the great Emily, she has, too, a considerable talent for comedy. This is sometimes, and I think, unfortunately, expressed in satire.

H. C. Harwood. OutL. Nov. 11, 1922, p. 406

The pity was that, though her books are full of wise and witty sayings, she did not sufficiently exploit her humour. Yet, withal, in her first four books at least, one recognises that she was one of the few real humorists of the twentieth century. We have had, we still have, plenty of funny men; but hers is the humour that springs from creation of character. Her humour has kinship with the humour of Dickens, which trusts not in clowning and buffoonery—excellent qualities in their way and time and place—but relies wholly for its effects on the observation and study of average human types. It is impossible to convey that humour, or to do it faint justice, as it is impossible to convey Dickens's humour. . . .

Her wit is so elusive and at the same time so profound that even now . . . I can never dip into her pages without lighting upon fresh examples. . . . And to her wit she brought a power of imagery unexcelled by any modern work. Only an author endowed with an equally acute sense of beauty and proportion, born of humour, could have put such gems of fancy into words without seeming a bit high-flown.

Edwin Pugh. BkmL. July, 1928, p. 194

The strength of the book is not in its insight into human character, though that is not lacking. Nor does it lie in the inevitability with which the drama is unfolded and the sin of an all-absorbing and selfish ambition punished. It lies in the fusion of the elements of nature and man, as observed in this remote countryside by a woman even more alive to the changing moods of nature than of man. Almost any page at random will furnish an illustration of the blending of human passion with the fields and skies. . . .

One reviewer compared *Precious Bane* to a sampler stitched through long summer evenings in the bay window of a remote farmhouse. And sometimes writers of Welsh and Border origin, like William Morris, have had their work compared to old tapestries. But while these comparisons suggest something of the harmonies of color they fail to convey the emotional force which glows in these pages. Nature to Mary Webb was not a pattern on a screen. Her sensibility is so acute and her power over words so sure and swift that one who reads some passages in Whitehall has almost the physical sense of being in Shropshire cornfields.

Precious Bane is a revelation not of unearthly but of earthly beauty in one bit of the England of Waterloo, the Western edge, haunted with the shadows of superstition, the legendary lore and phantasy of neighbours on the Border, differing in blood and tongue. This mingling of peoples and traditions and turns of speech and proverbial wisdom is what Mary Webb saw with the eye of the mind as she stood at her stall in Shrewsbury market, fastened in her memory, and fashioned for us in the little parcel of novels which is her legacy to literature.

Stanley Baldwin. Introd. in Mary Webb, Precious Bane
(Jonathan Cape, 1929), pp. 10–11

With this heart to love and mind to labour, Mary Webb had in her service rarely delicate senses. All poets are for their own purposes good "observers"; though most of their "notes," maybe, take themselves. But by no means all poets are very exact and comprehensive observers. Mary Webb, whose world was "a place of almost unbearable wonder," had senses almost microscopic in their delicacy. She could—most rewardful of feats—seize the momentary. "It may be all illumined, like a sombre pine at the advent of wood pigeons." That for sight. And for sound: "The peewits wheel and call continually, and from amid the ripple of their wings their cry sounds lost and lovely as some Naiad's voice beneath running water." And this of the wind—with how far a journey: "It is like a whisper in the night, when you cannot tell whether a child or a man is speaking. . . . We never see the gates of its dark house swing open, nor watch it fall beyond the waters into its tomb beneath the yellow sunset." And for scent she tells of the resinous sweetness of agrimony on a dusty highway in July; the curious redolence of a rock in hot weather.

In these moods she had no need of "fine" writing—the writing that is pitched above the voice. Her imagination went abreast with her feeling, and her words embodied both. *The Spring of Joy* wells over with a grave and sweet happiness, the happiness "of the minds of the simple-hearted, who are the Magi of the world." Trees, leaves, buds, flowers, fruits; country scenes and ways and work and pleasures; wind and waters, cloud, meadow and woodland; these are its never-failing joy.

Walter de La Mare. Introd. in Mary Webb. *Poems and The Spring of Joy* (Jonathan Cape, 1933), pp. 15–16

Mary Webb's poems have been extolled for their music—but as that word is capable of many interpretations, we should like to ask, before we accept the verdict, in what way her poems conform to that mysterious law which is the essence of music? Mr. Robert Lynd truly refers to the "imaginative energy" of her writings, but this energy is a result as well as a cause. Mr. Walter de la Mare in describing her appearance has called her "bird-like," and she also possessed the poet's "wood-bird soul," but he does not reveal the secret of her flight and song. Mr. Baldwin has praised her "acute sensibility," but this very quality of acuteness has its hidden springs which we would try to discover. . . .

Poetic art has its own "countless variations," and may give us the highly trained technique of a Robert Bridges or a de la Mare (which one may call scholastic or rational poetry), or the naïve song of a singer who has an untrained but instinctive ear for his music—such as we find in the work of Mary Webb (which one may call natural or intuitional poetry). Such a singer may truly be termed "bird-like," for his song is as dependent as that of a bird upon the inspiration of the moment. All forms of poetry, however, whether trained, or spontaneous, include three chief factors—beauty of imagination, energy of expression, and rhythm of form, and all three are evidenced in the poems of Mary Webb. Surely it is rhythm in its widest sense which at the same time distinguishes and unites her verse and prose?

Lorna Collard. *CR*. April, 1933, pp. 456, 458

Mary Webb died just over twenty years ago at the comparatively early age of 46. Her contribution to English literature consists of but six novels, a volume of essays and poems, and more recently a further selection of hitherto unpublished poems have been printed. During her lifetime Mary Webb's writings received little recognition, and were known only to a small circle of appreciative readers. In 1926 The Right Hon. Stanley Baldwin was given a copy of *Precious Bane* for a Christmas gift, by one of his secretaries, and he read the book with keen delight, and a week or two later sent the author a letter expressing his admiration. Mary Webb was deeply touched by this recognition, especially in view of scanty acknowledgement which the wider public had given to the book. The following year the Prime Minister when presiding at the Royal Literary Fund Dinner referred to her as a "literary genius who had recently died without public mention," and at last public interest was awakened, and a special edition of her works became imperative. Ironically Mary Webb had passed beyond "the world's blames and praises." . . .

When one turns to criticism of Mary Webb it can be said that her range was limited, for she frequently introduces the same characters in differing guise. There is a use of symbolism which leads her into inconsistencies, and a tendency to become vague and verbose. Sometimes she plays the part of the rustic philosopher, and story and dialogue are but the vehicle of her meditations. Her strength lay not in invention, but in imagination. While we readily grant that she may lack originality as a story-teller, in perception, in feeling she excels. She has a noble conception of human nature, a love for the homely, and is wholly sensitive to the mystery of life, and its fortitude born of beauty, love, and laughter. She is a true creative artist in that she portrays the oceanic storms which rage in the lives of the lowly, the way in which the suffering spirit transforms the homespun and the commonplace.

Wilfred Shepherd. *LQHR*. Oct., 1949, p. 305

WEDGWOOD, C. V. (1910–   )

Few political figures are lucky enough to find a skilful and sympathetic biographer close at hand within the family circle, but perhaps Lord Wedgwood as the originator of a great plan for a History of Parliament deserves his good fortune. Miss Wedgwood has decided not to plunge too deeply into the problems of contemporary history, although she includes a deal of interesting political material, mainly in the form of extracts from letters [*The Last of the Radicals*]. She has preferred to write what is primarily a personal sketch, in which only the outlines of political changes are traced. It is doubtful whether a fuller treatment would have been worth while, for Wedgwood was essentially a simple man, and always too much of an individualist to be representative of his times.

H. M. Pelling. *CJ*. July, 1952, p. 641

Miss Wedgwood has written a superb book [*The King's Peace*]. I do not know whether to admire more the easy perfection of the scholarship or the maturity of judgment, the perception and sympathy of her understanding of people or the skill with which she recounts the first steps of the ominous, familiar story of the Civil War. She has chastened her style so that the book is beautifully written: there lies a charm upon it. And I have no doubt at all that she makes the onset of the Civil War more intelligible and real to us than any historian before her. If she goes on like this she is going to achieve one of the historical masterpieces of her generation and of our time.

One reason why she carries such conviction is that she writes without any discoverable *parti-pris:*

> I have tried to describe the variety, vitality and imperfections as well as the religion and government of the British Isles in the seventeenth century, deliberately avoiding analysis and seeking rather to give an impression of its vigorous and vivid confusion.

How right she is, as against the fashionable analytical historians who are so determined to show how clever they are at the expense of history. Her beguilingly modest attitude is really cleverer and more subtle.

A. L. Rowse. *TT*. Jan. 8, 1955, p. 49

The reader of Miss Wedgwood's new historical work [*The King's Peace*] will find himself fortunate in every way. Not only will he be enchanted with what he reads, but he will lay the book down in the comfortable knowledge that there is more to come. For *The King's Peace,* covering the years 1637 to 1641, is only the beginning of the story of the Great Rebellion. I do not know how many other volumes we are to expect, but I hope that they will be numerous. For Miss Wedgwood's way of writing is delightful as well as informative. . . .

But I should be doing Miss Wedgwood an injustice if I failed to mention other qualities besides this very important one of being able to see and to describe clearly and distinctly both what we imagine a most perceptive observer would have seen at the time and what a more knowledgeable, but still perceptive, observer can discover later. There is a remarkable rapidity and concision of style; both wit and humour; a restrained but evident excitement in narrative; a freeness and ease in dealing with such complicated events and in the wearing of so much learning. No side has been taken except the side of humanity, and that has been taken with understanding, sympathy and, whenever possible, with precision.

Rex Warner. *L.* May, 1955, pp. 103, 105

There can be, then, no doubt of the importance of C. V. Wedgwood's theme. How has she treated it in this second volume [*The King's War 1641-1647*] of a work with the over-all title of *The Great Rebellion*?

The answer must be, brilliantly. In her first volume, *The King's Peace,* Miss Wedgwood was working her way into her theme. The result was a very satisfactory book but this is a still more satisfactory one. . . .

One way that Miss Wedgwood achieves this success is by her portraits of individuals. We are made to see the quite decisive role of the great parliamentarian, John Pym. We are made to see the role of the King, nearly uniformly disastrous. We are made to see the role of the pugnacious Queen, Henrietta Maria, patroness of Maryland, worthy for courage but not for good sense. We are made to see (and this is something of a novelty) Prince Rupert not merely as a dashing cavalry officer, a kind of Jeb Stuart, but as a serious, judicious and admirable soldier and royal servant, not adequately appreciated by his uncle. We are made to see (and it is important that we should see) the disastrous role of the insolent courtiers who followed the King to Oxford where he set up his rival Government, in opposition to that of the rebels in London. The Court alone is nearly enough to account for the royal defeat.

D. W. Brogan. *NYT.* April 19, 1959, p. 5

Dr. Wedgwood sticks to her own period in this survey of seventeenth-century verse as a vehicle of topical comment [*Poetry and Politics Under the Stuarts*]. Her book is modest in size as well as in scope. . . . But for all its rather specialised and limited compass, it is unique in its approach. It is rare indeed to look at verse through the focus of a professional historian. Dr. Wedgwood, writing with special authority and perception of her period, is particularly well qualified to illuminate the social and political background against which the poets cut and thrust.

John Pudney. *JOL.* March, 1960, p. 286

The "revaluation" in the subtitle of Miss Wedgwood's biography [*Thomas Wentworth, First Earl of Strafford, 1593-1641: A Revaluation*] is in particular of her own first book, *Strafford,* initially published in February, 1935. She has retained the structure and used much of the writing of her earlier work, but her new book is far more than what normally constitutes a revised edition. It is not only very much longer; what was originally a fine biography has now become a more profound and subtle one. . . . "In her searching analysis of Wentworth," Miss Wedgwood has achieved what she hoped: "not merely better history but a more interesting and in some ways a more tragic portrait."

Willson H. Coates. Am. Hist. R. July, 1963, p. 1114

The Trial of Charles I is one of the most successful of Miss Wedgwood's many successful books. She has interrupted her work on the English Revolution, of which two volumes have already appeared, for a detailed examination of the most revolutionary event of the period—the execution of Charles I as "a tyrant, traitor, murderer and a public enemy." Her treatment is mainly narrative, but by looking closely at the events she throws much light on some perplexing problems.

Christopher Hill. NS. Aug. 28, 1964, p. 283

WELCH, DENTON (1917–1948)

To write an autobiography in one's early twenties is both a bold and a cautious decision. Bold because a whole army of irritable elders will be ready with their ridicule; cautious because this, after all, is the only material to which one can claim an absolute monopoly. Mr. Welch has written the boldest kind of autobiography, and his courage has been rewarded by a work of outstanding originality and merit. There is no self-consciousness in his self-absorption, and little reticence; better still, there is no disloyalty to his recent past. No attitude is commoner or more odious than the patronage of an adult towards his own adolescence, the complacent assurance of present superiority. Mr. Welch takes himself seriously, though humour is not lacking, and when he finds his actions discreditable he treats them with cold severity rather than whimsical disassociation. . . .

Maiden Voyage will shock some people by its level relentless tone, by the author's instinctive hatred of illusion and pretence. Without a hint of toughness, without the least false note of cynicism, there is a feline unsentimentality about Mr. Welch which is immensely stimulating. I do not agree with Miss Edith Sitwell who speaks in her foreword of "a moving and youthful quality." Youth is usually clouded, imitative and insecure, whereas Mr. Welch, even in his most defenceless moments, seems to be armoured by his alert and honest mind. But I agree with Miss Sitwell's conclusion that he "may easily prove to be not only a born writer but a very considerable one."

Philip Toynbee. NSN. June 12, 1943, p. 390

He is a subjective, impressionistic writer, aware of dualism, paradoxes, and the truth which escapes any definition of it. His concern is largely with the wonderful, the deviate, the strange—not with the so-called "realism" which rejects the adventure of the dreamlike creation of language. Beauty goes hand in hand with terror, formal elegance with informal brutality, the archaic with the modern.

In Youth Is Pleasure has the distinction of style and vision which characterize *Maiden Voyage*—and it may be more complex in theme and symbol than the earlier volume. Welch's work shows, in both volumes, the influence of sensationalistic psychology and of other writers who have been influenced by it such as Joyce, Virginia Woolf, Alex Comfort. There is no escape into any general, vague statement. Every reality has to be broken down into smaller and smaller parts. For Welch, as for perhaps the best stylists in the tradition of the sensationalistic, reality is minute, made up of many diverse fragments, never wholly realizable.

Marguerite Young. NYT. March 31, 1946, p. 6

Just a year ago . . . I wrote of Mr. Denton Welch's first book, *Maiden Voyage,* that it was "rare, these days, to read a new author and feel impatient to see his next book." *In Youth Is Pleasure* is Mr. Welch's next book, and it is a sad disappointment. It is a disappointment to find in an author's "second" book more of the faults, fewer of the virtues, than there were in his "first." The reader's sole consolation, in this case, is his probable conclusion that though the volume under review is published after *Maiden Voyage,* it must surely have been written before that book. . . .

It is significant that *In Youth Is Pleasure* also precedes *Maiden Voyage* in time; the events of the former book lead up to those of the latter. . . . At the end of this very slim volume Orvil Pym [the narrator], I regret to say, becomes an awful bore. . . . Intensely narcissistic, he is filled with obsessions and fears. Of himself he writes far too much and with shocking amateurishness. . . .

When I had read *In Youth Is Pleasure* I had a nasty vision. I saw a figure with a waxed moustache and a four-letter name leaping through the glass of a Fifth Avenue window. Nevertheless Mr. Welch wrote *Maiden Voyage,* and I still feel impatient to see his next book. Let's hope it will have been written *after* the two already in print.

James Stern. NR. April 1, 1946, pp. 452, 454

Cycling through Kent on a Whitsun afternoon some fifteen years ago, Denton Welch, then a boy of eighteen, was badly injured by a carelessly-driven car. *A Voice through a Cloud,* now posthumously published, has as its framework the accident and the year of slow recovery that followed. In the precarious remaining years of his life—he was thirty-one when he died in 1948—Denton Welch worked at it intermittently, laying it aside over periods to write his collection of short stories; he was trying to complete it, in conditions of extraordinary pain and difficulty, at the time of his death. So we learn from the Foreword by his friend Eric Oliver; for the book's careful style shows no sign of these difficulties, nor of the sense of urgency that obsessed its writer in his last months.

To call *A Voice through a Cloud* a novel, as Mr. Oliver does, seems an odd and wilful misconception. For the very reason that it is not fiction it shows most admirably Denton Welch's particular gifts, which were not of invention but of imagination. What it does convey, with exceptional vividness and clarity, is the transforming power of illness—the invalid's vision, in fact.

Naomi Lewis. Colophon. May, 1950, p. 28

WELLESLEY, DOROTHY (? –1956)

The poetry of Dorothy Wellesley has been neglected because it is not in the nineteenth century tradition: it should be welcomed because it gives evidence of a poetic equipment which can assimilate knowledge, coordinate experience and select and refine it into virile and satisfying poetry. In 1925 she published *Lost Lane.* Anyone who gave it the most cursory examination would have found evidence of . . . [rare] knowledge. Viniculture, the working of diamond mines, the manufacture of cotton goods, the names and habits of shells and fishes, birds and snakes appeared equally familiar to the authoress. To those who have not read the poems such a bare summary of the subjects treated will naturally sound less attractive than alarming. They will think of Armstrong on the *Art of Medicine* and of Erasmus Darwin on *The Loves of the Plants,* and conclude that so bluestocking a writer could never prove congenial. But John Donne wrote fine lines on The Flea, and Byron on George III, subjects on the face of them not very susceptible to poetry. And those who turn from pretty melodies and tuneful emotions to Dorothy Wellesley's concrete and definite poetry will find that it is as stimulating as to turn from the misty . . . *paysage* of Corot to the sharply defined winter landscape of . . . Breughel. For she has discovered the hard grandeur of material life and the dignity of facts.

R. McNair Scott. LM. Nov., 1931, p. 48

WELLESLEY, DOROTHY

Dorothy Wellesley presents the actual child, not merely in such amusing snatches as "Great-grandmama," "Sheep," "England," but in descriptions like that in "The Lost Forest," where the green light of the leaves is seawater flowing among the trunks, while congers nose the daffodils, a flight of fishes perch upon a cherry bough.

I sent somebody to Bumpus's [book store] for *Poems of Ten Years,* found that this selection of picturesque detail, this going back, was not a mere literary device, but a love that seemed a part of character for undisturbed Nature, a hatred for the abstract, the mechanical, the invented. This love, this hatred, gave its own intensity to poems often beautiful, often obscure, sometimes ill-constructed, but seemed without purpose or philosophy. Then I came upon *Matrix,* a long meditation, perhaps the most philosophic poem of our time . . . and discovered that it was moving precisely because its wisdom, like that of the sphinx, was animal below the waist. In its vivid, powerful, abrupt lines, passion burst into thought without renouncing its uterine darkness.

W. B. Yeats. Introd. in *Selections from the Poems of Dorothy Wellesley* (Macmillan, 1936), p. xi

Dorothy Wellesley's selected poems [*Selected Poems*] are the ruins, or the sketches, of a very considerable opus. There are massively splendid passages . . . and there is everywhere a wonderful grasp of scene and object and a wonderful, if bewildering, vocabulary to convey these: flacking water, scuted snakes, rudding snails, in a landscape of swales and cledges. There are the moments that Yeats noted, of obscurely piercing intuition. . . . And it is not a matter just of occasional striking badness. Even the best poems seem often not to have reached their final drafts, and there is everywhere the strangest slaphappiness about technique: rhymes, good, bad, and indifferent, peppered in as they come: music-hall rhymes—now that we talk of Cockneys—like "mortar" and "water," "forty" and "naughty": a rich rhyme like "soul" and "console"—and rich rhyme is always awkward in English—in a fine passage where no rhyme is needed at all. Only in England could a poet of such great natural gifts have remained so much, in the worst sense, an amateur. Where Mr. Reeves is a model, for the young poet, of scrupulous economy, Miss Wellesley is an example (dangerous, because attractive in spite of everything) of splendid waste. That has not prevented her from producing noble, imperfect poems.

G. S. Fraser. *NSN*. April 9, 1949, p. 362

WELLS, H. G. (1866–1946)

I suggest that Mr. Wells' life and activity may be taken as symbolical of the life of his time. He has told his own story again and again in his novels; it is his own story that he has been telling when he unfolds his ideas about the society in which we live. He, more than any other considerable living writer, seems to have been born to realise within the microcosm of his own experience the social evolution which most of us see in the macrocosm of the nation—an evolution which has been *observed* by Mr. Bennett with equal clearness, but in a less personal and subjective way, with more detachment. All of us know from the study of history in what way England has changed in the last hundred years—how scientific thought suddenly gained a new importance when it was applied to industry—how the shell of feudalism survived its vitality when the great factory towns began to dominate the country—how all the classes were shuffled and left unsettled—how the cities spread out in disorderly suburbs and slums, without plan or direction—how men and women became factory workers and office workers without knowing why, most of them scantily educated, housed as the competing jerry-builders thought fit, and flung into the maelstrom of competitive labour. All this we knew in a certain sense, but it was Mr. Wells more than anyone else who made us aware of this national life by presenting it in the only possible effective way, the imaginative way. It may almost be said that he gave it to us as an impressionistic account of his own life. He had lived in all this; the social system, or lack of system, had expressed itself in him; and finally he became conscious of all those elements about him and in him which had left their deep impression.

R. A. Scott-James. *Personality in Literature* (Martin Secker, 1913), pp. 152–53

As an artist, and more particularly as a writer, Wells has an almost unequalled power of vivid reproduction of those things which he has seen and experienced. His vision is remorseless—his descriptive power unfailing. He has invention in the highest measure, and unlimited ingenuity. As a recorder of his own impressions he is vivid to an extraordinary degree. He catches and renders the superficial aspects of things with amazing, illusive positiveness. At his best he gives an illusion of concrete reality to all readers not more imaginative than himself. And these are very few. One result of this power is that his foregrounds are frequently almost ridiculously clear. He has a rich vein of humour which, in some of his books, pervades the whole of the canvas. There is a playful humour in *The Wonderful Visit,* and *The Wheels of Chance.* The tramp annexed by the *Invisible Man* is a humorous creation of signal originality. The sophisticated medium, Chaffery, in *Mr. Lewisham* is another delightful, humorous conception. A lambent humour plays all over the *Sea Lady.* In some of his novels, however, especially *Ann Veronica, Marriage,* and *The Passionate Friends,* and even in *Kipps,* the prophetic element in the author takes its revenge upon the artist by pumping all the humour out of the story a good while before the descent of the curtain. There is subtle humour in the contrast of character and pretension between the clear-minded abstract thinker, Cavor, and the pseudo-practical blunderer, Bedford in *The First Men in the Moon.* The drollery of *Mr. Polly* is delightful, especially to newcomers; those who know their "H. G." really well recognise some elements in it which have done duty before. The delights of his sympathetic humour are seen at their best in the first three quarters of *Kipps.*

Wells also has considerable dramatic force and the endowments enumerated, added to his very considerable powers of characterisation ... ought manifestly to constitute Mr. Wells one of the novelists of all time. Unfortunately, his pre-occupation with social philosophy inevitably forces most of his best fiction into the same category with that of George Eliot, and Henry Bordeaux—that of the problem novel, or the novel with a purpose. Peacockian eccentricities are just permissible in novels, in strict moderation; but philosophies in petticoats and trousers are impossible. Many of Mr. Wells's characters tend to become talking machines with taps labelled "H.G. January 1914," "H.G. February 1914," and so on illimitably. Talk about the confessional! There never was such a deponent as Mr. Wells.

Thomas Seccombe. *BkmL.* April, 1914, p. 23

The Time Machine, despite certain obvious faults of imagination and style, is a brilliant fantasy; and it affords a valuable picture of the young Wells looking at the world, with his normal eyes, and finding it, more particularly, incomplete. At the age of twenty-seven or so, he has freed himself very completely from the bonds of conventional thought, and is prepared to examine, and to present life from the detached standpoint of one who views it all from a respectable distance; but who is able, nevertheless—an essential qualification—to enter life with all the passion and generosity of his own humanity.

And in *The Wonderful Visit*—published in the same year as *The Time Machine*—he comes closer to earth. That ardent ornithologist, the Rev. H. Hilyer, Vicar of Siddermouth, who brought down an angel with a shot-gun, is tenderly imagined; a man of gentle mind, for all the limitations of his training. The mortalised angel, on the other hand, is rather a tentative and simple creature. He may represent, perhaps, the rather blank mind of one who sees country society without having had the inestimable privilege of learning how it came about. . . . And in *The Wonderful Visit,* that exuberance we postulated, that absorption in the development of idea, is more marked; in the unfolding of the story we can trace the method of the novelist.

Indeed, the three romances that follow discover hardly a trace of the social investigator. *The Island of Dr. Moreau, The Invisible Man* and *The War of the Worlds* are essays in pure fantasy, and although the first of the three is influenced by biology I class it unhesitatingly among the works of sheer exuberance. Each of these books is, in effect, an answer to some rather whimsical question, and the problem that Dr. Moreau attempted to solve was: "Can we, by surgery, so accelerate the evolutionary process as to make man out of a beast in a few days or weeks?" And within limits he found that the answer was: "Yes."

J. D. Beresford. *H. G. Wells* (Nisbet, 1915), pp. 23–25

Both Wells and Bernard Shaw have confessed that throughout their most active intellectual careers they believed instinctively that progress was mainly a matter of chronology. To discover the future Wells considered it necessary merely to set his imagination at work on Chicago and multiply it by a thousand; while the famous remark of Shaw that he was "better than Shakespeare" sprang from his assumption that, living three centuries later, he naturally stood (as a dwarf, in his own phrase) upon Shakespeare's shoulders. This naiveté placed them at the mercy of literature, as they soon discovered. Everyone knows the change that came over Bernard Shaw's cosmos when for the first time, a few years ago, he read two or three pre-Darwinian philosophers: one could almost have heard a pin drop when he stopped talking about being better than Shakespeare. A similar experience, exhibited in his books, has befallen Wells, and there is no doubt that reading has contributed to the progressive modesty of his point of view. Each monument of historic experience that he has absorbed has left its mark on him. Rabelais, Machiavelli, Plato, incorporated at regular intervals in his own work, have certainly contributed to make him less agile and less dramatic. . . .

After the fashion of Cato, Bernard Shaw and H. G. Wells have come lately to the study of Greek. Bernard Shaw read Plato at fifty, and in his latest book Wells has insisted that in the Great State everyone will study Greek. Nothing could signify more plainly that these outriders of the Modern Mind have come to a halt and wish to connect themselves with tradition, with history, with literature, with religion, with the grand current of human experience. Having been for so long experimenting with new and untried forces, sharply separated from what is received and understood, they should be related to the familiar landmarks and connected with the main stream of English thought and literature.

Van Wyck Brooks. The World of H. G. Wells
(N.Y., Mitchell Kennerley, 1915), pp. 12–14

It is the business of the Catholic, among the many other tasks he has to handle in the modern world, to analyse this Modern Thought patiently and to explain it to itself. . . .

The process will have the more value if it deals with the particular and the concrete; so let us take what is the best, and at the same time the most typical example, of the mood in this country and at this moment. It is not an example of great weight nor likely to endure for long; it is not one which the most of Europe would take seriously, but, still, it is of very great interest as a symptom and as an example—Mr. Wells's *Outline of History*.

This particular and concrete example has the added value that it is in itself good. It is a first-rate example of the thing with which we have to deal. It would be a poor compliment to Mr. Wells as a writer, to repeat here what all the world has justly said of him for now the better part of a generation. I know not whether more to admire the elasticity of his mind, his power of exposition, or, what is rarer and sometimes more valuable than either, the poise of his judgment. It is the latter quality which has given him so well-merited a fame in the foresight of mechanical development. And to these great qualities as a writer and as an exponent must be added the sincere, living, unfatigued interest which he takes in all things presented to his mind, and especially in the fate and arrangement of mankind. We may be certain that in dealing with this very high type of the thing opposed to us, we are at the heart of the matter, and at grips with the essential quarrel between his side and ours.

Hillaire Belloc. DR. May, 1920, pp. 184–85

It can scarcely be said of Mr. Wells that he is a materialist in the sense that he takes too much delight in the solidity of his fabric. His mind is too generous in its sympathies to allow him to spend much time in making things shipshape and substantial. He is a materialist from sheer goodness of heart, taking upon his shoulders the work that ought to have been discharged by Government officials, and in the plethora of his ideas and facts scarcely having leisure to realise, or forgetting to think important, the crudity and coarseness of his human beings. Yet what more damaging criticism can there be both of his earth and of his Heaven than that they are to be inhabited here and hereafter by his Joans and his Peters? Does not the inferiority of their natures tarnish whatever institutions and ideals may be provided for them by the generosity of their creator?

Virginia Woolf. *The Common Reader* (Hogarth Pr., 1925), pp. 186–87

Though Wells, in the count of years, is nearly as old as was Scott when polishing up his novels, he is so much younger biologically that it is rather disconcerting to see him casting even a casual glance towards the Elysian Fields. Still, his decision to run no further risks with time must give satisfaction to a multitude of readers as they view the superb Atlantic Edition of his works, which the Scribners are publishing.

Happily, time still favors Wells. Thackeray once told Motley that he intended to give the world, before he left it, a big novel which should key up all the rest. Never written was that masterpiece which, he remarked, no one would ever read anyway. More fortunate than the great Victorian, Wells has turned the trick against fate by gathering up in a novel of eight hundred pages all that he has tried to teach his generation, editing and revising the reactions of the age upon his mind in a sort of summary that he is willing to stick by. The implication is that, though he may still carry on, the world now has him in all essentials complete. For an impartial re-valuation of his achievements he has had to read over again, he says, all the books and essays he has ever published. If much was cast aside when he assembled his works, as of "temporary interest," he has let stand, after all excisions, some thirty volumes, being, he is inclined to think, somewhat too generous with himself. In a last look backwards, he feels that, despite many defects, he has "done well" by himself, that he "would live and write in rather the same way" if he had to live over again. Though, as here, the edge of his humor appears now and then worn down a bit, he has in fact done extraordinarily well by himself.

Wilbur Cross. *YR*. Jan., 1927, pp. 298–99

So far, anyhow, this work [*The World of William Clissold*] is not a novel, because it contains none of the passionate and emotional reactions which are at the root of all thought, and which must be conveyed in a novel. This book is all chewed-up newspaper, and chewed-up scientific reports, like a mouse's nest. But perhaps the novel will still come: in Vols. II and III.

For after all, Mr. Wells is not Mr. Clissold, thank God! And Mr.

Wells has given us such brilliant and such very genuine novels that we can only hope the Clissold "angle" will straighten out in Vol. II. [1927]
D. H. Lawrence in *Phoenix, The Posthumous Papers of D. H. Lawrence*, ed. Edward D. McDonald (N.Y., Viking, 1936), p. 350

All our youth they hung about the house of our minds like Uncles, the Big Four: H. G. Wells, George Bernard Shaw, John Galsworthy and Arnold Bennett. They had the generosity, the charm, the loquacity of visiting uncles. Uncle Wells arrived always a little out of breath, with his arms full of parcels, sometimes rather carelessly tied, but always bursting with all manner of attractive gifts that ranged from the little pot of sweet jelly that is *Mr. Polly,* to the complete meccano set for the mind that is in *The First Men in the Moon.* And he brought all the scientific fantasies, and the magic crystals like *Tono-Bungay* and *The New Machiavelli,* in which one could see the forces of the age sweep and surge like smoke about brightly coloured figures that were blinded by them, that saw through them, that were a part of them, that were separate from them and were their allies, and illustrated as well as it has ever been done the relationship between man and his times.

This impression of wild and surpassing generosity was not in the least one of youth's illusions.

Rebecca West. *The Strange Necessity* (N.Y., Doubleday, 1928), p. 215

Wells had lately published *Ann Veronica,* closely followed by *The New Machiavelli,* and was not very popular in consequence. He had something on his mind that made him resentful at times, and he complained of old friends who had turned against him. But this was a passing mood only. He could always be gaily vituperative, but he was rarely bitter. There was something frank and unashamed in Wells, a vigorous enjoyment of life, that disarmed criticism. He was perhaps a little greedy in his zest for life, I thought; as some are greedy over the pleasures of the table. Yes, Wells was greedy, but how much better appetite is than apathy! It was this lusty appetite for every phase of life, for work and for play as well, which I liked so much in Wells. And when he played, he played to win. Badminton was a favourite game with both of us, and Wells had tricky little strokes: he couldn't resist them—he couldn't bear not to win. Yet he was quite aware of his weakness, for in one of his books, I remember, he commented on this kind of play.

But Wells's weaknesses give him an uncanny insight into other peoples' minds, and what is more, a forgiving understanding. He doesn't want to change people so much as to tidy up their surroundings. There is in Wells the writer, together with his genial understanding of human nature, an undeviating idealism which, in Wells the man, is often hidden behind a cloud of laughter. There is a good deal of the research-student left in him from the time when his ideal of a world was a perfectly-ordered laboratory, and everything about him must therefore be clean, tidy and ready for use; and with a grasp of detail, he has retained the scientist's habit of generalizing from single facts.

I think of Wells as a great literary cartoonist, who depicts what is happening in the world, and in men's minds, and when I re-read his books, many things I had forgotten come back to me. And what a teeming brain he has! Ideas pass through his head as coins through a banker's fingers, to be invested at once so as to bring in the highest possible interest: and such amusing ideas too, with which Wells plays delightfully. His idealism he keeps for his books; there is none of it in his talk; nor, indeed, does his temper encourage idealism in anyone else; his response to it in others is rather a teasing facetiousness; though this may well be because Wells likes to think things out for himself; or that his sense of fun is uppermost.

William Rothenstein. *Men and Memories* (N.Y., Coward-McCann, 1932), pp. 100–2

It can be said for H. G. Wells what cannot be said for any of his contemporaries . . . that he changed the mental outlook of more than one generation, and not in his own country alone. The young men and women who brought themselves up on H. G. Wells thought about the present and future in a completely different way from the way in which their parents and professional teachers had intended they should think. . . . Historians in the future will doubtless be as fond of labels as historians now. One of their labels is waiting, already written—"The H. G. Wells Age."

Storm Jameson. *Adam.* Nov., 1941, pp. 1–2

His long distant flight of imagination, his staunchness in defending his own views, the range and vigour of his mind in scientific exposition, have all won the respect of a younger generation of writers.

C. Day Lewis. *Adam.* Nov., 1941, p. 17

To H. G. Wells my mind, such as it is, owes the greater part of its freedom. His books burst on me when I was a schoolboy. They stimulated, nudged, prodded, shook, assured and cheered me. They drew from me possible agreement and shocked protest. They liberated me, they set me thinking for myself. The younger generation have little notion how much had to be won for them, how much they owe even of the very premises and axioms of their thought to this courageous pioneer.

L. A. G. Strong. *Adam*. Nov., 1941, p. 6

Wells, it seems to me, had greater genius than any other novelist of his time in England; . . . for lack of any serious concern for his art, before he was halfway through his career [he] gave up for mankind what was meant for the novel—I cannot help thinking to mankind's ultimate loss.

Wells's work falls broadly in three phases in roughly chronological sequence. Before 1900 most of his fiction consisted of scientific romances; after 1900, though he continued on occasion to write them, until about 1910 the main stress is on comedy; and then from about 1910 his interest for the most part was in the novel of ideas. The *New Machiavelli, Joan and Peter,* and *Mr. Britling Sees It Through* had a topical value in their day, but little literary interest now; while no one is likely again to read *The World of William Clissold* (in three volumes), the fictitious autobiography of a character closely resembling Wells himself, when he can read the *Experiment in Autobiography,* which is not fiction.

The scientific romances are still unsurpassed of their kind. They are intellectual *jeux d'esprit; The First Men in the Moon* (1901) may be taken as typical. Wells works out, in all its implications, what would happen, on current knowledge, if men reached the moon. It is fantasy based on logic.

Walter Allen. *The English Novel* (N.Y., Dutton, 1958
[c. 1954]), pp. 376–77

[Arnold] Bennett also had a tremendous respect for Wells's mind. He undoubtedly considered him a genius both as a novelist and as a social philosopher. Early in the correspondence [between them] Bennett writes, "No one knows more about the *craft* of fiction than you do," and, more than half seriously, that it was his ambition "after 25 years of study, meditation and prayer, to attempt an elaborate monograph on you and let this be the climax of my career." As late as 1926, long after Wells's novels had taken a direction with which Bennett could not have sympathized, Bennett writes concerning *William Clissold:* "This is an *original* novel. My novels never are." And *The Outline of History* "staggered" Bennett. He wrote Mrs. Wells in 1920, "I cannot get over it. It's a life work." In 1929, in an article for the *Realist,* Bennett states: "No imaginative author of modern times has exerted an influence equal to that of Wells."

Harris Wilson. *Arnold Bennett and H. G. Wells:*
A Record of a Personal and a Literary Friendship,
ed. Harris Wilson (Rupert Hart-Davis, 1960), pp. 17–18

WESKER, ARNOLD (1932–   )

The dramatist [*Roots*] is trying to show, at a time when the horrors of a "rootless society" are often debated, that some of the roots we prize without considering them too closely need to be grubbed up at once. I have not explored the farther areas of Norfolk, but we need not suppose that Mr. Wesker is talking explicitly of one county, one area: I imagine that he chose Norfolk because he worked there for sixteen months. . . .

It is a contentious, exhilarating piece from the theatre of ideas: one, I agree, to annoy those who cannot believe that Mr. Wesker's earth-encrusted families exist, and those who will regret both his naturalism and his repetitive dialogue. His resolute naturalism can be a bit tiresome, for example a first-act passage of messy "local colour" that is a pointless Cold Comfort decoration. But the verbal repetitions seem to me to be well judged, and as satisfying in their way as C. K. Munro's used to be in moderation, though Mr. Wesker never goes to Munro's lengths.

J. C. Trewin. *ILN*. Aug. 22, 1959, p. 92

Arnold Wesker is one of the latest of these young playwrights [social realists] to arrive on the English stage. In June and July of this year his trilogy was performed at the Belgrade Theatre, Coventry, and, now, three months later these three plays are published in one volume. . . . Wesker is clearly drawing heavily in these plays on his personal life—Ronnie, for instance, carries to a large degree the unity of the plays as a character and as a chorus—but the point that Wesker wishes to emphasize at the outset is the intimacy of his involvement with the life and people who, as a dramatist, he is committed to exhibit. His attitude is not imposed upon the plays with distance and detachment but is allowed to evolve; to emerge gradually and painfully through the actual development of the play itself so that—in a sense—Wesker and his audience carry the burden of the dramatic experience together and find its coherence as an artistic statement simultaneously. The trilogy is an exploration in dramatic terms and through it, eventually and with great honesty, Wesker defines his attitude—however inconclusively—towards his background, himself and the society to which he belongs. He is an idealist whose passionate concern is to regenerate people and society and, perhaps, only those who want to change society care desperately enough for society—or they would never bother to try. Certainly, Ronnie, the idealist moves through the trilogy from disillusionment to disillusionment but he emerges in the end, his ideals only slightly impaired, with a firmer grasp of life's exigencies and a more deliberate and purposeful sense of urgency. Perhaps, however, Wesker's chief virtues as a dramatist stem from two main sources; firstly, from the way in which his passionate concern for individuals transforms what otherwise might have been puppet figures into people of life and substance about whom we are too intensely concerned; and, secondly, from the severe and often terrifying honesty with which he pursues his theme, without compromise or favour, without permitting his ideals to subvert his material or his politics to tempt him to easy or clear-cut solutions. . . .

Wesker's plays are full of incident and dramatic interest, however domestic. His world is one of the family, an intimate group bound by affection and experience; moving through social changes and being changed by them. He is sometimes clumsy with inexperience, unable quite to handle the sheer wealth that his themes throw up; his characters are not altogether clearly conceived or fully projected and his dramatic situations are often over-contrived to the point where the theatrical machinery creaks. He has not yet learnt to handle direct conflict and his trilogy has a certain ingrown quality the potential of which is not entirely brought out in dramatic terms. But to say that he is promising would be insulting; the trilogy represents a real achievement. Wesker and his contemporaries have taken the initiative in drama, and the life of theatre might well compensate us for the death of, say, the novel as an art form.

A. R. Jones. *CQ*. Winter, 1960, pp. 367–70

"Then where do we look for our new vision?" The question is proposed . . . by Ronnie at the end of *I'm Talking About Jerusalem,* the last play in Arnold Wesker's trilogy. In *Chicken Soup with Barley, Roots,* and *Jerusalem* Wesker chronicles the struggles of the Kahn family to live the good Communist life. . . . What this trilogy says is not that Communism is false but that even the "truth" of Communism, if it were to obtain, would not automatically make a man free or whole. If visions don't work, the failure is a human failure, don't blame life: "Free agents, Sammy boy." This strikes me as an adult acknowledgment, and it largely accounts for the resonance of the trilogy which persists after one has forgotten Ronnie's remarks about the Labour Party and Sir Winston's Sunday paintings. The play is concerned with man's own resources when the dream and the ball are over. Ronnie is trying to write a socialist novel, but Wesker has written a sturdy trilogy which should ring bells for anyone, Harold Macmillan included. Even Tories try to build Jerusalem, some kind of Jerusalem. Wesker's trilogy is a humane imitation of an action; it has the same kind of force as that splendid moment in *The Entertainer* by John Osborne when Archie Rice, explaining his own failure, invokes the memory of a great negress, in a bar, standing up and singing and defining her entire being in the song. These are not cheery-beery affirmations, slogans painted on a humanist bandwagon; they are precise formulations, acts in a human scene.

Denis Donoghue. *HdR*. Spring, 1961, pp. 96–97

Preposterously high and absurdly low assessments have been made of the three plays by Arnold Wesker somewhat grandiloquently labelled the "Wesker Trilogy"—*Chicken Soup with Barley, Roots,* and *I'm Talking About Jerusalem.* . . . Exacerbated by the solemn hosannas of his more chuckle-headed fans (and also, no doubt, by his own earnest proclamations) Mr. Wesker's enemies dismiss him as a mere brand-name oversold by the theatrical Left. Why, they ask indignantly, should they pay homage to a writer who has not yet learned to construct a piece; who takes three acts to get to the point of a play, and three plays to tell a story; who fills the stage with boring, sordid, lower-class people talking continually about Socialism; who has a disgusting preoccupation with incontinence (in two of these plays Mr. Wesker presents semi-paralysed men unable to control their bowels)? On the other side, Mr. Wesker's idolaters seem to be mesmerized by the sheer arithmetic of his work, as if three plays must be better than one. With awestruck reverence they point out that no one else *under thirty* has written a *trilogy,* an argument which only a sterile, youth-worshipping age like ours could be asked to take seriously as a sufficient reason for admiration. With no less irrelevance they invite us to kneel before the trilogy because it is a unique exposition of the political dilemmas of our time.

. . . On the credit side, first of all, Arnold Wesker has—at his best—a refreshingly accurate ear for what ordinary people say and how they say it. In the English theatrical context, moreover, their language is almost exotically unusual, for it is the idiom of Norfolk farm labourers (in *Roots*) and East End Jews (in the other two plays . . .). This freshness of language, rubbing the familiarity off everyday talk and feeling, helps the dramatist to camouflage the staleness of the fourth-wall naturalism within whose forms he works. Socially, his plays are important because they introduce members of the "working class"—and, in particular, the *rural* working class—as human beings with rights of their own on the stage, instead of as comic silhouettes and stereotypes. . . . *Roots* may be considered as a milestone in the modern English drama, on linguistic and sociological grounds alone. What is more important, however, is Wesker's attitude towards his characters: a burning moral concern, fuelled by compassion and forgiveness, blazing up in a flare of theatrical life force. This author labours to show the love between people, especially people in a family; to affirm their essential individual value, as members of mankind, and to remind the audience that they belong to it, too. As a dramatist, he has the courage of his inexperience. He is not afraid of looking sentimental in trying to illustrate kindness and generosity or of looking "pi" in his attempt to dramatize ideas, and at his best his characters project a stirring emotional power which helps to make good theatre *and* good life. He is a major dramatist in the making, with one play of lasting value already to his credit.

Richard Findlater. *TC*. Sept., 1960, pp. 234, 236

Sending up the Air Force may mean different things at different times—in war and in peace for instance. Also at different theatres. Because we have just had Mr. [Henry] Livings's worm's eye view of an RAF station at the Arts Theatre, some people in last night's audience assumed that Mr. Wesker was on the same tack and went on tittering at scenes of square bashing which, like most things Mr. Wesker writes, were in fact intensely earnest, and about as far from Mr. Livings's Fred Carno army jokes as could well be imagined. Not that the play [*Chips With Everything*] has not its funny moments; the raid on a coke dump is a beautifully timed dumbshow and there is good natural reporting of the talk to be heard in any hut or NAAFI. But Mr. Wesker's airmen are the truest I have seen on any stage and make Mr. Rattigan's *Ross* melodramatic and Mr. Livings's like comic postcards compared to documentary film. . . .

I find the first half of the play irritating, but I think what I rejected was the audience's facile assumption that this was simply a not very amusing exposé of the way recruits are broken in. What Wesker was saying came over eventually with great conviction. All the same, I believe we should have had less stamping and a more explicit characterisation from an earlier point in time but I incline to think that as a whole, this is Wesker's best play, moving away from the particular and autobiographical towards a larger study of the disillusion which betrays the nonconformist.

Philip Hope-Wallace. *G*. April 28, 1962, p. 5

Cries from the heart we doubt ever got cried (we hope they didn't, anyway) stud . . . [Wesker's] pages. They foster the notion that Mr. Wesker's eye and ear for experience are dulled. He cannot even run up a convincing pop lyric; his attempt in *Roots* fatally resembles the folk songs his characters are perpetually singing to one another. His Jewish families constantly fall into the accents of a TV comedy series—less funny than most; his removal men in *I'm Talking About Jerusalem* are like Hancock bit-players—only less funny. In particular, the corporal in *Chips With Everything* is far less funny than many real individuals of the type presumably aimed at—the surly, eccentric, egotistical long-service NCO. And we are far now from lamenting a detachable stylistic shortcoming. Mr. Wesker denigrates by his practice the interestingness and intelligence of the life he purports to know and care about.

Kingsley Amis. *Spec.* Aug. 10, 1962, p. 190

WEST, ANTHONY (1914–   )

All the people in Mr. West's book [*On a Dark Night**] are dead this is depressing because they are so sinful and lively, especially the hero, J. M. Wallis, who committed suicide in Occupied Germany. So here they all are milling sinfully around, self-deceived, devil-deceived, driven into patently man-made concentration camps, geared to false laughter in man-made seaside resorts, earth-bound. There is the added horror of forced association. . . .

The author's removal of . . . [his] hero on the last page to the "eternal awareness of the mind of God" has an almost blasphemous effect. This book is a good sort of failure. The author's thought is not quite up to the theme; his imagination is good; his intelligence limps behind.

Stevie Smith. *Spec.* Oct. 28, 1949, p. 584

It [*The Vintage*] is a deftly told and provocative story. Its after-death locale is an effective device, enabling the author to penetrate the essence of his characters' personalities without the heavy grinding of psychiatric machinery, and to project the jumbled anxiety and guilt of modern man without any literal limitations of time or space. But it is essentially a book of life, one man's thoughtful reflections on the question—what is it all for?

Carol H. Weiss. *Com.* Feb. 10, 1950, p. 491

I will confine myself to remarking that the character given the name Max Town who dominates *Heritage,* if he is not Mr. West's Portrait of H. G. Wells, well, he is the spittin' image. The novel is the story of a successful writer of genius and a successful actress of genius who have a son together but not a marriage ceremony. The story is told by the son, with a tolerant implication that such relationships are not nearly as destructive as the Text Book Parent would insist.

One immense difficulty outstares the author from his chosen subject, that is, the creation of a fictitious genius—actually two fictitious geniuses, but he, rightly, tends to neglect the actress for the writer of novels and histories. The reader tends to be stubborn about having characters put

*English title of *The Vintage*

upon him as geniuses. If they are scientists or painters he may accept them on a minimum of data and fuss. But of literary genius he demands proof. Oblique reference to impressively titled publications will not do. Nor is the author's good faith in his fabricated genius nearly enough. Nor yet a bunch of other characters going around implying the genius of their central figure.

Mr. West does all of these things, and further, surrounds his genius with a furore of Mercedes-Benzes, eccentrically adoring mistresses, and villas the right distance outside Cannes. All these encumbrances, however, do not suggest the atmosphere of genius so much as that of a writer whose books sell well. . . .

The book represents a strongly sympathetic view of human affairs, a view that has not been romanticized as it might have been, nor moralized over as many may think it preferably should have been. The author has treated his subject with devotion and pride, while determinedly submitting these qualities to a scrutinizing honesty, and if scrutinizing honesty in the hands of some novelists has rendered the novel by now pretty groggy, this grogginess is no doubt a desired effect. But these honesty-obsessed writers should realize that it is not as easy as it might appear to remove the nervous system for examination and leave the animal alive and throbbing. There is the risk of their being left holding a corpse. If all that they are after is the way things work, they must at least know how to trim an obstreperous truth to a delighting fact.

Cashenden Cass. NR. Oct. 17, 1955, pp. 19–20

Anthony West's problem in *On a Dark Night* is formidable, for he invites the complete unreality of fantasy in his narrative of existence after death. . . . After an uncertain beginning marred by an attempt at American soldiers' diction, West proceeds with style and taste to solve the problem that has defeated Graham Greene in his sombre gospels, and Charles Williams in his fantasies: the presentation of a religious theme without the trappings of sectarian theology; an impressive accomplishment. The novel is limited by the amount of cleverness West must exert to create literary actuality—the undue demand upon the imagination that fantasy always makes. But like Rex Warner's novels, *On a Dark Night* is important as a rare example in the contemporary English novel of the serious confrontation of a serious theme. It is free of Huxley's façade of intellectualism and of Waugh's flippancy, and it departs from the tradition of manners and social realism that limits the writing of L. P. Hartley and much of Elizabeth Bowen.

John McCormick. Catastrophe and Imagination
(Longmans, 1957), pp. 291–92

WEST, MORRIS (1916–   )

Mr. Morris West, an Australian writer whose last book gave a disturbing picture of childhood in the slums of Naples [*Children of the Sun*], has now published a novel in which he portrays another aspect of Italian life that the tourist tends to overlook. *The Devil's Advocate* is set in Calabria, a region of dire poverty and superstition, where a cult has grown up round the memory of Giacomo Nerone, reputed saint, martyr and miracle worker. . . .

The author, a Roman Catholic who spent several years as a teaching brother in a monastery, depicts in Nerone a "saint" who lacks the more obvious attributes of saintliness. . . .

Though the author does his best to rouse our interest in Nerone, the character most likely to remain in the reader's memory is Meredith. A dying man, too sceptical to risk asking a miracle for himself, he develops . . . from a withdrawn and chilly intellectual into a man who understands his humanity's need for love. . . .

The book, broad in outline and emotional in style, is likely to appeal to a popular market. The author is critical of his Church: there are, he tells us, too many holy medals and not enough medicine; too many churches and not enough schools.

TLS. Oct. 23, 1959, p. 614

. . . A novel—one might think—is known by its words. And I can only describe *The Devil's Advocate* as a sort of *Green Hat* with benefit of clergy. A similar staginess afflicts the writing.

D. J. Enright. *Spec.* Nov. 13, 1959, p. 679

Mr. West has made full use of the trial symbol to expose the moral weaknesses, and conflicts of his characters in *Daughter of Silence*. He sets the scene, with somewhat hackneyed skill, in the drowsy, dusty, primitive Tuscan landscape which seems to hold such an extraordinary fascination for English and American novelists. . . .

Mr. West is not one to be scared by . . . frank contemplation of the human predicament, and being a profoundly Catholic writer he has the didactic urge to suggest answers. Sometimes his answers sound a little too like the catechism—a catechism fully aware of Jung, of course, but neatly arranged to offer the reader both sin and salvation, justice and love, in convenient equations. And none of the characters has the power to move us as deeply as the hero-victim of *The Devil's Advocate*. But Mr. West continues to deserve respect and interest precisely because he can make the unfashionable question of the soul's health an exciting and dignified theme for his novels.

TLS. Nov. 24, 1961, p. 837

None of this disparate material [in *The Shoes of The Fisherman*] comes alive. The characters are crudely conceived; pages of unassimilated information constantly impede from the narrative flow. When the Pope begins acting liaison between Kamenev and the American President, one is irresistibly reminded of the capers of Upton Sinclair's superman, Lanny Budd. Mr. West should quietly write off *The Shoes of the Fisherman* as a loss. Purged of temptation to handle "great" events and "great" ideas, he should return to the direct, garish, popular narratives he stage-manages so expertly.

John L. Brown. *NYT.* Oct. 17, 1963, p. 27

WEST, REBECCA (1892–   )

The conjunction of Miss West and Henry James is a curious one; for Miss West has precisely the kind of acute, modern, probing, flippant, traditionless, open mind that seems so alien to the mind of Mr. James. Miss West, I imagine, abhors reticence, while Mr. James, I also imagine, detested revelation. The oddity of this conjunction of very dissimilar minds is extraordinarily apparent in Miss West's book [*Henry James*]; for she has remarkable difficulty in concealing her dislike of most of her author's writing, and is only able to allay the reader's suspicion of her attitude towards him by periodically bepraising him with a generosity that is entirely beyond his merits. . . . All these sentences lifted casually here and there from Miss West's book do denote that on the whole Miss West thinks that Mr. James was a tedious old gentleman even when he was a youth; and it was probably her sense of this irritation with him that induced her to such generosity as her final sentence: "He died, leaving the white light of his genius to shine out for the eternal comfort of the mind of man." It is as if she wished the reader to forget that she had been praising Mr. James with faint damns, and had tried to accomplish this purpose by damning him with loud praise.

St. John Ervine. *BkmL.* Sept., 1916, p. 169

Miss West's long-expected novel [*The Judge*] impresses one first as being beautifully written. That of itself would not take one far, but the rich and humourous imagery, the signal vitality of her style, are used to construct a most sympathetic portrait of a young Scotch girl. . . . All the elements of a great novel are here, if they are not quite satisfactorily combined. To applaud the sympathy and intelligence of the author I can find no sufficient words. But when she is content to try to do either test at once, or is able to compose more cleverly, she will, I think, so deeply impress the delighted reader that *The Judge* will be dismissed as immature.

H. C. Harwood. *OutL.* July 1, 1922, p. 14

Her literary reputation has till now been resting upon a high-spirited little book on Henry James, the best psychoanalytical novel yet published; and the best regular reviews now appearing of current fiction. Admirers of her *Return of the Soldier,* and her critical articles in the English *New Statesman* are at last given the work which they have so long been promised, a long and important novel entitled *The Judge*.

Before the reader has finished three pages of it, he will settle himself more comfortably in his chair, and surrender himself to the powerful and lamentably rare pleasure of reading a writer who can write. Miss West does not use the *staccato* style *As Now Worn by Leading Literary Ladies;* her writing is rich, closely packed, highly coloured, and individual. It seems impossible for her to be careless, to take the easy, faded word, or to fall short of precision. Her imagination is primarily visual, and her landscapes stand out with mineral hardness and brilliance. Her style reflects her subjects like a metal mirror varying with their colours, but burnishing them all to an ardent, almost truculent, loveliness.

Raymond Mortimer. *Dial.* Oct., 1922, p. 441

It must be obvious to anyone who reads the work of Miss West that in her is to be found what I may call a germ of grim brilliancy. She is brilliantly conversant with the more serious side of life. Miss West writes as if she was rather angry with humanity, as if she viewed the mass of people amongst whom she moves and has her being with a slightly malicious smile. Perhaps at present, and I say this advisedly (for Miss West is comparatively young), she cannot see the sun because the clouds obscure it, yet she would do well to remember that though not seen the sun is still there. Miss West has of course had a remarkable success in a comparatively short literary career and in every way she deserves it, for if Miss West is as yet somewhat uncertain of her own feet and much more certain of the feet of other people, she has every chance of a most distinguished career in the world of letters. But Miss West would do very well to beware of the newspapers. Lately she has written many superficial articles, in which she attacks men, in an extremely cheap kind of way. Miss West is too good an artist, she has too brilliant gifts, she has too great powers of really fine writing, to develop into a kind of woman, to whom the Editors of the cheaper press write, when they wish to secure an article that is merely written to cause correspondence.

Patrick Braybrooke. *Novelists: We Are Seven* (C. W. Daniel, 1926), p. 141

. . . Miss Rebecca West's rather vapourish little expedition into the realms of fantasy, *Harriet Hume,* has made me regret the ponderous but respectable feminism of her earlier novels.

LL. Nov., 1929, p. 482

Miss Rebecca West's *The Thinking Reed* is a big book, both in bulk and in subject; there is a good deal more matter than the afflictions of wealth here. Her writing covers a really immense field with an air of athletic ease: intellectual writing, in the exact sense, but at the same time flexible, vivid and never cold. *The Thinking Reed* seems to me to be a classic novel, such as is not often written today: imagination (or vision) and sheer top-form professional ability now seldom go together; it is hard to find a mean between satire and good faith. The settings have depth, they are not only painted; they are not abstract, or there to illustrate moods. . . . The book as a book appears to me to have almost no imperfections; it rounds itself off, it is impossible to think beyond it.

Elizabeth Bowen. *NSN.* April 11, 1936, p. 571

Why Miss Rebecca West calls her novel *The Thinking Reed* is a mystery, because hardly any of her characters are capable of thinking at all. It produces on the reader an impression of waste.

Why should so much wit and brilliance be wasted on such boring people? Cleverness there is in plenty, but all its scintillations fly off into the deep night of dullness.

SR. April 11, 1936, p. 471

Miss West's book [*The Meaning of Treason*] is rich in argument and impression and one elaborates the other. She is satirical but on the side of authority, scornful, at times even snobbish about her victims, sizing them up with the drastic wit of an undeceived hostess and yet unexpectedly, surprisingly fair, and even compassionate. No doubt there is a touch of strain and rhetoric in her moralisings. We are not always sure when we hear the words of common sense that the voice is free of the tremor of the extremist. Like many brilliant writers, she has a mind that is too incessantly being made up; it is like listening to doors slamming one after the other through a house. If I could have been an American rebel or a Sinn Feiner, I would have been puzzled to know what her

advice to me would have been. But there is no doubt of the people she portrays with such alarming moral verve—the mad, the simple, the frightened, the liars, the shameless, the eccentrics, the conceited, caught in a world that was shabbier and more exacting than they suspected.
V. S. Pritchett. *NSN*. Sept. 24, 1949, p. 332

The Meaning of Treason is the title: but I am not sure what is the meaning of the title. I can only suppose that Miss West thinks that she has provided a psychological explanation of treason in her occasional analyses of the characters and minds of various traitors of the last war. For myself, I cannot derive any coherent "reason for treason" from her pages, for all the various Freudian diagnoses of compensation, mother-complex and what not.
Sir John Squire. *ILN*. Oct. 1, 1949, p. 490

This is the fundamental dilemma which is hidden in all Rebecca West's writings, the problem of God dying in the cookery class. Her most complete statement is in the terrifying and marvelous essay called *Letters to a Grandfather*. Few people seem to know of this work. It has probably alienated the religious by its extraordinary symbolism, a transcendent God appearing as a tired Negro in a worn scarlet dress suit, and the Holy Ghost as the light reflected from the whites of his eyes. The irreligious probably realized that this was a deeply religious work and rejected it. It is however exceedingly important. . . . The final vision of the *Letter to a Grandfather* is in fact stated to be essentially the same thing as the Crucifixion, and the crucified Christ acquires splendor by being an explorer, stretched out in space trying from one point to embrace and understand all, and therefore the supremely worthy object of the devotion of the lady hung on the opposite wall.
G. E. Hutchinson. *The Itinerant Ivory Tower*
(Oxford Univ. Pr., 1953), p. 253

Actually, rather more fatiguing than Miss West's occasional overabundance in *A Train of Powder* is the endemic ascendancy of her intellection over her feeling. Although there is evidence that Miss West would herself be the first to announce that no cause is searched out and no justice allotted by the mind alone, operating without the support of natural emotion, throughout her essays emotion shows itself as the self-consciousness of education rather than as the free impulse of the heart.

Miss West's pictures of Mrs. Hume, of the parents of Marshall, of the families of the Greenville lynchers are all portraits which, although shrewd, lack the kind of truth which is finally supplied only by simple warmth and compassion—the wall of her superior powers would seem to rise between Miss West and these suffering human beings. Of course, if tenderness were also within her gift, it might incapacitate Miss West as a reporter. It is quite possible she must do without this one more talent in order to make such full use of her superb intellectual gifts.

Diana Trilling. *NYT*. March 20, 1955, p. 3

Miss Rebecca West dwells, and has dwelt for many years on the summits. Intellectually and morally, in temperament and outlook as much as in practical achievement, she towers above contemporary practitioners in popular journalism. She is one of the few really great reporters of our time. Her latest book [*A Train of Powder*] is a collection of a few of her essays in reporting over the past troubled decade—studies in crime, ranging from the greatest of the Nuremberg trials, through a lynching in South Carolina, the case of the hapless Mr. Setty (the Warren Street motor trader, bits of whom were cast up on an Essex marsh), and the even more hapless youth, William Martin Marshall, the Foreign Office radio operator who gave information to an official in the Soviet Embassy. The unity of the book—and it is a remarkable unity in spite of the wide diversity of experience recorded—is supplied by Miss West's maintenance and exposition of the feminine principle.

John Connell. *TT*. June 4, 1955, p. 740

If Jonathan Edwards were living in our time, and if he were a gifted literary critic, he might well have written this volume of Rebecca West's . . . the chapters of *The Court and the Castle* indicate to us what a very "high" Calvinist Miss West has become—a supralapsarian even, one suspects, of a more rigorous sort than John Calvin himself. She is studying here a series of writers, mostly but not entirely English—beginning with Shakespeare and including Proust, Henry James, Kipling, Trollope, Kafka—from the point of view of their acceptance or rejection of two Calvinist dogmas, that of total depravity and that of predestination or absolute decrees. . . .

This is a great theme, and since the issues of corruption versus innocence and of predestination (or determinism) versus free will are as profound as any with which great writers deal, Miss West's concentration on the theme makes it possible for her to get well under the surface of most of the works she deals with. In general, she is guiltless of the vice of distorting a writer's picture of things for the sake of demonstrating a thesis triumphantly, and in general, too, she is quite free from the small vice of undervaluing a writer because he is guilty of some theological or social heresy. Of some of her terribly mistaken Pelagians, such as Fielding and Emily Brontë, she writes with the liveliest appreciation.

Newton Arvin. *NYT*. Nov. 3, 1957, p. 28

Miss West, by writing this book [*The Court and the Castle*], has joined ... [a] very small company of critics. I do not know how long it took her to write, but its three sections must surely be the fruits of years of meditation. Wondering, as we all wonder, "whether the universe is good or bad," Miss West has attentively read the great writers of Western Europe—not going to them for easy formulations, for "answers," but accepting them as companions in the search. As a result, her criticism of their work, though it is subordinated to a purpose, is not unbalanced; there is no trace of the squashing, distorting and lopping common among critics who write to a thesis. . . .

In reviewing this book, the temptation is to quote and quote again. It is so full of passages which are too striking to be hurried over, too beautifully expressed for paraphrase to be possible. What I have written is not a review in any critical sense, for the book is too profound and densely packed for me to be able to assess it until I have had time to live with it, to keep it beside me as a companion to my reading, as one keeps *The Sacred Wood* or *Countries of the Mind* or *The Wound and the Bow*. Meanwhile, I hope I have at least conveyed my sense of the book's importance and my feeling of obligation to its author.

John Wain. *L.* Dec., 1958, pp. 62–63, 65

WHITE, T. H. (1906–1964)

T. H. White has made, in fact, the same assumption which Tolstoy made in writing *War and Peace:* that there are no essential differences between historical characters and people living to-day. For that reason *The Sword in the Stone* is not just a boy's book about monsters, or a funny book about knights in armour, nor a purely whimsical book like Kenneth Grahame's *Wind in the Willows*. It has something in common with all these, but has the life and solidity that they lack. The best bits of it indeed are the direct descriptions of nature, of country life, of the behaviour and appearance of bird, beast, and fish. Like Tolstoy, still more like Rostov, or Levin, White has a passion for all country sports and crafts. He can describe haymaking because he has obviously worked in the hayfield, or an owl eating a mouse, because he has fed owls on mice. Thus he enters into the soul of a hawk, of a grass-snake, of a badger, of a fish, because he has kept them, tamed them, spent months of his life learning to know them. It is not idle whimsicality which leads him to translate their characters into terms which all his readers may understand, but poetic insight. He has thus without magic equipped himself to describe Arthur's training as though he himself had been

Merlin's pupil. It will be remembered that Arthur was turned into a fish, a bird, etc. These chapters in *The Sword in the Stone* show, in my opinion, real poetic imagination which is all the more moving because they are broken up by passages of great comic buffoonery. . . . *The Sword in the Stone* is, in short, the most delightful book for old and young. Those who don't like King Pellinore will like the grass snake.

David Garnett. *NSN*. Sept. 3, 1938, p. 349

Lewis Carroll knew exactly when to stop, and that in this kind of tale particularly, quality means more than quantity. Mr. White [*The Sword in the Stone*] is less discriminating: his best chapters are delightful, and had he cut out the others—the less imaginative, the Robin Hood episode for instance—he would have increased enormously the value of the whole. . . .

. . . quotation will show the kind of novel Mr. White has written. It hovers somewhere between *Through the Looking Glass* and Mark Twain's *The Mysterious Stranger,* being less a dream tale than the former, and lacking the philosophic purpose of the latter. We are at once in Arthurian and modern times: the Wart, in fact, is eventually revealed as the youthful Arthur. Mr. White clearly enjoyed writing the book, and a good many people, young and old, will enjoy reading it.

Forrest Reid. *Spec.* Sept. 2, 1938, p. 382

That scholarly, witty and enthusiastic medievalist, Mr. T. White, has produced a third fine book devoted to the Arthurian legends. Sir Lancelot of the Lake, the "Chevalier Mal Fet," is the central figure, and the darkly mystic, thwarted character which Mr. White finds him to be dominates the book. Hence *The Ill-Made Knight* is a more thoughtful, adult and subdued piece of writing than *The Sword in the Stone* or *The Witch in the Wood.* It has its fits of farce and comedy—its irreverent poking of fun at some of the solemnities of the days of chivalry—but not the out-and-out joyful boisterousness of the earlier volumes. . . . It ranks with *The Sword in the Stone* but is a different sort of book, more mystical than magical, more a novel than a prime fairy story. . . .

A great part of the story's charm, as in its predecessors, is the rich background of medieval lore—odd bits of information, long lists of heraldic terms, a lovely collection of items in one course of a meal—rhythmic and resounding words that impart their medieval color even though the reader doesn't know exactly what they all mean. Details of weight and construction of armor—or of Guenever's bathroom in the castle—are illuminating and interesting.

Beatrice Sherman. *NYT*. Nov. 10, 1940, p. 6

It had better be admitted at once (since the habit of using an author's best work as a yardstick is unfair but almost unavoidable) that *Mistress Masham's Repose* has not the wisdom and valor which shine out in *The Sword and Stone*. . . . But then, why should one expect it? This is an exquisite filagree, with all the bright charm of the miniature. Mr. White thoroughly understands the art of this sort of fantasy, which is to keep a number of balls in the air, and always to offer a fresh theme before the first can become monotonous or can appear artificial. . . .

Of course one can cavil. Mr. White, who has a sound ear for the language of the Houhyhnhms, seems to have lost his *Sprachgefühl* in dealing with the speech of Lilliput. He imputes to his Lilliputians such names as Gradgnag and Blambrangrill. In the Lilliputian speech as reported by Gulliver, there is a very high proportion of short vowels and liquid consonants, suited to the tiny mouths that spoke it; surely such names as those cited belong to Brobdingnag. . . .

But these are cavils. When all is said, *Mistress Masham's Repose* is a book like no other. All its extravagances hang together, like the rococo and chinoiserie in which the builders of Malplaquet delighted. As its Lilliputians would say, it is a Work to be held in high Esteem by all true Persons of Quality.

Basil Davenport. *Sat.* Sept. 28, 1946, p. 7

It is difficult not to do this extraordinary book a disservice by praising it with extravagant enthusiasm. In a world which is overgenerous with its superlatives, the use of such terms as great and good may well be questioned. They should not be questioned in this case. *Mistress Masham's Repose* is a masterpiece of narration, literary ingenuity, humor and satire and Mr. White, on the basis of this book, deserves to be mentioned in the company of Evelyn Waugh, C. S. Lewis, and George Orwell as one of the few fortunate possessors of a splendid prose style.

Francis X. Connolly. *Com.* Nov. 15, 1946, p. 125

The real gratification, as in T. H. White's former novels, comes from the author's personality and his mode of conveying it, a mode that seems particularly English in its assumption and corresponding avoidance of certain things—bravery, loyalty, sex and so forth—and its appearance— despite these limitations—of absolute intellectual freedom, which comes from its unself-conscious abruptness and its inconsequential poetic drift around arresting topics, like the expression of a puffin's eye or the fact that one shouts a warning to *oneself* if one is pushed over a cliff. As also in the writing of Richard Hughes and Arthur Ransome there is an added twist of pleasurable fraudulence in the spectacle of someone so obviously intelligent keeping up so determinedly English a *persona!*

I recommend *The Master* wholeheartedly, not least because Mr. White and his two brisk and practical child heroes maintain this brave and refreshing pretence of not knowing why hollowed-out islands and caverns under-sea have such fascination for us. There are many critics today to tell them, but fortunately they are still too busy on *The Tempest* and *Kubla Khan* to get around to the adventure story.

John Bayley. *Spec.* March 1, 1957, p. 290

But the problem of every epic remains the same. What end had the chase in view? Even the quest for the Grail has an edge of absurdity: *what then?* the whisper sounds. Or else: it was Galahad's private Game, and nobody cares for Galahad. And what had Merlin's marvellous education done, at the last, for the King? Mr. White soon finds himself with questions like these on his hands. The danger lies, of course, in the new dimension that the teller gives to the figures of pageantry: at once the limitations rise of logic, life and time. What began as a schoolboy frolic ends with an old man, "inventor of civilisation," trying to find the great reasons why he has greatly failed. Kipling's Gramarye has turned into modern war-torn England. . . .

The White Arthuriad does not ignore the difficulties of the old story as so many versions for the young are bound to do, but it is for other reasons than this that it is so much more than a juvenile book. The lesson it seems to teach—since Merlin knows it all from the start—is that what must be must be; the real and exhilarating business of life is the battle against the inevitable. Or perhaps the telling itself is the trouble. This extraordinary and often magical volume may or may not lead a young Milton to the defence of virgins: that depends on the reader's temperament. But from a literary and aesthetic view it will certainly impose its picture for a long time after, perhaps for always, on any later version that may be read.

Naomi Lewis. *NS.* July 12, 1958, p. 51

WILLIAMS, CHARLES (1886–1945)

Even of the chaos he loves to create, for instance, Mr. Charles Williams is obliged to give a well-rounded version in *The Greater Trumps,* for what he does not contribute none could contribute for him, in that outrageous jumbling of the commonplace and the supernatural—the little suburban parent and the magic pack of cards—with which this writer plunges into the fine, defiant use of his imagination.

Viola Meynell. *LL.* June, 1932, p. 247

This book [*Reason and Beauty in the Poetic Mind*] would be excellent as a present from parents who wish to ensure that their children will detest poetry for their whole lives. Mr. Williams explains in his preface that the four corners of his book lie at such points as the use of the word "Reason" by Wordsworth in *The Prelude,* &c. Actually, for the most part, his arguments amount to no more than a paraphrase of *The Prelude,* parts of *Paradise Lost,* and Keats' "Odes," expressed in a suggestive way which might be helpful to students who are anxious to know what these poems are "about." Scattered through his book there are some definitions which would also perhaps be useful to examination candidates, such as that "prose pretends and tends to subdue its own method of existence to its business of dealing with the reader, but poetry desires and determines to subdue the reader to its own method of existence." . . .

This is the kind of criticism which goes far to explain why so many people detest poetry. It speaks of poets as though they were superior beings incapable of experiencing the feelings of ordinary people; it translates simple and direct poetry, which easily explains itself, into high-flown and indirect language. In trying to elevate poetry, it puts it on the shelf.

Stephen Spender. *Spec.* Dec. 22, 1933, pp. 941–42

This book [*The Descent of the Dove*] is not quite what you expect it to be; but nothing by Mr. Charles Williams—nothing, at least, that he has written because he wanted to—ever is; and the sort of people who would object that Proteus does not observe the rules of all-in wrestling, the very literal-minded, may sometimes complain of Mr. Williams that he is playing a game of his own. The easiest way to try to prove a foul is to accuse Mr. Williams of heresy. To those who believe that orthodoxy is for the Church to determine, not for the individual writer to expect to arrive at until his views have been published and tested, this will not appear a deadly accusation. One may even go so far as to maintain that a heresy from Mr. Williams would be, in its result (and Mr. Williams does assume that intelligent and educated minds exist), a real contribution to the explication of orthodoxy.

Of three classes of Mr. Williams's writings: his romantic thrillers, from *War in Heaven* to *Descent into Hell,* his later poetry, and his theological works (*He Came down from Heaven* and the present book) it may be said that while they can all be enjoyed separately, they can only be partly understood unless they are considered together.

T. S. Eliot. *NSN.* Dec. 9, 1939, p. 864

WILLIAMS, CHARLES

Something must here be said to those who may ask "Who was Charles Williams?" He had spent most of his life in the service of the Oxford University Press at Amen House, Warwick Square, London. He was a novelist, a poet, a dramatist, a biographer, a critic, and a theologian: a "romantic theologian" in the technical sense which he himself invented for those words. A romantic theologian does not mean one who is romantic about theology but one who is theological about romance, one who considers the theological implications of those experiences which are called romantic. The belief that the most serious and ecstatic experiences either of human love or of imaginative literature have such theological implications, and that they can be healthy and fruitful only if the implications are diligently thought out and severely lived, is the root principle of all his work. His relation to the modern literary current was thus thoroughly "ambivalent." He could be grouped with the counter-romantics in so far as he believed untheologized romanticism (like Plato's "unexamined life") to be sterile and mythological. On the other hand, he could be treated as the head of the resistance against the moderns in so far as he believed the romanticism which they were rejecting as senile to be really immature, and looked for a coming of age where they were huddling up a hasty and not very generous funeral. He will not fit into a pigeon-hole.

The fullest and most brilliant expression of his outlook is to be found in his mature poetry, and especially in *Taliessin through Logres* and *The Region of the Summer Stars*. . . . I must here content myself with saying that they seem to me, both for the soaring and gorgeous novelty of their technique and for their profound wisdom, to be among the two or three most valuable books of verse produced in the century. Their outstanding quality is what I would call glory or splendour; a heraldic brightness of colour, a marble firmness of line, and an arduous exaltation.

C. S. Lewis. Introd. in *Essays Presented to Charles Williams,* ed. C. S. Lewis (Oxford Univ. Pr., 1947), pp. vi–vii

In the last six years or so something like a *cultus* of the late Charles Williams has grown up in Anglican literary circles. T. S. Eliot's approval and C. S. Lewis's championship have assisted in promoting the cause, but it has been left to Miss Dorothy Sayers to give final, unequivocal formulation to the myth of Williams the great writer. "All the works of his maturity," she tells us, "—novels, plays, poems, and essays in theology or literary criticism—illumine one another, and illumine also *those other great writers* of the central tradition from whom their author himself derived illumination. If Williams is a pregnant interpreter of Dante, Dante is equally a pregnant interpreter of Williams. So, too, with Shakespeare, Milton, Wordsworth. They and he are 'set on the marble of exchange.' "

It is an astonishing claim. That Williams had undoubted abilities as a literary critic may be gathered from such an essay as "The Cycle of Shakespeare" in *The English Poetic Mind*. The wonder is indeed that he should have got as far as he did, for he seems to have regarded literature as something existing in itself, which he could plunge into and use in his own right without the checks of either literary or other discipline; nor is it irrelevant to point out here how badly he could write. . . .

The irony is that a man whose creative writings all in some form or other celebrate what he called "holy fact" should lack the imaginative writer's grasp of that one thing. Of Williams's verse I will content myself with remarking that he did not practise what he preached. As he himself truly affirmed: "This is the law of symbolism—that the symbol must be utterly itself before it can be a symbol." Williams's fondness for treating of people already out of the body has been generally commented on. The trouble is that he never knows quite what he means by the death region in *Descent into Hell* and *All Hallows' Eve*. Falling between the theological and the symbolical stools, he presents us with something not unlike the world of *Outward Bound*. And there is no fusion between the Dantean or other references and latter day *mise-en-scène;* the association is not imaginatively caught but foisted on from outside. . . .

Perhaps I should have said something of *The Descent of the Dove*, but I have hunted my heretic sufficiently. Williams was critic, novelist, poet, playwright, and theologian (of a sort), and all to a greater or lesser extent *manqué*. He had liveliness of mind and energy, but his famed "originality" was basically a matter of indiscipline of spirit. What can it have been in him that so impressed his friends and literary supporters? No doubt we shall better understand when we have read his biography.

H. P. Hanshell. *Month.* Jan., 1953, pp. 14, 24–25

Charles Williams believes in the supernatural. But his mind is at the same time highly rational, even (in a sense) sceptical. However bizarre the events that occur in his novels may be, they are always, essentially, logical, and subject to the same laws which apply to our everyday experience. And the people to whom they occur are everyday people—middle-class people for the most part, who work in shops and offices, or as professional men or clergymen, and who live in London, its suburbs, and the home-counties. Charles Williams himself lived and worked among such people (as an employee of the Oxford University Press's London Office, and a lecturer in the City Literary Institute) and he believed in their fundamental decencies. It is among such people that he has mostly found his readers rather than among the "intellectuals" (whom he tended to distrust). His novels belong, it may be, to "middlebrow" literature. They were written partly, it would appear, for entertainment, partly to bring in money. But in turning, only half-seriously, to the novel form, Charles Williams employed ideas which he held with profound seriousness. These ideas are most fully developed in his other prose-writings—literary critical, historical, and religious in character, and above all, in his poetry and plays. The corpus of his published work is large, and some acquaintance with its varied aspects is necessary if we are to gain a correct estimate of his stature. But primarily, he was a poet. All his work is to be understood in terms of his conception of the poet's experience, and its relationship to spiritual truth.

John Heath-Stubbs. *Charles Williams*
(BC/Longmans, 1955), p. 8

Perhaps the most remarkable thing about Charles Williams . . . is what one might call the orthodoxy of his imagination, as distinct from his beliefs, for this is very rare in our technological culture. In describing the life of the body and its finite existence in time, most contemporary writers, whatever their beliefs, show a Manichaean bias, an emphasis on the drab and the sordid. If they are materialists they place the beautiful and the exciting in some temporal future; if they are professing Christians the only road to salvation they can imagine is the Negative Way of ascetic renunciation. Even the few who, like D. H. Lawrence, do not suffer from this bias, cannot find anything in the contemporary world to their relish and turn for sustenance to preindustrial societies.

Chesterton, a writer by whom, I think, Charles Williams was influenced, did try to keep his balance and his nerve, but in his praise of wonder and wine there is a shrillness of tone, an exaggerated heartiness which betrays an inner strain. In the work of Charles Williams I can detect no strain whatever; he can imagine Beatrice in the Finchley Road as easily as in 13th century Florence.

W. H. Auden. *CC*. May 2, 1956, p. 553

C. W.'s highest point, in terms of utterance, was reached in 1945, with *The Figure of Beatrice, What the Cross Means to Me* and with the general completion of the poems which appeared next year in *The Region of the Summer Stars*. The pattern of his life, which had been created by his enormous energy, remained the same, office work, lectures, conversations, letters, articles, poetry but there was no more thrust. The affirmation of the goodness of life in all its images was maintained, the coinherence with his many friends and with the life of poetry and love was secure.

A. M. Hadfield. *An Introduction to Charles Williams*
(Robert Hale, 1959), p. 100

It has been amply shown, I think, that Charles Williams, in his novels, has taken ordinary unreligious people, mainly young women, and for the most part has sought to reveal how in the tremendous spiritual conflict in which the whole world is involved willy-nilly they may, if they are in love, perform the greatest miracles of love. That is to say, eros and agape are really one. Eros does not become agape, as in the great plays of Claudel; eros *is* agape. Indeed, eros transcends agape; it opens the way to divine power itself, which is made manifest through the transfigured lover. Of course, there is usually the doctrine of Substitution at work as well, so that we cannot categorically say ever that the miracle has been exclusively performed by the power of eros; Williams never makes his issues so simple. Yet, at the end of most of these novels, there seems to us an unbridgeable gap between the tremendous supernatural achievement and the very ordinary person responsible for it. One is aware that this is part of Williams's intention: to show what power the Christian really has, if he but use it, and how behind him is the whole Communion of Saints; and Christian, in this connexion, is every person of good will, however spiritually ignorant. . . . What Williams has failed to do is to convey adequately, except in *Descent into Hell,* where in fact the doctrine is over-explained, the notion that spiritual action may be exerted by one through another in an endless process of exchange, and the basic idea that the lover's vision is really and truly paradisiacal, restoring to the lover the pure gaze of man made in the image of God, renovating his whole nature. It is indeed only through reading his other works that one comes to understand what actually happens in the novels. . . .

It is to the credit of Charles Williams that he has attempted to consecrate the ordinary and the homely, human love and married life. The ideal of the anchorite has, after all, often enough been expounded and Williams's effort to relate the majority of mankind to spiritual life is a tribute to his intelligence and his charity. Moreover, his vision is expressed through a powerful poetic imagination. Nevertheless, it cannot be said that the result is fully satisfactory.

Ernest Beaumont. *DR.* Spring, 1959, pp. 72–73

Charles Williams' Arthurian poems constitute his own recasting of the Arthurian myth as he derived it from earlier sources, principally Malory. His unfinished prose essay, *The Figure of Arthur,* is however, a retracing of the myth through all the principal early texts and, though undated, can, I think, be presumed to follow the poetry in Williams' career.

The Figure of Arthur is in many ways a puzzling document. It is apparently a partial first draft, filled with Williams' notes for later additions and corrections. Moreover, there are indications that the completed work would have been a vastly more complex book than the present version would indicate.

Charles Moorman. Arthurian Triptych
(Berkeley, Calif., Univ. of California Pr., 1960), p. 38

WILLIAMS, EMLYN (1905–)

It is a rare pleasure to find a writer who has realized the value of an indirect approach to a subject that has been treated purely directly on previous occasions, and has thereby succeeded in lending it a new and greater dramatic interest. The theme of *Night Must Fall* concerns a murder, but Mr. Emlyn Williams, instead of using the conventional method of approach and starting audience and players on the frantic pursuit of clues and criminals, has set himself to disclose the psychology of a murderer whose identity becomes apparent to the audience soon after the curtain has risen. Suspense is faultlessly preserved as the play moves to a crisis of action, but the interest of the audience is held less by the tension of the plot than by the skill with which the complexities of mind and motive in its central character are unravelled. So completely has Mr. Williams succeeded in his aim that in comparison with this play all other modern plays with murder as their theme that come to mind seem in retrospect as flat as the proverbial pasteboard.

Derek Verschoyle. Spec. June 7, 1935, p. 974

That *The Corn Is Green* is a good little play, and what this good little play is all about, and who acts in it, and how they fare—all these things were the talk of London's smartest grill-room half an hour after the curtain fell, and were doubtless bruited all over the country by breakfast time next morning. *The Corn is Green* is a simple little story about how a noble-minded woman—who incidentally isn't a fool—decides to bring education to a remote Welsh mining village. Discovering a genius, she grasps her nettle and brings it to flower. . . . The simplicity of the story can be relied on to throw the spectator into a mood of acceptance of make-believe, from which he need make very occasional sorties to admire this bit of pathos pressed home but not too far home, and the skirting of that bathos which, ever round the corner, never arrives. For this Mr. Williams has to thank a sense of wit and humour which is as uncanny as Miss Dodie Smith's sense of how to make characters move naturally among tables and chairs.

>James Agate. *The Amazing Theatre*
>(George G. Harrap, 1939), p. 182

The title of this play about war and people under invasion is *The Morning Star*. The implications of the very idea of that star are vast; the glory and tenderness it means to man, the finality of its splendor and return in legend and song. There is nothing about the story or the style of Mr. Emlyn Williams' latest play that suits its title. The mere choice of the title gives his play away. . . .

Essentially this play of *The Morning Star* is only a British not-quite-silly piece of fiction—not quite silly because of the fact that the British audiences, whatever their bravery and box-office outside art, have seemingly accepted this sort of noveletting as true to the moment—it has box-office truth also, apparently, for *The Morning Star* is enjoying a London run. Be that as it may. It is doubtless absurd of us here in America to take *The Morning Star* seriously at all. The fundamental problem involved esthetically is the relation of form to content; the eternal principle here is that the form must proceed organically, out of the identical substance, must come straight from the content, or idea. In other words, taking the issue with the greatest seriousness, the idea inescapably must find, if it is to discover its full urgency, the means, tone, values and impact that express it. Alas!

>Stark Young. *NR*. Sept. 28, 1942, pp. 381–82

Emlyn Williams brought Wales to the stage most effectively in *The Corn Is Green,* which had an enormous success in America as well as this country; but this brilliant actor-author is the exception that proves the rule. In the entire history of Wales he is the one solitary figure on the plane of first-rate dramatists to write a play in English that is essentially Welsh in essence. More recently he has repeated the feat in *The Druid's Rest.*

>Eric Johns. *TW*. Sept., 1944, p. 28

Emlyn Williams will be forty-six this autumn. We shall have much more from him, and I imagine that most of the plays will have his distinctive marks: intensity, sometimes over-wrought (he has a Celtic enthusiasm); a strong flare of theatrical speech; a complicated plot of multiple ingenuities. There should also be a Welsh flavour, for Emlyn Williams writes best when he writes of his own people. What I said of him nearly seven years ago still holds: in any play by this dramatist we look for originality of theme, knowing that we shall be spared the grosser clichés: he starts with half the battle gained. Nothing in his most recent plays, *Trespass* or *Accolade*—not among his major works—would make me alter this, though both of these pieces are too anxiously contrived. (Williams may have won half the battle, but here he loses on points.) We shall honour him first as the dramatist of *The Corn Is Green* and *Night Must Fall,* where the mechanics are adroitly managed and the theatrical quality never falters. Many have high regard for *Spring 1600* which is the Shakespearean spring, not a telephone number. And it is sometimes forgotten, too, that Emlyn Williams, back in 1933, adapted *The Late Christopher Bean* from *Prenez Garde à la Peinture* of René Fauchois and transformed it into his own play.

In spite of the qualities they share, nobody will confuse one of Williams's plays with the next. They are not tape-machine strips. He has never waned to a lounge-hall dramatist, a tinkerer with the impolite nothing, the brittle tittering of the tea-table, the shoeshine epigram. Instead, we think of the house-boy of *Night Must Fall,* with his menacing charm; of the discerning teacher, the Welsh pit-boy, the village school, of *The Corn Is Green;* the musical landlord of *The Druid's Rest,* who engaged his maids by ear; the old farmer of *The Wind of Heaven;* the little Cockney sparrow, amoral moppet, from Rotherhithe in *Accolade*. Atmosphere, suspense—any amount of it.

True, and it is a demerit, we feel sometimes that Williams—*The Corn Is Green* excepted—stands outside any scene he presents to us; that he moves his people back and forth as one would move them in a toy theatre. Yet when the manipulation is as cunning as it is at *his* best, it would be sad to carp. Certainly no Williams's drama is a litter-bin, a raffle of scraps. He constructs his plays—even Pinero might have admitted this—and his craft never fails to surprise us at a time when so much playmaking sags glumly like pastry that has refused to rise. . . .

He may exaggerate; he may embarrass; he may over-write. But always he makes us want to know the end. He is a dramatist of the theatre theatrical.

J. C. Trewin. *Adel*. Nov., 1951, pp. 432–33, 437

WILLIAMS, RAYMOND (1921–   )

Mr. Williams's intention [*Drama from Ibsen to Eliot*]—and what could be better?—is to discuss drama as literature. He believes the two have been losing touch for a century, and in order to restore communication between them it is necessary to replace naturalism by convention (which should include verse) and regain, if we can, a language with roots in a life of action.

This is the thesis, but even in this summary a popular fallacy is discernible. Whoever makes an antithesis between naturalism and convention prepares confusion. Naturalism is one convention among others. Mr. Williams goes a step farther for in getting rid of naturalism he proposes, in D. H. Lawrence's phrase, to get rid of "the old stable ego of the character." Before this discussion has advanced more than a page or two, we see that Mr. Williams is confusing "characters and principals." . . .

But Mr. Williams is right in his discussion of Synge, and Mr. O'Casey —and, elsewhere, of the Elizabethans—in looking for active community as the source of richness in language.

How shall we get it? Not by "minority culture" which is Mr. Williams's only proposal. The theatre does not become literature by moving up to the top shelf. This is where Mr. Williams's argument leads—and where it breaks down.

Montagu Slater. NSN. Jan. 3, 1953, pp. 16–17

. . . *Culture and Society* is admirably positive in spirit, is informed by an energetic but patient optimism. Thus, Mr. Williams discusses with a kind of high and sober good sense the inadequacy of some fashionable rejections of the value of political action, of the responsibility to work *with* social machinery so as to make that machinery better. He is therefore particularly effective in his observations on some aspects of "the outsider." . . .

It is, in fact, a proof of the power of Mr. Williams's examination that he does throw us right back to the very sources of our own energy and purposes—because, for his own position, he gives a fine meaningfulness and application: he gives a positive and humane restatement of social purpose, free of the limiting trappings of class; he does the same in redefining culture as a way of life, free of our common narrow conceptions. He thus clarifies our knowledge of much that may be built upon. *Culture and Society* is therefore a considerable contribution to the understanding and evaluation of our own sources of strength and our own best possibilities.

Richard Hoggart. EC. April, 1959, pp. 173, 179

Mr. Williams's work [*Culture and Society*] is important, often brilliant, and a healthy change from the tiresome fear of our expanding society that is now so common among intellectuals. The book is uneven in style, and varies from a fairly stiff schoolmasterish prose to passages of remarkable passion and illumination. It is of real value, but it has one obvious limitation for an American reader. Mr. Williams, as he himself explains, comes from the working class, went to Cambridge on scholarships, and in his personal circumstances and general outlook is entirely typical of the first-generation of British intellectuals who have been educated at the expense of the state, have never felt themselves to be part of the Establishment or even of normal commercial middle-class society, and who have a profound and almost mystical attachment to the working class as a *community*. This feeling for community, for tradition, for local usages and settled habits (all of which represent the other meaning of culture, a total way of life), counts for much more in the ranks of British Socialism than does Marxist class antagonism. Although Mr. Williams, like so many intellectuals in Britain, calls himself a "Socialist," he is certainly no Marxist. The Marxist version of "class" is too abstract a term for someone with Mr. Williams's social experience to apply to the hearty realities of the British village and countryside, and the whole idea of radical and destructive opposition to "bourgeois" culture by an aroused working class offends his belief in society as a *common* culture. Besides, the Marxist idea also sets "culture," in the self-conscious and superior sense that Mr. Williams disapproves of, over and against existing society. Marx, as he shows, is on this side of his thinking very much a contemporary (as of course he was a neighbor) of the Victorian prophets of "culture."

What interests Mr. Williams is a national culture in which all classes can share. He does not want to revolutionize society but to see that the "masses" enter more and more into the common culture. He really believes in society as the solidarity of all classes within it.

Alfred Kazin. *Contemporaries*
(Boston, Little, Brown, 1962), pp. 428–29

The suspicion grows that Mr. Williams conceals the lack of any acute or sober analysis of our current situation by daring and unsupported announcements, almost page by page, that he has discovered a breakthrough, a long crisis (this after, only a year ago, he discovered a long revolution: how long, O, Lord, how long?), a mounting crisis, forces of growth, drives of expansion, a deadlock (which he has broken at the level of theory), and, of course, clear challenge. To say the least, it seems to me an over-stimulated condition in which to conduct a serious inquiry [*Britain in the Sixties: Communication*].

But it is more ominous than that. The most interesting feature of Mr. Williams's writing is its violence. He seems incapable of talking of any change, movement or effort except in violent language. Tightening, breakthrough, crisis, struggle, revolution, pressures, drives, forces, tensions, stresses: these are the descriptive words which come naturally to him; and, to anyone who is used to reading social and political theory, they are warning signals. Those who habitually see political or social situations, or political or social movements, in such terms usually end as either apostles of despair or apologists of authoritarianism. Mr. Williams is a knitted figure, greyer than most of them, and his argument, certainly, is not a blueprint for an authoritarian regime. But it is a handy knitting pattern for it.

Henry Fairlie. *Enc.* Aug., 1962, p. 82

WILLIAMSON, HENRY (1897–   )

His attitude to himself is a mixture of modesty and self-assertion; to the world one of playful disillusionment. "They have been in the sunlight. Since the days of ancient Greece the doves have remained in the sunlight; we who have laboured have found nothing." So books are only an excuse for and an aid to meditation, and to a projection into the past—a past of past Williamson books and the war. Mr. Williamson means that he has found nothing (or little) in the world of men. Even in the New World, in the southern sun where the negroes pleased him, being always "deeply humorous and content" he was pining for the old. He has an advantage here over many writers of novels about the countryside, for he is left with no illusions about the goodness and superior wisdom of country people (in this age of industrialism), and is therefore not tempted to romanticize about them. His present is a world peopled by animals. He observes with phenomenal precision, and writes down straightforwardly what he has observed, but his animals, birds and fishes do not become the dead objects of his observation, but the actual beings of a world which he sees and presents dramatically.

B. H. de C. Ireland. *FR.* Jan., 1935, p. 124

These fragments were part of *Tarka the Otter* until the tenth or eleventh version of that story: the published version, terrifically overwritten, was the seventeenth. Even that one did not stand; the publisher's bibliographical details on later editions reveal that the book has been pawed over a score of times. Now the dangerous age is passed, thank heaven; the book has settled down for the term of its natural life, however long or short it be, and its creator has for it a happy state of benevolent indifference.

The earlier versions, those immediately preceding the seventeenth, were written in what can only be described as a state of mental anguish. Unfortunately it persisted with other books. Organization, for those who walk on their own feet, is the only salvation for us now that the last illusory vapours about the rickety little age are being licked up by the sunshine. How I long for an organized mind, like that of Arnold Bennett! Tarka turned my world sour from morning until late at night. My food, too. At last I could bear the fog and maze no longer: every scene and incident must be recast from actuality, except one—that of the prolonged winter, which remained with slight additions, from the original draft, in spite of certain blue pencilled suggestions that it was vague and unreal, and inferior to the other chapters. With this purpose I visited the rivers again, making sketches and notes which afterwards were wedged into the general mosaic—how the twin ash trees above the Orleigh Mill holt were grown with moss and ivy respectively: how the rising on Cranmere of the Taw river was different from that of his sister Torridge (or that branch which has chanced to be called Ockment), the brother running bright at his earliest beginning, and the sister stirring out of the silence and mystery of a peat tarn.

Henry Williamson. *Adel.* April-June, 1949, p. 217

The work of Henry Williamson remains unknown among many readers of wide and catholic taste, in spite of the fact that his famous book, *Tarka the Otter,* won the Hawthornden Prize for 1928. The majority of his books fall sharply into two categories—the purely nature tales, like *Tarka,* and the novels. The nature stories have always been fairly well received, though often critically as is natural with such work, but the novels have been attacked and criticised as much as they have been praised—and they have been praised by such writers as T. E. Lawrence, Arnold Bennett, Sir John Squire, and Thomas Hardy.

It would appear that, as Lawrence remarked, the more popular critics have found him "unclassifiable," and have therefore tended to dismiss him with a few well chosen, destructive clichés. Nevertheless, with each book he is becoming more widely read, and *The Phasian Bird,* which appeared in 1948, was singled out for special mention by the more discerning critics.

Williamson's work derives largely from that of Richard Jefferies—and he himself has admitted that he is a disciple of Jefferies. His aim is to see, and to teach others to see, "as the sun sees, plainly, without shadows." That, he says, is his life's work.

Perhaps the book which has most nearly expressed his philosophy, excepting *The Phasian Bird* which was an obvious step forward in his development, is *The Flax of Dream*. This long work consists of four books, *The Beautiful Years, Dandelion Days, The Dream of Fair Women,* and *The Pathway;* these are now appearing in separate volumes in Penguin Books. In it Williamson traces the life of Willie Maddison from childhood, expressing through the character his own beliefs. It was completed when he was thirty—a considerable achievement when one considers that during the time when it was written, between 1920 and 1930, a number of other titles appeared regularly, including *Tarka*. He is, however, a slow worker, and several years elapse between each [sic] new book.

The nature books, *Tarka* and the one most akin to it, *Salar the Salmon,* and the three volumes of stories, *The Peregrine's Saga, The Old Stag,* and *The Lone Swallows,* are mostly set in north Devon—that part of the country where Williamson has spent almost all his life. They are unique, for no living writer has attempted to portray nature in all its ways of life in such detail as has Williamson. It is to his credit that he has few imitators.

Anthony Gower. *Colophon*. Oct., 1950, p. 40

The greatest made book of our time is Henry Williamson's *Salar the Salmon.* Mr. Williamson wrote it to meet a demand, following the success of *Tarka the Otter.* He didn't enjoy writing it; but, in fact, it is even *better* than "Tarka," it is a tremendous *tour-de-force.* One day it will be recognised as the greatest piece of prose poetry of our age, the very greatest book ever written about the natural world. This is not its author's opinion, but I stick to it.

Maurice Wiggin. *JOL*. Dec. 17, 1959, p. 346

WILLIAMSON, HUGH ROSS (1901–   )

This is another little book [*The Poetry of T. S. Eliot*] for the "plain reader." As an explanation of Mr. Eliot's poetry, it is thorough and straightforward. Mr. Williamson's view of Eliot corresponds closely, one presumes, with Mr. Eliot's view of himself; he takes the line, already familiar from the critical essays of Mr. I. A. Richards and Mr. F. R. Leavis, of Eliot as a major poet. The Georgians come in for their usual blast of criticism in an early chapter. . . . The importance of Mr. Eliot's theory and its influence on his poetry—the two are in fact indivisible— are sustained by Mr. Williamson throughout this book. He keeps close to his subject, and if there is nothing very new in what he has to say, he says it clearly and persuasively, and amplifies very usefully the comments of previous critics.

NSN. Dec. 10, 1932, pp. 772, 774

In his latest book, *The Gunpowder Plot,* Mr. Hugh Ross Williamson invites us to question the traditional story of that celebrated attempt to blow up Parliament, although former attempts to throw doubt on it were pretty effectively refuted by no less an authority on seventeenth-century fiction than Samuel Rawson Gardiner. It must be confessed that Mr. Williamson's methods are a little confusing to his readers. . . .

Mr. Williamson's book would in fact have been better if he had confined himself to retelling a tale which is dramatic enough and would assuredly have made an excellent play or radio script. In trying to prove that somehow King James I and Sir Robert Cecil were the real villains of the piece he has fallen over backwards. Moreover he ought to beware of himself applying those methods of smearing a victim which he condemns in others.

Maurice Ashley. *Spec.* Oct. 5, 1951, pp. 446–47

It is a pity that this [*Jeremy Taylor*] book has to begin with a possibly not quite sincere sermon on the Gunpowder Plot, and end with the *Dissuasive,* which Gosse is quoted as calling "this multiplication of insulting diatribes against the ancestral religion of his country," because we are rightly inclined to think of Taylor as a sympathetic though isolated and tormented figure, and as a writer of dignified English, despite the abyss into which apparently he plunged when trying to write hymns. . . . The author steers a well-balanced course amid all . . . the shoals, though he certainly sees the Puritan regime as a tyranny yet has no preference for royal absolutism. The book is more valuable as a reference to an all-but forgotten English Catholic, Christopher Davenport, than as a sorrowful reminder of what our poor country once endured and a hint of what troubles may yet lie ahead of us.

Month. Jan., 1953, p. 188

It is no uncommon journey from Manse to Mass, but Mr. Ross Williamson has taken it uncommonly. The choice of a title for his autobiography [*The Walled Garden*] is significant. The most formative events of his childhood occurred in the garden of a house which backed on to the ancient abbey of Romsey, in which town his father was Congregationalist minister. This house with its somewhat abnormal inhabitants was something more than a home to him; here he learnt those lessons which the rest of his life has proved he never forgot—that human beings are capable of breaking faith; that majority opinion is wrong; that history is timeless and that of England an exercise in anti-Protestant polemic; that everything for which his father stood is to be rejected.

Gerald Irvine. *TT*. Dec. 8, 1956, p. 1532

I fear that in our age of petty rebellions . . . an age when one is invited to believe only in disbelief, such a play as *Teresa of Avila* can hardly be popular. It is a portrait of courage, not of exhibitionism. It does not snarl. Its dramatist, Hugh Ross Williamson, will not pretend that he has brought to the stage the full Saint of Avila. But it is, I think, a courageous adventure governed by a civilised mind. . . . True, it is without squalor. True, it has to be rather a sober document in saintliness than a work of springing inspiration; but . . . Mr. Williamson has never been a belittling dramatist, and, compared with some of the wildly advertised little pieces—almost forgotten already—that we have had to face in recent years, *Teresa* is like Congreve's pearl of orient to a dead whiting's eye.

J. C. Trewin. *ILN*. Nov. 4, 1961, p. 788

WILSON, ANGUS (1913–)

Angus Wilson's *The Mulberry Bush* is rather like a pale, detached sketch of J. B. Priestley's far more expert (and more sentimental) *The Linden Tree*. Old do-gooders, Rose and James Padley (a sort of Webbian Couple) find all the skeletons in the cupboard and all the crows come home to roost on the last day in the old college home. They have cleared their minds of cant and fought the good fight all their liberal lives and can't see the harm they've done right under their own noses. Their slogans, their freedoms have become the millstones, the cages of the next generation. . . .

Are we to mock or to feel sympathy? Like Turgeniev in *A Month in the Country* (who exposed the effects of Bovary-ism in a sad household) this does not quite tell us how to react. We audiences like to know. It is a way novelists have in the theatre, that vulgar place, where success is what matters, not truth; where a line, which *reads* so wittily, goes mysteriously for nothing when spoken and where a dull and obvious gesture sets the audience in a glow of delight.

Philip Hope-Wallace. *TT*. April 7, 1956, p. 387

Mr. Angus Wilson's first collection was published in 1949, when, with a return to more normal living conditions, the short story was once more in disfavour with public and publishers alike; many little reviews had already ceased publication, and of the twelve stories included in the volume only three had appeared previously in periodicals. Moreover, the author did not derive from Kafka, Sartre, Camus, or any of the influences fashionable at that period; and his attitude towards his subject-matter was mordantly satirical: not, one would have thought, conducive to success in a country where satire has often been regarded with suspicion and distrust.

In spite of these apparent drawbacks—and possibly because the stories dealt with people rather than abstractions—*The Wrong Set* achieved immediate popularity. Mr. Séan O'Faolain described it as "one of the outstanding books of this twenty years," and prophesied that, within another decade, Mr. Wilson would be "as well known and admired as Evelyn Waugh, Elizabeth Bowen, A. E. Coppard, or Ernest Hemingway." This prediction seemed likely to be fulfilled with the publication of *Such Darling Dodos,* a second collection which bore out abundantly the promise of the earlier volume, and *Hemlock and After,* whose ruthless yet compassionate treatment of a difficult theme made it one of the most discussed novels of 1952.

At the same time, it is possible to detect, on re-reading *Hemlock and After,* weaknesses not readily perceptible in Mr. Wilson's handling of the shorter form, but more amply revealed both in his recent play *The Mulberry Bush* and his latest novel *Anglo-Saxon Attitudes*. Certain obsessive preoccupations also become apparent when the stories are considered in relation to the later work. . . .

Not only physical but psychological patterns are often repeated: the possessive mother, . . . the lonely unwanted boy, compensating with dangerous daydreams, . . . the conflict between humanistic principles and the cruel atavistic urge. . . .

One of the stories' many outstanding merits was the fact that, while they were primarily concerned with the hidden mainsprings of character, they were also extremely rich in situation and plot: though this sometimes led to an effect of overcrowding, as if Mr. Wilson were in reality writing potted novels. But the glib, rapid, hectic manner which carried the reader breathlessly towards the appointed end concealed defects that become only too obvious when the author has more space at his command. A penchant for melodrama, for instance, already demonstrated by the holocaust which brought "Totentanz" to a conclusion, and indulged to the full in *The Mulberry Bush*. . . .

Anglo-Saxon Attitudes is by no means free from the same fault. Mr. Wilson, evidently determined to disprove the theory that short-story writers are unable to write novels on "the grand scale," has produced a book more than 400 pages long and containing forty-five main characters. . . . It must reluctantly be stated that this large cast is not controlled with the assurance which one would expect from a writer who has hitherto proved himself so adroit. The author has obviously attempted to include as many kinds of life as possible: to construct a novel of Dickensian or Zolaesque complexity; but the main plot-foundation is, alas, too frail to support the elaborate edifice built upon it.

Already, in *Hemlock and After,* Mr. Wilson's earlier dry, deft, clipped style was becoming encrusted with a growth of metaphors, but now the strict discipline imposed by the short-story medium has been altogether relaxed, with unfortunate results: there are definite signs of careless writing and passages of awkwardly phrased dialogue, while much of the text would not pass Mr. Wyndham Lewis's Taxi-Driver Test. *Anglo-Saxon Attitudes* is the current Book Society Fiction Choice, with a first printing of 35,000 copies: Mr. Wilson is therefore assured of the success which Mr. O'Faolain predicted for him, and there are still three years to go during which he may yet prove himself the equal of those writers mentioned in the other part of the critic's prophecy.

TLS. May 18, 1956, p. 296

Such a collection of characters [in *Hemlock and After*] is promising, especially when they are vividly realised and morally involved. Mr. Angus Wilson understands this and dives into their lives with alacrity and intelligence and sympathy. He is garrulous and epigrammatic but he moves quickly and at the right moment from person to person. The novel is closely patterned; indeed, one of its great pleasures is in its construction. But he is a personal novelist, filling out his characters by opinionating and also, of course, taking from them some of their autonomy in so doing. In this he is like D. H. Lawrence and not like George Eliot, our great duty-monger. He has no great care for style, is more for English truculence than English urbanity. He is wicked in epigram though less sharp in his satire in this novel than he was in his short stories. He succeeds in the portrayal of character, is rather parsimonious of scenes (there is more opinionating reminiscence and talk). There are one or two very good scenes, of course. . . .

In every generation one or two novelists revise the conventional picture of English character. Mr. Wilson does this. There was morbidity, madness, even sourness in his stories—precisely qualities which our sociable tradition eschewed. They needed to be introduced by someone with humanity. We needed to recover our broadness without losing our moral sense. He has also bedded out in our rank social soil some of the hot-house blooms of our Dickensian tradition. Mrs. Salad, for example, is a perennial London joy. This poetic old dear is nastier than Mrs. Gamp, for she is close to crime and is thoroughly shady. She was—she is—a lavatory attendant and no shame to her; but that is a life, not a fantasy. Mr. Wilson is subtle in conveying the social foundations of egocentricity. Mrs. Salad is not a middle-class joke. He has given his people moral natures. He sees England with what looks like a foreign eye. That, for me, is an important virtue in a novel which, in any case, impresses by its range and its power of stating issues.

V. S. Pritchett. *The Griffin.* Oct., 1956, pp. 18–19

There is nothing new, much less "foreign" in the style of Mr. Wilson or in his angle of vision; it is all "camp" of the sort to which British literature has accomodated itself for decades now. But *what* Mr. Wilson sees, as opposed to how he sees it, is a world quite different from that entered by, say, Mr. Waugh's Basil Seal; and his cast of characters [*Anglo-Saxon Attitudes*] is the product of quite special and recent events. . . . The point beneath the satire is a familiar one, the upper-class contempt for the "seriousness" and the thirst for "significance" of the disinherited, American or lower class, now moving into the universities to claim their share in a culture formerly reserved for gentlemen. . . . In this novel he has attempted to go beyond the scope of his early work . . . to create a major novel—complete with all the outward symbols of the Victorian thickness of texture for which he is evidently trying. . . .

In the end it all seems factitious, a manufactured frame not quite counterfeiting a full vision of life. . . . And at the moment of the Happy Ending (even this Mr. Wilson has not been able to eschew) it becomes not only factitious but false. . . . Such dénouement-juggling and moral-mongering are not really Mr. Wilson's forte; but I am pleased to say that around and above plot and point the amiable nastiness we know and admire in his stories continues to play.

Leslie Fiedler. *Cmty.* March, 1957, pp. 296–98

It must be apparent by now that a significant shift in fiction during the decade has been towards a renewal in the influence on contemporary writers of the Victorians. Or perhaps it would be more accurate to say that admiration for the amplitude and plenitude of the great Victorians has led some contemporary novelists to question what has often seemed the main tradition of the modern novel from James to Joyce and Virginia Woolf and attempt a return to something like nineteenth-century modes.

Snow and Cooper are examples of this. Another is Angus Wilson. . . . His first novel *Hemlock and After,* would, in any event, have created a sensation, since there is in it a much more open recognition of homosexuality than we have been used to in English fiction. The theme is the inadequacy of liberal values in the face of the evil in society. . . . It is a most ambitious novel, with a very large gallery of characters. As an exposure of the underworld and its inhabitants brought into being by the law relating to homosexuality in England, it is brilliantly terrifying. Judged by the highest standards, however—and these are the standards the book invokes—the novel, it seems to me, fails. Any novel that sets out to criticize society and man's fate in it must contain a representation of society that convinces, that we feel can stand for the actual society being criticized. Here Wilson is unsuccessful, partly because he falls into the old trap of the moralist, the habit of seeing human beings in hues of crude black and white. At times *Hemlock and After* seems no more than a moral melodrama; and the trouble is that very often the writing is at its most powerful precisely where the action is most melodramatic. . . .

Wilson, in fact, is a very literary writer, as became increasingly plain with *The Middle Age of Mrs. Eliot*. In this novel the rival he has set himself up against—one can scarcely say model—is not Dickens but George Eliot. In the character of Meg Eliot he is attempting, as becomes explicit during the course of the book, to create a heroine of a distinct kind that has engaged the talents of some of our greatest writers. She has been in her various avatars Jane Austen's Emma, George Eliot's Maggie Tulliver and Dorothea Brooke, Meredith's Clara Middleton and Henry James's Isabel Archer. . . .

The Middle Age of Mrs. Eliot is told in massive detail, in extremely slow motion, and Meg Eliot never emerges from the detail with the significance her author clearly intends her to have. There are many good things in the novel, brilliant snapshots of the contemporary scene; but it is as nearly a dull book as it is possible for Wilson to write. And in the last part of the book one has the disconcerting impression that he is taking with deadly seriousness what he would be satirizing and turning into heartless comedy in a short story. Wilson's real success still lies in his short stories. All the same, he is one of the very few of our contemporaries whose novels deserve to be judged by the highest standards. Powerful and original minds are always rare, and Wilson's is one.

Walter Allen. *The Novel Today*
(BC/Longmans, 1960), pp. 29–31

INTERVIEWER: Do you find writing comes easily to you?

WILSON: Yes. I write very easily. I told you *Hemlock* took four weeks. *Anglo-Saxon Attitudes* took four months, and an awful lot of that time was taken up just with thinking. The play—*The Mulberry Bush,* the only thing I've rewritten several times—was different again. My latest book of short stories, *A Bit off the Map,* took longer too, and my new novel is proving a bit difficult. But I'm not unduly worried. When one starts writing it's natural for the stuff to come rolling off the stocks—is that the right image?—rather easily. And, of course, the fact that it comes harder doesn't necessarily mean that it's worse. When Dickens published his novels in serial form he always added in his letter to the reader: "I send you this labor of love." After *Bleak House* he couldn't; it hadn't been a labor of love. But the later Dickens novels are certainly none the worse for that. . . . I wasn't aware of using any techniques, except that the book [*Anglo-Saxon Attitudes*] was concerned with echoes of memory. I think the reader should be unaware of techniques, though it's the critic's job to see them, of course. . . . the techniques used in *Anglo-Saxon Attitudes* are not just flashbacks as in the cinema, nor just episodic as in *Point Counter Point*—I've recently re-read that and can see no shape in it at all. If you examine the flashbacks in *Anglo-Saxon Attitudes*—and they took me a lot of trouble, I may say—you'll see that it is an ironic picking up of phrases. Marie Hélène says, "Life consists, I believe, in accepting one's duty, and that means often to accept the second best." This leads Gerald to remember his courtship of Ingeborg: he accepted the second best then, and it has ruined both his life and hers. This is an ironic comment on the cynical realism of Marie Hélène. It's not just cinema, you see, it's very carefully planned, though I say it myself. . . .

INTERVIEWER: Some people think you have an unnecessarily large number of vicious characters.

WILSON: I really don't know why people find my characters unpleasant. I believe—perhaps it would be different if I were religious—that life is very difficult for most people and that most people make a fair job of it. The opportunities for heroism are limited in this kind of world: the most people can do is sometimes not to be as weak as they've been at other times. When Evelyn Waugh reviewed *Hemlock and After* he was very percipient about techniques, but described the characters as "young cad," "mother's darling," and so on—terms it would never occur to me to use. I told him I thought the people he described in those terms had behaved rather well. Terence—the "young cad"—is on the make, certainly, but he behaves rather well in spite of that. And Eric does half break away from his mother—which is quite an achievement in the circumstances.

Of course, all my characters are very self-conscious, aware of what they are doing and what they are like. There's heroism in going on at all while knowing how we are made. Simple, naïve people I'm impatient of, because they haven't faced up to the main responsibility of civilized man —that of facing up to what he is and to the Freudian motivations of his actions. Most of my characters have a Calvinist conscience, and this is something which in itself makes action difficult. The heroism of my people, again, is in their success in making a relationship with other human beings, in a humanistic way, and their willingness to accept some sort of pleasure principle in life as against the gnawings of a Calvinist conscience and the awareness of Freudian motivations.

Writers at Work: The Paris Review Interviews,
ed. Malcolm Cowley (N.Y., Viking, 1958),
pp. 255, 259, 261

As to an author's attempt to discover what he can do about himself from what he has written, he is in a worse position than anybody else because of the far greater temptation to take liberties with the text! (It is his own, after all, he may feel.) Mr. Wilson . . . has fallen into this trap [in the Ewing lectures given at the University of California at Los Angeles in 1960 and published as *The Wild Garden*]. He discovers in his work a symbolism of "wild gardens" and "clearings in the wild" that he links up headily with his own late-flowering love of gardening and the fact that on one side of the family he is of colonial, pioneering stock from South Africa. The result—as the "meaning" of the symbolism thickens—is not to illuminate but seriously to blur our impression of the novels. In its smaller way, it is as though Shakespeare had written not only his plays but also the commentaries of Mr. Wilson Knight on them. . . . Mr. Wilson might have done better to keep his material for a straight autobiography.

TLS. Nov. 21, 1963, p. 947

WILSON, COLIN (1931–)

I must say I find Mr. Wilson's book [*The Outsider*] a disturbing addition to the prevailing anti-rational mode, feeling as I do that one is better off with too much reason than with none at all. I hate the idea of the kind of people who may already hanker after behaving like Stephen Dedalus being persuaded that there is fashionable authority for doing so, that they were right all along in attributing their folly and apathy to a source outside themselves and their control. And I hope Mr. Wilson is right when he says that those who have already volunteered for the Legion of the Lost would welcome demobilisation. How this is to be achieved I know no more than he does, and I agree that a course of PT and cross-country running, or a good dose of salts, would not quite meet the case. Perhaps there are curative properties in the notion that ordering up another bottle, attending a jam session, or getting introduced to a young lady, while they may solve no problems at all, are yet not necessarily without dignity, and while they may indicate no sensitivity at all, are yet not irreconcilable with it. Right: Legion of the Lost . . DIS-*MISS!*

Kingsley Amis. *Spec*. June 15, 1956, p. 831

Actually *The Outsider* is a kind of scrapbook, or an anthology with a thesis. Mr. Wilson has selected a point of view, which he calls that of the "Outsider," and has written what is in effect a linking commentary on literary illustrations of it. The illustrations range from Blake to Camus, and there are some biographical illustrations from George Fox to Nijinsky. Most of the examples are in fact from the nineteenth century, which makes the "mid-twentieth century malaise" even more difficult to swallow. To his tasks of selection and commentary Mr. Wilson has brought great enthusiasm, a certain expository clarity, and a seemingly genuine conviction. Moreover, the Outsider's "fundamental attitude: non-acceptance of life, of human life by human beings in a human society" (p. 18) is, in theory, quite widely held, so that both the examples and the commentary can be associated with a body of serious and important writing. Yet, if criticism now means anything, this is exactly the kind of book which might notably benefit from it; it is this process, as always, that the fixed alliance impedes.

The Outsider is *not* a critical work. Mr. Wilson uses, in his examples, work as different as Wells's pamphlet *Mind at the End of its Tether* and Dostoievski's *Brothers Karamazov,* without seriously considering whether differences of intention and success modify (as they must do) the apparent thesis. Further, in his analyses of particular works, he is not free from the familiar error of detaching extracts from their dramatic context, or of failing to take this whole context into account. . . . And, if it is not a critical work, it is hardly, in any serious sense, a philosophical work. Certainly it expounds an attitude, makes classifications within it, and recommends it. But the classifications are in fact vague, and the central attitude itself is, by the end of the book, rather miscellaneous.

Raymond Williams. *EC*. Jan., 1957, p. 69

Wilson's diagnosis of our disoriented society should be read because while often contradictory it is also adventurous and relevant, and I am going to predict that in five years' time, long after these recent incestuous squabblings have been forgotten, *The Outsider* and *Religion and the Rebel* will still be in and out of the public libraries all over the country, and will quietly be increasing and formulating thought. However, I hope they will never be swallowed whole, I hope that they will be read to be criticised—because, after supporting Wilson up to this point, I too now depart from him.

It is not Wilson's pessimism that bothers me at all—that seems to me comparatively mild and justifiable as far as it goes. It is his reasons for optimism which are not only morally unacceptable but which should be seen not to be accepted. After Mankowitz, Mortimer and others had charged him with Hitlerian strong man yearnings, Wilson seemed to steady up. He described himself to me as a "socialist," and said he detested cruelty and injustice. I am not disputing these claims, merely pointing out that, as far as I am aware, it was the first time he had made them—and this was after *Religion and the Rebel* appeared.

Meanwhile, there, in that book for evermore, are described attitudes that, if the book was honestly written, you have to accept as being his honest opinions. What does he say? He says that Sartre's doctrine of "commitment" is essential. The Outsider hates modern civilisation for its materialism: therefore he must not flee from it into an ivory tower, but *"seek power over it."* Again: he must "strive to become a moving force behind society; to acquire power for one's fellow men by becoming a power among them." Even more nakedly: "the Outsiders must achieve political power over the hogs."

Kenneth Allsop. *The Angry Decade*
(N.Y., British Book Centre, 1958), p. 180

Mr. Colin Wilson's latest book is an attempt to develop the theme of *The Lonely Crowd* by David Reisman of Harvard, who distinguishes between three types of men: the inner-directed man whose behaviour is largely determined by his own conception of what is right, the other-directed man whose ambition is to conform to what his neighbours expect, and the tradition-directed man. Mr. Wilson urges us to resist mass pressures and to become heroes. The theme of his opening chapter is "the Vanishing Hero," and he makes it clear that he is repelled by the fashionable modern "cult of the ordinary chap." And yet his own phenomenal success is mainly due to this cult. The century of the Common Man would also seem to be the century of the Common Thinker. The title of this book, *The Age of Defeat,* is faintly reminiscent of *The Decline of the West,* and Mr. Wilson's popular success after the Second World War was comparable with that of Spengler's after the First World War, a fact which is in itself significant of a certain deterioration of standards. Spengler was not only one of the most erudite but also one of the most original thinkers of this century, but it would be difficult to suggest any idea which Mr. Wilson has originated, and though he has read widely his many misquotations, summarised some time ago in a long letter to *The Times Literary Supplement,* irritate the scholarly. His own public, however, are unperturbed for they do not read *The Times Literary Supplement*. What they want is what Mr. Wilson so admirably provides, a popular digest of contemporary thought by "an ordinary chap." The populariser of philosophy has an important role to play at a time when it is difficult to lure people from television, and it is not the least of Mr. Wilson's merits that he may in time succeed to the position of that great populariser, the late C. E. M. Joad. In time, for Joad took a First in Greats, but Mr. Wilson is an insatiable reader and he is still young.

Sir Arnold Lunn. *EC.* March, 1960, pp. 142–43

There is, in fact, precious little to be said in favor of this four-hundred-and-forty-two page novel [*Ritual in the Dark*] except that it hasn't got a four-hundred-and-forty-third page.

Anthony West. *TNY.* Aug. 20, 1960, p. 108

I suspect . . . that Mr. Wilson is inclined to generalise confidently about an author when he has read only a small part of his output. It would be easy enough to dismiss his book [*The Strength to Dream*] as superficial and muddled. But I am reluctant to do this, for there is something decidedly attractive about Mr. Wilson's literary personality; he has an original mind, even if it doesn't produce very original conclusions. There are enough good and lively observations in his book to make one wish it added up to rather more.

Bernard Bergonzi. *MGW.* April 26, 1962, p. 7

WODEHOUSE, P. G. (1881–   )

The most lighthearted book of the season—one is almost tempted to say of *any* season—is to hand in Mr. Wodehouse's latest story [*The Prince and Betty*]. It would be idle to compare it with Mike or the immortal Psmith, or even with *Love Among the Chickens,* since it bears about the same proportion to those finished productions as does the harlequinade scene in a pantomime to light comedy. It does not pretend to be a true picture of life, at least we hope not. But it takes a far-fetched theme and rollicks and frolicks and effervesces about it to a quite delightful extent. It is funny. Just that. And when one thinks of all the dreary attempts to attain that end that have been made by professional and unprofessional humourists all the world over, we feel under a distinct debt of gratitude to the man who can make us laugh.

OutL. June 1, 1912, p. 807

The Girl in the Boat is the best of all Mr. Wodehouse's farces. Why go into details? The neatness with which absurdity is linked to absurdity, the unfading humour of his phrases, and the gaiety of his imagination put him in a class apart. And this time he has gone one better than himself. Mere recollection of the part played by John Peters in Sam's wooing is enough to make a man cut himself shaving or be removed for his chuckles from church.

H. C. Harwood. *OutL.* June 24, 1922, p. 510

If Plato has been called the Master of those who think, and Aristotle the Master of those who know, then how can Wodehouse fail to be the Master of those who laugh? What is the secret of this charm, so widely and so deeply felt? Some elements in the success of Wodehouse are easily seen. He blends English and American slang in so happy a way that he is as a humorist equally intelligible on both sides of the Atlantic; and his ambidexterity in this respect is not merely linguistic. . . . Further, all writing intended to amuse must, if it is to have more than the most transitory of appeals, possess a kind of formal perfection. Comic verse has to be very sound metrically; only a man of the very highest moral purpose can make Chablis and Rabelais rhyme. In amusing prose the appearance of spontaneity is the result of a self-discipline which the literary critic does not need to apply. The humorist loses his reader at once if the wheels are heard to creak; he is like a man telling a funny story after dinner who fumbles for words. Wodehouse never fails us in this:

Others abide our question: thou art Jeeves.

Some day there will be composed a "Beauties of Wodehouse," like the now forgotten work entitled "The Beauties of Shakespeare." It will include much of rare charm which lies in other parts of the Master's work. It will represent adequately all that portrayal of clerical life in which Wodehouse is the lineal and only successor of Trollope; it will give a selection (and what a tantalizing task its making will be, where all is *première cru*?) of the incomparable vignettes of life as it is lived elsewhere, in an editor's office, by an estate agent, by the keeper of a village drugstore, by peddlers of stock in nonexistent oil companies, by film actors, by members of the Junior Lipstick and the Senior Bloodstain Clubs and if there be any other clubs. It may draw on the Ukridgiana and the golfing stories, which, although my admiration can hardly be described as this side of idolatry I personally group with *Much Ado About Nothing* and *Timon of Athens* as parallels to Homer's alleged tendency to nod. But the center of the stage must always be occupied by the figure of Bertie Wooster, the Till Eulenspiegel of our time.

Arthur D. Nock. *Sat.* July 25, 1936, p. 5

WODEHOUSE, P. G.

A thing that people often forget about P. G. Wodehouse's novels is how long ago the better-known of them were written. We think of him as in some sense typifying the silliness of the nineteen-twenties and nineteen-thirties, but in fact the scenes and characters by which he is best remembered had all made their appearance before 1925. Psmith first appeared in 1909, having been foreshadowed by other characters in earlier school-stories. Blandings Castle, with Baxter and the Earl of Emsworth both in residence, was introduced in 1915. The Jeeves-Wooster cycle began in 1919, both Jeeves and Wooster having made brief appearances earlier. Ukridge appeared in 1924. When one looks through the list of Wodehouse's books from 1902 onwards, one can observe three fairly well-marked periods. The first is the school-story period. It includes such books as *The Gold Bat, The Pothunters,* etc., and has its high-spot in *Mike* (1909).... The next is the American period. Wodehouse seems to have lived in the United States from about 1913 to 1920, and for a while showed signs of becoming Americanised in idiom and outlook. Some of the stories in *The Man with Two Left Feet* (1917) appear to have been influenced by O. Henry, and other books written about this time contain Americanisms (*e.g.* "highball" for "whisky and soda") which an Englishman would not normally use *in propria persona.* Nevertheless, almost all the books of this period—*Psmith, Journalist; The Little Nugget; The Indiscretions of Archie; Piccadilly Jim* and various others—depend for their effect on the *contrast* between English and American manners. English characters appear in an American setting, or *vice versa:* there is a certain number of purely English stories, but hardly any purely American ones. The third period might fitly be called the country-house period. By the early nineteen-twenties Wodehouse must have been making a very large income, and the social status of his characters moved upwards accordingly, though the Ukridge stories form a partial exception. The typical setting is now a country mansion, a luxurious bachelor flat or an expensive golf club.

George Orwell. Windmill. Sept., 1945, pp. 12–13

If variety of achievement and gradual extension of scope are to be demanded as criteria of literary greatness, Mr. Wodehouse cannot be accorded a high rank. He developed his particular perfection early in his career, and has retained it for nearly forty years without divagation or experiment. In fact, part of his popularity depends upon his guaranteed consistency. In a world of shock and change, the Wodehouse novels are almost the only phenomena that can be trusted to remain true to an imperishable identity.

It is, indeed, by means of this intrepid consistency that Mr. Wodehouse has acquired one of his chief claims to be accounted among the permanent contributors to English literature—his creation of two or three characters which have become gradually familiar to the whole reading public. From Don Quixote to Sherlock Holmes, there are only a handful of fictitious personages who thus take on an existence of their own in the popular mind; Bertie Wooster and Jeeves seem to be the latest recruits to this select band. Some significance, then, may be found in the fact that the themes and characters in Mr. Wodehouse's stories have their predecessors in English drama and fiction at intervals for more than three hundred years. . . .

His chief characters are elegant, affected young men-about-town, whose vacuous manner can conceal considerable shrewdness. The secondary personages are practical and discreet servants, eccentric fathers or uncles, strong-minded dowagers, and husband-hunting young ladies. The action of the stories depends largely upon one type of situation, the "hoax"—sometimes verbal, in the form of elaborate and brazen lying, sometimes physical, as the "practical joke," or again what might be termed as the "hoax of fate," when misunderstanding and coincidence overwhelm a hapless victim with an accumulation of illusory disasters. The embellishment of wit ranges from epigram through exaggerated metaphor to the sheer insistence of colloquial catch-phrases.

Tracing these types and devices back through the centuries, one comes to the comedies of Ben Jonson, with corroborative material in the prose satires on contemporary London life, such as *The Gull's Hornbook*.

Lionel Stevenson. *AQ*. Autumn, 1949, pp. 226–27

The literary phenomenon concerning P. G. Wodehouse is not that he has been publishing books for nearly half a century (his first was about 1910) but that he is still writing from a frame of reference adopted during the first World War, and which draws from an even earlier era of English society.

His reading public went along happily with Wodehouse's initial supposition that Edwardian high society was alive and subject to kidding—as long as the author played that premise strictly for laughs. When social leveling in England progressed at a rate to make even the supposition ridiculous, Wodehouse, who hasn't seen much of England since the mid-Twenties, anyway, quickly shifted his stock in trade to Hollywood, a place of sufficient high incomes to make his books plausible once more. . . .

If anybody hears creaks in the ancient Wodehouse machine, I hope he will try to overlook it. Considering Wodehouse's long service of good-natured and well-meant entertainment, surely we can go along with him a while longer. At least another half-century.

Harrison Kinney. *NYT*. Nov. 4, 1951, p. 36

P. G. Wodehouse has been publishing for nearly sixty years. I have been reading him for forty. I have been a fan since boyhood. He seems to me a master of the ludicrous. He hit his stride in farce in the early 1920s, and is still going strong at the age of eighty. Among the top ten books of his whole output, I would include at least four that have appeared since the Second World War. If I had to pick one as his happiest, best constructed and most jewel-encrusted, I'd say *Joy in the Morning,* a Bertie Wooster-Jeeves novel which he published at the age of sixty-six. . . .

A criticism of Wodehouse's books . . . is that they repeat themselves. They do. In eighty books there are many repetitions of characters (under different names), situations and jokes. Wodehouse has chosen to till a fairly small field, and he has rotated his crops in a fairly tight cycle. In situation comedy, with recurrent characters, there is as much to be said for repetition as against it. Kipling didn't incessantly produce novels about artists who became war correspondents and went blind. Hardy didn't incessantly produce novels about pure farm girls seduced by gentleman rotters. But Kipling and Hardy weren't in the game of situation comedy. Ronald Searle, with his St. Trinian's girls, was, and we loved the repeated joke. If Tony Hancock has left his seedy lodgings at Railway Cuttings, East Cheam, we long wistfully for his return. We loved the old Ben Travers Aldwych farces, and expected each to repeat the pattern of the last; with Tom Walls barking, Ralph Lynn dithering, Mary Brough disapproving, Winifred Shotter fetching in pyjamas and Robertson Hare doubting and de-bagged. Situation comedy in good hands can stand a great deal of repetition and, when you get a good cast of actors together, their sameness from story to story can be half the fun. That is Wodehouse's line of country, and he has stuck to it with relish.

Richard Usborne. *Wodehouse at Work*
(Herbert Jenkins, 1961), pp. 13, 28

. . . I want to suggest an entirely new approach to Wodehouse: to claim him as a social realist of a high order—of, indeed, the higher orders. I realise, of course, that it is fashionable to consider social realism a matter exclusively of poverty and grime: Leila Yorke is herself under that very misapprehension, and it is only the brilliant plotting of Mr. Wodehouse, aided and abetted by Freddie Widgeon, Mr. and Mrs. Thomas G. Molloy and others, which puts her right. For an earl is as real a social phenomenon as a prostitute: a pity, perhaps, but there it is. Mr. Wodehouse's originality, and our pleasure, has been to realise that any earl is pottier than any ponce you care to name. . . . Mr. Wodehouse, seeing England from long distances of time and space, has constructed an imaginary world whose very ludicrousness prevents us from recognising it as our own here and now.

Julian Mitchell. Spec. Oct. 20, 1961, p. 550

Where Jeeves and Wooster are concerned, Mr. Wodehouse has hitherto, perhaps, been more at home in the short story rather than the novel form; but *Stiff Upper Lip, Jeeves* shows fewer signs of flagging than some of its predecessors. Indeed, the author's fertility of invention and ability to conduct his story at a spanking pace have never been more in evidence. Now in his eighty-second year, Mr. Wodehouse, for the entertainment he has given us alone, has as much claim as any to be considered (as Bertie Wooster might put it) the Grand Old Man of English L.

TLS. Aug. 9, 1963, p. 605

WOLFE, HUMBERT (1885–1940)

Mr. Wolfe is a very interesting poet. He is unusually spontaneous: the swift succession of his perceptions, the blithe and untrammelled way in which he throws them off, recall the more pleasing side of Rupert Brooke. He has, like Brooke, a rather dreamy, transcendental attitude to things; varied by that not altogether mature type of humour and urbanity that one associates with our older universities. To our thinking, he has a more delicate sensibility and a surer technique than his predecessor; but this judgment is not likely to be endorsed. So, by arriving in a decade that has grown more jaded and sophisticated emotionally, he has possibly missed "immortality"—though he has literally been broadcasted. But, to be serious about either of these writers, one would have to start by recalling the dictum of a French critic, that a poet needs feet as well as wings. Mr. Wolfe's manner, though we find it graceful, fresh, easy, quite individual, is not *personal* in the way that makes for durability. It is not the adequate, inevitable expression of a *whole* personality.

H. P. Collins. Crit. July, 1925, pp. 585–86

... I really believe Mr. Wolfe's grief is a fiction, and if he did not want me to, he should not dress up as Pierrot. He is to be congratulated on having troubled to make the fifty or so poems of *Humoresque* into a *book*. I can never see why poets should imagine that any order, any jumble of poems, so long as it is chronological or the titles look nice in the index, will do. Poems may result from the reaction after a wide space of years, with seemingly contradictory reactions doing the same in between; all these have to be correlated into some sort of whole. Mr. Wolfe has done this, but by a most unfortunate device. Who cares, or can be expected to care, a dried fig for Pierrot? Does not all this business of Moon and Pantaloon preclude any hope of sincerity? And heavens, what a title! The book as a whole is disappointing, and if I linger over its faults it is because it annoys me to see those wise ones who first dethroned Brooke, now lauding his insufficient disciple. It would be kinder to pass them over, but Mr. Wolfe ought to want something more than kindness. There are beautiful things in *Humoresque,* but nothing to touch the earlier, and Mr. Wolfe seems to be at pains to conventionalise his lyrical gift; "Boy in the Dusk" and "Harlequinade" (O dear!) alone retain the pleasant, unexpected lilt, like the swaying of a laden lilac bough, that gave so much freshness to last spring. Of course a poet must change; he should not stand still, *should* reach out and try—but Mr. Wolfe does not seem to reach out, he *is* standing still. . . .

Robert Herring. LM. May, 1926, p. 89

Mr. Humbert Wolfe is certainly no professor, but his pamphlet on *Romantic and Unromantic Poetry* was delivered as a lecture at the University of Bristol. It would be profitless to display the opinions decked out in Mr. Wolfe's sprightly and whipped-up style; it is less fatiguing to enjoy this artless artfulness, this innocently opulent development of the schoolboy's fine writing, for its own sake. After rushing us on an admiring Cook's Tour through the Georgian poets, Mr. Wolfe turns to make timorous and unrelated attack on the modern "unromantics." He achieves some bizarre couplings—Allen Tate, T. S. Eliot and Marianne Moore are dismissed with the same robust curtness. There is a final conciliatory gesture to Mr. Eliot when Mr. Wolfe stoops to "claim the best of the unromantic poets for the romantic." He takes his leave with a poem of his own composition which he hopes will clinch his argument. It does.

Gorley Putt. Scy. Sept., 1933, p. 208

. . . Some writers prove that the heroic couplet is still the most potent vehicle of social indictment. Humbert Wolfe's *News of the Devil* (1926) wielded loose run-on couplets in a shrewd if diffuse satire on the Press which at times had something of Samuel Butler's wit and fluency.

Geoffrey Bullough. The Trend of Modern Poetry
(Oliver and Boyd, 1934), p. 105

No contemporary career has been more barometric than Mr. Wolfe's. He came to the contest comparatively late in life. As he confesses in these essays [*Portraits by Inference*], "what I wrote first is of no moment or interest, except to me who had had to wait for my thirties to see my first proof." And that is not so long ago.

Since that time he has become that rare miracle, a poet who is a bestseller. By some trick of fate, personality, or by a perversity larger than his own conscious nature he has, like Heine, roused a storm of antagonists, one of whom stung too deeply. . . .

There are some critics who have not been able to join in the hue and cry against Mr. Wolfe; who, though unable to appreciate his literary window-dressing and too frequent up-stage tricks with the poetic limelight, nevertheless saw gleams in his work of an uncommon humanity, a wide and magnanimous insight into human motives and an appreciation of human heroism.

They shared too with the larger public a pleasure in his gift for expressing the nostalgias of the grown-up for the never-never lands of childhood and youth; a gift of the same kind as that of Hans Andersen. They felt too that he had introduced into modern letters a puckishness, a speed, and a technique of elision and allusiveness; qualities whose novelty made the reader gasp and experience almost a sense of physical giddiness when reading his verse.

It was obvious to them that such originality could not be snuffed out by a lampoon.

Their confidence was justified when Mr. Wolfe published *The Uncelestial City* and *Now a Stranger*. . . . Here was a writer, like his larger prototype Heine, realistic enough in his insight into social and personal problems, to be able to forget to attitudinize about them.

In these *Portraits by Inference* Mr. Wolfe develops the power of quick dramatization of the moment. He might call them *Portraits by Lightning Inference,* for though they are deliberate enough in their preparation, the sudden exposure of personality is done by a turn of wit that recalls Mr. Wolfe's naughtier and self-destructive methods whose audacity could not always be justified.

LL. Nov., 1934, pp. 231–32

WOODCOCK, GEORGE (1912–)

The young anarchist poet George Woodcock started a magazine *Now,* at first a most unpretentious poetry sheet, and later a quite influential paper. Originally purely literary, it gradually came to encompass most of the aspects of the new tendency and its catholicity of editorial policy was probably a shock to those who expect of a radical publication the

heresy hunting and dogmatism of the Marxist journals. Similarly, Woodcock's own poetry has been anything but tendentious.
Kenneth Rexroth. Introd. in The New British Poets,
ed. Kenneth Rexroth (N.Y., New Directions, 1949),
p. xxviii

The traditional view is that there is little of Wilde's literary work which is worth much, that Wilde the conversationalist and behaver is the significant figure. Tradition is often wrong and it is important that the facts should from time to time be re-examined to check it. This Mr. Woodcock has painstakingly done but the results of his re-examination of Wilde's writing and ideas [*The Paradox of Oscar Wilde*] seem to confirm, even, I suspect, for Mr. Woodcock himself, the traditional view. . . .

Mr. Woodcock who is, one gathers, an anarchist, does his best to show us what Wilde's ideas on Religion, Art, and Politics were, and to make of him an apostle of individualism, but it is difficult to take ideas as serious or contradictions as important paradoxes which seem so clearly to be simply strategies for an occasion. . . .

Concerning the one work of Wilde's upon the excellence of which we can all agree, *The Importance of Being Earnest,* Mr. Woodcock's own social interests make him see in Lady Bracknell "a satire on the snobbish values of the upper classes" and in Miss Prism and Dr. Chasuble respectively "Wilde's contempt for the educational system and the Church of his day." This seems to me a complete misrepresentation of what Wilde is trying to do, namely to portray the Garden of Eden as a spot quite different from the pagan island of the blest.
W. H. Auden. PR. April, 1950, pp. 390–94

Travel in Peru is cheap, if nothing else is, and Mr. Woodcock was enterprising [*Incas and Other Men*]. He took life as it came. He went over the Andes into the tropics, he came back to the fantastic desert, he saw the mountain mines. He studied the witchdoctors' cures in the Indian markets, he risked any kind of food and when he went down with South American dysentery it was mild and traceable to the food of the good hotels, not to the dirty places he and his wife found themselves in. . . . Mr. Woodcock's great virtue is that he is an educated traveller, going his own way, learning and seeing, not pretending to an intimacy or knowledge where he did not have them, never superficial in the jaunty know-all way of the rapid traveller who has been fed on booklets. He is never boring and he has the art of putting his travels before us, hour by hour.
V. S. Pritchett. NS. May 23, 1959, p. 728

Mr. Woodcock traces the origin of modern anarchism [*Anarchism*] from the Diggers, through Godwin, Proudhon, Bakunin, Kropotkin and Tolstoy. After a section which is mainly devoted to the great individual thinkers and their ideas he follows the international and the various national movements in great and separate detail. This is not a satisfactory way of organising the book since it involves both repetition and a sense of certain vital disconnections. . . .

Yet, apart from this organisational mistake it seems to me that this is a model of how such a book would have been written. Mr. Woodcock intrudes his own views so little that we are left in some doubt as to whether he himself is an anarchist or not, at least until the final and most personal chapter of the book. Yet he holds none the less a delicate moral thread from beginning to end, intervening just sufficiently to keep our senses alerted and a moral argument in being.

Philip Toynbee. *Obs.* June 30, 1963, p. 20

WOODHOUSE, C. M. (1917–)

. . . a word must be said about a book of singular promise published in 1950—*One Omen* by C. M. Woodhouse (born 1917). Among the imaginative books produced by young writers since the war none has impressed me more or given me more pleasure. His earlier book, *Apple of Discord* (1948) was an excellent account of the intricacies of Greek politics which he studied when he was wandering in Greek mountains with the tough men of the Resistance from 1942 to 1944, and afterwards when he held official posts in Athens. This second book, presented in the form of twelve "stories," shows that he has studied the technique of Russian writers. Here, giving rein to his imagination, he reveals a literary talent which should serve him in good stead as an imaginative writer on any theme that may attract him. He did fine work as a soldier. He is now doing fine work, intellectual and imaginative, as a writer.

R. A. Scott-James. *Fifty Years of English Literature:*
1900-1950 (Longmans, 1951), p. 187

In his introduction [to *British Foreign Policy Since the Second World War*] Mr. Woodhouse announces to reviewers that his book is superficial. One cannot quarrel with this statement, but his further description of his work as a critical examination of British foreign policy in the fifteen years under review is, unfortunately, not very apt. . . . It is a pity that this former director-general of the Royal Institute of International

Affairs, who has been a distinguished soldier, able businessman, and successful politician, should have written such a routine book. Clearly the reticence of high position is often a handicap to scholarship.

Henry R. Winkler. *Am. Hist. R.* Jan., 1963, p. 514

It has been said that this biography [*Rhodes*] is definitive, and it greatly enlarges without essentially changing our picture of Rhodes. J. G. Lockhart, and the Hon. C. M. Woodhouse, who completed the book after Lockhart's death, have made "full use of Rhodes Papers at Rhodes House, Oxford," and these are particularly valuable in relation to the negotiations for mining concessions in Southern Rhodesia, to the Jameson Raid . . ., and to the farcical intervention of Princess Radziwill in the last years of Rhodes's life. . . .

The weakness of this biography is its psychological naivety, and the authors' obvious feeling that Rhodes's stature would be diminished if it were admitted that he was by temperament homosexual. Rhodes's emotional feeling about his young secretaries, and in particular about Neville Pickering, to whom in one will he left "My worldly wealth," is well known, and to say that "there is no reason to doubt his later explanation that he was quite simply too busy to seek a wife in his youth, and that marriage would have distracted him from his ambitions," will hardly do at this time of day. Mystical idealism, that quality in Rhodes so highly valued by his contemporaries, is no less interesting when it is seen to have its roots in emotional frustration.

TLS. Sept. 20, 1963, p. 699

WOOLF, LEONARD (1880–)

One cannot be too grateful for the genuine literary criticism [*Essays on Literature, History, Politics*] contained in these essays, which differ profoundly from so many ephemeral jottings, piously preserved in the guise of books. Mr. Woolf is acute, penetrating, and, above all, intellectually sincere in his judgments, while the range of his imaginative sympathy is wide enough to include Ben Jonson and Mr. T. S. Eliot, Hazlitt and Miss Edith Sitwell. He can detect—and this perhaps is most rare of all—the failing of life in authors whose reputations continue to grow. Pages and pages of floundering dissection fail to disclose the real nerve as a few sentences of Mr. Woolf disclose it again and again. . . . All the literary essays may be said to present new aspects. . . .

J. A. T. Lloyd. *FR.* Oct., 1927, p. 576

Mr. Woolf has written a remarkable beginning to what promises to be a book of the first importance [*After the Deluge*]; and one reader, at least, will wait with eager anxiety for its sequel. Few recent works of this magnitude have combined so many attractive qualities. He writes with a crystal clarity. His reading is wide, his illustrations singularly happy; and he has what is very nearly genius for the apposite quotation. I do not know whether it is the residential proximity of Mr. Lytton Strachey which is responsible for Mr. Woolf's felicitous use of the supreme weapon of irony. I can only record my impression that rarely in modern times has it been so skillfully employed.

Mr. Woolf deals with a complex theme; and it is not easy to state briefly the thesis he is examining. In one sense he is writing the history of the democratic idea since the eighteenth century. In another he is seeking to explain how the ideas of a community form a kind of matrix from which the life-history of an individual at any given period receives its form. His theme is the mighty one that idea-systems beget their children in partial independence of actual events, so that these are always being shaped and twisted by traditions from which they are seeking to escape. I can, perhaps, best explain the vastness of his system if I say that the explanation he is making of the contour of our lives includes not merely that Marxian analysis which is the main clue to the whole, but shows also how the economic environment of some given generation begets ideas which, so to say, come to have hands and feet. It is a gigantic task; and Mr. Woolf himself would be the first to agree that it is too early to predict that he will be successful in accomplishing it. To construct a really satisfactory philosophy of history is, after all, one of the supreme intellectual adventures. But whatever the ultimate outcome, the sense of excitement one has in reading Mr. Woolf's pages deserves emphatic gratitude.

My anxiety is that Mr. Woolf should be read; and I therefore desire here merely to name some of the things in his book which seem to me of quite exceptional interest. There is a remarkable picture of the difference between the mind of Europe in 1789 and that mind in 1900; and the discussion there of the influence of the philosophers upon the French Revolution is quite masterly.

Harold J. Laski. *NSN*. Oct. 17, 1931, p. 486

In Mr. Leonard Woolf's estimates of what is good and bad [*Principia Politica*], what is important and what is unimportant, I have found only one thing to query, and that is his very high estimate of the ancient Greeks in the political and ethical spheres. Intellectually and artistically, I could acquiesce in almost any degree of praise; but in practical affairs they made much the same mistakes as are being made at the present day. . . .

WOOLF, LEONARD

The title of the book, *Principia Politica,* is somewhat misleading. The book is not a general treatise on the theory of politics in the style of Aristotle or Hobbes. It is, one gathers, one of a number of volumes, some published, others not yet written, which, in their entirety, will be worthy of the title. But this volume is concerned almost entirely with a narrower question, namely: Can a technically advanced society be stable under a totalitarian dictatorship? This question is of the most urgent present-day importance, and Mr. Woolf's discussion of it is at once broad and penetrating.

Bertrand Russell. *Enc.* Nov., 1953, p. 75

Mr. Woolf is not, and was never, a silly. The society of these friends at Cambridge and later has been the most important thing in his life; yet he had other friends and interests outside theirs. He is intellectually tough as well as sensitive. He prides himself on a congenital absence of a sense of sin. He persists in thinking that our society has made progress in his lifetime. Though he was caught up in all that excitement, he is not a man to believe that a life can be a work of art; he calls himself, from the age of ten, "a fully developed human being, mean, cowardly, untruthful, nasty, and cruel." But, cool and unillusioned as he is, he would not allow anybody to traduce that experiment in civility. We may look back to it, perhaps, as in its way one of those moments in which life, as in Yeats's Byzantium, takes on a formed, brimming perfection like that of art, and appears for an instant motionless before it flows over the basin's rim. For time, whether real or not, has elapsed, and although, in Lowes Dickinson's view, the springs of action "lie deep in ignorance and madness," acts have occurred, acts unthinkable in Trinity Great Court in 1903; yet this civility is also a matter of history, and it is a great pleasure to read Mr. Woolf's account [*Sowing*] of it.

Frank Kermode. *Spec.* Sept. 9, 1960, p. 378

Leonard Woolf was one of Bloomsbury's founding fathers. Now in his eightieth year, for close on half a century he has been one of England's most distinguished radical journalists, editors, and political thinkers. He is equally distinguished as a publisher; with his wife, Virginia Woolf, he founded The Hogarth Press, for many years the most continuously exciting of British publishing firms. Though the first volume [*Sowing*] of his autobiography takes him only to his twenty-fifth year, when he went down from Cambridge University, it makes a perfect introduction to the spirit and tone of Bloomsbury at its best, for Bloomsbury, despite its name, was rooted in the Cambridge of the beginning of the century.

At the book's end the author is leaving for Ceylon to take up a post in the Colonial service.

Sowing is written with great distinction. The prose is vigorous and clear, an admirable vehicle for the expression of downright opinions. . . . But his prose is also an admirable vehicle for the description of a late nineteenth-century middle-class neighborhood in London. He may not recreate his childhood as a poet would, but his memories of himself as a child he sets down with a vivid clarity.

Walter Allen. NYT. Oct. 2, 1960, p. 5

Mr. Woolf has powers of attentive memory of particulars and an inspired naiveté and love of truth which at moments make his descriptions of childhood, and some of his observations, remind one of Tolstoy's account of his Childhood, Boyhood, and Youth. Indeed there is something Tolstoyan about Mr. Woolf's view [*Sowing*] that everyone is, or was, in childhood, the same creature, behind the mask of acquired characteristics which he assumes at a certain age in order to confront his fellow-adults, or adolescents. . . .

Mr. Woolf does not believe in original sin yet he understands the subjective truth of each person's loneliness, inferiority, and animal nature. He is religious without having a religion, in modern terms a liberal, but with a past like a halo surrounding him with shining qualities of Hebrew and Greek civilisations.

His penetration rarely fails, yet his descriptions of his Cambridge friends, those Apostles who afterwards became the demi-gods of Bloomsbury, fall just short of being finally convincing.

Stephen Spender. Enc. Jan., 1961, p. 72

WOOLF, VIRGINIA (1882–1941)

But what of the subject that she regards as of the highest importance: human beings as a whole and as wholes? She tells us (in her essays) that human beings are the permanent material of fiction, that it is only the method of presenting them which changes and ought to change, that to capture their inner life presents a different problem to each generation of novelists; the great Victorians solved it in their way; the Edwardians shelved it by looking outwards at relatives and houses; the Georgians must solve it anew, and if they succeed a new age of fiction will begin. Has she herself succeeded? Do her own characters live?

I feel that they do live, but not continuously, whereas the characters of Tolstoy (let us say) live continuously. With her, the reader is in a state of constant approval. "Yes that is right," he says, each time she implies something more about Jacob or Peter: "yes that would be so: yes." Whereas in the case of Tolstoy approval is absent. We sink into André, into Nicolay Rostoff during the moments they come forth, and no more endorse the correctness of their functioning than we endorse our own. And the problem before her—the problem that she has set herself, and that certainly would inaugurate a new literature if solved—is to retain her own wonderful new method and form, and yet allow her readers to inhabit each character with Victorian thoroughness. Think how difficult this is. If you work in a storm of atoms and seconds, if your highest joy is "life; London; this moment in June" and your deepest mystery "here is one room; there another," then how can you construct your human beings so that each shall be not a movable monument but an abiding home, how can you build between them any permanent roads of love and hate? There was continuous life in the little hotel people of *The Voyage Out* because there was no innovation in the method. But Jacob in *Jacob's Room* is discontinuous, demanding—and obtaining—separate approval for everything he feels or does. And *Mrs. Dalloway?* There seems a slight change here, an approach towards character-construction in the Tolstoyan sense; Sir William Bradshaw, for instance, is uninterruptedly and embracingly evil. Any approach is significant, for it suggests that in future books she may solve the problem as a whole. She herself believes it can be done, and, with the exception of Joyce, she is the only writer of genius who is trying. All the other so-called innovators are (if not pretentious bunglers) merely innovators in subject matter and the praise we give them is of the kind we should accord to scientists. ... But they do not advance the novelist's art. Virginia Woolf has already done that a little, and if she succeeds in her problem of rendering character, she will advance it enormously. [1925]

E. M. Forster. *Abinger Harvest*
(Edward Arnold, 1936), pp. 110–11

To the Lighthouse is a story about Mrs. Ramsay, but in a sense her death is a minor incident brought in to show how her influence lived after her; things centre round her in the third part just as continuously, with just as little natural climax, as they did in the first. You might indeed say that it is hopeless to look for an orderly plot about such a heroine, because the things that are interesting about her make a plot irrelevant. And yet it is a mistake to suppose that you can say even those things in a novel without a plot.

Mrs. Woolf's later style is very beautifully adapted to the requirements of this subject; so much so as to attack very directly the problem of motivation. Indeed I think it is for this that she will chiefly be remembered; in this administrative but domestic setting, by the very structure of the sentences, we are made to know what it felt like for the heroine to make up her mind. Of course in itself this is not new; it is the main business of a novelist to show his reader, by slow accumulations, all the elements and proportions of a decision, so that the reader knows how the character felt about it; but Mrs. Woolf, so as to be much more immediately illuminating, can show how they are at the back of a decision at the moment it is taken.

We arrive, for instance, with some phrase like "and indeed" into a new sentence and a new specious present. Long, irrelevant, delicious clauses recollect the ramifications of the situation (this part corresponds to the blurring of consciousness while the heroine waits a moment to know her own mind; and it is here, by the way, that one is told most of the story); then by a twist of thought some vivid but distant detail, which she is actually conscious of, and might have been expected to finish the sentence, turns her mind towards the surface. From then on the clauses become shorter; we move towards action by a series of leaps, each, perhaps, showing what she would have done about something quite different, and just at the end, without effort, washed up by the last wave of this disturbance, like an obvious bit of grammar put in to round off the sentence, with a partly self-conscious, wholly charming humility in the heroine (how odd that the result of all this should be something so flat and domestic), we get the small useful thing she actually did do. . . . All one can say against the wilful and jumping brilliance of Mrs. Woolf's descriptive passages is that, as part of a design, they come to seem unsatisfying; however delicate and brightly coloured they seem cut in low relief upon the great block she has taken for her material, and even when you are sure that some patch is really part of the book you often cannot (as you can in my two examples) see why it should be. Of course her methods catch intensely a sense of period, of setting, of the immediate person described; are very life-like, in short; and I do not know how far it may be due to just this quality; to the fact that so many of her images, glittering and searching as they are, spreading out their wealth of feeling, as if spilt, in the mind, give one just that sense of waste that is given by life itself. ". . . the great revelation perhaps never did come. Instead, there were little daily miracles, illuminations, matches struck unexpectedly in the dark."

"How far that little candle sheds its beams"; but still it is the business of art to provide candelabra, to aggregate its matches into a lighthouse of many candlepower. If only (one finds oneself feeling in re-reading these novels), if only these dissolved units of understanding had been co-ordinated into a system; if only, perhaps, there was an index, showing what had been compared with what; if only these materials for the metaphysical conceit, poured out so lavishly, had been concentrated into crystals of poetry that could be remembered, how much safer one would feel.

William Empson in Scrutinies, II, coll. Edgell Rickword
(Wishart, 1931), pp. 210–11, 215–16

Because it is in an almost continuous state of moral and intellectual relaxation that Mrs. Woolf's characters draw out their existence, they can be projected only through a more or less direct transcription of their consciousness. Such a qualification is necessary, however, for the method here is rarely if ever as direct as that of Joyce or his followers. Between the consciousness and the rendition of it there is nearly always interposed a highly artificial literary style. This style remains practically uniform for all the characters; it is at once individual and traditional. The effect of its elegant diction and elaborately turned periods is to make one feel at times as if these sad and lonely people were partly compensated for the vacuity of their lives by the gift of casting even their most random thoughts in the best literary tradition. . . .

Here also Mrs. Woolf is pre-eminently the poet; for as an unwillingness to use motives and actions led to her substitution of poetic symbols in their stead so is she also compelled to use a metaphorical rather than a narrative style. In this practice of course she is not without precedent; other novelists have relied on metaphor to secure their finest effects of communication. But while such effects are ordinarily used to heighten the narrative, they are never extended to the point where they assume an independent interest. In Mrs. Woolf's books metaphorical writing is not occasional but predominate; from the beginning it has subordinated every other kind; and it was inevitable that it should one day be segmented into the purely descriptive prose-poems of *The Waves*. [1932]

William Troy in Literary Opinion in America,
ed. Morton Dauwen Zabel, Vol. I
(N.Y., Harper Torchbooks, 1962), pp. 333–34

Virginia Woolf seemed to have the worst defect of the Mandarin style, the ability to spin cocoons of language out of nothing. The history of her literary style has been that of a form at first simple, growing more and more elaborate, the content lagging far behind, then catching up, till, after the falseness of *Orlando,* she produced a masterpiece in *The Waves.*

Her early novels were not written in an elaborate style. Her most significant early book is *Monday or Tuesday* (1921) and demonstrates the rule that Mandarin prose is the product of those who in their youth were poets. In short it is romantic prose. Not all poets were romantic prose writers (e.g. Dryden) but most romantic prose writers have attempted poetry.

The development of Virginia Woolf is the development of this lyrical feeling away from E. M. Forster, with his artlessness and simple, poetical, colloquial style, into patterns of her own. The reveries of a central character came more and more to dominate her books. In *The Waves* she abandoned the convention of the central figure and described a group of friends, as children, as young people and finally in late middle age. In a series of tableaux are contrasted the mystery of childhood, the promise of youth, the brilliance of maturity and the complex, unmarketable richness of age. If *The Years* seems an impressionist gallery with many canvases, landscapes, portraits, and conversation pieces, then *The Waves* is a group of five or six huge panels which celebrate the dignity of human life and the passage of time. It is one of the books which comes nearest to stating the mystery of life and so, in a sense, nearest to solving it. [1938]

Cyril Connolly. *Enemies of Promise*
(N.Y., Macmillan, 1948), p. 49

Perhaps of all writers on literature, Virginia Woolf is the least "critical" in the day-of-judgment meaning of the word. She writes plastically, molding little busts and cameos of people, times and places; her every word is a revelation of her individual sensibility, and one might suspect that she has no regard for general principles at all, so little does she parade them and so modestly does she qualify the range and validity of her wider judgments. When speaking of Russian or American literature, for instance, she is careful to stress the fact that she is a foreigner, an Englishwoman, a lover of gardens, quiet, and Jane Austen. But this does not prevent her from seeing that Miss Austen may be likened to the Greek tragedians, "though with a thousand differences of degree: she, too, in her modest, everyday prose, chose the dangerous art where one slip means death." She is one of the few imaginative writers who can apply their own artistic methods to criticism without ever violating its first canon: to bring the reader closer to the book, the particular, than he could have come unaided—to "make it new," as Pound tried to do, and so often ended by making it Pound. She can instill a deeper awareness of the nature of writing by analyzing a page of Flaubert, as she does in "Re-reading Novels" in this new volume, than you could get from an entire treatise, even a good one, on truth and value in art, or contemporary significance in fiction. No writer about books surpasses her in immediacy, in the ability to convey "knowledge of" as distinguished from "knowledge about."

Frank Jones. *PR*. May, 1948, p. 592

Now come the extracts from the diary [*A Writer's Diary*] she kept, irregularly, from 1915 to within four days of her death in 1941, a deliberate revelation and pitiless self-examination of that strange make-up which was her mind. She regarded it as good practice, rather as an athlete regards his exercises for limbering up. . . .

No-one could seem dull to her, with her capacity for making people up; the portrait might bear no relation to reality, or perhaps she had a reality of her own. Yet people were a worry, for she was much sought after, and the interruption got between her and what she most wanted to do: she has again been held up by her accursed love of talk. "Incessant company," she writes in a moment of excerbation, "is as bad as solitary confinement." For there was only one thing she wanted to do, and that was to live her own arduous inner life as a writer. It is here that we begin to reach the depths and to uncover both the anguish and the ecstasy. To lead this life was perhaps harder for her than for most writers, not only for reasons of health but because the balance of what she wanted to say and the way in which she wanted to say it was so exceedingly precarious; how to keep the flight of the mind, as she puts it, and yet to be exact. A false step, and she will be off the stretched wire. It is the problem of seeing with the intensity natural to her, and at the same time of exercising the craftsman's control; the eternal problem of the artist, in her case rendered the more acute by her peculiar temperament and the ever-experimental character of her work. What she was reaching after we shall never quite know, and perhaps she did not quite know it herself. There is a groping, and from time to time a hint, a moon of light at the end of a tunnel; but of the intensity there can be no question. . . .

We may smile at her uncertainties, but there is no smiling at the profound sense of tragedy which underlay her high spirits and her fun. Outright she says that no one knows how she suffers, walking up a London street, nor how deep is her great lake of melancholy. . . .

. . . as the years go by the diary makes it clearer and clearer that she had no desire to follow obediently in the accepted tradition of narrative and characterisation. She is in pursuit of something far more elusive, which could be attained only by oblique methods of her own. She was trying to do something very difficult, trying to express the inexpressible, like someone gifted with seeing a colour not visible to human eyes, or hearing a sound not audible to human ears. She was perfectly well aware that her interests as a writer—she calls it her *only* interest—lay in "some queer individuality of my own, not in strength, or passion, or anything startling, but then I say to myself, is not 'some individuality' precisely the quality I respect?" And then, her acumen as a critic suddenly shooting out its chameleon tongue, she captures Donne and Peacock into the same company as herself.

V. Sackville West. Enc. Jan., 1954, pp. 71–72, 74

Virginia, holding a cigarette, would lean forward before speaking and clear her throat with a motion like that of a noble bird of prey, then, as she spoke, excitement would suddenly come as she visualized what she was saying and her voice would crack, like a schoolboy's, on a higher note. And in that cracked high note one felt all her humour and delight in life. Then she would throw herself back in her chair with a hoot of laughter, intensely amused by her own words. . . .

When Virgiina came over from Asheham she brought the wind off the Downs into the house with her. She had a warmth and good-fellowship which set people at their ease; she had the gift for sudden intimacy which I had found so charming in D. H. Lawrence when I had first met him. Her voice and her glance were filled with affection, mockery, curiosity, comradeship. She would put a hand on one's shoulder and as she propelled one about the garden, between the flower beds, she would ask some reckless question which flattered and disturbed. Her interest was exciting and left one tingling with satisfied vanity or doubts about oneself. . . .

Virginia was a wonderful raconteur—she saw everyone, herself included, with detachment, and life itself as a vast Shakespearian Comedy. She loved telling stories at her own expense—some of them as ribald as anything in Chaucer—for all her personal vanity was forgotten in the storyteller's art. . . .

There was much of the same reckless imagery in her conversation that gives such individuality to her novels.

David Garnett. L. Sept., 1955, pp. 54–55

Virginia Woolf's conceptions of form and self owe a great deal to ideas she had absorbed in her wide reading of both the English romantic poets and Proust and the *fin de siècle* French writers. Her readings enriched her ambivalent conscience, which strained simultaneously toward a projection of the world as a symbolic image and toward its vision as a distinct entity with which the self must come to terms. For this reason, her fusion of novel and poem did not lead, as might be expected, to a dilution of the novel. Rather, it intensified the novelist's task of making, with Jane Austen, "the moment to glow." The elements of each novel became images in a picture that reflects "facts" in their universal dimensions. . . .

The manner in which the interior monologue is used is an additional source of the lyrical design. Mental associations proceed independently of time or cause and facilitate the interweaving of motifs. But although inner speech was of great importance to her narrative, Virginia Woolf's main object was to use the stream of consciousness poetically and to integrate it into the design as a whole in conjunction with other images. On a lyrical level, therefore, the interior monologue served a peculiar aesthetic end. It converted association into formal soliloquies, imposing controlled imagery on inner speech. The significance of her stream of consciousness is not only that it is logical and planned, as David Daiches has shown, but also that it is used obliquely, transposing each thought into an image that expresses the thought. . . .

The Waves is the only novel in which Mrs. Woolf found a complete expression of her aims. Restless as any writer must be who searches for perfection, she turned to a relatively more conventional form in *The Years* (1937), in which time is both more loosely rendered and more externally perceived. Only in *Between the Acts,* posthumously published in 1941, might a reconciliation have been found had she lived to complete it. . . . In *Between the Acts,* the problems of *The Waves* approach their solution. The moment of illumination in life is juxtaposed with an archetypal image of time; the social world is transfixed by a mythical world through the intervention of art. Both levels are brought together by the performance of a play which acts simultaneously as the content of the novel and as a symbolic motif.

Ralph Freedman. *The Lyrical Novel* (Princeton, N. J., Princeton Univ. Pr., 1963), pp. 201–2, 218–19, 268–69

In its structural severity **Between the Acts** resembles a musical composition, or a poetic drama. Like these it rewards vigilant attention and increasing familiarity and yet gives immediate pleasure at a first reception. Few novels have this kind of form. In some ways **Between the Acts** is an advance upon **Mrs. Dalloway, To the Lighthouse** or **The Waves** because, without loss of depth, it has greater width of interest and greater variety of effect than they have. It owes more to the comic spirit. All her novels include the humour that depends upon fantasy and a perception of the grotesque, but the later and more characteristic work does not elsewhere include as much of the comedy of manners. At the surface the book is predominantly about contrasted manners and values. The characters, shrewdly observed and amusingly presented, are juxtaposed so as to offset one another, the scenes are comic, at times even farcical, as often as they are moving. It is a picture of present-day English life and manners in a setting which evokes the past history of England and forebodings of the future. But the full significance of the book depends, as in all her characteristic work, upon the sequence of scenes, the juxtaposition of experiences which throw light on one another, the recurrent images or symbols and (even more here than elsewhere) the variations of rhythm.

At the heart of the book lie the ageless paradoxes: man's insatiable thirst for the ideal and his constant preoccupation with the trivial; the "dateless limit" of human history and the "brief candle" of an individual life.

Joan Bennett. *Virginia Woolf* (N.Y., Harcourt Brace, 1945), p. 150

YEATS, WILLIAM BUTLER (1865-1939)

Mr. Yeats is the only one among the younger English poets who has the whole poetical temperament, and nothing but the poetical temperament. He lives on one plane, and you will find in the whole of his work, with its varying degrees of artistic achievement, no unworthy or trivial mood, no occasional concession to the fatigue of high thinking. It is this continuously poetical quality of mind that seems to me to distinguish Mr. Yeats from the many men of talent, and to place him among the few men of genius. . . . And that, certainly, is the impression which remains with one after a careful reading of the revised edition of Mr. Yeats' collected poems and of his later volume of lyrics, *The Wind Among the Reeds*. . . .

The lyric, in its first, merely personal stage, a symbol, it can be expressed only by symbol; and Mr. Yeats has chosen his symbolism out of Irish mythology, which gives him the advantage of an elaborate poetic background, new to modern poetry. I am not sure that he does not assume in his readers too ready an acquaintance with Irish tradition, and I am not sure that his notes, whose delightfully unscientific vagueness renders them by no means out of place in a book of poems, will do quite all that is needed in familiarising people's minds with that tradition. But after all, though Mr. Yeats will probably regret it, almost everything in his book can be perfectly understood by any poetically sensitive reader who has never heard of a single Irish legend, and who does not even glance at his notes. For he has made for himself a poetical style which is much more simple, as it is much more concise, than any prose style; and, in the final perfecting of his form, he has made for himself a rhythm which is more natural, more precise in its slow and wandering cadence, than any prose rhythm. It is a common mistake to suppose that poetry should be ornate and prose simple. It is prose that may often allow itself the relief of ornament; poetry, if it is to be of the finest quality, is bound to be simple, a mere breathing, in which individual words almost disappear into music. Probably, to many people, accustomed to the artificiality which they mistake for poetical style, and to the sing-song which they mistake for poetical rhythm, Mr. Yeats' style, at its best, will seem a little bare, and his rhythm, at its best, a little uncertain. They will be astonished, perhaps not altogether pleased, at finding a poet who uses no inversions, who says in one line, as straightforward as prose, what most poets would dilute into a stanza, and who, in his music, replaces the aria by the recitative. How few, it annoys me to think, as I read over this simple and learned poetry, will realise the extraordinary art which has worked these tiny poems, which seem as free as waves, into a form at once so monumental and so alive! Here, at last, is poetry which has found for itself a new form, a form really modern, in its rejection of every artifice, its return to the natural chant out of which verse was evolved; and it expresses, with a passionate quietude, the elemental desires of humanity, the desire of love, the desire of wisdom, the desire of beauty. [1900]

Arthur Symons. *Studies in Prose and Verse* (Dent., n.d.), pp. 230, 234–35

This book [*Later Poems*] is anything but a duplicate of its predecessor, or even a twin. Mr. Yeats's poetry is other than it was. The observation is frequently made, and it is often coupled with a suggestion that his art has deteriorated. People want him to go on writing "Innisfree." One sometimes suspects that such critics are more familiar with Mr. Yeats in anthologies than in the series of his published volumes. So far as that goes, it may be conjectured that the anthologists of the future will draw more upon this second collection than upon the first. . . . Much of the finest work in it is of a new kind and less obvious in its appeal. Perhaps the difference might be roughly indicated if one said that when people did not understand one of Mr. Yeats's old poems they thought it nevertheless charming, but that when they do not understand one of his new poems they think it dull. . . . still, in many essentials Mr. Yeats has not changed. His preoccupation with religion remains. His attitude towards civilisation is what it has always been: . . . He still, and in his poetry, stands for two cultures and two traditions, the aristocratic scholarly and the popular, both sustained by ceremony and fed by the free imagination; he has always cared about the world and Ireland and has not changed his opinions about their diseases. . . .

. . . he is on the whole to be ranked with the learned and the intellectual poets, the cryptic and the hierophantic, the philosophers who explore strange regions of thought, the contemplatives who burrow into the recesses of the mind, the questioners who accept nothing which they have not closely examined, the scholars who make references of which the savour is reserved for those equal in knowledge, the experimentalists who are not satisfied with anything ready made in picture or rhythm, the craftsmen who labour for a perfection the nature of which few will comprehend. [1921]

J. C. Squire. *Essays on Poetry* (N.Y., George H. Doran, n.d.), pp. 162–63, 169

We hardly go to Yeats in search of information. This is Dodona, and we are privileged to sit under the eaves on the oracle's dog-days, watching the private exfoliation of a solitary mind, a peacock at a pool. If we could avoid the irritation of being made appear deaf, and a little vulgar, it would be a wholly profitable entertainment. It would be more: for though we may find very little, if anything, in these reprints of reviews or prefaces [*Essays: 1931-36*], that adds to what we know already (from *Ideas of Good and Evil*) about the composition of Yeats's poetry it is grand to find the first poet of our time declaring yet once again for the fluid personality, a condition of fire, spiritual, inspiring, as against the mechanical dialectic of the post-romantic materialists. There is no fighter so grand as an old fighter.

But to make the critical point—I have read the essay on Berkeley three times over, with care and interest; and what it says might be said in one page. Even then it would be a series of glissades from one point to another barely connected. . . .

Yet even without being analytical, there are many passing references, and wide generalizations that distend the mind rather than fill it, that have to be jettisoned by the way. . . . So it is through nine-tenths of Yeats's prose. I remember an account of a meeting in Boston, between Santayana and Yeats, when Yeats spread his cloths of gold and the coldly sceptical philosopher was a little bored; and how AE used to say that Yeats did not care two pins about Truth—all he wanted was a phrase. . . .

But it *is* enough if these essays be thought of as a solemn frolic of the mind. . . . No poet's prose can be much more than that—a gloss on his poetry and its composition.

Seán O'Faoláin. *LM*. Feb., 1938, pp. 434–35

Yeats never—rarely if we look through the whole body of the collected poems, never if we look at that segment of them which seems destined to stand—requires much editorial gloss to explain a symbol because it is the property of an occult sodality or because it is private to himself alone. (In this he contrasts with Mr. Eliot.) The symbol is objective and easy, or else it is actually developed a little way so that the "impartial spectator" who reads (and who stands in our mind for the test of the poem's objectivity) can go on and obtain a sufficiently clear and exciting image to answer to it. There is an interesting point of biography here which it would be a service in some historian to clear up. Much of the prose of Yeats is far more difficult than any of the verse, being crowded with obscure and unaided symbols. It is as if his scruple in the poetry were his sense of a professional responsibility, while his prose is for his own consumption. Florid Neo-Platonism, theosophy, even a little astrology, for his privacy, but in his poetry only symbols fit for the public currency. [1939]

> J. C. Ransom in *The Permanence of Yeats,*
> ed. James Hall and Martin Steinmann
> (N.Y., Macmillan, 1950), p. 101

Certainly, for the younger poets of England and America, I am sure that their admiration for Yeats's poetry has been wholly good. His idiom was too different for there to be any danger of imitation, his opinions too different to flatter and confirm their prejudices. It was good for them to have the spectacle of an unquestionably great living poet, whose style they were not tempted to echo and whose ideas contradicted those in vogue among them. You will not see, in their writing, more than passing evidences of the impression he made, but the work, and the man himself as poet, have been of the greatest significance to them for all that. . . . Yeats would not have this influence had he not become a great poet; but the influence of which I speak is due to the figure of the poet himself, to the integrity of his passion for his art and his craft which provided such an impulse for his extraordinary development. When he visited London he liked to meet and talk to younger poets. People have sometimes spoken of him as arrogant and over-bearing. I never found him so; in his conversations with a younger writer I always felt that he offered terms of equality, as to a fellow worker, a practitioner of the same mystery. It was, I think, that, unlike many writers, he cared more for poetry than for his own reputation as a poet or his picture of himself as a poet. Art was greater than the artist; and this feeling he communicated to others; which was why younger men were never ill-at-ease in his company.

This, I am sure, was part of the secret of his ability, after becoming unquestionably the master, to remain always a contemporary.

The points that I particularly wish to make about Yeats's development are two. The first . . . is that to have accomplished what Yeats did in the middle and later years is a great and permanent example—which poets-to-come should study with reverence—of what I have called Character of the Artist: a kind of moral, as well as intellectual excellence. The second point, which follows naturally after what I have said in criticism of the lack of complete emotional expression in his early work, is that Yeats is preeminently the poet of middle age. By this I am far from meaning that he is a poet only for middle-aged readers: the attitude towards him of younger poets who write in English, the world over, is enough evidence to the contrary. . . . But in fact, very few poets have shown this capacity of adaptation to the years. It requires, indeed, an exceptional honesty and courage to face the change. Most men either cling to the experiences of youth, so that their writing becomes an insincere mimicry of their earlier work, or they leave their passion behind, and write only from the head, with a hollow and wasted virtuosity. There is another and even worse temptation: that of becoming dignified, of becoming public figures with only a public existence—coat-racks hung with decorations and distinctions, doing, saying and even thinking and feeling only what they believe the public expects of them. Yeats was not that kind of poet: and it is, perhaps, a reason why young men should find his later poetry more acceptable than older men easily can. [1940]

                T. S. Eliot in *The Permanence of Yeats,*
                ed. James Hall and Martin Steinmann
                (N.Y., Macmillan, 1950), pp. 332–33, 337

Measured by potentiality, by aspiration, and by the achievement of a few poems, it is as an heroic failure that one is forced to consider Yeats's poetic career as a whole. The causes were complex. Something, no doubt, must be attributed to defects of "character"; and a very great deal must be attributed to the literary tradition of the nineteenth cenury which, as he came to see so clearly, offered the very opposite of an incitement to maturity. But, since "the death of language . . . is but a part of the tyranny of impersonal things" (*Essays*), that tradition itself appears as the symptom of a deeper disease. Yeats wrote . . . of himself as a young man, already half-conscious that "nothing so much matters as Unity of Being": "Nor did I understand as yet how little that Unity, however wisely sought, is possible without a Unity of Culture in class or people that is no longer possible at all" (*Autobiographies*). These passages, representative of many others, are part of a diagnosis that is valuable not merely for the light that it throws on Yeats's poetry. For those who would understand our divided and distracted civilization, in which the "passionate intensity" of partial men offers itself as a substitute for the vitality that springs from the whole consciousness, few things are more profitable than a study of Yeats's poetry and prose together. "The mischief," he said, "began at the end of the seventeenth century when man became passive before a mechanized nature."

                L. C. Knights. *SoR*. Winter, 1941, pp. 440–41

Yeats commonly hovered between myth and philosophy, except for transcending flashes, which is why he is not one of the greatest poets. His ambition was too difficult for accomplishment, or his gift too small to content him. His curse was not that he rebelled against the mind of his age, which was an advantage for poetry, considering the mind, but that he could not create, except in fragments, the actuality of his age, as we can see Joyce and Mann and it may be Eliot, in equal rebellion, nevertheless doing. Yeats, to use one of his own lines, had "to wither into the truth." That he made himself into the greatest poet in English since the seventeenth century was only possible because in that withering he learned how to create fragments of the actual, not of his own time to which he was unequal, but of all time of which he was a product. [1942]

R. P. Blackmur. *Language as Gesture*
(N.Y., Harcourt, Brace, 1952), pp. 122–23

The man who emerges from his poetry is a modern man though his name be Cuchulain or Naisi. He walks a tightrope between false choices, he is torn by an inner division and undermined by preternatural forces which he is not in a position to assess nor has sufficient power given him to dominate. If he cries out his cry of the infinite power of man it is in the teeth of the facts, not because of them. As a result Yeats's work is full of overtones even when he appears to be shouting. Every poem is a battleground and the sounds of gunfire are heard throughout.

What saves him, though like Baudelaire he is *"toujours du vertige hanté,"* from making merely a case history of crisis is the tremendous organization that informs the poems and the poet; every crisis is mastered, and every poem comes out of years of preparation. He looked the poet, and he lived the poet. He has justified and reinforced everything by autobiography, essay, and public speech, has written the history of the movements that he joined or began and the biographies of his friends to bring all into coherence; nothing is left to chance. He keeps asking the same questions over and over until they have become profound: what is truth? what is reality? what is man? His answers are symbolic, but fully in harmony one with another, for they spring from a rich, unified consciousness. During a lifetime of bitter toil Yeats constantly advanced and penetrated until he had evolved a world which has more solidity than that of any poet since Wordsworth. Few poets have found mastery of themselves and of their craft so difficult or have sought such mastery, through conflict and struggle, so unflinchingly.

Richard Ellmann. *Yeats: The Man and the Masks*
(N.Y., Macmillan, 1948), pp. 294–95

However diverse our fundamental beliefs may be, the reaction of most of us to all that occult is, I fancy, the same: How on earth, we wonder, could a man of Yeats's gifts take such nonsense seriously? I have a further bewilderment, which may be due to my English up-bringing, one of snobbery. How *could* Yeats, with his great aesthetic appreciation of aristocracy, ancestral houses, ceremonious tradition, take up something so essentially lower-middle class—or should I say Southern Californian—so ineluctably associated with suburban villas and clearly unattractive faces? A. E. Housman's pessimistic stoicism seems to me nonsense too, but at least it is a kind of nonsense that can be believed by a gentleman—but mediums, spells, the Mysterious Orient—*how* embarrassing. In fact, of course, it is to Yeats's credit, an example to me, that he ignored such considerations, nor, granted that his *Weltanschauung* was false, can we claim credit for rejecting what we have no temptation to accept, nor deny that the poetry he wrote involving it is very good. . . . The Celtic legends Yeats used were woven into his childhood—he really went to seances, he seriously studied all those absurd books. . . .

Yeats has effected changes which are of use to every poet. . . . His main legacies to us are two. First, he transformed a certain kind of poem, from being either an official performance of impersonal virtuosity or a trivial *vers de société* into a serious reflective poem of at once personal and public interest. . . . Secondly, Yeats released regular stanzaic poetry, whether reflective or lyrical, from iambic monotony; the Elizabethans did this originally for dramatic verse, but not for lyric or elegiac. [1948]

W. H. Auden in *The Permanence of Yeats*,
ed. James Hall and Martin Steinmann
(N.Y., Macmillan, 1950), pp. 345–46, 349–50

The plays are always produced under difficulties because they require a special type of player, who concentrates primarily not on acting but on beauty of tone and sensitiveness of rhythm. Very rarely are they produced as they should be produced but, nevertheless, they continue to be produced. *The Collected Plays of W. B. Yeats* is something more than the complete theatrical work of our greatest theatrical poet. It is the story of the Poet Who Made Good.

Poets rarely make good in the modern theatre. They are too fond of their own verses. Now, verse in a play is only a musical accompaniment to the action; it is necessary because the action is so concentrated, so fabricated, so intense that only poetry can fully express it. Yeats gave every indication of following this pattern—the pattern of Browning, Shelley, Keats, Tennyson. In these collected plays you can even see the unregenerate Yeats of *The Countess Cathleen;* a string of vaguely related scenes, like frescoes from the life of some medieval saint strung out all over the walls of an Italian church. The later Yeats had a detestation of that play. He knew it was merely a one-act play, that the whole action should have been concentrated into one scene.

Then you can turn to the wonderful scene in *The Only Jealousy of Emer* where Cuchulain's wife cries: . . . "I renounce Cuchulain's love."

That is why Yeats is our greatest theatrical poet, for the line can chill your blood like some line of Shakespeare. I once asked him how he came by his extraordinary understanding of the stage and he replied distantly, "Oh, I took away a play of Corneille, and studied it till I'd mastered every trick of the dramatist." I think that this was probably a bit of Yeats' romancing. What really happened, I fancy, was that finding himself in charge of a theatre which he couldn't fill single-handed, he set out to find dramatists, and then discovered that he must teach them their job. Nothing makes a man learn faster than the necessity for teaching. . . .

He was a master of the one-act play. It was his particular medium and he used it magnificently, but I never felt that he could sustain a full-length play.

Frank O'Connor. NYT. May 31, 1953, pp. 1, 16

The world of the *Autobiographies* is very different from that of *The Celtic Twilight*. The scene is, for the most part, London. The actors—and they were actors—are Lionel Johnson, Wilde, Morris, George Russell and all the literary and Irish-political figures of that time. These people are not in the least idealized, very few of them are fairies, and then only in a worldly sense; they are seen in a hard, clear, but undramatic light, and the sordid aspect of their lives—their drink, dope and debts—is not concealed.

Yeats's attitude to what he calls the "Tragic Generation," the generation of *The Yellow Book* and the Rhymers' Club, was that of one who felt that their destiny was his own, and who yet felt dissatisfied with them and critical. The central point of his criticism was what involved him most deeply in his own work: the relation of their emotional, unbalanced lives to their accomplished, trancelike poetry. . . .

So that he was not only in contact with the literary movement of his time, he was also deeply involved with the people who made it. He took his tradition, not so much from books (as he had at first imagined he should do), as from the lives of those people who created his cultural environment, and whose lives presented a picture of civilization to him in its most vivid form. Their lives, deeply rooted in the lives of their ancestors, saturate his later poetry; especially the poetry of *The Tower*. I only wish sometimes that he had allowed his interest to extend still further, outside the immediate circle of his friends, into the social life that surrounded him.

I believe that what distinguished Yeats from those other writers is not so much—as Dr. Leavis has said—his power of self-criticism, as his realism. He is far too rhetorical a writer to be self-critical. It is clear from the style of his prose that he must constantly be presenting himself to himself in a dramatic manner; and his conversation gives the same impression. . . . Indeed one might say that it was Yeats's sense of reality which made him exploit his gift as a romantic poet; but he is certainly not a master of self-criticism, as Eliot is.

Yeats was strengthened in his attitude to the life around him by certain of his intellectual experiences. The chief of these were the three influences of the Irish Literary Renaissance, Magic and Symbolism, and his interest in contemporary politics, which seem in the last years to have broadened into a prophetic concern (which resembles that of Stefan George, during and after the war) with the destiny of Europe.

At first sight the Irish Renaissance, so venomously featured by George Moore in his *Hail and Farewell,* seems inextricably tangled with the Magic and Symbolism. But actually it played a conflicting rôle in his work, directing it towards the Irish legends and the Celtic Twilight, whereas the Magic and Symbolism became essentially part of his approach to the world around him. One also has to distinguish between the Symbolism which had to do with the Magic and the Symbolism which was part of the symbolist movement in poetry. This close connexion between the mystery of magical symbols and the literary movement of H. D., Ezra Pound and their followers, is typical of Yeats. However mysterious and shadowy it is, his poetry has always the stamp of success, and his magic invocations always have a slightly public air.

Stephen Spender. *The Destructive Element*
(Phila., Penna., Albert Saifer, 1953), pp. 119–21

Yeats was introduced to the Japanese Nō by Ezra Pound, who was translating excerpts with the help of Ernest Fenellosa. He saw the relation to his own work, and of course admired the plays as the work of dedicated artists done for a class of cultivated warrior-aristocrats—this was for Yeats the true heroic situation for poetry, life being all action and courtesy, poetry all contemplation and style. . . .

Every aspect of the technique and presentation of Nō must have struck Yeats as certain proof of the soundness of his own theory of drama, which in itself stems from the Romantic Image. Above all these were dance-plays, and so antithetical to the realism that was, in Yeats's view, draining the force of the theatre, so hostile indeed to the whole mimetic tradition of the West, that the players went masked. The Nō answered, better than Wagner or any merely synaesthetic experiment, the prayer of a Symbolist poet for a fitting theatre—Mallarmé had desired a Symbolist drama but was put off by the prospect of irrelevant *expressions* in the actors' faces—and though they came too late to coincide with Yeats's earlier mood of heroic vision they provided him with a drama-medium in which he at last fully found himself as a poet for the theatre.... His actors would have the blank, inward faces of the wooden Japanese masks; they would not necessarily even speak their own lines. Musicians would frame the action, and comment in song. All would be inexplicit, suggestive, but faultless in design; and often the climax of the play would be a dance like Salome's. There would be no separable meaning; the verses would be spoken as the dance was danced, and would dispense with that kind of expression that points "meaning."

Frank Kermode. *Romantic Image*
(Routledge and Kegan Paul, 1957), pp. 78–80

The received opinion among readers of Yeats is that the classic poems are in *The Tower* and *The Winding Stair*. And yet by comparison with *The Wild Swans at Coole* the human image in those spectacular books is curiously incomplete; remarkably intense, but marginal; a little off-centre. Does this matter? Yes, it does; intensity is not enough. It matters greatly that *The Wild Swans at Coole* is at the very heart of the human predicament, groping for values through which man may define himself without frenzy or servility.

This book is concerned with the behaviour of man in the cold light of age and approaching death. The ideal stance involves passion, self-conquest, courtesy, and moral responsibility. Yeats pays the tribute of wild tears to many personages and to the moral beauty which they embody; the entire book is crammed with moral life. Most of the poems were written between 1915 and 1919, and it is significant that those were the years in which Yeats was perfecting his dance-drama; because the dancer was the culmination of the efforts which Yeats made in *The Wild Swans at Coole* to represent the fullness of being as a dynamic action.

Denis Donoghue. *L*. Dec., 1961, pp. 59–60

YOUNG, FRANCIS BRETT (1884–1954)

... neglect has allowed Mr. Brett Young a free hand to experiment, and so interesting has been each one of these experiments, at any rate so far as his prose and verse are concerned—I cannot speak of his plays—that his varied production might serve as a text to illustrate the tendencies of our time.

Tendencies are as infectious as influenzas; even with rigid isolation the subject is not immune but he is safer than he would be by frequenting various literary groups, which are the worst disseminators of such infection. Mr. Brett Young, who was a doctor before he became a writer, probably learned in the exercise of his earlier profession the wisdom of avoiding infected areas unless compelled to visit them professionally. Literature has not summoned him professionally into such infected areas, and, with the exception of an excellent book on Robert Bridges, in which he gave a model diagnosis of a completely uninfectious patient, he has not been called upon to administer the consolating criticism.

At the same time, one feels that Mr. Brett Young has indulged in a certain amount of research among the infectious tendencies of the present day; so much so, that occasionally he seems to have felt it was his duty to inoculate himself, however mildly, in each serum in turn. The first tendency of this kind was toward a type of Welsh influenza which has remained endemic in the Marches, and which, under the influence of Mr. Arthur Machen, almost grew into a pandemic. The result was *Undergrowth*. . . .

Well, here is an end of my poor attempt to remind people that Mr. Brett Young is a novelist who has shown by his industry and steady progress, by his versatility and romantic outlook, by his technical accomplishment and by a kind of graceful modesty which is the very essence of his individuality as a writer that he is worthy of much more attention than he has received. Yet I come back to my opinion that he is . . . moving honorably toward that high place in the literature of the next decade for which he is marked out.

Compton Mackenzie. *Bkm*. Aug., 1920,
pp. 635–36, 640–41

Mr. Young's people . . . incur their misfortunes with open eyes, by frequenting too often average human situations. Their beauty it is that brings them to nothing; they are not visited by thunderbolts, they simply cannot flourish in ordinary air. It does not need argument to show that this is essentially the mood of a lyric poet, and that it yet cannot be expressed at length in lyric poetry. When the dirty devices encamp with their ado in the mind they rouse heavier music. So Mr. Young took to writing novels which should be shadow-masques enacting selected episodes from his private mythology. Though he had by nature all the ingeniousness of the poet, and none of the cunning of the novelist born, he attained novelist's status with remarkable ease. He had to rein in his tendency to easy excitement and to overwork the surface of his mind. This he did gallantly; indeed they are the two bravest virtues of his necessity which have been so doggedly mistaken by the reviewers, the one for a will-o'-the wisp of promise, the other for a disqualifying technical ability. His vivid embodiments of the dirty devices have been supposed to be promising touches of realism; and the curious uneven light which pervades his novels and has so often been supposed to arise from a decay of the formulating power, or to be the refraction from a flaw in vision, is really a deliberate effect, designed to cast a haze of quasi-apotheosis over whoever stands for Beauty in the story, and at the same time to reveal sharply and uninvitingly the people and things which play her opponents. This mastery of lighting never relaxes from *Undergrowth* onwards. For the rest, down to *The Tragic Bride,* he was, like most novelists with the lyrical instinct, a little "unnovelistic" in his tricks, a little over-cunning in contrivances. *The Young Physician,* which is happy hunting ground for the deprecatory critic, is full of examples of this.

E. G. Twitchett. *LM.* May, 1924, pp. 397-98

Mr. Brett Young is one of the younger novelists whose work has been favourably mentioned by competent judges. We observe that he has already published some dozen novels. This story is a "ghost" story of no great interest; we do not suppose that it is representative of Mr. Brett Young's work, but if so, the novels that he has written are a great many too many.

There are several kinds of horror story possible: the straight tale, such as the were-wolf story in Petronius and the witch stories in Apuleius, the scientific story of H. G. Wells, the romantic story of Poe, and the "psychological" story of Hawthorne and James. Mr. Brett Young's publishers mention *The Turn of the Screw* in connection with *Cold Harbour;* but there is this fundamental difference—that Mr. Brett Young builds up an over-elaborate setting for a very weak thrill at the end, whereas James uses the minimum of external apparatus to convey an authentic impression of human evil.

Crit. July, 1925, p. 476

To have been a General Practitioner is surely to know the inside of man, and to have been a ship's doctor, too, should be guarantee enough that he knows the outside of him as well. Francis Brett Young has done all these things, so it is not surprising that his novels are beginning to be so widely read. For though it is obviously absurd to suggest that the more an author has done in life, the more interesting his novels will be, there must be something in the statement that given equal potentialities the man who knows most of life will write the best stories about it. . . .

Success has been a long time in coming, but the world awakens slowest to the recognition of the artists whom it will end by admiring the longest. This is a truism needing no obvious examples for its proof, but it serves to explain why it is only now that there is any wide feeling of curiosity in the air about Brett Young, whose first novel was published about eighteen years ago. . . .

Another reason for the solidity of this success is undoubtedly the obvious fact of his Englishness. He may write of South Africa, Egypt, or the Orient, he may publish his projected Neapolitan novel, but the fact remains that everything he sees, he sees with English eyes, and all his thoughts on matters, no matter how foreign, are English thoughts. Always he will be a truly English author, utterly in sympathy with the English mind. And though it is perhaps natural that English eyes may be more quickly attracted by writers whose manners or points of view are foreign, it is obvious that the English people will in the end love best the authors who have their own habit of mind.

Arnold Gyde. World Today. Dec., 1928, pp. 14, 17

My Brother Jonathan . . . has all the unfashionable virtues, and for these is likely, I am afraid, to be made to pay more dearly at the hands of modern critics than for any positive demerit. An extremely long book, perhaps unnecessarily long, given its content, it is "well-constructed" in the nowadays unpopular meaning of the word; it is solid, honestly written and shows the same steady advance which has been noticeable in Mr. Brett Young's work ever since he wrote *The Tragic Bride*. . . . Mr. Brett Young keeps all his promises; that the kind of promises he makes are precisely those in whose performance the present generation feels least interest is, I dare say, our fault and not the novelist's.

LL. Jan., 1929, p. 57

White Ladies would have been improved vastly if Mr. Brett Young had put a little of Mr. Perrin into his Worcester sauce instead of sticking to his recipe (by a gentleman of the country). It is seven hundred uninspired pages long, a father-to-son house-and-family narrative. Mr. Brett Young is a doctor, like Somerset Maugham, and a writer, like R. H. Mottram. I was asked the other day why I inveighed against middlebrows since it would never lead to their writing any better. The reason is that I think the train of fiction is already hopelessly overcrowded, and that all the comfortable seats are occupied by people with third-class tickets. My mission is to evict them to make room for those few, sad, unappreciated vocational artists whose books are so much better and so much more entertaining. This does not apply to *White Ladies,* which Mr. Mossbross has chosen for the boys as their holiday task. "It's a lovely little thing," he says, "a broad field of English wurzels with the evening sun on it."

Cyril Connolly. NSN. Aug. 3, 1935, pp. 166–67

Both as poet and as novelist Francis Brett Young has for long occupied a high place among modern English writers. His latest novel *Far Forest*

... is suffused with local colour, but the story is one of individuals, not of a community, and there is nothing of gloom or of sordidness in it. ... The author has captured the real genius of the countryside in all the varying seasons; with a veritable charm he can describe the forests and the fields, the hop-gardens and the rural lanes, and always he finds just the right word to arouse a feeling of response in the reader. His writing is never tedious, for he knows how to exercise the art of restraint—a saving grace in a novelist. For the descriptive passages alone the book would be notable; but there is also the human element. The characters are not complex, nor are they, for a modern novel, many in number, but they are drawn with marvellous understanding and insight. ... In this skilful mingling of scene and character, of nature and humanity one is reminded of the novels of Mary Webb.

Frederick T. Wood. ES. Aug., 1937, pp. 134–35

YOUNG, G. M. (1882–1959)

It is true that there comes a time very early in the reading of Gibbon when the artifices of the style begin to tease; but it is a stage which a true Gibbonian soon learns to get over. It is easy to analyse those artifices, and at bottom they are very simple, like the details of some contemporary front-elevation. Far less obvious is the justness of the broader plan of the whole work, appreciation of which demands a deeper knowledge of the multifarious subject-matter and of possible alternatives to Gibbon's treatment of it than the majority possess. This is one of Mr. Young's strongest points; he gives the impression [*Gibbon*] that he has qualified himself for judging the *Decline and Fall* by reading it through and through many times.

TLS. Dec. 15, 1932, p. 958

Mr. G. M. Young's essay at the end of *Early Victorian England,* a summing up as brilliant as it was judicious, received from critics the applause which it deserved. The first 102 pages of his new book [*Victorian England: Portrait of an Age*] are a reprint of this essay: in the remaining 85 pages he describes, considers and judges the Late Victorian Age. He explains shortly, moreover, his conception of what history would be. He is so old-fashioned as to believe in the desirability, and even, it seems, in the possibility, of "the disinterested mind."

> In the daily clamour for leadership, for faith, for a new heart or a new cause, I hear the ghost of late Victorian England whimpering on the grave thereof. To a mature and civilised

man no faith is possible except faith in the argument itself, and what leadership therefore can he acknowledge except the argument whithersoever it goes.

I fancy that I detect in him a nostalgia for the old agricultural society, with squire and parson as the focal points of its orderly ellipse. But any prejudices that he has he keeps in admirable control, and I could find hardly a detail on which to challenge him, unless it were his theory that the Dilke divorce deprived Liberalism of the leader it required. . . .

Mr. Young's book is remarkable alike for its concision and its comprehensiveness: it covers public health and private morals, education and agriculture, art and economics. It is packed with fascinating illustrations of his theme. . . . The erudition which enables Mr. Young to draw upon an apparently inexhaustible supply of such details is allied with an admirable talent for summarising an action. . . .

Victorianism is a subject dangerously vast for a short book, impossibly vast for a short review. But . . . *Victorian England* is a book which all who are interested in history or literature must read. And they will find this obligation a pleasure.

Raymond Mortimer. *NSN*. Dec. 12, 1936, pp. 986, 991

In this collection of essays [*Last Essays*] which concludes all that Mr. Young has to say in this form there is a consideration of the criticism of Longinus and Dionysius of Halicarnassus; the subject might appear academic, but Mr. Young is a writer always sensible to historic continuity, and the essay may be linked closely with Virginia Woolf's article on modern criticism. . . . Mrs. Woolf brilliantly overstated her case, but Mr. Young makes some modest proposals which he bases on his study of classical criticism. To arrive at an accurate estimate of a book, he says, the critic must put it through a series of tests. . . . This insistence on an orderly approach to literature is one of the keys to the understanding of the temper of Mr. Young's own mind; in quietly elegant prose he carefully feels his way through the subject in hand with an exemplary regard for logic and consistency. . . . One might say that Mr. Young is a contemporary Dionysius of Halicarnassus, determined to see all in its due proportions and to direct, as far as he is able, the various contributions in a way which will be beneficial to the national culture. There are not many men whose training, wide sympathies, and unemotional temper of mind fit them for this kind of work. Mr. Young fulfills his responsibilities admirably.

List. Jan. 18, 1951, p. 112

BIBLIOGRAPHY

GENRE ABBREVIATIONS

a	autobiography	p	poetry
b	biography	pd	poetic drama
c	criticism	r	reminiscence
d	drama	rd	radio drama
e	essay	s	short stories
h	history	sk	sketches
m	memoir	t	travel or topography
misc	miscellany	tr	translation
n	novel		

For explanatory note on Bibliography see page 437.

PETER QUENNELL
1905-

Masques & Poems, 1922 (p); *Poems*, 1926 (p); *Inscription on a Fountain Head*, 1929 (p); *Baudelaire and the Symbolists*, 1929 (repr. 1954) (c); *Memoirs of the Comte de Gramont*, 1930 (tr); *The Phoenix-Kind*, 1931 (n); *A Superficial Journey Through Tokyo and Peking*, 1932 (t); *A Letter to Mrs. Virginia Woolf*, 1932 (e); *Sympathy*, 1933 (s); *Byron*, 1934 (b); *Byron: The Years of Fame*, 1935 (repr. 1950) (b); *Victorian Panorama*, 1937 (h); *Caroline of England*, 1939 (b); (with George Paston, pseud.) *"To Lord Byron." Feminine Profiles, Based upon Unpublished Letters, 1807-1824*, 1939 (b); *Byron in Italy*, 1941 (b); *Four Portraits* [Boswell, Gibbon, Sterne, John Wilkes], 1945 (b); *John Ruskin*, 1949, (b); *The Singular Preference*, 1952 (e); *Spring in Sicily*, 1952 (t); *Hogarth's Progress*, 1955 (b); *The Sign of the Fish*, 1960 (e); *Shakespeare*, 1964 (b)

ARTHUR QUILLER-COUCH
1863-1944

Athens, 1881 (p); *Dead Man's Rock*, 1887 (n); *The Astonishing History of Troy Town*, 1888 (*Troy Town*, 1928); *The Splendid Spur*, 1889 (n); *The Blue Pavilions*, 1891 (n); *Noughts and Crosses*, 1891 (s); *The Warwickshire Avon*, 1892 (t); *"I Saw Three Ships"*, 1892 (s); *Green Bays: Verses and Parodies*, 1893 (enlgd. 1930) (p); *The Delectable Duchy*, 1893 (s); *Fairy Tales Far and Near, Re-told by Q*, 1895; *Wandering Heath*, 1895 (s); *Adventures in Criticism*, 1896 (c); *Ia*, 1896 (n); *Poems and Ballads*, 1896 (p); *St. Ives, Being the Adventures of a French Prisoner in England by Robert Louis Stevenson (completed by A. T. Quiller-Couch)*, 1897 (n); *The Ship of Stars*, 1899 (n); *Historical Tales from Shakespeare*, 1899 (s); *Old Fires and Profitable Ghosts*, 1900 (s); *The Laird's Luck*, 1901 (s); *The Westcotes*, 1902 (n); *The White Wolf*, 1902 (s); *Two Sides of the Face*, 1903 (s); *The Adventures of Harry Revel*, 1903 (pub. as *Harry Revel*, 1931) (n); *Hetty Wesley*, 1903 (n); *Fort Amity*, 1904 (n); *The Mayor of Troy*, 1905 (n); *Shining Ferry*, 1905 (n); *Shakespeare's Christmas*, 1905 (s); *Sir John Constantine*, 1906 (n); *From a Cornish Window*, 1906 (e); *Major Vigoureux*, 1907 (n); *Poison Island*, 1907 (n); *Merry-garden*, 1907 (s); *True Tilda*, 1909 (n); *Lady Good-for-nothing, a Man's Portrait of a Woman*, 1910 (n); *Corporal Sam*,

1910 (s); *The Sleeping Beauty and other Fairy Tales from the Old French Retold,* 1910; *The Roll Call of Honour, a New Book of Golden Deeds,* 1911 (b); *Brother Copas,* 1911 (n); *The Vigil of Venus,* 1912 (p); *Hocken and Hunken, a Tale of Troy,* 1912 (n); *In Powder & Crinoline, Old Fairy Tales Retold,* 1913 (pub. as *The Twelve Dancing Princesses,* 1923); *News From the Duchy,* 1913 (s); *Poetry,* 1914 (c); *Nicky-Nan, Reservist,* 1915 (n); *On the Art of Writing,* 1916 (e); *Mortallone and Aunt Trinidad, Tales of the Spanish Main,* 1917 (s); *Notes on Shakespeare's Workmanship, from Lectures,* 1917; *Memoir of Arthur John Butler,* 1917 (m); *Shakespeare's Workmanship,* 1918 (c); *Studies in Literature,* 1918 (c); *Foe-Farrell,* 1918 (n); *On the Art of Reading,* 1920 (c); *Selected Stories,* 1921; *Studies in Literature, Second Series,* 1922 (c); *Charles Dickens and Other Victorians,* 1925 (c); *Honorable Men* (Livingston, Lincoln, Gordon, from *The Roll Call of Honour*), 1925 (b); *The Age of Chaucer,* 1926 (h); *A Lecture on Lectures,* 1927; *Polperro Privateers, or, The Capture of the Burgomeister Van der Werf,* 1927 (s); *Victors of Peace: Florence Nightingale, Pasteur, Father Damien* (previously pub. in *The Roll Call of Honour*), 1927 (b); *The Duchy Edition of Tales and Romances by Q,* 3 vols., 1928-29; *Studies in Literature, Third Series,* 1929 (c); *Poems,* 1929 (p); *Paternity in Shakespeare,* 1932 (Shakespeare lecture for Brit. Academy); *The Poet as Citizen,* 1934 (e); *A Further Approach to Shakespeare,* 1934 (c); *Mystery Stories: Twenty Stories,* 1937 (s); *Cambridge Lectures,* 1943 (selection); *Shorter Stories,* 1944 (selection); *Memories and Opinions: an Unfinished Autobiography,* ed. S. C. Roberts, 1945; *Q. Anthology,* 1948; (with Daphne du Maurier) *Castle d'Or,* 1962 (n)

Fred Brittain, *Arthur Quiller-Couch: a Biographical Study of Q,* 1948

KATHLEEN RAINE
1908-

Stone and Flower, Poems 1935-43, 1943 (p); Denis de Rougement, *Talk of the Devil [La Part du Diable],* 1945 (tr); *Living in Time,* 1946 (p); Balzac, *Cousine Bette,* 1948 (tr); *The Pythoness,* 1949 (p); *William Blake,* 1951 (c); Balzac, *Lost Illusions,* 1951 (tr); *The Year One,* 1951 (p); *Selected Poems,* 1952 (p); *Coleridge,* 1953 (c); *The Collected Potems,* 1956; *Blake and England,* 1960 (Founder's Memorial Lecture, Girton College, Cambridge Univ.)

TERENCE RATTIGAN
1911-

French Without Tears, 1937 (d); *After the Dance,* 1939 (d); *Flare Path,* 1942 (d); *While the Sun Shines,* 1944 (d); *Love in Idleness,* 1945 (Am. ed. *O Mistress Mine*) (d); *The Winslow Boy,* 1946 (d); *The Browning Version,* 1949 (d); *Harlequinade,* 1949 (d); *Playbill* (the two preceding titles), 1949 (2d); *Adventure Story,* 1950 (d); *Who Is Sylvia?,* 1951 (d); *The Deep Blue Sea,* 1952 (d); *Collected Plays,* 2 vols., 1953; *The Sleeping Prince,* 1954 (d); *Separate Tables (Table by the Window, Table Number Seven),* 1954 (2d); *Variation on a Theme,* 1959 (d); *Olivia,* 1960 (d); *Ross: A Dramatic Portrait,* 1960 (d); *Man and Boy,* 1963 (d)

HERBERT READ
1893-

Songs of Chaos, 1915 (p); *Naked Warriors,* 1919 (p); *Eclogues,* 1919 (p); *Mutations of the Phoenix,* 1923 (p); *In Retreat,* 1925 (sk); *English Stained Glass,* 1926 (e); *Reason and Romanticism,* 1926 (c); *Collected Poems, 1913-25,* 1926; *English Prose Style,* 1928 (c); *Phases of English Poetry,* 1928 (c); *The Sense of Glory,* 1929 (c); *Julien Benda and the New Humanism,* 1930 (e); *Ambush,* 1930 (sk); *Wordsworth,* 1930 (c); *The Meaning of Art* (Am. ed. *The Anatomy of Art*), 1931 (c); *The End of a War,* 1931 (p); *Form in Modern Poetry,* 1932 (c); *Art Now,* 1933 (rev. enlgd. 1961) (e); *The Innocent Eye,* 1933 (a); *Art and Industry,* 1934 (c); *Poems, 1914-34,* 1935 (p); *The Green Child,* 1935 (n); *In Defence of Shelley,* 1936 (c); *Art and Society,* 1937 (e); *Collected Essays in Literary Criticism,* 1938 (c); *Poetry and Anarchism,* 1938 (c); *Annals of Innocence and Experience,* 1940 (rev. 1946) (a); *Thirty-Five Poems,* 1940 (p); *Education Through Art,* 1943 (c); *The Politics of the Unpolitical,* 1943 (e);

The Education of Free Men, 1944 (e); *A World Within a War*, 1944 (p); *A Coat of Many Colours*, 1945 (e); *Collected Poem*, 1946; *The Grass Roots of Art*, 1947 (e); *Coleridge as Critic*, 1949 (c); *Education for Peace*, 1950 (e); *Contemporary British Art*, 1951 (c); *Byron*, 1951 (b,c); *The Philosophy of Modern Art*, 1952 (e); *Collected Poems*, 1953; *The True Voice of Feeling*, 1953 (c); *Anarchy and Order*, 1954 (e); *Icon and Idea*, 1955 (e); *Moon's Farm*, 1955 (p); *The Art of Sculpture*, 1956 (e); *The Tenth Muse*, 1957 (c); *A Concise History of Modern Painting*, 1959 (h); *Kandinsky*, 1959 (b); *The Parliament of Women*, 1960 (d); *Aristotle's Mother*, 1960 (d); *The Forms of Things Unknown*, 1960 (e); (with Edward Dahlberg) *Truth is More Sacred*, 1961 (c); *A Letter to a Young Painter*, 1962 (e); *The Contrary Experience*, 1963 (a); *Selected Writings*, 1963 (p,c)

Francis Berry, *Herbert Read*, rev. 1961

FORREST REID
1876-1947

The Kingdom of Twilight, 1904 (n); *The Garden God*, 1905 (n); *The Bracknels*, 1911 (rev. as *Denis Bracknel*, 1947) (n); *Following Darkness*, 1912 (rev. as *Peter Waring*, 1937) (n); *The Gentle Lover*, 1913 (n); *W. B. Yeats*, 1915 (c); *At the Door of the Gate*, 1915 (n); *The Spring Song*, 1916 (n); *A Garden by the Sea*, 1918 (s); *Pirates of the Spring*, 1919 (n); *Pender Among the Residents*, 1922 (n); *Apostate*, 1926 (r); *Demophon*, 1927 (n); *Illustrators of the Sixties*, 1928 (c); *Walter de la Mare*, 1928 (c); *Uncle Stephen*, 1931 (n); *Brian Westby*, 1934 (n); *The Retreat*, 1936 (n); *Private Road*, 1940 (r); *Retrospective Adventures*, 1941 (e,s); *Notes and Impressions*, 1942 (e); *Poems from the Greek Anthology*, 1943 (tr); *Young Tom*, 1944 (n); *The Milk of Paradise*, 1946 (c)

Russell Burlingham, *Forrest Reid, a Portrait and a Study*, 1953

I. A. RICHARDS
1893-

(with C. K. Ogden and James Wood) *The Foundations of Aesthetics*, 1922 (e); (with C. K. Ogden) *The Meaning of Meaning, a Study of the Influence of Language upon Thought*, 1923 (e); *Principles of Literary Criticism*, 1924 (e); *Science and Poetry*, 1926 (e); *Practical Criticism*, 1929 (c); *Mencius on the Mind*, 1932 (e); *Basic Rules of Reason*, 1933 (e); *Coleridge on Imagination*, 1934 (e); *Interpretation in Teaching*, 1938 (c); *How to Read a Page*, 1943 (c); *Basic English and its Uses*, 1943 (e); *The Wrath of Achilles; The Iliad of Homer*, 1951 (abgd.) (tr); *Speculative Instruments*, 1955 (e); *Goodbye Earth*, 1958 (p); *The Screens*, 1960 (p); *Tomorrow Morning, Faustus!*, 1962 (d)

DOROTHY RICHARDSON
1872-1957

The Quakers, Past and Present, 1914 (e); *Pilgrimage*, consisting of the following novels: *Pointed Roofs*, 1915; *Backwater*, 1916; *Honeycomb*, 1917; *Tunnel*, 1919; *Interim*, 1919; *Deadlock*, 1921; *Revolving Lights*, 1923; *Trap*, 1925; *Oberland*, 1927; *Dawn's Left Hand*, 1931; *Clear Horizon*, 1935; *Dimple Hill*, 1938; *John Austen and the Inseparables*, 1930 (c)

EDGELL RICKWORD
1898-

Behind the Eyes, 1921 (p); *Rimbaud, the Boy and the Poet*, 1924 (b); *Invocations to Angels and The Happy New Year*, 1928 (p); *Love One Another*, 1929 (n); *Twittingpan and Some Others*, 1931 (p); Marcel Coulon, *Poet Under Saturn*, 1932 (tr); *Collected Poems*, 1947

ANNE RIDLER
1912-

Poems, 1939 (p); *The Nine Bright Shiners*, 1943 (p); *Cain*, 1943 (pd); *The Shadow Factory*, 1946 (pd); *Henry Bly*, 1950 (pd); *The Golden Bird*, 1951 (p); *The Trial of Thomas Cranmer*, 1956 (pd); *A Matter of Life and Death*, 1959 (p); *Who is My Neighbour? and How Bitter the Bread*, 1963 (2pd)

MICHAEL ROBERTS
1902-1949

These Our Matins, 1930 (p); *Newton and the Origin of Colours*, 1934 (e);

Critique of Poetry, 1934 (c); *Poems*, 1936 (p); *The Modern Mind*, 1937 (e); *T. E. Hulme*, 1938 (b); *Orion Marches*, 1939 (p); *The Recovery of the West*, 1941 (e); *The Estate of Man*, ed. J. B. A. Smith, 1951 (e); *Collected Poems*, 1958

T. W. Eason and R. Hamilton, *A Portrait of Michael Roberts*, 1949

LENNOX ROBINSON
1886-1958

The Cross-Roads, 1910 (d); *Two Plays: Harvest, The Clancy Name*, 1911 (2d); *Patriots*, 1912 (d); *The Dreamers*, 1915 (d); *A Young Man from the South*, 1917 (repr. 1945) (n); *Dark Days* [life in Ireland], 1918 (sk); *The Lost Leader*, 1918 (repr. 1954) (d); *The Whiteheaded Boy*, 1920 (repr. 1925) (d); *Eight Short Stories*, 1920 (s); *Crabbed Youth and Age*, 1924 (d); *The Round Table*, 1924 (d); *The White Blackbird, Portrait*, 1926 (2d); *The Big House*, 1928 (d); *Plays*, 1928 (d); *Give a Dog—*, 1928 (d); *Ever the Twain*, 1930 (d); *The Far-Off Hills*, 1931 (d); *Bryan Cooper*, 1931 (b); *Is Life Worth Living?*, 1933 (rev. 1938) (d); *More Plays (All's Over, Then?* and *Church Street* [latter repr. 1955]), 1935 (2d); (with Tom Robinson and Nora Dorman) *Three Homes*, 1938 (r); *Killycreggs in Twilight and Other Plays*, 1939 (3d); *Curtain Up*, 1942 (a); *Towards an Appreciation of the Theatre*, 1945 (c); *Pictures in a Theatre: a Conversation Piece*, 1947 (r); *The Lucky Finger*, 1948 (d); *Palette and Plough* [Desmond O'Brien], 1948 (b); *Ireland's Abbey Theatre, 1899-1951*, 1951 (h); *Drama at Irish*, 1953 (d); *Never the Time and the Place* and *Crabbed Youth and Age*, 1953 (2d); *I Sometimes Think*, 1956 (e)

Michael J. O'Neill, *Lennox Robinson*, 1964

W. R. RODGERS
1909-

Awake, 1941 (p); *The Ulstermen and their Country*, 1947 (e); *Portrait of James Joyce*, 1950 (radio script); *Europa and the Bull*, 1952 (p); *Ireland in Colour*, 1957 (e)

FREDERICK ROLFE
(BARON CORVO)
1860-1913

Stories Toto Told Me, 1898 (s); *In His Own Image*, 1901 (repr. 1924) (s); *Chronicles of the House of Borgia*, 1901 (Am. ed. *A History of the Borgias*, 1931) (h); *The Rubaiyat of Umar Khaiyam*, 1903 (tr); *Hadrian the Seventh*, 1904 (repr. 1950) (n); *Don Tarquinio*, 1905 (repr. 1957) (n); *Don Renato*, 1909 (repr. 1963) (n); *The Desire and Pursuit of the Whole*, ed. A. J. A. Symons, 1934 (repr. 1953) (n); (with C. H. C. Pirie-Gordon) *Hubert's Arthur*, ed. A. J. A. Symons, 1935 (n); *The Songs of Meleager*, 1937 (tr); *Three Tales of Venice*, 1950 (s); *Amico di Sandro, A Fragment of a Novel*, 1951 (n); *Letters to Grant Richards*, 1952; *The Cardinal Prefect of Propaganda*, 1957 (s); *Nicholas Crabbe, or The One and the Many*, 1958 (n); *Letters to C. H. C. Pirie-Gordon*, ed. Cecil Woolf, 1959

Cecil Woolf, *A Bibliography of Frederick Rolfe, Baron Corvo*, 1957

ISAAC ROSENBERG
1890-1918

Night and Day, 1912 (p); *Youth*, 1915 (p); *Moses*, 1916 (pd); *Poems*, ed. Gordon Bottomley, 1922; *Collected Works*, ed. Gordon Bottomley, and Denys Harding, 1937; *Collected Poems*, ed. Gordon Bottomley and Denys Harding, 1949

ALAN ROSS
1922-

The Derelict Day, 1947 (p); *Time was Away*, 1948 (t); *The Forties*, 1950 (e); *The Gulf of Pleasure*, 1951 (t); *Poetry, 1945-50*, 1951 (c); *The Bandit on the Billiard Table*, 1954 (rev. enlgd. as *South to Sardinia*, 1960) (t); *Something of the Sea*, 1954 (p); *To Whom it May Concern, Poems 1952-1957*, 1958 (p); *African Negatives*, 1962 (p)

A. L. ROWSE
1903-

Politics and the Younger Generation, 1931 (e); (with G. B. Harrison) *Queen*

Elizabeth and Her Subjects, 1935 (e); *Sir Richard Grenville of the Revenge,* 1935 (repr. 1963) (b); *Poems of a Decade, 1931-41,* 1941 (p); *Tudor Cornwall: Portrait of a Society,* 1941 (repr. 1963) (e); *A Cornish Childhood,* 1942 (a); *The Spirit of English History,* 1943 (e); *The English Spirit,* 1944 (e); *Poems Chiefly Cornish,* 1944 (p); *West Country Stories,* 1945 (s); *Poems of Deliverance,* 1946 (p); *The Use of History,* 1946 (e); *The End of an Epoch,* 1947 (e); *The West in English History,* (e); *The England of Elizabeth. The Structure of Society,* 1950 (h); *The English Past,* 1951 (e); *An Elizabethan Garland,* 1953 (e); L. Romier: *L'Ancienne France,* 1953 (tr); *The Expansion of Elizabethan England,* 1955 (h); *The Early Churchills,* 1956 (b); *The Elizabethans and America,* 1958 (h); *The Later Churchills,* 1958 (b); *Poems, Partly American,* 1959 (p); *All Souls and Appeasement,* 1961 (e); *Raleigh and the Throckmortons,* 1962 (b); *William Shakespeare,* 1963 (b); *Marlowe: a Critical Study,* 1964 (c)

NAOMI ROYDE-SMITH
? -1964

A Private Anthology, 1924 (p); *The Tortoiseshell Cat,* 1925 (n); *The Housemaid,* 1926 (d); *A Balcony,* 1927 (d); *John Fanning's Legacy,* 1927 (n); *Skin Deep, or Portrait of Lucinda,* 1927 (n); *The Lover,* 1928 (s); *Children in the Wood* (Am. ed. *In the Wood*), 1928 (n); *Summer Holiday, or Gibraltar* (Am. ed. *Give Me My Sin Again*), 1929 (n); *Mafro, Darling,* 1929 (d); *The Island,* 1930 (n); *Pictures and People,* 1930 (r); *The Delicate Situation,* 1931 (n); *The Mother,* 1931 (n); *Mrs. Siddons,* 1931 (d); *The Double Heart, a Study of Julie de Lepinasse,* 1931 (b); *Madame Julia's Tale,* 1932 (s); *The Bridge,* 1932 (n); *The Incredible Tale,* 1932 (n); *Pilgrim from Paddington,* 1933 (p); *The Private Life of Mrs. Siddons* (Am. ed. *Portrait of Mrs. Siddons*), 1933 (b); *David,* 1933 (n); *The Queen's Wigs,* 1934 (p); *Private Room,* 1934 (d); *Jake,* 1935 (n); *All Star Cast,* 1936 (n); *For Us in the Dark,* 1937 (n); *Miss Bendix,* 1938 (n); *The Altar-Piece,* 1939 (n); *Urchin Moor,* 1939 (n); *The Younger Venus,* 1939 (n); *Jane Fairfax,* 1940 (n); *Outside Information,* 1941 (e); *The Unfaithful Wife,* 1941 (n); *Mildensee,* 1943 (n); *Fireweed,* 1944 (n); *The State of Mind of Mrs. Sherwood,* 1946 (b); *Love in Mildensee,* 1948 (s); *The Iniquity of Us All,* 1949 (n); *The Idol and the Shrine* [the Life of M. de Guérin], 1949 (b); *Rosy Trodd,* 1950 (n); *The New Rich,* 1951 (n); *She Always Caught the Post,* 1953 (n); *All Night Sitting,* 1954 (d); *Melilot,* 1955 (n); *Love at First Sight,* 1956 (n); *The Whistling Chambermaid,* 1957 (n); *How White is my Sepulchre,* 1958 (s); *A Blue Rose,* 1959 (s); *Love and a Birdcage,* 1960 (n)

BERTRAND RUSSELL
1872-

Selective Bibliography: the works most apt to interest a student of literature.

A Critical Exposition of the Philosophy of Leibniz, with an appendix of leading passages, 1900 (repr. 1937); *The Principles of Mathematics,* 1903; *Philosophical Essays,* 1910 (e); (with Alfred North Whitehead) *Principia Mathematica,* 1910-1913; *The Problems of Philosophy,* 1912; *Our Knowledge of the External World as a Field for Scientific Method in Philosophy,* 1914; *The Philosophy of Bergson,* 1914; *Mysticism and Logic,* 1918 (repr. 1953) (e); *Roads to Freedom: Socialism, Anarchism and Syndicalism,* 1918 (Am. ed. *Proposed Roads to Freedom*) (e); *The Analysis of Mind,* 1921; (with Dora Russell) *The Prospects of Industrial Civilization,* 1923 (e); *Icarus, or, The Future of Science,* 1924 (e); *The ABC of Relativity,* 1925; *What I Believe,* 1925 (e); *On Education Especially in Early Childhood,* 1926 (Am. ed. *Education and the Good Life*) (e); *The Analysis of Matter,* 1927; *An Outline of Philosophy,* 1927 (Am. ed. *Philosophy*); *Selected Papers of Bertrand Russell,* sel. by author, 1927; *Why I Am Not a Christian,* 1927 (e); *Sceptical Essays,* 1928 (e); *Marriage and Morals,* 1929 (e); *The Conquest of Happiness,* 1930 (e); (with John Cowper Powys) *Debate! Is Modern Marriage a Failure?,* 1930; (with others) *Divorce as I See It,* 1930 (Am. ed. *Divorce*) (e); *The Scientific Outlook,* 1931 (e); *Education and the Social Order,* 1932 (Am. ed. *Education* and the Modern World) (e); Freedom and Organization, 1814-1914, 1934 (Am. ed. Freedom versus Organization, 1814-1914) (h); (with others) The Meaning of Marx, a Symposium, 1934; Religion and Science, 1935 (e); In Praise of Idleness, 1935 (e); Power. A New Social Analysis, 1938 (e); An Inquiry into Meaning and Truth, 1940 (e); A History of Western Philosophy and its Connection with Political and Social Circumstances from the Earliest Times to the Present Day, 1945 (h); The Faith of a Rationalist, 1947 (e); Philosophy and Politics, 1947 (e); Human Knowledge: Its Scope and Limits, 1948 (e); Authority and the Individual, 1949 (the Reith lectures); Unpopular Essays, 1950 (e); New Hopes for a Changing World, 1951 (e); The Impact of Science on Society, 1952 (e); What Is Freedom?, 1953 (e); What Is Democracy, 1953 (e); Satan in the Suburbs, 1953 (s); History as an Art, 1954 (Herman Ould Memorial lecture); Human Society in Ethics and Politics, 1954 (e); Nightmares of Eminent Persons, 1954 (s); Portraits from Memory, 1956 (r); Logic and Knowledge: Essays, 1901-1950, ed. Robert Charles Marsh, 1956 (e); Fact and Fiction, 1961 (e)

H.W. Leggett, Bertrand Russell, 1950 [lists principal works]; Alan Dorward, Bertrand Russell. A Short Guide to His Philosophy, 1951 [select bibliog.]

GEORGE WILLIAM RUSSELL (AE) 1867-1935

[The numerous political essays and pamphlets omitted.]

Homeward: Songs by the Way, 1894 (p); The Future of Ireland and the Awakening of the Fires, 1897 (e); The Earth Breath, 1897 (p); Ideals in Ireland: Priest or Hero?, 1897 (e); Literary Ideals in Ireland—Nationality and Cosmopolitanism in Literature, 1899 (e); An Artist of Gaelic Ireland, 1902 (e); The Nuts of Knowledge, 1903 (p); The Divine Vision, 1903 (p); Controversy in Ireland, 1904 (e); The Mask of Apollo, 1904 (s); By Still Waters, 1906 (p); Some Irish Essays, 1906 (e); Deidre, 1907 (d); The Hero in Man, 1909 (e); The Renewal of Youth, 1911 (e); Collected Poems, 1913 (sec. ed. 1926); Gods of War, 1915 (p); Imaginations and Reveries, 1915 (e); The Candle of Vision, 1918 (e); Michael, 1919 (p); Open Letter to the Irish People, 1922 (e); The Interpreters, 1922 (e); Voices of the Stones, 1925 (p); Midsummer Eve, 1928 (p); Dark Weeping, 1929 (p); Enchantment, 1930 (p); Vale, 1931 (p); Song and its Fountains, 1932 (e); The Avatars, a Futurist Fantasy, 1933 (s); The House of the Titans, 1934 (p); Selected Poems, 1935 (p); Some Passages from the Letters of AE to W. B. Yeats, 1936; AE's Letters to Minanlabain, 1937; The Living Torch, ed. Monk Gibbon, 1937 (e); Letters from AE, ed. Alan Denson, 1961

Alan Denson, Printed Writings by George William Russell (AE): A Bibliography, 1961

EDWARD SACKVILLE-WEST 1901-1965

Piano Quintet, 1925 (n); The Ruin, a Gothic Novel, 1926 (n); The Apology of Arthur Rimbaud: a Dialogue, 1927 (c); Mandrake over the Water-Carrier: a Recital, 1928 (n); Simpson, a Life, 1931 (rev. 1951) (n); (with V. Sackville-West) Rainer M. Rilke, Duineser Elegien, 1931 (tr); The Sun in Capricorn: a Recital, 1934 (n); A Flame in Sunlight: The Life and Work of Thomas De Quincey, 1936 (b); The Rescue, 1945 (rd); Inclinations, 1949 (e)

VICTORIA SACKVILLE-WEST 1892-1962

Poems of West and East, 1917 (p); Heritage, 1919 (n); Orchard and Vineyard, 1921 (p); The Dragon in Shallow Waters, 1921 (n); The Heir, 1922 (s); Knole and the Sackvilles, 1922 (h); Challenge, 1923 (n); Grey Wethers, 1923 (n); Seducers in Ecuador, 1924 (s); Passenger to Teheran, 1926 (t); The Land, 1926 (p); Aphra Behn, the Incomparable Astrea, 1927 (b); Twelve Days: An Account of a Journey Across the Bakhtiari Mountains in South-Western Persia, 1928 (t); Andrew Marvell, 1929 (b); King's Daughter, 1929 (p); The Edwardians, 1930 (n); (with Edward Sackville-West) Rainer M. Rilke, Duineser Elegien, 1931 (tr); All Passion Spent, 1931 (n); Sissinghurst,

1931 (p); *V. Sackville-West* [Selected Poems], 1931 (p); *Invitation to Cast Out Care*, 1931 (p); *The Death of Noble Godovary, and Gottfried Künstler*, 1932 (s); *Thirty Clocks Strike the Hour*, 1932 (s); *Family History*, 1932 (n); *Collected Poems*, 1933-; *The Dark Island*, 1934 (n); *Saint Joan of Arc*, 1936 (rev. 1948) (b); *Pepita*, 1937 (b); *Some Flowers*, 1937 (e); *Solitude*, 1938 (p); *Country Notes*, 1939 (e); *Country Notes in Wartime*, 1940 (e); *English Country Houses*, 1941 (e); *Selected Poems*, 1941; *Grand Canyon*, 1942 (n); *The Eagle and the Dove: A Study in Contrasts, St. Teresa of Avila and St. Thérèse of Lisieux*, 1943 (b); *The Garden*, 1946 (p); *In Your Garden*, 1951 (e); *In Your Garden Again*, 1953 (e); *The Easter Party*, 1953 (n); *Daughter of France* [la Grande Mademoiselle, 1627-93], 1959 (b); *No Signposts in the Sea*, 1961 (n)

Jean Muriel Wines, *A Bibliography of the Writings of V. Sackville-West*, 1958

GEORGE SAINTSBURY
1845-1933

A Short History of French Literature, 1866 (repr. to 1917) (h); *Primer of French Literature*, 1880 (h); *Dryden*, 1878 (b,c); *Marlborough*, 1886 (b); *A History of Elizabethan Literature*, 1887 (h); *Essays on French Novelists*, 1891 (c); *Corrected Impressions: Essays on Victorian Writers*, 1895 (c); *Essays in English Literature, 1780-1860*, 1895 (c); *A History of 19th-Century Literature, 1780-1895*, 1896 (h); *The Flourishing of Romance and the Rise of Allegory*, 1897 (c,e); *A Short History of English Literature*, 1898 (h); *A History of Criticism and Literary Taste in Europe*, 3 vols., 1900-04 (repr. 1929-34) (h); *The Earlier Renaissance*, 1901 (e); *Loci Critici, Selections and Notes*, 1903 (c); *A History of English Prosody*, 3 vols., 1906 (h); *Historical Manual of English Prosody*, 1910 (h); *A History of English Criticism*, 1911 (rev. enlgd. 1949) (h); *A History of English Prose Rhythm*, 1912 (h); *The English Novel*, 1913 (rev. 1919) (h); *The Peace of the Augustans: A Survey of 18th-Century Literature*, 1916 (repr. 1946) (h); *A History of the French Novel to the Close of the 19th Century*, 1917 (h); *Notes on a Cellar-Book*, 1920 (e); *A Letter Book*, 1922 (e); *A Scrap Book*, 1922; *A Second Scrap Book*, 1923; *A Last Scrap Book*, 1924; *A Consideration of Thackeray*, 1931 (c); *Prefaces and Essays*, sel. and ed. Oliver Elton, 1933; *A Last Vintage: Essays and Papers*, ed. John W. Oliver et al [with bibliography], 1950 (e)

George Saintsbury, The Memorial Volume: Essays, Papers and Portraits, by Oliver Elton, Sir Herbert Grierson, etc. Biographical memoir by A. Blyth Webster. Ed. A. M. Clark and A. Muir, 1945 (Am. ed. *A Saintsbury Miscellany*)

SAKI (H. H. MUNRO)
1870-1916

The Rise of the Russian Empire, 1900 (h); *The Westminster Alice*, 1902, (s); *Reginald*, 1904 (s); *Reginald in Russia*, 1910 (s); *The Chronicles of Clovis*, 1911 (repr. 1948) (s); *The Unbearable Bassington*, 1912 (repr. 1947) (n); *When William Came*, 1913 (repr. 1941) (n); *Beasts and Super-Beasts*, 1914 (repr. 1950) (s); *The Toys of Peace*, 1919 (e); *The Square Egg and Other Sketches, with Three Plays*, 1924; *The Short Stories of Saki*, 1930 (s); *The Novels and Plays of Saki*, 1933

WILLIAM SANSOM
1912-

Jim Braidy, 1943 (e); *Fireman Flower*, 1944 (s); *Three*, 1946 (s); *Westminster at War*, 1947 (e); *The Equilibriad*, 1948 (e); *South: Aspects and Images from Corsica, Italy and Southern France*, 1948 (t); *Something Terrible, Something Lovely*, 1948 (s); *The Body*, 1949 (n); *The Passionate North*, 1950 (s); *The Face of Innocence*, 1951 (n); *A Touch of the Sun*, 1952 (n); *It Was Really Charlie's Castle*, 1953 (n); *Pleasures Strange and Simple*, 1953 (e); *A Bed of Roses*, 1954 (s); *Lord Love Us*, 1954 (s); *A Contest of Ladies*, 1956 (s); *The Loving Eye*, 1956 (n); *Among the Dahlias*, 1957 (s); *The Cautious Heart*, 1958 (n); *The Icicle and the Sun*, 1958 (t); *Blue Skies, Brown Studies*, 1961 (t); *Collected Short Stories*, 1960 (s); *The Last Hours of Sandra Lee*, 1961 (n); *The Stories of William Sansom*, 1963 (s); *Away To It All* (Europe), 1964 (t)

SIEGFRIED SASSOON
1886-

[anon] *Poems*, 1906 (p); [anon] *Orpheus in Dilyoeryum*, 1908 (p); [anon] *Sonnets* 1909 (p); [anon] *Twelve Sonnets*, 1911 (p); [anon] *An Ode for Music*, 1912 (p); [anon] *Hyacinth*, 1912 (p); [anon] *Melodies*, 1912 (p); [Saul Kain, pseud.] *The Daffodil Murderer*, 1913 (Chantrey Prize poem, parody of Masefield, *The Everlasting Mercy*); *Apollo in Diloeryum*, 1913 (p); [anon] *Discoveries*, 1915 (p); [anon] *Morning-Glory*, 1916; *The Redeemer*, 1916 (p); *The Old Huntsman*, 1917 (p); *Counter-attack*, 1918 (p); *Four Poems*, 1918 (p); *Picture Show*, 1919 (p); *The War Poems of Siegfried Sassoon*, 1919; [anon] *Recreations*, 1923 (p); *Selected Poems*, 1925 (p); *Lingual Exercises for Advanced Vocabularians*, 1925 (p); *Satirical Poems*, 1926 (new ed. enlgd. 1933) (p); [*Thirty-Two Poems*], 1926 (p); *The Heart's Journey*, 1927 (p); *Nativity*, 1927 (p); *To My Mother*, 1918 (p); [anon] *Memoirs of a Fox-Hunting Man*, 1928 (repr. 1954) (a,n); *In Sicily*, 1930 (p); *Memoirs of an Infantry Officer*, 1930 (a,n); [Pinchbeck Lyre, pseud.] *Poems*, 1931 (p); *To the Red Rose*, 1931 (p); *Prehistoric Burials*, 1932 (p); *The Road to Ruin*, 1933 (p); *Vigils*, 1934 (p); *Sherston's Progress*, 1936 (a,n); *The Complete Memoirs of George Sherston*, (*Memoirs of a Fox-Hunting Man*, *Memoirs of an Infantry Officer*, with the preceding title), 1937 (a,n); *The Old Century and Seven More Years*, 1938 (r); *On Poetry*, 1939 (Memorial lecture, Univ. of Bristol); *Poems Newly Selected, 1916-35*, 1940; *Rhymed Ruminations*, 1940 (p); *The Flower Show Match*, 1941 (e); *The Weald of Youth*, 1942 (r); *Siegfried Sassoon* [*Selected Poems: Augustan Poets*], 1943 (p); *Siegfried's Journey, 1916-20*, 1945 (r); *Collected Poems*, 1947; *George Meredith*, 1948 (b,c); *Common Chords*, 1950 (p); *An Adjustment*, 1955 (p); *Sequences*, 1956 (p); *The Path to Peace, Selected Poems*, 1960 (p); *Collected Poems, 1908-56*, 1961

Geoffrey Keynes, *A Bibliography of Siegfried Sassoon*, 1962

D. S. SAVAGE
1917-

The Autumn World, 1939 (p); *Don Quixote*, 1939 (p); *A Time to Mourn; Poems, 1934-43*, 1943 (p); *The Personal Principle*, 1944 (c); *Hamlet and the Pirates*, 1950 (c); *The Withered Branch*, 1950 (c)

DOROTHY SAYERS
1893-1957

Opus I, 1916 (p); *Catholic Tales and Christian Songs*, 1918 (s,p); *Whose Body*, 1923 (n); *Clouds of Witness*, 1926 (n); *Unnatural Death*, 1927 (n); *The Unpleasantness at the Bellona Club*, 1928 (n); *Lord Peter Views the Body*, 1928 (s); *Thomas, the Troubadour, Tristan in Brittany*, 1929 (tr); [with Robert Eustace, pseud.] *The Documents in the Case*, 1930 (n); *Strong Poison*, 1930 (n); *The Five Red Herrings*, 1931 (n); *Have His Carcase*, 1932 (n); *Hangman's Holiday*, 1933 (s); *The Dorothy L. Sayers Omnibus*, 1933 (3n); *Murder Must Advertise*, 1933 (n); *The Nine Tailors*, 1934 (n); *Gaudy Night*, 1935 (n); *Busman's Honeymoon*, 1937 (n and, with M. Saint Clare Byrne, d); *The Zeal of Thy House*, 1937 (d); *The Greatest Drama Ever Staged* [on Easter], 1938 (e); *In the Teeth of the Evidence*, 1939 (s); *He That Should Come*, 1939 (d); *The Devil to Pay*, 1939 (d); (with others) *Double Death*, 1939 (s); *Strong Meat*, 1939 (e); *Love All*, 1940 (d); *Golden Cockerel*, 1941 (rd); *The Mind of the Maker*, 1941 (e); *The Man Born to Be King*, 1941 (repr. 1951) (rd); *The Just Vengeance*, 1946 (d); *Unpopular Opinions*, 1946 (e); *Four Sacred Plays* (*The Zeal of Thy House, The Devil to Pay, He That Should Come, The Just Vengeance*), 1948 (4d); *The Comedy of Dante Alighieri the Florentine*, 1949 (tr); *The Emperor Constantine*, 1951 (d); *Introductory Papers on Dante*, 1954 (c); *The New Sayers Omnibus*, 1956; *Further Papers on Dante*, 1957 (c); *The Song of Roland*, 1957 (tr)

FRANCIS SCARFE
1911-

Inscapes, 1940 (p); *Forty Poems and Ballads*, 1941 (p); *Auden and After*,

1942 (c); *W. H. Auden*, 1949 (b,c); *Underworlds*, 1950 (p); *Promises*, 1950 (n); *Single Blessedness*, 1951 (n); Paul Valéry, *Reflections on the World Today*, 1951 (tr); *Unfinished Woman*, 1954 (n); *The Art of Paul Valéry*, 1954 (c)

ERNEST DE SELINCOURT
1870-1943

English Poets and the National Ideal, 1915 (e); *The Study of Poetry*, 1918 (e); *Keats*, 1921 (c); *Poetry*, 1929 (e); Editor of William Wordsworth, *The Prelude*, 1932; *Dorothy Wordsworth: A Biography*, 1933 (b); *Oxford Lectures on Poetry*, 1934 (e); Editor of *Letters of William and Dorothy Wordsworth*, 6 vols., 1935-9; *The Early Wordsworth*, 1936 (b); Editor (with Helen Darbishire) of William Wordsworth, *Poetical Works*, 5 vols., 1940-9; Editor of Dorothy Wordsworth, *Journals*, 2 vols., 1941; *Wordsworthian and Other Studies*, 1947 (c)

Helen Darbishire, *Ernest de Selincourt*, from *Proceedings of the British Academy*, Vol. 29, 1944

EDWARD SHANKS
1892-1953

Songs, 1915 (p); *Poems*, 1916 (p); (with C. C. Mandell) *Hilaire Belloc, the Man and His Work*, 1916 (b,c); *The Queen of China*, 1919 (p); *The Old Indispensables*, 1919 (n); *The People of the Ruins*, 1920 (n); *The Island of Youth*, 1921 (p); *Fête Galante, a Dance-Drama . . . after Maurice Baring's Story of that Name* (dramatiz. by Ethel Smyth), 1923 (pd); *The Richest Man*, 1923 (n); *First Essays on Literature*, 1923 (c); *Bernard Shaw*, 1924 (b,c); *The Shadowgraph*, 1925 (p); *Twenty Poems*, 1926 (p); *The Beggar's Ride*, 1926 (d); *Collected Poems, 1909-25*, 1926; *Second Essays on Literature*, 1927 (c); *Bo and His Circle*, 1931 (e); *Queer Street*, 1932 (n); *Poems, 1912-32*, 1933 (p); *The Enchanted Village*, 1933 (n); *Tom Tiddler's Ground*, 1934 (n); *Old King Cole*, 1936 (Am. ed. *The Dark Green Circle*) (n); *Edgar Allan Poe*, 1937 (b,c); *My England*, 1938 (t); *Rudyard Kipling*, 1940 (c); *Elizabeth Goes Home*, 1942 (e); *The Night Watch for England*, 1942 (p); *Poems, 1939-52*, 1954

GEORGE BERNARD SHAW
1856-1950

(Selective Bibliography)

The many reprints of separate plays are not indicated. Only a sampling is given of Shaw's almost innumerable essays and tracts on the subjects that interested him, such as Fabianism, socialism, censorship, the English language and its spelling, war, the Irish question. Also, this list includes only some of the selected and collected works.

Cashel Byron's Profession, 1886 (n) (rev. 1901, contains *The Admirable Bashville, or, Constancy Unrewarded*, d based on the novel, *Cashel Byron's Profession*); *An Unsocial Socialist*, 1887 (n); *The Quintessence of Ibsenism*, 1891 (enlgd. 1913) (c); *Widowers' Houses*, 1893 (d); *Plays Pleasant and Unpleasant* (Pleasant: *Arms and the Man, Candida, The Man of Destiny, You Never Can Tell*; Unpleasant: *Widowers' Houses, The Philanderer, Mrs. Warren's Profession*), 1898; *The Perfect Wagnerite*, 1898 (c); *Love Among the Artists*, 1900 (n); *Three Plays for Puritans* (*The Devil's Disciple, Caesar and Cleopatra, Captain Brassbound's Conversion*), 1901 (3d); *Man and Superman*, 1903 (d); *The Irrational Knot*, 1905 (n); *Dramatic Opinions and Essays*, 1906 (c); *John Bull's Other Island, Major Barbara*; also *How He Lied to Her Husband*, 1907 (3d); *The Sanity of Art*, 1908 (c); *Press Cuttings*, 1909 (d); *The Shewing-up of Blanco Posnet*, 1909 (d); *Misalliance*, 1910 (d); *Brieux: A Preface*, 1910 (c); *The Doctor's Dilemma, Getting Married, and The Shewing-up of Blanco Posnet*, 1911 (3d); *Androcles and the Lion*, 1914 (d); *Misalliance, The Dark Lady of the Sonnets, Fanny's First Play. With a Treatise on Parents and Children*, 1914 (3d,e); *Androcles and the Lion, Overruled, Pygmalion*, 1916 (3d); *Heartbreak House*, 1917 (d); *Heartbreak House, Great Catherine, and Playlets of the War* (*O'Flaherty, V.C., The Inca of Perusalem, Augustus Does His Bit, Annajanska*), 1919 (6d); *Back to Methuselah*, 1921 (d); *Saint Joan*, 1924 (d); *Translations and Tomfooleries* (*Jitta's Atonement*, tr. from the German of Seigfried Trebitsch; *The Admirable Bashville, Press Cuttings, The Glimpse of Reality, Passion, Poison and

Petrification, The Fascinating Foundling, The Music-Cure), 1926 (7d); *The Intelligent Woman's Guide to Socialism and Capitalism*, 1928 (rev. enlgd. 1937 as *The Intelligent Woman's Guide to Socialism, Capitalism, Sovietism and Fascism*) (e); *Bernard Shaw and Karl Marx. A Symposium, 1884-1889*, ed. R. W. Ellis, 1930 (e); *The Apple Cart*, 1930 (d); *Ellen Terry and Bernard Shaw: A Correspondence*, ed. Christopher St. John, 1931; *Complete Works* (standard edition), 1931-50; *Immaturity*, 1931 (written 1879) (n); *What I Really Wrote About the War*, 1931 (e); *Pen Portraits and Reviews*, 1932 (c); *Essays in Fabian Socialism* (includes *The Fabian Society. What It Has Done and How It Has Done It*, 1892; *The Impossibilities of Anarchism*, 1893; *The Common Sense of Municipal Trading*, 1904), 1932 (e); *Doctors' Delusions, Crude Criminology and Sham Education*, 1932 (e); *Our Theatres in the Nineties*, 1932 (c); *Music in London, 1890-94*, 1932 (c); *Major Critical Essays* (*The Quintessence of Ibsenism, The Perfect Wagnerite, The Sanity of Art*), 1932 (c); *The Adventures of the Black Girl in Her Search for God*, 1932 (n); *Prefaces*, 1934 (enlgd. 1938) (e); *Too True to be Good, Village Wooing, On the Rocks*, 1934 (3d); *Short Stories, Scraps and Shavings*, 1934 (s); *The Simpleton of the Unexpected Isles, The Six of Calais, The Millionairess*, 1936 (3d); *London Music in 1888-89*, 1937 (c); *In Good King Charles's Golden Days*, 1939 (d); *Geneva: A Fancied Page of History*, 1939 (d); *Shaw Gives Himself Away*, 1939 (a); *Everybody's Political What's What*, 1944 (e); *Geneva, Cymbeline Refinished and Good King Charles*, 1946 (3d); *The Crime of Imprisonment*, 1946 (e); *Sixteen Self Sketches*, 1949 (a); *Shaw on Vivisection*, ed. G. H. Bowker, 1949; *Buoyant Billions, Farfetched Fables, Skakes Versus Shav.* 1950 (3d); *The Complete Plays*, 1950; *Bernard Shaw and Mrs. Patrick Campbell: Their Correspondence*, ed. Alan Dent, 1952; *Selected Prose*, ed. Diarmuid Russell, 1953; *Advice to a Young Critic*, 1955 (letters); *My Dear Dorothea*, 1956 (written 1877) (e); *The Illusions of Socialism. With, Socialism: Principles and Outlook*, 1956 (e); *Bernard Shaw's Letters to Granville Barker*, ed. C. B. Purdom, 1956; *An Unfinished Novel*, ed. Stanley Weintraub, 1958 (n); *Shaw on Theatre* (includes *The Dying Tongue of Great Elizabeth, The Art of Rehearsal*), ed. E. J. West, 1958 (e); *How to Become a Musical Critic*, ed. Dan H. Laurence, 1960 (c); *Shaw on Shakespeare*, ed. Edwin Wilson, 1961 (c); *To a Young Actress; Letters to Molly Tompkins*, ed. Peter Tompkins, 1961 (letters); *Complete Plays with Prefaces*, 1962; *Platform and Pulpit*, ed. Dan H. Laurence, 1962 (e); *The Matter With Ireland*, ed. Dan H. Laurence and David H. Greene, 1962 (e); *Religious Speeches*, ed. Warren Sylvester Smith, 1963; *The Rationalization of Russia*, ed. Harry M. Geduld, 1964 (e)

William Irvine, *The Universe of G.B.S.*, 1949; Alfred C. Ward, *Bernard Shaw, a Biography*, 1951 [selected bibliog.]

ROBERT C. SHERRIFF
1896-

Journey's End, 1929 (d); *Badger's Green*, 1930 (d); (with Vernon Bartlett) *Journey's End*, 1931 (n); *The Fortnight in September*, 1931 (n); (with Jeanne de Casalis) *St. Helena*, 1934 (d); *Two Heart's Doubled*, 1935 (d); *The Hopkins Manuscript*, 1939 (rev. as *The Cataclysm*, 1958) (n); (with others, from novel by James Hilton) *Goodbye Mr. Chips*, 1940 (screenplay); *Chedworth*, 1944 (n); *Another Year*, 1948 (n); (from stories by W. Somerset Maugham) *Quartet*, 1948 (screenplay); *Miss Mabel*, 1949 (d); *Home at Seven*, 1950 (d); (with W. S. Maugham, and Noel Langley, from stories by Maugham) *Trio*, 1950 (screenplay); (with Frederick L. Green) *Odd Man Out*, 1950 (screenplay); *The White Carnation*, 1954 (d); *King John's Treasure*, 1954 (n); *The Long Sunset*, 1956 (d); *A Shred of Evidence*, 1961 (d); *The Wells of St. Mary's*, 1961 (n)

NEVIL SHUTE
1899-1960

Pied Piper, 1924 (n); *Marazan*, 1926 (repr. 1952) (n); *So Disdained*, 1928 (repr. 1951) (n); *Lonely Road*, 1932 (repr. 1962) (n); *Ruined City*, 1938 (repr. 1951) (n); *Kindling*, 1938 (n); *What Happened to the Corbetts*, 1939 (repr.

1952) (n); *Ordeal*, 1940 (n); *Landfall*, 1940 (repr. 1962) (n); *An Old Captivity*, 1940 (n); *Pastoral*, 1944 (repr. 1964) (n); *Most Secret*, 1945 (n); *Vinland the Good*, 1946 (film play); *The Chequer Board*, 1947 (n); *No Highway*, 1948 (n); *A Town like Alice*, 1950 (Am. ed. *Legacy*) (n); *Round the Bend*, 1951 (n); *The Far Country*, 1952 (n); *So Disdained*, 1952 (n); *In the Wet*, 1953 (n); *Slide Rule, The Autobiography of an Engineer*, 1954 (a); *Requiem for a Wren*, 1955 (also pub. as *The Breaking Wave*) (n); *Beyond the Black Stump*, 1956 (n); *On the Beach*, 1957 (n); *The Rainbow and the Rose*, 1958 (n); *Trustee from the Toolroom*, 1960 (n); *Stephen Morris*, 1961 (n); *Three of a Kind*, 1962 (n)

ETHEL SIDGWICK
1877-

Promise, 1910 (n); *Le Gentleman, an Idyll of the Quarter*, 1911 (n); *Herself*, 1912 (n); *Succession, a Comedy of the Generations* (seq. to *Promise*), 1913 (n); *A Lady of Leisure*, 1914 (n); *Duke Jones* (seq. to *A Lady of Leisure*), 1914 (n); *The Accolade*, 1915 (n); *Hatchways*, 1916 (n); *Jamesie*, 1918 (n); *Madam*, 1921 (n); *Restoration, the Fairy Tale of a Farm*, 1923 (n); *Laura, a Cautionary Story*, 1924 (n); *The Bells of Shoreditch*, 1928 (Am. ed. *When I Grow Rich*) (n); *Dorothy's Wedding, a Tale of Two Villages*, 1931 (Am. ed. *A Tale of Two Villages*) (n); *Mrs. Henry Sidgwick, a Memoir*, 1938 (m). Also plays for children.

JON SILKIN
1930-

The Portrait, 1951 (p); *The Peaceable Kingdom*, 1954 (p); *The Two Freedoms*, 1958 (p); *The Re-ordering of the Stones*, 1961 (p); *Flower Poems*, 1964 (p)

ALAN SILLITOE
1928-

Without Beer or Bread, 1957 (p); *Saturday Night and Sunday Morning*, 1958 (n); *The Loneliness of the Long-Distance Runner*, 1959 (s); *The General*, 1960 (n); *The Rats*, 1960 (p); *The Key to the Door*, 1961 (n); *The Ragman's Daughter*, 1963 (s); *Road to Volgograd*, 1964 (t)

MAY SINCLAIR
1865-1946

Nakiketas, n.d. (p); *Essays in Verse*, 1892 (p); *Audrey Craven*, 1897 (n); *Mr. and Mrs. Nevill Tyson*, 1898 (Am. ed. *The Tysons*, 1906) (n); *Two Sides of a Question*, 1901 (n); *The Divine Fire*, 1904 (n); *Superseded*, 1906 (n); *The Helpmate*, 1907 (n); *The Judgment of Eve*, 1907 (Am. ed. *The Return of the Prodigal*) (s); *Kitty Tailleur*, 1908 (Am. ed. *The Immortal Moment*) (n); *The Creators*, 1910 (n); *The Flaw in the Crystal*, 1912 (n); *Feminism*, 1912 (e); *The Three Brontës*, 1912 (b); *The Combined Maze*, 1913 (n); *The Three Sisters*, 1914 (n); *Tasker Jevons, the Real Story*, 1916 (Am. ed. *The Belfry*) (n); *The Tree of Heaven*, 1917 (n); *A Defence of Idealism, Some Questions and Conclusions*, 1917 (e); *Mary Olivier, a Life*, 1919 (n); *The Romantic*, 1920 (n); *Mr. Waddington of Wyck*, 1921 (n); *Anne Severn and the Fieldings*, 1922 (n); *Life and Death of Harriett Frean*, 1922 (n); *The New Idealism*, 1922 (e); *Uncanny Stories*, 1923 (s); *A Cure of Souls*, 1924 (n); *Arnold Waterlow, a Life*, 1924 (n); *The Dark Night*, 1924 (p); *The Rector of Wyck*, 1925 (n); *Far End*, 1926 (n); *The Allinghams*, 1927 (n); *History of Anthony Waring*, 1927 (n); *Fame*, 1929 (s); *Tales Told by Simpson*, 1930 (s); *The Intercessor*, 1931 (s)

EDITH SITWELL
1887-1964

The Mother, 1915 (p); (with Osbert Sitwell) *Twentieth Century Harlequinade*, 1916 (p); *Clowns' Houses*, 1918 (p); *The Wooden Pegasus*, 1920 (p); *Façade*, 1922 (enlgd. 1949) (p); *Bucolic Comedies*, 1923 (p); *The Sleeping Beauty*, 1924 (p); (with Osbert and Sacheverell Sitwell) *Poor Young People*, 1925 (p); *Troy Park*, 1925 (p); *Poetry and Criticism*, 1925 (e); *Edith Sitwell [Poems]*, 1926 (p); *Elegy on Dead Fashion*, 1926 (p); *Rustic Elegies*, 1927 (p); *Five Poems*, 1928 (p); *Popular Song*, 1928 (p); *Gold Coast Customs*, 1929 (p); *Alexander Pope*, 1930 (b,c); *Collected*

Poems, 1930; *Jane Barston, 1719-1746*, 1931 (p); *Bath*, 1932 (h); *The English Eccentrics*, 1933 (b); *Five Variations, on a Theme*, 1933 (p); *Aspects of Modern Poetry*, 1934 (c); *Victoria of England*, 1934 (b); *Selected Poems*, 1936; *I Live Under a Black Sun*, 1937 (n); (with Osbert and Sacheverell Sitwell) *Trio*, 1938 (e); *Poems New and Old*, 1940 (p); *Street Songs*, 1942 (p); *English Women*, 1942 (e); *A Poet's Notebook*, 1943 (c); *Green Song*, 1944 (p); *The Song of the Cold*, 1945 (p); *Fanfare for Elizabeth*, 1946 (b); *The Shadow of Cain*, 1947 (p); *A Notebook on William Shakespeare*, 1948 (c); *The Canticle of the Rose: Selected Poems 1920-1947*, 1949 (p); *Poor Men's Music*, 1950 (p); *Façade and Other Poems 1920-1935*, 1950 (p); *Selected Poems*, 1952 (p); *A Book of Flowers*, 1952 (e); *Gardeners and Astronomers*, 1953 (p); *The Collected Poems*, 1957; *The Pocket Poets: Edith Sitwell*, 1960 (p); *The Outcasts*, 1962 (p); *The Queens and the Hive* [Elizabeth I], 1962 (b)

Geoffrey Singleton, *Edith Sitwell: The Hymn to Life*, 1960

OSBERT SITWELL
1892-

(with Edith Sitwell) *Twentieth Century Harlequinade*, 1916 (p); *The Winstonburg Line, Three Satires*, 1919 (p); *Argonaut and Juggernaut*, 1919 (p); *At the House of Mrs. Kinfoot*, 1921 (p); *Who Killed Cock-Robin*, 1921 (c); *Out of the Flame*, 1923 (p); *Triple Fugue*, 1924 (s); *Discursions on Travel, Art and Life*, 1925 (e); (with Edith and Sacheverell Sitwell) *Poor Young People*, 1925 (p); *Before the Bombardment*, 1926 (n); *Winter the Huntsman*, 1927 (p); *England Reclaimed*, 1927 (repr. 1949) (p); (with Sacheverell Sitwell) *All At Sea*, 1927 (d); *The People's Album of London Statues*, 1928 (e); *The Man Who Lost Himself*, 1929 (n); *Miss Mew*, 1929 (p); *Dumb Animal*, 1930 (s); *The Collected Satires and Poems of Osbert Sitwell*, 1931; *Three-Quarter Length Portrait of Michael Arlen*, 1931 (p); *Three-Quarter Length Portrait of the Viscountess Wimbourne*, 1931 (p); *Dickens*, 1932 (c); *Winters of Content*, 1932 (enlgd. 1950) (t); *Miracle on Sinai*, 1933 (n); *Brighton*, 1935 (h); *Penny Foolish*, 1935 (e); *Mrs. Kimber*, 1937 (p); *Those were the Days*, 1938 (n); (with Edith and Sacheverell Sitwell) *Trio*, 1938 (e); *Escape With Me!*, 1939 (e); *Open The Door*, 1941 (s); *A Place of One's Own*, 1941 (n); *Gentle Caesar*, 1943 (d); *Selected Poems Old and New*, 1943; *Left Hand, Right Hand!* (Vol. I of autobiog.), 1944 (a); *Sing High! Sing Low!* 1944 (e); *A Letter to My Son*, 1944 (e); *The True Story of Dick Whittington*, 1946 (n); *The Scarlet Tree* (Vol. II of autobiog.), 1946 (a); *Alive— Alive Oh!*, 1947 (s); *Great Morning!* (Vol. III of autobiog.), 1947 (a); *The Novels of George Meredith*, 1947 (c); *Laughter in the Next Room* (Vol. IV of *Left Hand, Right Hand!*, autobiog.), 1948 (a); *Four Songs of the Italian Earth*, 1948 (p); *Demos the Emperor*, 1949 (pd); *Death of a God*, 1949 (s); *England Reclaimed and Other Poems*, 1949 (p); *Noble Essences*, 1950 (a); *Wrack at Tidesend* (Vol. II of *England Reclaimed*), 1952 (p); *Collected Stories*, 1953; *The Four Continents*, 1954 (e); *On the Continent* (Vol. III of *England Reclaimed*), 1958 (p); *Fee Fi Fo Fum!*, 1959 (n); *A Place of One's Own*, 1961 (s); *Tales My Father Taught Me*, 1962 (r); *Pound Wise*, 1963 (e)

Richard Fifoot, *A Bibliography of Edith, Osbert, and Sacheverell Sitwell*, 1963

SACHEVERELL SITWELL
1897-

The People's Palace, 1918 (p); *Dr. Donne and Gargantua, First Canto*, 1921 (p); *The Hundred and One Harlequins*, 1922 (p); *Dr. Donne and Gargantua, Canto The Second*, 1923 (p); *The Parrot*, 1923 (p); *Southern Baroque Art*, 1924 (c); *The Thirteenth Caesar*, 1924 (p); (with Edith and Osbert Sitwell) *Poor Young People*, 1925 (p); *Exalt the Eglantine*, 1926 (p); *All Summer In A Day*, 1926 (a); *Dr. Donne and Gargantua, Canto The Third*, 1926 (p); *The Cyder Feast*, 1927 (p); *German Baroque Art*, 1927 (c); *A Book of Towers . . . of Southern Europe*, 1928 (t); *Sacheverell Sitwell* [Selected Poems], 1928 (p); *The Gothick North, A Study of Medieval Life, Art and*

Thought, 1929-30 (h); *Two Poems. Ten Songs*, 1929 (p); *Dr. Donne and Gargantua, The First Six Cantos*, 1930 (p); *Beckford and Beckfordism*, 1930 (e); *Far From My Home*, 1931 (e); *Spanish Baroque Art*, 1931 (c); *Mozart*, 1932 (b); *Canons of Giant Art*, 1933 (p); *Liszt*, 1934 (b); *Touching The Orient*, 1934 (sk); *A Background For Domenico Scarlatti 1685-1757*, 1935 (e); *Dance of the Quick and the Dead*, 1936 (e); *Collected Poems*, 1936; *Conversation Pieces*, 1936 (e); *Narrative Pictures*, 1937 (e); *La Vie Parisienne, A Tribute to Jacques Offenbach*, 1937 (e); *Roumanian Journey*, 1938 (t); (with F. Bamford) *Edinburgh*, 1938 (h); *German Baroque Sculpture*, 1938 (c); (with Edith and Osbert Sitwell) *Trio*, 1938 (e); *Mauretania*, 1940 (e); *Poltergeists*, 1940 (e); *Sacred and Profane Love*, 1940 (e); *Valse des Fleurs*, 1941 (sk); *Primitive Scenes and Festivals*, 1942 (e); *The Homing of the Winds*, 1942 (e); *Splendours and Miseries*, 1943 (e); *British Architects and Craftsmen*, 1945 (e); *The Hunters and the Hunted*, 1947 (e); *The Netherlands*, (e); *Selected Poems*, 1948; *Morning, Noon and Night in London*, 1948 (e); *Theatrical Figures in Porcelain*, 1949 (e); *Spain*, 1950 (t); *Cupid and Jacaranda*, 1952 (e); *Truffle Hunt with Sacheverell Sitwell*, 1953 (e); *Selected Works*, 1953; *Portugal and Madeira*, 1954 (t); *Selected Works*, 1955; *Denmark*, 1956 (t); *Arabesque and Honeycomb*, 1957 (e); *Malta*, 1958 (t); *Journey to the Ends of Time*, 1959 (a); *Bridge of the Brocade Sash* 1959 (t); *Golden Wall and Mirador*, 1961 (t); *The Red Chapels of Banteai Srei*, 1962 (e)

Richard Fifoot, *A Bibliography of Edith, Osbert, and Sacheverell Sitwell*, 1963

LOGAN PEARSALL SMITH
1865-1946

The Youth of Parnassus, 1895 (repr. 1909) (s); *Trivia, Printed from the Papers of Anthony Woodhouse, Esq.*, 1902 (many repr.) (e); *The Life and Letters of Sir Henry Wotton*, 1907 (b); *Songs and Sonnets*, 1909 (p); *The English Language*, 1912 (repr. 1952) (h); *A Few Practical Suggestions* [on the Work of the Society for Pure English], 1920 (e); *More Trivia*, 1922 (e); *English Idioms*, 1923 (e); *Four Words: Romantic, Originality, Creative, Genius*, 1924 (e); *Words and Idioms: Studies in the English Language*, 1925 (e); *The Prospects of Literature*, 1927 (e); *Needed Words*, 1928 (e); *Afterthoughts*, 1931 (aphorisms); *Robert Bridges. Recollections*, 1931 (r); *On Reading Shakespeare*, 1933 (c); *All Trivia (Trivia, More Trivia, Afterthoughts, Last Words)*, 1933 (e); *Reperusals and Re-collections*, 1936 (e); *Unforgotten Years*, 1938 (r); *Milton and His Modern Critics*, 1940 (c); *A Portrait of Logan Pearsall Smith, Drawn from His Letters and Diaries and Introduced by John Russell*, 1950

Robert G. Hardy, *Recollections of Logan Pearsall Smith*, 1949

STEVIE SMITH
1902-

[The books of poetry, except the last listed, are illustrated by the author.]

A Good Time Was Had By All, 1937 (p); *Novel on Yellow Paper*, 1937 (repr. 1951) (n); *Over the Frontier*, 1938 (n); *Tender Only to One*, 1937 (p); *Mother, What is Man?*, 1942 (p); *The Holiday*, 1949 (n); *Harold's Leap*, 1950 (p); *Not Waving But Drowning*, 1957 (p); *Some Are More Human than Others; Sketchbook*, 1958 (illustrations); *Cats in Colour*, 1959 (illustrations); *Selected Poems*, 1962 (p)

SYDNEY GOODSIR SMITH
1915-

Skail Wind, 1941 (p); *The Wanderer*, 1943 (p); *The Deevil's Waltz*, 1946 (p); *Carotid Cornucopius, the First Four Fitts*, 1947 (p); *Selected Poems*, 1947 (p); *Under the Eildon Tree*, 1948 (p); *A Short Introduction to Scottish Literature*, 1951 (h); *So Late Into the Night: Fifty Lyrics 1944-48*, 1952 (p); *Cokkils*, 1953 (p); *A Collection of Poems*, 1954; *Omens*, 1955 (p); *Orpheus and Eurydice*, 1955 (p); *The Merrie Life and Dowie Death of Colickie Meg, the Carlin Wife of Ben Nevis*, 1956 (p); *Figs and Thistles*, 1959 (p); *The Wallace*, 1960 (pd)

CHARLES PERCY SNOW
1905-

Death Under Sail, 1932 (rev. 1959) (n); New Lives for Old, 1933 (n); The Search, 1934 (rev. 1958) (n); Strangers and Brothers, sequence of novels: Strangers and Brothers, 1940, The Light and the Dark, 1947, Time of Hope, 1949, The Masters, 1951, The New Men, 1954, Homecomings, 1956, The Conscience of the Rich, 1958, The Affair, 1960, Corridors of Power, 1964; (with Pamela Hansford Johnson, the following plays, 1951): Family Party, Her Best Foot Forward, The Pigeon With the Silver Foot, Spare the Rod, The Supper Dance, To Murder Mrs. Mortimer; The Two Cultures and the Scientific Revolution, 1959 [Cambridge, Rede Lecture]; Science and Government, 1961 [Harvard, Godkin Lecture]; Recent Thoughts on the Two Cultures, 1961 [Birbeck College, lecture]; Magnanimity, 1962 [Univ. of St. Andrews, rectorial address]; A Postscript to "Science and Government", 1963 (e)

William Cooper (pseud.), C. P. Snow, 1959; Robert Graecen, The World of C. P. Snow, with bibliog. by Bernard Stone, 1962

CHARLES HAMILTON SORLEY
1895-1915

Letters from Germany and from the Army, ed. W. R. Sorley, 1916; Marlborough, 1916 (sec. ed. enlgd. 1919, repr. to 1932) (p); The Letters of Charles Sorley, with a chapter of biography [by Mrs. Janet Sorley], 1919; Charles Hamilton Sorley [Selected Poems], 1931 (p)

MURIEL SPARK
1918-

Child of Light: A Reassessment of Mary Wollstonecraft Shelley, 1951 (b); The Fanfarlo, 1952 (p); (with Derek Stanford) Emily Brontë, 1953 (b); John Masefield, 1953 (c); The Comforters, 1957 (n); The Go-away Bird, 1958 (s); Robinson, 1958 (n); Memento Mori, 1959 (n); The Bachelors, 1960 (n); The Ballad of Peckham Rye, 1960 (n); The Prime of Miss Jean Brodie, 1961 (n); Voices at Play, 1961 (d,s,e); Doctors of Philosophy, 1963 (4d,6s); The Girls of Slender Means, 1963 (n)

Derek Stanford, Muriel Spark: A Biographical and Critical Study, with bibliog. by Bernard Stone, 1963

BERNARD SPENCER
1909-1963

Aegean Islands, 1946 (p); (with others) George Sepheres, The King of Asine, 1948 (tr); The Twist in the Plotting, 1961 (p); With Luck Lasting, 1963 (p)

STEPHEN SPENDER
1909-

Nine Entertainments, 1928 (p); Twenty Poems, 1930 (p); Poems, 1933 (sec. ed. 1934 (p); Vienna, 1934 (p); The Destructive Element, 1935 (c); The Burning Cactus, 1936 (s); Forward from Liberalism, 1937 (e); Trial of a Judge, 1938 (d); The Still Centre, 1939 (p); (with J. B. Leishman) Rainer Maria Rilke, Duino Elegies, 1939 (tr); (with Goronwy Rees) Danton's Death by Georg Büchner, 1939 (tr); Poems for Spain, 1939 (p); The New Realism, 1939 (e); Selected Poems, 1940 (p); The Backward Son, 1940 (n); Ruins and Visions, 1942 (p); Life and the Poet, 1942 (e); (with J. L. Gili) Selected Poems of Federico Garcia Lorca, 1943 (tr); Poetry Since 1939, 1946 (c); European Witness [Impressions of Germany in 1945], 1946 (e); Poems of Dedication, 1947 (p); Returning to Vienna, 1947 (p); Botticelli, 1948 (b); The Edge of Being, 1949 (p); (with F. Cornford) Paul Eluard, Le Dur Désir de Durer, 1950 (tr); World Within World, 1951 (a); Rainer Maria Rilke, The Life of the Virgin Mary, 1951 (tr); Learning Laughter [A Study of Children in Israel], 1952 (e); Shelley, 1952 (c); Ed., Encounter, 1953-; The Creative Element, 1953 (e); Sirmione Peninsula, 1953 (p); Collected Poems, 1928-1953, 1955; The Making of a Poem, 1955 (e); Engaged in Writing, and The Fool and the Princess, 1958 (s); Inscriptions, 1958 (p); Schiller, Mary Stuart, 1958 (tr); The Struggle of the Modern, 1963 (c)
Also trs. of Toller and Wedekind

J. C. SQUIRE
1884-1958

Socialism and Art, 1907 (e); Poems and Baudelaire Flowers, 1909 (p); Imaginary Speeches, and Other Parodies, 1912 (p,e); William the Silent, 1912 (b); The Three Hills, 1913 (p); Steps to Parnassus, and Other Parodies and Diversions, 1913 (p,e); The Survival of the Fittest, 1916, (p); Twelve Poems, 1916 (p); The Lily of Malud, 1917 (p); The Gold Tree, 1918 (e); Tricks of the Trade, 1917 (p,e); Poems: First Series, 1918 (p); (Solomon Eagle, pseud.) Books in General, First Series, 1918 (c); The Birds, 1919 (p); Ed., London Mercury, 1919-1934; The Moon, 1920, (p); (Solomon Eagle, pseud.) Books in General, Second Series, 1920 (c); Life and Letters, 1920 (e); (Solomon Eagle, pseud.) Books in General, Third Series, 1921 (c); Collected Parodies, 1921 (p,e); Poems, Second Series, 1922 (p); Books Reviewed, 1922 (c); (Solomon Eagle, pseud.) Essays at Large, 1922 (e); American Poems, 1923 (p); Essays on Poetry, 1923 (c); A New Song of the Bishop of London and the City Churches, 1924 (p); The Grub Street Nights Entertainments, 1924 (s); Poems in One Volume, 1926 (p); Life at the Mermaid, 1927 (e); (with John L. Balderston) Berkeley Square, 1928 (d); (with Joan R. Young) Robin Hood, 1928 (d); (adapted from Jane Austen, with Eileen H. A. Squire) Pride and Prejudice, 1929 (d); Sunday Mornings, 1930 (e); A Face in the Candlelight, 1932 (p); Outside Eden, 1933 (s); Reflections and Memories, 1935 (r); Shakespeare as a Dramatist, 1935 (c); Weepings and Wailings, 1935 (p); Flowers of Speech, 1935 (e); The Honeysuckle and the Bee, 1937 (a); Water Music, 1939 (e); Poems of Two Wars, 1940 (p); Selected Poems, 1948 (p); Collected Poems, 1959

Patrick J. F. Howarth, Squire: 'Most Generous of Men', 1963

ROBERT STANDISH
1898-

The Three Bamboos, 1942 (n); Bonin, 1943 (n); The Small General, 1945 (n); Mr. On Loong, 1946 (n); The Gulf of Time, 1947 (n); Elephant Walk, 1948 (n); Gentleman of China, 1949 (n); Follow the Seventh Man, 1950 (n); Storm Centre, 1951 (n); A Worthy Man, 1951 (n); A Long Way from Pimlico, 1954 (n); Private Enterprise, 1954 (s); Honourable Ancestor, 1956 (n); Blind Tiger, 1957 (n); The Prince of Storytellers [Life of E. Phillips Oppenheim], 1957 (b); African Guinea Pig, 1958 (n); The Radio-active General, 1959 (s); The First of Trees, The Story of the Olive, 1960 (h); The Big One Got Away, 1960 (n); The Talking Dog, 1961 (s); The Cruise of "The Three Brothers", 1962 (n); Singapore Kate, 1964 (n)

DEREK STANFORD
1918-

The Freedom of Poetry, Studies in Contemporary Verse, 1947 (e); Music for Statues, 1948 (p); Christopher Fry, 1951 (c); Christopher Fry Album, 1952 (e); (with Muriel Spark) Emily Brontë, 1953 (b,c); Dylan Thomas, 1954 (rev. 1964) (c); (with Ada Harrison) Anne Brontë, 1959 (b,c); Movements in English Poetry, 1900-1958, 1959 (h); John Betjeman, 1961 (c); Muriel Spark, 1963 (b,c)

FREYA STARK
1893-

Bagdad Sketches, 1932 (sk); The Valleys of the Assassins and Other Persian Travels, 1934 (t); The Southern Gates of Arabia, 1936 (t); Seen in the Hadhramaut, 1938 (t); A Winter in Arabia, 1940 (t); Letters from Syria, 1942 (t); East is West, 1939-1943, 1945 (Am. ed. The Arab Island) (h); Perseus in the Wind, 1948 (e); Traveller's Prelude, 1950 (a); Beyond Euphrates, 1951 (a); The Coast of Incense, 1933-1939, 1953 (a); The Freya Stark Story (condensation of autobiog. to 1939), 1953 (a); Ionia, A Quest, 1954 (t); The Lycian Shore, 1956 (t); Alexander's Path, 1958 (t); Riding to the Tigris, 1959 (t); Dust in the Lion's Paw, 1939-1946, 1961 (a); The Journey's Echo: Selections, 1963 (t)

JAMES STEPHENS
1882-1950

Insurrections, 1909 (p); The Lonely God, 1909 (p); The Adventures of

Seumas Beg: The Visit from Abroad, In The Orchard, Treasure Trove, 1910 (p); *The Spy,* 1910 (p); *The Hill of Vision,* 1912 (repr. 1922) (p); *The Charwoman's Daughter,* 1912 (Am. ed. *Mary, Mary*) (n); *The Crock of Gold,* 1912 (repr. 1954) (n); *Five New Poems,* 1913 (p); *Here Are Ladies,* 1913 (s); *The Demi-Gods,* 1914 (n); *The Adventures of Seumas Beg, The Rocky Road to Dublin,* 1915 (p); *Songs from the Clay,* 1915 (p); *The Insurrection in Dublin,* 1916 (e); *Green Branches,* 1916 (p); *Reincarnations,* 1918 (p); [James Esse, pseud.] *Hunger,* 1918 (n); *Irish Fairy Tales,* 1920 (s); *Arthur Griffith, Journalist and Statesman,* 1922 (b); *Deirdre,* 1923 (repr. 1962) (n); *Little Things,* 1924 (p); *In the Land of Youth,* 1924 (n); *A Poetry Recital,* 1925 (p); *Collected Poems,* 1926 (rev. enlgd. 1954); *On Prose and Verse,* 1928 (e); *Etched in Moonlight,* 1928 (s); *Dublin Letters,* 1928 (e); *Julia Elizabeth,* 1929 (d); *The Outcast,* 1929 (p); *Theme and Variations,* 1930 (p); *Strict Joy,* 1931 (p); *Kings and the Moon,* 1938 (p); *A James Stephens Reader,* sel. Lloyd Frankenberg, 1962

Birgit Bramsbäck, *James Stephens,* 1959

G. B. STERN
1890-

Pantomime, 1914 (n); *"See-Saw",* 1914 (repr. 1931) (n); *Twos and Threes,* 1916 (n); *Grand Chain,* 1917 (n); *A Marrying Man,* 1918 (n); *Children of No Man's Land,* 1919 (Am. ed. *Debatable Ground*) (n); *Larry Munro,* 1920 (Am. ed. *The China Shop,* 1921) (n); *The Room,* 1922 (n); *The Back Seat,* 1923 (repr. 1949) (n); *Smoke Rings,* 1923 (s); *Tents of Israel,* 1924 (Am. ed. *The Matriarch*) (n); *Thunderstorm,* 1925 (n); *A Deputy Was King* (continues *Tents of Israel*), 1926 (n); (with Geoffrey Holdsworth) *The Happy Meddler,* 1926 (n); *The Dark Gentleman,* 1927 (n); *Bouquet* (travels in the wine-producing regions of France), 1927 (t); *Jack a'Manory,* 1927 (Am. ed. *The Slower Judas*), 1927 (s); *Debonair,* 1928 (n); *Petruchio,* 1929 (Am. ed. *Modesta*) (n); *Mosaic* (continues *Tents of Israel*), 1930 (n); *The Shortest Night,* 1931 (d); *The Man Who Pays the Piper,* 1931 (d); *The Matriarch,* 1931 (d); *Little Red Horses,* 1932 (Am. ed. *The Rueful Mating*) (n); *Long-Lost Father,* 1932 (n); *The Rakonitz Chronicles (Tents of Israel, A Deputy Was King, Mosaic),* 1932 (n); *The Augs,* 1933 (Am. ed. *Summer's Play*) (n); *Pelican Walking,* 1934 (s); *Shining and Free: A Day in the Life of the Matriarch,* 1935 (n); *Monogram,* 1936 (r); *Oleander River,* 1937 (n); *The Ugly Dachshund,* 1938 (s); *The Woman in the Hall,* 1939 (repr. 1961) (n); *Long Story Short,* 1939 (s); *A Lion in the Garden,* 1940 (n); *Another Part of the Forest,* 1941 (r); *Dogs in an Omnibus,* 1942 (n); *The Young Matriach,* 1942 (n); (with Sheila Kaye-Smith) *Talking of Jane Austen,* 1943 (c); *Trumpet Voluntary,* 1944 (n); *The Reasonable Shores,* 1946 (n); *No Son of Mine,* 1948 (n); *Benefits Forgot,* 1949 (r); *A Duck to Water,* 1949 (n); *Ten Days of Christmas,* 1950 (n); (with Rupert Croft-Cooke) *Gala Night at "The Willows",* 1950 (d); (with Sheila Kaye-Smith) *More Talk of Jane Austen,* 1950 (c); *The Donkey Shoe,* 1952 (n); *Robert Louis Stevenson,* 1952 (b,c); *A Name to Conjure With,* 1953 (a); *Raffle for a Bedspread,* 1953 (d); *Johnny Forsken,* 1954 (n); *He Wrote "Treasure Island",* 1954 (b); *All in Good Time,* 1954 (a); *The Way It All Worked Out* (seq. to preceding), 1956 (a); *For All We Know,* 1956 (n); *And Did He Stop and Speak to You?,* 1957 (r); *Seventy Times Seven,* 1957 (n); *The Patience of a Saint,* 1958 (n); *Unless I Marry,* 1959 (n); *One is Only Human,* 1960 (e); *Bernadette,* 1960 (b); *Dolphin Cottage,* 1962 (n); *Promise Not to Tell,* 1964 (n)

LYTTON STRACHEY
1880-1932

Some New Plays in Verse, 1908 (pd); *Light Verse,* 1909 (p); *Landmarks in French Literature,* 1912 (c); *Eminent Victorians,* 1918 (b); *Queen Victoria,* 1921 (b); *Books and Characters, French and English,* 1922 (c); *Pope,* 1925 (Leslie Stephen lecture); *Elizabeth and Essex,* 1928 (b); *Portraits in Miniature,* 1931 (e); *Characters and Commentaries,* 1933 (e); *The Collected Works,* 1948, 6 vols.

Charles R. Sanders, *Strachey, His Mind and Art,* 1957 [no bibliog.]

L. A. G. STRONG
1896-1958

Dallington Rhymes, 1919 (p); Dublin Days, 1921 (p); Twice Four, 1921 (p); Says the Muse to Me, Says She, 1922 (p); Eight Poems, 1923 (p); The Lowery Road, 1923 (p); Doyle's Rock, 1925 (s); Difficult Love, 1927 (p); At Glenan Cross, 1928 (p); The English Captain, 1929 (s); Dewer Rides, 1929 (repr. 1949) (n); The Jealous Ghost, 1930 (n); Christmas, 1930 (p); Northern Light, 1930 (p); Common Sense About Poetry, 1931 (c); Selected Poems, 1931 (p); The Big Man, 1931 (s); The Garden, 1931 (repr. 1947) (n); The Brothers, 1932 (repr. 1946) (n); Don Juan and the Wheelbarrow, 1932 (s); March Evening, 1932 (p); A Defence of Ignorance, 1932 (e); A Letter to W. B. Yeats, 1932 (e); (with Monica Redlich) Life in English Literature, 1932 (e); Sea Wall, 1933 (n); Corporal Tune, 1934 (n); The Seven Arms, 1935 (n); Tuesday Afternoon, 1935 (s); The Hansom Cab and the Pigeons, 1935 (e); The Last Enemy, 1936 (n); Call to the Swan, 1936 (p); Common Sense About Drama, 1937 (c); The Fifth of November, 1937 (repr. 1956) (n); The Swift Shadow, 1937 (n); Laughter in the West, 1937 (n); The Minstrel Boy, A Portrait of Tom Moore, 1937 (b); Odd Man In, 1938 (s); Shake Hands and Come Out Fighting, 1938 (r); The Open Sky, 1939 (n); Trial and Error, 1939 (d); The Absentee, 1939 (d); Sun on the Water, 1940 (s); English for Pleasure, 1941 (radio talks to schools); The Bay, 1941 (n); John Millington Synge, 1941 (b); House in Disorder, 1941 (n); John McCormack, 1941 (b); Slocombe Dies, 1942 (n); Authorship, 1944 (e); The Unpractised Heart, 1942 (n); The Director, 1944 (n); All Fall Down, 1944 (n); A Tongue in Your Head [on speaking English], 1945 (e); Sink or Swim, 1945 (n); Othello's Occupation, 1945 (n); Travellers, 1945 (s); Light Through the Cloud (The Story of The Retreat, York, 1796-1946), 1946 (h); The Doll, 1946 (s); Trevannion, 1948 (n); The Sacred River [James Joyce], 1949 (c); Maud Cherrill, 1949 (b); Which I Never, 1950 (n); Three Novels: The Garden, Corporal Tune, The Seven Arms, 1950 (3n); Darling Tom, 1952 (s); John Masefield, 1952 (b); The Writer's Trade, 1953 (e); The Hill of Howth, 1953 (n); Personal Remarks, 1953 (e); It's Not Very Nice, 1954 (d); The Story of Sugar, 1954 (h); Dr. Quicksilver 1660-1742, [Thomas Dover, M.D.], 1955 (b); Deliverana, 1955 (h); Flying Angel, 1956 (e); The Rolling Road, 1956 (e); The Body's Imperfection, Collected Poems, 1957; Treason in the Egg, 1958 (n); Light Above the Lake, 1958 (n); Instructions to Young Writers, 1958 (e); Green Memory, 1961 (a)

See John Gawsworth, Ten Contemporaries, 1933

FRANCIS STUART
1902-

We Have Kept the Faith, 1923 (p); Women and God, 1931 (n); The Coloured Dome, 1932 (n); Pigeon Irish, 1932 (n); Glory, 1933 (n); Try the Sky, 1933 (n); Things to Live For, 1934 (a); In Search of Love, 1935 (s); The Angel of Pity, 1935 (n); The White Hare, 1936 (n); Racing for Pleasure and Profit in Ireland . . . , 1937 (e); The Bridge, 1937 (n); Julie, 1938 (n); The Great Squire, 1939 (n); The Pillar of Cloud, 1948 (n); Redemption, 1949 (n); The Flowering Cross, 1950 (n); Good Friday's Daughter, 1952 (n); The Chariot, 1953 (n); The Pilgrimage, 1955 (n); Victors and Vanquished, 1958 (n); Angels of Providence, 1959 (n)

ALFRED SUTRO
1863-1933

Maurice Maeterlinck, Aglavaine and Selysette, 1897 (tr); Maeterlinck, The Treasure of the Humble, 1897 (tr); Maeterlinck, Wisdom and Destiny, 1898 (tr); Maeterlinck, Alladine and Palomides, Interior [tr. William Archer], and The Death of Tintagiles, 1899 (tr); The Cave of Illusion, 1900 (d); Maeterlinck, The Life of the Bee, 1901 (repr. 1929) (tr); Maeterlinck, The Buried Temple, 1902 (tr); Women in Love, 1902 (8d); The Foolish Virgins, 1904 (d); Maeterlinck, Monna Vanna, 1904 (tr); A Marriage Has Been Arranged: a Duologue, 1904 (d); Ella's Apology: a Duologue, 1905 (d); Mollentrave on Women, 1905 (repr. 1921) (d); A Game of Chess: a Duologue, 1905 (d); The Gutter of Time: a Duologue, 1905 (d);

A Maker of Men: a Duologue, 1905 (d); *Mr. Steinman's Corner*, 1905 (d); *The Salt of Life*, 1905 (d); *The Walls of Jericho*, 1906 (d); *The Open Door: a Duologue*, 1906 (d); *The Fascinating Mr. Vanderveldt*, 1906 (d); *John Glayde's Honour*, 1906 (d); *The Barrier*, 1907 (d); *The Man on the Kerb: a Duologue*, 1908 (d); *The Builder of Bridges*, 1909 (repr. 1921) (d); *The Man in the Stalls*, 1911 (d); *The Firescreen*, 1912 (d); *The Bracelet*, 1912 (d); *Five Little Plays*, 1912 (5d); *The Perplexed Husband*, 1913 (d); *The Two Virtues*, 1914 (d); *Freedom*, 1914 (d); *The Marriage ... Will Not Take Place*, 1917 (d); *The Choice*, 1919 (d); *Uncle Anyhow*, 1919 (d); *The Perfect Lover*, 1921 (d); *The Laughing Lady*, 1922 (d); *The Great Well*, 1922 (d); *Far Above Rubies*, 1924 (d); *A Man with a Heart*, 1925 (d); Maeterlinck, *Ancient Egypt*, 1925 (tr); *The Desperate Lovers*, 1926 (d); Maeterlinck, *The Life of the White Ant*, 1927 (tr); *Living Together*, 1929 (d); *The Blackmailing Lady*, 1929 (d); Maeterlinck, *The Magic of the Stars*, 1930 (tr); *About Women*, 1931 (e); *Which: Lord Byron or Lord Byron, a Bet*, 1932 (e); *Celebrities and Simple Souls*, 1933 (r)

FRANK SWINNERTON
1884-

The Merry Heart, 1909 (n); *The Young Idea*, 1910 (repr. 1922) (n); *The Casement*, 1911 (n); *The Happy Family*, 1912 (n); *George Gissing*, 1912 (repr. 1924) (c); *R. L. Stevenson*, 1914 (repr. 1948) (c); *On the Staircase*, 1914 (repr. 1948) (n); *The Chaste Wife*, 1916 (n); *Nocturne*, 1917 (repr. 1948) (n); *Shops and Houses*, 1918 (n); *Women*, 1919 (e); *September*, 1919 (n); *Coquette*, 1921 (n); *The Three Lovers*, 1922 (n); *Young Felix*, 1923 (n); *The Elder Sister*, 1925 (n); *Summer Storm*, 1926 (n); *Tokefield Papers*, 1927 (new enlgd. ed. 1949) (e); *A Brood of Ducklings*, 1928 (n); *A London Bookman*, 1928 (e); *Sketch of a Sinner*, 1929 (n); *Authors and the Book Trade*, 1932 (e); *The Georgian House*, 1933 (n); *Elizabeth*, 1934 (n); *The Georgian Scene*, 1934 (English ed. *The Georgian Literary Scene*, 1935) (rev. 1950) (c); *Swinnerton, An Autobiography*, 1936 (a); *Harvest Comedy*, 1937 (n); *The Reviewing and Criticism of Books*, 1939 (Dent Memorial lecture); *The Two Wives*, 1940 (n); *The Fortunate Lady*, 1941 (n); *Thankless Child*, 1942 (n); *A Woman in Sunshine*, 1944 (n); *English Maiden*, 1946 (n); *A Faithful Company*, 1948 (n); *The Doctor's Wife Comes to Stay*, 1949 (n); *Arnold Bennett*, 1950 (c); *A Flower for Catherine*, 1950 (n); *The Bookman's London*, 1951 (t); *Londoner's Post*, 1952 (e); *Master Jim Probity*, 1952 (n); *An Affair of Love*, 1953 (n); *A Month in Gordon Square*, 1953 (n); *The Summer Intrigue*, 1955 (n); *The Adventures of a Manuscript*, 1956 (e); *Authors I Never Met*, 1956 (e); *Background with Chorus: a Footnote to Changes in English Literary Fashion between 1901 and 1917*, 1956 (e); *The Woman from Sicily*, 1957 (n); *A Tigress in Prothero*, 1959 (Am. ed. *A Tigress in the Village*) (n); *The Grace Divorce*, 1960 (n); *Death of a Highbrow*, 1961 (n); *Figures in the Foreground: Literary Reminiscences 1917-1940*, 1963 (r)

ARTHUR SYMONS
1865-1945

An Introduction to the Study of Browning, 1886 (rev. 1906) (c); *Days and Nights*, 1889 (p); *Silhouettes*, 1892 (sec. ed. enlgd. 1898) (p); Zola, *L'Assomoir*, 1894 (n,tr); *London Nights*, 1895 (rev. 1897) (p); *Collected Poems*, 1895; *Studies in Two Literatures* [English and French], 1897 (c); *Amoris Victima*, 1897 (p); Verhaeren, *Les Aubes*, 1898 (tr); *Aubrey Beardsley*, 1898 (rev. 1905) (c); *The Symbolist Movement in Literature*, 1899 (rev. 1908, 1919; repr. 1958) (c); *Images of Good and Evil*, 1899 (p); G. d'Annunzio, *The Dead City*, 1900 (n,tr); *Poems*, 2 vols., 1901; *Plays, Acting and Music*, 1903 (rev. 1909) (c); *Cities*, 1903 (e); *Lyrics*, 1903 (p); *Studies in Prose and Verse*, 1904 (c); Baudelaire, *Poems in Prose*, 1905 (tr); *Spiritual Adventures*, 1905 (s); *The Fool of the World*, 1906 (p); *Studies in Seven Arts*, 1906 (rev. 1925) (c); *Great Acting in English*, 1907 (e); *William Blake*, 1907 (c); *Lyrics*, 1907 (p); *Cities of Italy*, 1907 (t); *A Book of Parodies*, 1908 (p,e); *The Romantic Movement in English Poetry*, 1909 (c); *London*, 1909 (t); *Knave of Hearts, 1894-1908*, 1913 (p); *Gabriel* d'Annunzio, 1914 (c); Poems, 1914 [1889-99] (p); *Figures of Several Centuries*, 1916 (c); *Tragedies*, 1916 (pd); *Barbara Roscorla's Child*, 1917 (d); *Tristan and Iseult*, 1917 (pd); *Cities and Sea-Coasts and Islands*, 1918 (t); *Colour Studies in Paris*, 1918 (e); *The Toy Cart*, 1919 (d); *Studies in the Elizabethan Drama*, 1920 (c); *Charles Baudelaire*, 1920 (c); *Lesbia*, 1920 (p); *Cesare Borgia, Iseult of Brittany, The Toy Cart*, 1920 (3d); *Love's Cruelty*, 1923 (p); *Dramatis Personae*, 1923 (c); *The Café Royal*, 1923 (e); *Collected Works*, 9 vols., 1924; Baudelaire, *Les Fleurs du Mal, Petits Poèmes en Prose, Les Paradis Artificiels*, 1925 (tr); *Notes on Joseph Conrad, with Some Unpublished Letters*, 1925 (r); *Studies on Modern Painters*, 1925 (c); *From Catullus*, 1925 (tr); Villiers de l'Isle-Adam, *Claire Lenoir*, 1925 (tr); *Eleonora Duse*, 1926 (b); *Parisian Nights*, 1926 (e); *A Study of Thomas Hardy*, 1927 (c); *The Letters of Charles Baudelaire to His Mother*, 1927 (tr); *From Toulouse-Lautrec to Rodin with Some Personal Impressions*, 1929 (r,c); *Studies in Strange Souls* [D. G. Rosetti, A. C. Swinburne], 1929 (c); *A Study of Oscar Wilde*, 1930 (c); *Confessions, A Study in Pathology*, 1930 (r,c); *Mes Souvenirs* [on Verlaine], 1931 (r); *Wanderings*, 1931 (t); *Jezebel Mort*, 1931 (p); *A Study of Walter Pater*, 1932 (c)

Roger Lhombreaud, *Arthur Symons*, 1963 [partial bibliog.]

JULIAN SYMONS
1912-

Confusions About X, 1939 (p); *The Second Man*, 1943 (p); *The Immaterial Murder Case*, 1945 (n); *A Man Called Jones*, 1947 (n); *Bland Beginning*, 1949 (n); *A. J. A. Symons, His Life and Speculations*, 1950 (b); *The 31st of February*, 1950 (n); *Charles Dickens*, 1951 (b,c); *Thomas Carlyle*, 1952 (b,c); *The Broken Penny*, 1953 (n); *The Narrowing Circle*, 1954 (n); *Horatio Bottomley*, 1955 (b); *The Paper Chase*, 1956 (n); *The Colour of Murder*, 1957 (n); *The General Strike*, 1957 (e); *The Gigantic Shadow*, 1958 (n); *The Thirties*, 1960 (e); *Buller's Campaign* [Boer War], 1963 (h); *The End of Solomon Grundy*, 1964 (n)

JOHN MILLINGTON SYNGE
1871-1909

In the Shadow of the Glen, 1904 (d); *In the Shadow of the Glen and Riders to the Sea*, 1905 (2d); *The Well of the Saints*, 1905 (d); *The Playboy of the Western World*, 1907 (many repr.) (d); *The Aran Islands*, 1907 (e); *The Tinker's Wedding*, 1908 (d); *Poems and Translations*, ed. W. B. Yeats, 1909 (p); *Deirdre of the Sorrows*, 1910 (d); *The Works*, 4 vols., 1910; *In Wicklow, West Kerry and Connemara*, 1911 (t); *Plays by John M. Synge* (incl. extracts from notebooks and unpub. letter), 1932; *The Complete Works*, 1935; *Plays, Poems and Prose*, 1941; *Translations* (from Petrarch, Villon, etc.), ed. Robin Skelton, 1961 (tr); *Collected Works*, ed. Robin Skelton, 1962

David H. Greene and Edward M. Stephens, *J. M. Synge, 1871-1909*, 1959 [book list]

ANGELA THIRKELL
1890-1961

Three Houses, 1931 (r); *Ankle Deep*, 1933 (n); *High Rising*, 1933 (n); *Wild Strawberries*, 1934 (n); *The Demon in the House*, 1934 (n); *O These Men, These Men*, 1935 (n); *The Grateful Sparrow*,* 1935 (tr); *August Folly*, 1936 (n); *The Fortunes of Harriette: The Surprising Career of Harriette Wilson*, 1936 (Am. ed. *Tribue for Harriette*) (b); *Coronation Summer*, 1937 (n); *Summer Half*, 1937 (n); *Pomfret Towers*, 1938 (n); *The Brandons*, 1939 (n); *Before Lunch*, 1939 (n); *Cheerfulness Breaks In*, 1940 (n); *Northbridge Rectory*, 1941 (n); *Marling Hall*, 1942 (n); *Growing Up*, 1943 (n); *The Headmistress*, 1944 (n); *Miss Bunting*, 1945 (n); *Peace Breaks Out*, 1946 (n); *Private Enterprise*, 1947 (n); *Love Among the Ruins*, 1948 (n); *The Old Bank House*, 1949 (n); *County Chronicle*, 1950 (n); *The Duke's Daughter*, 1951 (n); *Happy Returns*, 1952 (n); *Jutland Cottage*, 1953 (n); *What Did It Mean?*, 1954 (n); *Enter Sir Robert*, 1955 (n); *Never Too Late*, 1956 (n); *A Double Affair*, 1957 (n); *Close Quarters*, 1958 (n); *Love at All Ages*, 1959 (n); *Three Score and Ten*, 1961 (n)
*from the German

DYLAN THOMAS
1914-1953

18 Poems, 1934 (p); *Twenty-Five Poems*, 1936 (p); *The Map of Love*, 1939 (p,s); *The World I Breathe*, 1939 (p,s); *Portrait of the Artist as a Young Dog*, 1940 (s); *New Poems*, 1943 (p); *Deaths ands Entrances*, 1946 (p); *Selected Writings*, ed. J. L. Sweeney, 1946; *Twenty-Six Poems*, 1950 (p); *In Country Sleep*, 1952 (p); *Collected Poems, 1934-1952*, 1952; *The Doctor and the Devils* (from story by Donald Taylor), 1953 (film script); *Quite Early One Morning*, 1954 (broadcasts); *Under Milk Wood*, 1954 (pd); *A Child's Christmas in Wales*, 1954 (rev. 1959) (r); *Adventures in the Skin Trade*, 1955 (s); *A Prospect of the Sea*, ed. Daniel Jones, 1955 (misc.); *Letters to Vernon Watkins*, ed. Vernon Watkins, 1957; *The Beach of Falesá* (based on a story by R. L. Stevenson), 1963 (s)

J. Alexander Rolfe, *Dylan Thomas: a Bibliography*, 1956; John Ackerman, *Dylan Thomas: His Life and Work*, 1964

EDWARD THOMAS
1878-1917

The Woodland Life, 1897 (t,a); *Horae Solitariae*, 1902 (e); *Oxford*, 1903 (rev. 1922, repr. 1932) (t); *Rose Acre Papers*, 1904 (repr. 1910, incl. essays from *Horae Solitariae*) (e); *Beautiful Wales*, 1904 (new ed. 1924) (t); *The Heart of England*, 1906 (repr. 1932) (t); *Richard Jeffries*, 1909 (repr. 1938) (b,c); *The South Country*, 1909 (repr. 1938) (t); *Rest and Unrest*, 1910 (e); *Feminine Influence on the Poets*, 1910 (e); *Windsor Castle*, 1910 (repr. 1939) (t); *The Isle of Wight*, 1911 (t); *Light and Twilight*, 1911 (e); *Maurice Maeterlinck*, 1911 (e); *Celtic Stories*, 1911 (repr. 1922) (s); *Keats*, 1912 (b); *Algernon Charles Swinburne*, 1912 (b); *George Borrow*, 1912 (b); *Lafcadio Hearn*, 1912 (b); *Norse Tales*, 1912 (s); *The Icknield Way*, 1913 (t); *The Country*, 1913 (e); *The Happy-Go-Lucky Morgans*, 1913 (n); *Walter Pater*, 1913 (c); *In Pursuit of Spring*, 1914 (e); *Four-and-Twenty Blackbirds*, 1915 (s); *The Life of the Duke of Marlborough*, 1915 (b); *A Literary Pilgrim in England*, 1917 (t); *Poems*, 1917 (p); *Last Poems*, 1918 (p); *Collected Poems*, 1920 (new ed. 1928; Faber ed. 1936, 1949); *Cloud Castle*, 1922 (e); *Edward Thomas* [Selected Essays], 1926 (e); *Chosen Essays*, sel. Ernest Rhys, 1926 (e); *Selected Poems*, 1926 (p); *Selected Poems*, introd. Edward Garnett, 1927 (p); *The Childhood of Edward Thomas: A Fragment of Autobiography*, 1938 (a); John C. Moore, *The Life and Letters of Edward Thomas*, 1939; *The Trumpet*, 1940 (p); *The Prose of Edward Thomas*, sel. Roland Grant, 1948

Robert P. Eckert, *Edward Thomas: A Biography and a Bibliography*, 1937; Henry Coombes, *Edward Thomas*, 1956 [no bibliog.]

R. S. THOMAS
1913-

The Stones of the Field, 1946, (p); *An Acre of Land*, 1952 (p); *The Minister*, 1953 (p); *Song at the Year's Turning: Poems 1942-1954*, 1955 (p); *Poetry for Supper*, 1958 (p); *Tares*, 1961 (p); *The Bread of Truth*, 1963 (p); *Words and the Poet*, 1964 (e)

SYLVIA THOMPSON
1902-

The Rough Crossing, 1921 (n); *A Lady in Green Gloves*, 1924 (n); *The Hounds of Spring*, 1926 (n); *The Battle of the Horizons*, 1928 (n); *Chariot Wheels*, 1929 (n); *Winter Comedy*, 1931 (Am. ed. *Portrait by Caroline*) (n); *Summer's Night*, 1932 (n); *Helena*, 1933 (Am. ed. *Unfinished Symphony*) (n); *Breakfast in Bed*, 1934 (n); (with Victor Cunard) *Golden Arrow*, 1935 (d); *A Silver Rattle*, 1935 (n); *Third Act in Venice*, 1936 (n); *Recapture the Moon*, 1937 (n); *The Adventures of Christopher Columin*, 1939 (n); *The Gulls Fly Inland*, 1941 (n); *Empty Heart*, 1945 (n); *The People Opposite*, 1948 (n); *The Candle's Glory*, 1953 (n)

TERENCE TILLER
1916-

Poems, 1941; *The Inward Animal*, 1943 (p); *Unarm, Eros*, 1947 (p); *Reading a Medal*, 1957 (p); John Gower, *Confessio Amantis*, 1963 (tr)

RUTHVEN TODD
1914-

Over the Mountain, 1939 (n); The Laughing Mulatto [Alexandre Dumas], 1940 (b); Ten Poems, 1940 (p); Until Now, 1942 (p); The Lost Traveller, 1943 (n); The Acreage of the Heart, 1944 (p); The Planet in My Hand, 1946 (p); Tracks in the Snow, 1946 (e); Two Poems, 1951 (p); Loser's Choice, 1953 (n); A Mantelpiece of Shells, 1954 (p); Garland for the Winter Solstice, 1961 (p)

J. R. TOLKIEN
1892-

A Middle-English Vocabulary, 1922 (textbook); Beowulf, The Monsters and the Critics, 1936 (Gollancz Memorial lecture); The Hobbit, 1937 (repr. 1951) (child's bk.); Fairy Stories: a Critical Study, 1946 (c); Farmer Giles of Ham, 1949 (repr. 1951) (child's bk.); The Lord of the Rings (trilogy: The Fellowship of the Ring, The Two Towers, The Return of the King), 1954-55 (3n); The Adventures of Tom Bombadil, 1962 (p); Tree and Leaf, 1964 (e)

CHARLES TOMLINSON
1927-

Relations and Contraries, 1951 (p); The Necklace, 1955 (p); Solo for a Glass Harmonica, 1957 (p); Seeing Is Believing, 1958 (p); A Peopled Landscape, 1963 (p)

H. M. TOMLINSON
1873-1958

The Sea and the Jungle, 1912 (repr. to 1956) (t); Old Junk, 1918 (rev. 1933); London River, 1921 (rev. enlgd. 1951) (sk); Waiting for Daylight, 1922 (sk); Tidemarks [The Moluccas and the forest of Malaya in 1923], 1924 (t); Under the Red Ensign, 1926 (Am. ed. The Foreshore of England) (e); Gifts of Fortune, 1926 (t); Gallions Reach, 1927 (repr. 1952) (n); Illusion, 1915, 1928 (e); Côte d'Or, 1929 (e); Thomas Hardy, 1929 (c); All Our Yesterdays, 1930 (n); Norman Douglas, 1931 (rev. enlgd. 1952) (c); Out of Soundings, 1931 (e); The Snows of Helicon, 1933 (n); South to Cadiz, 1934 (t); (with H. Charles Tomlinson) Below London Bridge, 1934 (t); Mars His Idiot, 1935 (e); All Hands! (Am. ed. Pipe All Hands), 1937 (n); The Day Before, 1939 (n); The Wind is Rising, 1941 (war diary); The Turn of the Tide, 1945 (t,e); Morning Light, 1946 (n); The Face of the Earth, 1950 (t); Malay Waters, 1951 (h); The Haunted Forest, 1951 (child's bk.); A Mingled Yarn, 1953 (a); H. M. Tomlinson: A Selection from his Writings, sel. Kenneth Hopkins, 1953 (misc.); The Trumpet Shall Sound, 1957 (s)

Isadore L. Baker, H. M. Tomlinson: Gallions Reach, 1953 [no bibliog.]

PHILIP TOYNBEE
1916-

The Savage Days, 1937 (n); School in Private, 1941 (n); The Barricades, 1943 (n); Tea with Mrs. Goodman, 1947 (Am. ed. Prothalamium) (n); The Garden to the Sea, 1953 (n); Friends Apart, a Memoir of Esmond Romilly and Jasper Ridley in the Thirties, 1954 (m); The Fearful Choice, 1958 (e); Pantaloon, or The Valediction, 1961 (novel in verse form); Underdogs: Eighteen Victims of Society, 1961 (e); (with Arnold Toynbee) Comparing Notes, 1963 (e); Two Brothers, 1964 (novel in verse form)

HENRY TREECE
1912-1966

Thirty-eight Poems, 1940; Towards a Personal Armageddon, 1941 (p); Invitation and Warning, 1942 (p); (with Nicholas Moore and F. Hendry) Sailing Tomorrow's Seas, 1944 (p); The Black Seasons, 1945 (p); Collected Poems, 1946; I Cannot Go Hunting Tomorrow, 1946 (s); How I See Apocalypse, 1946 (e); The Haunted Garden, 1947 (p); Dylan Thomas, 1949 (rev. 1956) (e); The Exiles, 1952 (p); The Dark Island, 1952 (n); The Rebels, 1953 (n); Legions of the Eagle, 1954 (child's bk.); The Eagles Have Flown, 1954 (child's bk.); Desperate Journey, 1954 (n); Ask for King Billy, 1955 (n); Carnival King, 1955 (d); Hounds of the King, 1955 (s); The Golden Strangers, 1956 (n); The Great Captains, 1956 (n); Red Queen, White Queen, 1958 (n); Don't Expect Any Mercy, 1958 (n); The Master of

Badger's Hall, 1959 (n); *The Bombard*, 1959 (s); *A Fighting Man*, 1960 (n); *The Golden One*, 1961 (s); *Jason*, 1961 (n); *The Crusades*, 1962 (h); *Electra*, 1963 (Am. ed. *Amber Princess*) (n); *Fighting Men: How Men Have Fought Through the Ages*, 1963 (h)

HERBERT TRENCH
1865-1923

Deirdre Wed, 1901 (p); D. S. Merezhokovsky, *The Death of the Gods*, 1901 (tr); *Souvenir of the Blue Bird* [contains esssay on life and work of Maeterlinck, with account of some scenes of the play], 1910 (b,c); *Lyrics and Narrative Poems*, 1911 (p); *Ode from Italy in Time of War: Night on Mottarone*, 1915 (p); *Poems with Fables in Prose*, 1918 (p,s); *Napoleon*, 1919 (d); *The Collected Works*, 3 vols., 1924

Abel Chevalley, *Herbert Trench: Notice sur sa Vie et ses Oeuvres*, 1925

GEORGE MACAULAY TREVELYAN
1876-1962

England in the Age of Wycliffe, 1899 (h); *England Under the Stuarts*, 1904 (repr. 1960) (h); *The Poetry and Philosophy of George Meredith*, 1906 (c); *Garibaldi's Defence of the Roman Republic, 1848-49*, 1907 (repr. 1933 etc.) (h); *Garibaldi and the Thousand, Naples and Sicily 1859-60*, 1909 (repr. 1928) (h); *Garibaldi and the Making of Italy*, 1911 (sev. repr.) (h); *The Life of John Bright*, 1913 (b); *Clio: A Muse, and Other Essays Literary and Pedestrian*, 1913 (also pub. as *The Recreations of a Historian*, 1919) (e); *Scenes from Italy's War*, 1919 (r); *British History in the Nineteenth Century, 1782-1901* (new ed. to 1919, 1962), 1922 (h); *History of England*, 1926 (repr. 1937, 1945) (h); *Walking*, 1928 (e); *England Under Queen Ann*, 3 vols., 1930-34 (h); *Sir George Otto Trevelyan, a Memoir by His Son*, 1932 (m); *Garibaldi* [includes *Garibaldi's Defence of the Roman Republic, Garibaldi and the Thousand*,and *Garibaldi and the Making of Italy*], 1933 (h); *Grey of Fallodon*, 1937 (b); *The English Revolution, 1688-1689*, 1938 (h); *A Shortened History of England*, 1942 (h); *English Social History: A Survey of Six Centuries*, 1942 (h); *History and the Reader*, 1945 (e); *Trinity College, an Historical Sketch*, 1946 (h); *An Autobiography and Other Essays*, 1949 (a,e); *English Literature and Its Readers*, 1951 (Pres. address, Eng. Assoc.); *A Layman's Love of Letters*, 1954 (Clark lectures)

JAMES TURNER
1909-

Jono: a Collection of Prose and Verse, 1932 (misc.); *Mass of Death*, 1937 (n); *Pastoral*, 1942 (p); *The Alien Wood*, 1945 (p); *The Hollow Vale*, 1947 (p); *My Life with Borley Rectory*, 1950 (n); *Murder at Landred Hall*, 1954 (n); *Rivers of East Anglia*, 1954 (h,t); *A Death by the Sea*, 1955 (n); *The Dolphin's Skin: Six Studies in Eccentricity*, 1956 (b); *Strange Little Snakes*, 1956 (n); *The Frontiers of Death*, 1957 (n); *The Crystal Wave*, 1957 (n); *The Shrouds of Glory: Six Studies in Martyrdom*, 1958 (b); *The Dark Index*, 1959 (n); *The Deeper Malady*, 1959 (n); *The Interior Diagram*, 1960 (p); *The Glass Interval*, 1961 (n); *Condell*, 1961 (n); *The Crimson Moth*, 1962 (n); *The Nettle Shade*, 1963 (n); *The Long Avenues*, 1964 (n)

W. J. TURNER
1889-1946

The Hunter, 1916 (p); *The Dark Fire*, 1918 (p); *The Dark Wind*, 1920 (p); *In Time Like Glass*, 1921 (p); *Paris and Helen*, 1921 (p); *Music and Life*, 1921 (e); *The Man Who Ate the Popomack*, 1922 (d); *Smaragda's Lover*, 1924 (p); *Variations on the Theme of Music*, 1924 (e); *Marigold*, 1926 (p); *Orpheus, or The Music of the Future*, 1926 (e); *Select Poems*, 1926 (p); *The Aesthetes*, 1927 (e); *Beethoven*, 1927 (b); *Musical Meanderings*, 1928 (e); *A Trip to New York and a Poem*, 1929; *Miss America*, 1930 (p); *Pursuit of Psyche*, 1931 (p); *Music: A Short History*, 1932 (sec. ed. enlgd. 1949) (h); *Facing the Music: Reflections of a Music Critic*, 1933 (e); *Wagner*, 1935 (b); *Jack and Jill*, 1934 (p); *Berlioz*, 1934 (b); *Blow for Balloons*, 1935 (n); *Henry Airbubble* (seq. to preceding), 1936 (n); *Mozart*, 1936 (b); *Music: an Introduction to its Nature and Appreciation*, 1936 (e); *Songs and

Incantations, 1936 (p); *Selected Poems, 1916-1936*, 1939 (p); *The Duchess of Popacatapetl*, 1939 (n); *English Music*, 1941 (e); *Fables, Parables and Plots*, 1943 (misc.); *English Ballet*, 1944 (e); *Fossils of a Future Time?*, 1946 (p); *Exmoor Village: a General Account by W. J. Turner, based on Factual Information from Mass-Observation*, 1947 (e)

KATHARINE TYNAN
1861-1931
(Selective Bibliography)

From 1895 to her death K.T. published two, three, or four novels a year and in a few years as many as six. Six were published posthumously. None of the novels is included here, but her other works, excluding children's books, are listed.

Louise de la Vallière, 1885 (p); *Shamrocks*, 1887 (p); *Ballads and Lyrics*, 1891 (p); *Cuckoo Songs*, 1894 (p); *A Cluster of Nuts*, 1894 (sk); *An Isle in the Water*, 1895 (s); *The Land of Mist and Mountain*, 1895 (s); *Miracle Plays: Our Lord's Coming and Childhood*, 1895 (d); *A Lover's Breastknot*, 1896 (p); *The Wind in the Trees*, 1898 (p); *The Land I Love Best, 1899 (e); Poems*, 1901 (p); *The Handsome Quaker*, 1902 (s); *Innocencies*, 1905 (p); *The Yellow Domino*, 1906 (s); *Book of Memory, Birthday Book of the Blessed Dead*, 1906 (sk); *A Little Book for John O'Mahony's Friends*, 1906 (e); *A Little Book of XXIV Carols*, 1907 (p); *The Rhymed Life of Saint Patrick*, 1907 (p); *Twenty-One Poems*, sel. W. B. Yeats, 1907 (p); *Experiences*, 1908 (p); *The Lost Angel*, 1908 (s); *Men and Maids, or, The Lover's Way*, 1908 (s); (with Frances Maitland) *The Book of Flowers*, 1909 (e); *Cousins and Others*, 1909 (s); *Ireland*, 1909 (e); *Lauds*, 1909 (p); *New Poems*, 1911 (p); *Irish Poems*, 1913 (p); *Twenty-Five Years, Reminiscences*, 1913 (r); *The Flower of Peace, a Collection of the Devotional Poetry of Katharine Tynan*, 1914 (p); *Flower of Youth*, 1915 (p); *The Holy War*, 1916 (p); *Lord Edward* [Fitzgerald]*: a Study in Romance*, 1916 (b); *The Middle Years*, 1916 (r); *Herb o' Grace, Poems in War-Time*, 1918 (p); *The Years of the Shadow*, 1919 (r); *Evensong*, 1922 (p); *The Wandering Years*, 1922 (r); *Memories*, 1924 (r); *A Dog Book*, 1926 (s); *Twilight Songs*, 1927 (p); *Collected Poems*, 1930; *Twenty-Four Poems*, 1931 (p)

KENNETH TYNAN
1927-

He That Plays the King, 1950 (c); *Alec Guinness*, 1953 (e); (with Cecil Beaton) *Persona Grata* [short biographies of actors], 1953 (b); *Bull Fever*, 1955 (e); (with Harold Lang) *The Quest for Corbett*, 1960 (rd); *Curtains*, 1961 (c)

PETER USTINOV
1921-

House of Regrets, 1943 (d); *Beyond*, 1944 (d); *The Banbury Nose*, 1945 (d); *Top Secret*, 1945 (d); *Paris Not so Gay*, 1947 (d); *Plays about People*, 1950 (3d); *The Love of Four Colonels*, 1951 (d); *The Moment of Truth*, 1953 (d); (with Eric Ambler) *The Way Ahead*, 1956 (d); *Romanoff and Juliet*, 1957 (d); *Add a Dash of Pity*, 1959 (s); *Ustinov's Diplomats*, 1960 (e); *We Were Only Human*, 1961 (e); *The Loser*, 1961 (s); *Photo Finish*, 1962 (d)

Geoffrey Williams, *Peter Ustinov*, 1957 [no bibliog.]

HORACE ANNESLEY VACHELL
1861-1955

The Model of Christian Gay, 1895 (e); *The Romance of Judge Ketchum*, 1896 (n); *The Quicksands of Pactolus*, 1896 (n); *A Drama in Sunshine*, 1898 (n); *The Procession of Life*, 1899 (n); *John Charity*, 1900 (n); *Life and Sport on the Pacific Slope*, 1900 (t); *The Shadowy Third*, 1902 (n); *The Pinch of Prosperity*, 1903 (n); *Brothers*, 1904 (repr. 1928) (n); *The Hill*, 1905 (repr. 1925) (n); *The Face of Clay*, 1906 (n); *Her Son*, 1907 (n); *The Waters of Jordan*, 1908 (n); *The Paladin*, 1909 (repr. 1925) (n); *An Impending Sword*, 1909 (repr. 1932) (n); *The Other Side*, 1910 (repr. 1927) (n); *John Verney*, 1911 (n); *Jelf's*, 1912 (d); *Blinds Down*, 1912 (n); *Bunch Grass*, 1912 (n); *Loot from the Temple of Fortune*, 1913 (n); *Quinneys'*, 1914 (repr. 1942) (n); *Spragge's Canyon*,

1914 (n); *Quinneys'*, 1915 (d); *Searchlights*, 1915 (d); *The Triumph of Tim*, 1916 (n); *The Case of Lady Camber*, 1916 (d); *Fishpingle*, 1917 (n); *Some Happenings*, 1918 (n); *The Soul of Susan Yellam*, 1918 (n); *Whitewash*, 1920 (n); *The Fourth Dimension*, 1920 (n); *Blinkers*, 1921 (n); *Change of Partners*, 1922 (n); *Fellow-Travellers*, 1923 (r); *The Yard*, 1923 (n); *Quinneys' Adventures*, 1924 (n); *Leaves from Arcady*, 1924 (s); *Watling's for Worth*, 1925 (n); *A Woman in Exile*, 1926 (n); (with A. H. Marshall) *Mr. Allen*, 1926 (n); *Dew of the Sea*, 1927 (s); *Miss Torrobin's Experiment*, 1927 (n); *The Actor*, 1928 (n); *The Homely Ant*, 1928 (e); *Virgin*, 1929 (n); *The Enchanted Garden*, 1929 (s); *The Best of England*, 1930 (e); *Out of Great Tribulation*, 1930 (n); (with H. Simpson) *Plus Fours*, 1930 (d); *At the Sign of the Grid*, 1931 (n); *Fishpingle*, 1931 (d); *Into the Land of Nod*, 1931 (n); *The Fifth Commandment*, 1932 (n); *Experiences of a Bond Street Jeweller*, 1932 (n); *This was England*, 1933 (e); *Vicars' Walk*, 1933 (n); *The Old Guard Surrenders*, 1934 (n); *The Disappearance of Martha Penny*, 1934 (n); *Moonhills*, 1935 (n); *When Sorrows Come*, 1935 (n); *Arising Out of That*, 1935 (n); *Joe Guinney's Jodie*, 1936 (n); *My Vagabondage*, 1936 (e); *The Golden House*, 1937 (n); *Distant Fields*, 1938 (a); *Lord Samarkand*, 1938 (r); *Where Fancy Beckons*, 1938 (r); *Quinneys for Quality*, 1938 (n); *Phoebe's Guest House*, 1939 (n); *Great Chameleon*, 1940 (n); *Little Tyrannies*, 1940 (e); *Black Squire*, 1941 (n); *Gift from God*, 1942 (n); *Hilary Trent*, 1944 (n); *Averil*, 1945 (n); *Eve's Apples*, 1946; (n); *Farewell Yesterday*, 1946 (n); *Now Came Still Evening On*, 1946 (r); *Rebels*, 1947 (n); *Quiet Corner*, 1948 (n); *Twilight Grey*, 1948 (r); *Children of Sin*, 1948 (n); *In Sober Livery*, 1949 (r); *Methuselah's Diary*, 1950 (a); *More from Methuselah*, 1951 (a); *The Lamp of Golconda*, 1952 (n); *Quests*, 1954 (e)

JOHN VAN DRUTEN
1901-1957

Young Woodley, 1925 (d); *The Return of the Soldier* (adapted from Rebecca West's novel), 1928 (d); *Diversion*, 1928 (d); *After All*, 1929 (d); *Young Woodley*, 1928 (n); *A Woman On her Way*, 1930 (n); *London Wall*, 1931 (d); *There's Always Juliet*, 1931 (d); (with Benn Wolf Levy) *Hollywood Holiday*, 1931 (d); *Behold, We Live*, 1932 (d); *Somebody Knows*, 1932 (d); *The Distaff Side*, 1933 (d); *Flowers of the Forest*, 1934 (d); *Parnell*, 1936 (d); *And Then You Wish*, 1936 (n); *Most of the Game*, 1936 (d); *Gertie Maude*, 1937 (d); *The Way to the Present*, 1938 (a); *Intermezzo*, 1939 (d); *Raffles*, 1939 (d); *Leave Her to Heaven* (adapted from Ben Ames Williams' novel), 1940 (d); *Ballerina*, 1940 (d); *Old Acquaintance*, 1941 (d); *Solitaire* (adapted from Edwin Corle's novel), 1942 (d); (with Lloyd Morris) *The Damask Cheek*, 1943 (d); *McLeod's Folly*, 1943 (d); *The Voice of the Turtle*, 1944 (d); *I Remember Mama* (adapted from Kathryn Forbes's sketches, *Mama's Bank Account*), 1944 (d); *The Mermaids Singing*, 1946 (d); *The Druid Circle*, 1948 (d); *Make Way for Lucia*, 1949 (d); *Bell, Book and Candle*, 1951 (d); *I Am a Camera* (based on stories of Christopher Isherwood), 1951 (d); *I've Got Sixpence*, 1953 (d); *Playwright at Work*, 1953 (a); *The Vicarious Years*, 1955 (n); *The Widening Circle*, 1957 (a)

C. E. VULLIAMY
1886-

Charles Kingsley and Christian Socialism, 1914 (e); *Our Prehistoric Forerunners*, 1925 (h); *Unknown Cornwall*, 1925 (t); *Immortal Man: a Study of Funeral Customs and of Beliefs in Regard to the Nature and Fate of the Soul*, 1926 (e); *The Archæology of Middlesex and London*, 1930 (h); *Voltaire*, 1930 (b); *John Wesley*, 1931 (b); *Rousseau*, 1931 (b); *James Boswell*, 1932 (b); *William Penn*, 1933 (b); *Judas Maccabeus*, 1934 (e); *Aspasia. The Life and Letters of Mary Granville, Mrs. Delany, 1700-1788*, 1935 (b); *Mrs. Thrale of Streatham*, 1936 (b); *Royal George* [George III], 1937 (b); *Outlanders: A Study of Imperial Expansion in South Africa, 1877-1902*, 1938 (h); *Crimea: The Campaign of 1854-1856*, 1939 (h); *Calico Pie*, 1940 (a); *A Short History of the Montagu Puffins*, 1941 (b); *The Polderoy Papers*, 1943 (b); *Doctor Philigo, His Journal and

Opinions, 1944 (b); *Edwin and Eleanor*, 1945 (n); *English Letter Writers*, 1945 (e); *Ursa Major: A Study of Dr. Johnson and His Friends*, 1946 (b); *Man and the Atom*, 1947 (e); *Clerical Error*, 1947 (e); *Byron*, 1948 (c); *Prodwit's Guide to Writing*, 1949 (e); *The Anatomy of Satire*, 1950 (e); *Henry Plumdew*, 1950 (n); *Rocking Horse Journey: Some Views of the British Character*, 1952 (e); *Don among the Dead Men*, 1952 (n); *The Onslow Family, 1528-1874*, 1953 (h); *The Proud Walkers*, 1955 (n); *Body in the Boudoir*, 1956 (n); *Cakes for Your Birthday*, 1959 (n); *Little Arthur's Guide to Humbug*, 1960 (e); *Justice for Judy*, 1960 (n); *Tea at the Abbey*, 1961 (n); *Floral Tribute*, 1963 (n)

JOHN WAIN
1925-

Hurry On Down, 1953 (Am. ed. *Born in Captivity*) (n); *Living in the Present*, 1955 (n); *A Word Carved on a Sill*, 1956 (p); *Preliminary Essays*, 1957 (c); *The Contenders*, 1958 (n); *A Travelling Woman*, 1959 (n); *Nuncle*, 1960 (s); *Weep Before God*, 1961 (p); *Strike the Father Dead*, 1962 (n); *Sprightly Running*, 1962 (a); *Essays on Literature and Ideas*, 1963 (e); *The Living World of Shakespeare*, 1964 (c)

A. B. WALKLEY
1855-1926

Playhouse Impressions, 1892 (c); *Frames of Mind*, 1899 (e); *Dramatic Criticism*, 1903 (3 lectures at Royal Institution); *Drama and Life*, 1907 (c); *Pastiche and Prejudice*, 1921 (c); *More Prejudice*, 1923 (c); *Still More Prejudice*, 1925 (c)

EDGAR WALLACE
1875-1932
(Selective Bibliography)

The Mission That Failed, 1898 (p); *Writ in Barracks*, 1900 (p); *Unofficial Despatches*, 1901 (e); *The Four Just Men*, 1905 (n); *"Smithy"*, 1906 (sk); *Smithy Abroad: Barrack-Room Sketches*, 1909; *Sanders of the River*, 1911 (s); *The People of the River*, 1912 (s); *Bosambo of the River*, 1914 (s); *Smithy's Friend Nobby*, 1914 (sk); *"Smithy", Not to Mention Nobby Clark and Spud Murphy*, 1914 (sk); *Tam o' the Scouts*, 1918 (s); *People: a Short Autobiography*, 1926 (a); *Edgar Wallace: a Short Autobiography*, 1929 (a); (with Delos W. Lovelace and Marian C. Cooper) *King Kong*, 1932 (n); *My Hollywood Diary: The Last Work of Edgar Wallace*, 1932 (a)

Also, from 1919 on, very numerous mystery or detective stories (e.g., 20 in 1926, 14 in 1927, 12 in 1928, 23 in 1929)

Margaret Lane, *Edgar Wallace*, 1938 (rev. 1964) [no bibliog.]

HUGH WALPOLE
1884-1941

The Wooden Horse, 1909 (n); *Maradick at Forty*, 1910 (n); *Mr. Perrin and Mr. Traill*, 1911 (Am. ed. *The Gods and Mr. Perrin*) (n); *The Prelude to Adventure*, 1912 (n); *Fortitude*, 1913 (n); *The Duchess of Wrexe (The Rising City: I)*, 1914 (n); *The Golden Scarecrow*, 1915 (n); *The Dark Forest*, 1916 (n); *Joseph Conrad*, 1916 (c); *The Green Mirror (The Rising City: II)*, 1917 (n); *The Secret City* (seq. to *The Dark Forest*), 1919 (n); *Jeremy*, 1919 (n); *The Captives*, 1920 (n); *The Art of James Branch Cabell*, 1920 (c); *A Hugh Walpole Anthology*, sel. by the author, with a note by Joseph Conrad, 1921; *The Young Enchanted*, 1921 (n); *The Thirteen Travellers*, 1921 (s); *The Cathedral*, 1922 (n); *Jeremy and Hamlet*, 1923 (n); *The Old Ladies*, 1924 (n); *Portrait of a Man with Red Hair*, 1925 (n); *The English Novel*, 1925 [The Rede lecture, 1925] (c); *Harmer John*, 1926 (n); *Reading*, 1926 (e); *A Stranger*, 1926 (n); *Jeremy at Crale*, 1927 (n); *Wintersmoon*, 1928 (n); *The Silver Thorn*, 1928 (s); *Anthony Trollope*, 1928 (c); *My Religious Experience*, 1928 (e); (with J. B. Priestley) *Farthing Hall*, 1929 (n); *Hans Frost*, 1929 (n); *Rogue Herries (Herries Chronicles: I)*, 1930 (n); *Above the Dark Circus* (Am. ed. *Above the Dark Tumult*), 1930 (n); *Judith Paris (Herries Chronicles: II)*, 1931 (n); *A Letter to a Modern Novelist*, 1932 (e); *The Apple Trees*, 1932 (r); *The Fortress (Herries Chronicles: III)*, 1931 (n); *Vanessa (Herries Chronicles: IV)*, 1933 (n); *All Souls' Night*, 1933 (s); *Captain Nicholas*, 1934 (n); *The Inquisitor*, 1935 (n); *Mr. Huffman*, 1935 (s); *A Prayer for My Son*, 1936 (n); *John Cornelius*, 1937 (n); *The Cathedral*, 1937 (d); *Head in Green Bronze*, 1938 (e); *The Joyful Delaneys*, 1938 (n); *The Haxtons*, 1939 (d); *The Sea Tower*, 1939 (n); *The Herries Chronicle (Rogue Herries, Judith Paris, The Fortress, Vanessa)*, 1939 (4n); The Cumberland Edition of *The Works*, 30 vols., 1939-40; *The Bright Pavilions*, 1940 (n); *The Freedom of Books*, 1940 (e); *Roman Fountain*, 1940 (t); *The Blind Man's House*, 1941 (n); *The Killer and the Slain*, 1942 (n); *Katherine Christian*, 1943 (n); *Women are Motherly*, 1943 (s)

Rupert Hart-Davis, *Hugh Walpole*, 1952 (repr. 1963) [bk list]

REX WARNER
1905-

Poems, 1937 (rev. as *Poems and Contradictions*, 1945) (p); *The Wild Goose Chase*, 1937 (n); *The Aerodrome*, 1941 (n); *Why Was I Killed? A Dramatic Dialogue* (Am. ed. *Return of the Traveller*), 1943 (e); *The Medea of Euripides*, 1944 (tr); *English Public Schools*, 1954 (e); *The Cult of Power*, 1946 (e); *The Prometheus Bound of Aeschylus*, 1947 (tr); *Men of Stones*, 1949 (n); *The Hippolytus of Euripides*, 1949 (tr); Xenophon, *The Persian Expedition*, 1949 (tr); *John Milton*, 1949 (b,c); *Views of Attica*, 1950 (t); *E. M. Forster*, 1950 (rev. 1960) (c); *Men and Gods* [Stories from Ovid], 1950 (tr); *Greeks and Trojans*, 1951 (e); *The Helen of Euripides*, 1961 (tr); (with pictures by Martin Hürlimann) *Eternal Greece*, 1953 (repr. 1961) (e); *Escapade*, 1953 (n); Thucydides, *The History of the Peloponnesian War*, 1954 (tr); *The Vengeance of the Gods*, 1954 (s); (with others) *New Poems*, 1954 (p); [Plutarch] *The Fall of the Roman Republic: Six Lives*, 1958 (tr); *The Young Caesar*, 1958 (n); *The Greek Philosophers*, 1958 (c); *Imperial Caesar* (seq. to *The Young Caesar*), 1958 (n); *War Commentaries of Caesar*, 1960 (tr); George Seferis, *Poems*, 1960 (tr); *Pericles the Athenian*, 1963 (n)

SYLVIA TOWNSEND WARNER
1893-

The Espalier, 1925 (p); *Lolly Willowes*, 1926 (n); *Mr. Fortune's Maggot*, 1927 (n); *Time Importuned*, 1928 (p); *The True Heart*, 1929 (n); *Some World Far From Ours and "Stay Corydon"*, 1929 (s); *Elinor Barley*, 1930 (s); *A Moral Ending*, 1931 (s); *Opus 7*, 1931 (p); *The Salutation*, 1932 (s); *Rainbow*, 1932 (p); (with Valentine Ackland) *Whether a Dove or Seagull*, 1933 (p); *More Joy in Heaven*, 1935 (s); *Summer Will Show*, 1936 (n); *After the Death of Don Juan*, 1938 (n); *The Cat's Cradle-Book*, 1940 (s); *A Garland of Straw*, 1943 (s); *The Museum of Cheats*, 1947 (s); *The Corner That Held Them*, 1948 (n); *Somerset*, 1949 (t); *Jane Austen, 1775-1817*, 1951 (b); *The Flint Anchor*, 1954 (s); *Winter in the Air*, 1955 (s); Marcel Proust [*Contre Sainte-Beuve*] *By Way of Sainte-Beuve*, 1958 (Am. ed. *Marcel Proust on Art and Literature*) (tr); *A Spirit Rises*, 1962 (n)

VERNON WATKINS
1907-

Ballad of the Mari Lwyd, 1941 (p); *The Lamp and the Veil*, 1945 (p); *The Lady with the Unicorn*, 1948 (p); *Selected Poems*, 1948 (p); Heinrich Heine, *The North Sea*, 1951 (tr); *The Death Bell*, 1954 (p); *Cypress and Acacia*, 1959 (p); *Affinities*, 1962 (p)

WILLIAM WATSON
1858-1935

The Prince's Quest, 1880 (p); *Epigrams of Art, Life and Nature*, 1884 (p); *Wordsworth's Grave*, 1889 (p); *Lachrymae Musarum*, 1892 (p); *Poems*, 1892 (p); *The Eloping Angels*, 1893 (p); *Five Sonnets*, 1893 (p); *Excursions in Criticism*, 1893 (c); *Odes*, 1894 (p); *The Father of the Forest*, 1895 (p); *Hymn to the Sea*, 1895 (p); *The Purple East*, 1896 (p); *A Sonnet to Thomas Bailey Aldrich*, 1896; *The Lost Eden*, 1897 (p); *The Year of Shame*, 1897 (p); *The Hope of the World*, 1898 (p); *The Collected Poems*, 1899; *The Tomb of Burns*, 1900 (p); *Ode on the Day of the Coronation of King Edward VII*, 1902; *Selected Poems*, 1903; *For England*, 1903 (p); *Eight Poems*, 1904; *Some Poems*, 1904; *The*

Poems of William Watson, ed. J. A. Spender, 1905 (p); *New Poems*, 1909 (p); *Sable and Purple*, 1910 (p); *The Heralds of the Dawn*, 1912 (d); *The Muse in Exile*, 1913 (p); *Retrogression*, 1916 (p); *Pencraft*, 1916 (e); *The Man Who Saw*, 1917 (p); *The Superhuman Antagonists*, 1919 (p); *Ireland Arisen*, 1921 (p); *Ireland Unfreed*, 1921 (p); *A Hundred Poems* [sel. from his various vols.], 1922 (p); *Poems Brief and New*, 1925 (p); *Selected Poems*, sel. by the author, 1928; *The Poems of Sir Williams Watson, 1878-1935*, 1936; *I Was an English Poet*, selection, comp. by Lady Maureen Pring Watson, 1941 (p)

Cecil Woolf, *Sir William Watson*, 1956

ALEC WAUGH
1898-

The Loom of Youth, 1917 (repr. 1929, 1941) (n); *Resentment*, 1918 (p); *The Prisoners of Mainz*, 1919 (sk); *Pleasure*, 1921 (s); *Public School Life*, 1922 (e); *The Lonely Unicorn* (Am. ed. *Roland Whately*), 1922 (n); *Myself When Young*, 1923 (r); *Card Castle*, 1924 (n); *Kept*, 1925 (n); *Love in These Days*, 1926 (n); *On Doing What One Likes*, 1926 (e); *Nor Many Waters* (Am. ed. *Portrait of a Celibate*), 1928 (n); *The Last Chukka*, 1928 (s); *Three Score and Ten*, 1920 (n); *". . . 'Sir,' She Said"*, 1930 (n); *The Coloured Countries* (Am. ed. *Hot Countries*), 1930 (t); *So Lovers Dream*, 1931 (Am. ed. *That American Woman*) (n); *"Most Women"* . . . , 1931 (t); *Leap Before You Look*, 1932 (rev. enlgd. 1934) (n); *No Quarter* (Am. ed. *Tropic Seed*), 1932 (n); *Thirteen Such Years*, 1932 (r); *Wheels Within Wheels* (Am. ed. *The Golden Ripple*), 1933 (n); *Playing with Fire*, 1933 (n); *The Balliols*, 1934 (n); *Pages in Woman's Life*, 1934 (s); (with Adrian Alington, et al.) *Beginnings*, 1935 (e); *One Man's Road*, 1935 (a); *Jill Somerset*, 1936 (n); *Eight Short Stories*, 1937 (s); *Going Their Own Ways*, 1938 (n); *No Truce with Time*, 1941 (n); *His Second War*, 1944 (e); *Galaxy*, ed. E. Myers, 1944 (e); *Unclouded Summer*, 1948 (n); *The Sunlit Caribbean*, 1948 (Am. ed. *The Sugar Islands: A Caribbean Travelogue*) (t); *The Lipton Story*, 1950 (b); *Where the Clocks Chime Twice*, 1951 (t); *Guy Renton*, 1953 (n); *Island in the Sun*, 1955 (n); *Merchants of Wine* [The House of Gilbey], 1957 (h); *The Sugar Islands: a Collection of Pieces Written about the West Indies between 1928 and 1953*, 1958 (Am. ed. *Love and the Caribbean: Tales, Characters and Scenes of the West Indies*) (t); *In Praise of Wine*, 1959 (e); *Fuel for the Flame*, 1960 (n); *My Place in the Bazaar*, 1961 (s); *The Early Years*, 1962 (a); *A Family of Islands: a History of the West Indies from 1492 to 1898*, 1964 (h)

EVELYN WAUGH
1903-1966

Decline and Fall, 1928 (n); *Rossetti, His Life and Works*, 1928 (b,c); *Vile Bodies*, 1930 (n); *Labels*, 1930 (Am. ed. *A Bachelor Abroad: a Mediterranean Journal*) (t); *Remote People*, 1931 (Am. ed. *They Were Still Dancing*) (t); *Black Mischief*, 1932 (n); *A Handful of Dust*, 1934 (n); *Ninety-Two Days: The Account of a Tropical Journey Through British Guiana and Part of Brazil*, 1934 (t); *Edmund Campion*, 1935 (b); *Waugh in Abyssinia*, 1936 (t); *Mr. Loveday's Little Outing*, 1936 (s); *Scoop*, 1938 (n); *Robbery Under Law*, 1939 (Am. ed. *Mexico: an Object Lesson*) (t); *Work Suspended: Two Chapters of an Unfinished Novel*, 1942; *Put Out More Flags*, 1942 (n); *Brideshead Revisited*, 1945 (n); *When the Going Was Good* [author's selection from *Labels, Remote Peaople, Ninety-Two Days* and *Waugh in Abyssinia*], 1946 (t); *Scott-King's Modern Europe*, 1947 (n); *The Loved One*, 1948 (n); *Wine in Peace and War*, 1949 (e); *Helena*, 1950 (n); *Men at Arms* (Vol. I of trilogy), 1952 (n); *Love Among the Ruins*, 1953 (n); *Tactical Exercise*, 1954 (s); *Officers and Gentlemen* (Vol. II of trilogy), 1955 (n); *The Ordeal of Gilbert Pinfold*, 1957 (n); *The Life of the Right Reverend Ronald Knox*, 1959 (b); *A Tourist in Africa*, 1960 (t); *Unconditional Surrender* (Vol. III of trilogy), 1961 (Am. ed. *The End of the Battle*) (n); *A Little Learning*, 1964 (a)

Frederick J. Stopp, *Evelyn Waugh*, 1958

MARY WEBB
1881-1927

The Golden Arrow, 1916 (n); *Gone to Earth*, 1917 (n); *The Spring of Joy*, 1917 (enlgd. 1937) (e); *The House in Dormer Forest*, 1920 (n); *Seven for a Secret*, 1922 (n); *Precious Bane*, 1924 (n); *Poems and The Spring of Joy*, 1928 (p,e); *Collected Works*, 7 vols., 1928; *Armour Wherein He Trusted*, 1929 (n,s); *In Dark Weather*, 1933 (p); *The Chinese Lion*, 1937 (s); *A Mary Webb Anthology*, ed. H. B. L. Webb, 1939; *Fifty-One Poems*, 1946 (p); *The Essential Mary Webb*, ed. Martin Armstrong, 1949

Thomas Moult, *Mary Webb*, 1932 [no bibliog.]

C. V. WEDGWOOD
1910-

Stafford, 1593-1641, 1935 (b); *Oliver Cromwell*, 1939 (repr. 1962) (b); *The Thirty Years War*, 1938 (h); *William the Silent*, 1944 (repr 1960) (b); *Battlefields in Britain*, 1944 (h); *Velvet Studies*, 1946 (e); (with others) *King Charles I*, 1949 (h); *Richelieu and the French Monarchy*, 1949 (h); *Reading History*, 1950 (e); *Seventeenth-Century English Literature*, 1950 (h); *The Last of the Radicals: Josiah Wedgwood, M.P.*, 1951 (b); *Montrose*, 1952 (b); *Edward Gibbon*, 1955 (b); *The Great Rebellion: The King's Peace, 1637-1641*, 1955 (h); *Literature and the Historian*, 1956 (e); *The Common Man in the Great Civil War*, 1957 (e); *The Sense of the Past*, 1957 (e); *The King's War, 1641-1647*, 1958 (h); *Poetry and Politics under the Stuarts*, 1960 (c); *Truth and Opinion*, 1960 (e); *The Trial of Charles I*, 1964 (Am. ed. *A Coffin for King Charles*) (h); *History and Hope*, 1964 (e)

DENTON WELCH
1917-1948

Maiden Voyage, 1943 (a); *In Youth is Pleasure*, 1944 (n); *Brave and Cruel*, 1948 (s); *A Voice Through a Cloud*, 1950 (n); *A Last Sheaf, Stories, Poems, Pictures*, ed. Eric Oliver, 1951; *The Denton Welch Journals*, ed. Jocelyn Brooke, 1952; *Denton Welch: Extracts from his Published Works*, ed. Jocelyn Brooke, 1963

DOROTHY WELLESLEY
?-1956

[M.A.] *Early Poems*, 1913 (p); *Poems*, 1920 (p); *Pride*, 1923 (p); *Lost Lane*, 1925 (p); *Genesis: An Impression*, 1926 (p); *Matrix*, 1928 (p); *Deserted House*, 1930 (p); *Jupiter and the Nun*, 1932 (p); *Sir George Goldie, Founder of Nigeria*, 1934 (m); *Poems of Ten Years, 1924-1934*, 1934 (p); *Selections from the Poems of Dorothy Wellesley*, Introd. by W. B. Yeats, 1936 (p); *Lost Planet*, 1942 (p); *The Poets*, 1943 (p); *Desert Wells*, 1946 (p); *Selected Poems*, 1949 (p); *Far Have I Travelled*, 1952 (r); *Rhymes for Middle Years*, 1954 (p); *Early Light: The Collected Poems*, 1955

H. G. WELLS
1866-1946

(Selective Bibliography)

Included are all short-story collections and all novels, which are of various kinds: autobiographical, propagandist, sociological utopian, and some resembling science fiction. The many reprints of the more popular novels are not indicated. Of the very numerous pamphlets, tracts, and essays, only a sampling is included, to show the breadth of Wells's interests. Two principal collected editions of Wells's work are: *The Atlantic Edition*, 28 vols., 1924-27; *The Essex Edition*, 24 vols., 1926-27

(with R. A. Gregory) *Honours Physiography*, 1893 (e); *Textbook of Biology*, 1893; *The Time Machine*, 1895 (n); *The Wonderful Visit*, 1895 (n); *Select Conversations with an Uncle*, 1895 (sk); *The Stolen Bacillus*, 1895 (s); *The Wheels of Chance*, 1896 (n); *The Island of Doctor Moreau*, 1896 (n); *The Red Room*, 1896 (s); *The Invisible Man*, 1897 (n); *Thirty Strange Stories*, 1897 (s); *Certain Personal Matters*, 1897 (e); *The Plattner Story*, 1897 (s); *The War of the Worlds*, 1898 (n); *When the Sleeper Wakes*, 1899 (rev. as *The Sleeper Awakes*, 1910) (n); *A Cure for Love*, 1899 (s); *Tales of Space and Time*, 1899 (s); *The Vacant Country*, 1899 (s); *Love and Mr. Lewisham*, 1900 (n); *The First Men in the Moon*, 1901 (n); *The Sea Lady*, 1902 (n); *Twelve Stories*, 1903 (s); *Mankind in the Making*, 1903 (e); *The Food of the Gods*, 1904 (n); *Kipps*, 1905 (n); *A Modern Utopia*, 1905 (n); *In the Days of the Comet*, 1906 (n); *The Future in America*, 1906 (e); *Socialism and the Family*, 1906 (e);

Faults of the Fabian, 1906 (e); *Reconstruction of the Fabian Society*, 1906 (e); *Will Socialism Destroy the Home?*, 1907 (e); *The War in the Air*, 1908 (n); *First and Last Things*, 1908 (rev. 1917) (e); *New Worlds for Old*, 1908 (e); *Ann Veronica*, 1909 (n); *Tono-Bungay*, 1909 (n); *The History of Mr. Polly*, 1910 (n); *The New Machiavelli*, 1911 (n); *The Country of the Blind*, 1911 (s); *The Door in the Wall*, 1911 (s); *Marriage*, 1912 (n); (with others) *The Great State*, 1912 (Am. ed. *Socialism and the Great State*) (e); *The Passionate Friends*, 1913 (n); *The Wife of Isaac Harman*, 1914 (n); *The World Set Free*, 1914 (n); *An Englishman Looks at the World*, 1914 (Am. ed. *Social Forces in England and America*) (e); *Bealby*, 1915 *The Research Magnificent*, 1915 (n); *Boon*, 1915 (sk); *Mr. Britling Sees It Through*, 1916 (n); *What Is Coming*, 1916 (e); *The Soul of a Bishop*, 1917 (n); *God, the Invisible King*, 1917 (e); *Joan and Peter*, 1918 (n); *In the Fourth Year: Anticipation of World Peace*, 1918 (e); *The Undying Fire*, 1919 (n); *Russia in the Shadows*, 1920 (e); *The Outline of History*, 1920 (h); *The Salvaging of Civilisation*, 1921 (e); *The Secret Places of the Heart*, 1922 (n); *Washington and the Hope of Peace*, 1922 (Am. ed. *Washington and the Riddle of Peace*) (e); *A Short History of the World*, 1922 (h); *Men Like Gods*, 1923 (n); *The Dream*, 1924 (n); *A Year of Prophesying*, 1924 (e); *The Story of a Great Schoolmaster, Sanderson of Oundle*, 1924 (b); *The World of William Clissold*, 1926 (n); *Meanwhile*, 1927 (n); *The Short Stories of H. G. Wells*, 1927 (s); *Democracy Under Revision*, 1927 (e); *Blettsworthy on Rampole Island*, 1928 (n); *The Open Conspiracy*, 1928 (rev. 1930 as *What Are We to Do With our Lives?*) (e); *The Way the World is Going*, 1928 (e); *The King Who Was a King, the Book of a Film*, 1929; *The Treasure in the Forest*, 1929 (n); (with Julian Huxley and others) *The Science of Life Series*, 6 vols. 1929-1935; *The Autocracy of Mr. Parham*, 1930 (n); *The Valley of Spiders*, 1930 (s); *The Way to World Peace*, 1930 (e); *The Work, Wealth and Happiness of Mankind*, 1931 (e); *After Democracy*, 1932 (e); *The Bulpington of Blup*, 1933 (n); *The Scientific Romances of H. G. Wells*, 1933 (Am. ed. *Seven Famous Novels*) (7n); *The Shape of Things to Come*, 1933 (e); *Experiment in Autobiography*, 1934 (a); *Stalin-Wells Talk, the Verbatin Record and a Discussion by Shaw, Wells, Keynes, Ernst Toller and Others*, 1934 (e); *The New America*, 1935 (t); *Things to Come*, 1935 (d); *Human Happiness*, 1936 (e); *The Man Who Could Work Miracles*, 1936 (film play based on s); *The Croquet Player*, 1936 (s); *The Brothers*, 1936 (s); *The Idea of a World Encyclopaedia*, 1936 (lecture at Royal Institution); *The Anatomy of Frustration*, 1936 (e); *The Camford Visitation*, 1937 (e); *Star Begotten*, 1937 (n); *Brynhild*, 1937 (n); (with others) *Biology of the Human Race, How Animals Behave, Man's Mind and Behaviour*, 1937 (h,e); *The Brothers*, 1938 (n); *World Brain*, 1938 (e); *Apropos of Dolores*, 1938 (n); *The Fate of Homo Sapiens*, 1939 (Am. ed. *The Fate of Man*) (e); *The Holy Terror*, 1939 (n); *Travels of a Republican Radical*, 1939 (e); *The Rights of Man*, 1940 (e); *Babes in the Darkling Wood*, 1940 (s); *All Aboard for Ararat*, 1940 (e); *The New World Order*, 1940 (e); *Short Stories*, 1940; *Guide to the New World*, 1941 (e); *You Can't Be Too Careful*, 1941 (s); *The New Rights of Man*, 1942 (e); *The Conquest of Time*, 1942 (e); *Phoenix, A Summary of the Inescapable Conditions of World Reorganisation*, 1942 (e); *Science and the World-Mind*, 1942 (e); *Crux Ansata, An Indictment of the Roman Catholic Church*, 1943 (e); *A Thesis on the Quality of Illusion . . .*, 1944 (e); *The Happy Turning*, 1945 (e); *Mind at the End of Its Tether*, 1945 (e); *The Short Stories*, 1948

G. H. Wells, [Geoffrey West], *A Bibliography of H. G. Wells*, 1925 (enlgd. 1926); Vincent Brome, *H. G. Wells, a Biography*, 1951 [selected bk. list]

ARNOLD WESKER
1932-

Chicken Soup With Barley (Part I of trilogy), 1959 (d); *Roots* (Part II of trilogy), 1959 (d); *I'm Talking About Jerusalem* (Part III of trilogy), 1960 (d); *The Wesker Trilogy*, 1960 (3d); *The Kitchen*, 1961 (d); *Chips With Everything*, 1962 (d)

ANTHONY WEST
1914-

On a Dark Night, 1949 (Am. ed. *The Vintage*) (n); *D. H. Lawrence*, 1950 (c); *Another Kind*, 1951 (n); *Heritage*, 1955 (n); *Principles and Persuasions*, 1958 (c); *The Trend Is Up*, 1960 (n)

MORRIS WEST
1916-

Gallows on the Sand, 1956 (n); *The Big Story*, 1957 (n); *Kundu*, 1957 (n); *Children of the Sun* [the depressed classes in Naples], 1957 (Am. ed. *Children of the Shadows*) (e); *The Second Victory*, 1958 (n); *The Devil's Advocate*, 1959 (n); *Daughter of Silence*, 1961 (n, also d, 1961); *The Shoes of the Fisherman*, 1963 (n)

REBECCA WEST
1892-

Henry James, 1916 (c); *The Return of the Soldier*, 1918 (repr. 1940) (n); *The Judge*, 1922 (repr. 1947) (n); [pseud. Lynx] (with David Low) *Lions and Lambs*, 1928 (e); *The Strange Necessity*, 1928 (c); *Harriet Hume*, 1929 (n); *War Nurse*, 1930 (n); *D. H. Lawrence*, 1930 (c); *Arnold Bennett Himself*, 1931 (e); *Ending in Earnest*, 1931 (c); *A Letter to a Grandfather*, 1933 (e); *St. Augustine*, 1933 (b); (with David Low) *The Modern "Rake's Progress"* [paintings Low, words R. West], 1934 (s); *The Harsh Voice*, 1935 (repr. 1948) (4n); *The Thinking Reed*, 1936 (n); *Black Lamb and Grey Falcon, The Record of a Journey Through Yugoslavia in 1937*, 1942 (t); *The Meaning of Treason* [trials of William Joyce and others], 1949 (e); *A Train of Powder* [criminal cases incl. Nuremberg trials], 1955 (e); *The Court and the Castle*, 1957 (e); *The Fountain Overflows*, 1957 (n); *The Event and Its Images*, 1962 (e); *The Vassall Affair*, 1963 (e)

T. H. WHITE
1906-1964

Loved Helen, 1929 (p); *The Green Bay Tree*, 1929 (p); (with Ronald M. Scott) *Dead Mr. Nixon*, 1931 (n); *Darkness at Pemberley*, 1932 (n); *Farewell Victoria*, 1933 (n); *Earth Stopped*, 1934 (n); *Gone to Ground*, 1935 (n); *Song Through Space*, 1935 (p); *England Have My Bones* [a diary of country life], 1936 (e); *Burke's Steerage*, 1938 (e); *The Sword in the Stone*, 1938 (repr. 1950) (n); *The Witch in the Wood*, 1939 (n); *The Ill-Made Knight*, 1941 (n); *Mistress Masham's Repose*, 1946 (n); *The Elephant and the Kangaroo*, 1947 (n); *The Age of Scandal*, 1950 (h); *The Goshawk* [falconry], 1951 (e); *The Scandalmonger* [on life and scandal in 18th and early 19th century England], 1952 (e); *The Book of Beasts* [Latin bestiary], 1954 (tr); *The Master*, 1957 (n); *The Godstone and the Blackymor* [Ireland], 1959 (t); *The Once and Future King*, 1959 (n)

CHARLES WILLIAMS
1886-1945

The Silver Stair, 1912 (p); *Poems of Conformity*, 1917 (p); *Divorce*, 1920 (p); *Poems of Home and Overseas*, 1921 (p); *Windows of Night*, 1925 (p); *The Masque of the Manuscript*, 1927 (d); *A Myth of Shakespeare*, 1929 (d); *The Masque of Perusal*, 1929 (d); *Poetry at Present*, 1930 (c); *Heroes and Kings*, 1930 (p); *War in Heaven*, 1930 (repr. 1947) (n); *Three Plays*, 1931 (d,p); *The Place of the Lion*, 1931 (new ed. 1952) (n); *Many Dimensions*, 1931 (repr. 1952) (n); *The Greater Trumps*, 1932 (new ed. 1954) (n); *The English Poetic Mind*, 1932 (c); *Shadows of Ecstasy*, 1933 (n); *Bacon*, 1933 (b); *Reason and Beauty in the Poetic Mind*, 1933 (c); *James I*, 1934 (b); *Rochester*, 1935 (b); *Queen Elizabeth*, 1936 (b); *Thomas Cranmer of Canterbury*, 1936 (d); *The Rite of the Passion*, 1936 (e); *Henry VII*, 1937 (b); *Seed of Adam*, 1937 (d); *Stories of Great Names*, 1937 (b); *Descent into Hell*, 1937 (n); *He Came Down from Heaven*, 1938 (repr. 1950) (e); *Taliessin through Logres*, 1938 (p); *Judgement at Chelmsford*, 1939 (d); *The Passion of Christ*, 1939 (e); *The Descent of the Dove: A Short History of the Holy Spirit in the Church*, 1939 (new ed. 1950) (e); *Religion and Love in Dante*, 1941 (e); *The New Christian Year*, 1941 (e); *Witchcraft*, 1941 (e); *The Forgiveness of Sins*, 1942 (e); *The Figure of Beatrice: a Study in Dante*, 1943 (c);

The House of the Octopus, 1945 (d); *Solway Ford*, 1945 (p); *All Hallows' Eve*, 1945 (n); *Flecker of Dean Close*, 1946 (b); *Seed of Adam*, 1948 (4d); (with C. S. Lewis) *Arthurian Torso* [includes a posthumous fragment of Williams' *The Figure of Arthur*], 1948 (p); *The Image of the City*, 1958 (c); *Collected Plays*, 1963

John Heath-Stubbs, *Charles Williams*, 1955 (including bibliog. by Linden Huddlestone); Mary Shideler, *The Theology of Romantic Love: a Study in the Writings of Charles Williams*, 1962

EMLYN WILLIAMS
1905-

A Murder Has Been Arranged, 1930 (d); *The Late Christopher Bean* (adapt. of René Fauchois, *Prenez garde à la peinture*), 1933 (d); *One Goes Alone*, 1935 (12d); *Night Must Fall*, 1935 (d); *He Was Born Gay*, 1937 (d); *The Corn Is Green*, 1937 (d); *The Light of Heart*, 1940 (Am. ed. *Yesterday's Magic*) (d); *The Morning Star*, 1942 (d); Ivan Turgenev, *A Month in the Country* (adapt.), 1943 (d); *The Druid's Rest*, 1944 (d); *The Wind of Heaven*, 1945 (d); *Guest in the House*, 1945 (d); *Spring, 1600*, 1946 (d); *Thinking Aloud*, 1946 (d); *Trespass*, 1947 (d); *Pepper and Sand: a Duologue*, 1948 (d); *The Corn Is Green*, 1950 (3d); *Accolade*, 1951 (d); *Readings from Dickens*, 1953; *Someone Waiting*, 1954 (d); *Beth*, 1959 (d); *George, an Early Autobiography*, 1961 (a); *The Collected Plays*, Vol. I, 1961

Richard Findlater [pseud.], *Emlyn Williams*, 1956 [no bibliog.]

RAYMOND WILLIAMS
1921-

Reading and Criticism, 1950 (c); *Drama from Ibsen to Eliot*, 1952 (c); (with Michael Orrom) *Preface to Film*, 1954 (e); *Drama in Performance*, 1954 (c); *Culture and Society, 1780-1950*, 1958 (h); *Advertising*, 1960 (e); *Border Country*, 1960 (n); *The Long Revolution*, 1961 (h); *Britain in the Sixties: Communications*, 1962 (e); *The Existing Alternatives in Communications*, 1962 (e)

HENRY WILLIAMSON
1897-

The Beautiful Years (The Flax of Dream: I), 1921 (repr. 1949) (n); *Dandelion Days (The Flax of Dream II)*, 1922 (repr. 1950) (n); *The Lone Swallows*, 1922 (e); *The Peregrine's Saga* (Am. ed. *Sun Brothers*), 1923 (s); *The Dream of Fair Women (The Flax of Dream: III)*, 1924 (rev. ed. 1931) (n); *The Incoming of Summer*, 1924 (e); *A Midsummer Night*, 1924 (e); *The Old Stag*, 1926 (repr. 1946) (s); *Tarka the Otter*, 1927 (repr. 1949) (s); *The Pathway (The Flax of Dream: IV)*, 1928; *The Flax of Dream*, rev., 4 vols., 1929-31 (n); *The Linhay on the Downs*, 1929 (enlgd. 1934) (2s); *The Wet Flanders Plain*, 1929 (r); *The Patriot's Progress*, 1930 (n); *The Village Book*, 1930 (e); *The Wild Red Deer of Exmoor*, 1931 (e); *The Labouring Life*, 1932 (e); [Anon] *The Golden Falcon, or The Haggard of Love*, 1933 (repr. 1947, with author's name) (n); *On Foot in Devon*, 1933 (t); *Devon Holiday*, 1935 (r); *Salar, the Salmon*, 1935 (s); *Goodbye, West Country*, 1937 (diary); *The Children of Shallowford* [on author's children], 1939 (rev. enlgd. 1959) (a); *As the Sun Shines*, 1941 (sel.); *Genius of Friendship: T. E. Lawrence*, 1941 (m); *The Story of a Norfolk Farm*, 1941 (e); (with Lilias R. Haggard) *Norfolk Life*, 1943 (e); *The Sun in the Sands*, 1945 (a); *Tales of a Devon Village*, 1945 (s); *Life in a Devon Village*, 1945 (e); *The Phasian Bird*, 1948 (n); *The Star-Born*, 1948 (n); *The Dark Lantern*, 1951 (n); *Donkey Boy*, 1952 (n); *Tales of Moorland and Estuary*, 1953 (s); *Young Philip Maddison*, 1953 (n); *How Dear Is Life?*, 1954 (n); *A Fox Under My Cloak*, 1955 (n); *The Golden Virgin*, 1957 (n); *A Clear Water Stream*, 1958 (e); *Love and the Loveless*, 1958 (n); *A Test to Destruction*, 1960 (n); *The Henry Williamson Animal Saga*, 1960 (s); *In the Woods*, 1961 (misc.); *The Innocent Moon*, 1961 (n); *It was the Nightingale*, 1962 (n); *The Power of the Dead*, 1963 (n)

I. W. Girvan, *A Bibliography and a Critical Survey of the Works of Henry Williamson*, 1931

HUGH ROSS WILLIAMSON
1901-

The Poetry of T. S. Eliot, 1932 (c); *John Hampden*, 1933 (b); *The Rose and the Glove*, 1934 (d); *After the Event*, 1935 (d); *King James I*, 1935 (b); *Cinderella's Grandchild*, 1936 (d); *Gods and Mortals in Love*, 1935 (e); *The Seven Deadly Virtues, In a Glass Darkly, Various Heavens*, 1936 (3d); *Mr. Gladstone*, 1937 (d); *Stories from History: Ten Plays for Schools*, 1938 (10d); *Who Is for Liberty?*, 1939 (e); *George Villiers*, 1940 (b); *A.D. 33, a Tract for the Times*, 1941 (e); *Captain Thomas Schofield*, 1942 (n); *China Among the Nations*, 1943 (e); *Paul, a Bond Slave*, 1945 (rd); *Charles and Cromwell*, 1946 (b); *Queen Elizabeth*, 1947 (d); *The Story without an End* [dramatized meditations on the life, death, and resurrection of Jesus], 1947 (d); *The Arrow and the Sword* [on the deaths of William Rufus and Thomas Becket], 1947 (e); *Were You There: The Cardinal's Learning*, 1948 (d); *The Silver Bowl*, 1948 (repr. 1962) (n); *The Seven Christian Virtues*, 1949 (e); *Four Stuart Portraits* [Sir Balthazar Gerbier, Lancelot Andrewes, Sir John Eliot, Col. Thomas Rainsborough], 1949 (b); *Conversation with a Ghost*, 1950 (d); *Diamond Cut Diamond*, 1951 (d); *The Gunpowder Plot*, 1951 (h); *Sir Walter Raleigh*, 1951 (b); *Jeremy Taylor*, 1952 (b); *His Eminence of England*, 1953 (d); *Canterbury Cathedral*, 1953 (e); *The Ancient Capital: an Historian in Search of Winchester*, 1953 (t); *King Claudius*, 1954 (d); *Fool's Paradise*, 1954 (d); *James, By the Grace of God* [James II], 1955 (n); *Historical Whodunits*, 1955 (h); *The Great Prayer: Concerning the Canon of the Mass*, 1955 (e); *The Walled Garden*, 1956 (a); *The Day They Killed the King* [Charles I], 1957 (e); *Enigmas of History*, 1957 (h); *The Beginning of the English Reformation*, 1957 (h); *The Mime of Bernadette*, 1958 (d); *The Sisters*, 1958 (n); *The Challenge of Bernadette*, 1958 (e); *Sixty Saints of Christendom*, 1960 (b); *A Wicked Pack of Cards*, 1961 (n); *The Day Shakespeare Died*, 1962 (b); *The Flower-in Hawthorn* [St. Joseph of Arimathea and Glastonbury], 1962 (e)

ANGUS WILSON
1913-

The Wrong Set, 1949 (repr. 1960) (s); *Such Darling Dodos*, 1950 (s); *Hemlock and After*, 1952 (n); *Emile Zola*, 1952 (c); (with Philippe Jullian) *For Whom the Cloche Tolls, A Scrapbook of the Twenties*, 1953; *Anglo-Saxon Attitudes*, 1956 (n); *The Mulberry Bush*, 1956 (d); *A Bit Off the Map*, 1957 (e); *The Middle Age of Mrs. Eliot*, 1958 (n); *The Old Men at the Zoo*, 1961 (s); *The Wild Garden, or, Speaking of Writing*, 1963 (r,c); *Late Call*, 1964 (n)

COLIN WILSON
1931

The Outsider, 1956 (e); *Religion and the Rebel*, 1957 (e); *The Age of Defeat*, 1959 (e); *Ritual in the Dark*, 1960 (n); *Adrift in Soho*, 1961 (n); (with Patricia Pitman) *Encyclopaedia of Murder*, 1961; *The Strength to Dream: Literature and the Imagination*, 1962 (c); *Man Without a Shadow*, 1963 (n); *Origins of the Sexual Impulse*, 1963 (e); *The World of Violence*, 1963 (n); *Necessary Doubt*, 1964 (n); *Rasputin and the Fall of the Romanovs*, 1964 (h); *Brandy of the Damned*, 1964 (c)

Sidney Ronald Campion, *The World of Colin Wilson: a Biographical Study*, 1962 [no bibliog.]

P. G. WODEHOUSE
1881-

(Selective Bibliography)

A number of plays, mostly in collaboration; the "Mulliner" series of collected short stories; about two humorous novels a year since 1910, a few of which, including in their titles the names of some of his best known characters, are: *Enter Psmith*, 1909; *Psmith in the City*, 1910; *Leave It to Psmith*, 1923; *The Inimitable Jeeves*, 1924; *Very Good, Jeeves*, 1930; *Brinkley Manor, a Novel about Jeeves* (Am. ed. *Right Ho, Jeeves*), 1934; *Bertie Wooster Sees It Through*, 1955; *Jeeves in the Offing*, 1960.

Performing Flea: a Self-Portrait in Letters, 1953 (a); *America I Like You*, 1956 (e); *Over Seventy*, 1957 (a)

Richard Usborne, *Wodehouse at Work*, 1961

HUMBERT WOLFE
1885-1940

London Sonnets, 1920 (p); Shylock Reasons with Mr. Chesterton, 1920 (p); Circular Saws, 1923 (s); Labour Supply and Regulation, 1923 (e); Kensington Gardens, 1924 (p); Lampoons, 1925 (p); The Unknown Goddess, 1925 (p); Humoresque, 1926 (p); News of the Devil, 1926 (p); Cursory Rhymes, 1927 (p); Requiem, 1927 (p); The Silver Cat, 1928 (p); This Blind Rose, 1928 (p); Troy, 1928 (p); The Craft of Verse, 1928 (e); Dialogues and Monologues, 1928 (c); Notes on English Verse Satire, 1929 (e); Early Poems, 1930 (p); The Uncelestial City, 1930 (p); A Winter Miscellany, ed. with original poems by Wolfe, 1930; Tennyson, 1930 (c); Snow, 1931 (p); Poems, 1931 (p); George Moore, 1931 (c); Requiem, 1931 (e); Signpost to Poetry, 1931 (c); A, B, C, of the Theatre, 1932 (p); Now a Stranger, 1933 (a); Reverie of Policeman, 1933 (pd); Romantic and Unromantic Poetry, 1933 (c); Portraits by Inference, 1934 (r); Ronsard and French Romantic Poetry, 1935 (The Zaharoff lecture); The Fourth of August, 1935 (p); Stings and Wings, 1935 (p); X at Oberammergau, 1935 (p); P.L.M.: Peoples, Landfalls, Mountains [France], 1936 (t); Edmond Rostand, Cyrano de Bergerac, 1937 (d,tr); Don J. Ewan, 1937 (p); The Upward Anguish, 1938 (a); Out of Great Tribulation, 1939 (p); Kensington Gardens in Wartime, 1940 (p)

Also translations of Greek Anthology, Heine, Ronsard, etc.

GEORGE WOODCOCK
1912-

The White Island, 1940 (p); New Life to the Land, 1942 (e); The Centre Cannot Hold, 1943 (p); Railways and Society, 1943 (e); Anarchy or Chaos, 1944 (e); Homes or Hovels, !944 (e); William Godwin, 1946 (b); The Basis of Communal Living, 1947 (e); Imagine the South, 1947 (p); A Hundred Years of Revolution, 1848 and After, 1948 (h); The Incomparable Aphra [Aphra Behn], 1948 (b); The Writer and Politics, 1948 (e); The Paradox of Oscar Wilde, 1949 (b); (with I. Avakumovic) The Anarchist Prince [Peter Kropotkin] 1950 (b); British Poetry Today, 1950 (c); Ravens and Prophets: an Account of Journeys in British Columbia, Alberta and South Alaska, 1952 (t); Pierre-Joseph Proudhon, 1956 (b); To the City of the Dead [Mexico], 1957 (t); Incas and Other Men, 1959 (t); Anarchism, 1962 (h); Faces of India, 1964 (t); Miniature Steam Locomotives, 1964 (e)

C. M. WOODHOUSE
1917-

Apple of Discord: A Survey of Recent Greek Politics, 1948 (e); One Omen, 1950 (n); Dostoievsky, 1951 (c); The Greek War of Independence, 1952 (h); Britain and the Middle East, 1959 (e); British Foreign Policy Since the Second World War, 1961 (h); (with John Gilbert Lockhart) Rhodes, 1963 (b)

LEONARD WOOLF
1880-

The Village in the Jungle, 1913 (repr. 1926) (n); The Wise Virgins, 1914 (n); International Government, 1916 (e); (with Virginia Woolf) Two Stories, 1917 (s); The Future of Constantinople, 1917 (e); Co-operation and the Future of Industry, 1918 (e); Empire and Commerce in Africa, a Study in Economic Imperialism, 1919? (e); International Economic Policy, 1919? (e); The Control of Industry by the People Through the Co-operative Movement, 1920 (e); Economic Imperialism, 1920 (e); Mandates and Empire, 1920 (e); Stories of the East, 1921 (s); Socialism and Co-operation, 1921 (e); The Savagery of Man, 1925 (e); Fear and Politics, 1925 (e); Essays on Literature, History, Politics, etc., 1927; Hunting the Highbrow, 1927 (e); Imperialism and Civilization, 1928 (e); The Way of Peace, 1928 (e); After the Deluge: a Study of Communal Psychology, 1931 (e); Quack, Quack, 1935 (e); The League and Abyssinia, 1936 (e); Barbarians at the Gate, 1939 (Am. ed. Barbarians Within and Without) (e); The Hotel, 1939 (d); After the Deluge, Vol. II: 1830 and 1832, 1939 (e); The Future of International Government, 1940 (e); Utopia and Reality, 1940 (e); The War for Peace,

1940 (e); *Foreign Policy*, 1947 (e); *Principia Politica*, Vol. III of *After the Deluge*, 1953 (e); *Sowing: an Autobiography of the Years 1880-1904*, 1960 (a); *Growing: an Autobiography of the Years 1904-1911*, 1961 (a); *Beginning Again: an Autobiography of the Years 1911-1918*, 1964 (a)

VIRGINIA WOOLF
1882-1941

The Voyage Out, 1915 (n); (with Leonard Woolf) *Two Stories*, 1917 (s); *Night and Day*, 1919 (n); *Kew Gardens*, 1919 (s); *The Mark on the Wall*, 1919 (sk); *An Unwritten Novel*, 1920 (sk); *Monday or Tuesday*, 1921 (sk); *Jacob's Room*, 1922 (n); *Mr. Bennett and Mrs. Brown*, 1924 (c); *Mrs. Dalloway*, 1925 (n); *The Common Reader*, 1925 (c); *To the Lighthouse*, 1927 (n); *Orlando*, 1928 (n); *A Room of One's Own*, 1929 (e); *Beau Brummell*, 1930 (e); *On Being Ill*, 1930 (e); *Street Haunting*, 1930 (e); *The Waves*, 1931 (n); *The Common Reader, 2nd Series* (Am. ed. *The Second Common Reader*), 1932 (c); *A Letter to a Young Poet*, 1932 (e); *Flush*, 1933 (b); *Walter Sickert: a Conversation*, 1934 (e); *The Roger Fry Memorial Exhibition Address*, 1935 (e); *The Years*, 1937 (n); *Three Guineas*, 1938 (e); *Reviewing*, 1939 (e); *Roger Fry*, 1940 (b); *Between the Acts*, 1944 (n); *The Death of the Moth*, 1942 (e); *A Haunted House*, 1943 (s); *The Moment*, 1947 (e); *The Captain's Death Bed*, 1950 (e); *A Writer's Diary*, ed. Leonard Woolf, 1953; *Virginia Woolf and Lytton Strachey: Letters*, 1958

Brownlee Jean Kirkpatrick, *A Bibliography of Virginia Woolf*, 1957

WILLIAM BUTLER YEATS
1865-1939

Mosada, 1886 (p); *The Wanderings of Oisin*, 1889 (p); *The Countess Cathleen*, 1892 (pd); *The Celtic Twilight*, 1893 (misc.); *The Land of Heart's Desire*, 1894 (pd); *Poems*, 1895; *The Secret Rose*, 1897 (s); *The Tables of the Law, The Adoration of the Magi*, 1897 (s); *The Wind Among the Reeds*, 1899 (p); *The Shadowy Waters*, 1900 (p); *Cathleen ni Houlihan*, 1902 (pd); *Where There is Nothing*, 1902 (pd); *In the Seven Woods*, 1903 (p); *The Hour-Glass*, 1903 (pd); *Ideas of Good and Evil*, 1903 (e); *The King's Threshold and On Baile's Strand*,1904 (2pd); *Stories of Red Hanrahan*, 1904 (s); *Poems, 1899-1905*, 1906; *The Poetical Works*, 2 vols., 1906-7; *Deirdre*, 1907 (pd); *Discoveries*, 1907 (e); *The Golden Helmet*, 1908 (pd); (with Lady Gregory) *The Unicorn from the Stars*, 1908 (pd); (with Lionel Johnson) *Poetry and Ireland*, 1908 (e); *The Green Helmet*, 1910 (p); *Synge and the Ireland of His Time*, 1911 (e); *The Cutting of an Agate*, 1912 (e); *Responsibilities*, 1914 (p,d); *Reveries over Childhood and Youth*, 1915 (a); *The Wild Swans at Coole*, 1917 (pd); *Per Amica Silentia Lunae*, 1918 (e); *Two Plays for Dancers*, 1919 (pd); *Michael Robartes and the Dancer*, 1920 (p); *Four Plays for Dancers*, 1921 (pd); *Later Poems*, 1922; *The Player Queen*, 1922 (pd); *Plays and Controversies*, 1923 (misc.); *The Cat and the Moon and Certain Poems*, 1924 (p); *The Bounty of Sweden*, 1925 (e); *A Vision*, 1925 (rev. 1937) (e); *Autobiographies: Reveries over Childhood and Youth and The Trembling of the Veil*, 1926 (a); *October Blast*, 1927 (p); *The Tower*, 1928 (p); *The Death of Synge*, 1928 (m); *The Winding Stair*, 1929 (p); *A Packet for Ezra Pound*, 1929 (e); *St. Patrick's Breast-plate*, 1929 (e); *Stories of Michael Robartes and his Friends* (with *The Resurrection*), 1931 (misc.); *Words for Music Perhaps*, 1932 (p); *The Winding Stair*, 1933 (p); *The King of the Great Clocktower*, 1934 (e,p); *Wheels and Butterflies*, 1934 (e,d); *Letters to the New Island*, 1934 (e); *A Full Moon in March*, 1935 (misc.); *Dramatis Personae*, 1935 (r); *Modern Poetry*, 1936 (e); *Essays, 1931-1936*, 1937; *The Herne's Egg*, 1938 (pd); *New Poems*, 1938; *The Autobiography* (*Reveries, The Trembling of the Veil, Dramatis Personae*), 1938; *Last Poems and Two Plays*, 1939; *On the Boiler*, 1939 (misc.); *Letters on Poetry to Dorothy Wellesley*, 1940 (repr. 1964); *Last Poems and Plays*, 1940; *If I Were Four-and-Twenty*, 1940 (e); *Pages from a Diary*, 1944 (r); *Tribute to Thomas Davis*, 1947 (e); *The Collected Poems*, 1950; (with George Moore) *Diarmuid and Grania*, 1951 (d); *The Collected*

Plays, 1952; *The Variorum Edition of the Poems,* 1957; *Selected Criticism,* ed. Norman Jeffares, 1964 (c)

Allen Wade, *A Bibliography of the Writings of W. B. Yeats,* 1958

FRANCIS BRETT YOUNG
1884-1954

(with E. Brett Young) *Undergrowth,* 1913 (n); *Deep Sea,* 1914 (n); *Robert Bridges,* 1914 (c); *The Dark Tower,* 1915 (n); *The Iron Age,* 1916 (n); *Five Degrees South,* 1917 (p); *Marching on Tanga,* 1917 (sk); *The Crescent Moon,* 1918 (n); *The Young Physician,* 1919 (n); (with W. Edward Stirling) *Captain Swing,* 1919 (d); *Poems, 1916-1918,* 1919; *The Tragic Bride,* 1920 (n); *The Black Diamond,* 1921 (n); *The Red Knight,* 1921 (n); *Pilgrim's Rest,* 1922 (n); *Woodsmoke,* 1924 (n); *Cold Harbour,* 1924 (n); *Sea Horses,* 1925 (n); *Portrait of Clare,* 1927 (Am. ed. *Love is Enough*) (n); *The Key of Life,* 1928 (n); *My Brother Jonathan,* 1928 (n); (with William Armstrong) *The Furnace,* 1928 (d); *Black Roses,* 1929 (n); *Jim Redlake,* 1930 (Am. ed. *The Redlakes*) (n); *Mr. and Mrs. Pennington,* 1931 (n); *The House Under Water,* 1932 (n); *Blood Oranges,* 1932 (s); *The Cage Bird,* 1933 (s); *This Little World,* 1934 (n); *White Ladies,* 1935 (n); *Far Forest,* 1936 (n); *They Seek a Country,* 1937 (n); *Portrait of a Village,* 1937 (n); *Doctor Bradley Remembers,* 1938 (n); *The Christmas Box,* 1938 (s); *The City of Gold,* 1939 (n); *Mr. Lucton's Freedom,* 1940 (Am. ed. *The Happy Highway*) (n); *The Ship's Surgeon's Yarn,* 1940 (s); *Cotswold Honey,* 1940 (s); *A Man About the House,* 1942 (n); *The Island,* 1944 (p); *In South Africa,* 1952 (t); *Wistanslow,* 1956 (n)

Jessica Brett Young, *Francis Brett Young: A Biography,* 1962 [no bibliog.]

G. M. YOUNG
1882-1959

Gibbon, 1932 (b); *The Origin of the West-Saxon Kingdom,* 1934 (h); *Early Victorian England, 1830-1865,* 1934 (h); *Charles I and Cromwell,* 1935 (h); *Victorian England: Portrait of an Age,* 1936 (h); *Daylight and Champaign,* 1937 (e); *The Technique of Criticism,* 1938 (e); *The Age of Tennyson,* 1939 (h); *The Government of Britain,* 1941 (e); *Basic* [English], 1943 (e); *Why Not Prosperity,* 1943 (e); *Mr. Gladstone,* 1944 (b); *Ourselves,* 1944 (e); *Rights and Duties in the Modern State,* 1946 (e); *Shakespeare and the Termers,* 1947 (Shakesp. lecture of Brit. Academy); *Today and Yesterday,* 1948 (e); *Last Essays,* 1950 (e); *Stanley Baldwin,* 1952 (b); (with others) *The Good Society,* 1953 (e); *Victorian Essays,* 1962 (c)

Except in a few cases, each specified in a headnote, the editors have attempted to list all the separate publications of the authors, excluding only (1) privately printed works and those issued in very small limited editions; (2) ephemeral works such as wartime propaganda. Date of publication given is the earliest, whether of English or American edition. Title of an American edition is noted when it differs markedly from the English title. Reprints are noted only when, occurring twenty years or more after the original publication, they indicate continuing popularity or suggest (though, of course, they do not guarantee) availability. Wherever possible, a bibliography or, if none has been published in book form, a recent biographical study, usually including bibliography, has been added for each author.

For further information about the Bibliography, see Introduction in Volume I.

COPYRIGHT ACKNOWLEDGMENTS

The editors and the publishers are grateful to many individuals, literary agencies, periodicals, and publishers for permission to include copyrighted material. Every effort has been made to trace and to acknowledge properly all copyright owners. If any acknowledgment has been inadvertently omitted, the necessary correction will be made in the next printing.

The source of each selection is given in the text.

In the list that follows, an asterisk indicates a British or Irish publisher or literary agent.

ROBERT AICKMAN. For excerpt from his article on Clifford Bax.

WALTER ALLEN. For excerpts from his articles on Leonard Woolf, Louis MacNiece, W. Somerset Maugham.

ADPRINT LTD.* See William Collins Sons.

THE AMERICAN SCHOLAR. For excerpts from *"Finnegans Wake:* An Anthropological Study" by Richard V. Chase (reprinted from *The American Scholar,* vol. 13, no. 4, Autumn, 1944, copyright © 1944 by the United Chapters of Phi Beta Kappa, by permission of the publishers).

APPLETON-CENTURY-CROFTS. For excerpts from chapters by George Freedley in *A History of Modern Drama,* ed. Barrett H. Clark and George Freedley (copyright, 1947, D. Appleton-Century Co., Inc., reprinted by permission of Appleton-Century-Crofts); for excerpts from *The Time of Yeats* by Cornelius Weygandt.

THE ARIZONA QUARTERLY. For excerpt from "The Antecedents of P. G. Wodehouse" by Lionel Stevenson, vol. 5, no. 3 (Autumn, 1949).

EDWARD ARNOLD (PUBLISHERS) LTD.* For excerpts from *Abinger Harvest* and *Two Cheers for Democracy* by E. M. Forster.

MRS. E. S. ARUNDEL. For excerpt from *Gods of Modern Grub Street* by Arthur St. John Adcock.

ASSOCIATED ILIFFE PRESS LTD.* For excerpts from *Theatre World* on Emlyn Williams by Eric Johns; on Roger MacDougall by H. G. M.; on Frederick Lonsdale by F. S.

THE ATHENEUM HOUSE INC. For excerpts from *Curtains* by Kenneth Tynan (copyright © 1961 by Kenneth Tynan, reprinted by permission of Atheneum Publishers).

440 COPYRIGHT ACKNOWLEDGMENTS

THE ATLANTIC MONTHLY. For excerpts from articles: on Hall Caine by Max Beerbohm; on Arthur Koestler by Raymond Mortimer; on Laurence Housman by Agnes Repplier; on Anthony West by Charles J. Rolo; on Lytton Strachey by Virginia Woolf.

W. H. AUDEN. For excerpts from his articles on Ford Madox Ford, Robert Graves, and George Woodcock.

JOHN BARKHAM. For excerpts from his article on John Masters.

DONALD BARR. For excerpts from his article on Vernon Lee.

BARNES AND NOBLE, INC. For excerpt from *The Achievement of E. M. Forster* by John Bernard Beer.

BARRIE AND ROCKLIFF.* For excerpt from *T. F. Powys* by H. Coombs.

GEORGINA BATTISCOMBE. For excerpt from her article on Dorothy Richardson.

ERNEST BENN LTD.* For excerpts from *From Marlowe to Shaw* by Havelock Ellis and from *Old and New Masters* by Robert Lynd.

MRS ARNOLD BENNETT. For excerpt from *Frank Swinnerton* by Arnold Bennett.

MISS JANICE BIALA. For excerpts from *It Was the Nightingale* by Ford Madox Ford.

R. P. BLACKMUR. For excerpts from his articles on T. E. Lawrence and L. H. Myers.

BASIL BLACKWELL.* For excerpts from *Sowing the Spring* by J. G. Southworth and from *Modern Poetic Drama* by Priscilla Thouless. For excerpts from articles in *Essays in Criticism:* on F. R. Leavis by F. W. Bateson; on T. F. Powys by H. P. Collins; on John Wain by Stanley Gardner; on Joyce Cary by Barbara Hardy; on Raymond Williams by Richard Hoggart; on John Cowper Powys by G. Wilson Knight; on Colin Wilson by Arnold Lunn; on J. R. Tolkien by Mark Roberts; on John Middleton Murry by Derek Stanford; on F. R. Leavis by Kenneth Trodd; on George Orwell by Raymond Williams; on Colin Wilson by Raymond Williams.

THE BODLEY HEAD LTD.* For excerpts from *Poems and Plays* by Gordon Bottomley, ed. Claude C. Abbott; from *Poets of the Younger Generation* by William Archer; from *The Beardsley Period* by Osbert Burdett; from *More Authors and I* by C. Lewis Hind; from *A Study of George Orwell* by Christopher Hollis; from *Attitudes and Avowals* by Richard Le Gallienne; from *Maurice Baring* by Laura Lovat; from *Figures in Modern Literature* by J. B. Priestley; from *Bernard Shaw, Frank Harris and Oscar Wilde* by Robert Harborough Sherard; from the Introduction by John Strachey to Christopher Caudwell's *Studies in a Dying Culture*.

WILLIAM MCKNIGHT BOWMAN. For excerpt on Emlyn Williams by Stark Young.

ELIZABETH BOWEN. For excerpt from her article on William Sansom.

SIR MAURICE BOWRA. For excerpt from his essay in *A Celebration for Edith Sitwell*.

BRANDT & BRANDT, INC. For excerpts from the essay on Osbert Sitwell in *The New Republic*; from *Scepticisms* by Conrad Aiken; from *Cargoes for Crusoes* by Grant Overton.

THE BRITISH ACADEMY. For excerpt on J. W. Mackail by Cyril Bailey in *Proceedings of the British Academy*, XXXI (1945).

COPYRIGHT ACKNOWLEDGMENTS 441

THE BRITISH BOOK CENTRE. For excerpt from *The Angry Decade* by Kenneth Allsop.

THE BRITISH COUNCIL. For excerpts from the following titles in the series *Writers and Their Work* (see individual excerpts for edition dates): *Joyce Cary* by Walter Allen; *Herbert Read* by Francis Berry; *L. P. Hartley* by Paul Bloomfield; *C. P. Snow* by William Cooper; from *Poets of the 1939-1945 War* by R. N. Currey; *C. Day Lewis* by Clifford Dyment; *Osbert Sitwell* by Roger Fulford; *Katherine Mansfield* by Ian Gordon; *Evelyn Waugh* by Christopher Hollis; *Charles Williams* by John Heath-Stubbs; *I. Compton-Burnett* by Pamela Hansford Johnson; *Edith Sitwell* by John Lehmann; *G. M. Trevelyan* by J. H. Plumb; *Lytton Strachey* by R. A. Scott-James; *Robert Graves* by Martin Seymour-Smith; *Christopher Fry* by Derek Stanford; *John Masefield* by L. A. G. Strong; *Arnold Bennett* by Frank Swinnerton; *Wyndham Lewis* by E. W. F. Tomlin; *Graham Greene* by Francis Wyndham; *Ford Madox Ford* by Kenneth Young. Also for excerpts from *The Novel Today* by Walter Allen, from *The Year's Work in Literature 1949* by Walter Allen; from *Poetry To-day (1957-1960)* by Elizabeth Jennings; from *Poetry To-day* by Geoffrey Moore; from *The Novel 1945-1950* by P. H. Newby.

VERA BRITTAIN. For excerpt from her *Testament of Friendship*.

CURTIS BROWN LTD.* For excerpts from *Essays Presented to Charles Williams*, ed. C. S. Lewis; from *The Novels of Ivy Compton-Burnett* by Robert Liddell; from *Vive Moi!* by Séan O'Faoláin. Also for excerpts from articles first published in *The Observer* by A. Alvarez on Norman MacCaig, on Hugh MacDiarmid, on John Lehmann, and on Charles Tomlinson.

JOHN MASON BROWN. For excerpt from his *Broadway in Review*.

BURNS AND OATES LTD.* For excerpt from *Some Victorian and Georgian Catholics* by Patrick Braybrooke.

UNIVERSITY OF CALIFORNIA PRESS. For excerpts from *Postwar British Fiction* by James Gindin.

CAMBRIDGE UNIVERSITY PRESS. For excerpts from *Virginia Woolf: Her Art as a Novelist* by Joan Bennett; from *Arthur Quiller-Couch* by Fred Brittain; from *Essays and Reflections* by H. H. Child; from *The Concise Cambridge History of English Literature* by George Sampson.

H. J. CAPE ESTATE. For excerpt from essay from Jonathan Cape in *T. E. Lawrence by His Friends*, ed. A. W. Lawrence.

JONATHAN CAPE LTD.* For excerpts from *Poets and Pundits* by Hugh I'Anson Faussett; from *Lawrence and the Arabs* by Robert Graves; from *John Middleton Murry* by Rayner Heppenstall; from essay by Jonathan Cape in *T. E. Lawrence by His Friends*, ed. A. W. Lawrence; from *The Craft of Fiction* by Percy Lubbock; from *Barrie* by Thomas Moult; from *Reminiscences of D. H. Lawrence* by John Middleton Murry; from *The Destructive Element* by Stephen Spender.

FRANK CASS LTD.* For excerpt from *The Lamp and the Lute* by Bonamy Dobrée.

CASSELL AND CO. LTD.* For excerpts from *Aspects and Impressions* by Edmund Gosse; from *The Early Years of Alec Waugh* by Alec Waugh.

CHAPMAN AND HALL LTD.* For excerpts from *Contemporary Theatre 1925* by James Agate; from *Thus to Revisit* by Ford Madox Ford; from *J. E. Flecker: An Appreciation* by Douglas Goldring.

442 COPYRIGHT ACKNOWLEDGMENTS

CHATTO AND WINDUS LTD.* For excerpts from *The Shaping Spirit* by A. Alvarez; from *The Achievement of E. M. Forster* by John Bernard Beer; from *Looking Backward* by Norman Douglas; from *A Critical History of English Poetry* by H. C. Grierson and J. C. Smith; from *Auden* by Richard Hoggart; from *The Olive Tree* by Aldous Huxley; from *New Bearings in English Poetry* by F. R. Leavis; from *Authors Dead and Living* by F. L. Lucas; from Foreword by Siegfried Sassoon to *Collected Works of Isaac Rosenberg;* from *Characters and Commentaries* by Lytton Strachey; from *The English Novelists,* ed. Derek Verschoyle; from *Drama from Ibsen to Eliot* by Raymond Williams.

CHICAGO TRIBUNE. For excerpt from review of L. A. G. Strong by Frank Swinnerton (July 28, 1934, p. 12).

UNIVERSITY OF CHICAGO PRESS. For excerpts on I. A. Richards by R. S. Crane, published in *Ethics*; from *Dylan Thomas* by Elder Olsen.

CHILMARK PRESS. For excerpts from *Puzzles and Epiphanies* by Frank Kermode (copyright Frank Kermode 1962; Chilmark Press 1962); from *Romantic Image* by Frank Kermode (copyright Routledge and Kegan Paul Ltd. 1957, 1961; Chilmark Press 1963).

THE CHRISTIAN CENTURY FOUNDATION. For excerpts from "Charles Williams" by W. H. Auden in *The Christian Century* (May 21, 1956) (copyright 1956 The Christian Century Foundation, reprinted by permission of *The Christian Century*); from unsigned review of *Christian Behavior* by C. S. Lewis in *The Christian Century* (Jan. 26, 1944) (copyright 1944 The Christian Century Foundation, reprinted by permission of *The Christian Century*).

THE CLARENDON PRESS, OXFORD.* For excerpts from *Modern Poetry* by Louis MacNeice; from *Poetry at Present,* by Charles Williams; from Preface by W. B. Yeats to *The Oxford Book of Modern Verse,* ed. W. B. Yeats.

SIR KENNETH CLARK. For excerpt from his essay in *A Celebration for Edith Sitwell.*

CLONMORE AND REYNOLDS LTD.* For excerpt from the Introduction by W. B. Yeats to *Letters to Katharine Tynan,* ed. Roger McHugh.

MORTON COHEN. For excerpts from his article on H. Rider Haggard and on Rudyard Kipling.

MISS D. E. COLLINS. For excerpt from *Autobiography* by G. K. Chesterton.

PADRAIC COLUM. For excerpt from *Life and the Dream* by Mary Colum.

WILLIAM COLLINS AND SONS LTD.* For excerpts from *Old Gods Falling* by Malcolm Elwin; from *Aspects of Literature* by John Middleton Murry in the "Britain in Pictures" series (copyright by Adprint Ltd.); from *First Essays in Literature* by Edward Shanks.

COLUMBIA UNIVERSITY PRESS. For excerpt from *Hardy of Wessex* by Carl J. Weber.

THE COMMONWEAL. For its generous permission to quote from many studies and reviews.

THE CONTEMPORARY REVIEW. For its generous permission to quote from several studies and reviews.

RICHARD A. CORDELL. For excerpts from his *Henry Arthur Jones and the Modern Drama;* from his *Somerset Maugham: A Biographical and Critical Study.*

COPYRIGHT ACKNOWLEDGMENTS 443

CORNELL UNIVERSITY PRESS. For excerpt from *Modernism in Modern Drama* by Joseph Wood Krutch.

R. S. CRANE. For excerpt from his article on I. A. Richards.

THE CRESSET PRESS LTD.* For excerpts from *The Present Age from 1920* by David Daiches (Am. edition *The Present Age in British Literature*); from *A Visit to Mrs. Wilcox* by Naomi Lewis; from *Graham Greene and The Heart of the Matter* by Marie Mesnet; from *The Present Age from 1914* by Edwin Muir.

THE CRITICAL QUARTERLY SOCIETY. For excerpts on John Middleton Murry by John Bernard Beer; on William Golding and on Philip Larkin by C. B. Cox; on Evelyn Waugh by A. E. Dyson; on Arnold Wesker by A. R. Jones; on R. S. Thomas by W. Moelwyn Merchant.

MRS. ROBERT CURTIS. For excerpt from *Edgar Wallace—Each Way* by Robert G. Curtis.

DAVID DAICHES. For excerpt from his article on C. Day Lewis.

THE DALHOUSIE REVIEW. For excerpts on H. Rider Haggard and on Rudyard Kipling by Morton Cohen; on Lord Dunsany by J. P. D. Llwyd.

THE C. W. DANIELS CO. LTD.* For excerpts from *Novelists: We are Seven* by Patrick Braybrooke.

J. M. DENT & SONS LTD.* For excerpts on Hugh Walpole from *Appreciations* by Joseph Conrad (on behalf of the Trustees of the Estate); from *Books and Writers* by Robert Lynd; from *Studies in Prose and Verse* by Arthur Symons.

DENNIS DOBSON LTD.* For excerpts from essays on Christopher Isherwood by G. H. Bantock and on Aldous Huxley by D. S. Savage in *The Novelist as Thinker*, ed. B. Rajan.

DODD, MEAD & CO. For excerpts from Burns Mantle's Introduction to *The Best Plays of 1931-32*, ed. Burns Mantle.

DOUBLEDAY AND CO., INC. For excerpts from *Frank Swinnerton* by Arnold Bennett; from *Poetry in our Time* by Babette Deutsch; from *The Theater of the Absurd* by Martin Esslin (copyright © 1961 by Martin Esslin; reprinted by permission of Doubleday and Co., Inc.).

DRAMA. For excerpts on Frederick Lonsdale by W. Bridges-Adams; on J. M. Barrie by W. A. Darlington; on Sean O'Casey by Albert Hunt; on Terence Rattigan, William Golding, Graham Greene and Benn Levy by J. W. Lambert; on John Osborne and Peter Ustinov by Audrey Williamson.

THE DUBLIN REVIEW. For excerpts on Charles Williams by Ernest Beaumont and on Maurice Baring by David Lodge.

GERALD DUCKWORTH & CO. LTD.* For excerpts from *Ronald Firbank: A Memoir* by Ifan Kyrle Fletcher; from *Aspects of Modern Poetry* by Edith Sitwell.

E. P. DUTTON AND CO., INC. For excerpts from *The Modern Novel* by Walter Allen; from Richard Ellmann's Introduction to *The Symbolist Movement in Literature* by Arthur Symons; from *Thus to Revisit* by Ford Madox Ford; from *The Last Pre-Raphaelite* by Douglas Goldring.

LEON EDEL. For excerpt from his article on Dorothy Richardson.

WILLIAM EMPSON. For excerpt from his article on Virginia Woolf.

444 COPYRIGHT ACKNOWLEDGMENTS

ENCORE. For excerpts on Kenneth Tynan by Penelope Gilliatt; on John Osborne by Michael Hastings; on R. C. Sherriff by Albert Hunt; on Harold Pinter by Irving Wardle; on Sean O'Casey by Colin Wilson.

THE ENGLISH ASSOCIATION. For excerpts from the following articles in *English:* on James Turner by Adam Fox; on E. H. W. Meyerstein by Wilfrid Gibson and by Laurence Binyon; on L. A. G. Strong by George Rostrevor Hamilton; on Michael Roberts and on Vernon Watkins by Ralph Lawrence; on A. T. Quiller-Couch and John Wain by Hermann Peschmann; on Siegfried Sassoon by Vivian de Sola Pinto; on Wilfred Owen by Howard Sergeant; on Alfred Noyes by Derek Stanford; on J. R. Tolkien by D. M. Stuart; on John Osborne by "Thespis"; on W. S. Maugham by Paul West; on C. S. Lewis and on Norman Nicholson by Margaret Willy; and from *Essays and Studies* (1952) by Margaret Willy on Lilian Bowes-Lyon.

THE ENGLISH REVIEW. For excerpts on J. M. Synge by Lady Gregory and by George Moore; on Edward Thomas by E. S. P. Hynes; on Charles Sorley by T. Sturge Moore; on Caradoc Evans by Herman Ould; on John van Druten by Horace Shipp; on J. M. Barrie by Horace Thorogood; on George Bernard Shaw by H. M. Walbrook.

ENGLISH STUDIES. For excerpts on Charles Morgan, J. B. Priestley and Francis Brett Young by Frederick T. Wood.

D. J. ENRIGHT. For excerpts from his articles on Frank O'Connor, Seán O'Faoláin, L. A. G. Strong, and Francis Stuart.

EPWORTH PRESS. For excerpts from articles published in *London Quarterly Review* and *London Quarterly and Holborn Review:* on J. M. Barrie and William Watson by Henry Bell; on Mary Webb by Wilfred Shepard.

ST. JOHN G. ERVINE. For excerpts from his *Some Impressions of My Elders* and from his articles on James Stephens and Rebecca West.

EYRE AND SPOTTISWOOD LTD.* For excerpts from *The Theatre of the Absurd* by Martin Esslin; from *The Vanishing Hero* by Seán O'Faoláin.

FABER AND FABER LTD.* For excerpts from *Critical Essays* by Osbert Burdett; from *Forrest Reid* by Roger Burlingham; from *Selected Essays* and essay in *A Choice of Kipling's Verse* by T. S. Eliot; from *Yeats: The Man and the Masks* by Richard Ellmann; from *Vision and Rhetoric* by G. S. Fraser; from *Collected Essays in Literary Criticism* by Herbert Read.

FARRAR, STRAUS & GIROUX, INC. For excerpts from *T. S. Eliot: A Symposium for His 70th Birthday,* ed. Neville Braybrooke; from *The Bloomsbury Group* by J. K. Johnstone, copyright 1954 by The Noonday Press, reprinted by permission of Farrar, Straus & Giroux, Inc.; from *A Reader's Guide to the Contemporary English Novel* by Frederick R. Karl; from *Sights and Spectacles, 1937-1958* by Mary McCarthy; from *The Early Years of Alec Waugh* by Alec Waugh.

LESLIE FIEDLER. For excerpts from his articles on V. S. Pritchett and Angus Wilson.

ADAM FOX. For excerpt from his article on James Turner.

G. S. FRASER. For excerpts from his *The Modern Writer and His World* and from his essay in *T. S. Eliot: A Symposium for His 70th Birthday,* ed. Neville Braybrooke.

DONALD GALLUP. For excerpt on Arthur Machen by Carl Van Vechten.

COPYRIGHT ACKNOWLEDGMENTS 445

STEPHEN GILBERT. For excerpt from his essay in *Forrest Reid Memorial.*

MISS JENNIFER GOSSE. For excerpt from *Aspects and Impressions* by Edmund Gosse.

JOHN GRADDON. For excerpt from his article on T. S. Eliot.

HORACE GREGORY. For excerpts from his articles on Winifred Bryher, T. S. Eliot, Edwin Muir, and Edith Sitwell.

GROVE PRESS, INC. For excerpts from *Dylan Thomas* by T. H. Jones (published by Grove Press Inc., copyright © 1963 by T. H. Jones); from *Samuel Beckett: A Critical Study* by Hugh Kenner (published by Grove Press, Inc., copyright © 1961 by Hugh Kenner).

HOWARD GRIFFIN. For excerpt from his "Dialogue with W. H. Auden" in *Accent.*

THOM GUNN. For excerpt from his article on J. C. Squire.

SIR GEORGE ROSTREVOR HAMILTON. For excerpt from his article on L. A. G. Strong.

HARCOURT, BRACE & WORLD, INC. For excerpts from *The Lion and the Honeycomb* by R. P. Blackmur (copyright 1955 by Richard P. Blackmur); from an essay on W. B. Yeats by R. P. Blackmur (copyright 1952 by Richard P. Blackmur) in *Language as Gesture* and in the same volume an essay on T. S. Eliot (copyright 1951 by Richard P. Blackmur); from *Selected Essays of T. S. Eliot* (copyright 1932, 1936, 1950 by Harcourt, Brace & World, Inc., renewed 1960, 1964 by T. S. Eliot); from *Two Cheers for Democracy* by E. M. Forster (copyright 1951 by E. M. Forster); from *Abinger Harvest* by E. M. Forster (copyright 1936, renewed 1964, by E. M. Forster); from *The Drama and the Stage* by Ludwig Lewisohn; from *Dickens, Dali and Others* by George Orwell (copyright 1946, by George Orwell); from *Characters and Commentaries* by Lytton Strachey (copyright 1933, © 1961 by James Strachey); from *Sowing* by Leonard Woolf (© 1960 by Leonard Woolf). All the preceding reprinted by permission of Harcourt, Brace & World, Inc.

DESMOND HARMSWORTH LTD.* For excerpt from *Wyndham Lewis* by Hugh Gordon Porteus.

HARPER & ROW PUBLISHERS, INC. For excerpts from *Memories and Impressions* by Ford Madox Hueffer [Ford]; from *A Mirror for Anglo-Saxons* by Martin Green; from *Collected Essays* and *On the Margin* by Aldous Huxley; from *Reading, Writing and Remembering* by E. V. Lucas; from *Joyce Cary: A Preface to His Novels* by Andrew Wright.

GEORGE G. HARRAP & CO. LTD.* For excerpts from *The Amazing Theatre* by James Agate; from *Studies of Contemporary Poets* by Mary C. Sturgeon.

RUPERT HART-DAVIS LTD.* For excerpts from *Around Theatres* by Max Beerbohm; from *J. B. Priestley* by David Hughes; from *A. E. Housman* by George Watson.

L. P. HARTLEY. For excerpt from his article on Edward Sackville-West.

HARVARD UNIVERSITY PRESS. For excerpts from *Mythology and the Romantic Tradition in English Poetry* by Douglas Bush; from W. B. Yeats's *Letters to the New Island,* ed. Horace Reynolds.

A. M. HEATH & CO. LTD.* For excerpts from *Imagination and Reveries* and *The Living Torch* by "AE" (George William Russell).

446 COPYRIGHT ACKNOWLEDGMENTS

WILLIAM HEINEMANN LTD.* For excerpts from *The Life and Letters of Sir Edmund Gosse* by Evan Charteris; from *Silhouettes* by Edmund Gosse; from *The Life and Letters of John Galsworthy* by H. V. Marrott; from *A Number of People* by Sir Edward Marsh; from *The Emperor's Clothes* by Kathleen Nott.

DAVID HIGHAM ASSOCIATES LTD.* For excerpts from *The Modern Novel* by Walter Allen; from *The Open Night* by John Lehmann; from article on William Sansom by Ronald Mason; from *Great Morning* and *Noble Essences* by Osbert Sitwell.

HODDER AND STOUGHTON LTD.* For the excerpt from *English Portraits* by John Freeman.

THE HOGARTH PRESS LTD.* For excerpts from *Essays on Literature and Society* by Edwin Muir; from *The Common Reader* and *The Death of the Moth* by Virginia Woolf.

HOLT, RINEHART & WINSTON, INC. For excerpts from *Bernard Shaw* by Richard Burton (all rights reserved, reprinted by permission of Holt, Rinehart and Winston, Inc.); from *The Georgian Scene* by Frank Swinnerton (copyright 1934, copyright renewed © 1962 by Frank Swinnerton, reprinted by permission of Holt, Rinehart and Winston, Inc.).

THE JOHN HOPKINS PRESS. For excerpt from essay by Mark Van Doren in *Four Poets on Poetry*, ed. Don Cameron Allen.

HORIZON. For its generous permission to quote from numerous studies and reviews.

THE HUDSON REVIEW. For excerpts from articles on Arnold Wesker by Denis Donoghue (reprinted by permission of *The Hudson Review*, vol. XIV, No. 1 [Spring, 1961] copyright 1961 by The Hudson Review, Inc.); on Joyce Cary by Sidney Monas (reprinted by permission of *The Hudson Review*, vol. III, No. 3) [Autumn, 1950] copyright 1950 by The Hudson Review, Inc.

HUMANITIES PRESS, INC. For excerpt from *Imagism and The Imagists* by Glenn Hughes.

HUTCHINSON & CO. LTD.* For excerpts from *Autobiography* by G. K. Chesterton; from *Eden Phillpotts* by Waveny Girvan; from *Visions and Revisions* by John Cowper Powys; from *The Georgian Literary Scene* by Frank Swinnerton (Am. ed., *The Georgian Scene*); from *The Modern Novel* by Paul West; for essays by James Bridie, Laurence Housman and Dr. Daniel Jones, in *G. B. S. 90*, ed. Stephen Winsten.

THE ILLUSTRATED LONDON NEWS. For excerpts on Hugh Ross Williamson, Arnold Wesker, John van Druten, and R. C. Sherriff by J. C. Trewin; on Rebecca West by J. C. Squire.

INDIANA UNIVERSITY PRESS. For excerpts from *Somerset Maugham: A Biographical and Critical Study* by Richard Cordell; from *The Present Age in British Literature* by David Daiches; from *The Emperor's Clothes* by Kathleen Nott.

JOSEPHINE JACOBSEN. For excerpt from her article on Anne Ridler.

G. INGLI JAMES. For excerpt from his article on C. S. Lewis.

ELIZABETH JANEWAY. For excerpts from her articles on Rosamund Lehmann and Alec Waugh.

JOINER AND STEELE.* For excerpts from *Five Novelist Poets of Today* by R. L. Mégroz; from *Dorothy Richardson* by J. C. Powys.

COPYRIGHT ACKNOWLEDGMENTS 447

ALUN R. JONES. For excerpts from his articles on Ronald Firbank and Philip Larkin.

HUGH KENNER. For excerpt on Charles Tomlinson.

THE KENYON REVIEW. For excerpt on Frank O'Connor by John Peter.

ALFRED A. KNOPF, INC. For excerpts from *Collected Impressions* by Elizabeth Bowen; from *The Armed Vision* by Stanley Edgar Hyman (copyright 1947, 1948 Alfred A. Knopf, Inc. reprinted by permission); from *First Impressions* by Llewelyn Jones.

JOSEPH WOOD KRUTCH. For excerpt from his *Modernism in Modern Drama*.

RALPH LAWRENCE. For excerpts from his articles on Michael Roberts and Vernon Watkins.

LAWRENCE & WISHART. For their generous permission to quote from numerous articles published in *Scrutinies I* and *II*.

SIR SHANE LESLIE. For excerpt from his article on Baron Corvo.

EXECUTORS OF THE ESTATE OF C. S. LEWIS. For excerpt from *Essays Presented to Charles Williams,* ed. C. S. Lewis.

THE LISTENER. For its generous permission to quote from numerous studies and reviews.

LITTLE BROWN AND CO. For excerpts from *Contemporaries* by Alfred Kazin (copyright © 1961 by Alfred Kazin, copyright © 1959 by Alfred Kazin, by permission of Little, Brown and Co.-Atlantic Press); from *Vive Moi!* by Seán O'Faoláin (copyright © 1963, 1964 by Seán O'Faoláin, by permission of Atlantic-Little, Brown & Co.); from *The Vanishing Hero* by Seán O'Faoláin, (copyright © 1956, 1957 by Seán O'Faoláin, reprinted by permission of Atlantic-Little, Brown & Co.).

LIVERIGHT PUBLISHING CORP. For excerpt from *Personal Remarks* by L. A. G. Strong. By permission of Liveright, Publishers, New York. Copyright © 1953 by L. A. G. Strong.

LONDON MAGAZINE. For its generous permission to quote from numerous studies and reviews.

JOHN LONG LTD.* For excerpt from *Edgar Wallace—Each Way* by Robert Curtis.

LONGMANS, GREEN AND CO. LTD.* For excerpts from *The Price of an Eye* by Thomas Blackburn; from *Edward Marsh* by Christopher Hassall; from *Catastrophe and Imagination* by John McCormick; from *Fifty Years of English Literature* by R. A. Scott-James; from *Curtains* by Kenneth Tynan; and for the many excerpts from the publications listed under The British Council.

RICHARD DE LA MARE. For excerpt from *Forrest Reid Memorial* and from Introduction to *John Freeman's Letters,* both works written by Walter de La Mare.

MACDONALD AND CO. (PUBLISHERS) LTD.* For excerpt from *The Last Pre-Raphaelite* by Douglas Goldring.

MACGIBBON AND KEE LTD.* For excerpt from the Foreword to *Memories* by Lord David Cecil; from *Humanities* and from *Memories* by Desmond MacCarthy; from Raymond Mortimer's Foreword to *Humanities* by Desmond MacCarthy; for excerpt by G. B. Shaw from *Shaw on Theater,* ed. E. J. West.

448 COPYRIGHT ACKNOWLEDGMENTS

JACKSON MAC LOW. For excerpt from his article on Sidney Goodsir Smith.

MACMILLAN & CO. LTD., LONDON.* For excerpts from *The Art of Adventure* by Erik Linklater; from *Essays on Literature and Ideas* by John Wain; from articles by Edward Shanks in *The London Mercury* and *The Saturday Review* on behalf of Mrs. Edward Shanks.

THE MACMILLAN COMPANY, NEW YORK. For excerpts from *Enemies of Promise* by Cyril Connolly; from *Yeats, the Man and the Masks* by Richard Ellmann; from *Old Gods Falling* by Malcolm Elwin; from *John Millington Synge* by David Greene and Edward Stephens; from *Descent from Parnassus* by Dilys Powell.

S. P. B. MAIS. For excerpts from his *Some Modern Authors*.

THE MANCHESTER GUARDIAN [later THE GUARDIAN] and THE MANCHESTER GUARDIAN WEEKLY. For their generous permission to quote from numerous studies and reviews.

T. S. MATTHEWS. For the excerpt from his article on Sybille Bedford.

J. C. AND R. G. MEDLEY. For the excerpt from *Ave* by George Moore.

R. L. MÉGROZ. For the excerpt from his article on L. A. G. Strong.

VIVIAN MERCIER. For the excerpt from his article on "AE" (George William Russell).

METHUEN & CO. LTD.* For excerpts from *English Literature between the Wars* by B. Ifor Evans; from *Reading, Writing and Remembering* by E. V. Lucas; from *Dramatic Values* by C. E. Montague; from *Twentieth-Century English Literature* by A. C. Ward.

UNIVERSITY OF MICHIGAN PRESS. For excerpt from *New Bearings in English Poetry* by F. R. Leavis.

THE MONTH. For excerpts on Edward Sackville-West by Jocelyn Brooke; on Shane Leslie by J. H. C.; on Charles Williams by H. P. Hanshell; on Seán O'Faoláin by D. L. K.; on Percy Lubbock by Derek Stanford; on Evelyn Waugh by Frederick J. Stopp.

ARTHUR V. MOORE. For excerpts on T. S. Eliot by Ezra Pound.

MARIANNE MOORE. For excerpts from her reviews in *The Dial* and *Poetry*.

RAYMOND MORTIMER. For excerpt from his article on Richard Hughes.

THOMAS MOULT. For excerpt from his article on Richard Church.

MRS. WILLA MUIR. For excerpt on Arnold Bennett by Edwin Muir.

THE NATION. (New York). For its generous permission to quote from numerous studies and reviews.

NATIONAL COUNCIL OF TEACHERS OF ENGLISH. For excerpts from Edward Davison's article "Three Irish Poets" (May 1926 in *The English Journal,* reprinted with the permission of the National Council of Teachers of English.)

THOMAS NELSON AND SONS LTD.* For excerpt from *The Modern Short Story* by H. E. Bates.

NEW DIRECTIONS. For excerpts from *Bernard Shaw* by Eric Bentley (copyright 1947, 1957 by New Directions, reprinted by permission of New Directions, Publishers); from *Joseph Conrad* by Albert Guérard, Jr.; from *Polite Essays* by Ezra

COPYRIGHT ACKNOWLEDGMENTS 449

Pound (all rights reserved, reprinted by permission of the publishers, New Directions, New York).

THE NEW REPUBLIC. For its generous permission to quote from numerous studies and reviews.

NEW SALTIRE. For excerpt on Eric Linklater by W. G. Henderson.

THE NEW STATESMAN, THE NEW STATESMAN AND NATION. For their very generous permission to quote from numerous studies and reviews.

THE NEW YORK HERALD TRIBUNE. For excerpts on Graham Greene by Enid Baird; on Anthony Powell by Elizabeth Bowen; on Nevil Shute and on John Masters by James Hilton; on Nancy Mitford by Phyllis McGinley; on L. A. G. Strong by James Stern.

THE NEW YORK TIMES. For its very generous permission to quote from numerous studies and reviews. (Date indicated in credit line of each excerpt, copyright by the New York Times Company, reprinted by permission.)

NEW YORK UNIVERSITY PRESS. For excerpt from *The Great Tradition* by F. R. Leavis; from *Joyce: The Man, The Work, The Reputation* by Marvin Magalaner and Richard Kane.

THE NEW YORKER. For excerpts on James Hilton by Clifton Fadiman; on Paul Vincent Carroll by Wolcott Gibbs; on Colin Wilson, Joyce Cary, and William Sansom by Anthony West.

NORTHWESTERN UNIVERSITY PRESS. For excerpt from *D. H. Lawrence: The Failure and the Triumph of Art* by Eliseo Vivas (copyright 1960 by Northwestern University Press).

W. W. NORTON AND CO., INC. For excerpt from *The Making of a Poem* by Stephen Spender.

SEAN O'FAOLAIN. For excerpts from several of his articles.

CHARLTON OGBURN, JR. For excerpt from his article on John Masters.

UNIVERSITY OF OKLAHOMA PRESS. For excerpt from *Imagism: A Chapter for the History of Modern Poetry* by Stanley K. Coffmann, Jr. (copyright 1957 by The University of Oklahoma).

OLIVER AND BOYD LTD.* For excerpts from *The Trend of Modern Poetry* by Geoffrey Bullough.

OXFORD UNIVERSITY PRESS.* For excerpts from *The Letters of Gerard Manley Hopkins to Robert Bridges,* ed. Claude C. Abbott; from *Tradition and Experiment in Present Day Literature* by J. D. Beresford; from *James Joyce* by Richard Ellmann (© 1959 by Richard Ellmann, reprinted by permission of Oxford University Press, Inc.); from *Vernon Lee* by Peter Gunn; from *The Modern Poets: A Critical Introduction* by M. L. Rosenthal (© 1960 by M. L. Rosenthal, reprinted by permission of Oxford University Press, Inc.); from *Drama from Ibsen to Eliot* by Raymond Williams (Oxford University Press, Inc., 1953, reprinted by permission).

THE PARIS REVIEW. For excerpt from "An Interview with T. S. Eliot on the Art of Poetry" (no. 21).

PARTISAN REVIEW. For excerpts on George Woodcock by W. H. Auden; on Elizabeth Bowen by Elizabeth Hardwick; on Lytton Strachey by Stephen Spender;

450   COPYRIGHT ACKNOWLEDGMENTS

on Virginia Woolf by Frank Jones; on David Jones by John Hollander; on William Sansom by Isaac Rosenfeld.

PENGUIN BOOKS LTD.* For excerpts from *The Modern Writer and His World* by G. S. Fraser; from the essay on F. R. Leavis by Andor Gomme in *The Modern Age,* ed. Boris Ford.

HERMANN F. PESCHMANN. For excerpts from his articles on A. T. Quiller-Couch and John Wain.

A. D. PETERS & Co.* For excerpts from *A Short View of the English Stage* and *More First Nights* by James Agate; from *Modern English Fiction* by Gerald Bullett; from *Freddy Lonsdale* by Frances Donaldson; from *Thoughts in the Wilderness* by J. B. Priestley; from *The Creative Element* by Stephen Spender; from *Wodehouse at Work* by Richard Usborne. Also for excerpts on Liam O'Flaherty, Naomi Mitchison, Oliver Onions, Robert Lynd and Percy Lubbock by J. B. Priestley; on Ronald Firbank by V. S. Pritchett; and on Alec Waugh by Evelyn Waugh.

VIRGILIA PETERSON. For excerpt from her article on Rose Macaulay.

DRYDEN L. PHELPS. For excerpt from *The Twentieth-Century Theater* by William Lyon Phelps.

VIVIAN DE SOLA PINTO. For excerpt from his article on Siegfried Sassoon.

POETRY. For excerpts from reviews of John Pudney's *Flight Above Cloud* by Nelson Algren; of Michael Roberts's *Orion Marches,* W. R. Rodgers's *Awake! and Other Poems,* and W. J. Turner's *Fossils of A Future Time* by David Daiches; of Edward Shanks's *Edgar Allan Poe* by John Gould Fletcher; of J. C. Squire's *Collected Poems* by Thom Gunn; of Anne Ridler's *The Trial of Thomas Cranmer* by Josephine Jacobsen; of Charles Tomlinson's *Seeing Is Believing* by Hugh Kenner; of Sidney Goodsir Smith's *Figs and Thistles* by Norman Mac Caig; of Sidney Goodsir Smith's *So Late into the Night* by Jackson Mac Low; of Gordon Bottomley's *Poems and Plays* by John H. Meyer; of Bryher's *Gate to the Sea* by Marianne Moore; of Rex Warner's *Poems* by Samuel French Morse; of Alan Ross's *Something of the Sea* by Ernest Sandeen; of Denise Levertov's *With Eyes at the Back of our Heads* by Eve Triem; of Stevie Smith's *Not Waving But Drowning* by David Wright.

LAURENCE POLLINGER LTD.* For excerpts from *Eight for Immortality* by Richard Church; from *Sights and Spectacles* by Mary McCarthy.

J. B. PRIESTLEY. For excerpt from his article on H. M. Tomlinson.

PRINCETON UNIVERSITY PRESS. For excerpt from *The Lyrical Novel* by Ralph Freedman; from essay by John Crowe Ransom in *The Intent of the Critic,* ed. Donald Stauffer.

V. S. PRITCHETT. For excerpt from his article on Rex Warner.

PURDUE RESEARCH FOUNDATION. For excerpt on Dorothy Richardson by Leon Edel.

G. P. PUTNAM'S AND COWARD-MCCANN. For excerpt from *Books and Authors* by Robert Lynd.

HENRY REGNERY CO. For excerpts from *T. S. Eliot: A Symposium for His 70th Birthday,* ed. Neville Braybrooke; from *A Study of George Orwell* by Christopher Hollis.

MRS. EVA REICHMANN. For excerpts from *Around Theatres* by Max Beerbohm.

COPYRIGHT ACKNOWLEDGMENTS 451

THE REVIEW. For excerpts on William Empson by Ian Hamilton; on Roy Fuller by Graham Martin; on William Empson by Christopher Ricks.

KENNETH REXROTH. For several excerpts from *New British Poets*, ed. Kenneth Rexroth.

FIELD ROSCOE & CO.* For extract from *Ave* by George Moore.

SIR WILLIAM ROTHENSTEIN. For numerous passages from *Men and Memories* by William Rothenstein.

ROUTLEDGE AND KEGAN PAUL LTD.* For excerpts from *The Condemned Playground* by Cyril Connolly; from *Speculations* by T. E. Hulme, ed. Herbert Read; from *Thought in Twentieth Century Poetry* by Raymond Tschumi.

JOHN RUSSELL. For excerpt from his *A Portrait of Logan Pearsall Smith*.

G. W. RUSSELL ESTATE. For excerpts from *Imaginations and Reveries* by "AE" (George William Russell).

ERNEST SANDEEN. For excerpt from his article on Alan Ross.

THE SATURDAY REVIEW (New York). For excerpts on Sacheverell Sitwell by Julian Huxley; on Peter Ustinov by Richard E. Meyers; on Malcolm Bradbury by C. P. Snow; on G. B. Stern and on Angela Thirkell by Pamela Taylor.

FRANCIS SCARFE. For excerpt from his article on Dylan Thomas.

SCHOCKEN BOOKS, INC. For excerpts from Foreword by Siegfried Sassoon in *Collected Poems of Isaac Rosenberg* (reprinted by permission of Schocken Books, Inc., copyright 1949 by Schocken Books, Inc.).

CHARLES SCRIBNER'S SONS. For excerpts from the Preface to *Letters from America* by Rupert Brooke (used by permission of Charles Scribner's Sons); from *George Bernard Shaw* by Edmund Fuller (used by permission of Charles Scribner's Sons); from *Barrie* by Thomas Moult; from *James Joyce* by William Y. Tindall.

SECKER & WARBURG LTD.* For excerpts from *Grand Men* by Harold Acton and Mary Cunard; from *Writers at Work,* ed. Malcolm Cowley; from *Critical Essays* by George Orwell; from *Inclinations* by Edward Sackville-West.

HOWARD SERGEANT. For excerpt from his article on Wilfred Owen.

SHEED AND WARD, INC. For excerpts from *Autobiography* by G. K. Chesterton (copyright 1936, reprinted by permission of Miss D. E. Collins and Sheed and Ward, Inc., New York).

SIDGWICK & JACKSON LTD.* For excerpts from *Modern English Writers* by Harold Williams.

THE SEWANEE REVIEW. For excerpt on Lennox Robinson by N. O'Connor.

WILLIAM KEAN SEYMOUR. For excerpts from his articles on George Barker and Ted Hughes.

SIMON & SCHUSTER, INC. For excerpts from *Around Theatres* by Max Beerbohm.

THE SOCIETY OF AUTHORS. For excerpts on James Stephens and Rebecca West by St. John Ervine; from *Private View* by Walter de La Mare; from the Introduction by Walter de La Mare to *John Freeman's Letters,* ed. Gertrude Freeman and Sir John Squire; from *Aspects of Literature* and *Reminiscences of D. H. Lawrence* by John Middleton Murry.

452 COPYRIGHT ACKNOWLEDGMENTS

SOUTHERN ILLINOIS UNIVERSITY PRESS. For excerpts from "A Single State of Man" by A. Alvarez in *A D. H. Lawrence Miscellany,* ed. Harry T. Moore; from "Things to Come" in *George Orwell: Fugitive from the Camp of Victory* by Richard Rees (copyright © 1962 by Southern Illinois University Press, reprinted by permission of Southern Illinois University Press).

THE SOUTHERN REVIEW. For excerpts on W. B. Yeats by L. C. Knights; on Louis MacNeice by H. J. Miller.

NEVILLE SPEARMAN LTD.* For excerpt from *Arthur Koestler* by John Atkins.

THE SPECTATOR. For its very generous permission to quote from numerous essays and reviews.

STEPHEN SPENDER. For his generous permission to quote from several of his articles.

DEREK STANFORD. For excerpts from his *The Freedom of Poetry;* from his *Christopher Fry;* and from his article on Alfred Noyes.

ZEPH STEWARD. For excerpt from *The Art of Wodehouse* by Arthur D. Nock.

ST. MARTIN'S PRESS, INC. For excerpt from *The Experiments of Sean O'Casey* by Robert Hogan.

STAPLES PRESS.* For excerpt from *Dramatists of Today* by J. C. Trewin.

ENID STARKIE. For excerpt from her article on Joyce Cary.

STEWART & KIDD PUBLISHING CO. For excerpt from *G. B. Shaw* by Archibald Henderson.

MILDRED SUTTON. For excerpt from *Some Contemporary Dramatists* by Graham Sutton.

THAMES & HUDSON LTD.* For excerpts from *A Reader's Guide to the Contemporary English Novel* by Frederick R. Karl.

GILBERT THOMAS. For excerpt from his *John Masefield.*

LOWELL THOMAS. For excerpt from his article on T. E. Lawrence.

TIME AND TIDE. For its generous permission to quote from various reviews in this journal and in *John O'London's Weekly.*

TIMES LITERARY SUPPLEMENT. For its very generous permission to quote from numerous reviews and articles (for complete list, see Index to Critics).

DIANA TRILLING. For excerpt from her review of Rebecca West's *A Train of Powder.*

LIONEL TRILLING. For excerpts from his articles on C. P. Snow and F. R. Leavis.

THE TWENTIETH CENTURY. For excerpts on Clifford Bax by Robert Aickman; on Dorothy Richardson by Georgina Battiscombe; on R. C. Sherriff by C. O. G. Dovie; on Arnold Wesker by Richard Findlater; on Lytton Strachey by Rosalind Nash; on Graham Greene by Derek Traversi; on Rex Warner by A. A. De Vitis; on Samuel Beckett by Roy Walker.

THE VIKING PRESS. For excerpts from interviews with E. M. Forster and Angus Wilson in *Writers at Work: The Paris Interview Series,* ed. Malcolm Cowley (copyright © 1957, 1958 by The Paris Review Inc., reprinted by permission of the Viking Press, Inc.); from *The Lost Childhood* by Graham Greene (copyright

COPYRIGHT ACKNOWLEDGMENTS 453

1951 by Graham Greene, reprinted by permission of The Viking Press, Inc.); from *Phoenix* by D. H. Lawrence, ed. Edward MacDonald; from *Transition* by Edwin Muir (copyright 1926, 1954 by Edwin Muir, reprinted by permission of The Viking Press, Inc.); from *The Liberal Imagination* by Lionel Trilling; from *The Strange Necessity* by Rebecca West, from *Craft and Character in Modern Fiction* by Morton Dauwen Zabel.

THE VIRGINIA QUARTERLY REVIEW. For excerpts on Edith Sitwell by Horace Gregory; on Joyce Cary by Enid Starkie.

ROY WALKER. For excerpt from his article on Samuel Beckett.

JOYCE WEINER ASSOCIATES.* For excerpt from *Literature in My Time* by Sir Compton Mackenzie.

PAUL WEST. For excerpt from his article on W. Somerset Maugham.

THE WESTERN HUMANITIES REVIEW. For excerpt on Philip Larkin by Alun R. Jones.

MARGARET WILLY. For excerpts from her articles on C. S. Lewis and on Norman Nicholson published in *English;* on Lilian Bowes-Lyon in *Essays and Studies* (1952).

EDMUND WILSON. For his generous permission to quote from several of his writings.

WILLIS KINGSLEY WING. For excerpts from *Lawrence Vindicated* by Robert Graves (published in *The New Republic,* March 22, copyright 1955 by International Authors, N. Y.).

LEONARD WOOLF. For excerpts from *The Death of the Moth* and *The Common Reader* by Virginia Woolf.

THE WORLD PUBLISHING CO. For excerpts from *The Writer Observed* by Harvey Breit; from *The Lonely Voice* by Frank O'Connor.

YALE UNIVERSITY PRESS. For excerpts from *Wyndham Lewis* by Geoffrey Wagner; from *Concepts of Criticism* by René Wellek.

THE YALE REVIEW. For excerpts on May Sinclair by Jean de Bosschère; on Elizabeth Jennings by Thom Gunn; on A. L. Rowse by Wallace Notestein; on P. H. Newby by Paul Pickrel.

CROSS-REFERENCE INDEX TO AUTHORS

Only significant references are included.

ABERCROMBIE, Lascelles
  (Marsh) II, 285
AGATE, James
  (Lucas, E. V.) II, 238; (O'Casey) II, 387, 388, 389; (Ustinov) III, 264
ALDINGTON, Richard
  (Lewis, Percy Wyndham) II, 213-14
AMIS, Kingsley
  (Braine) I, 118-19; (Cooper) I, 186; (Larkin) II, 140; (Osborne) II, 409-10; (Powell) II, 443; (Wain) III, 274-75
ANGRY YOUNG MEN, The
  (Amis) I, 11-12; (Murdoch) II, 351; (Osborne) II, 411-12, 412-13, 414; (Wain) III, 275
ARCHER, William
  (Agate) I, 3-4; (Moore) II, 330; (Phillips) II, 420; (Pinero) II, 427, 428
ARLEN, Michael
  (West, Morris) III, 333
AUDEN, W. H.
  (Graves) I, 371; (Grierson) I, 389; (Day Lewis) II, 200, 201-2, 204; (MacNeice) II, 272, 273, 274; (Madge) II, 276; (Spender) III, 170, 171-72; (Symons, Julian) III, 208; (Thomas, Dylan) III, 219; (Toynbee) III, 244; (Warner, Rex) III, 288, 290

BARING, Maurice
  (Lee, Vernon) II, 185
BARKER, George
  (Watkins) III, 294
BARRIE, J. M.
  (Bridie) I, 126; (Hardy) II, 11; (Jameson) II, 96; (Lonsdale) II, 230
BATESON, F. W.
  (Leavis) II, 170

BECKETT, Samuel
  (Joyce) II, 117; (Lyle) II, 242
BEERBOHM, Max
  (Belloc) I, 60; (Douglas) I, 226; (Kipling) II, 129
BELLOC, Hillaire
  (Guedalla) I, 392; (Kaye-Smith) II, 118; (Lucas, F. L.) II, 241; (Madge) II, 276; (Snow) III, 160
BENNETT, Arnold
  (Galsworthy) I, 334; (Kipling) II, 123; (Lang) II, 138; (Macaulay) II, 250; (Moore) II, 332; (Powys, T. F.) II, 454; (Swinnerton) III, 202, 203; (Wells) III, 319, 324, 326; (Williamson, Henry) III, 354
BETJEMAN, John
  (Firbank) I, 294; (Smith, Stevie) III, 152
BLUNDEN, Edmund
  (Hassall) II, 23; (Read) III, 14
BLUNT, Wilfred Scawen
  (Trench) III, 252
BOTTRALL, Ronald
  (Leavis) II, 174; (Madge) II, 276
BOWEN, Elizabeth
  (Lessing) II, 196; (West, Anthony) III, 332
BRIDGES, Robert
  (Bottomley) I, 104; (Eliot) I, 265; (Hopkins) II, 46; (Squire) III, 172; (Webb) III, 311; (Young, Francis Brett) III, 398
BROOKE, Rupert
  (Owen) II, 416-17; (Sorley) III, 161, 163; (Wolfe) III, 371
BUTLER, Samuel
  (Cannan) I, 146; (Douglas) I, 224-25; (Isherwood) II, 83; (Shaw) III, 101; (Sinclair) III, 129; (Wolfe) III, 372

CAINE, Hall
(Corelli) I, 190-191; (Kaye-Smith) II, 119; (Powys, John Cowper) II, 447

CAMPBELL, Roy
(Lyle) II, 242

CARY, Joyce
(Allen) I, 8; (Hartley) II, 20; (Murdoch) II, 351

CAUDWELL, Christopher
(Bowra) I, 117

CHESTERTON, G. K.
(Beerbohm) I, 57-58; (Belloc) I, 61-62, 64; (Gregory) I, 388; (Hardy) II, 11; (Kaye-Smith) II, 119; (Lewis, C. S.) II, 211-12; (Lucas, F. L.) II, 241; (Williams, Charles) III, 346

COMPTON-BURNETT, Ivy
(Bowen) I, 109-10; (Sinclair) III, 129

CONNOLLY, Cyril
(Leavis) II, 177; (Lubbock) II, 235; (Powell) II, 440-41

CONRAD, Joseph
(Ford) I, 302, 303; (Galsworthy) I, 332; (Greene) I, 385; (Hanley) II, 7; (Hardy) II, 12; (Hudson, W. H.) II, 59; (Joyce) II, 107; (Kipling) II, 128; (Maugham) II, 304; (Meynell, Viola) II, 316; (Powys, John Cowper) II, 454; (Tomlinson) III, 241-42

COOPER, William
(Wilson, Angus) III, 360

COPPARD, A. E.
(Strong) III, 194

CORELLI, Marie
(Haggard) II, 2; (Powys, John Cowper) II, 447

COWARD, Noel
(Maugham) II, 301; (Milne) II, 319-20; (Myers) II, 363; (Robinson) III, 41; (Ustinov) III, 264

CUNNINGHAME-GRAHAM, R. B.
(Conrad) I, 181

DAVIE, Donald
(Leavis) II, 179; (Wain) III, 275

DAVIES, Rhys
(Jones, Gwyn) II, 103

DAVIES, W. H.
(Flecker) I, 296; (Gibson) I, 342; (Noyes) II, 381

DAY LEWIS (See under LEWIS)

DE LA MARE, Walter
(Freeman) I, 322; (Hassall) II, 23; (Hodgson) II, 35; (Noyes) II, 382; (Squire) III, 172; (Webb) III, 311

DOUGHTY, Charles
(Lawrence, T. E.) II, 166; (MacDiarmid) II, 257

DOUGLAS, Norman
(Huxley) II, 73; (Menen) II, 305

DURRELL, Lawrence
(Spencer) III, 165-66

EGLINTON, John
(Joyce) II, 117

ELIOT, T. S.
(Binyon) I, 90; (Bottrall) I, 107; (Grierson) I, 389; (Hulme) II, 67; (Huxley) II, 73-74; (James) II, 94; (Leavis) II, 172, 177, 179; (MacDiarmid) II, 257; (MacNeice) II, 274; (Murry) II, 358; (Noyes) II, 384; (O'Casey) II, 391; (Sitwell, Osbert) III, 137; (Waugh, Evelyn) III, 304; (Williams, Charles) III, 344; (Williamson, Hugh Ross) III, 355; (Wolfe) III, 372; (Woolf, Leonard) III, 376; (Yeats) III, 390, 392-93, 396

EMPSON, William
(Hamilton) II, 6; (Leavis) II, 174, 179; (Madge) II, 276; (Richards) III, 25

FIRBANK, Ronald
(Green) I, 378; (Hichens) II, 32; (Huxley) II, 73-74

FORD, Ford Madox
(Duggan) I, 240

FORSTER, E. M.
(Benson, Stella) I, 79-80; (Isherwood) II, 81-82; (Newby) II, 370; (Powys, T. F.) II, 454; (Woolf, Virginia) III, 383

FRY, Christopher
(Nicholson) II, 377; (Stanford) III, 178

GALSWORTHY, John
(Bennett) I, 65, 67; (Jameson) II, 96; (Kaye-Smith) II, 118; (Kipling) II, 124; (Masefield) II, 289; (Maugham) II, 304; (Snow) III, 158-59; (Wells) III, 324

GIBSON, Wilfrid
(Marsh) II, 285

CROSS-REFERENCE INDEX

GISSING, George
(Moore) II, 332; (Swinnerton) III, 199-200, 201

GOLDING, William
(Murdoch) II, 353; (Spark) III, 165

GOSSE, Edmund
(Shanks) III, 90

GRAHAME, Kenneth
(White) III, 339

GRAVES, Robert
(Empson) I, 276; (Hughes) II, 62; (Larkin) II, 141; (Thomas, Dylan) III, 219

GREEN, Henry
(Murdoch) II, 352; (Powell) II, 440-41; (Sansom) III, 77

GREENE, Graham
(Ford) I, 305; (Powell) II, 440-41; (West, Anthony) III, 332

GREGORY, Lady
(O'Casey) II, 389; (Synge) III, 212-13

GUEDALLA, Philip
(Strachey) III, 186

HAGGARD, H. Ryder
(Kipling) II, 123-24, 128-29; (Lang) II, 138

HARDY, Thomas
(Butler) I, 138-39; (Housman, A. E.) II, 51; (Joyce) II, 107; (Kaye-Smith) II, 118; (Larkin) II, 141; (Lawrence, T. E.) II, 169; (Lucas, F. L.) II, 241; (Phillpotts) II, 424, 425; (Powys, John Cowper) II, 447, 451; (Powys, T. F.) II, 454; (Richards) III, 27; (Strong) III, 192; (Warner, Sylvia Townsend) III, 290-91; (Wodehouse) III, 370

HARTLEY, L. P.
(Compton-Burnett) I, 174; (Lawrence, D. H.) II, 160; (West, Anthony) III, 332

HEWLETT, Maurice
(Kaye-Smith) II, 118

HOPE, Anthony
(Lang) II, 138

HOPKINS, Gerard Manley
(Bridges) I, 121, 121-22; (Doughty) I, 221; (Eliot) I, 256-57; (Lyon) II, 246

HOUSMAN, A. E.
(Kipling) II, 124; (Powys, T. F.) II, 454; (Yeats) III, 394

HUDSON, W. H.
(Housman) II, 48

HUGHES, Richard
(White) III, 341

HUXLEY, Aldous
(MacCarthy) II, 254-55; (Menen) II, 305; (Myers) II, 363; (Powell) II, 443; (Pritchett) II, 461; (Russell, Bertrand) III, 56; (Waugh, Evelyn) III, 307, 308; (West, Anthony) III, 332; (Wilson, Angus) III, 362

ISHERWOOD, Christopher
(Auden) I, 19; (Spender) III, 171-72

JAMES, Henry
(Bowen) I, 109; (Compton-Burnett) I, 172, 174, 175; (Ford) I, 303; (Guedalla) I, 392; (Hardy), II, 11; (Hartley) II, 20; (Heppenstall) II, 26; (Kipling) II, 122-23; (Lee, Vernon) II, 184; (MacCarthy) II, 255; (Muir) II, 345; (Myers) II, 364; (Pinter) II, 430; (Powys, T. F.) II, 454; (Richardson) III, 31; (Sidgwick) III, 116-17; (Sinclair) III, 126; (Smith, Logan Pearsall) III, 148; (West, Rebecca) III, 334; (Young, Francis Brett) III, 399

JEROME, Jerome K.
(Wallace) III, 279

JOYCE, James
(Beckett) I, 47, 48, 50; (Hudson, W. H.) II, 58; (James) II, 92; (Jones, David) II, 101-2; (Lawrence, D. H.) II, 160; (Lewis, Percy Wyndham) II, 215, 221-22; (Moore) II, 336-37; (O'Casey) II, 389; (O'Connor) II, 393, 395; (Powys, John Cowper) II, 450-51; (Richardson) III, 29; (Shaw) III, 100; (Sitwell, Sacheverell) III, 141; (Strong) III, 195-96; (Thomas, Dylan) III, 218; (Wilson, Colin) III, 363; (Yeats) III, 392-93

KAYE-SMITH, Sheila
(Tynan) III, 259

KER, W. P.
(Grierson) I, 390

KIPLING, Rudyard
(Gibson) I, 340-41; (Greene) I, 385; (Haggard) II, 2-3; (Mansfield) II, 280; (Noyes) II, 384; (Powys, T. F.) II, 452-53, 454; (Shute) III, 115; (Wodehouse) III, 370

CROSS-REFERENCE INDEX

LANG, Andrew
(Mason) II, 293
LARKIN, Philip
(Wain) III, 275
LAWRENCE, D. H.
(Davidson) I, 203; (Ford) I, 305; (Forster) I, 311, 318; (Gibbons) I, 338; (Hardy) II, 16-17; (Hartley) II, 21; (Housman, A. E.) II, 52; (Hudson, Stephen) II, 58; (Huxley) II, 70; (Jones, Gwyn) II, 103-4; (Leavis) II, 172-73; (Lucas, F. L.) II, 240; (Murry) II, 358-59, 361; (Nicholson) II, 376; (Plomer) II, 435; (Powys, John Cowper) II, 446, 449, 450-51; (Powys, T. F.) II, 453, 454; (Pritchett) II, 461, 462; (Savage) III, 84; (Silkin) III, 119; (Stuart) III, 198; (Swinnerton) III, 202; (Wilson, Angus) III, 359; (Woolf, Virginia) III, 385
LAWRENCE, T. E.
(Aldington) I, 6-7; (Rattigan) III, 11
LEAVIS, F. R.
(Connolly) I, 177; (Lewis, C. S.) II, 211; (Snow) III, 158
DAY LEWIS, C.
(Graves) I, 371; (MacNeice) II, 272, 273, 274; (Spender) III, 171-72
LEWIS, C. S.
(Sayers) III, 86-87; (White) III, 341
LEWIS, Percy Wyndham
(Comfort) I, 168; (Grigson) I, 391; (Plomer) II, 435

MACAULAY, Rose
(Ford) I, 316
MACDIARMID, Hugh
(Smith, Sydney Goodsir) III, 149-150
MACNEICE, Louis
(Auden) I, 18-19; (Grierson) I, 389; (Spender) III, 171-72
MANSFIELD, Katherine
(Bentley) I, 82-83
MARSH, Edward
(Hassall) II, 24
MASEFIELD, John
(Bennett) I, 73; (Binyon) I, 89; (Gibson) I, 340-41; (Sorley) III, 161-62
MAUGHAM, W. S.
(Isherwood) II, 82; (Macaulay) II, 250; (Moore) II, 332; (Osborne) II, 409-10

MEW, Charlotte
(Warner, Sylvia Townsend) III, 291
MOORE, George
(Bennett) I, 75, 76; (Freeman) I, 332; (Galsworthy) I, 332; (Gosse) I, 356-57; (Synge) III, 213; (Waugh, Alec) III, 299; (Yeats) III, 396
MOORE, Nicholas
(Stanford) III, 177
MOORE, T. Sturge
(Hulme) II, 67
MORGAN, Charles
(Lawrence, D. H.) II, 160
MOVEMENT, The
(Gunn) I, 393; (Jennings) II, 97; (Morgan) II, 343
MURDOCH, Iris
(Compton-Burnett) I, 174; (Hartley) II, 22; (Wain) III, 274
MURRY, John Middleton
(Heppenstall) II, 26, 27; (Huxley) II, 70; (Stanford) III, 177

NICHOLSON, Norman
(Lyon) II, 245
NOYES, Alfred
(Priestley) II, 455

O'CASEY, Sean
(Johnston) II, 101
O'CONNOR, Frank
(Stuart) III, 197
O'FAOLAIN, Seán
(Stuart) III, 197, (Wilson, Angus) III, 358
ORWELL, George
(Chesterton) I, 162; (Heppenstall) II, 26; (White) III, 341
OSBORNE, John
(Pinter) II, 431; (Wesker) III, 328-29

POWELL, Anthony
(Newby) II, 371
POWYS, T. F.
(Gibbons) I, 338
PRIESTLEY, J. B.
(Myers) II, 365-66; (O'Casey) II, 387; (Ustinov) III, 264; (Wilson, Angus) III, 357
PRINCE, F. T.
(Tomlinson) III, 238
PRITCHETT, V. S.
(O'Connor) II, 394

QUILLER-COUCH, Arthur
(Bennett) I, 73; (Haggard) II, 1; (Priestley) II, 455

RAINE, Kathleen
(Madge) II, 276
RATTIGAN, Terence
(Ustinov) III, 265
READ, Herbert
(Comfort) I, 169; (Heppenstall) II, 27; (Hulme) II, 67; (Muir) II, 346-47
RICHARDS, I. A.
(Empson) I, 274-75, 276; (Hamilton) II, 6; (Hulme) II, 67; (Leavis) II, 170, 172; (Madge) II, 276; (Read) III, 12
RICHARDSON, Dorothy
(Sinclair) III, 125
ROBINSON, Lennox
(O'Faoláin) II, 397
RUSSELL, Bertrand
(Lawrence, D. H.) II, 157, 159
RUSSELL, George William
(Priestley) II, 455; (Stephens) III, 181-82; (Tynan) III, 259, 260; (Yeats) III, 390, 395

SAINTSBURY, George
(Bennett) I, 73-74; (Daiches) I, 198-99; (Priestley) II, 455
SAKI
(Wesker) III, 327
SASSOON, Siegfried
(Owen) II, 415, 416, 417, 418; (Sitwell, Osbert) III, 135
SCARFE, Francis
(Stanford) III, 177
SHAW, George Bernard
(Beerbohm) I, 57; (Dennis) I, 217; (Galsworthy) I, 333; (Golding) I, 352; (Granville-Barker) I, 368; (Greene) I, 381; (Gregory) I, 386; (Harris) II, 20; (Jameson) II, 96; (Joyce) II, 110; (Lonsdale) II, 228-29; (Maugham) II, 299; (O'Casey) II, 385-86; (Squire) III, 173; (Ustinov) III, 264, 265, 266; (Walkley) III, 277; (Wells) III, 321-22, 324
SHUTE, Nevil
(Forester) I, 306
SILLITOE, Alan
(Hanley) II, 7

SITWELL, Edith
(Sitwell, Osbert) III, 137; (Sitwell, Sacheverell) III, 142; (Thomas, Dylan) III, 219; (Wain) III, 275; (Welch) III, 315; (Woolf, Leonard) III, 376
SITWELL, Osbert
(Sitwell, Edith) III, 129; (Strong) III, 194
SITWELL, Sacheverell
(Sitwell, Edith) III, 129; (Sitwell, Osbert) III, 137
SMITH, Logan Pearsall
(Priestley) II, 455
SNOW, C. P.
(Cooper) I, 186; (Leavis) II, 176; (Wilson, Angus) III, 360
SPARK, Muriel
(Murdoch) II, 354
SPENDER, Stephen
(Graves) I, 371; (Grierson) I, 389; (Day Lewis) II, 202; (MacNeice) II, 272, 273; (O'Connor) II, 394; (Scarfe) III, 88
SQUIRE, J. C.
(Shanks) III, 90
STEPHENS, James
(Hodgson) II, 34; (Priestley) II, 455
STRACHEY, Lytton
(Beerbohm) I, 54; (Guedalla) I, 391; (Leslie) II, 191; (MacCarthy) II, 255; (Woolf, Leonard) III, 377
SYMONS, Arthur
(Davidson) I, 201-2; (Gosse) I, 359; (Gould) I, 359
SYNGE, John Millington
(Colum) I, 166-67; (Gregory) I, 386; (Lucas, F. L.) II, 241; (Masefield) II, 289; (Robinson) III, 39-40; (Stephens) III, 181

THOMAS, Dylan
(Clarke) I, 165; (Evans) I, 285; (Heppenstall) II, 26; (Leavis) II, 174; (Stanford) III, 178; (Treece) III, 247; (Wain) III, 275; (Watkins) III, 294
THOMAS, Edward
(Spencer) III, 166-67
TILLER, Terence
(Spencer) III, 165-66
TODD, Ruthven
(Symons, Julian) III, 208

TREECE, Henry
(Fraser) I, 319
TYNAN, Katharine
(Stanford) III, 178

USTINOV, Peter
(MacDougall) II, 260-61

WAIN, John
(Braine) I, 118-19; (Larkin) II, 140
WALKLEY, A. B.
(Agate) I, 3
WALLACE, Edgar
(Galsworthy) I, 333
WALPOLE, Hugh
(Thirkell) III, 215
WARNER, Rex
(West, Anthony) III, 332
WATKINS, Vernon
(Scarfe) III, 88; (Tiller) III, 233
WATSON, William
(Noyes) II, 382
WAUGH, Alec
(Nichols, Beverley) II, 372
WAUGH, Evelyn
(Laski) II, 142; (Manning) II, 278; (Newby) II, 370, 371; (Powell) II, 440-41, 443, 444; (White) III, 341; (Wilson, Angus) III, 362
WEBB, Mary
(Young, Francis Brett) III, 401
WEDGWOOD, C. V.
(Macaulay) II, 251
WELLS, H. G.
(Belloc) I, 64; (Bennett) I, 65, 67, 70-72, 77; (Galsworthy) I, 334; (Garnett) I, 334-35; (Hardy) II, 11; (Lee, Vernon) II, 184; (Mansfield) II, 280; (Pritchett) II, 462-63; (Swinnerton) III, 203; (West, Anthony) III, 331-32; (Wilson, Colin) III, 364
WESKER, Arnold
(Pinter) II, 431
WEST, Rebecca
(Macaulay) II, 250
WILLIAMS, Charles
(West, Anthony) III, 332
WODEHOUSE, P. G.
(Waugh, Evelyn) III, 308
WOLFE, Humbert
(Warner, Sylvia Townsend) III, 290
WOOLF, Virginia
(Bowen) I, 115; (Lessing) II, 195-96; (Lewis, Percy Wyndham) II, 215; (Lucas, F. L.) II, 241; (MacCarthy) II, 255; (Murdoch) II, 353; (O'Connor) II, 393; (Sackville-West, V.) III, 69; (Sitwell, Sacheverell) III, 141; (Woolf, Leonard) III, 378; (Young, G. M.) III, 402

YEATS, William Butler
(Blunt) I, 101; (Clarke) I, 165; (Eliot) I, 267-68; (Jones, David) II, 102; (Joyce) II, 117; (Lewis, Percy Wyndham) II, 221; (MacNeice) II, 274; (O'Casey) II, 386, 387-88, 389; (Owen) II, 418, 419; (Priestley) II, 455; (Spender) III, 169; (Stuart) III, 197; (Synge) III, 210, 211-12, 213-14, 214; (Trench) III, 249; (Tynan) III, 260; (Watkins) III, 292, 293, 294
YOUNG, G. M.
(Kipling) II, 129

INDEX TO CRITICS

Passage begins on the page listed.

Selections from the *Times Literary Supplement*, always unsigned, are indexed under the publication title.

ABBOTT, Claude C.
  Bottomley, I, 104
ACTON, Harold
  Douglas, I, 231
ADAMS, Phoebe
  Russell, B., III, 58
ADCOCK, Arthur St. John
  Mackenzie, II, 270; Maugham, II, 297; Noyes, II, 381
AFFABLE Hawk (Desmond MacCarthy)
  Hulme, II, 65; Lehmann, R., II, 189
AGATE, James
  Drinkwater, I, 237; Dunsany, I, 249; Lonsdale, II, 228; Maugham, II, 298; Munro, II, 351; O'Casey, II, 386; Priestley, II, 456; Robinson, III, 40; Shaw, III, 97; Williams, E., III, 348
AIKEN, Conrad
  Gibson, I, 340; Sitwell, O., III, 135
AIKMAN, Robert Fordyce
  Bax, I, 45
ALDINGTON, Richard
  Lawrence, D. H., II, 158; Sitwell, O., III, 134; Sitwell, S., III, 139
ALGREN, Nelson
  Pudney, II, 465
ALLEN, Walter
  Bowen, I, 113; Cary, I, 153; Dennis, I, 217; Duggan, I, 240; Empson, I, 279; Enright, I, 281; Grigson, I, 391; Hudson, S., II, 57; Jones, Gwynn, II, 103; Lewis, P. W., II, 218; Lowry, II, 231; MacNeice, II, 274; Maugham, II, 304; Monsarrat, II, 328; O'Connor, II, 395; Powell, II, 442; Sillitoe, III, 121; Sinclair, III, 128; Swinnerton, III, 202; Wain, III, 274; Wells, III, 326; Wilson, A., III, 360; Woolf, L., III, 378
ALLSOP, Kenneth
  Amis, I, 10; Wilson, C., III, 364

ALVAREZ, A.
  Auden, I, 23; Empson, I, 275; Lawrence, D. H., II, 157; Lehmann, J., II, 188; MacCaig, II, 253; MacDiarmid, II, 259; Tomlinson, C., III, 238; Watkins, III, 294
AMIS, Kingsley
  Compton-Burnett, I, 171; Wesker, III, 330; Wilson, C., III, 363
ANAND, Mulk Raj
  Lawrence, T .E., II, 167
APERTYX
  Cannan, I, 145
ARCHER, William
  Housman, L., II, 52; Jones, H. A., II, 105; Quiller-Couch, III, 4; Robinson, III, 40; Symons, A., III, 203
ARROWSMITH, J. E. S.
  Arlen, I, 17; Cronin, I, 195; Delafield, I, 210
ARVIN, Newton
  West, R., III, 338
ASHLEY, Maurice
  Williamson, H. R., III, 356
ASQUITH, Cynthia
  Barrie, I, 38
ATKINS, John
  Greene, I, 381; Orwell, II, 406; Treece, III, 246
AUDEN, W. H.
  Ford, I, 304; Graves, I, 373; Hopkins, II, 44; James, II, 89; Jones, David, II, 101; Lewis, C. S., II, 206; MacNeice, II, 275; Tolkien, III, 235; Williams, C., III, 346; Woodcock, III, 374; Yeats, III, 393

BAILEY, Cyril
  Mackail, II, 266
BAINES, Jocelyn
  Lewis, P. W., II, 219

INDEX TO CRITICS

BAIRD, Enid
  Greene, I, 378
BAKER, Carlos
  Johnson, II, 99
BALDWIN, Stanley
  Webb, III, 310
BANTOCK, G. H.
  Isherwood, II, 80
BARFIELD, Owen
  Koestler, II, 134
BARKER, George
  MacNeice, II, 271; Rodgers, III, 41; Spender, III, 170; Symons, J., III, 208; Watkins, III, 292
BARKHAM, John
  Masters, II, 295
BARNES, T. R.
  Auden, I, 19; Orwell, II, 403
BARR, Donald
  Lee, V., II, 183
BARROWS, John
  Manning, II, 277; Murry, II, 361
BATES, H. E.
  Coppard, I, 187; Moore, G., II, 333; O'Flaherty, II, 400
BATESON, F. W.
  Leavis, II, 179; Lewis, C. S., II, 210
BATTISCOMBE, Georgina
  Benson, S., I, 81
BAYLEY, John
  Ford, I, 304; Forster, I, 317; White, III, 341
BEAUMONT, Ernest
  Williams, C., III, 347
BEECHAM, Audrey
  Madge, II, 275
BEER, John Bernard
  Forster, I, 315; Murry, II, 361
BEERBOHM, Max
  Archer, I, 15; Baring, I, 28; Barrie, I, 32; Caine, I, 141; Galsworthy, I, 330-1; Granville-Barker, I, 367; Jerome, II, 98; Jones, H. A., II, 104; Kipling, II, 122; Lang, II, 136; Moore, G., II, 330; Phillips, II, 420; Pinero, II, 426; Shaw, III, 92; Symons, A., III, 204
BELL, Graham
  Gerhardi, I, 337; Hutchinson, II, 68
BELLOC, Hillaire
  Wells, III, 322
BENNETT, Joan
  Woolf, V., III, 386

BENNETT, Arnold
  Sitwell, S., III, 140; Swinnerton, III, 200
BENTLEY, Eric
  O'Casey, II, 387; Shaw, III, 104
BENTLEY, Nicolas
  Milne, II, 320
BERESFORD, J. D.
  Richardson, III, 29; Wells, III, 320
BERGER, John
  Read, III, 16
BERGONZI, Bernard
  Bottrall, I, 107; Fuller, I, 329; Lewis, C. S., II, 210; Powell, II, 446; Wilson, C., III, 366
BERRY, Francis
  Read, III, 17
BERRY, Gerald
  Agate, I, 3
BETT, Henry
  Barrie, I, 34; Watson, III, 297
BICKLEY, Francis
  Synge, III, 210; Watson, III, 295
BIERSTADT, Edward Hale
  Dunsany, I, 247
BINYON, Lawrence
  Fausset, I, 287; Meyerstein, II, 311; Rosenberg, III, 47
BIRRELL, Francis
  Sutro, III, 198
BIRMINGHAM, William
  Greene, I, 380
BISHOP, Reginald (with John Lewis)
  Koestler, II, 131
BLACKBURN, Thomas
  Day Lewis, II, 203; MacNeice, II, 274
BLACKMUR, R. P.
  Aldington, I, 5; Eliot, I, 264; Lawrence, T. E., II, 167; Myers, II, 364; Yeats, III, 392
BLAKESTON, Oswell
  Day Lewis, II, 202; Quennell, III, 3
BLISS, William
  Freeman, I, 320
BLOOMFIELD, Paul
  Hartley, II, 21; Menen, II, 305; O'Flaherty, II, 400
BLUNDEN, Edmund
  Sackville-West, E., III, 65
BOOTH, Philip
  Davie, I, 206

INDEX TO CRITICS 463

BOTTERILL, Denis
Graham, I, 364; Rickword, III, 34; Smith, S. G., III, 150; Stanford, III, 177

BOTTOME, Phyllis
Murray, II, 356; Shute, III, 114; Waugh, A., III, 300

BOURNE, John
Leavis, II, 173

BOWEN, Elizabeth
Barrie, I, 37; Gwynn, I, 396; Powell, II, 440; Sansom, III, 80; West, R., III, 336

BOWLES, Patrick
Beckett, I, 48

BOWRA, Maurice
Sitwell, E., III, 132

BOYD, Ernest A.
Colum, I 166; Dunsany, I, 246; Eglinton, I, 254; Gregory, I, 386; Russell, G. W., III, 60; Shaw, III, 95; Stephens, III, 182

BOYLE, Kay
Monsarrat, II, 329

BRADBURY, Malcolm
Ford, I, 303; Wain, III, 276

BRADDOCK, Joseph
Lyle, II, 241

BRAHMS, Caryl
Osborne, II, 412

BRAYBOOKE, Neville
Grahame, I, 366

BRAYBROOKE, Patrick
Noyes, II, 382; Tynan, Katharine, III, 259; Walpole, III, 283; West, R., III, 335

BREIT, Harvey
Coward, I, 194; Forester, C. S., I, 305; Green, I, 375; Thomas D., III, 220

BRIDIE, James
Shaw, III, 102

BRIDGES-ADAMS
Lonsdale, II, 230

BRIEN, Alan
Laski, II, 143

BRIGHOUSE, Harold
Dane, I, 201; Robinson, III, 41

BRITTAIN, Fred
Quiller-Couch, III, 7

BRITTAIN, Vera
Holtby, II, 37

BROGAN, D. W.
Wedgwood, III, 314

BROOKE, Jocelyn
Bowen, I, 114; Huxley, II, 76; Lawrence, T. E., II, 169; Powell, II, 443; Powys, J. C., II, 448; Rolfe, III, 46; Sackville-West, E., III, 67; Swinnerton, III, 202

BROOKS, Van Wyck
Wells, III, 321

BROWN, Elizabeth L.
Thompson, III, 231

BROWN, Ivor
Gould, I, 360; Lewis, C. S., II, 209; Nicholson, II, 376; Royde-Smith, III, 54

BROWN, John L.
West, M., III, 334

BROWN, John Mason
Carroll, I, 149

BROWN, Stuart Gerry
Grierson, I, 389

BROWNE, E. Martin
Johnston, II, 100

BRUNINI, John Gilland
Lewis, C. S., II, 206

BRUSTEIN, Robert
Osborne, II, 414

BRYDEN, Ronald
Greene, I, 385; Pinter, II, 433

BRYHER
Mackenzie, II, 270

BUCKLER, Ernest
Bates, H. E., I, 43

BULLETT, Gerald
Coppard, I, 187; Golding, L., I, 349; O'Connor, II, 392; Powys, T. F., II, 452; Strong, III, 192; Walpole, III, 284

BULLOCK, George
Corelli, I, 191

BULLOUGH, Geoffrey
Nichols, R., II, 375; Owen, II, 415; Sassoon, III, 81; Sayers, III, 86; Sitwell, O., III, 136; Wolfe, III, 372

BURDETT, Osbert
Armstrong, I, 17; Belloc, I, 62; Jameson, II, 96; Meynell, A., II, 313; Moore, G., II, 331; Smith, L. P., III, 145; Symons, A., III, 205

BURLINGHAM, Roger
Reid, III, 21

BURTON, G. L.
　Drinkwater, I, 239
BURTON, Richard
　Shaw, III, 95
BUSH, Douglas
　Abercrombie, I, 1; Aldington, I, 7; Bridges, I, 122; Empson, I, 277; Murray, II, 355
BUTTS, Myra
　Huxley, II, 71

CAMPBELL, Roy
　Lewis, D. B. W., II, 212
CAPE, Jonathan
　Lawrence, T. E., II, 166
CAREW, Dudley
　Priestley, II, 457
CARY, Joyce
　Cary, I, 152
CASS, Cashenden
　West, A., III, 331
CASSON, Edmund
　Gibson, I, 341
CAUDWELL, Christopher
　Lawrence, T. E., II, 166
CAVENDISH, Henry
　Standish, III, 177
CAZAMIAN, Madeleine L.
　Cannan, I, 146
CECIL, David
　MacCarthy, II, 255
CECIL, Lady Eleanor
　Sinclair, III, 123
CHAMBERS, Harry
　Larkin, II, 141
CHAPMAN, F.
　Barker, I, 30; MacNeice, II, 271
CHARQUES, R. D.
　Bentley, I, 83; Meyerstein, II, 311; Sassoon, III, 81; Standish, III, 176; Walpole, III, 285
CHARTERIS, Evan
　Gosse, I, 356
CHASE, Richard
　Joyce, II, 110
CHESTERTON, G. K.
　Davidson, I, 204; Gosse, I, 358; Shaw, III, 94
CHEVALLEY, Abel
　Cannan, I, 146
CHEW, Samuel C.
　Granville-Barker, I, 368

CHILD, H. H.
　Barrie, I, 37
CHRISTIE, J. T.
　Noyes, II, 383
CHRYSTAL, Sir George
　Saintsbury, III, 73
CHUBB, Thomas Caldecot
　Duggan, I, 240
CHURCH, Richard
　Blunden, I, 93; Chesterton, I, 161; Clarke, I, 164; Davies, W. H., I, 209; Gibson, I, 342; Graves, I, 370; Macaulay, II, 250; Mackenzie, II, 270; Priestley, II, 459; Roberts, III, 36; Sackville-West, V., III, 70; Sitwell, S., III, 140; Turner, W. J., III, 256
CLARK, Kenneth
　Sitwell, E., III, 131
CLARKE, Austin
　Binyon, I, 89; Gogarty, I, 347; Gwynn, I, 395; Moore, T. S., II, 339; Rickword, III, 34; Russell, G. W., III, 61; Trench, III, 250
CLURMAN, Harold
　Osborne, II, 414
COATES, Willson H.
　Wedgwood, III, 314
COFFMAN JR., Stanley K.
　Hulme, II, 66
COHEN, J. M.
　Goldring, D., I, 355
COHEN, Morton N.
　Haggard, II, 3; Kipling, II, 128
COLE, M. D.
　Pudney, II, 465
COLEMAN, John
　Sillitoe, III, 122
COLLARD, Lorna
　Webb, III, 311
COLLINS, H. P.
　Powys, T. F., II, 453; Wolfe, III, 371
COLLINS, J. P.
　Vachell, III, 268
COLUM, Mary
　Blunt, I, 100; Gregory, I, 388; Russell, G. W., III, 62
CONNELL, John
　Masters, II, 295; West, R., III, 338
CONNOLLY, Cyril
　Baring, I, 28; Bennett, I, 75; Benson, S., I, 78; Eliot, I, 258; Forster, I, 307; Housman, A. E., II, 48; Hux-

INDEX TO CRITICS 465

ley, II, 73; Isherwood, II, 79; James, II, 90; Joyce, II, 107; Lewis, P. W., II, 215; Milne, II, 319; Stephens, III, 183; Waugh, E., III, 304; Woolf, V., III, 382; Young, F. B., III, 400
CONNOLLY, Francis X.
  White, III, 341
CONRAD, Joseph
  Galsworthy, I, 330; Walpole, III, 282
COOKE, Alistair
  Lewis, C. S., II, 205
COOMBES, H.
  Powys, T. F., II, 453
COOPER, Frederick Taber
  Corelli, I, 189
COOPER, William
  Snow, III, 153
CORDELL, Richard A.
  Jones, H. A., II, 105; Maugham, II, 303
CORKE, Hilary
  Durrell, I, 251; Mew, II, 309; O'Faolain, II, 396; Snow, III, 157
COULSON, John
  Russell, B., III, 58
COURTNEY, Janet E.
  Gosse, I, 357
COWLEY, Malcolm
  Koestler, II, 130
COX, C. B.
  Larkin, II, 139
COX, R. G.
  Auden, I, 24; Potter, II, 437
CRAIG, Maurice James
  Moore, N., II, 337
CRANE, R. S.
  Richards, III, 28
CRANE, Walt
  Strong, III, 195
CRANSTON, Maurice
  Murdoch, II, 351; Russell, B., III, 57
CROSS, Wilbur
  Wells, III, 323
CUNLIFFE, J. W.
  Hudson, W. H., II, 61
CURREY, R. N.
  Caine, I, 144
CURTIS, Robert G.
  Wallace, III, 280

DAICHES, David
  Barker, I, 31; Barrie, I, 40; James, II, 94; Day Lewis, II, 202; MacDiarmid, II, 259; Roberts, III, 37; Rodgers, III, 42; Scarfe, III, 88; Turner, W. J., III, 258
DALLAS, Ian
  Osborne, II, 410
DANE, Clemence
  Walpole, III, 284
DANIEL, John
  Beerbohm, I, 57
DARBISHIRE, Helen
  De Selincourt, I, 218
DARLINGTON, W. A.
  Barrie, I, 38
DAVENPORT, Basil
  Symons, J., III, 208; White, III, 341
DAVENPORT, John
  Bedford, I, 51
DAVIE, Donald
  Blunt, I, 101; Eliot, I, 270; Owen, II, 418; Tomlinson, C., III, 237; Wain, III, 276
DAVISON, Edward
  Stephens, III, 183
DAWSON-SCOTT, C. A.
  Sinclair, III, 125
DE BOSSCHERE, Jean
  Sinclair, III, 127
DE LA MARE, Walter
  Freeman, I, 321; Reid, III, 20; Thomas, E., III, 229; Webb, III, 310
DENNIS, NIGEL
  Tynan, Kenneth, III, 262; Wain, III, 276; Waugh, E., III, 301
DEUTSCH, Babette
  Fraser, I, 319
DE VILLOSE, Henry
  MacCarthy, II, 254; Orwell, II, 404
DEVITIS, A. A.
  Warner, R., III, 290
DEVREE, Howard
  Lewis, P. W., II, 220
DOBREE, Bonamy
  Agate, I, 2; Eliot, I, 257; Forster, I, 306; Hardy, II, 11; Koestler, II, 130; Lehmann, J., II, 186; Lewis, P. W., II, 214; Logue, II, 227
DOCK, E. K. T.
  Lewis, C. S., II, 207
DONALDSON, Frances
  Lonsdale, II, 229
DONOGHUE, Denis
  Wesker, III, 328; Yeats, III, 397

INDEX TO CRITICS

DOUGLAS, Norman
  Brooke, Rupert, I, 128; Lawrence, D. H., II, 152; Thomas, E., III, 227
DOUIE, C. O. G.
  Sherriff, III, 110
DRINKWATER, John
  Abercrombie, I, 1; Lucas, F. L., II, 238
DUCHENE, Anne
  Johnson, II, 99; Spark, III, 164
DUFFIELD, Brett
  O'Casey, II, 390
DUFFIN, Henry Charles
  Barrie, I, 39; Gould, I, 362
DURKAN, John
  MacDiarmid, II, 258
DURRELL, Lawrence
  Larkin, II, 139; Sassoon, III, 84; Spencer, III, 166
DYMENT, Clifford
  Day Lewis, II, 201; Pudney, II, 464
DYSON, A. E.
  Waugh, E., III, 308

EARP, T. W.
  Lewis, D. B. W., II, 212
EASTMAN, Max
  Gogarty, I, 348
EBERHART, Richard
  Levertov, II, 196; Todd, III, 234
EDEL, Leon
  Richardson, III, 32
EDELSTEIN, J. M.
  Lowry, II, 232
EDWARDS, Betty
  Lyle, II, 242
ELIOT, T. S.
  Kipling, II, 126; Murray, II, 354; Murry, II, 358; Symons, A., III, 206; Williams, C., III, 343; Yeats, III, 391
ELLIS, Havelock
  Shaw, III, 93
ELLIS, S. M.
  Lucas, E. V., II, 236; Nichols, B., II, 372
ELLMANN, Richard
  Joyce, II, 113; Symons, A., III, 207; Yeats, III, 393
ELWIN, Malcolm
  Caine, I, 141; Corelli, I, 190; Doyle, I, 234; Haggard, II, 2; Hewlett, II, 30; Kipling, II, 123; Lang, II, 137

EMPSON, William
  Lewis, C. S., II, 204; Woolf, V., III, 380
ENGLAND, Denzil
  Pinero, II, 429
ENRIGHT, D. J.
  Auden, I, 23; Cooper, I, 186; De La Mare, I, 214; O'Connor, II, 393; O'Faolain, II, 395; Owen, II, 416; Snow, III, 159; Stuart, III, 197; West, M., III, 333
EPSTEIN, Jacob
  Hulme, II, 66
ERVINE, St. John G.
  Maugham, II, 298; Shaw, III, 98; Stephens, III, 181; Walkley, III, 278; West, R., III, 334
ESSLIN, Martin
  Pinter, II, 431
EVANS, B. Ifor
  Lawrence, T. E., II, 168; Lucas, F. L., II, 240; MacNeice, II, 273; Maugham, II, 299; Priestley, II, 457
EVANS, C. S.
  Phillpotts, II, 424

FADIMAN, Clifton
  Hilton, II, 33; Lehmann, R., II, 189
FAINLIGHT, Harry
  MacCaig, II, 253
FAIRLEY, Barker
  Doughty, I, 221
FAIRLIE, Henry
  Williams, R., III, 352
FARRAR, John
  Lucas, E. V., II, 236
FASSETT, I. P.
  Macaulay, II, 249
FAUSSETT, Hugh I'Anson
  Blunden, I, 95
FAY, Gerard
  Behan, I, 59; Osborne, II, 413
FFRENCH, Yvonne
  Campbell, I, 143
FIEDLER, Leslie A.
  Pritchett, II, 464; Wilson, A., III, 360
FIGGIS, Darrell
  Trench, III, 249
FINDLATER, Richard
  Wesker, III, 329
FINN, James
  O'Connor, II, 394

INDEX TO CRITICS 467

FISCHER, Max
　Koestler, II, 131
FITZGIBBON, Constantine
　Rattigan, III, 11
FLEMING, Peter
　Sherriff, III, 112; Smith, L. P., III, 146; Vulliamy, III, 272
FLETCHER, Ifan Kyrle
　Firbank, I, 292
FLETCHER, J. G.
　Plomer, II, 435; Quennell, III, 1; Shanks, III, 90; Sitwell, S., III, 141; Warner, S. T., III, 291
FORD, Ford Madox [see also Hueffer]
　Conrad, I, 180; Galsworthy, I, 332; Hardy, II, 9; Harris, II, 18; Hudson, W. H., II, 59; James, II, 86
FORMAN, Joan
　Lewis, C. S., II, 208
FORSTER, E. M.
　Blunt, I, 99; Carpenter, I, 147; Eliot, I, 256; Firbank, I, 293; Fry, R., I, 326; MacCarthy, II, 255; Reid, III, 18; Sitwell, E., III, 130; Woolf, V., III, 379
FOULKE, Adrienne
　Lehmann, R., II, 190
FOX, Adam
　Turner, J., III, 254
FRASER, G. S.
　Balchin, I, 27; Campbell, I, 143; Eliot, I, 267; Empson, I, 276; Hassall, II, 24; Jennings, II, 97; Madge, II, 139; Spark, III, 165; Spencer, III, 165; Spender, III, 171; Wellesley, III, 318
FREEDLEY, George
　Ervine, I, 282; Levy, II, 202; Sayers, III, 85; Van Druten, III, 270
FREEDMAN, Ralph
　Woolf, V., III, 385
FREEMAN, John
　Mackenzie, II, 268; Meynell, A., II, 313; Murray, II, 354; Priestley, II, 455; Tomlinson, H. M., III, 240
FREMANTLE, Anne
　Godden, I, 345; Mitford, II, 325; Stuart, III, 197
FRIED, Michael
　Gunn, I, 394
FULFORD, Roger
　Sitwell, O., III, 138
FULLER, Edmund
　Shaw, III, 106

FULLER, John
　Garnett, I, 336
FULLER, Ronald
　Hassall, II, 23
FULLER, Roy
　Amis, I, 12; Fuller, I, 327; Larkin, II, 138; MacCaig, II, 252; Richards, III, 27; Ross, III, 51
FURBANK, P. N.
　Amis, I, 13; Clarke, I, 165; Forester, C. S., I, 306; *Forster, I, 312; Johnston, II, 100
*With Haskell, F. J. H.
FYVEL, T. R.
　Lehmann, J., II, 187

GARDNER, Helen
　Eliot, I, 263
GARMAN, Douglas
　De La Mare, I, 212; Lewis, P. W., II, 217
GARNETT, David
　White, III, 339; Woolf, V., III, 384
GARNETT, Edward
　Hudson, W. H., II, 58; Monkhouse, II, 326
GEISMAR, Maxwell
　Savage, III, 84
GEORGE, R. E. Gordon
　Trench, III, 251
GIBBS, Woolcott
　Carroll, I, 150
GIBSON, Wilfrid
　Meyerstein, II, 310
GILBERT, Stephen
　Reid, III, 21
GILLETT, Eric
　Bax, I, 45; Belloc, I, 64; Delafield, I, 210
GILLIATT, Penelope
　Tynan, Kenneth, III, 261
GILMAN, Richard
　Pinter, II, 432
GINDIN, James
　Lessing, II, 193
GIRVAN, Waveny
　Phillpotts, II, 425
GOLDRING, Douglas
　Flecker, I, 297; Ford, I, 301
GOMME, Andor
　Leavis, II, 174
GORDON, Ian A.
　Mansfield, II, 282

GOSSE, Edmund
  Butler, I, 137; Lang, II, 136
GOSSE, Helen
  Du Maurier, I, 242
GOULD, Gerald
  Macaulay, II, 248; Meynell, V., II, 316; Myers, II, 362
GOWER, Anthony
  Williamson, H., III, 354
GRADDON, John
  Eliot, I, 267
GRAECEN, Robert
  Morgan, II, 343
GRANDE, Luke M.
  Golding, W., I, 354
GRANDSEN, K. W.
  Manning, II, 278; Read, III, 18; Tiller, III, 233
GRAVES, Robert
  Aldington, I, 7; Lawrence, T. E., II, 164
GREEN, Martin
  Holtby, II, 39; Leavis, II, 172
GREENBERG, Martin
  Leavis, II, 169
GREENE, David H. (with Edward Stephens)
  Synge, III, 214
GREENE, Graham
  Bowen, I, 108; Buchan, I, 134; De La Mare, I, 214; Doyle, I, 235; Ford, I, 300; Ford, I, 301; Golding, L., I, 350; Hope, II, 40; James, II, 87; Read, III, 15; Richardson, III, 31
GREENWELL, Tom
  Ustinov, III, 266
GREGORY, Horace
  Bryher, I, 131; Eliot, I, 269; Muir, II, 349; Sitwell, E., III, 134
LADY GREGORY
  Synge, III, 210
GRIERSON, H. C. (with J. C. Smith)
  Bridges, I, 123; Hodgson, II, 34; Hulme, II, 66
GRIFFIN, Howard
  Auden, I, 21
GRIGSON, Geoffrey
  Auden, I, 24; Durrell, I, 253; Lewis, P. W., II, 218; Sitwell, E., III, 129; Sitwell, S., III, 145
GROSS, John
  James, II, 94

GROSSKURTH, Phyllis
  Lee, V., II, 184
GRUBB, Frederick
  Forster, I, 314
GUERARD, Albert, Jr.
  Conrad, I, 183
GUEST, John
  Stanford, III, 178
GUNN, Peter
  Lee, V., II, 184
GUNN, Thom
  Jennings, II, 96; Silkin, III, 119; Squire, III, 175
GUNSTON, David
  Thomas, E., III, 228
GUTWILLIG, Robert
  Hughes, R., II, 62
GYDE, Arnold
  Young, F. B., III, 399

HADFIELD, A. M.
  Williams, C., III, 346
HALE, E. E.
  Sidgwick, III, 117
HAMBURGER, Michael
  Muir, II, 347
HAMILTON, Clayton
  Phillips, II, 421; Sutro, III, 198
HAMILTON, Cosmo
  Gibbs, I, 339
HAMILTON, Iain
  Douglas, I, 232; Empson, I, 278; Heath-Stubbs, II, 25; Hughes, T., II, 65; Day Lewis, II, 203
HAMPSHIRE, Stuart
  James, II, 95
HANLEY, James
  Lewis, A., II, 199
HANSHELL, H. P.
  Williams, C., III, 344
HARDIE, Alec M.
  Blunden, I, 98
HARDING, J. M. and D. W.
  Read, III, 14
HARDING, D. W.
  Myers, II, 363; Rosenberg, III, 48
HARDING, Joan N.
  Morgan, II, 342
HARDWICK, Elizabeth
  Bowen, I, 111
HARDY, Barbara
  Cary, I, 153

INDEX TO CRITICS 469

HARRIS, Frank
   Shaw, III, 100
HARRISON, G. B.
   Strachey, III, 187
HART-DAVIS, Rupert
   Walpole, III, 286
HARTLEY, Anthony
   Graham, I, 364
HARTLEY, L. P.
   Harris, II, 18; Sackville-West, E., III, 65; Thompson, III, 231
HARWOOD, H. C.
   Firbank, I, 291; Linklater, II, 224; Machen, II, 262; Mansfield, II, 280; Marriott, II, 284; Monkhouse, II, 326; Nichols, B., II, 372; Russell, B., III, 56; Sidgwick, III, 118; Waugh, A., III, 298; Webb, III, 309; West, R., III, 334; Wodehouse, III, 367
HASSALL, Christopher
   Marsh, II, 286
HASTINGS, Michael
   Osborne, II, 411
HAWKINS, Desmond
   Bentley, I, 83; Gibbons, I, 338; Ridler, III, 35
HAZLITT, Henry
   Smith, L. P., III, 146
HEATH-STUBBS, John
   Williams, C., III, 345
HELLMAN, Geoffrey T.
   Vulliamy, III, 272
HENDERSON, Archibald
   Shaw, III, 94
HENDERSON, Philip
   Day Lewis, II, 200; MacNeice, II, 272
HENDERSON, W. G.
   Linklater, II, 226
HENRY, Robert
   Fausset, I, 287
HEPPENSTALL, Rayner
   Lucas, F. L., II, 241; Murry, II, 359
HERGESHEIMER, Joseph
   Walpole, III, 282
HERRING, Robert
   Agate, I, 2; Lewis, A., II, 199; Lucas, F. L., II, 238; Scarfe, III, 88; Wolfe, III, 371
HILL, Christopher
   Wedgwood, III, 315
HILTON, James
   Masters, II, 294; Shute, III, 113

HIMMELFARB, Gertrude
   Buchan, I, 135
HIND, C. Lewis
   Anstey, I, 13; Machen, II, 262
HOGAN, Robert
   O'Casey, II, 391
HOGGART, Richard
   Allen, I, 9; Auden, I, 22; Wain, III, 274; Williams, R., III, 351
HOLLANDER, John
   Jones, David, II, 103
HOLLIS, Christopher
   Haggard, II, 3; Orwell, II, 408; Waugh, E., III, 305
HOLLOWAY, John
   Enright, I, 280; Logue, II, 227
HOLT, Edgar
   Pinero, II, 428
HOPE, Francis
   Murdoch, II, 351
HOPE-WALLACE, Philip
   Dennis, I, 217; Wesker, III, 330; Wilson, A., III, 357
HOPKINS, Gerard Manley
   Bridges, I, 120; Hopkins, II, 41
HOPKINS, J. G. E.
   Milne, II, 319
HORCHLER, R. T.
   Bryher, I, 132
HOUGH, Graham
   Moore, G., II, 336
HOUSE, Humphry
   Blunden, I, 94
HOUSMAN, Laurence
   Shaw, III, 102
HOUSTON, Ralph
   Lewis, A., II, 199
HOWARD, Brian
   Brown, I, 131
HOWE, Irving
   Lessing, II, 195; Orwell, II, 408; Sillitoe, III, 120
HOWE, P. P.
   Mackenzie, II, 268; Maugham, II, 297; Phillpotts, II, 423; Pinero, II, 428
HUDSON, Stephen
   Hudson, S., II, 57
HUEFFER, Ford Maddox [see also Ford]
   Dunsany, I, 245; Kipling, II, 122; Lee, V., II, 182; Lewis, P. W., II, 213

HUGHES, David
   Lee, L., II, 181; Priestley, II, 458
HUGHES, Glenn
   Flint, I, 299; Hulme, II, 67
HUGHES, Riley
   Sayers, III, 86
HUGHES, Ted
   Owen, II, 418
HUGHES, William
   Warner, R., III, 289
HUMPHRIES, Rolfe
   Lee, L., II, 182; Watkins, III, 292
HUNEKER, James
   Shaw, III, 93
HUNT, Albert
   O'Casey, II, 389; Sherriff, III, 112
HUTCHINSON, G. E.
   West, R., III, 337
HUTCHINSON, Percy
   Walpole, III, 286
HUXLEY, Aldous
   Lawrence, D. H., II, 148; Thomas, E., III, 226
HUXLEY, Julian
   Sitwell, S., III, 144
HYMAN, Stanley Edgar
   Caudwell, I, 157; Empson, I, 274; Hulme, II, 67; Leavis, II, 171
HYNES, E. S. P.
   Thomas, E., III, 226

IRELAND, B. H. de C.
   Williamson, H., III, 353
IRVINE, Gerald
   Williamson, H. R., III, 356
IRVINE, Lyn Ll.
   Hughes, R., II, 61

JACKSON, Holbrook
   Shaw, III, 96
JACOBSON, Dan
   Leavis, II, 178; Lee, L., II, 182
JACOBSEN, Josephine
   Ridler, III, 35
JAMES, G. Ingli
   Lewis, C. S., II, 209
JAMES, Henry
   Brooke, R., I, 127
JAMESON, Storm
   Wells, III, 325
JANEWAY, Elizabeth
   Lehmann, R., II, 190; Waugh, A., III, 299

JARRELL, Randell
   Auden, I, 19; Pitter, II, 434
JEBB, Gladwyn
   Lewis, P. W., II, 216
JEBB, Julian
   Toynbee, III, 244
JENNINGS, Elizabeth
   Betjeman, I, 88; Durrell, I, 252; Gunn, I, 392
JENNINGS, Richard
   Fry, R., I, 326; Van Druten, III, 270
JOAD, C. E. M.
   Russell, B., III, 56; Shaw, III, 105
JOHN, K.
   Du Maurier, I, 243
JOHNS, Eric
   Williams, E., III, 349
JOHNSON, Pamela Hansford
   Cary, I, 152; Compton-Burnett, I, 171; Shute, III, 114
JOHNSON, R. Brimley
   Mackenzie, II, 269; Sidgwick, III, 118; Walpole, III, 283
JOHNSTONE, J. K.
   Bell, I, 60
JONAS, Klaus W.
   Maugham, II, 303
JONES, A. R.
   Wesker, III, 327
JONES, Alun
   Firbank, I, 294; Larkin, II, 140
JONES, Dr. Daniel
   Shaw, III, 103
JONES, E. B. C.
   Pritchett, II, 461; Quennell, III, 1
JONES, Ernest
   Machen, II, 264
JONES, Frank
   Woolf, V., III, 383
JONES, Henry Arthur
   Shaw, III, 99
JONES, Llewelyn
   Moore, T. S., II, 339
JONES, T. H.
   Thomas, D., III, 223
JONES, W. S. Handley
   Shaw, III, 106

KARL, Frederick R.
   Green, I, 377; Isherwood, II, 83; Johnson, II, 100; Newby, II, 371

INDEX TO CRITICS 471

KAVAN, Anne
   Lehmann, R., II, 190
KAZIN, Alfred
   Tynan, Kenneth, III, 261; Williams, R., III, 352
KEE, Robert
   Brooke, J., I, 126
KELL, Richard
   Comfort, I, 170
KELLETT, E. E.
   Sackville-West, V., III, 69
KENDON, Frank
   Machen, II, 263
KENNER, Hugh
   Beckett, I, 50; Heath-Stubbs, II, 25; Tomlinson, C., III, 238
KENYON, Charles Frederick
   Marriott, II, 283
KERMODE, Frank
   Beckett, I, 50; Betjeman, I, 87; Durrell, I, 250; Golding, W., I, 352; Gunn, I, 393; Hughes, R., II, 63; Jones, David, II, 102; Lewis, P. W., II, 222; Symons, A., III, 206; Waugh, E., III, 308; Woolf, L., III, 378; Yeats, III, 396
KERNAHAN, Coulson
   Masefield, II, 290; Newbolt, II, 367; Noyes, II, 379
KILMER, Joyce
   Gould, I, 359
KINGSMILL, Hugh
   Barrie, I, 35; Kipling, II, 124
KINNEY, Harrison
   Wodehouse, III, 369
KNIGHT, G. Wilson
   Powys, J. C., II, 450
KNIGHTS, L. C.
   Roberts, III, 36; Yeats, III, 392
KNOWLES, David
   Trevelyan, III, 253
KOCH, Vivienne
   Graham, I, 362; Hamilton, II, 6
KOHN, Hans
   Nichols, B., II, 373
KRAUSE, David
   O'Casey, II, 390
KRONENBERGER, Louis
   Linklater, II, 225
KRUTCH, Joseph Wood
   MacCarthy, II, 254; Shaw, III, 108; Smith, L. P., III, 147

KUNITZ, Stanley
   Graves, I, 375

LAMBERT, J. W.
   Golding, W., I, 352; Greene, I, 383; Levy, II, 198; Rattigan, III, 11
LANE, Margaret
   Wallace, III, 280
LASK, Beth Z.
   Rosenberg, III, 47
LASKI, Harold J.
   Ervine, I, 283; Woolf, L., III, 377
LAWRENCE, D. H.
   Galsworthy, I, 331; Wells, III, 323
LAWRENCE, Margaret
   Hall, II, 5
LAWRENCE, Ralph
   Roberts, III, 38; Watkins, III, 294
LAWS, Frederick
   Linklater, II, 226
LEAVIS, F. R.
   Conrad, I, 184; De La Mare, I, 213; Eliot, I, 265, I, 310; Hopkins, II, 44; James, II, 90; Lawrence, D. H., II, 155
LEES, F. N.
   Greene, I, 381
LE GALLIENNE, Richard
   Phillips, II, 421
LEHMANN, John
   Sitwell, E., III, 133; Thomas, E., III, 228
LEHMANN, Rosamond
   Hanley, II, 6
LEJEUNE, C. A.
   Thirkell, III, 216
LESLIE, Andrew
   Bedford, I, 53
LESLIE, Shane
   Rolfe, III, 44
LEVENTHAL, A. J.
   Beckett, I, 47
LEVIN, Bernard
   MacInnes, II, 265
LEVIN, Harry
   Joyce, II, 117
DAY LEWIS, C.
   Wells, III, 325
LEWIS, C. S.
   Williams, C., III, 344
LEWIS, John (with Reginald Bishop)
   Koestler, II, 131

472 INDEX TO CRITICS

LEWIS, Naomi
  Meynell, A., II, 315; Welch, III, 316; White, III, 342
LEWISOHN, Ludwig
  Dane, I, 199
LIDDELL, Robert
  Compton-Burnett, I, 173
LINDSAY, Jack
  Joyce, II, 108
LINDSAY, Maurice
  MacDiarmid, II, 258
LINKLATER, Eric
  Waugh, E., III, 303
LISTER, Richard
  Powell, II, 441
LLOYD, J. A. T.
  Dunsany, I, 248; Mottram, II, 344; Stern, III, 184; Woolf, L., III, 376
LLWYD, J. P. D.
  Dunsany, I, 248
LODGE, David
  Baring, I, 29
LOVAT, Laura
  Baring, I, 29
LUBBOCK, Percy
  James, II, 86
LUCAS, Audrey
  Lucas, E. V., II, 238
LUCAS, E. V.
  Archer, I, 16
LUCAS, F. L.
  Belloc, I, 61; Bottomley, I, 102; Davies, W. H., I, 208; De La Mare, I, 211; De Morgan, I, 216; Graves, I, 369; Trench, III, 251; Warner, S. T., III, 290
LUCAS, Naomi
  Macaulay, II, 251
LUNN, Sir Arnold
  Wilson, C., III, 365
LYND, Robert
  Bennett, I, 72; Cunningham-Graham, I, 196; Douglas, I, 223; Eliot, I, 255; Flecker, I, 295; Gregory, I, 386; Kipling, II, 127; Synge, III, 212; Tomlinson, H. M., III, 239

MACAULAY, Rose
  Forster, I, 308; Liddell, II, 223; Plomer, II, 437; Walpole, III, 287; Waugh, E., III, 302
MACBETH, George
  Betjeman, I, 86

MACCAIG, Norman
  Smith, S. G., III, 151
MACCARTHY, Desmond [see also Affable Hawk]
  Ellis, I, 270; Garnett, I, 344; Hall, II, 4; Huxley, II, 71; Joyce, II, 108; Lawrence, D. H., II, 146; Leslie, II, 191; Maugham, II, 300; Robinson, III, 40; Sassoon, III, 83; Squire, III, 173
MACDIARMID, Hugh
  Smith, S. G., III, 152; Thomas, D., III, 220
MACDONAGH, Donagh
  Joyce, II, 115
MACDONALD, II, Dwight
  Newby, II, 370
MACDONELL, A. G.
  Mason, II, 294; Sherriff, III, 110
MACKENZIE, Compton
  Aldington, I, 6; Arlen, I, 17; Butler, I, 138; Caine, I, 141; Hall, II, 5; Kaye-Smith, II, 119; Kennedy, II, 120; MacDiarmid, II, 256; Young, F. B., III, 397
MACKENZIE, Orgill
  Mansfield, II, 282
MACLEISH, Fleming
  Lee, L., II, 180
MACLOW, Jackson
  Smith, S. G., III, 150
MACNEICE, Louis
  Aldington, I, 5; Bowra, I, 117; Mottram, II, 345; Spender, III, 167
MAGALANER, Marvin
  Joyce, II, 112
MAHOOD, M. M.
  Cary, I, 155
MAIS, S. P. B.
  Sackville-West, V., III, 68; Squire, III, 173; Sutro, III, 198; Swinnerton, III, 201
MALLET, Sir Charles
  Hope, II, 39
MALLET, Isabelle
  Thirkell, III, 217
MALONE, Andrew E.
  Kaye-Smith, II, 118
MANNING, Olivia
  Warner, S. T., III, 291
MANSFIELD, Katherine
  Monkhouse, II, 326; Stern, III, 183

MANTLE, Burns
  Levy, II, 198
MARRIOTT, Charles
  Lowry, II, 231
MARSH, Edward
  Monro, II, 328
MARSHALL, Arthur
  Tynan, Kenneth, III, 260
MARTIN, E. W.
  Scarfe, III, 88; Warner, R., III, 288
MARTIN, Graham
  Fuller, I, 328; Holloway, II, 36
MARTIN, Olga
  Bridie, I, 125
MASEFIELD, John
  Synge, III, 211
MASON, H. A.
  Spender, III, 168
MASON, Ronald
  Sansom, III, 77
MATTHEWS, T. S.
  Bedford, I, 52; Hilton, II, 33
MAYNE, Richard
  Aldington, I, 7; Pritchett, II, 463
MCCARTHY, Desmond
  Moore, G., II, 230
MCCARTHY, Mary
  Greene, I, 384; Van Druten, III, 271
MCCORMICK, John
  West, A., III, 332
MCDOWALL, Arthur
  Moore, T. S., II, 338; Turner, W. J., III, 255
MCGINLEY, Phyllis
  Mitford, II, 323
MCGREEVY, Thomas
  Moore, G., II, 330
MCHUGH, Roger
  Tynan, Katharine, III, 260
MCLAREN, Moray
  Linklater, II, 226
MCLAUGHLIN, Richard
  Aldington, I, 5
MCQUILLAND, Louis
  Wallace, III, 279
MEGROZ, R. L.
  Armstrong, I, 17; Blunt, I, 99; Bottomley, I, 103; Shanks, III, 89; Sitwell, O., III, 136; Strong, III, 193
MELLERS, W. H.
  Benson, S., I., 79

MERCHANT, W. Moelwyn
  Thomas, R. S., III, 230
MERCIER, Vivian
  Russell, G. W., III, 64
METCALF, John
  Shute, III, 114
MEYER, John H.
  Bottomley, I, 106
MEYER, Richard E.
  Ustinov, III, 264
MEYNELL, Viola
  Morgan, II, 341; Sayers, III, 85; Thompson, III, 231; Williams, C., III, 342
MICHIE, James
  Graves, I, 372; Warner, S. T., III, 292
MILLER, Karl
  Beckett, I, 49; Davie, I, 206; Sillitoe, III, 122
MIRSKY, D. S.
  Read, III, 13
MITCHELL, Julian
  Lessing, II, 194; Wodehouse, III, 370
MOIRER, Philip
  Murry, II, 360
MONAS, Sydney
  Cary, I, 152
MONRO, Alida
  Mew, II, 308
MONRO, Harold
  Davies, W. H., I, 207; Doughty, I, 220; Graves, I, 369; Leslie, II, 191; Mew, II, 307; Meynell, A., II, 313; Nichols, R., II, 374; Noyes, II, 380; Sassoon, III, 81; Sinclair, III, 128
MONTAGUE, C. E.
  Shaw, III, 95; Synge, III, 210
MOORE, Geoffrey
  Read, III, 16
MOORE, George
  Eglinton, I, 254; Gregory, I, 387; Synge, III, 211
MOORE, Marianne
  Bryher, I, 133; Housman, L., II, 53
MOORE, Reginald
  Golding, W., I, 351
MOORE, T. Sturge
  Sorley, III, 161
MOORMAN, Charles
  Williams, C., III, 348
MORAN, Helen
  Delafield, I, 210; Kennedy, II, 120

MORGAN, Charles
  Moore, G., II, 334; Walkley, III, 278
MORGAN, Edwin
  Graham, I, 363
MORGAN, W. John
  Evans, I, 285
MORLAND, M. A.
  Davidson, I, 203
MORLEY, Christopher
  Saki, III, 75
MORLEY, Edith J.
  Vulliamy, III, 272
MORRIS, John
  Lawrence, T. E., II, 170; Liddell, II, 223
MORSE, Samuel French
  Warner, R., III, 288
MORTIMER, Raymond
  Dane, I, 200; Douglas, I, 226; Hughes, R., II, 62; Koestler, II, 134; MacCarthy, II, 256; Sinclair, III, 126; Sitwell, S., III, 141; Stuart, III, 196; West, R., III, 335; Young, G. M., III, 401
MOSES, Montrose J.
  Dane, I, 200
MOULT, Thomas
  Barrie, I, 33; Mansfield, II, 281
MUGGERIDGE, Malcolm
  Chesterton, I, 162
MUIR, Edwin
  Bennett, I, 66; Davie, I, 205; Eliot, I, 261; Gould, I, 361; Graves, I, 370; Hamilton, II, 6; Hardy, II, 15; Hudson, S., II, 56; Lawrence, D. H., II, 144; Richards, III, 24; Silkin, III, 120; Strachey, III, 185; Walpole, III, 287
MUIR, Kenneth
  Masefield, II, 292
MUIR, Willa
  Dobrée, I, 219
MULK, Raj
  Lawrence, T. E., II, 167
MULLER, H. J.
  Daiches, I, 198; MacNeice, II, 273
MURRAY, D. L.
  Guedalla, I, 392
MURRY, J. M.
  Lawrence, D. H., II, 150; Masefield, II, 288; Newbolt, II, 367; Swinnerton, III, 201

NASH, Rosalind
  Strachey, III, 186
NATHAN, George Jean
  Carroll, I, 149; Ustinov, III, 265
NEVINSON, Henry W.
  Thomas, E., III, 227
NEWBY, P. H.
  Green, I, 376; Hartley, II, 20; Stark, III, 179
NICHOLS, Wallace B.
  Noyes, II, 382
NICOLSON, Benedict
  Orwell, II, 406
NICOLSON, Harold
  Douglas, I, 228; Forster, I, 312
NOCK, Arthur D.
  Wodehouse, III, 367
NORRIE, Ian
  Braine, I, 119
NORWOOD, Gilbert
  Dane, I, 201; Lonsdale, II, 228
NOTESTEIN, Wallace
  Rowse, III, 53
NOTT, Kathleen
  Ross, III, 51; Sayers, III, 86; Silkin, III, 120; Snow, III, 155

O'BRIEN, Kate
  Allen, I, 8; Thompson, III, 232; Toynbee, III, 243
O'CONNOR, Frank
  Coppard, I, 189; Mansfield, II, 283; Yeats, III, 394
O'CONNOR, N.
  Robinson, III, 38
O'CONNOR, Ulick
  O'Casey, II, 389
O'FAOLAIN, Seán
  Holtby, II, 37; Huxley, II, 75; O'Faolain, II, 397; O'Flaherty, II, 399; Thirkell, III, 213; Waugh, E., III, 306; Yeats, III, 390
OGBURN, Charlton Jr.
  Masters, II, 296
OLSEN, Elder
  Thomas, D., III, 221
O'NEILL-BARNA, Anne
  O'Faolain, II, 396
ORWELL, George
  Koestler, II, 133; Sitwell, O., III, 138; Wodehouse, III, 368

INDEX TO CRITICS 475

OSBORNE, Charles
  Behan, I, 58
OULD, Hermon
  Evans, I, 284
OVERTON, Grant
  Gibbs, I, 338; Swinnerton, III, 201

PAINTER, George D.
  Duncan, I, 244; Durrell, I, 249-50
PALMER, John
  Robinson, III, 38
PARTRIDGE, Ralph
  Howard, II, 55
PAYNE, William M.
  Trench, III, 249
PEARSON, Hesketh
  Shaw, III, 101
PELLING, H. M.
  Wedgwood, III, 312
PESCHMANN, Hermann
  Quiller-Couch, III, 5; Wain, III, 275
PETER, John
  O'Connor, II, 394
PETERSON, Virgilia
  Macaulay, II, 252
PFEIFFER, Karl G.
  Maugham, II, 302
PHELPS, William Lyon
  Phillips, II, 423
PICKREL, Paul
  Newby, II, 369
PINTO, V. De Sola
  Sassoon, III, 82
PIPER, Myfanwy
  Armstrong, I, 18
PIPPETT, Aileen
  Cronin, I, 196
PIPPETT, Roger
  Wain, III, 275
PLOMER, William
  Betjeman, I, 85; O'Flaherty, II, 399; Prince, II, 460; Pritchett, II, 462; Stuart, III, 196; Thomas, R. S., III, 229
PLUMB, John H.
  Trevelyan, III, 252
POLLOCK, John
  Milne, II, 317; Pinero, II, 427
PORTER, Katherine Anne
  Thomas, D., III, 221
PORTEUS, Hugh Gordon
  Lewis, P. W., II, 217

POSS, Stanley
  Isherwood, II, 81
POUND, Ezra
  Eliot, I, 254
POWELL, Anthony
  Powell, II, 444; Sackville-West, V., III, 71
POWELL, Dilys
  Sitwell, E., III, 130
POWYS, J. C.
  Hardy, II, 8; Richardson, III, 30
PRICE, J. B.
  Bridges, I, 124
PRIESTLEY, J. B.
  Bridie, I, 125; Brown, I, 131; De La Mare, I, 210; Hewlett, II, 29; Housman, A. E., II, 48; Jacobs, II, 84; Lubbock, II, 234; Lynd, II, 243; Mitchison, II, 320; O'Flaherty, II, 397; Onions, II, 401; Saintsbury, III, 72; Shaw, III, 109; Squire, III, 174; Tomlinson, H. M., III, 240
PRITCHETT, V. S.
  Davies, R., I, 207; Doughty, I, 222; Firbank, I, 294; Ford, I, 300; Greene, I, 383; Huxley, II, 77; Jacobs, II, 84; Joyce, II, 116; Powell, II, 440; Reid, III, 20; Ross, III, 50; Rowse, III, 52; Warner, R., III, 288; West, R., III, 336; Wilson, A., III, 359; Woodcock, III, 374
PRYCE-JONES, Alan
  Grahame, I, 365
PUDNEY, John
  O'Casey, II, 388; Wedgwood, III, 314
PUGH, Edwin
  Evans, I, 283; Waugh, A., III, 298; Webb, III, 309
PUMPHREY, Arthur
  Hichens, II, 32
PUTT, Gorley
  Wolfe, III, 372

QUENNELL, Peter
  Bates, H. E., I, 41; Huxley, II, 73; Jones, Glyn, II, 103; Lawrence, D. H., II, 154; O'Connor, II, 392; Royde-Smith, III, 55; Russell, B., III, 56; Sitwell, S., III, 143; Smith, L. P., III, 147
QUIGLEY, Isabel
  Amis, I, 10; Stern, III, 185

476 INDEX TO CRITICS

QUINTON, Anthony
  Braine, I, 119; Hartley, II, 21; Spark, III, 163

RAINE, Kathleen
  Binyon, I, 91; Eliot, I, 262; Gascoyne, I, 337; Ridler, III, 35; Spender, III, 169
RANSOM, John Crowe
  Richards, III, 25; Yeats, III, 390
RATTRAY, Robert F.
  Shaw, III, 108
RAU, Santha Rama
  Menen, II, 305
RAY, David
  Milne, II, 320
RAYMOND, Ernest
  Mottram, II, 344
RAYMOND, John
  Allen, I, 9; Bates, R., I, 44; Bottome, I, 102; Hutchinson, II, 69; Sayers, III, 87
READ, Herbert
  Hopkins, II, 43; Hulme, II, 66; James, II, 88; Muir, II, 346
REDFERN, James
  Anstey, I, 14; Carroll, I, 150
REED, Henry
  Compton-Burnett, I, 172; Davies, R., I, 207; Mitford, II, 323; Sitwell, O., III, 137
REES, Richard
  Murry, II, 358; Orwell, II, 409
REEVES, James
  Bridges, I, 124; Eliot, I, 262
REID, Forest
  Royde-Smith, III, 55; White, III, 340
REPPLIER, Agnes
  Housman, L., II, 54
REXROTH, Kenneth
  Madge, II, 276; Rodgers, III, 43; Savage, III, 84; Treece, III, 247; Woodcock, III, 373
RICHARDS, I. A.
  Hopkins, II, 41
RICHARDSON, Maurice
  Ellis, I, 272; Laski, II, 143; Menen, II, 306; Shute, III, 113
RICKS, Christopher
  Burgess, I, 136; Empson, I, 278; Grigson, I, 391

RICKWORD, C. H.
  Powys, T. F., II, 451
RIDLER, Anne
  Raine, III, 8
ROBERTS, Brian
  Lehmann, R., II, 189; Royde-Smith, III, 55
ROBERTS, Mark
  Tolkien, III, 236
ROBERTS, Michael
  Auden, I, 18
ROBERTS, Morris
  James, II, 91
ROBERTS, R. E.
  Macaulay, II, 249; MacCarthy, II, 254
ROLO, Charles J.
  Laski, II, 142
ROMILLY, Giles
  Fraser, I, 318
ROPES, Arthur B.
  Drinkwater, I, 238
ROSENFELD, Isaac
  Sansom, III, 78
ROSENTHAL, M. L.
  Levertov, II, 196; MacDiarmid, II, 259
ROSS, A. C. Gordon
  Van Druten, III, 269
ROTHENSTEIN, William
  Beerbohm, I, 54; Conrad, I, 181; Field, I, 289; Fry, R., I, 325; Galsworthy, I, 332; Gosse, I, 357; Housman, A. E., II, 48; Hudson, W. H., II, 60; Wells, III, 324
ROUECHE, Berton
  Huxley, II, 75
ROUTH, H. V.
  Potter, II, 438
ROWSE, A. L.
  Wedgwood, III, 313
RUSSELL, Bertrand
  Roberts, III, 37; Woolf, L., III, 377
RUSSELL, G. W.
  Stephens, III, 180
RUSSELL, John
  Smith, L. P., III, 147; Strachey, III, 188

SACKVILLE-WEST, Edward
  Bowen, I, 109; Bowra, I, 116; Compton-Burnett, I, 172; Conrad, I, 182; James, II, 91

INDEX TO CRITICS 477

SACKVILLE-WEST, V.
  Stark, III, 178; Symons, A., III, 204; Woolf, V., III, 384
SAINTSBURY, George
  Gosse, I, 356
SALTER, William
  Bridie, I, 125
SAMPSON, George
  Eliot, I, 259; Lucas, E. V., II, 235
SANDEEN, Ernest
  Ross, III, 50
SASSOON, Siegfried
  Hassall, II, 24; Rosenberg, III, 49
SAVAGE, D. S.
  Huxley, II, 75; Lowry, II, 231
SCARFE, Francis
  Symons, J., III, 208; Thomas, D., III, 218; Treece, III, 245
SCHOLES, Robert
  Liddell, II, 224
SCOTT, J. D.
  Balchin, I, 27
SCOTT, Nathan A. Jr.
  Auden, I, 25
SCOTT, R. McNair
  Wellesley, III, 317
SCOTT, V. M. L.
  Orwell, II, 403
SCOTT-JAMES, R. A.
  Green, I, 380; Pitter, II, 434; Raine, III, 8; Richardson, III, 30; Smith, S., III, 149; Strachey, III, 189; Watson, III, 296; Wells, III, 319; Woodhouse, III, 375
SCOTT-JAMES, Violet
  Holtby, II, 37
SCOTT-KILVERT, Ian
  Warner, R., III, 289
SEATON, Ethel
  Quiller-Couch, III, 6
SECCOMBE, Thomas
  Wells, III, 319
SELDES, Gilbert
  Lubbock, II, 233
SENCOURT, R.
  Binyon, I, 91
SERGEANT, Elizabeth Shepley
  Sidgwick, III, 116
SERGEANT, Howard
  Owen, II, 416
SEYMOUR, William Kean
  Barker, I, 32; Hughes, T., II, 64

SEYMOUR-SMITH, Martin
  Graves, I, 371
SHAHANI, Ranjee G.
  Lyon, II, 246; Pitter, II, 433; Turner, W. J., III, 257
SHAND, P. Morton
  Caine, I, 140
SHANKS, Edward
  Coppard, I, 186; Freeman, I, 319; Linklater, II, 224; Lucas, E. V., II, 236; Lynd, II, 242; Mansfield, II, 280; Marriott, II, 284; Masefield, II, 289; Mason, II, 293; Meynell, V., II, 316; Milne, II, 318; Murry, II, 357; Nichols, R., II, 375; Nicolson, II, 378; O'Flaherty, II, 398; Squire, III, 172; Stern, III, 184; Thomas, E., III, 225
SHAPIRO, Harvey
  Tomlinson, C., III, 237
SHAW, Charles B.
  Lucas, E. V., II, 237
SHAW, G. B.
  Bell, I, 59; Butler, I, 137; Ervine, I, 282; Gregory, I, 388; Harris, II, 19
SHAWE-TAYLOR, Desmond
  Benson, E. F., I, 78; Todd, III, 233
SHEPARD, Wilfred
  Webb, III, 311
SHERARD, Robert Harborough
  Harris, II, 18
SHERMAN, Beatrice
  White, III, 340
SHERRY, Norman
  Enright, I, 281
SHIPP, Horace
  Van Druten, III, 269
SHRAPNEL, Norman
  Brooke-Rose, I, 129; Coward, I, 195; Fielding, I, 290; Manning, II, 278
SIBLEY, Carroll
  Hilton, II, 33
SINCLAIR, May
  Flint, I, 298; Richardson, III, 28
SINGER, Burns
  Morgan, II, 342; Watkins, III, 293
SINGLETON, Geoffrey
  Sitwell, E., III, 134
SITWELL, Edith
  Auden, I, 18; Bottrall, I, 106; Empson, I, 274; Sitwell, S., III, 143; Thomas, D., III, 218

INDEX TO CRITICS

SITWELL, Osbert
Fry, R., I, 327; Gosse, I, 357; Moore, G., II, 333

SKELTON, Robin
Lessing, II, 193

SLATER, Robin
Duncan, I, 244; Williams, R., III, 351

SMITH, Janet Adam
Grierson, I, 390

SMITH, Logan Pearsall
Field, I, 288

SMITH, Stevie
Godden, I, 346; West, A., III, 331

SNOW, C. P.
Bradbury, I, 117

SOUTHRON, Jane Spence
Cary, I, 151

SOUTHWORTH, James G.
Binyon, I, 90

SPARROW, John
Galsworthy, I, 333; Lucas, F. L., II, 239; Quennell, III, 2

SPENDER, Stephen
Auden, I, 20; Betjeman, I, 85; Binyon, I, 91; Blunden, I, 94; Caudwell, I, 156; Comfort, I, 168; Eliot, I, 260; Forster, I, 311; Fraser, I, 318; Fry, C., I, 323; Grigson, I, 390; Housman, A. E., II, 50; James, II, 94; Lawrence, D. H., II, 155; Lee, L., II, 180; Moore, N., II, 337; Muir, II, 345, 346; Nicholson, II, 377; Pitter, II, 434; Prince, II, 460; Read, III, 14; Rodgers, III, 43; Strachey, III, 189; Thomas, D., III, 219; Tiller, III, 232; Toynbee, III, 244; Williams, C., III, 343; Woolfe, L., III, 379; Yeats, III, 395

SQUIRE, J. C.
Housman, A. E., II, 46; Mansfield, II, 279; Marsh, II, 286; Meynell, A., II, 314; Monro, II, 328; Murry, II, 356; Owen, II, 414; Priestley, II, 455; Rickwood, III, 33; West, R., III, 337; Yeats, III, 389

STANFORD, Derek
Cecil, I, 158; Comfort, I, 168; Fielding, I, 290; Fry, C., I, 324; Gascoyne, I, 336; Lubbock, II, 234; Moore, N., II, 337; Murry, II, 360; Nicholson, II, 376; Noyes, II, 383; Raine, III, 8; Todd, III, 234

STARK, Freya
Ker, II, 121

STARKIE, Enid
Cary, I, 155

STARRETT, Vincent
Machen, II, 261

STEINER, George
Lowry, II, 231

STEPHENS, Edward (with David H. Greene)
Synge, III, 214

STERN, James
Aldington, I, 6; Newby, II, 370; O'Connor, II, 393; Silkin, III, 120; Strong, III, 195; Welch, III, 316

STEVENSON, Lionel
Saki, III, 74; Wodehouse, III, 368

STEWART, J. I. M.
Brooke-Rose, I, 129; Nicolson, II, 379

STIRLING, W. F.
Lawrence, T. E., II, 166

STOKES, Sewell
Carroll, I, 150

STONIER, G. W.
Barker, I, 31; Bates, H. E., I, 42; Bates, R., I, 43; Bridges, I, 121; Brooke, J., I, 127; Linklater, II, 225; Mitchison, II, 322; Myers, II, 364; Pitter, II, 434; Pritchett, II, 461; Shanks, III, 91; Spender, III, 168; Toynbee, III, 243

STOPP, Frederick J.
Waugh, E., III, 305

STRACHEY, John
Caudwell, I, 156

STRACHEY, Julia
Newby, II, 369; Sansom, III, 78

STRACHEY, Lytton
Hardy, II, 7

STRACHEY, R.
Vulliamy, III, 272

STREET, G. S.
Mansfield, II, 278

STRONG, L. A. G.
Cary, I, 151; Colum, I, 167; Gibbons, I, 338; Joyce, II, 109; Liddell, II, 223; Masefield, II, 292; Myers, II, 365; Royde-Smith, III, 54; Shanks, III, 90; Synge, III, 213; Wells, III, 325

STUART, Dorothy Margaret
Newbolt, II, 368; Tolkien, III, 235

STURGEON, Mary C.
Drinkwater, I, 237; Macaulay, II, 247; Masefield, II, 288; Monro, II, 327

INDEX TO CRITICS 479

STURGESS, Henry
 Godden, I, 345
SUMMERSON, John
 Macaulay, II, 249
SUTTON, Graham
 Dane, I, 199
SWINNERTON, Frank
 Aldington, I, 4; Belloc, I, 61; Bennett, I, 68; Bennett, I, 74; Chesterton, I, 160; Coward, I, 192; Cunningham-Graham, I, 196; Douglas, I, 225; Galsworthy, I, 334; Garnett, I, 335; Herbert, II, 27; Hudson, W. H., II, 61; Kaye-Smith, II, 119; Moore, G., II, 332; Onions, II, 402; Strong, III, 195
SYKES, Christopher
 Bedford, I, 52
SYMONS, A. J. A.
 Rolfe, III, 45
SYMONS, Arthur
 Bridges, I, 121; Conrad, I, 179; Watson, III, 296; Yeats, III, 388
SYPHER, Wylie
 Todd, III, 234

TATE, Allen
 Richards, III, 26
TAUBMAN, Robert
 Brophy, I, 130; Hartley, II, 22; James, II, 93; Jameson, II, 96
TAYLOR, A. J. P.
 Snow, III, 160
TAYLOR, Pamela
 Stern, IIII, 185; Thirkell, III, 215
TEMPLE, Ruth Zabriskie
 Gosse, I, 358; Moore, G., II, 335
THOMAS, Gilbert
 Fausset, I, 287; Guedalla, I, 391; Lynd, II, 244; Masefield, II, 291; Strong, III, 192
THOMAS, Lowell
 Lawrence, T. E., II, 164
THOMPSON, Rosemary
 Treece, III, 247
THOROGOOD, Horace
 Barrie, I, 33
THOULESS, Priscilla
 Abercrombie, I, 1; Binyon, I, 89; Bottomley, I, 104; Davidson, I, 202; Flecker, I, 296; Moore, T. S., II, 340
THWAITE, Anthony
 Gunn, I, 393; Priestley, II, 458; Silkin, III, 119

TIMES LITERARY SUPPLEMENT (*TLS*)
 Vol. I: Agate, 3; Amis, 13; Arlen, 16; Bates, 42; Bateson, 44; Beerbohm, 56; Bell, 59, 60; Bennett, 77; Benson, 78; Bentley, 84; Beresford, 85; Binyon, 92; Blunden, 96; Bottome, 102; Bowra, 116; Braine, 118; Brooke, R., 128; Brophy, 130; Brown, I., 131; Bryher, 133; Burgess, 136; Butler, S., 139; Campbell, 144; Cecil, 159; Chambers, 159; Church, 163, 164; Collier, 166; Colum, 167; Comfort, 168, 169; Compton-Burnett, 174; Conrad, 185; Coppard, 188; Cronin, 195; Daiches, 198; Davie, 205; Davies, R., 207; De Selincourt, 218; Douglas, N., 229; Doyle, 236; Drinkwater, 239; Duggan, 242; Du Maurier, 243; Duncan, 244, 245; Durrell, 251; Enright, 280; Gissing, 344; Godden, 346; Goldring, 355; Gosse, 355; Graham, 364. *Vol. II*: Haggard, 2; Harris, 19; Hartley, 21; Hassall, 24; Heath-Stubbs, 25; Heppenstall, 26, 27; Herbert, 28; Hilton, 32; Hodgson, 35; Holloway, 36; Hope, 40; Housman, A. E., 50; Howard, 56; Hughes, T., 64; Jerome, 98; Jones, Glyn, 103; Jones, Gwyn, 104; Joyce, 113, 114; Kennedy, 120; Ker, 121; Kipling, 130; Laver, 144; Lawrence, D. H., 160, Leavis, F. R., 176; Lehman, J., 187, 188; Lessing, 193; Lewis, C. S., 211; Lowry, 232, Lucas, F. L., 240; Madge, 277; Menen, 305; Meyerstein, 310; Mitchison, 322; Monsarrat, 329; Owen, 417; Powys, J. C., 450, 451; Prince, 460; Pritchett, 462. *Vol. III*: Richards, 23, 24, 27; Robinson, 41; Russell, B., 59; Sackville-West, E., 66; Sackville-West, V., 71; Saki, 76; Sansom, 79; Sayers, 87; Sillitoe, 121; Snow, 154; Spark, 164; Spencer, 166; Symons, J., 207; Thirkell, 215; Tomlinson, H. M., 240; Treece, 248; Waugh, E., 305; West, M., 331, 332; Wilson, A., 356, 361; Wodehouse, 369; Woodhouse, 374; Young, G. M., 399
TINDALL, W. Y.
 Joyce, II, 111; Spender, III, 170
TOMLIN, E. W. F.
 Lewis, P. W., II, 218
TOMLINSON, Charles
 Empson, I, 276
TOMLINSON, H. M.
 Doughty, I, 220; Douglas, I, 224

480 INDEX TO CRITICS

TOYNBEE, Philip
   Forester, C. S., I, 305; Hutchinson, II, 68; Rowse, III, 53; Standish, III, 176; Welch, III, 315; Woodcock, III, 375

TRAVERSI, Derek
   Greene, I, 379

TREWIN, J. C.
   MacDougall, II, 260; Rattigan, III, 9; Sherriff, III, 112; Ustinov, III, 264; Van Druten, III, 271; Wesker, III, 327; Williams, E., III, 349; Williamson, H. R. III, 357

TRIEM, Eve
   Levertov, II, 197

TRILLING, Diana
   West, R., III, 337

TRILLING, Lionel
   Kipling, II, 126; Leavis, II, 176; Orwell, II, 404; Snow, III, 157

TRODD, Kenneth
   Leavis, II, 179

TROY, William
   O'Connor, II, 393; Woolf, V., III, 382

TSCHUMI, Raymond
   Day Lewis, II, 201; Russell, G. W., III, 63

TUCKER, Martin
   Bradbury, I, 118; Rowse, III, 54

TURNELL, Martin
   Eliot, I, 259; Lewis, D. B. W., II, 213

TURNER, W. J.
   Milne, II, 318; Munro, II, 349

TWITCHETT, E. G.
   Read, III, 13; Young, F. B., III, 398

TYNAN, Katherine
   Bottomley, I, 102; Macaulay, II, 247; Monkhouse, II, 325

TYNAN, Kenneth
   Beckett, I, 47; Behan, I, 58; Dennis, I, 217; Greene, I, 381; Osborne, II, 409; Rattigan, III, 10

UNDERHILL, Evelyn
   Murry, II, 358

URQUHART, Fred
   Manning, II, 277; Potter, II, 439

USBORNE, Richard
   Wodehouse, III, 370

USSHER, Arland
   Shaw, III, 108

VAN DOREN, Mark
   Hardy, II, 15

VANSON, Frederic
   Carpenter, I, 147

VAN THAL
   Nicolson, II, 379

VAN VECHTEN, Carl
   Machen, II, 263

VERSCHOYLE, Derek
   Ervine, I, 282; Gogarty, I, 346; Hardy, II, 12; Isherwood, II, 79; Nichols, B., II, 373; Williams, E., III, 348

VIVAS, Eliseo
   Lawrence, D. H., II, 158

VULLIAMY, C. E.
   Beerbohm, I, 55; Potter, II, 438

WAGNER, Geoffrey
   Lewis, P. W., II, 220

WAIN, John
   Connolly, I, 176; Greene, I, 385; Hopkins, II, 46; Leavis, II, 177; Meyerstein, II, 312; Snow, III, 158; Thomas, D., III, 222; Toynbee, III, 244; West, R., III, 339

WALBROOK, H. M.
   Shaw, III, 100

WALDMAN, Milton
   Lee, V., II, 183; Levy, II, 197; Morgan, II, 341; Munro, II, 350; Myers, II, 363; O'Casey, II, 385; Powys, J. C., II, 446

WALKER, Roy
   Beckett, I, 48

WALL, Bernard
   Heppenstall, II, 27

WALPOLE, Hugh
   Sackville-West, V., III, 68

WALSH, Michael
   Tynan, Katharine, III, 258

WALTON, Geoffrey
   MacNeice, II, 272

WARD, A. C.
   Chesterton, I, 161; Coward, I, 193; Cunningham-Graham, I, 197; Hewlett, II, 30; Richards, III, 24

WARD, R. H.
   Powys, J. C., II, 448

WARDLE, Irving
   Pinter, II, 430

INDEX TO CRITICS 481

WARREN, C. Henry
  Spender, III, 167; Strong, III, 193; Turner, W. J., III, 257

WARNER, Rex
  Bateson, I, 44; Stark, III, 179; Trevelyan, III, 253; Wedgwood, III, 313

WATSON, Francis
  Orwell, II, 403

WATSON, George I.
  Houseman, A. E., II, 49

WATTS, Stephen
  Rattigan, III, 11

WAUGH, Alec
  Maugham, II, 301; Waugh, A., III, 300

WAUGH, Evelyn
  Bedford, I, 51; Duggan, I, 241; Firbank, I, 292; Quennell, III, 3; Sitwell, S., III, 144; Waugh, A., III, 299

WEALES, Gerald
  Menen, II, 306

WEATHERBY, W. J.
  Compton-Burnett, I, 174; Fry, C., I, 325; Powys, J. C., II, 450

WEBER, Carl J.
  Hardy, II, 13

WEBSTER, Owen
  Golding, W., I, 353

WEDGWOOD, C. V.
  Lee, L., II, 181; Macaulay, II, 250; Plomer, II, 436; Ross, III, 50

WEISS, Carol H.
  West, A., II, 331

WELBY, T. Earle
  Symons, A., III, 205

WELCH, Colin
  Lawrence, D. H., II, 160

WELLEK, René
  Bateson, I, 45; Empson, I, 278; Leavis, II, 177; Richards, III, 28

WELLS, H. G.
  Bennett, I, 70; Gissing, I, 342; Swinnerton, III, 199

WEST, Anthony
  Cary, I, 154; Collier, I, 166; Ellis, I, 272; Sansom, III, 79; Wilson, C., III, 366

WEST, Geoffrey
  Russell, G. W., III, 61; Swinnerton, III, 202

WEST, Paul
  Green, I, 378; Hanley, II, 7; Isherwood, II, 82; Maugham, II, 302

WEST, Rebecca
  Coward, I, 192; Lawrence, D. H., II, 162; Sherriff, III, 111; Sinclair, III, 126; Stern, III, 184; Tomlinson, H. M., III, 241; Wells, III, 324

WESTWOOD, Jane
  Eliot, I, 268

WEYGANDT, Cornelius
  Freeman, I, 322

WHITE, Antonia
  Brooke, J., I, 126; Du Maurier, I, 243; Laski, II, 142

WHITEHORN, Katharine
  Murdoch, II, 353; Spark, III, 165

WIGGIN, Maurice
  Williamson, H., III, 355

WILLIAMS, Charles
  Masefield, II, 290; Powys, J. C., II, 447; Sitwell, S., III, 142

WILLIAMS, Harold
  Anstey, I, 14; Cannan, I, 145; Ervine, I, 282; Field, I, 288; Hichens, II, 31; Housman, L., II, 54; Newbolt, II, 368

WILLIAMS, I. A.
  Quennell, III, 1

WILLIAMS, Orlo
  De Morgan, I, 215; Murry, II, 357; Plomer, II, 435

WILLIAMS, Raymond
  Hardy, II, 16; Huxley, II, 77; Lawrence, D. H., II, 162; Orwell, II, 407; Synge, III, 214; Wilson, C., III, 364

WILLIAMSON, Audrey
  Osborne, II, 412; Ustinov, III, 266

WILLIAMS-ELLIS, A.
  Blunden, I, 92

WILLIAMSON, Henry
  Williamson, H., III, 353

WILLINGHAM, John R.
  Mitford, II, 324

WILLIS, Irene Cooper
  Hardy, II, 13

WILLY, Margaret
  Lewis, C. S., II, 208; Lyon, II, 245; Nicholson, II, 376

WILSON, Angus
  Bates, H. E., I, 42; Golding, W., I, 351; Murdoch, II, 352; Powys, J. C., II, 451

WILSON, Colin
  O'Casey, II, 389
WILSON, Edmund
  Beerbohm, I, 57; Connolly, I, 175; Doyle, I, 235; Eliot, I, 266; Potter, II, 439; Saintsbury, III, 73; Waugh, E., III, 301
WILSON, Harris
  Wells, III, 326
WINKLER, Henry R.
  Woodhouse, III, 375
WINKLER, R. O. C.
  Bottrall, I, 106
WINTERS, Yvor
  Bridges, I, 122; Hopkins, II, 42
WINWAR, Frances
  Mitford, II, 324
WOLFE, Humbert
  Gould, I, 361; Moore, G., II, 331; Sitwell, S., III, 142; Squire, III, 175
WOOD, Frederick T.
  Morgan, II, 341; Priestley, II, 455; Young, F. B., III, 400
WOODHOUSE, C. M.
  Stark, III, 180
WOOLF, Leonard
  Corelli, I, 189; Dobrée, I, 219; Forster, I, 315; Koestler, II, 132; Shaw, III, 101; Strachey, III, 191
WOOLF, Virginia
  Beerbohm, I, 53; Belloc, I, 60; Bennett, I, 65; Conrad, I, 178; Forster, I, 308; Gissing, I, 343; Hardy, II, 10; James, II, 85; Joyce, II, 106; Moore, G., II, 332; Strachey, III, 187; Wells, III, 322
WORDSWORTH, Christopher
  Hanley, II, 7
WORSLEY, T. C.
  Eliot, I, 264; Fry, C., I, 323; Granville-Barker, I, 368; Pinter, II, 431
WRIGHT, Andrew
  Cary, I, 154
WRIGHT, David
  Smith, S., III, 149; Watkins, III, 292
WYNDHAM, Francis
  Cooper, I, 186; Golding, W., I, 350; Greene, I, 382; MacInnes, II, 265; Newby, II, 370; Sansom, III, 80; Snow, III, 153

YEATS, William Butler
  Colum, I, 166; Davidson, I, 201; Gregory, I, 386; Sitwell, E., III, 131; Synge, III, 212; Wellesley, III, 318
YOUNG, G. M.
  Sitwell, S., III, 143
YOUNG, Kenneth
  Ford, I, 303
YOUNG, Marguerite
  Treece, III, 246; Welch, III, 316
YOUNG, Stark
  Carroll, I, 148; Williams, E., III, 349

ZABEL, Morton Dauwen
  Ford, I, 303